CW01432205

Edward J. Dent

Edward J. Dent

A Life of Words and Music

Karen Arrandale

THE BOYDELL PRESS

First published 2023
The Boydell Press, Woodbridge

ISBN 978 1 78327 205 1

The Boydell Press is an imprint of Boydell & Brewer Ltd
PO Box 9, Woodbridge, Suffolk IP12 3DF, UK
and of Boydell & Brewer Inc.
668 Mt Hope Avenue, Rochester, NY 14620-2731, USA
website: www.boydellandbrewer.com

A CIP catalogue record for this title is available
from the British Library

This publication is printed on acid-free paper

Printed and bound in Great Britain by
TJ Books Limited, Padstow, Cornwall

Contents

Illustrations vi

Preface and Acknowledgements viii

Abbreviations xii

Dramatis Personae xv

Introduction: Edward J. Dent – Another Kind of Genius 1

1 The Ribston Pippin 1876–1895 6

2 The Bumptious Undergraduate 1895–1899 19

3 The Accidental Scholar 1899–1901 59

4 The Travelling Fellow 1902–1906 86

5 The Wanderer 1906–1907 128

6 The New Spirit 1907–1910 140

7 The Impresario 1910–1914 177

8 The Pacifist 1914–1918 212

9 The Journalist 1919–1922 273

10 The International Musician 1922–1926 327

11 The Professor 1926–1931 367

12 The Juggler 1931–1934 387

13 The Beleaguered Diplomat 1935–1936 428

14 The Colonial Doctor 1936–1939 445

15 Titurel 1939–1945 464

16 Tityvillus 1946–1957 499

Afterword 514

Appendix: Dent's Ulcer 519

Select Bibliography 521

Index 529

Illustrations

1	Eight-year-old Edward Dent at Bilton Grange. By kind permission of the Governors of Bilton Grange School.	13
2	Edward Dent c.1900. Photograph taken by J. Palmer Clarke. By kind permission of the Provost and Fellows of King's College, Cambridge.	20
3	Gibbs Building, King's College, c.1898. By kind permission of the Provost and Fellows of King's College, Cambridge.	21
4	Dent sailing back from Germany in 1896, with his sister Isabel, Ted Haynes, Sir Walter Parratt, and Hilda Kekewich. By kind permission of the Provost and Fellows of King's College, Cambridge.	39
5	Cartoon of Dent ('Prof Pears') at the 1903 Rome IMG Congress from the *Giornale di Sicilia*.	99
6	Letter from Dent to Clive Carey, illustrated with music. By kind permission of the Provost and Fellows of King's College, Cambridge.	108
7	Programme of *The Magic Flute*, December 1911. Clive Carey as Papageno. By kind permission of the Provost and Fellows of King's College, Cambridge.	192
8	Page from the *Cambridge Magazine*, April 1916. Cambridge University Library.	235
9	'The Willow-Tree Bough', by Dent, to words by Charles Scott-Moncrieff. By kind permission of the Provost and Fellows of King's College, Cambridge.	263
10	Hotel Bucintoro, Venice. Author's photograph.	346
11	Dent and J.B. Trend in Salzburg, 1924, taken by Sydney Loeb. Reproduced by kind permission of Jessica Loeb and Caroline Watts.	354
12	Frankfurt ISCM, 1927. Dent with his head in a noose in the Hirsch garden; from left to right, Gian-Francesco Malipiero, Paul Hirsch, Dent, Paul Pisk, Erwin Schulhoff, Max Butting. By kind permission of the Provost and Fellows of King's College, Cambridge.	375
13	Zurich ISCM jury in a Geneva funfair aeroplane, 1928: Willem Pijper, Heinz Tiessen, Bozidar Sirola, Ravel and Dent. © The British Library Board. Add. 71144, p. 33.	381

14 Oxford–London ISCM jury meeting in Dent's King's College rooms, Cambridge, 1931. Charles Koechlin, Alfredo Casella, Adrian Boult, Alban Berg, Dent, Gregor Fitelberg, Désiré Defauw. By kind permission of the Provost and Fellows of King's College, Cambridge. 394

15 Postcard to Arnold Schoenberg, signed by Dent, Roberto Gerhard, and others, 1933. By kind permission of the Provost and Fellows of King's College, Cambridge. 401

16 Programme of the Cambridge ISMR Congress, 1933. By kind permission of the Provost and Fellows of King's College, Cambridge. 408

17 Dent and Wolfgang Frommel, Berlin, c.1932. By kind permission of the Provost and Fellows of King's College, Cambridge. 417

18 Hans Raab in his Nazi uniform. On the back written: 'A man who is dead – forever! 31/10/35'. By kind permission of the Provost and Fellows of King's College, Cambridge. 418

19 Programmes of the Barcelona ISCM and ISMR joint Congress and Festival. By kind permission of the Provost and Fellows of King's College, Cambridge. 442

The author and publisher are grateful to all the institutions and individuals for permission to reproduce the materials in which they hold copyright. Every effort has been made to trace the copyright holders; apologies are offered for any omission, and the publisher will be pleased to add any necessary acknowledgement in subsequent editions.

Preface and Acknowledgements

Some years ago I was given a battered keyboard instrument, part of the estate of a refugee Catalan composer called Roberto Gerhard who had lived here in Cambridge. It had once been an elegant square pianoforte straight out of a Jane Austen novel, a Stodart of 1807, in a flame mahogany case, with brass trim and tiny drawers underneath. At some point it had been turned into an ersatz clavichord by chopping off an octave or so from its keyboard and carefully replacing its hammers with nails. It certainly wasn't at all the kind of instrument you might associate with a pupil of Arnold Schoenberg. Inside the case was a tattered piece of card addressed to 'Mr Dent, King's College'. I went to King's.

That first visit to the Dent archive at King's was more than revelation; it was dumbfounding. Twenty-six years of diaries and thousands of letters, all only recently catalogued and mostly unread. This respectable and respected Professor of Music, it transpired, had helped his old friend Gerhard to escape from Nazi-occupied Paris, organised a place for him at King's with a small stipend: everything, in fact, any refugee needed for official refugee status. Moreover, it appeared that Dent had done the same for quite a few others, assisting a substantial chunk of musical Europe on the run, but that was only a tiny part of his story. Many of the names scattered throughout the diaries and letters might have been expected from an eminent musicologist: Vaughan Williams and Hubert Parry, Hugh Allen, William Walton; then Ferruccio Busoni, Alban Berg, Egon Wellesz, Gian Francesco Malipiero, Manuel de Falla and so on, but why E.M. Forster, Rupert Brooke, Hugh Dalton, George Mallory, John Maynard Keynes, Edward Carpenter, Siegfried Sassoon, Osbert Sitwell, Edward Gordon Craig, Albert Rothenstein, Magnus Hirschfeld, Wilhelm Herzog and many others? Startling little vignettes presented themselves: Dent's pity at seeing how ill 'poor little Mrs Murry'[1] appeared, sitting in the offices of the *Athenaeum*; Dent bumping into 'the Craiglockhart poet'[2] on the steps of the hospital where they were both visiting the wounded Siegfried Sassoon; Dent and Clive Carey inspecting Mrs Strindberg's Cabaret Theatre Club and its 'Cave of the Golden Calf' as a possible venue for opera;[3] Dent at Busoni's Berlin flat when Futurists Marinetti and Boccioni

1 Katherine Mansfield, who was suffering from the tuberculosis which killed her shortly after. Her husband John Middleton Murry was then editor of the *Athenaeum* when Dent was writing for it, and Dent had been asked to write for their earlier *Rhythm*. Murry sent Dent out to write about music in postwar Weimar Germany, a move which eventually resulted in Dent helping to found the International Society for Contemporary Music.

2 Wilfred Owen, who had been helped by two of Dent's friends, Sassoon and Philip Bainbrigge.

3 The ex-wife of the playwright: she had commissioned artists like Eric Gill and Jacob Epstein to decorate the place. The cabaret didn't really work out for opera, but Dent and

dropped by to try to sell him a massive painting.[4] There was much more; an almost overwhelming mass of familiar and less familiar people and events gradually revealed in decades of unpublished diaries and thousands of letters with a vast network of friends and associates, which taken as a whole presents an alternative view of twentieth-century cultural history, a secret history of music, opera, theatre, literature, fine art, sexuality and how so much now taken for granted actually came into being. Behind it all is the extraordinary, elusive figure of Edward J. Dent. I was enchanted.

That was more than a decade ago, and I would like to express immeasurable thanks to the many generous people and institutions who helped me along the way. I am very grateful to the Hinrichsen Foundation for giving me a grant for research in the UK, and to the Wingate Foundation for a two-year scholarship to travel to European archives. At King's College, Cambridge, the Provost and Fellows kindly granted me a Senior Associateship, with unstinting support from Professor Iain Fenlon, Professor Nick Marston, Librarian Peter Jones, the late Dr Hal Dixon, with his extensive knowledge of college history, the Reverend Richard Lloyd Morgan, and the wonderful, patient people in the Archive Centre, Dr Patricia McGuire and Peter Monteith. The college Development Office supported various Dent events. Richard Andrewes at the university library helped with the Bliss and Sassoon archives there and introduced me to George Dannatt, who had known Dent's close friend and correspondent Jack Gordon. The Manuscripts Room staff were beyond helpful in digging out endless dusty boxes full of treasures. Thanks are due too to Bilton Grange, Dent's prep school, who kindly allowed me to reproduce early photographs of young Dent and wander around the beautiful premises.

Other academics have been extremely generous with their time and trouble, especially Dr Valerie Langfield, who introduced me to Winton Dean, Nigel Fortune and Katharine Thomson, gave me access to the Jack Gordon and the Thomson letters, and shared her wide knowledge of the period. Nick Robinson at the Fitzwilliam Museum showed me some of Dent's contributions to the collections. Long conversations with E.M. Forster's biographer, Professor Wendy Moffatt, helped clarify Dent's friendship with Forster, while another Forster scholar, Dr Glen Leonard, uncovered Dent's broadcasts at the BBC and posed several provocative questions. Professor Rachel Cowgill, Dr Kate Kennedy, Professor Alison Sinclair, Professor Anne Schreffler, Dr Tess Atkins, Hugh Taylor, Professor Tim Cribb, Timothy Day, the late Christopher Hogwood, Dame Margaret Anstee, who had studied with J.B. Trend, and Meirion Bowen, friend and biographer of Roberto Gerhard, all gave immensely valuable support and helpful perspective. Great thanks to Dr Judith Murray-Rust and Dr Carol Evans, who diagnosed Dent's chronic ulcer. Antony Beaumont was very kind and helpful with regard to Dent's relationship with Busoni. Others who generously gave much appreciated advice or information are Bruce Phillips, with his vast knowledge of the music and people of the period, Penny Hatfield at Eton, Paul Banks at the Royal College of Music, Nicholas Bell

Carey later went to the Old Vic instead, which did.

4 Dent later wrote the biography of his old friend, the composer Ferruccio Busoni, who did buy one of Marinetti's pictures and posed for a portrait by Boccioni.

at the British Library, Timothy Day, Milo Keynes, Thomas Holme Hansen, Toby Thacker, Professor Roger Savage, Professor Julian Rushton, and Denis Browne's great-nephew Nick Peacey.

Dent's family at Ribston Hall, Charles and Anne Dent, kindly showed me around the house where he grew up. At nearby Harewood House, there was a delightful afternoon with the late Earl of Harewood, George Lascelles, who copied Dent's letters for me and talked about his 'old friend Dent' while his little dog sat on my lap. I was lucky enough to interview people who had known Dent and were happy to talk about him: the late George Dannatt, Winton Dean, Christopher Raeburn, Sir David Willcocks, Professor Robin Orr, John Amis, Katharine Thomson and Nigel Fortune; Dominic Vlasto, whose mother, Dent's pupil Jill Vlasto, rescued Dent's papers from dissemination.

Dr Marga Estanyol at Biblioteca de Catalunya, Barcelona, helped immensely to open up the Higini Anglès archive for me there, besides cooking magnificent paella, and Dr Eike Feiss of the Schoenberg Institut, Vienna, was most generous with the material there. Ralf Dose and his team at the Magnus-Hirschfeld-Gesellschaft in Berlin were unfailingly helpful and wonderfully informative about the background there. Dr Jorge and Dr Gertrud Muraro at Winterthur showed me Werner Reinhart's house and archive, with warm hospitality on top. In Vienna, Dr Biber at the Gesellschaft der Musikfreunde in Vienna gave me access to its archives and some understanding of Dent's Vienna experiences. The staff at the Österreichische Nationalbibliothek were very helpful and accommodating, and I am grateful for their permission to quote from unpublished letters of Egon Wellesz and Guido Adler there. Harald and Geli Haymerle and their wonderful family gave me boundless hospitality, help and advice in navigating Viennese libraries beside the timeless glories of Viennese cafés, as did Claus-Christian Schuster. The Fondazione Giorgio Cini on San Giorgio in Venice were kind enough to copy for me Dent's correspondence with Malipiero, Chilesotti and Casella, to grant permission to quote one of its letters, and it has one of the best views in Venice. Dr Andrea Stadter and her family helped me to sort out my complicated German train travels. Many friends have helped simply by listening to me talk endlessly about Dent, often providing unexpected insights or ideas.

For permission to use the main unpublished sources, I would like to thank the Provost and Fellows of King's College, Cambridge for permission to copy the Lawrence Gowing portrait of Dent in the Combination Room, to use photographs in the Dent archive and to quote from the E.M. Forster and Rupert Brooke archives, while Professor Laura Gowing generously allowed the portrait to be used for the cover. For permission to use Sydney Loeb's contemporary photographs, and for a fascinating insight into Loeb, I am grateful to Caroline Watts and Jessica Loeb. Thanks to the Master and Fellows of Magdalene College, Cambridge for permission to quote from the unpublished diaries of A.C. Benson in the Pepys Library. The heirs of the estate of J.B. Trend have kindly allowed me to quote from Trend's and Dent's unpublished and published work and letters. For permission to quote from Ralph Vaughan Williams, I am grateful to Hugh Cobbe and the Ralph Vaughan Williams Trust. Thanks to the Bliss Trust for permission to quote from Arthur Bliss's unpublished letters to Dent, and to Nick Peacey and the heirs of Denis Browne for permission to quote from his letters, beside the chance to hear some of Browne's music performed. Thanks to the Barbara Levy Literary Agency for permission to quote Siegfried Sassoon's letters to Dent, and to the estate of the late George Dannatt for permission to quote Jack Gordon's correspondence; to the Britten–Pears Library, Snape, for permission to quote from the Britten letters. Thanks to the British Library for permission to use the postcard of Dent and several eminent composers in a funfair aeroplane. For permission to quote from their published work, I would like to thank Lord Skidelsky, Professor Samuel Hynes, Professor Anne Schreffler, Professor Pamela Potter and the Yale University Press, Susie Gilbert and Professor Jeremy Dibble.

But mostly, I would like to thank my patient friends, and Stuart, who read every word.

Abbreviations

Institutions

AAC	Academic Assistance Council
BL	British Library
BM	British Museum
BNOC	British National Opera Company
BSSSP	British Society for the Study of Sexual Psychology
CEMA	Committee for the Encouragement of Music and the Arts
CUL	Cambridge University Library
CUMC	Cambridge University Musical Club
CUMS	Cambridge University Musical Society
DTC	Day Training College
ENSA	Entertainments National Service Association
IMG/IMS/SIM	Internationale Musikgesellschaft / International Musical Society / Société Internationale de la Musique
IGMW/ISMR/SIM	post–WWI revival of above: Internationale Gesellschaft für Musikwissenschaft / International Society for Musical Research (later International Musicological Society) / Société Internationale de la Musique
ISCM	International Society for Contemporary Music
KC	King's College, Cambridge
KCA	King's College, Cambridge, Archive Centre
KCMS	King's College Musical Society
MDS	Marlowe Dramatic Society
ÖNB	Österreichische Nationalbibliothek
RAM	Royal Academy of Music
RCM	Royal College of Music

Books, Periodicals and Publishers

ATFE	*A Theatre for Everybody*
CM	*Cambridge Magazine*
CR	*Cambridge Review*
CUP	Cambridge University Press
DMMM	*Dictionary of Modern Music and Musicians*
Grove's	*Grove's Dictionary of Music and Musicians* (editions specified)
LM	*London Mercury*
MA	*Musical Antiquary*
M&L	*Music & Letters*
MMR	*Monthly Musical Record*
MQ	*Musical Quarterly*
MT	*Musical Times*
N&A	*The Nation and The Athenaeum*
OUP	Oxford University Press

Dent's Main Correspondents

HA	Higini Anglès
PB	Philip Bainbrigge
ATB	Theo Bartholomew
ACB	Arthur Christopher Benson
AB	Arthur Bliss
KB	Kennard Bliss
BB	Benjamin Britten
RB	Rupert Brooke
DB	Denis Browne
OB	Oscar Browning
FB	Ferruccio Busoni
CC	Clive Carey
WD	Winton Dean

AE	Alfred Einstein
EE	Edwin Evans
EMF	Edwin Morgan Forster
JG	Jack Gordon
TG	Tyrone Guthrie
LH	Lawrence Haward
JMK	John Maynard Keynes
PL	Percy Lubbock
RO	Robin Orr
SS	Siegfried Sassoon
CS	Charles Sayle
KT	Katharine Thomson
JBT	John Brand Trend
EW	Egon Wellesz
RVW	Ralph Vaughan Williams
JSW	James Steuart Wilson

Dramatis Personae

Allen, Sir Hugh Percy (1869–1946), organist at Ely Cathedral, then New College, Oxford; Director of the Royal College of Music, conductor of the Bach Choir

Anglès, Higini (1888–1955), Catalan musicologist and cleric

Bainbrigge, Philip Gillespie (1890–1918), poet, teacher, musician

Bartholomew, Augustus Theodore 'Theo' (1882–1933), librarian and bibliographer, editor of Samuel Butler, pioneer of gay studies

Baylis, Lilian (1874–1937), founder of the Old Vic/Sadler's Wells

Beecham, Sir Thomas (1879–1961), conductor

Bliss, Sir Arthur (1891–1975), composer

Bliss, Francis Kennard (1892–1916), artist, musician

Boult, Sir Adrian Cedric (1889–1983), conductor

Bridges-Adams, William (1889–1965), producer and director

Britten, Benjamin (1913–1976), composer

Brooke, Rupert Chawner (1887–1915), founder of Marlowe Dramatic Society, poet, writer

Browne, William Denis (1888–1915), musician, love of Dent's life

Browning, Oscar (1837–1923), dilettante historian and musician, Fellow of King's College

Busoni, Ferruccio (1866–1924), composer and piano virtuoso

Carey, Francis Clive Savill (1883–1968), singer, teacher at the Royal College of Music and at Adelaide Conservatory, opera producer at the Old Vic/Sadler's Wells, folk-dancer, one of Dent's closest friends

Craig, Edward Henry Gordon (1872–1966), theatre producer

Dalton, Edward Hugh John Neale, later Baron Dalton (1887–1962), Labour politician, later Chancellor of the Exchequer

Dean, Winton Basil (1916–2013), musicologist, Handel scholar

Einstein, Alfred (1880–1952), musicologist, editor of *Acta Musicologica*

Evans, Edwin (1874–1945), music critic, co-founder and President of ISCM (International Society for Contemporary Music)

Forster, Edwin Morgan (1878–1970), writer, librettist and critic

Foss, Hubert James (1899–1953), music editor at Oxford University Press

Friedlaender, Max (1852–1934), German singer, writer and music historian specialising in Schubert's songs

Goodhart-Rendel, Harry Stuart 'Hal' (1887–1959), musician, architect, writer, Slade Professor at Oxford

Gordon, John Barrit 'Jack' (1898–1978), opera producer

Guthrie, Sir William Tyrone (1900–1971), theatre producer and director

Haward, Lawrence Warrington (1978–1957), music critic at *The Times*, art critic and collector, later curator of Manchester Art Galleries, Dent's closest friend

Haynes, Edmund Sidney Pollock 'Ted' (1877–1949), lawyer, writer on civil liberties, publisher

Hirsch, Paul (1881–1951), German-born music collector, whose collection became the basis of the British Library music collection

Hirschfeld, Magnus (1868–1935), pioneering German sexologist, founder of the Wissenschaftlich–humanitäres Komitee (Scientific–Humanitarian Committee)

Jekyll, Francis 'Timmy' (1882–1965), librarian, nephew and biographer of gardener Gertrude Jekyll

Keynes, John Maynard (1883–1946), celebrated economist, Fellow of King's College

Kraus, Alessandro (1853–1931), Florentine collector of early musical instruments

Lascelles, George Henry Hubert, 7th Earl of Harewood (1923–2011), founder of *Opera* magazine, board member of the Royal Opera House and English National Opera

Lubbock, Percy (1879–1965), writer and critic; friend of Clive Carey and A.C. Benson

Monro, Harold Edward (1879–1932), poet, owner of the Poetry Bookshop

Murry, John Middleton (1889–1957), writer, editor, especially of *The Athenaeum*

Ogden, Charles Kay (1889–1957), polymath linguistic philosopher, founder of the *Cambridge Magazine*

Orr, Robert Kensley 'Robin' (1909–2006), composer, Professor of Music at Cambridge

Paget, Violet, aka 'Vernon Lee' (1856–1935), writer, musician, part of the expatriate community outside Florence

Purves, Patrick John Chester Jervis Laidlaw (1890–1960), official in the secretariat, League of Nations

Reinhart, Werner (1884–1951), Swiss philanthropist and amateur musician

Sassoon, Siegfried Loraine (1884–1968), poet, writer

Sayle, Charles Edward (1864–1924), bibliographer and Uranian poet

Scherchen, Hermann (1891–1966), conductor, editor

Seyssel, Claudio di, Marchese di Aix e di Sommariva del Bosco (1874–1930), Dent's longtime friend

Squire, William Barclay (1855–1927), early music scholar and editor

Stanford, Sir Charles Villiers (1852–1924), Irish-born composer, Professor of Music at Cambridge, later also Professor at the Royal College of Music, knighted 1901

Stewart, Reverend Hugh Fraser (1863–1948), Fellow of Trinity College, whose extended family, including his sister 'Daisy' (wife of Francis Jenkinson) and three of his daughters, Jean, Katherine 'Katten', and Frideswide 'Frida', were serious musicians

Summers, Augustus Montague (1880-1948), occult scholar and anthologist

Thomson, Katharine Fraser Stewart (1906–2006), political activist and musician

Toye, John Francis (1883–1964), music critic and writer; he and his brother Geoffrey worked with Dent at the Old Vic/Sadler's Wells

Trend, John Brande 'JB' (1887–1958), first Professor of Spanish at Cambridge; Dent's partner

Wellesz, Egon (1885–1974), composer, musicologist

Williams, Ralph Vaughan (1872–1958), composer

Wilson, Sir James Steuart (1889–1966), singer, later Director-General of the BBC and of The Royal Opera House

Wolf, Johannes (1869–1947), German music scholar and teacher

He was a tall, weakly-built young man, whose clothes had to be judiciously padded on the shoulder in order to make him pass muster. His face was plain rather than not, and there was a curious mixture in it of good and bad. He had a fine forehead and a good large nose, and both observation and sympathy were in his eyes. … All the energies and enthusiasms of a rather friendless life had passed into the championship of beauty.

—E.M. Forster, *Where Angels Fear to Tread* (Penguin, 1975; first pub. 1905), p. 70.

He was medieval. Like a gothic statue. Tall and refined, with shoulders that seemed braced square by an effort of the will, and a head that was tilted a little higher than the usual level of vision, he resembled those fastidious saints who guard the portals of a French cathedral. Well educated, well endowed, and not deficient physically, he remained in the grip of a certain devil whom the modern world knows as self-consciousness, and whom the medieval, with dimmer vision, worshipped as asceticism.

—E.M. Forster, *A Room With A View* (Penguin, 1978; first pub. 1908), p. 106.

That mixture of culture and mischief.

—E.M. Forster, 'A View without a Room' (Penguin, 1978; first pub. 1958), p. 233.

Dent of course in a corner.

—Lytton Strachey to Dora Carrington, 1918, in *The Letters of Lytton Strachey*, ed. Paul Levy (New York, 2005), p. 424.

His importance in the musical hierarchy of Cambridge may perhaps be described as unofficial rather than official; he had a finger in all the choicest musical pies, but he rarely made them. Stanford was Professor of Music; Charles Wood the teacher of theory and composition; Mann organist of King's; Alan Gray the conductor of the Musical Society. Yet for nearly all of us younger men it was Dent, more than anyone else, who kindled our enthusiasm and held our allegiance.

—Francis Toye, *For What We Have Received* (London, 1950), p. 65.

I always imagine Dent as the Serpent telling Eve about the Apples. 'My dear Eve …' pointing out all the blemishes on them, with back-hits at God and Adam, and a rumour that the Holy ghost was *enceinte* [pregnant]. But so kindly.

—Rupert Brooke to Geoffrey Keynes, March 1911.

I can hardly hope to be myself the composer of the perfect English song, but if I can help somebody else to do it, it wd be something.

—Dent to Lawrence Haward, 24 July 1901.

INTRODUCTION

Edward J. Dent – Another Kind of Genius

Fame is a quixotic beast. It is an entirely mysterious process how and why some become household names while others often far more deserving vanish from the selective memory-banks of history. Few people now know who Edward J. Dent was, which is probably the way he would have liked it, since throughout his incredibly productive life he never sought celebrity however much he might have deserved it. After the Second World War, having seen through one of his lifelong ambitions, formal government support for the establishment of national opera, ballet and theatre as well as what became the Arts Council,[1] Dent refused a knighthood from the Attlee government.[2] It was a typical gesture, modest and perverse in equal measure; he knew his own worth. Briefly: Fellow of King's College, Cambridge, and Professor of Music 1926–41, Dent helped to found and to run what became English National Opera, the Royal Opera House, the National Theatre, the International Society for Contemporary Music (ISCM), the International Society for Musical Research (ISMR), and was in on the establishment of the Arts Council. He helped found *Musica Britannica*; his editions of early opera, his translations of about fifty-six operas into English, his productions of *The Magic Flute* (1911) and *The Fairy Queen* (1914/20), beside his work on the earliest productions of the Marlowe Dramatic Society or Handel operas, rescued early works from obscurity. He researched and wrote the first biographies of Alessandro Scarlatti and Ferruccio Busoni, wrote seminal books on Mozart, on opera and theatre, besides hundreds of articles on musical and non-musical subjects.[3] A founder member of the first gay rights organisation, the British Society for the Study of Sexual Psychology (BSSSP) in 1913, Dent was also a member of the British Academy; President of the Musical Association, the Philharmonic Society, the Purcell Society and the Liszt Society; a member of the Church Music Society; he helped to found the Drama League and the British Music Society; he was on the League of Nations music committee; and more.

But Dent's real genius was as a facilitator, providing the mind and energy underpinning some of the major cultural undertakings of the past century, while working behind the scenes or through his writings suited his subversive and mischievous spirit. His very apt nickname was 'The Old Serpent'; he loved watching people take up his ideas – which they generally did – and, having carefully laid all the foundations,

1 Robert Skidelsky, *John Maynard Keynes: Fighting for Britain 1937–1946* (London, 2000), pp. 296–8.

2 KCA, EJD/4/1.

3 See Lawrence Haward, *Edward J. Dent: A Bibliography* (Cambridge, 1956).

see these ideas take hold and grow as he tweaked the strings. He was never cruel, nor was it simple schadenfreude, but he enjoyed confirming his cynical views of basic human nature while energetically working to achieve the contrary. And since Dent was a manipulator of genius, those he manipulated often remained in genuine ignorance of their own true part in things, while those possessing the large or fragile egos abounding in the arts often simply did not give him due credit when recording their own life's works. One cannot entirely blame them; to be on the receiving end of 'the kindest heart and the wickedest tongue in Cambridge' must have brought up some very mixed emotions.

Manipulation – or facilitation – is by nature mostly a hidden activity, and people quickly forget. Dent's persistent veiled influence in the first half of the twentieth century eventually resulted in the high standards of theatrical and operatic productions enjoyed today as a matter of course, while his internationalist agenda has long since been vindicated. But how this all came to pass has up to now remained secreted away in unpublished correspondence, forgotten, the connections not made between people supposedly from different disciplines.[4] The problem is he was almost too accomplished an operator, and where the need has disappeared, so has the credit for its disappearance: Dent 'was so successful that his work is probably taken for granted. Now that the objects have been attained, it is hard to realise that so much needed to be attained.'[5]

Born into the landed gentry, seventh child of John Dent Dent of Ribston Hall, Yorkshire, Dent grew up in the cosy, comfortable upper-middle classes forming the rigid backbone of Victorian Britain, which ruled the British Empire with such devotion and certainty. He could easily have slid along the well-upholstered route via Eton and Cambridge into some professional sinecure; instead he chose music. Gentlemen then did not become musicians, while to be 'musical' carried a murky Wildean subtext. So two defining characteristics of Dent's life and persona – musicology and homosexuality,[6] the one disappointing and undefined, the other illegal and unspeakable – stamped him from the outset as an outsider, while his birth and upbringing gave him a public face which presented the opposite. This insider–outsider paradox at his core in fact suited Dent perfectly and forced him to improvise constantly in order to find a way forward without compromising either his musical ideals or his true self. He was born to privilege but voted Labour, pursued high culture but wanted above all for it to be part of the fabric of everyday life, not something rarefied and special, while excellence was never to be compromised at any level. He was a failed composer who became one of the country's leading academic musicians without ever having held an official academic post, before being begged to become Professor at Cambridge. If Dent's path had been less difficult, his life would have been far less interesting.

4 Although recent work has begun to address this. See Afterword.

5 Hugh Carey, *Duet for Two Voices: An Informal Biography of Edward Dent compiled from his letters to Clive Carey* (Cambridge, 1979), p. 1.

6 Both terms were coined in Dent's lifetime, one c.1926, the other c.1897.

The residual marks of his privileged birth and upbringing emerge as personal traits he wrestled with all his life: his prudery, his loathing of sentimentality, of piety, and his own deep need to preserve his privacy. Dent once described himself as a 'late Victorian', and recognised his own place on the cusp between the nineteenth and twentieth centuries, an identification which was not self-limiting, but acknowledgement of his own struggles in helping shift the one into the other. His was a life dedicated to opening up possibilities for outsiders in a way now recognised as being 'modernist', and parallels a modernism whose birth pangs were both hindered and helped by wars.

All his life he cultivated the oblique intimacy of chamber music or extensive letter-writing. Striking up a correspondence was the best way any buttoned-up man of Dent's class and background could continue less formal contact, and his letters allowed him a freedom well beyond what polite society normally found acceptable. His vast range of correspondents was an extension of the intimate, safe circles he nurtured at home, while the letters are invariably entertaining, and – even through the built-in habits of discretion – show off the writer's complex character and his inimitable view of his world.

Dent got into the habit of discretion in the post-Wildean world where homosexuals like himself had to be extremely discreet, were subject to public opprobrium, prosecution under the law and often blackmail. Much if not most of his early correspondence has been destroyed, probably deliberately, for obvious reasons; while some, like his correspondence with the sexologist Magnus Hirschfeld, was destroyed in the war, Dent's letters by the Nazis and Hirschfeld's probably by Dent himself. Explicit references to homosexuality are rare in his extant correspondence, and while he never actually denies his personal preferences, the closest he ever comes to discussing them publicly is via the accepted codes of a professed misogyny and confirmed bachelorhood. But discretion suited him, and he enjoyed playing the game while keeping his own cards very close, letting little hints slip out from time to time. A diary entry in 1916 records when Dent was asked at a dinner party point-blank if he was a 'Uranian',[7] he replied obscurely that he was rather a 'disciple of Edward Carpenter'. His early support for what would now be called gay rights was kept very quiet, like his membership of the BSSSP.[8] But behind the games of secrets and obfuscations lay the desire for clarity one day, beside the naughty impulse simply to stir things up. In 1938, Dent donated to the Cambridge University Library a collection of letters which lay ignored for eighty years, with little gems such as the letter to Dent from L.H.G. Greenwood which would have revealed in 1938 the existence and whereabouts of the manuscript of their mutual friend E.M. Forster's *Maurice*, his then unpublishable novel about homosexual love. Instead, it was to lie forgotten

7 'Uranian' is the term, possibly adopted from Karl Ulrichs' 'Urning', to describe men with feminine characteristics, a third sex. English Uranians professed a 'Greek' love of an older man for a younger man. The term was used in the writings on the subject by Edward Carpenter and John Addington Symonds.

8 Dent had met Magnus Hirschfeld in Berlin c.1903, and was probably responsible for Hirschfeld's connections in England when the BSSSP was getting off the ground. See Chapter 7.

for decades in Greenwood's old rooms in Emmanuel College. Letters from Siegfried Sassoon show how much Dent helped him improve his poetry and come to terms with his sexuality, and more.

Much of Dent's life was an exercise in necessary improvisation, finding fresh ways to express himself, to pursue a full personal life in spite of current laws, and a musical career in the teeth of constant institutionalised frustration. Even at King's College, Cambridge, where music was important and men had always found it relatively easy to slip from sexuality of 'the usual public-school' kind into what Dent's contemporary Lytton Strachey called 'the higher sodomy', Dent found his own way. As a freshman he suffered through several heart-wrenching, embarrassing crushes, which only confirmed to him that sexual relationships were perhaps better pursued abroad, especially in countries with the Code Napoléon,[9] rather than on home turf, avoiding the public humiliation he feared and hated as well as any legal difficulties. His musical research abroad dovetailed nicely into his cheerful pursuit of the right kind of young man, often in uniform, sometimes aristocratic, and he enjoyed exercising his considerable gift for languages by chatting them up of a warm evening in the piazza.

As Dent discovered, even becoming a 'musician' in late Victorian Britain was neither easy nor straightforward. When he went up to King's in 1895, the first musical hurdle was to get his degree in Classics.[10] The prevailing official attitude was dismissive, and Dent later liked to cite an elderly don's view: 'Music, Sir, is a very agreeable diversion for a man who cannot afford to hunt.'[11] He scraped a third in Classics, breezed through his Mus B and decided to float what he called a *balon d'essai* and apply for a Fellowship at King's offering a musical composition as a dissertation, a calculatedly provocative challenge, the first of many in his life: no one had ever before applied for a Fellowship in Music, much less been awarded one. The college was thrown by this outrageous application, and cast about for advice, finally coming up with the limp proposal that he submit the equivalent for a Master's degree, basically a school exercise rather than anything remarkable. Dent was outraged, and responded by presenting them with a huge piece for chorus and eighty-piece orchestra along with what became his seminal book on Alessandro Scarlatti,[12] for years the classic study of that composer. Even so he barely squeaked in, up against a major economist and a minor mathematician.

It was to be a defining feature of Dent's career that in spite of his conspicuous abilities he did not rise automatically to the top of his chosen profession, but instead had constantly to find other approaches, institutional side-doors. Cambridge provided Dent with more than a rough and uncertain ride; along the way he learnt how to navigate the vicious combination-room politics, 'where the tempers run so high because the stakes are so low', and in himself a capacity for making strong

9 In countries which kept the Code Napoléon – e.g., Italy – homosexuality, together with blasphemy, heresy and witchcraft, had remained decriminalised since the early 19th century.

10 See Chapter 2 for discussion of this apparent oddity.

11 Sedley Taylor, quoting a former Vice Provost of King's. Cited in Dent's obituary of Sedley Taylor, MT (1 May 1920).

12 The college had a terrible time trying to find someone to assess both, as Dent intended.

friendships with a wide range of people. Not quite unconsciously, he used his background – that impossible, inimitable combination of arrogance, charm and ruthlessness bred in the bone and encouraged by the established institutions which nurtured him – together with his formidable intellect to improvise his career.

It may seem odd, given his considerable international reputation, that no full biography has been written before or since Dent's death in 1957, Hugh Carey's 'Informal Biography' coming the closest. Carey had found the potential scope of Dent's biography so overwhelming that he decided to limit his field to Dent's correspondence with his uncle, the singer Clive Carey (who had himself left notes for a Dent biography). Equally daunting was the question of how to deal with Dent's sexuality, and the fact that by the end of his life, Dent had managed to upset or offend a lot of influential people. That there was a real need for a full biography was certainly in the minds of musicologists Philip Radcliffe, Winton Dean and Philip Brett, and while there is musicological justification alone for a biography, Dent is really a much bigger, more interesting, more complex player on the twentieth-century stage. How to encapsulate a man who can seriously recommend the composition of strict counterpoint as an alternative to knitting or smoking?

When he was a very young man travelling in Italy to research Alessandro Scarlatti, Dent was introduced into the rarified company so carefully selected by Mary Berenson to be presented to her husband, the art authority Bernard Berenson. Other such privileged young men had included Dent's friends Morgan Forster and Maynard Keynes. This was 1903, and Berenson was at the height of his fame and influence. The invitation must have been terrifying.

Tucked into the hillside above Florence, Villa I Tatti itself was the embodiment of *la bella vita* – the beautiful life – exquisitely furnished, its walls hung with old Masters, the pervasive tone one of hushed, funeral-director reverence. Hot and dusty from his long walk up from Florence, young Dent was intimidated by its self-conscious grandeur. Years later he recalled the clatter as his teaspoon dropped on the stone floor, his hostess' anxious looks cast at her 'priceless china' cups in the hands of this nervous young man. Secure and surrounded by their own established good taste, Berenson and his guests grilled him politely on his 'Ideal'. Flustered and hesitant, Dent replied that his ideal would be to understand 'all the music that had been, or would ever be, written'. 'All music?' His examiner 'turned pale', the exquisite company shuddered. But what about bad music? 'What would become of Taste?'

A 'sudden fit of recklessness' came upon Dent. 'Taste?' he said, 'We might get some new ideas about it …'

All music.

CHAPTER 1

The Ribston Pippin 1876–1895

> I shd like (if I were a novelist) to write a novel about someone who was brought up to all that and thankful to be quit of it.[1]

The Ribston Pippin is an old variety of apple, originating at Ribston Hall in the North Riding of Yorkshire, probably from French seeds sent to Sir Henry Goodricke (1642–1705), who admired French architecture as well as French apples. Having enjoyed a remarkably successful career as soldier and diplomat in volatile times, when he succeeded to the baronetcy in 1670 Sir Henry built himself a grand house in a French style, which still sits high on a bend in the River Nidd, rather less of it than appears in the Kipp engraving of c.1707, and lacking its original fortified garden wall, but a handsome and elegant establishment nevertheless.[2] By then Ribston, earlier 'Ripestane', already had a long and colourful past. It once marked the river crossing point of the Great North Road, and in the twelfth century those great protectors of important byways, the Knights Templar, established a place of refuge and respite there, of which only the austerely beautiful chapel remains, now attached to the house itself. It is the coldest as well as the oldest part of the house, and young Edward Dent often bitterly complained of its penetrating cold when forced to work in the room next to it. A lifelong aversion to damp and to institutionalised religion probably began at home.

Ribston was never home to the aristocracy; rather, throughout its long history it fostered under its various roofs a succession of landed gentry, the upwardly mobile middle classes who formed the bedrock of establishment England: bishops, diplomats, politicians, merchants, soldiers, less creative than acute and certainly strong-minded. The Dent family are only the most recent of these to take over house and estate, arriving there in 1834, just before Victoria came to the throne, and quietly, unobtrusively, they began take a hand in county affairs.

It was Dent's solid 'late Victorian' background, as he described it, which gave him both the built-in confidence of his class and the foundations for a lifelong rebellion against it. He used it, wore its protective mantle unconsciously and spent his life undermining its certainties. Edward Joseph Dent was born at Ribston on 16 July 1876, to John Dent Dent and Mary Hebden Woodall Dent, the seventh and last child of a conspicuously successful marriage. For nearly twenty years before his birth

1 LH 23/08/1945.

2 Gervase Jackson-Stops, 'Ribston Hall, Yorkshire–II' in *Country Life* (18 October 1973), p. 1142.

his siblings had already been running around the corridors at Ribston, galloping their ponies with the local hunt, playing music and silly parlour games, 'Spillikin Fright' and 'Up Jenkins', in the evenings, and batting for the family on their own cricket pitch. John William 'Jack' was born in 1857, the same year as Edward Elgar, followed by Francis 'Frank', Charles, Mary Catherine, Margaret Eleanor 'Maggie' and Isabel. The youngest Dent, always known to his family as 'Joe',[3] grew up in the idyllic surroundings of his family estate at the edge of the Vale of York, bounded by the bigger Harewood estate to the west, with distant views of the North York Moors. Everything, everyone around him was familiar, yet he always felt himself set apart, first by age and later, by inclination. He never could join his elder brothers off shooting with the neighbouring Lascelles men at Harewood House; country sports, even his mother's passion for bicycling, left him cold. As the youngest he was spoilt and indulged up to a point, kind intentions mixed with earnest late-Victorian religiosity, with duty stamped into the core of his being. But there was always a deep residual fondness for his well-intentioned relatives, especially a Dent family living 5 miles (8 km) to the east – his Uncle Joe, Rector of nearby St John the Baptist, Hunsingore, and his Aunt Laura (Freshfield), with their children constantly in and out of Ribston.

Like the Goodrickes before them, the Dents were bred of Yorkshire, Lincolnshire and Nottinghamshire farmers, latterly prosperous landed gentry on the rise in these favourable new times. In 1834 both status and fortune were established beyond question because of simple nomenclature. The original family name of Tricket was changed to Dent when Jonathan Dent of Winterton on the Humber estuary died at the age of ninety and made young Joseph Tricket, Edward Dent's grandfather, his heir on the condition that he change to his wife Catherine's family name to continue the line, an offer Tricket could scarcely refuse. Upon coming to his majority, Uncle Jonathan had discovered that there was no family money to inherit, so he spent the rest of his long life restoring the family fortunes, his acumen and parsimony accruing for his heirs the huge sum of half a million pounds.[4] With the fortune came a coat of arms and the motto 'Patientia et perseverantia'.[5] An apt motto: Ribston's history was an object lesson in the constant need for care and vigilance; succeeding generations of Dents remained characteristically thrifty and in Yorkshire parlance 'careful' with their money. Edward never bought new clothes if he could avoid it and always darned his own socks. The house itself was thus spared many Victorian improvements: 'All in all the Dents' changes were almost always sensitive and conservative, having enhanced, rather than detracted from, the historical and architectural interest of Ribston.'[6] It was with mixed feelings that Edward Dent could later joke about

3 Although his family called him 'Joe', for consistency he will be referred to as 'Dent' or 'Edward'. Very few people in his life called him 'Edward', only his American colleagues, but he often called close younger friends by their Christian names, e.g., 'Clive' or 'Denis', but 'JB', possibly influenced by the Eton practice of never using Christian names. He is still known in the Dent family as 'Great Uncle Joe'.

4 Over 30 million pounds in today's terms.

5 *Burke's Landed Gentry*, 18th edn, vol. 2, pp. 154–5. The crest includes a crane, 'in the beak a rose slipped, and resting the claw on a serpent nowed'.

6 Jackson-Stops, 'Ribston Hall', p. 1045.

how any redecoration might endlessly be discussed, but that nothing would ever happen, certainly little would actually change. Returning to his family home after his eldest brother Jack's death in 1944, Dent noted that there was still no telephone, a bath had been installed but didn't work, while 'brown' shaving water still came from the rooftop tank. But their father John Dent had built up an excellent wine cellar, so the mourners enjoyed 1887 claret for lunch, sitting in the faded 1840s furnishings from the famous sale of the Duc d'Amande.

The Dents throve. Joseph acquired more lands – for example the township and chapelry of Lissett, in the East Riding – and quickly established himself as a county personage, becoming Justice of the Peace (JP) and High Sheriff of Yorkshire in 1847. They multiplied: Joseph had four sons, John, Joseph, William and Henry, with one daughter Ellen Isabel, and the family began to spread itself around the county and beyond, marrying into surrounding county families. Family ties were important; family values paramount, together with a strong sense of civic duty. Joseph's eldest son, Edward's father John Dent Dent (1826–1894), was given the kind of start in life perfect for a man who would fulfil every Victorian father's best hopes. He went to Eton, then to Trinity College, Cambridge, where he read Law. He was a soldier, promoted to Captain of the Yorkshire Hussars, before returning to Ribston to settle down as a local JP, member of Parliament for Knaresborough and canny investor in the burgeoning railways. In 1855 he married a Scarborough girl, Mary Hebden Woodall, from a similar prosperous, rising, upper-middle-class family. The Hebden and Woodall families had been connected for several generations through marriage as well as their shipping, banking and railway interests. Mary's father John, a prosperous banker, was part-owner of Woodall and Hebden's Bank, and Mayor of Scarborough from 1851–52, donating to the town its Mayoral Chain of Office and eventually his own house, St Nicholas House, as the Town Hall. He funded the pier, he held high office in the local masonic lodge, he owned land. And most significantly, the Woodalls were musical. Edward Dent later talked of his grandfather's friendship with the composer William 'Billy' Shield, another Freemason who had lived and worked around Scarborough as well as further up north in Gateshead, and he was close to his Scarborough uncle and namesake Edward Woodall ('Uncle Ted') and his formidable aunts. When they later moved to a villa in the South of France it became for years a stopping-point for Edward on his frequent trips to and from Italy.

The Dents of Ribston were an exemplary Victorian family; the sons went to Eton and Trinity College, Cambridge, and into the army, the church, the law or farming. John Dent Dent provided a model of duty and public service, but this made him a distant figure to his youngest son, who later said that he only began to know his father as a person just before his death in December 1894, when Edward was warmly praised for his academic achievements. John's brother Henry Francis followed a similar path, going from Eton and Trinity into the army, the Hussars, before settling into the life of a country gentleman, Master of the Bedale Hounds near Malton, about 20 miles (32 km) from Ribston. Their sister Ellen Isabel in 1857 married the Reverend Lovelace Stamer (later 3rd Baronet) who became Rector of Stoke-on-Trent, and later suffragan bishop of Shrewsbury. There were Stamer, Buxton and Dent cousins, together with friends made at school, in the army or Parliament: the Kekewiches and Vansittarts. By the time Edward Joseph was born in 1876, he was connected by blood and/or marriage to several dozen other solid, prosperous families around this part of England, including the Greenwoods of Swarcliffe Hall, the Headlams and Freshfields, and on convivial terms with other important local families, especially the Lascelles at neighbouring Harewood House and the Worsleys at Hovingham. Such intense family ties both irritated Edward and gave him an unconscious sense of belonging and responsibility in almost equal measure. The seven Dent children survived to healthy adulthood, but in fact only three would marry and leave Ribston: Maggie married a Greenwood; Charles and Frank had families of their own; but Catherine and Isabel divided their time between Ribston and their widowed mother's London houses, first Brook Street, then Rutland Gate. Jack followed his father into the army and later became a bachelor country squire, concerned mostly about his lands and his hunting rather than the house. Edward would later complain that the only serious topic of conversation to be had after dinner at Ribston was of the mange in foxes.

To grow up in the teeming life of a Victorian country house meant that every moment was rigidly mapped out according to long-established ritual, with family visits and local obligations at the fore. Edward later said that he had been brought up to sit as if every chair had a stiff back, but he enjoyed taking his young cousins, nephews and nieces out to the elegant stable block to see a new litter of kittens or giving them piggyback rides around the garden. Religious observance was another strict routine. Ribston's chilly Templar chapel was in use daily for family prayers; Sundays, the family would drive the 5 miles (8 km) across the flat upper reaches of the Vale of York to Hunsingore, where Uncle Joe preached the sermon and, for several years in his college vacations, Edward played the organ and later conducted the choir. Sundays meant church twice and nothing more energetic than some modest music-making in the evening, in spite of Edward's naïve efforts to inject some more lively music or topics for discussion:

> I asked (Charles) for a definition of Sunday music – he said 'the sort of music that would give you cold shivers down your back if it was played on a violin'. … Mother gave a negative suggestion – it was not to be dance music – Isabel said she thought pace had a good deal to do with it – I wish they would arrive at the idea, 'if music is worth playing, let us have it every day: if not, don't let us hear it at all!'[7]

He was forced eventually to realise what he was up against. One miserably cold, snowy night, he trudged home across the frozen fields from Hunsingore choir practice, to find that he had been locked out of the house while the rest of the family was at prayers. He was made to stand outside, huddled in the freezing doorway until they finished.[8]

Though always sympathetic to his distant Quaker ancestry, Dent mutinied against what he called 'clericism', versions of the rigid, frosty piety he endured as a child at Ribston, but however much he later rebelled against his late-Victorian upbringing, much of Dent's early experience re-emerges in his later life. He

7 Diary 01/10/1896.

8 Diary 20/12/1896.

understood from a young age the importance of close personal relations, and how useful networks are created, while the importance placed on loyalty and duty sits beside the need for rules and knowing when to break them. As a man whose life was spent poised between conflicting aspects of his own personality, Dent spent his early years becoming grounded in one of them, that inimitable, indefinable self-assurance and self-possession rooted in family and property.

Dent's musicality had its roots in that same early experience at Ribston, even if it later became a real bone of contention when he declared his intention to become a professional musician. Gentlemen then did not become musicians, yet music-making was an essential part of country-house life, some big houses even possessing a music room, and at Ribston the Broadwood grand pianoforte of 'figured walnut' was kept in the saloon for such after-dinner entertainments.[9] Mary Dent played the piano well, and made sure that her children were given the chance to learn music. The girls all played and sang – for years Isabel conducted a small local choir – while young Edward showed real proficiency. As the youngest it was hardly surprising that his precocity was encouraged and indulged from an early age, especially since he never showed the slightest inclination for the sporting activities his brothers loved. In 1882, when he was six, Dent planned a musical soirée for the entertainment of the family in the saloon at Ribston,[10] a carefully handwritten programme presented to the audience:

VALSE. STRAUSS.
MR. E.J. DENT

GIGUE. HANDEL.
MISS I.A. DENT

LE PREMIER PAS. POLKA.
MISS M.C. DENT

INTERVAL OF 5 MINUTES.

DUET. DIABELLI.
MRS. DENT & MR.E.J. DENT

THE HARMONIOUS BLACKSMITH. HANDEL.
MRS. DENT

DUET. SPOHR.
MRS. DENT, & MISS I.A. DENT.

GOD SAVE THE QUEEN

9 Its length is 8 feet 2 inches (c.2.5 m) and it is still there. When Dent saw it after Jack's death in 1944, it had been sitting in the damp 'without any fires' for over thirty years but 'astonishingly' was still in tune. LH 12/05/1944.

10 Programme, 7 October 1882, KCA.

When Dent was growing up, his family supported local music festivals, at Leeds but especially at nearby Hovingham, where from 1887 to 1906 the Worsley family of Hovingham Hall gave over their eighteenth-century Riding School to a music festival, the brain-child of Canon Thomas Percy Hudson, a Yorkshire-born local clergyman, with some extraordinary musicians playing there.[11] Dent knew him well in later years, when he was on the Cambridge University Musical Board and heavily involved with university musical societies, but for now Canon Hudson had managed to establish a major festival in this rural part of Yorkshire, supported by local gentry but specifically including anyone who loved music, with concessions made to 'members of choirs and the like to whom the experience would be of value'.[12] This inclusive principle in itself was an object lesson to Dent, as important as the chance to hear such musicians of international stature as Joseph Joachim and Johann Kruse. The repertoire, too, was ambitious and often contemporary, with Sterndale Bennett, Parry, Elgar, Somervell and Stanford being performed beside Brahms, Gluck, Verdi and Wagner, and choral pieces composed by women, Mrs Tom Taylor and Miss Alexandra Thomson. The 'band' was made up of locals propped up by professionals imported from London, a tactic later employed by the Cambridge University Musical Society to make big orchestral pieces affordable.

So Dent's considerable musical discrimination began early on. Local brass bands left him cold: he could never bear 'loud' music, 'while the sound of any sort of brass instrument terrified me into hysterics',[13] but the late-Victorian taste for choral and orchestral music remained with him for years. The family all loved D'Oyly Carte Gilbert and Sullivan; Dent and his sisters went to early performances of both *The Yeomen of the Guard* and *The Gondoliers*, and like everyone else in Victorian England, sang the duets at home. Dent later swore that from the age of six he had loathed 'certain types of Sullivan song like "Tit-willow"', but he retained a great respect for Sullivan.

Dent's mother had given him music, but for years tried to control what he did with it. His later professed misogyny had its roots at Ribston, and the kind of women whose company he dreaded and avoided – rather than the robust 'new' women he later met at Cambridge – were of the Victorian 'Aunt Agatha' ilk, the monster later made famous by P.G. Wodehouse, whose ferocious certainties admitted no real truth, not entirely unlike his own mother. It was years before he could recognise her bullying for what it was; his meek sister Isabel also suffered:

> she was always snubbed & kept in the background & supposed to be quite without intelligence. And my mother ruined her voice … because she wanted her to

11 Antony Pemberton, 'A Trip Round my Dining Room Walls' (Cambridge, 2011). Canon Hudson (1832–1921), who changed his name to Pemberton, later rejected an offer to become Master of Magdalene College, Cambridge, on the grounds that his own place, Pemberton Hall, was far more comfortable.

12 MT (November 1903), cited in Percy Scholes, *The Mirror of Music 1844–1944* (London, 1947), vol. 1, p. 171.

13 LH 07/03/1942.

> be a high soprano when she was really a mezzo: but my mother thought contraltos 'professional' & unladylike.[14]

Isabel was closer both in age and artistic temperament, while his other sister Catherine, the more intelligent and independent of the two, was probably the closest of all his siblings, once Dent was old enough to appreciate her tart affection. They remained on good terms; even as a young man about town when he was in London, Dent would always dutifully escort one or other of his sisters to art exhibitions or concerts, or even, in Isabel's case, to watch Test cricket at Lord's.

For his first nineteen years, at home Dent continued to be nurtured in careful suffocation which encouraged his musical gifts while quelling anything odd or untoward in his creativity, a paradoxical dilemma which took him years to recognise. He suffered from residual prudery all his life, constantly fighting conventions ground into him from an early age, on the cusp between Victorian and the progressive Edwardian, his musical creativity exquisitely restrained rather than adventurous. Although his family encouraged his intellectual achievements and his music, young Dent was all along kept aware that such encouragement was limited to what was socially acceptable to its generation and its ambivalent attitude to music: as he wrote decades later, music was an 'accomplishment for ladies ... That a gentleman should become a real professional musician remained utterly unthinkable until almost the end of the Queen's reign.'[15] He also noted that 'the middle classes ... had not yet attained general artistic culture, far less the courage to enjoy it with the freedom that only comes of long experience of possession'.[16]

It was difficult enough for the youngest child to express himself when virtually everyone else around him was an authority figure, and although Dent's musical talent allowed him to escape and carve out his own special place at home and later at Eton, the act of escaping any perceived constraints became part of his make-up.

❧ ❧ ❧

In September 1884, at the age of eight, Edward was sent off to prep school, the intention being to follow his brothers in due course to Eton. His family chose very carefully for their youngest, sending him to Yarlett Hall School, near Stoke-on-Trent, not far from where his uncle the bishop Lovelace Stamer and his family were living at the time. Founded in 1873 by the Reverend Walter Earle, Yarlett Hall practised enlightened contemporary ideas for educating younger boys. Edward's cousin Arthur Stamer had been one of its first pupils before going on to Rugby School, and it was convenient to have family so nearby to look after their young cousin if necessary. Dent was very fond of his uncle Lovelace, and was grateful.

14 LH 23/08/1945.

15 E.J. Dent, 'Early Victorian Music', in G.M. Young, ed., *Early Victorian England 1830–1865* (London, 1934), pp. 249–64, here p. 253.

16 *Ibid.*, p. 252.

FIGURE 1. Eight-year-old Edward Dent at Bilton Grange.
By kind permission of the Governors of Bilton Grange School.

Yarlett Hall was one of many such schools founded out of the Clarendon Committee Report of 1864 concerning the education of younger boys, but Earle wanted his school to go well beyond the report's basic recommendations, and he widened the curriculum to include science and music.[17] In fact, music and sport would become as important as Classics had been, with proper facilities for both: boys were instructed in Latin and Greek, English, mathematics, music, singing, French, German (the German music master, Kühne, also taught German), drawing, gymnastics and 'drilling'. The new school was so successful that within a few years of its inception it was clear that expansion would be needed, so in 1887, Earle bought Bilton Grange, a magnificent Victorian fantasy of medieval splendour designed by Augustus Welby Pugin, the building only thirty years old and already abandoned, and the whole school, young Dent included, moved there.

Pugin's buildings were sturdy as well as eye-catching, and it is a testimony to his excellent materials that so much has survived 130 years of children running up and down its staircases and corridors. Until very recently, the theatre-cum-concert hall survived, where Bilton Grange pupils performed music and plays and recited poetry, and the foundations for Dent's lifelong love of the theatre and of performance came

17 W.S. Blackshaw, *'More Than a School to Us': A History of Bilton Grange* (Rugby, 1997), pp. 22ff.

from his happy Bilton experience; every vacation he performed his most recent pieces in the saloon back at Ribston. There was plenty of space for the manly outdoor activities considered essential for young Christian gentlemen's complete education, but it was not forced on them. At Bilton Grange, Edward, bespectacled, thin, gangly and uncoordinated, who loathed most organised sport, enjoyed swimming in the outdoor pool and walking around the extensive grounds, while his music was encouraged and indulged, his tastes expanded. He learnt German and French beside the standard Classics, and proved as natural a linguist as he was a musician. Like his father and brothers he was down to go to Eton; unlike them, he won a scholarship in 1890 which not only gave him a first taste of independence, but changed his rather distant relationship with his father. From being the indulged youngest child whose musical talents were viewed as charming but non-essential, young Dent had demonstrated serious achievement; moreover, he was paying for his expensive education himself through his abilities, a fact of which his father was proud and said so. John Dent died in 1895, knowing that his son had won his scholarship to King's College, Cambridge, as well.

❦ ❦ ❦

Founded in 1440, Eton's origins were based on music, education and religious practice. Its particular exclusivity has been written about endlessly, the barriers constructed over centuries not so much to keep outsiders out, as to reassure those inside of its own special identity, with its distinctive collars, top hats and tail-coats, its own impenetrable slang ('tugs', 'beaks', 'saps') which Dent was careful not to use outside school, and a massively complicated hierarchy starting with the division between most of the school, the Oppidans, who paid the fees and lived in various Houses around town, and the Collegers, the King's Scholars entitled to add K.S. after their names. As a Colleger or 'Tug', Dent wore the academic gown and a surplice for chapel which set him apart from the Oppidans, and he lived with the other Collegers in their privileged individual rooms in New Buildings, facing the School Yard, a far more beautiful aspect than its name implies, a world of their own 'at the heart of the school'.[18] For good or ill, such labels were an essential part of the Eton experience, an imposed identity to be lived up to: 'it is presumed that if you were a Colleger at Eton you must be quite impossibly clever'.[19] At the same time, '*Tugs* … were separated from Oppidans by the same gulf that lay between Professionals and Gentlemen in the world of sport … A Tug was something between a *scug* and a hireling chorister'.[20]

18 Robert Skidelsky, *John Maynard Keynes: Hopes Betrayed 1883–1920* (London, 1983), p. 77.

19 Esmé Wingfield-Stratford, *Before the Lamps Went Out* (London, 1945), p. 129, citing Major Christopher Stone. Probably the best account of Dent's Eton in c.1900 can be found in Shane Leslie's novel *The Oppidan* (London, 1922), dedicated to Dent's lifelong friend, E.S.P. Haynes.

20 Leslie, *The Oppidan*, p. 48.

Dent had very mixed feelings about his time at Eton, prefiguring the ambivalent attitude he would later develop towards most of the traditionalist institutions in his life, but mostly, the 'cerebral and unworldly'[21] life of a Colleger suited him perfectly: 'an intellectual elite thrust into the heart of a social elite'.[22] The divide went deep, but Eton was indulgent to its intellectual elite, with often gifted individual tutors quick to spot and nurture outstanding talents. As a 'sap', with his spectacles and his gangly frame, his music and his dislike of sport, Dent would have found Oppidan life with its elevation of the athletic over the intellectual very difficult, as his near-contemporary, the composer Roger Quilter did.[23] As another distinguished Old Etonian later wrote with some personal bitterness: 'if I had any voice in choosing what house to enter a boy for, my instinct would be to find out which were known to turn out the highest proportion of athletic luminaries, and avoid them like the plague', even calling some of the Eton Houses in his day 'forcing houses of virile toughness that are so essential a part of the Fascist and Nazi educational technique.'[24] A few years later in *Peter Pan*, J.M. Barrie made his villainous Captain Hook an Old Etonian. But even cocooned in College, for a time Dent felt keenly his own comparative ignorance and social naïvety:

> My whole life was perpetually hampered – and is still – by the total absence of intellectual stimulus in my youth: also by the fact that I was a solitary child, always expected somehow to know what was 'the right thing' instinctively, whereas most children learn that, probably without being much aware of it, from brothers & sisters a year or two older. I felt all this dreadfully when I went to Eton and most boys of my own age who knew such lots of things – not necessarily Latin & Greek – that I did not: and later in life, undergraduates & others who had been trained sensibly in the method of working and making the best use of time & materials.[25]

It took time before the gawky, uncomfortable adolescent managed to make a place for himself through his musical talents. At public school, daily survival and sanity often depended on separating the private from the public self, a lesson Dent quickly learnt; outward conformity and appearances were well developed in his Eton years, while his conspicuous achievements, the concerts and compositions, established an acceptable public persona, distinctive enough to stop the bullies. His music, whether physically up in the organ-loft or mentally in his composing, became an escape from most hateful daily pressures, while his own experience made him sensitive to the similar plight of younger pupils, especially E.S.P. 'Ted' Haynes, another Colleger a year younger, who became one of his most intimate lifelong

21 Skidelsky, *John Maynard Keynes: Hopes Betrayed*, p. 77.

22 *Ibid.*, quoting Bernard Crick.

23 Roger Quilter (1877–1953) studied in Germany together with Balfour Gardiner, Percy Grainger and Cyril Scott. He and Dent seldom saw eye to eye, though they knew each other well enough.

24 Wingfield-Stratford, *Before the Lamps Went Out*, p. 121. Also Leslie, *The Oppidan*, p. 83, where young Peter says he would rather 'get the Newcastle than make a century at Lord's' and his friend 'looks at him for a moment as a Mohammedan looks at a Hindoo'.

25 LH 25/12/1940.

friends.[26] Dent's Etonian friends – Haynes, Frank Buckley, Sydney Waterlow, Dick Hart-Davis, George Cyril Armstrong, Jack Pollock – were mostly Collegers like himself.[27] Some like Armstrong and later, Francis Jekyll and John Maynard Keynes, were Newcastle Scholars, the official cream of the Eton intelligentsia, and Dent always gravitated towards the best, building his own trusted circles.[28] Throughout his life, he had few close relationships with his exact contemporaries; while he was very young he tended to worship older men, father and older brother figures, and as he got older, moving from Eton to Cambridge, his closest relationships were with younger men, along the acceptable contemporary Paterian lines of a Greek romantic friendship, a pattern which probably arose from having been for so long a younger brother or a young pupil himself in need of guidance. In any relationship, though, Dent always preferred to be the alpha cat. His early relationships were certainly affected by that early family dynamic, dominated by women at home and at school, the stiff but friendly Eton Dames he encountered there, Miss Dupuis or Miss Hackett, the college matron.[29]

In Dent's years there, Eton was learning how to accommodate and encourage its musical prodigies, and its most talented musicians were provided with excellent opportunities for the time, given practical help, concerts and public performances of their compositions to fond and influential audiences. Thirty years before, composer Sir Hubert Parry had been the pioneer,[30] taking his Oxford Bachelor of Music degree while still at Eton, and he was something of a role model for Dent, who later came to know him very well and to appreciate his struggle to become a composer in the teeth of strong family objections. In a school specialising in mathematics and Classics, Dent was lucky to find in the college organist, Charles Harford Lloyd, a teacher of sensitivity and genius, who encouraged his musical abilities and became a lifelong friend. He passed on to young Edward a love of compositional form, strict counterpoint and fugue, and laid the groundwork for his later facility in reading and

26 'His first year at Eton was unhappy; he was badly bullied. Though he no longer suffered physically after his father had taught him to box, the experience left him with a recurrent conviction that every man's hand was against him, a conviction that welled up in him at times of strain or despondency and embittered his generous struggle for liberty in many fields.' Renée Haynes on her father E.S.P. Haynes, in *The Lawyer: A Conversation Piece Selected from the Lawyer's Notebooks and other writings by E.S.P. Haynes 1877–1949* (London, 1951), p. xiii.

27 Sir Sydney Philip Perigal Waterlow (1878–1944) diplomat and cousin of Elizabeth von Arnim, author of *Elizabeth and her German Garden* (1898). As a young man, before his first marriage, he was one of Dent's first serious loves. For more on him and Dent's other Etonian friends, see later chapters.

28 In their very different ways, younger men Keynes and Jekyll both became close lifelong friends (see later chapters passim).

29 Eton Dames were women who assisted the Heads of the various Houses, looking after the boys – Oppidans – in their charge.

30 Sir Charles Hubert Hastings Parry, 1st Baronet (1848–1918), contributor to *Grove's Dictionary of Music and Musicians*, succeeding Grove as Director of the Royal College of Music, then Professor of Music at Oxford. Parry would be one of Dent's examiners when he later applied to King's College, Cambridge, for the first ever Fellowship awarded for academic music.

understanding scores, but it was his friendship that Dent valued far more deeply. In his tribute to Lloyd years later, Dent referred to his self-effacing and kindly style: 'a gentle and steady flame may cast no brilliant beam, but many torches can be kindled at it … It is almost impossible for a man who concentrates his chief energies on composition to be a good teacher. For teaching, to be of any value, requires as much concentration as composition, and concentration not upon oneself, but upon one's pupils.'[31]

Dent was one of the first Etonians to help turn music from a gentleman's pastime into a profession, following in the wake of the pianist–composer prodigy Donald Tovey, a year older, the son of an Eton master. Roger Quilter, George Butterworth, F.S. Kelly soon followed.[32] In his day Parry had been forced to go to nearby St George's Chapel, Windsor, for his music lessons, and Dent went to the current Royal Organist there, the Master of the Queen's Music, Sir Walter Parratt, who became another intensely close friend and mentor.[33]

Dent's musical horizons quickly began to expand, with concerts at Eton and in London, where he could stay with the Kekewich family, distant cousins, very musical, very warm and friendly.[34] For four years he practised (his main instruments were the organ and the pianoforte, but he also played the violin and cello, and later the tympani),[35] played, went to concerts, saw his first operas, met musical people, read and composed, living in his music as much as possible while thinking about his future. For most aspiring British composers, Germany was the place to study: Parry, Stanford, most of the younger men of Dent's generation like Tovey and Quilter, all went to Germany, beside Ethel Smyth and Frederick Delius, with Brahms the generational model. To Dent's wicked delight, Tovey would later label Stanford's music as 'Brahms-and-water', and his own later rejection of that well-trodden route was considered and deliberate rather than simply rebellious. For a time he loved German music: his first great musical excursion was with an Eton party to Bayreuth in 1894, and for several years Wagner was a driving passion, Bayreuth a place of regular pilgrimage.

A concomitant growing love of poetry and words began to influence his music; he experimented with settings of poems, and over the next few years he set to

31 E.J. Dent, 'The Personality of a Teacher: In Memoriam Charles Harford Lloyd (1849–1919)' in *The Athenaeum*, vol. 31 (31 October 1919), pp. 1128–9.

32 Sir Donald Francis Tovey (1875–1940), composer, pianist, musicologist; George S.K. Butterworth (1885–1916), composer; F.S. Kelly (1881–1916), composer, pianist. Both Kelly and Butterworth became friends of Dent's and were killed in the First World War. See below, Chapter 8.

33 Sir Walter Parratt KCVO (1841–1924), Master of the Queen's Music, Heather Professor of Music at Oxford, President of the Royal College of Organists. Dent kept in touch with him all his life, often visiting.

34 Sir Arthur Kekewich (1832–1907), Judge in Chancery, married Marianne Freshfield and had two very musical daughters Dent would copy music and compose for.

35 Dent always used the more old-fashioned terms 'pianoforte' and, for a long time, 'violoncello'.

music Shelley, Byron, de Musset, Blake and William Watson.[36] His Overture in C minor (1895) was played for Queen Victoria at Osborne House, mostly through Sir Walter's influence, significant public recognition and heady stuff for a young man. Lloyd sent a copy of the score to Parry, whose warm response was not shown to Dent until decades later:

> I have been reading this distinguished Overture as well as the noise of singing and pianoforte lessons would allow, and am very glad to see such excellent work coming from the dear old school. It really is quite a remarkable piece of work from a boy. Nearly all of it will be quite effective, some of it very much so, and the ideas are definite and broad and excellently expressed.[37]

Dent's Eton career finished in June 1895, with a performance of his Overture in C minor at the Royal College of Music.[38] When he left Eton what he missed the most were the people who had taken such a personal interest in him and his music, his feelings for Lloyd and for Parratt far stronger than simple pupil–teacher affection. For years he corresponded with them regularly, consulting them about his music, often visiting in the vacations. In retrospect Dent was grateful for his Eton experience and often went out of his way to help any Old Etonians who crossed his path, a rare sentimental gesture on his part.

The Dent men had generally gone to Trinity, but Dent fell in love with King's College, Cambridge, smaller, more intimate and very musical, not simply because it was the sister institution to Eton, with a Provost and similar chapel; 'the college that cared for poetry, music and drama'[39] was young Dent's considered, possibly rebellious, choice. When Dent took his 'Little-Go' in 1894,[40] it was no surprise that King's offered him a scholarship. Young Edward was part of the new wave at a revitalised King's which offered its undergraduates a wide range of official – Tripos – and unofficial 'fringe' subjects like music, and a remarkably convivial atmosphere. For the next fifty years it would be his home.

36 The only MSS to survive in KCA are his settings of Longfellow's 'Hymn to the Night' and Shelley's 'Music, when soft voices die'.

37 Parry to Lloyd, 11/02/1895. Copy by EJD.

38 Diary 10/06/1896.

39 Noel Annan, *The Dons: Mentors, Eccentrics and Geniuses* (London, 1999), p. 98.

40 'Little-Go' was the nickname for the 'Previous', an entrance examination for Cambridge; the 'Great-Go' a nickname for finals.

CHAPTER 2

The Bumptious Undergraduate 1895–1899

I have loved Cambridge because there I have had a home of my very own and friends to see me.[1]

King's stood for the Muses *en masse*. It was reported in other colleges to have celebrated a Bump Supper by marching around the College singing the chorus of a Greek play. Even if the story was only *ben trovato*, no one ... would have told it of any other college.[2]

Certainly no politics are more real than those of academic life, no loves deeper, no hatreds more burning, no principles more sacred.[3]

1895–1896

Dent's walk through the Gatehouse at King's College that October, 1895 was not simply a rite of passage, more the first such step in a lifetime of travels that afforded escape and the fresh, foreign ideas that stimulated his boundless curiosity. 'Life only really begins at university': Dent often quoted Bismarck's view, remembering the tall, gangly[4] younger self who had entered King's with such purpose and sense of liberation. The purpose was not the one for which he had been awarded his Classics scholarship of 80 pounds per annum,[5] but music; the liberation was from his loving family, who – especially his mother – continued to disapprove of

1 LH 29/08/1899.

2 G.M. Trevelyan, quoted in L.P. Wilkinson, *A Century of King's* (Cambridge, 1980), p. 36.

3 Isaiah Berlin (1909–1997), letter to Freya Stark, 12/06/1944, quoted in the *Independent*, 22/07/2009.

4 He was about 6 feet 2 inches (c.1.9 m) tall, according to people who knew him. In his diary Dent recorded his weight from time to time, from the weighing machines on railway station platforms. He seldom goes much over 10 stone (63.5 kg). On 06/06/1897 he was 9 stone 7 pounds (c.60 kg). He kept the family nickname 'Joe' for only a little longer. 'J. Dent' soon becomes 'E.J. Dent' in the KCMS records.

5 King's awarded 24 scholarships, running concurrently: 12 open; 12 for Etonians. Dent's was paid during his minority to his mother at 20 pounds each quarter-day and was meant to cover tuition, lecture fees, rent, Hall (for formal dining), kitchen, buttery, milk, gyp and bedmaker (college servants), shoe-black, laundress, electric light (where available) and bicycle store; also tax, matriculation and examination fees (12–13 pounds) to the university. King's College Accounts Books.

FIGURE 2. Edward Dent c.1900. Photograph taken by J. Palmer Clarke. By kind permission of the Provost and Fellows of King's College, Cambridge.

his stated career choice. But Dent was separated from Ribston by more than the 150 miles (240 km); the family nickname 'Joe' was quickly ditched, and his Eton 'speaking bags' sold to Sydney Waterlow. King's was his first real taste of adult freedom; with his King's scholarship even more than his Eton scholarship Dent could enjoy some sense of independence, though until his majority most of the bills would still be sent to his mother. 'Madame', as he referred to her, found such loose ends vexing, and for years Dent would be on the receiving end of her constant disapprobation:

> after lunch received a lengthy oration from mother – in which she abused the two dearest objects of my affections – music & Cambridge – however she was too much out of temper to be open to conviction by argument – so I could only sit & blink at her in silence ... A letter from Mother mostly about clothes ... A letter from Mother to prepare me for possibly meeting more Buxtons! ... A letter from Mother urgently requiring me to have dancing lessons.[6]

For hundreds of years King's had been an automatic stepping-stone from Eton,[7] but by Dent's time this free ride had almost disappeared. As a result of

6 Diary, December 1896.

7 After having been sacked from Eton, Oscar Browning had simply exercised his rights and taken up a Fellowship at King's. King's occupied a special place in the university: 'some

FIGURE 3. Gibbs Building, King's College, c.1898. By kind permission of the Provost and Fellows of King's College, Cambridge.

government-imposed reforms the college statues in 1861 opened King's scholarships to non-Etonians, and Augustus Austen Leigh, first as Tutor, later as Provost, seized the chance to change things, not only trebling the intake but establishing a new intellectual rigour.[8] In Dent's year there were only five Etonians, the remainder of the forty-two freshmen having come from other public schools beside a few from Germany and India.[9] In less than a generation King's had moved from being a repository for Old Etonians to being at the forefront of a new educational order, with a number of distinguished scholars and teachers in situ and a more broadly based, brighter undergraduate intake. In Dent's official subject, Classics, for example, there were Walter Headlam, J.E. Nixon, A.A. Tilley, Nathaniel Wedd and A.H. Cooke, Charles Waldstein (later changed to the less Germanic Walston) and M.R. James. But these men were equally distinguished in other fields, such as producing the Greek Play, or writing ghost stories, or researching and performing obscure Elizabethan madrigals.

peculiar privileges appertain to this College. The Provost has absolute authority within the precincts … and … its Undergraduates are exempt from the power of the Proctors and other University Officers within the limits of the College.' *Cambridge University Calendar 1902–03*, p. 763.

8 Augustus Austen Leigh (1840–1905), Provost 1889–1904; Jane Austen's great-nephew.

9 John J. Withers, *A Register of Admission to King's College Cambridge 1797–1925 …* (London, 1929), pp. 249–61.

Dent was in the first wave of that golden period up to the Great War, probably one of the most exciting times to be an undergraduate at Cambridge, with bright young minds casting off Victorian baggage, helped by gifted and sympathetic teachers. Personal relationships, from the relatively informal ones between Fellows and pupils to those within the hidden college hierarchies, were both the backbone of college life and a source of its constant frictions. For Dent's friend E.M. Forster,[10] who came up to King's two years later, 'it was the place where things were valued for what they were in themselves, not for what use you could make of them'.[11] For Dent, far more self-confident than Forster, it was simply where he most wanted to be, joining the King's College Musical Society (KCMS) and immediately being elected to its committee, joining the Cambridge University Musical Club (CUMC)[12] and the Cambridge University Musical Society (CUMS).[13] He was snatched up by A.H. 'Daddy' Mann, the college organist who also ran the college choir,[14] and within a month was playing daily on its organ, a temptingly magnificent instrument, dominating the chapel itself, its gold-plated pipes contrasting with the bare stone fan vaulting.[15]

The life of the intellect has many odd and unpredictable facets, and Dent's horizons were being expanded in a remarkably progressive and eclectic institution, one which encouraged its polymaths while allowing its eccentrics the chance to roam free. Victorian King's, 'a society more entertaining by its oddity than impressive by its gusto'[16] had all but disappeared, though the old order died hard, and the 'strange mastodons' were not replaced so much as morphed into the magnificently dotty intellectual, who would combine extraordinary scholarship with extravagant personal characteristics and behaviour. Some of its more outrageous and interesting remnants, like Oscar Browning,[17] persisted well into Dent's time there and were very important to him, not least as an object lesson in the complex nature of human achievement.

10 His lifelong friendship with Dent began with their joint serious love of music and soon, a love of Italy.

11 P.N. Furbank, *E.M. Forster: A Life. Volume One: The Growth of the Novelist (1879–1914)* (London, 1977), p. 49.

12 Founded 1889, 'for the study and practice of chamber music'. Frida Knight, *Cambridge Music* (Cambridge, 1980), p. 85; CUMC XVI.1.1 minute book.

13 Founded 1843.

14 A.H. Mann (1850–1929) built up the college choir and the choir school into a forerunner of what it is today. He also ran ambitious concerts and festivals, but was constantly blocked by his own uncertain status in college. He had no dining rights, was not allowed to use the library or Fellows' Garden, and wrote sad little notes to Oscar Browning, who often took pity on him. I am grateful to Timothy Day, currently writing a history of the choir school, for pointing this out: 'The tensions between Mann and Dent – and Stanford – were both social and musical.' The notes are in the Browning archive in KCA.

15 Nestled in its loft in the screen is a massive four-manual beast with 79 stops – the names themselves evocative and mysterious: 'Double Ophicleide', 'Nazard', 'Larigot' – pedals and pistons, used for twice-daily services in term-time.

16 John Saltmarsh, *King's College: A Short History* (Cambridge, 1958), p. 66.

17 As seen (note 7), Browning took up an automatic Fellowship at King's. He wrote several histories of the world, and later retreated to his elegant flat in Florence.

Browning was 'not a scholar or a thinker; his strength was that, in his sanguine way, he diffused a vision of glory'.[18] A snob of awesome, ridiculous dimensions, he could talk with perfect sincerity about 'the nicest emperor I ever met',[19] but whatever one might think of his many absurdities, he did oversee genuine reforms and inspired his students with a love for their subjects. Under his eye History was taught as a Tripos subject;[20] in 1891 he instituted the Day Training College which gave many impoverished young men a real chance in life, with an education and teaching qualifications. At Browning's instigation Dent taught music for several years at its premises in Warkworth Street,[21] giving him first-hand appreciation of how important music could be at the grassroots. When Dent later went off to Italy, thanks to Browning he spoke some Italian and was armed with essential introductions to a number of important people. In many ways Browning embodied the complex nature of the King's experience, with its mix of the personal and the institutional dynamic, the egregious and the inspirational. Soon Dent was captured, playing duets with him, singing with him, and discussing with him his impressive if dusty collection of books and musical scores, his love of Italy and Germany,[22] and Mozart. At a time when Mozart was considered to be a slight composer, Browning was a passionate collector and advocate of his music. He loved to tell people things; in many ways he was an inspiring, consummate teacher, exposing the many young men who passed one way and another through his hands to ideas and worlds beyond their immediate surroundings, but his acquaintance, though it could open doors, was by no means easy:

> The strangeness of the creation of such a man, so fine, so gross, so public-spirited, so mean, so intellectual, so dull, so great, so little, is a perfect mystery ... I cannot defend him and yet I admire him; I cannot respect him and yet I like him ... There is no theory of God which will explain the existence of a man like O.B.[23]

Dent was grateful, and proved to be a tenacious and loyal friend, even through the later years of decline and fall.

18 Furbank, *E.M. Forster: A Life. Volume One*, pp. 53–4.

19 Wingfield-Stratford, *Before the Lamps Went Out*, p. 153.

20 'Tripos', from the Latin, meaning 'a three-footed stool' on which the 'Father' in the philosophy school sat while disputing with the prospective Bachelor of Arts, whose responses were classed as First, Second or Third. The 'Tripos' usually consists of two exams, taken at the end of the first and third years. In Dent's day the range of Tripos subjects was only beginning to open up from Mathematics, Classics, Law and Natural Sciences, with History, and Modern and Medieval Languages among the most recent additions. How Music finally became accepted as a Tripos subject in 1948 is part of Dent's history.

21 Browning was also President and Honorary Treasurer of Footlights, President of the University Bicycle Club, and an officer of the Swimming Club, the Hockey Club, the Musical Club and the Liberal Club.

22 When preparing to conduct Brahms's *Requiem*, Dent borrowed a score from him, with the great scholar Otto Jahn's bookplate in it. Diary 24/04/1897.

23 A.C. Benson, *Diary*, ed. P. Lubbock (London, 1927), pp. 119–20.

Only an exclusive, separate and quirky institution like King's could allow such a paradoxical creature as Browning to flourish in its hothouse climate, and in these formative years while he was gradually discovering his own identity as musician and man, Dent learnt to seek out the 'queer' company as much as the musicians. Often, he discovered, they coincided; through such friendships he learnt to embrace and exploit his own otherness, preferring to operate through closed, self-defined societies. College life was by definition separate, a paradoxical world, descendant and close relative of the old enclosed monastic institutions, but also a tiny self-contained universe which opened up unimaginable possibilities to young men raised in stuffy late-Victorian parlours, especially if those parlours had been dominated by mothers, sisters and aunts, and long, decorous silences. Dent was glad to escape into such an intensely masculine society, with other intelligent young men living in close proximity, uncomplicated by any restricting or confusing female presence.[24]

The hothouse kept its doors open. King's undergraduates were expected to read for an Honours degree in one of the Tripos subjects, but anyone could attend lectures, and there were a number of 'fringe' subjects on offer, like Music or Tropical Medicine.[25] But much of the real intellectual stimulus came from being in daily contact with great minds from all disciplines, the local 'intellectual aristocracy':[26] local clans Darwins, Fletchers, Keynes; resident philosophers or scientists, G.E. Moore, Bertrand Russell or J.J. Thomson. When asked why his Cambridge college had more Nobel prizewinners than most countries, Max Perutz replied, 'Lunch'.[27] In college there were formal and informal societies, KCMS 'smokers' or Goldsworthy ('Goldie') Lowes Dickinson's discussion society, Browning's Monday Political Society, his Thursday Mozart evenings, his mad Sunday At Homes, J.E. Nixon's Saturday and Tuesday night glee-singing after Hall with Tintara wine and cigars; readings of ghost stories over sherry with 'Monty' James in his dark rooms. One gave papers on the meaning of life, sang recherché glees from tattered manuscripts, or simply entertained one's acquaintance with a late breakfast of buttered eggs delivered to one's rooms from the college kitchens. And most importantly and most unlike the outside world, no subject was ever considered unfit for serious discussion: sexuality, socialism, feminism. The Conversazione Society, aka The Apostles, was made up largely of men from King's and Trinity whose names are still familiar,[28]

24 The female equivalents were still confined to Newnham College or the even remoter Girton College. Although women could attend most lectures and sit exams, until 1948 they were not officially allowed to take Cambridge degrees. Married dons lived out of college, and would invite undergraduates to a family Sunday lunch, sometimes a treat and sometimes a trial for both parties.

25 See Annan, *The Dons*, pp. 110–11.

26 *Ibid.*, pp. 304–41.

27 He meant that college lunch afforded the chance to air ideas and problems with very bright people from different disciplines; you had to explain it to them and they often had a fresh take on what you were trying to do.

28 Oscar Browning, E.M. Forster, Clive Bell, Leonard Woolf, John Maynard Keynes, Lytton Strachey, Jack Sheppard, Rupert Brooke, *inter alia*. All friends and acquaintances of Dent's.

probably because of the intellectual boost they got from its clandestine meetings, the papers and the discussions. Fifty years later Dent wrote to another King's undergraduate, George Lascelles, Lord Harewood:

> Some people achieve eminence in life after having been at Public School and then going direct into the army, diplomacy or business, but in all those cases they miss (and it shows in their actions) the attitude of mind which comes only from the intellectual freedom of University life.[29]

Although he might have appeared perfect Apostles material, Dent was not asked to join; they probably realised that this was a man who did not join any society he wouldn't eventually have a good chance of running. Instead, he preferred having the working influence of a secretary rather than a president, and he had an instinct for where any real power lay, constructing his own power bases around the kind of personal friendships advocated by Lowes Dickinson.[30] Consciously or not, he was setting a pattern for the rest of his life, and the complicated hidden political waters to be navigated in and around Cambridge colleges would be the perfect training-ground for later pursuits.

In that freshman year Dent lived on the second floor of Fawcett's Building, now demolished, the site now mostly occupied by the south range of Chetwynd Court and the Keynes building. Since 1873, as a result of the educational reforms, an intensive building programme housed the growing numbers of students, although even in 1895 most of these 'modern' rooms lacked running water and electricity. The fastidious Browning, living in some opulence in Wilkins, would for years possess the only en suite in college, sometimes receiving visitors in his bath. Undergraduates and some of the Fellows could be seen on cold mornings sprinting for the baths or lavatories, and in his diary Dent recorded the kind of cold days seldom experienced now, with ice and snow and excruciating draughts rattling the windows. He would always hate the cold. But college rooms – often shared sitting-room, bedroom and gyp room (a basic kitchen) – were spacious enough to accommodate (in Dent's case) a piano, his violin and cello, piles of books and streams of friends calling by, while the college servants saw to most daily needs. At King's, music was considered so important to college life that everyone had to contribute 10 shillings towards KCMS. Dent was particularly frugal; in most of his first year he barely spent his scholarship allowance, which went on books, music and travel.

Cambridge at the turn of the twentieth century was still a Fen market town of some forty thousand inhabitants with a major university at its heart, its medieval streets, although grimy from coal smoke, still largely intact and alive, not yet improved by civic vandalism. Town and gown lived in close proximity and some mutual dependence; every day through the college gates came local bedmakers, boot-blacks, waiters and purveyors of milk, bread, wines and meats, deliverers of

29 Dent to Lord Harewood 17/07/1947.

30 Goldsworthy ('Goldie') Lowes Dickinson (1862–1932), philosopher, political thinker, pupil of Oscar Browning, Fellow of King's, member of the Apostles, friend and mentor to E.M. Forster, who wrote his biography. His ideas would probably have been explored more if his handwriting was not so illegible.

coals.[31] Apart from its lost railings outside King's College, King's Parade appeared much the same, but the shops then more functional, serving the daily needs of undergraduates and locals rather than tourists. Ryder & Amies on the corner is virtually unchanged in appearance; Colin Lunn's the tobacconist was at number 15 (Dent took up smoking cigarettes that year), Severs the printer at 10 (where Dent later lodged upstairs), Buol's Restaurant at number 17, 'the most recherché in the Town' where Dent ate and drank its rich chocolate with his friends after concerts. Cunningham the dentist was at number 2, an address Dent came to know all too well.[32] The traffic in the streets consisted mainly of horse-drawn trams, some traps and bicycles, including the familiar oversized tricycles of several King's dons. The railway station was over a mile from the centre of town, so bicycles were useful and popular. Or you could take a tram drawn by a 'tired' horse to the corner of the 'new' Catholic Church, where another would take you across and up the old London coaching road, Hobson's Conduit running alongside, into town. When another Old Etonian named Rolls brought his new motor-car into town in 1896 it was an event.[33] Dent himself was a great walker all his life; he was uncomfortable on a bicycle and never learnt to drive a car.

Against this backdrop of ordinary bustle wafted the gowns of the transient undergraduate population, around three thousand in 1895, like dark blue butterflies with lives on a different plane. Undergraduates kept to their colleges or their lodgings for most daily requirements, where it was easy to nip into Hall or to order one's breakfast, dinner or tea in one's rooms, waited on by the college servants (gyps), and scholars like Dent were entitled to college rooms. There was even a number of pampered cats in and around college, probably offspring of Browning's own fecund cat, who would leave her kittens mewing piteously, parked by the Fountain, to be taken in by anyone who could walk across the grass to rescue them. Of course they went to good homes; only Fellows were allowed to walk on the grass. Dent was fond of the grey kitten who lived in the Porters' Lodge, and would give it milk.[34] Nearby were establishments catering for visiting sisters, mothers or aunts, former coaching-houses like the Bull Hotel, the façade of which can still be made out between King's and St Catherine's colleges, or the Red Lion in medieval Petty Cury. The Union Society, then more like a gentleman's club, was another university gathering-place for food and conversation as well as its excellent library; many of Dent's letters were written on its stationery.

Town life remained mostly in the background, but common points of interest and engagement, dramatic and especially musical, were on the increase. Thanks to

31 Like most of his contemporaries Dent never recorded any dealings with servants, however much a part of his daily life they were, until he got his own housekeeper, the devoted Hills.

32 Sir George Humphrey, *Guide to Cambridge: The Town, University & Colleges* (Cambridge, 1895).

33 'It strikes me that London crossings will be rather more appalling when they are more common' Dent wrote in his diary, 01/12/1896. Rolls got a half-blue in cycling.

34 Diary 27/05/1896. Dent liked cats, and his diary is full of references to various cats he met, and at that time there were a lot of them in college.

the current Professor of Music, Charles Villiers Stanford,[35] CUMS had for some years accepted local players and singers of both sexes, while besides the informal local chamber music going on, a recent surge of interest in early keyboard instruments facilitated experimentation in restoration and playing technique. Otherwise the main places of convergence were at concerts given in the nearby Guildhall, the Victoria Assembly Rooms (now a Marks & Spencer) or at the Masonic Hall on Corn Exchange Street; or at the theatres: the Amateur Dramatic Club in Jesus Lane, the Georgian Festival Theatre in Barnwell and the Theatre Royal in St Andrew's Street, virtually rebuilt in January 1896 to become the New Theatre.[36] Over the next twenty-five years, Dent came to know it and its entrepreneurial manager W.B. Redfern very well. Redfern's was one of the most successful ever Town–Gown collaborations: the staging of the first of the triennial Greek Plays in 1882 at his theatre led to a revision of the University Statutes, allowing undergraduates to attend the theatre, then considered to have a corrupting influence on youth, and by Dent's day major travelling companies like Carl Rosa Opera or D'Oyly Carte, or William Poel's Elizabethan Stage Society made prolonged visits to town, impacting strongly on the locals. The standards of the University Amateur Dramatic Club went up, and eventually the time was ripe for even more radical student drama in the shape of the Marlowe Dramatic Society in 1907[37] and Dent's own benchmark production of *The Magic Flute* in 1911.

❧ ❧ ❧

> I begin to think that no knowledge is worth having unless it is easily acquired – Thus – Latin, French, Italian & German (& English) gave me no difficulty – & are of the greatest use to me – Greek is utterly useless, & I always hated learning it from the very first.[38]

Throughout his three years, Dent's Classics tutors at King's[39] had their famously tolerant natures stretched to the limit. Dent had made it abundantly clear from the outset that his Classics scholarship was useful only to fund his musical activities; in the first instance, the Bachelor of Music exams, as soon as he was eligible to sit them. His tutorials with Cooke he referred to as 'impending torture', all his work done in haste at the last possible moment: 'I struggled alternately in the afternoon with Chopin's Preludes & Hexameters'.[40] On the whole his tutors seem to have accepted this intransigence with charm and a sense of humour, as long as he kept up a reasonable front. Only in his third year did he get a serious caveat, threatening to

35 See 'Dramatis Personae'. Hugely influential on Dent's generation of musicians. See below.

36 Knight, *Cambridge Music*, pp. 77–8.

37 Tim Cribb, *Bloomsbury & British Theatre: The Marlowe Story* (Cambridge, 2007), p. 8.

38 LH 14/10/1899.

39 A.H. Cooke, Walter Headlam and Nathaniel Wedd.

40 Diary 15/05/1896.

cut off his scholarship, while three years of Classics does not appear to have harmed or hindered him; the extra fees involved were not an issue, and the enforced delay might even have been beneficial. At nineteen, Dent was insufferably cocky.

So he attended Stanford's lectures, had composition lessons with Charles Wood at Gonville & Caius College and singing lessons from W.H. Wing.[41] Eventually, a piano in his rooms facilitated personal music-making. At first the organ had seemed a natural step, and for a few years Dent continued to enjoy his organ-playing before he dropped it altogether. Always attuned to any institutional dynamics, he quickly recognised the limitations of such a regular duty, especially as an agnostic, and certainly did not wish to be for ever labelled as an 'organist'. Yet the overall experience was extremely valuable, both musically and in terms of the daily discipline demanded from a chapel choir, beside his weekly stints conducting and singing with Mann's choir, which met at the nearby Leys School.

He could blithely ignore his family's continuing social objections, but Dent's ambition to become a 'musician' was both high-minded and inchoate, since as yet he had no real idea of what it meant, nor that it might prove more difficult than he imagined. For some years, swaddled in his assumptions, Dent entertained no doubts whatever that he was going to be a composer, preferably one like his idol Stanford, both composer and current Professor. Although new colleges of music were up and running, trained musicians were mostly limited to orchestras, or playing the organ in a local church or college, or teaching music privately or at a public school, none of which was really considered professional, much less 'gentlemanly' activity. The very terms 'musical' and 'musician' were already coded references to sexual ambiguity.[42] 'Musicology' did not exist as a subject or as a word until c.1926, while the academic study of music, what the Germans already called *Musikwissenschaft*, was still too foreign a concept. Years later, when he was himself Professor of Music at Cambridge, Dent wrote an article[43] explaining the differences between the continental and the English systems of academic music, a potted history, in effect, of the university teaching of music in Britain:

> The older generation of professional musicians assumed that the normal career of a musical graduate began with his being a chorister at some cathedral; if he showed talent he would be instructed in musical theory by the organist, and might perhaps attend a professional school of music such as the Royal Academy. He might then present himself at Oxford or Cambridge for a degree and with those letters after his name obtain a good post as a cathedral organist himself ... Thirty-five years ago most Bachelors of Music hoped to become cathedral organists, and the examination was more or less planned with a church career in view.[44]

41 For Charles Wood, see below, note 60. W.H. Wing BA advertised in the *Cambridge Review*, and gave lessons on Wednesdays and Thursday at 11 Green Street.

42 Philip Brett, 'Are You Musical?', MT, vol. 135 (1994), pp. 370–76.

43 E.J. Dent, 'The Scientific Study of Music in England', *Acta Musicologica*, vol. 2 (1930), pp. 83–92. Dent's purpose at the time was to puff English music to the sceptical continentals in order to get them to agree to having two major international congresses in England.

44 *Ibid.*, p. 88.

Although it would not be included in the Tripos exams until 1948, Music had actually been a university subject at Cambridge since 1463,[45] and, from the sixteenth century onwards, candidates for the degree of B Mus[46] were asked to submit an original composition. When in 1875 Stanford had returned to Cambridge from his studies in Germany, he found Music in a sorry state. With characteristic energy he set about changing all that, presenting to the Senate a set of recommendations which attempted to address in practical ways the contemporary British prejudice against Music as an academic subject: 'At the heart of Stanford's proposals was the principle that music should no longer languish as a "second class" subject in comparison with other academic disciplines.'[47] In March 1892, the Board of Studies attached a condition of residence to the B Mus degree, enhancing its status, so musicians coming from the Cambridge stable would be highly educated indeed, and holding the equivalent of an MA. Cynics saw it simply as a safety measure; aspiring musicians like young Dent, a nuisance, since most prospective B Mus students had first to do their Tripos in another subject.

Stanford himself personified the 'European tradition of being a performer, composer, conductor and pedagogue',[48] but from 1893 until his death in 1924, although he was still Professor, Stanford no longer actually lived in Cambridge but in London, and it was easy to forget how in his early days Stanford had revolutionised Cambridge music. His own German training made him far less parochial in outlook than many English musicians, and the Cambridge music scene benefited. Thanks to Stanford, Cambridge enjoyed regular visits from the Joachim Quartet and other musicians of international stature; for the CUMS Jubilee in 1893 he even managed to entice Max Bruch, Tchaikovsky, Saint-Saëns and Boïto to Cambridge. He completely rejuvenated the torpid CUMS, encouraging women to join it, thereby enormously expanding its repertoire:

> he probably did more for music in Cambridge University than any other single man; he had the gift of kindling enthusiasm, and with his backing many small Cambridge groups were formed for promoting chamber music of a semi-professional nature.[49]

Stanford's visions of a national, state-funded opera, of a 'national musical infrastructure',[50] and his teaching methods, 'hugely influential in the formation of the typical Anglo-Saxon style of musical degree, in which the notions of musica theoretica and musica practica were intended to exist side by side',[51] would be taken up by Dent and others, but it would be decades before any tangible and public results were

45 Knight, *Cambridge Music*, p. 1.

46 Although Dent usually referred to it as the 'Mus. Bac.', the more common form, 'B Mus' will be used here.

47 Jeremy Dibble, *Charles Villiers Stanford* (Oxford, 2002), pp. 246–7.

48 Paul Rodmell, *Charles Villiers Stanford* (Farnham, 2002), p. 168.

49 Knight, *Cambridge Music*, p. 83.

50 Dibble, *Charles Villiers Stanford*, p. 133.

51 *Ibid.*, p. 462.

seen. His lectures, although often poorly attended, were brilliant, illustrated with live musical examples – string quartets, piano, voice or even full orchestra.[52] Funding these would be a source of acrimonious debate until a new age of recorded music removed the problem. Famously difficult (according to a contemporary Grove's, 'the most disliked man in England'), Stanford had a fearsome temper and 'he loved to snub a pupil'.[53] Dent, in his undergraduate years often caught between Stanford and Mann, observed that 'the older academics … were in constant fear of having a row with him; but in view of the immense distinction he conferred on the university they put up with occasional outbursts'.[54] Dent certainly did, and would say in retrospect that Stanford was 'always right',[55] had pointed him again and again in the right direction. 'I am always trying to pass on to my composition pupils what he taught me, and I know that the immense respect in which Music … is now held by the Council of the Senate and similar authorities … is all due to Stanford's struggles in the face of opposition long ago.'[56] The many entries about Stanford in Dent's diary during these undergraduate years express mostly affectionate awe and some amusement. 'S. was most agreeable & rather amusing … I was rather tickled when after telling a story of some very notoriously rude man, he turned to us [Hugh Allen and Dent] & said, "I wonder who is the rudest man in the University now?".'[57] Dent's later friend Ralph Vaughan Williams (at Trinity College in 1892–95) read History and had to endure at the same time the most withering kind of criticism from both Stanford ('Damnably ugly, me bhoy; why do you write such things?')[58] and from Charles Wood, who coached him for his B Mus but said he held out 'no hope for him as composer'.[59]

By the time Dent came up, thanks largely to Stanford's groundwork over the previous twenty years, he was in solid if mostly unadventurous musical company: Charles Wood, Edward Naylor, Hugh Allen, Walford Davies, Cyril Rootham, Alan Gray, Nicholas Gatty as well as Vaughan Williams were still around.[60] But the status

52 *Ibid.*, pp. 208–9.

53 J.B. Trend, 'Dent', quoting Dent, in *The Score*, no. 22 (1958), pp. 49–55. Dent went on: 'He said I should be better at translating operas than at composition, and I have been.' Cf. Diary 24/05/1899.

54 Knight, *Cambridge Music*, p. 84.

55 Trend, 'Dent', quoting Dent.

56 Dent to singer Harry Plunket Greene, quoted in Rodmell, *Charles Villiers Stanford*, pp. 334–5.

57 Diary 29/05/1897.

58 Knight, *Cambridge Music*, p. 84.

59 *Ibid.*

60 Charles Wood (1866–1926), Irish composer, University Lecturer in harmony and counterpoint; just before his death was appointed Professor of Music after Stanford. Edward Woodall Naylor (1867–1934), born in Scarborough, organist of Emmanuel College, composer. Cyril Rootham (1875–1938), read Classics, took his B Mus in 1900, came back to St John's College as organist, then Fellow. Nicholas Comyn Gatty (1874–1946), friend of Vaughan Williams, composer of operas which Dent supported but which never had more than moderate success. Dent came to know the extended family well.

of local musicians varied from college to college, with little central authority apart from the Musical Board which met each term to set exams and lectures. Stanford's was a professorial fellowship, and had he not been Professor of Music, it is impossible to say whether Trinity would have elected him a Fellow; his relationship with the college and indeed the university was always stormy. At Gonville & Caius, Charles Wood was made far more welcome, and although Professor of Harmony at the Royal College of Music at the same time, he quickly became part of the college fabric, so much so that in 1894 the college took the unprecedented step of electing him a Fellow, an event reported with approval in the *Cambridge Review*,[61] and the source of much self-congratulation on the part of Caius.

Dent's music in that first year was joyful and liberating; for a while he was entirely enraptured. For one thing, he was simply too busy to think about the future, working around and with numerous smaller, informal musical circles where the odd, the difficult and the recherché would be played and discussed. Performance, part of Stanford's credo, characterised the lively Cambridge music scene, and performance in all its aspects would underpin Dent's later work and his scholarly principles.[62] Besides showing his compositions to Wood or Stanford, and attending Stanford's Saturday morning lectures on late Beethoven quartets, for example, Dent threw himself into playing music, devouring scores as if they were popular novels, singing and conducting, copying more scores and parts borrowed from the Fitzwilliam Museum.[63] Music was taken very seriously in Cambridge life, one of the points where town and gown worked in harness, at concerts and informal playing.

At King's, Dent was being given the languages of Italian and English madrigals from J.E. Nixon, Mozart from Browning, and the knowledge that comes from endless copying of music for playing at CUMC or CUMS. At Nixon's, for example, there would be familiar glees and madrigals, unaccompanied, 'Come live with me and be my love' beside unfamiliar English and Italian ones Nixon had dug up himself, 'Perfida Chlori' or 'Underneath the Myrtle Tree'.[64] Even at Browning's, with its thick, overheated fug and couples fondling in the window-seats, there was some musical education, from Browning's two pianos, an eclectic collection of instruments and the notorious 'obeophones',[65] besides the fat man himself singing in his wobbly

61 'Mr Charles Wood's election to a Fellowship at Caius College is a departure of uncommon interest, as being the first occasion on which a musician has been thus honoured by an English University … It is to be hoped that this enlightened proceeding on the part of Caius College may be the prelude to some more important departures in the direction of developing musical study in the Universities.'

62 This is still the case at Cambridge. Students at music colleges are often heard to complain that Cambridge students, in comparison, get so much more performance experience and thereby intense practical experience of repertoire.

63 Music was then kept in the old university library, now the library of Gonville & Caius, and in the Fitzwilliam Museum.

64 Diary 26/10/1896.

65 'mechanical miniature organs … [which made] a series of whines and groans' and were used to play the wind parts in Mozart symphonies, the rest being bashed out on the pianos. Browning had four of these: 'the noise … drove his neighbours nearly mad'. Ian Anstruther, *Oscar Browning* (London, 1983), pp. 55–6.

tenor 'La ci darem la mano' or 'The Baby on the Shore'. But Mozart was played and discussed seriously when he was still considered to be a composer of slight, pretty music. Through his music, his conducting, playing and eventually lecturing, Dent got to know local people outside his chosen discipline and to explore the dynamics of such partnerships, making friends with the local musical academic families like the Fletchers, the Allbutts, the Darwins, the Stewarts, the Comptons and the Mollisons. Later, there were the sociable musical circles centred around Francis Jenkinson the University Librarian and his wife Daisy, also keen on Mozart and early keyboard music, then only just re-emerging from obscurity.[66] Dent played chamber music at the Darwins' or the Gaskoins' soirées;[67] duets with friends or the various college organists like Alan Gray at Trinity and especially Hugh Allen at Christ's College.[68] In his freshman year, when Dent's musical life was a massive jigsaw puzzle, pleasant enough to keep him occupied, but with the true full picture still far from clear, he was grounded by two local musical institutions, the Cambridge University Musical Society (CUMS) and the Cambridge University Musical Club (CUMC).

CUMC met informally several times a week at 5 St Mary's Passage[69] to play chamber music and to try out new compositions from students and anything new its keen members wished to hear played. Members could borrow books and scores from its well-stocked library, or practise on its pianos. On Saturday nights in term the members, mostly students but with a number of regular older devotees, would give chamber concerts, often followed by sessions of less elevated singing. One of its founders, Sedley Taylor,[70] a jovial, elderly Trinity don fond of good food and rich stories, who had written serious books on music, became a close friend of Dent's, and was especially good at late-night comic turns, such as his parody of Sullivan's 'The Lost Chord', 'The Lost Ball':[71] 'I never saw such a grotesquely enthusiastic player as he is – he kept me in fits of laughter.'[72] Over the next twenty years Dent spent a great deal of his time at the CUMC premises, organising the library, copying music, rehearsing for the concerts, his experience

66 Francis Jenkinson (1853–1923), University Librarian from 1889, married Daisy Stewart, a keen harpsichordist whose regular Mozart evenings were a source of pain and pleasure to Dent.

67 The Darwins, especially the family of George Darwin, son of Charles, lived at Newnham Grange; their daughter Gwen, later Raverat, who wrote *Period Piece*, played the flute. The whole extended family were close friends of Dent's. Mrs C.J.B. Gaskoin, wife of the medieval historian, was a keen and sometimes overpowering musical hostess.

68 Alan Gray (1855–1935), from 1892, organist at Trinity College, composer. For Hugh Allen, see 'Dramatis Personae'.

69 Later moving to Downing Place (now a language centre). Dent was elected a member on 20 April 1897. The subscription was a guinea. CUMC XVI.1.1 minute book.

70 Sedley Taylor (1834–1920). As seen in the Introduction, Dent wrote his obituary in MT (1 May 1920). He was famously described by the economist Alfred Marshall as 'that owl in the ivy-bush', his spectacles peering above his thick beard.

71 Knight, *Cambridge Music*, p. 85.

72 Diary 20/10/1896.

there invaluable, experimenting with new or unfamiliar music and discovering the attractions of serious chamber music.

CUMS under Stanford's aegis had twice-weekly rehearsals, mostly taken by Hugh Allen, for orchestral and larger choral works to be practised and performed at the end of term. Its membership included any good local musicians, often semi-professionals, like its excellent leader Haydn Inwards, a tradition which lasts to the present day. There was no large concert hall, so rehearsals were often 'relegated to a small subterranean chamber'[73] or held in the chemistry labs, with residual smells from experiments and formulae scrawled on the boards. Dent sang bass and baritone in the CUMS chorus and soon would conduct rehearsals and play 'drums', becoming an accomplished tympanist.

By the end of his second (Lent) term in 1896, the scope of Dent's musical activities had become so overwhelming that he felt the need to keep a record of it all. 'The difficulty I have just found in putting a date to an early sketch of mine for an organ sonata has made me resolve to start a diary – in true Wilkie Collins style.'[74] Dent's is not one of the great diaries – he later labelled it 'childish' – but its fascination stems from an intimate and personal view of distant events. Over the next twenty-six years the diary would unevenly record daily doings, detailed accounts of plays and concerts he had been to, books he was reading, correspondence and travels and long walks, execrable jokes he had been told by Sedley Taylor or Sydney Waterlow or Ted Haynes. Soon he began using it to record details of the performances he was reviewing or as notes for his books and articles. But it has few passages of reflection; obvious omissions are often as interesting as the entries, while any dramas are mostly those manufactured by Dent himself. Some manner of eventual publication was evidently at the back of his mind, since the diary is annotated throughout in pencil by Dent, probably at a much later date. Although diaries kept by Dent's contemporaries – A.C. Benson or E.M. Forster – often did use the medium to express in private what could not be said in public,[75] this is not generally the case with Dent. At first he shows himself to be a self-conscious diarist, naïvely proud enough of his clever observations to allow selected friends a glimpse at its contents; like Benson's, Dent's diary in the first two years was 'a sort of personal indulgence', for his own benefit in the first instance, but with an eye out for posterity. Unlike Benson, Dent did not seem to feel the need for much private anatomising. He was a remarkably self-confident young man, and even while he is recording some source of anxiety – in these years his first serious sexual yearnings and his concerns about his future as a composer – it feels more like consciously restrained note-taking for future reference than spontaneous burst of feeling.

By this time Dent had more than an idea of his own sexual leanings, and more importantly that his homosexuality was probably not of the usual transient

73 Diary 15/10/1896.

74 Diary 13/05/1896.

75 Examples in KCA include diaries kept by E.M. Forster, Goldsworthy Lowes Dickinson and R.S. Moorsom. A.C. Benson's diary, he himself declared, was 'to get some of the venom out of my system'. David Newsome, *On the Edge of Paradise: A.C. Benson, Diarist* (London, 1980), p. 2.

public-school type, nor the often anguished versions which throve in 'homosocial' places like Oxbridge colleges (of which both Dickinson and Browning were different examples). The trial of Oscar Wilde barely a year before had made a terrible impact on the fragile beginnings of a more tolerant attitude to same-sex love, and the repercussions of private indiscretion being made public disgrace through sexual witch-hunts or blackmail made a lot of normally sensible people very nervous. There are very few indiscreet passages in Dent's diary, possibly because there was little need for such private outpourings in the liberal atmosphere of King's, but Dent himself was naturally discreet. He loved gossip and secrets, and at the heart of everything he did were strong personal relationships which fostered personal loyalties and discretion.

The diaries for 1896–97 are far more detailed than the later ones. With a degree of archness – there are several asides coyly addressed to 'one's biographer'[76] – Dent diligently recorded his daily chapel duties, nearly every person he had to tea, dinner or breakfast, with whom he played 'Russian chopsticks', his impressions of them, the descriptions rarely going beyond 'most amicable' or 'attractive', and showing occasional flashes of what would become his trademark sharp tongue: 'thence to the Club – a very delightful evening, though Capstick's horn solo rather suggested a dyspeptic cow'. He was a natural observer of any scene, and, as Hermione Lee noted in her biography of an even keener observer, Virginia Woolf, egotism and observation are always related.[77] But most of it is interesting simply because ordinary, and, in Dent's young, self-conscious voice, a real picture emerges of his daily college life.

> Saturday May 30, 1896. I succeeded in shaving without bloodshed this morning – a comparatively rare occurrence I am afraid! More concerto – though the result seems very little indeed … I wrote to Sir Walter [Parratt]. Coffee with Franklin – thence to the Club, where I played for Bate & heard the first movements of the Septett. Capstick was quite good – even in the trio of the minuet – it was altogether a very creditable performance. O.B. [Browning] came in for it, but was rather objectionable, sprawling in the biggest armchair and talking & beating time with his feet. Johnson made me rather jealous by going to Buol's with Gatty afterwards – I was not asked to join them.

> Thursday June 4, 1896. Mann at 9.30. I practised on till 11.30. When I came in I found Curtis had brought me 'Quaff with me the purple wine' by Shield to score for strings for the A.D.C. [Amateur Dramatic Club] but he took it away about 1.30. C.U.M.S. at 2.30. Allen more outrageous than ever – We muddled along in the usual style … letter from Mother at Cromer … in the midst of swarms of Gurneys & Buxtons. Chapel at 5 … Mann's Choir … a good practice; Mann very much pleased. I strolled around the Backs with Champion … half an hour afterwards – then he went to bed and I to Douglas, with whom I found Whitworth … (left at 11) after which I strummed Brahms Intermezzi.

Dent was also an indefatigable walker, and his diaries are full of details of his walks, which he enjoyed partly for the company and gossip, partly for exercise as relief from long hours spent copying, playing or trying to compose music, a chance

76 Diary 31/01/1897.

77 Hermione Lee, *Virginia Woolf* (London, 1997), pp. 5–7.

to think. With his Old Etonian friend Cyril Armstrong, he did the 'Grantchester Grind', a pleasant mile through the fields along the river out to Grantchester via Newnham, or a walk in the opposite direction, down along the river to Chesterton and the meadows beyond, 3 miles up to Bait's Bite lock. In a few years he would tramp out alone across the Italian Apennines, 30 miles (48 km) or more in a day. 'To Armstrong ... tea – very weak – in a large cup, with much sugar, and most delicious bread & butter, after which we went out ... We did not converse much, but I meditated again on the concerto with some success I hope.'[78]

To some extent Dent is showing off, performing for a later self to consider; he obviously felt it important to keep up regular diary entries, although it is clear that some entries are being made a day or two down the line. Behind it all is a need to view himself from a distance while exercising control over events, developing what later became his characteristic, ambiguous 'serpentine' style to express what could not be made public. While his musical education was being conducted at several levels, Dent's worldly education was proceeding along loosely similar lines, much of it recorded in his diary, the threads often interwoven and revealing his current preoccupations. Everything Dent did was interconnected, and the application and discipline he shows in keeping his daily diary made it easier when in 1898 he began to write on a regular basis for the *Cambridge Review*. His meticulous comments on every chapel service or club concert, references to his battered pewter coffee-pot, or the increasing difficulties he was finding with his composing not only depict his everyday concerns, but provided him with much useful practice at expressing himself clearly on paper. Writing rather than composing music would probably be his most important skill, what earned him a living in lean times, carried him over the uncertain times, and would in the end be one of the more tangible reasons he is remembered at all.

He loved being in the thick of a group – preferring 'we' to 'I' – and while his easy self-assurance and talents secured his social success, social intercourse was not always straightforward. Possibly all the socialising and music-making kept any real intimacy at bay while he could sort out what it was he really wanted from some of his friends, although as any musician knows, playing chamber music is in itself an intensely intimate experience. For several years yet Dent would be frustrated by his own sexual ignorance and inexperience, and ignorance was anathema. Browning trumpeted his belief in 'love as a force in the classroom', his biographer remarking on the personal rationalisation behind that professed belief: 'Any homosexual tendencies which he may have enjoyed in secret previously were suddenly given a code of practice which exactly suited his personal demands.'[79] But Dent was young and fastidious enough to find Browning's conspicuous example distasteful if not downright repellant,[80] while the thought of having his own deepest personal feelings exposed appalled him.

78 Diary 22/05/1896.

79 Anstruther, *Oscar Browning, pp. 55–6*

80 A few years later Lytton Strachey recorded in his letters some of Browning's 'smutty' stories, which even he – who loved shocking the prudish – found distasteful. *The Letters of Lytton Strachey*, p. 52.

So for the time being he retreated into the various accepted contemporary takes on homosexual attraction, the version of 'Greek' love which made a kind of religion of intense male friendships. Under this careful umbrella, attraction to handsome boys was tolerable as long as it remained 'pure' and chaste, and Dent was still young enough to be self-deluding about his motives while intelligent enough to know better, a dilemma of the sort his friend E.M. Forster later portrayed in *Maurice*. He read *Marius the Epicurean*, Walter Pater's hugely popular version of 'Greek' love, and began to read some of the 'Uranian' poets, including their spiritual grandfather, Walt Whitman. Later, he read Havelock Ellis and become friends with Edward Carpenter, one of the few contemporaries able to write openly about homosexuality and keep alive the bid for a more open-minded attitude.[81] Post-Wildean fears notwithstanding, 'the usual public-school sodomy' had been the experience of most of Dent's contemporaries, as Dent's younger friend Francis Toye makes clear in his own autobiography. But even in 1950, more than fifty years later, Toye still felt the need for disingenuousness when putting any experience of homosexuality into print; until 1967 it was still illegal:

> a conspiracy of silence and prudery has led to a great deal of mendacity about the whole thing, from total denial to ridiculous exaggeration. Public-school homosexuality, in ninety cases out of a hundred, dies a natural death when school days are over ... it is just an insidious and unpleasant habit, somewhat akin to the wetting of beds by babies, which, when discovered, must be severely punished to ensure discontinuance.[82]

Scattered throughout Dent's diary entries of 1896, especially in the last week of Easter term, are the kinds of wistful yearnings which would probably have astonished those who thought they knew him: 'I woke early & looked out my window about 4.30. There was a lovely light on the New Buildings, and in the sky – but I thought it was no good going out – as I should have to see the sunrise alone'.[83] In fact, Dent had been busy all that year carefully cultivating two men in particular, John St Anthony Johnson[84] and Hubert H. Champion ('Cham').[85]

81 Henry Havelock Ellis (1859–1939), Edward Carpenter (1844–1929). The Uranian poets are discussed in Timothy d'Arch Smith's *Love in Earnest: Some Notes on the Lives and Writings of English 'Uranian' Poets from 1889–1930* (London, 1970). The term 'homosexual' only came into use c.1897.

82 Toye, *For What We Have Received*, pp. 31–3.

83 Diary 20/05/1896.

84 John St Anthony Johnson (born 03/04/1876), Trinity College, Stewart of Rannoch scholar 1896; choral scholar and organist at Trinity; studied composition at the RCM; singer. Although the friendship faded, they kept in touch down the years, mostly initiated by Johnson. Dent loaned him money and helped him in his career.

85 Hubert Hayward Champion (1874–1932), KC choir school, chorister 1883–89; Clifton, scholar; H.M. Inspector of Secondary Schools from 1919. Failed his B Mus although considered the cleverest man in his year. Dent helped him at all stages throughout his career. Withers, *A Register of Admission*.

> Johnson was there & we made each other's acquaintance & compared musical enthusiasms … I walked with him to his rooms, but he followed [deleted] came on with me as far as King's which shows that he has taken to me … I think he is a sincere & enthusiastic artist – he rather reflects my own character I think, which shows me my weak points.[86]

Johnson was more in the mould of Dent's school friends, an 'attractive' young man from a similar background and with similar interests, the friend he could discuss and play music with, argue with, but the strong impression remains that Dent has weighed him up and found him lacking. He rarely agreed with Johnson's musical judgements, but through Johnson he expanded his own repertoire of music (e.g., Brahms Intermezzi) and his circle of friends to include Trinity people like Nicholas Gatty. Though hardly recognising the fact, Dent was making a distinction between what he considered a friend and something else, far less clear.

For Dent, it seemed only natural that his musical and his sexual needs should dovetail neatly: both Johnson and Champion were good musicians, so the borrowing and lending of scores furnished the excuse for much of what he could pretend was innocent visiting, other motives being easily woven into the usual musical exchanges. But the diary entries reveal that Dent knew what he was about, producing piano compositions, his 'Champion Variations' in F minor,[87] to lay at his 'idol's' feet. Cham also worked with Mann, and probably through proximity, what had begun early that term as a mild attraction quickly became infatuation. By the end of May Week 1896, Dent was recording every tiny encounter with Champion, wallowing in the little dramas along the way:

> I stupidly managed to miss Champion … At 2.30 C.U.M.S. … Champion came for once in a way – but went away early with Curtis … Chapel at 5. Champion in the loft … overtaken by C. on his way down to bicycle with the races, cheerfully suggesting that I should do the same … I walked down to New Buildings with C. we discussed Brahms as a piano writer.[88]

The descriptions of Cham in the diaries show a clever but rather louche character, unable to bring himself to work hard enough to get his B Mus first time round, careless of his appearance, always casually dressed either in his 'old threadbare Norfolk' with cloth cap and tie, or barefooted in his rooms, and sometimes nothing on at all.[89] But Dent was too inexperienced to recognise either his own lovesick blindness or the nature of Cham's evasiveness: 'he persisted in talking acoustics – which was stupid – does the man think that I care about nothing else? … but to talk to him for 3/4 of an hour on any subject was a joy'.[90] As term ended, Dent's obsession only grew worse,

86 Diary 18/05/1896.

87 These have disappeared; the only surviving similar composition is a set of variations in E minor, 1895. KCA, EJD/1/3/8.

88 Diary 11/06/1896. Famously, May Week is in June, a post-exam celebration.

89 'Why so surprised at finding Cham naked?' Dent wrote to LH 29/08/1899. 'It's his normal condition & I think he is rather a fine sight.'

90 Diary 22/08/1897.

comparing notes with Ted, who had an 'idol' at Oxford, even to the point of standing under Cham's window several nights in a row, moping in rehearsals and taking long, ruminating walks to Chesterton with Mather, another college friend.

> There was a most lovely sunset about which I am afraid I expressed myself rather morbidly ... I was inclined to brood over the fact that I shall this evening have to say with de Musset 'Adieu! je crois que'en cette vie Je ne te reverrai jamais' [Farewell! I believe that in this life I'll never see you again] ... it is my last chance of attaining the object which the Variations in F minor failed to attain ... I went down to C. about 10, and found him dressing – he said he would not be in till about 12 – so I took Studies in Modern Music & pretended not to be able to find the Brahms; as he left me abruptly to find a 10 1/2 collar somewhere I went back to my rooms.[91]

In the end Dent simply left a note before catching the train down to London, where he took lodgings opposite Chappell's while his mother and Isabel stayed at the small London house they leased at 31 Brook Street.

His separation from Cham for the summer was turned into manufactured, self-indulgent drama of the kind he later reviled, all carefully set down in his diary, laced with clever quotes from poetry and song, a satisfying combination of poetry and anguish. Of course it was not Cham he was in love with, but the perfect idea of being in love with a good musician; conflating his love of music with his emerging sexual self, Dent had focused the whole show on poor Cham, hoping to 'attain the object' as he phrased it, but what exactly he meant by 'object' is not clear. Probably Cham had recognised that Dent really did not know his own mind, and flattering though the attentions might have been from such a remarkable young man, a lack of clarity on either part could be dangerous.

Dent was still too young and ignorant to understand the realities of such wish-fulfilment, but the thrill of forbidden pleasures is part of growing up. Although he never really shed his prudishness, Dent later loved to flirt with bad boys from the 'right' backgrounds, observing the naughtiness he could not quite let himself indulge in.

Within a week, his ability to live in the present asserted itself, and he plunged boyishly into London life, with visits to the Lumière Cinematographe, escorting Isabel to *Tannhäuser* (sung in French with choruses in Italian), *Tristan, The Mikado,* to plays, the Temple church, the Royal Academy and to Lord's. He caught up with Ted Haynes and Hugo Bell, went out to Eton to see Miss Hackett, the Parratts and Lloyd.

Already Cambridge had changed him and his attitudes; his trip to Bayreuth that summer of 1896 was Dent's last as a boy, in the company of his sister Isabel and Hilda Kekewich, meeting up with Etonians Lloyd, Parratt and Goodhart. It was the first time he deliberately set himself to target attractive young men while travelling, this time, Philip Webb, part of their wider Bayreuth party. Dent was still a self-conscious traveller, primly recording the sights and concerts he felt he should be doing, noting that 'unlike England nobody talked!', admiring the railways, the local food, giving equal weight to Conradi Becker's *Geschichte* and Strauss's *Die Fledermaus*: 'very

91 Diary 17/06/1896.

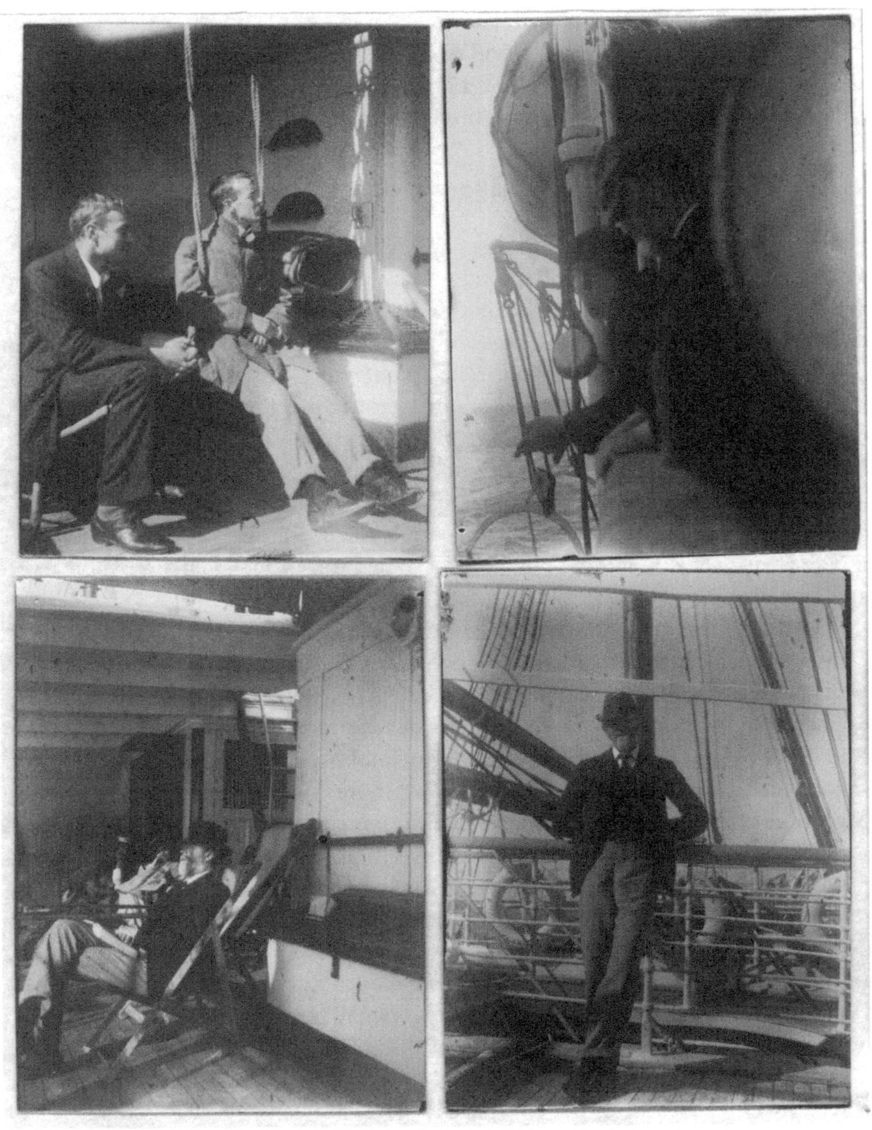

FIGURE 4. Dent sailing back from Germany in 1896, with his sister Isabel, Ted Haynes, Sir Walter Parratt, and Hilda Kekewich. By kind permission of the Provost and Fellows of King's College, Cambridge.

funny when we could understand it … music … bright & pretty & cleverly scored … We came away at 11.30 as we found Act III rather dull & vulgar'.[92]

A pattern had been set which Dent loosely followed for years, escape from the constraints of English life through continental travel, music and flirtations.

1896–1899

Dent's decision to sit his B Music part i beside his Classics exams in that year 1896–97 was a bold statement of intent and a mark of his determination after the long family summer at Ribston and Bayreuth. He could successfully juggle two entirely different subjects while maintaining the standard necessary to keep his scholarship and the growing regard he was so carefully cultivating. The meticulous diary-keeping was gradually integrated with Dent's numerous other time-consuming activities, until the diary began to turn into more of an aide-memoire. There was a lot to keep track of: every day beside his studies in two demanding subjects, Dent was reading, playing, rehearsing, composing, copying music, socialising around music, jotting down conversations about music with Hugh Allen, Johnson, Nixon or Cham. 'I was so saturated with music … that I went to bed early – feeling it impossible to do anything else.'[93]

Turned down by KCMS, 'rather a shock to my vanity not becoming secretary',[94] Dent moved instantly into the bigger pool, becoming an energetic and efficient secretary for CUMS. Slackers had no excuse, since their secretary had sent out streams of postcards to remind them of rehearsals or meetings; any falling off of standards would not be his fault. Dent was discovering in himself a talent for efficient organisation behind the scenes, while 'horrifying' its more conservative members when he gave some boys a shilling each to advertise the concerts by walking around the town with sandwich boards. Soon, he was helping Hugh Allen to conduct rehearsals and proposing repertoire, correcting and copying parts, the real beginnings of his long relationship with CUMS. At the same time, he turned his attentions to CUMC, making his presence felt, trying out his own compositions and those of others; by April 1897 – in between exams – being elected onto its committee. As with CUMS, Dent briskly redefined the club, organising its small but interesting library, copying out scores and parts for practice as well as the weekly performances; little escaped his attention, from tuning the club piano to programming. The chamber music being played was mostly new, either composed by students or imported, often by Dent as he travelled more widely and began to collect continental music. As its standards lifted, the club attracted more new members, and the Saturday chamber concerts Dent helped to organise increasingly became the proving ground for budding composers, an antidote to the prevailing late-Victorian taste for oratorio and big

92 Diary 28/07/1896, 30/07/1896.

93 Diary 16/02/1897.

94 Diary 15/10/1896. The KCMS people were probably terrified of him.

orchestral music. Its devoted president Sedley Taylor was thrilled; its prickly librarian, Charles Sayle,[95] resigned in a huff.

On 29 November, 'I had a bad attack of deafness in the morning but it passed off during chapel'. Three days later it was worse, but syringing of the ears temporarily restored the hearing he had apparently been losing for over a year.[96] It sounds as if there was something more fundamentally wrong; Dent records that he couldn't hear a word of Wedd's lecture, nor what he was himself singing.[97] While he was in Bayreuth the summer of 1897, his teeth began to give him trouble as well, with several trips to a local dentist whose angora kitten sat on his lap while the painful process went on.[98] Later, back in Cambridge he would pay the first of many, many visits to Cunningham, the dentist on King's Parade. His hearing and his teeth gave him serious trouble for most of his life.

In spite of his confident appearance and his constant musical socialising, Dent was too intelligent not to be aware of his deficiencies. In December 1896, he totted up his 'musical influences', Nixon, Charles Wood and W.T. Southward;[99] the 'new branch of music' he had so diligently studied and practised – Schubert's *Winterreise* and piano sonatas, Brahms's piano music and *Four Serious Songs*, Schumann's Piano Concerto, Handel's *Samson* and *Theodora*, some Mozart lieder, Beethoven, Chopin – his 'solo singing and choir training', ending with a very long list of the concerts and operas he has heard. Besides all this came his own meagre output, 'Weep you no more sad fountains' and the first movement of a concerto he had been struggling with for months: 'a rather poor show for 7 1/2 months'.[100] The concerto never materialised, probably evolving into the Serenade Dent produced the following summer. Composition, central to the Music degree, was really Dent's weak spot; he possessed compositional technique but not the essential creative inspiration that drove it, and all the careful listings were only an empirical sop to this basic lack.

Moreover, as charming people so often do, he still needed approval, and all that Lent term in 1897 he sounded his various mentors out about his abilities and prospects. Alan Gray told him flatly that he thought his compositions 'clever but without

95 Charles Edward Sayle (1864–1924), son of the local draper Robert Sayle, Sayle had left Oxford under the cloud of a homosexual affair. He catalogued both the St John's College Library and the Union Society Library; his great work was the catalogue of early English books in the CUL. Founder of the Baskerville Society. Although he applied to the British Museum and Edinburgh, he was turned down; when he finally did get a post at the CUL it was as an unpaid under-sub-librarian. Why a man of such obvious talents failed in this way is not clear, but homophobia is a real possibility, for Sayle was a published 'Uranian' poet. His friendship with Dent was strong but stormy. See below and Chapter 6.

96 Diary 29/11/1896 and 01/12/1896. Apparently deafness ran in the family.

97 J.B. Trend felt that Dent had hearing problems for much of his life, once noting that long before Dent went completely deaf, there were episodes when he couldn't tell the difference between G and G sharp; J.B. Trend, 'Dent', p. 55.

98 Diary 10/08/1897.

99 Rev. Walter T. Southward (1855–1919), Fellow of St Catherine's College: 'he is even more of a pedant than myself – & wanted to reduce all music to nothing but pure beauty – without any emotion'.

100 Diary December 1896.

feeling', but dropped strong hints that he himself might be leaving for York, leaving his post at Trinity vacant.[101] Wing confided that when he first took him on he thought he had never met anyone with so little voice, 'and … almost told me that it was no good my trying to sing'.[102] Thrown, Dent considered giving up his composition lessons with Wood, or even take a big side-step and doing some reviewing for the *Bookselling* magazine.[103] But Hugh Allen grounded him. One day on a chilly walk, as they both watched in fascination a Trinity don named Walker practising his boomerang, Dent was 'cheered' to find that Allen regarded him as the most likely 'person to take up his musical work here … I have … the faculty of arranging rhythms to suit words, & thinking out graceful rhythms dependent on stray triplets'.[104] Allen also offered practical help, that March introducing him to the lively Bindloss family running the Choral Society[105] in Melbourn, south of Cambridge.[106] Dent instantly adored them all, especially the children, and for several years he and Allen ran the society, going down on the train every Tuesday night for practices and trying out unfamiliar pieces on the local voices, from Stanford's new opera *Phadraig Crohoorne* to Bach. Then, after Brahms's death in April, for the May Week concert, encouraged by Allen, Dent pushed the committee to choose the Brahms *Requiem*, which involved a huge amount of work in the middle of his exams, copying parts and scoring, beside rehearsing.[107] At the time, such music was difficult to come by; copies of parts often had to be specially made for the chorus and orchestra, and Dent was also correcting parts which had been badly or erroneously copied previously. But it was all useful experience, especially the tact required to carry his ideas through committee, while the discipline of copying and studying different versions became the earliest foundations of his later scholarship. For years, Allen continued to be one of Dent's most useful and supportive friends; even after he moved to Ely, then to Oxford, his advice, his energy and ideas were always welcomed.

Perhaps the first casualty of his growing and often uncomfortable self-knowledge was Dent's relationship with Mann. While he enjoyed and appreciated the Manns' warm hospitality, he also felt suffocated by them, their kind, inflexible certainties so like his own family's; Mann himself detested 'modern' music, and had a child-like passion for steam-trains.[108] His diary entries track Dent's pity at Mann's uncer-

101 Diary 11/02/1897. Shortly after his return to Cambridge at the end of April a chance remark made by Mrs Gray scotched any such ambitions. 'I discovered that G[ray] has absolutely no intention of ever leaving Trinity to go to York or anywhere else, except the next world.' It was a useful object lesson, if irritating at the time; he was probably far better off having to sort out for himself more novel career paths. Gray settled into the kind of placid career which would have driven Dent mad.

102 Diary 11/02/1897.

103 Diary 15/02/1897.

104 Diary 24/02/1897.

105 Knight, *Cambridge Music*, p. 66.

106 Allen even persuaded the London North Eastern Railway to stop there specially, so he could get back into college before the gates were shut. *Ibid.*, p. 85.

107 Diary 24/04/1897.

108 Knight, *Cambridge Music*, p. 108.

tain college status beside a growing exasperation; the rigid and defensive musical judgements were becoming a trial, while Mann's famously florid style of organ-playing was driving Dent nearly demented.

> I was perhaps rather more outspoken than I ought to have been, but the way he played would have made Mendelssohn & Bach rise from their graves to strangle him – I very nearly did – we nearly came to blows & I with difficulty kept my temper when he ascribed WP's [Walter Parratt] position at Windsor to his chess-playing and his engagement for the Bach festival & at the R.C.M. to a clique.[109]

With great circumspection, he began the long and tricky process of distancing himself, using the excuse of his exams. Mann never for an instant suspected; with typical generosity he later gave Dent his 'old harpsichord'[110] on the condition that he have it restored, and is certainly one source of Dent's initial interest in old keyboard instruments.[111]

Johnson was another 'boring' discard, over the next two years gently set adrift, but Dent was invariably generous to people who had been 'friends', even those he had dropped, and he later recommended him for the post of organist to the English colony at Nice. But Johnson provided some important introductions to other Trinity men, including Nicholas Gatty and Ralph Wedgwood.[112] W.A. Barratt, a friend of the composer Isaac Albéniz, and Louis Paul,[113] who quickly became one of Dent's first really close homosexual friends, a fresh mentor to whom he was strongly attracted:

> most fascinating – he seems to be almost taking the place of Champion in my mind.[114]
>
> I think – in fact I feel almost certain – from the way he looked at me sometimes – when I looked at him in almost the same way – that my affection for him is in an appreciable degree reciprocated – What a lucid sentence![115]

'Fascinating', 'intriguing', 'interesting', 'attractive' were all code words for men Dent was attracted to sexually. His language for pretty women was quite different. Paul appears to have become the sexual mentor Dent needed and a source of worldly wisdom; up until his early death in 1900, they kept up a regular correspondence and visits. It would take many conversations with men like Louis Paul before he pos-

109 Diary 28/02/1897.

110 Diary 18/05/1898. Probably the Longman & Broderip Dent had later. He took it to an as yet unidentified restorer in Brecknock Road, London, in July 1898.

111 Although Dent himself only wrote one article on such early instruments, his was a lifelong interest, and he would later advise Rosamond Harding on her pioneering book *The Piano-Forte: its History traced to The Great Exhibition of 1851* (Cambridge, 1933, rev. 1978). From c.1890 onwards there was a strong undercurrent of interest in Cambridge in collecting early keyboard instruments; many of Harding's examples were local, especially from Moore's of Bridge Street, a massive local hoard sold off in c.1970.

112 Ralph Wedgwood (1874–1956), Apostle, later 1st Baronet, later Chair of the London and North Eastern Railway, which was how he knew Dent's family.

113 A.L. 'Louis' Paul, Old Etonian, son of the publisher Kegan Paul. Died 15 April 1900, while Dent was in Italy. He named young Dent his executor, asking him to burn all his papers.

114 Diary 07/12/1896.

115 Diary 31/01/1897.

sessed the sensitivity gay[116] men needed to understand the charged daily dynamics and invisible boundaries. Dent's blind spot remained his obsession with Cham, the thin and unconvincing label of 'friendship' covering his own inchoate but powerful sexual desires, and the fantasy persisted for years.

Now, wanting to go to Paris with Ted Haynes, and barely noting his Greek exams that March, Dent was forced instead to present himself at Ribston for the unveiling of his father's monument, 'in pious meditation at the paternal tombstone … I felt much annoyed'.[117] He side-stepped much of this by coaching the Hunsingore choir and entertaining the young Greenwood cousins: 'I had to gallop the whole length of the spare-bedroom passage first with Johnnie on my shoulders & then with Nam on my back – it was most exhausting!'[118] Dent always got on well with young children, enjoying their straightforward company and the chance to have a taste again of his own meagre childhood experience. His mother had hired another London house, in Rutland Gate, so after Easter, Dent and Isabel escaped to London for concerts of Paderewski playing Schumann and Henry Wood conducting Tchaikovsky, Sir Walter Parratt's Queen's Hall recital and the St Matthew Passion. And a curious seed was planted: 'In the afternoon we had a lecture from Mr. Drucker on the Scarlattis – there was not very much in it – but it was all new to me'.[119]

Dent's B Mus part i was almost too easy; the musical disciplines involved were by this time part of his established daily routines. The evening after his acoustics and counterpoint papers, and before his harmony and *viva voce*, he went to the CUMC to listen to very ordinary singing sessions of Brahms and Cobb, and stayed up late afterwards. The next day he cheekily asked Stanford what he had thought of the exams.[120] He was not in the least worried.

But the exams had been significant markers for him that year; he had more than proved his point that his musical ambitions were not out of order. In the weeks following he spent some time sorting out the CUMC records with Sayle: 'He gave me much of the history of his own connexion with the Club – I admired the way in which he contrived to bring out his own good points without appearing to do so.'[121] He went along to Tertius Noble's[122] organ recital, and talked with him afterwards. In spite of being, according to Wood, 'quite the cleverest man for the examination'

116 Of course the term 'gay' is anachronistic, but it serves the purpose here, and I think Dent might have approved it, much as he hated labels. The point is that there were no words then for gay men and women to describe themselves, and Dent himself was always searching for the words to describe himself and who he was. 'Homosocial', the term coined by Ben Pimlott in his biography of Hugh Dalton, is another such useful term, including straight or bisexual men who belonged to homosexual social circles.

117 Diary 18/03/1897.

118 Diary 19/04/1897.

119 Diary 08/04/1897.

120 Diary 22/05, 25/05 and 26/05/1897.

121 Diary 05/06/1897.

122 Tertius Noble (1867–1953), composer, then organist at Ely Cathedral.

Cham had failed it, as had Johnson. Francis Cornford[123] at Trinity introduced Dent to George Santayana from Harvard, 'a most interesting man; I hope I shall see more of him next term'.[124]

In the middle of a hectic May Week, in between rehearsals for CUMS, Dent was introduced to Ralph Vaughan Williams,[125] who had taken his B Mus the year before, 'whom I was much interested to meet … we discoursed on musical questions for about an hour and a half'. Dent would forget his face when he met him again two years later – he seems to have had a terrible memory for faces, possibly because of his poor eyesight – but Vaughan Williams (always 'VW' in the diary and letters) became a valuable lifelong friend, whose music Dent championed early on. Together with Hugh Allen, Vaughan Williams was one of the most influential of Dent's early friends; the three of them later ran a big annual choral competition at Petersfield, part of their serious approach to the propagation and dissemination of newer English music and the establishment of new standards.

Dent met up with Nicholas Gatty again in London for the Philharmonic Society concert of Glazunov's E flat symphony and a class at the Royal College of Music given by the composer: 'almost a second Schubert in his wealth of melody … rather loose structurally … but he does not tear one to pieces like Tschaikowsky'.[126] They went on to the Donaldson Collection,[127] where they found the Stanfords with Glazunov himself, egging on young Gustav von Holst[128] to play one of the serpents in the collection: 'he could only produce treble notes at first – but later gave the bottom ones'.[129] But as much as the company, the old instruments fascinated Dent, volumes of ancient music irresistible; he browsed the keyboard instrument collections in the South Kensington Museum, tentative beginnings to his serious lifelong pursuit of collecting unlikely music from unlikely corners.[130]

123 Francis Cornford (1874–1943), Classical scholar, Fellow of Trinity from 1899, who became a close friend and colleague. His experiences with the triennial Greek Play and Marlowe Dramatic Society productions helped Dent's early theatre and opera productions. His 1908 tract *Microcosmographia Academia* satirised the current stuffy academic dilemmas.

124 Diary 04/08/1897. George Santayana (1863–1952) taught at Harvard, was at King's when Dent met him and returned later. Influenced Bertrand Russell and a number of poet–philosophers, including T.S. Eliot. Dent got to know him later through other Harvard connections.

125 Ralph Vaughan Williams (1872–1958), composer, collector of folk-songs and melodies; compiled *The English Carol Book* and *The English Hymnal*. His own difficult path as a composer made him sympathetic to Dent's, while his experiences in Germany, the RCM and later with Ravel all helped Dent's own ideas and direction.

126 Diary 01/07/1896. Alexander Glazunov (1865–1936), Russian composer very popular at the time.

127 This is the musical instrument collection of the Royal College of Music, not to be confused with the John Donaldson Collection at Edinburgh.

128 Gustav von Holst (1874–1934), composer, friend of VW.

129 Diary 02/07/1896. This was one passage he later underlined.

130 The *Orpheus Britannicus* he bought at this time (diary 09/07/1897) is still in the Rowe Library at King's.

At Ribston, Dent's twenty-first birthday that July passed almost unnoticed. Uncle Ted sent him some Arensky pieces, while Carrie Stamer gave him 'a very charming pocket-book', and some letters. On 1 August 1897, his Deed of Release from his guardian Uncle Joseph Dent suddenly gave him an income, around 360 pounds a year on top of his scholarship, roughly 22,000 pounds in today's terms, on a par with some university lecturers.[131]

Bayreuth that August 1897 was a solitary trip, the first of many throughout his life, coming about by accident, since none of his suitable Old Etonian friends could come and Cham had said flatly that he was 'too busy'. When he later discovered that Cham had gone off to Switzerland with their mutual friend Macdougall, Dent was 'hurt', telling himself, 'I can make a pretext of writing to him from abroad – I have generally found that a correspondence started makes a friendship sound.' So he seized the chance to listen more carefully to the music, and his precise note-taking began to form the backbone of his serious musical criticism: 'I rather think the conductor took a few liberties not justified by the score & the drum episode in the scherzo was marred by the incredibleness of the A♭ in the strings & the fact that the drum was not in time.'[132]

Travelling alone became something he loved, but this first time Dent was nervous: 'I am almost unhappy about my journey … Am I getting like the old lady? quite incapable of amusing myself alone – & intolerant of solitude? I hope not – 21 is too young for that!' Overcrowded trains, a lack of due deference on the part of waiters and porters, any hold-ups rattled him, and he hated the fact that he was rattled. Dent preferred being in control of his surroundings, one of many reasons he learned languages, and his German was now up to 'quite sustained conversations with Frau Riechelt'.[133] Dent's French then was far better than his schoolboy German, and although Paris never had the attraction of Italy or Germany, he enjoyed a relaxing week there with Ted Haynes, going to the opera: Gounod's *Mireille* and Saint-Saëns' *Phryné* at the Opéra Comique, 'the best comic opera I have ever seen', and his first *Don Giovanni*, where he was pleased to spot Fauré in the audience next to the King of Siam. His sharp criticism picks out the tinkering which characterised most current productions, what even then felt wrong to him:

> they make 5 acts of it & introduce a good deal of music to take up the curtain which though Mozart is not Don Giovanni – besides a long ballet in the ball scene – where they danced to the Minuet from the G minor sym. & the Rondo alla Turca etc.[134]

Dent treated Ted to dinner at the Hotel de Paris, 'which he enjoyed very much – after which he lay in my bed while we discussed various subjects ranging from Parsifal to Sully Prudhomme'. He always found Ted attractive; in many ways they

131 That September he would give some of it to Johnson, to help him finish his B Mus, the first of many such gestures; Dent would always help friends in financial need.

132 Diary 14/08/1896. The work was Beethoven's 5th Symphony.

133 Dent's Bayreuth landlady. Diary 12/08/1897.

134 Diary 15/09/1897.

complemented each other, Ted's Rabelaisian gusto offsetting Dent's prudery. They spent a few more days in London, going to the theatre and to the Queen's Hall, but neither Forbes-Robertson as Hamlet nor Henry Wood's Tchaikovsky was as good as Paris. The two weeks of freedom ended on a sombre note, with Dent visiting Louis Paul in hospital, 'suffering from a disease of the spine'.[135]

The weeks at Ribston were tolerable only because his sister Catherine was keen to learn Italian before their projected trip in the spring before Dent's finals, so the two of them kept to a regular daily schedule of learning the language. But relations were still edgy; Dent was barely civil to the house-guests, the Vansittarts, good friends of his brother Jack, ignoring his mother's gushing attempts to engage his interest with their mandoline-playing daughter and retreating to the library to read Italian. The captain 'bored me to death' about his Etonian son, Robert, who was Captain of Oppidans and a keen cricketer.[136] He sat through a long sermon given by his uncle Lovelace Stamer, one of the choir telling him 'they were very sorry I was going to-morrow & that they liked somebody who took an interest in the music & put some spirit into it'.[137] He felt he had tried his best to engage his sisters, both intelligent women, in serious conversation about the *musical* function of the choir, arguing that it was simply an adjunct to the service, 'trained to assist the vocal effects of the rest of the people' and provoking them into vigorous disagreement: the choir had necessarily to be 'restricted to those who were of moral character' and shown to be separate from the congregation.

He showed his mother, 'Madame', his recent compositions, the letter from Sir Walter with a concert programme from Osborne House, where two of his pieces had been played to the Queen. The ever-practical Catherine dug out 'an old Norman French MS book', some metrical psalms and a 1641 collection of Amner's Hymns which had belonged to his grandfather, the friend of composer William Shield. Dent later showed them to Monty James and to Francis Jenkinson.[138] But the gesture marked a change in the family attitude, and that September he was tickled when his mother interrupted his playing a Rachmaninov Prelude to ask if this was part of his Serenade. He played bits of the real Serenade to her in the library, patiently talking her through it, communication of a kind.

Months later, larded with several lectures on his 'wickedness', his mother made a peace-offering. 'After tea I looked through some old music in the oak-room & turned up a copy of Schumann's 'Ballscenen' – dedicated to Miss Reichmann – the copy given by her to Mother, who gave it to me – & also the old books on music which belonged to her grandfather'.[139] Family connections took Dent's music more seriously; he continued to copy out music and compose for the Kekewich girls Emma,

135 Diary 05/08/1897.

136 Robert Gilbert Vansittart (1881–1957), later a famous diplomat who opposed Hitler. Dent would later find him a handful when called upon to look after him in Germany.

137 Diary 10/10/1897.

138 He later gave them to the CUL.

139 Diary 30/09/1898.

Isabel and Margaret, and the Gillett girls, Maud and Katherine with her 'new' Amati violin. The relatives who took the trouble to know him were very fond of him.

Buoyed by his B Mus part i success, Dent hoped to do even better in his finals year, but although he continued to wrestle with composing, his output remained very small.[140] His own high standards were only partly responsible for this; a frantically busy schedule left little time for creative work, and there was no obvious path to follow other than the prescribed one through composition, and few people capable of discussing the problem from a different perspective. When he broached with Mann the idea of continuing his studies at the Royal College of Music, Mann simply voiced his own prejudice about its having 'a rather commercial atmosphere about some of its products'. It was his problem, and he would have to find a solution himself.

Michaelmas term brought balmy walks with Sydney Waterlow, John Crace and Rainsley Moorsom,[141] tea at Walter Headlam's – now more of a friend than a tutor – Melbourn on Tuesday, Stanford's Saturday lectures and Dante lessons with Browning on Sundays. W. Figgis, the new editor of the *Cambridge Review*,[142] asked him to do the weekly music review, and possibly because of this new purpose, his diary entries are crisper and less self-indulgent. With the appearance on the scene of new young men like Waterlow, Dent became more open to other friendships, and two of the most significant were freshmen at King's that term, Morgan Forster, who joined the CUMC that October,[143] and Lawrence Haward.[144]

Dent had been in his rooms trying to get on with his Serenade and cataloguing the KCMS collection of music in its shabby boxes, when interrupted by a large young man in *pince-nez* who rather diffidently and formally requested to see what music the college had. They wound up chatting for hours, then playing Brahms, Haward impressing Dent with his sight-reading. He quickly attached himself to Dent, his admiration evident, while initially Dent found him a bit earnest, but very soon he ceased to be 'Haward', and usually referred to even in the diary as

[140] Between 1895 when he first came up to King's, and his submission for his Fellowship in 1901, Dent composed 14 songs, settings of poetry by Blake, Shakespeare, Byron, de Musset, Shelley, Dryden and Dante, of which his favourite was 'There be none of Beauty's daughters' (1896). There were the two serenades for small orchestra and his set of variations for piano in E minor. His contemporaries, for example, Donald Tovey or F.S. Kelly, both Old Etonians whose careers he followed with interest, had in the same time achieved a much higher public profile, since they were both performers as well as composers.

[141] More of Dent's King's friends. Moorsom kept a diary himself, far more explicit than Dent's.

[142] The CR was the weekly journal edited by students, more like a magazine than *Varsity*, its modern counterpart, and reporting on most of the university doings, plus reviews of current books and theatre. Its reviews were unsigned, but their authorship was common knowledge.

[143] For Forster, see 'Dramatis Personae'. He was also musical and homosexual. For a long time in their association Dent did not fully appreciate how much the novelist in Forster was bringing to his fiction from his immediate world. See below.

[144] For Haward, see 'Dramatis Personae'.

'Lawrence'. By June 1898 they were intimate enough for an easy correspondence, which lasted a lifetime.[145]

Another of Dent's unlikely lifelong friendships – with Club Librarian Charles Sayle – began this year, always an edgy relationship, since Sayle vacillated between defensive hissy fits and seasoned worldly advice. But like Browning, Sayle was a more openly gay role-model, and his small, elegant house in Trumpington Street became both a homosocial haven for the gilded youth of Cambridge, his 'Swans',[146] and a local masculine salon for ideas and music:

> The sofa runs at right angles, on the left hand side of the fire, and in front of the fire is a small Broadwood grand pianoforte, for though I do not play, I like to be the cause of music in others. Over the end of the pianoforte an old piece of embroidered work has been thrown, and on this was a bowl of autumn flowers which had been given me, a cherished photograph in a Florentine frame, a silver bowl of pot-pourri made from roses which had bloomed in Milton's cottage at Chalfont St. Giles, and behind all these stood the full-size plaster-cast bust of the young Augustus.[147]

He was probably harmless, but Sayle's diaries reveal tendencies towards little boys which would these days get him locked up. He collected photographs of small boys, especially titled ones, and pasted them in his diaries, while his mantelpiece was adorned with the photographs of all his 'Swans', the young men he nurtured and made much of, but most probably was far too timid and fastidious to approach in any overtly sexual way. His preciosity – one story has him thanking his hostess for her 'delicious salt'[148] – and his terrible poetry were sources of amusement and some contempt.[149] But as Dent came to appreciate, Sayle was also extremely well-connected, and his introductions, especially homosexual ones, included John Addington Symonds and Robert Nichols.

❧ ❧ ❧

In spite of three years of active obfuscation Dent seems always to have remained on cordial terms with his Classics tutors, a state of affairs maintained by his own personal charm and the kind of respect teachers always feel for their most gifted if wayward students. His lower second in the Classics part i exams in 1897 was barely enough to keep his scholarship, and possibly with this dismal result in mind, they kept a closer eye on his activities this term. The dean had pulled him up for neglect-

145 Miraculously, Haward would keep all of Dent's letters, and after his death, his widow Suzanne gave them to King's College.

146 Dent claims to be the source of this epithet: 'I told him all his geese were swans'.

147 'Angels of Earth', CM (16 November 1912), p. 470.

148 Paul Delany, *The Neo-Pagans: Friendship and Love in the Rupert Brooke Circle* (London, 1987), p. 17.

149 Most of his poetical work was published at his own expense. 'Bertha' became a local legend for its badness. Sayle and his poetry feature in d'Arch Smith's *Love in Earnest.*

ing to sign in,[150] and on 19 October, he was summoned by his tutor Cooke to explain why he had only attended one lecture. On the 31st he was late for his tutorial; a music meeting had run over. This was too much even for the easy-going Cooke: 'I afterwards heard vocal sounds more powerful than artistic', and Dent was soon hauled in again. 'I had to interview Cooke about translations etc not done – we discussed the possibilities of my tripos & of my resigning my scholarship – it was rather unpleasant'.[151] It shook Dent enough to consult Nixon, who was emphatic that he 'certainly not' resign. Losing his scholarship would have not been a major financial blow, but the sense of failure would have been intolerable, and it might blight any ambitions for a college Fellowship, the idea of which had begun to form in Dent's mind.[152]

The same energy and vision for change which had shaken up every musical society he joined Dent now ploughed into his reviewing. The *Cambridge Review* music section expanded to include remarks on Stanford's lectures and the quality of musical talent within the university. 'It is in some ways a healthy sign', Dent declared in one article, 'music in England has suffered too long from the indifference shown to the composition as compared with the adoration lavished on the executant.' The issue became one of his bugbears. Through the *Cambridge Review* he campaigned to reinstate the series of Wednesday Popular Concerts in the Guildhall, which had been stopped for financial reasons, and generally for more cheap seats for the public, advocating the use of the smaller concert room in the Guildhall as being more suitable for chamber music. He was learning about the power of the press; within a month he was at loggerheads with his editor and quite a few of the more conservative readers, who wrote letters heaving with barely suppressed rage.

The first clash was over music for the Greek Play, *The Wasps*, composed by Tertius Noble.[153] Dent's friends were involved, and from the outset he had sat in on rehearsals and read the score, so felt that he knew the music well enough to be able to voice an early opinion in his column, commenting freely on the quality of the music even before the full production had taken place.

> [Noble] had treated the play rather in the style of a modern comic opera. The result is that his rhythms are never too complicated to be intelligible, while the music is extremely bright and catching, and evidently the work of a well-read and eclectic musician.

150 It was probably an excuse to catch the elusive Dent; not signing in and out of college was a minor offence.

151 Diary 07/02/1898.

152 When he was about to take his Classics part ii Tripos exams, his tutors got a little of their own back, Davies asking him when presented with a sudden and unexpected burst of work if he were 'going in for a little death-bed repentance', and Cooke writing him a note to enquire rather caustically if there were any more music exams he might wish to have his name put down for.

153 Redfern's first staging of the Greek Play was in 1882, as seen above. It is still a Cambridge institution, taking place every two or three years – a classical Greek play in Greek, usually with music specially composed for it, the most famous example being Vaughan Williams' music for *The Wasps* in 1909. Cf. Knight, *Cambridge Music*, pp. 78–9.

Dent congratulated himself on his forbearance, but not everyone agreed.

By the time Dent submitted his copy – his premature review of the actual performance – for the edition of 25 November, Figgis was apoplectic; after an unsatisfactory 'rowing' in which he tried to get Dent to recant, Figgis seized the copy to tone it down himself. Dent simply did not understand Figgis' attitude, and when he read the final edited version was chagrined to find that Figgis had 'softened ... down considerably ... my censure ... is now so mild that my criticism reads much too favourable'. In his diary Dent concedes that he had found the performance 'on the whole good – Noble's orchestration surprisingly so', but to him that wasn't the only point at issue. He had used the review to tackle a number of serious musical questions, commenting on its inappropriateness for comedy, on the lack of necessary balance between the orchestral and choral writing, on the tiredness of the 'bassoon-joke' and on the marriage of words and music. Figgis must have come round to the idea that a bit of controversy was healthy, because when the next 'violent letter' came in, this one from John Willis Clark,[154] he sent it along to Dent to give him the chance to defend himself. 'It rather upset my equilibrium – though it was most unjust.' After a Founder's Day dinner and some 'derry-derry-dongs' or glee-singing at Nixon's, Dent went back to his rooms and spent the rest of the night drafting a reply. In the morning he took the draft to show to Sayle, who disapproved, and to Francis Cornford, who cheered him on, before handing it in to Figgis. His later articles in the *Cambridge Review* become much more polished, and before long he began to perfect his trademark ambiguous 'serpentine' style.

All this time Dent's friendship with Hugh Allen flourished, and when Allen took up his new post at Ely Cathedral, Dent often went up to consult him. Ever helpful, he was able to offer Dent 'the choice of getting the Serenade done by a small amateur orchestra at Chichester, but with incomplete wind, or of writing something else for them'. He recommended going to Vienna to hear lots of contemporary music, for 30 pounds all in,[155] and introduced Dent to some unlikely friends, Bishop Lord Alwyne Compton and his wife.[156] By this time Dent was resolutely anti-clerical and anti-church, but Compton was a new breed of cleric, more socially aware and liberal, besides being excellent company. Dent quickly became devoted to them, especially Lady Alwyne, who was everything that was missing in his own mother – warm, funny and sympathetic. They struck up a lively correspondence which lasted until her death.[157]

❧ ❧ ❧

Dent's first trip to Italy that spring was mostly a tourist jaunt, taking in the sights from Lucerne, Isola dei Pescatori and Milan, meeting up in Pisa with the lively Kekewich

154 John Willis Clark (1833–1910), eminent Cambridge historian, Fellow of Trinity, wrote, *inter alia,* the monumental 1886 *Architectural History of the University and Colleges of Cambridge* in four volumes. A frightening person to have offended.

155 LH 10/08/1898.

156 Lord Alwyne Compton (1825–1906), Bishop of Ely 1886–1905.

157 Diary 04/08/1898. Unfortunately, very little of this has survived, only hints from his diary.

girls, Margaret and Emma, before going on to Florence where they bumped into Browning and his entourage: 'M said she thought I was very rude to him!' They paid him a social call in his 'palatial rooms' at the Bonciani, with Dent and Browning's long-suffering secretary Fred playing duets on the piano while Browning 'held forth' on Florence, grandly offering to give Dent lessons on Dante back in Cambridge. They had Italian lessons from Signorina Cantagalli in Florence, who recommended Salorini's majolica factory and various Holy Week processions in and around the Duomo, the noise and music of which Dent thought rather like a football match.[158]

On the way home he visited Louis Paul in hospital before returning to Cambridge to cram for his finals, horsing around with Bernard Jones and Jerry Rickett,[159] going to Busoni's concert at the Philharmonic, conducted by Richter,[160] working on concerts for CUMS and KCMS, sitting up late with Haward: 'I discoursed on the English musical tradition handed down from Tallis etc to Wesley – lent him all my available madrigals & anthems etc to illustrate my little lecture.'[161] He barely mentions the May Classics Tripos exams, only his 'unspeakable relief' when it was all over. His lower third degree came as no surprise to anyone but Dent's angry mama, who fired off a 'stormy letter'.

At Cambridge that summer there were his newly restored harpsichord and trips to London to divert him; at Ribston, the Hovingham Festival with its promise of Joachim and Melba. In the first of many letters he would write over the course of his life to Lawrence Haward, Dent has found exactly the right outlet for his frustrations, adopting an engagingly bitchy style that also distanced him from his surroundings. In fact his easy correspondence with Lawrence freed him from the insufferable archness which was his besetting style sin, the style he assumed in his *Cambridge Review* articles or the equally self-conscious style he used early on in the diary. He had a sympathetic audience, a near-contemporary, not entirely uncritical, who shared his passions and appreciated his humour. His easy friendship with Lawrence was practically everything he had ever said he wanted, apart from the lack of physical attraction.[162]

Travel also diverted him. Germany again at the end of August – Bayreuth, via Frankfurt, Rothenberg and Munich – Dent more comfortable with the language this time, even finding 'the courage to cultivate' the acquaintance of some Germans. He reported smugly to Lawrence, 'I beg to inform you that one Englishman has mistaken me for a German & several Germans have mistaken me for an American'.[163] Travelling alone, he discovered, had its advantages. He could work on his string

158 Diary 08/04/1898.

159 Bernard Jones: organ scholar, part of Dent's wider homosocial circles; Dent later helped him find a post abroad.

160 Diary 04/06/1898. This was the first time Dent heard the man who became so important to him, whose life he wrote, but he had a headache at the time and was fussing more about the schoolgirl adulation going on behind him at Busoni's 'disgusting' rock-star status.

161 Diary 05/05/1898.

162 Diary 11/12/1898.

163 LH September 1898.

piece, and take time to visit the musical instrument collection at the Bavarian National Museum as well as going to what became his regular restaurant in Munich, the Heck, where he managed to pick up a music-loving oculist called Jacobsen who had once met Brahms, accompanying him to *La belle Hélène,* and discussing local opera with a native. He saw *Fidelio, Die Zauberflöte* and *Die Entführung aus dem Serail.* But what he enjoyed most was keenly observing everything around him: in Rothenberg, a model of the Rathaus which, when 10 pfennig was put into a slot, played Tilly's entry to the Meistertrunk (a local legend); walks in the surrounding fields 'with little streams & swarms & swarms of young frogs'. He inspected old pianofortes and harpsichords in the shops and played an old serpent in a museum. But: 'Cham's letter brings the greater happiness, in that I know by what he writes, that my end is accomplished, & that all I need do now is write letters in my best vein.'[164]

Even as he was becoming increasingly engaged with his travels, at the back of his mind was the ongoing dilemma: what to do next for any serious long-term musical career, whether to consider a doctorate. All that year in Cambridge Dent had been doing more teaching and coaching, discovering that he quite liked it: 'I almost think that the next vacant professorship at the Glasgow Athenaeum would suit me'.[165] That October C.H. Lloyd wrote to him, suggesting that he apply for the post of organist to the English Church at Algiers that winter: 'duties irksome, but place delightful & pay very good'.[166] Dent politely made enquiries, knowing full well that this short-cut was not what he wanted, his ambitions still high, if vague. Meanwhile, while working on his B Mus part ii, he continued to sideline, with a lot of performance, playing 'drums' for CUMS, while his reputation with the Melbourn choir inspired the Royston Choral Society to write to him asking that he 'revive' the society there. He had a successful audition for the Bach Choir,[167] then conducted by Stanford, which meant travelling to London every Tuesday for practice, so he could combine it with other activities in town. Twice a week now he read Dante with Sydney Waterlow, who introduced him to philosopher G.E. Moore and a beautiful young Old Etonian, Percy Lubbock.[168] Although he had been hovering in the background for a year now, Morgan Forster began to make more appearances in Dent's diary, with his music and his writing aspirations. Dent's restored harpsichord brought pleasure and discovery of how early keyboard music should sound; when he showed it to local music doyenne Mrs Gaskoin, 'she gloated over it like any bodysnatcher'.[169] Sedley Taylor brought Donald Tovey to the club concert on 19 November; although mildly jealous of Tovey's apparently effortless success, Dent was delighted to meet him again, 'I found him very pleasant, and asked him to play something of his own'. Tovey, always

164 Diary 08/09/1898.

165 Diary 15/08/1898.

166 Diary 20/10/1898.

167 The Bach Choir was founded in 1876, conducted at this time by Stanford. Parry had composed 'Blest Pair of Sirens' for it, and it included amongst its varied members Vaughan Williams and Adrian Boult.

168 See 'Dramatis Personae'.

169 Diary 03/12/1898.

affable, played his setting of 'Daffodils' and gratified his hosts by remarking on how much more 'infinitely superior' Cambridge music was to Oxford's. Now coming up to Dent's rooms, Tovey casually 'glanced' at some of Dent's music before playing the first movement of a trio of his own: 'very Brahmsy & intellectual but a bit stodgy, I thought', Dent sniffed.

Two episodes that term paved the way for Dent's future career. The first was a casual introduction to C.T. Gatty, the older cousin of Nicholas, working on church music at Trinity. Gatty was much more of a scholar than most of the musicians currently around, and this scholarly side caught Dent's interest, especially on the question of attribution. After talking about various kinds of church music, Gatty showed Dent some Michael Haydn:

> & also showed me a recent publication under M.H.'s name, of the Mass on Croatian Volkslieder mentioned by Hadow as attributed to J. Haydn: I have half a mind to write to Hadow about it. He also shattered my illusions with regard to Arcadelt's Ave Maria & Stradella's Pieta Signore: saying that the 1st was faked by Niedermeyer for Prince Poniatowski in 1840 – & the 2nd by Rossini: though I don't know what truth there was in his statements. [Dent later pencilled in: 'both true!'.][170]

His boundless intellectual curiosity, his pleasure in possessing inside knowledge in his chosen field were instantly sparked, and all that term, Dent began to sift more closely through the vast realms of uncatalogued music at the Fitzwilliam,[171] discovering Offenbach's *La Grande Duchesse,*[172] one of his first real forays into unknown opera. The second episode occurred during his much-anticipated Italian trip that spring, when things did not quite pan out in the way he hoped, and an irritating companion forced him to find an escape route.

On one of their regular 'Grantchester Grinds', he noticed that his companion, Cyril Armstrong,[173] was looking a little under the weather, 'too solitary a life', so to cheer him up Dent impulsively asked him to come along with him to Italy, 'half regretted it afterwards'. By mid-March, Dent was beginning especially to rue being on the receiving end of the Armstrong family approval: 'another long letter from Professor Armstrong – who will try my temper soon'.[174]

He had been looking forward to it for a long time, but this Italian trip was a very mixed bag, ultimately providing his friend Forster with inspiration for his Italian novels. On 26 March 1899, they were off, Dent armed with letters of introduction provided by Ted Haynes, to two members of the formidable expatriate community

170 Diary 23/01/1899.

171 At this time most of the music later housed in the Pendlebury Music Library was kept in the Fitzwilliam.

172 *La Grande Duchesse de Gérolstein* (1867).

173 George Cyril Armstrong (born 1876), Old Etonian, King's Scholar, Newcastle Scholar, later Fellow of Trinity. In spite of that disastrous holiday they remained friends. There is a letter from Armstrong in KCA, dated 1954 and signed 'affectionately'.

174 Diary 18/03/1899.

in Florence, Mrs Costelloe and Miss Gosselin.[175] When they entered their railway carriage, Armstrong suddenly dropped on his knees to pray, a 'startled' Dent looking on in amusement and horror. 'I am afraid that I shall find his virtue rather too much sometimes.' At the Pension Bonciani when Armstrong 'balked' at Italian food and drink, Dent was frankly appalled: 'I said I wanted dinner, & what was more, that I was going to have it'. 'He is good at worshipping', Dent wrote to Lawrence: 'You would be ten times as fussy, I know … but you would at least be appreciative over the right things – & not rave over every buttercup & every toad you saw when there was the Palazzo Vecchio or an Italian crowd to study'.[176] After this Dent made a point of travelling either alone or in more carefully selected company.

But life changes can turn on tiny pieces of serendipity. Almost as an afterthought, his Italian teacher Signora Cantagalli helped Dent to compose a formal letter of introduction she thought he might find useful, to Signor Alessandro Kraus at 10 Via Cerritani, housing his fabulous collection of musical instruments. He went alone, Armstrong being up in the hills. 'I was there 2 1/4 hours. His collection is marvellous: I specially admired an old organ of the early 18th cent – with beautiful diapasons. He has more at Fiesole, and invited me to come & see them tomorrow.' The very next day Dent called at the Villa Kraus, between Florence and the hill village of Fiesole, and was shown more instruments in the collection. 'After I had seen all I was given a glass of Marsala & introductions to Martucci of Bologna, Weckerlin of Paris & the heads of the libraries at S. Lorenzo & the Istituto Musicale.' Immediately he wrote to Lawrence: 'Being a pupil of Hipkins, you of course know that the only perfect Cristofori pianoforte is in the museum of the Signori Kraus at Florence.'

All at once Dent had gained privileged entry into a world he had barely considered up to now. The very next day, abandoning Armstrong to 'Ruskinize in the Cappella Spagnuola' and clutching his precious introductions, Dent hurried to the ancient libraries of Florence.

> with these I went & grubbed early Florentine operas in the Medici library & the library of the Reale Istituto Musicali – The librarian there Riccardo Gandolfi is delightful: I think Cherubini must have been like him in manner. I was horribly afraid of him at first – because I came as an idler. He made me sit down & work: & I got so interested that I spent 3 mornings there making notes & copying.[177]

Dent clearly made quite an impression on the serious scholars he encountered that day. What he had 'grubbed' up were 'original printed scores' of Jacopo Peri's *Euridice* and a manuscript copy of Milani's *Il potestà di Colognole* of 1657. He negotiated with Gandolfi to do more copying, of *La Tancia*, and, fuelled with inspiration from Kraus, went into the Laurenziana to consult with the second librarian there about editions of Florentine music assembled for an exhibition in Vienna in 1892. Soon he was copying everything he could lay his hands on and making arrange-

175 Diary 26/03/1899. Mrs Costelloe was Mary Costelloe, soon to become the wife of art critic and historian Bernard Berenson. Ted's connection had come via her brother, Logan Pearsall Smith, who also sent other Old Etonians Donald Tovey and F.S. Kelly out there.

176 LH 02/04/1899.

177 Diary, April 1899.

ments for copies of these rarities to be sent to the Cambridge University Library and the Fitzwilliam. 'I also discovered a drawing of a tomb of Francesco Landini a madrigalist & blind organist of S. Lorenzo and determined to take the first opportunity of hunting up the original.' So completely captivated was he by this new world of old music that his accounts of the few concerts he went to are unusually perfunctory, dismissing Eugen d'Albert's playing of Beethoven as 'sentimental … but he is better than Dohnanyi', while enjoying hearing Schumann's *Manfred* for the first time.

The return journey was via Bologna, where Dent immediately put Kraus's introductions to good use, going to the library, to Rossini's house and to the concert-room at the Liceo Musicale, with its 'hundreds of portraits of musicians – including one of Mozart presented by his father in 1770 & one of Dr Burney'. He was shown manuscripts of Dufay, Dunstable, Wagner, Mozart and of *Il barbiere di Siviglia*, and later, in the instrument collection at the Museo Civico, he remarked with some awe on the 'Archicembalo by Vito Tracentino of Venice 1606, with 31 notes to each octave – to give the enharmonic notes'.[178] After Bologna, they went to Milan, then up the Rhine falls at Neuhausen, Armstrong in raptures, Dent thinking only of the glories he had seen in Italy. Music, and his own place in the musical world, had suddenly opened up.

❧ ❧ ❧

A few weeks later Dent sailed through his B Mus part ii exams, beginning with Mann's counterpoint paper in the morning, and harmony for three hours in the afternoon, finishing early in spite of a barrel-organ playing outside. Perhaps the most useful part of his examinations was his *viva voce* with Stanford:

> a vile 8 part thing of Mendelssohn to read, with 4 soprano clefs, & part of the slow movement of Schubert's C major symphony … Mann sent me to the depths of despair by showing me some stupid mistakes in the counterpoint paper & picked holes in various things – [Sterndale] Bennett rather bothered me – though not so badly as I had expected.

It is one of the longest entries in Dent's diary, where he records what appears to have been, as far as Stanford was concerned, a tough formality, but one larded with gossip, information and the sense that Stanford had no doubts whatever about Dent's abilities. But it was direction which had worried Dent far more than any examination, and now Stanford gave him the first of several pieces of good advice; prescient, even. When Dent asked him about translations for operas, Stanford told him that they had had some 'very good ones done for the R.C.M.', but then shrewdly asked him if he had ever done any: 'he seemed to think I might. It was a happy thought & I determined to have a try.'[179]

The final papers on 25 May, in 'vocal composition and instrumental', were a final hurdle: 'I was rather pressed for time. I came out extraordinarily limp.' He cut

178 Diary 17/03/1899.

179 Diary 24/05/1899.

KCMS and went for a long walk instead, but was later talked into helping out with the Footlights production of *The Freshman*. The three musical Rubens brothers were all involved, Walter and Paul Rubens being responsible for the music, with Harry Rottenburg,[180] and the cast including a young Harold Monro.[181] Dent was 'tentatively' approached by Paul Rubens to help find some good musicians and wound up assembling the score, two days before the actual production. Dent loved it all – the frantic, last-minute scrambles, the silly but essential music, the camaraderie of production teams – and he would happily work with the Rubens brothers again. His actual degree had receded well into the background.

> I paid my fees in the morning for my degree. In the afternoon I took the degree – & had to wait a long time, as mine came last of all. The Vice-chancellor stumbled over his formula & had to be prompted by Southward or somebody. As I rose from my knees, he murmured anxiously 'It was what you came for, wasn't it?'[182]

For his next step, Dent had already decided to go to Germany for six months to work at composing, while taking up the introductions he had been given to various libraries there, at Dresden, the most conservative and beautiful of cities, and Munich, the most avant-garde and liberal. All his discussions over the past two years had only reinforced his desire to avoid the standard routes via the Royal College of Music (where Stanford taught), and after his own recent tantalising experiences abroad, he wanted to explore much more in Germany and Italy. His own concomitant need to explore his sexuality away from prying eyes was also a deciding factor. But Dent was still focused on composition, the scholarly side he had leapt at like a starving trout to a fly was still only a means to that end rather than a possible career goal in its own right. His obtuseness is perhaps excusable, and it would not be the last time he could not see what was so obvious in retrospect, that he was clinging to a personal fantasy not unlike his Cham obsession: stubbornly, youthfully confident of composing something substantial – an opera perhaps – to present to the college as a Fellowship offering, and another brilliant piece for the doctorate he needed for an academic career. His brother Charles advised him on the finances: 'he seemed to think mine unpromising – but I am content at present'. Instead of Bayreuth,[183] he planned to spend most of the long vacation in Cambridge, teaching some harmony now that he was qualified, and 'grubbing up' on as much music as possible.

Dent was moving on to new musical pastures, with Kraus's introduction to Weckerlin[184] at the Musée du Conservatoire and more than enough to occupy him in

180 Harry Rottenburg (1875–1955), another King's man, became one of the longest-serving members of the Cambridge institution Footlights, which nurtured so much theatrical and satirical talent.

181 Monro became a close friend 15 years later, when he was running the Poetry Bookshop.

182 Diary 15/06/1899.

183 A shame, really, since his Old Etonian friend Hugo Bell took his formidable sister, the explorer and Arabist Gertrude Bell along, who seems to have taken the place by storm. One cannot but wonder at such an encounter.

184 Jean Baptiste Weckerlin (1821–1910), studied under Halévy, professor of singing and librarian of the Conservatoire.

Paris for a short visit. He poured over the 'treasures' of the Musée, then binged at the Opéra Comique: Méhul's *Joseph*, Delibes' *Le roi l'a dit*, Mascagni's *Cavalleria rusticana*, 'beyond words disgusting – though only too well acted'; he read the libretto of *Carmen*, finding the character 'disgusting – & so are her lovers', 'but ... but I can't help admiring the skilful construction of the play'.[185] The current vogue for Edmond Rostand inspired him to consider using either *Cyrano de Bergerac* or *La Principe* for the opera he hoped to compose. Coming back via London, he stopped off at the Kekewiches, was introduced to Nigel Playfair,[186] and heard about Emma and Margaret singing for a lecture given by the family friend Violet Paget, aka Vernon Lee.[187] Then there was Hovingham with Lawrence, where they encountered a distracted Stanford conducting his *Te Deum*; he later 'played the big drum with frantic energy' in the *William Tell* Overture.

This was the last of the relatively idyllic and innocent summers spent at Ribston. Dent's perspective was already shifting abroad. Music was not limited to any single aspect of the art, and Dent's insatiable, lifelong journey in search of it and of himself was just beginning.

185 Diary 1–3/07/1899.

186 Nigel Playfair (1874–1934), ground-breaking producer, especially at the Lyric Theatre, Hammersmith. Dent would be involved with opera productions there after the First World War.

187 Violet Paget aka Vernon Lee (1856–1935), writer, musician, part of the expatriate community outside Florence. Dent often visited her at the Villa Palmerino there, and, once he recognised her lesbian sexuality, always referred to her as 'Vernon Lee'. She became a close friend, encouraging Dent in his early musical studies.

CHAPTER 3

The Accidental Scholar 1899–1901

> I had to fill out a form about myself. I did not know how to describe my occupation – so I hesitated between a Rentier [a person with an income from stocks and shares] and Tonkünstler – musician – generally composer I believe. I finally put down Rentier, as I thought it modest – But it apparently gives my landlady the impression of vast wealth – so she gets all out of me that she can.[1]

His brief trips to Germany had decided Dent on staying the first six months in Dresden, where there was a large and flourishing English colony he knew would welcome him, thanks to the essential letters of introduction furnished by Charles Sayle, Sedley Taylor, and his own family connections. His small independent income went much further abroad, but the idea of being so unencumbered had not quite sunk in yet: Dent was still enough of an inexperienced and nervous traveller to find such a conventional safety-net necessary, furnished with credentials he did not yet scorn, clothed in the remnants of his conventional upbringing.

It had started extremely well the first week in October 1899, with Dent joining Sedley Taylor and Hugh Allen at the chamber music festival in Meiningen, about 50 miles (80 km) west of Dresden.[2] On the boat crossing the Channel, Dent had already met up with Donald Tovey again, who performed his 'Bad Child's Book of Beasts' on the boat's piano, 'exquisitely funny, especially as he played & sang them'.[3] Meiningen was all that was civilised in Germany at the time, with a fairytale castle, Rembrandts in the local galleries and a serious music festival at its heart; Brahms had fallen in love with it and spent much of his declining years there. For Dent it was a revelation, with the Joachim Quartet playing Beethoven's String Quartet op. 131, 'which I confess is beyond me – except in some places', and Richard Mühlfeld playing clarinet in the trio written for him by Brahms, but most importantly, music-making of the highest order as part of the fabric of the place, with intelligent audiences and the company of friends. He loved it all. There was the Schubert C major Quintet, the Schumann A major Quartet, the Brahms B flat Sextet: 'an ideal performance – though rather long'. On the 10th, the weather turned quite cold as they set out for a performance of *Fidelio,* conducted by Fritz Steinbach, with Marie Joachim as Leonora 'magnificent':

1 LH 14/10/1899.

2 Sedley Taylor had been in on the festival from its inception, and wrote an article about it for the MT, vol. 36, no. 633, 'The First Saxe-Meiningen Musical Festival'.

3 Diary 04/10/1899.

> I am always overwhelmed by Fidelio whenever I see it: it upsets my emotions more than any other opera – & on this occasion I was very tearful – & so was most of the audience … even Allen who could see nothing but the incongruities of the 1st act – such as the new shoes & stockings of the prisoners & the fact that all the tenors came out at door & all the basses at the other door – even Allen was moved by the dungeon scene.[4]

By the following Saturday, Dent was busily establishing himself in Dresden, having found himself lodgings in the Altstadt and regular German lessons with a Fräulein Gottschald, recommended by Sydney Waterlow.[5] He hired himself a Schiedmeyer piano, but any attempts at composition would be interrupted by his immediate neighbours, one noisily thumping at Schumann's *Carnaval* on the piano while the other 'drowned that by singing biergarten songs with waltz refrains in a very syrupy voice'.[6]

He loved Dresden, the *Elbflorenz* or Florence on the Elbe, ancient seat of the Electors of Saxony, then at the height of its prosperity, charm and high culture, which attracted an international community. Along the northern bank of the river was the Neustadt, with its elegant avenues and self-consciously fine buildings. There were public gardens, and even the public transport was romantic, a small steam boat sailing up and down the river. Dent settled in remarkably quickly, finding several local restaurants which became his regular haunts, the Stadt Gotha, and the Residenz Café, chocolate at the Metropole, deciding that a vegetarian diet would do him good. It was also cheap: Dent fussed rather than worried about money, but he had a strong parsimonious streak, and took some pride in saving money on basics like food, while being lavish or generous in other areas. He had already made up his mind on one particular extravagance, though, and within days of his arrival went in to Klemm's bookshop to order fourteen volumes of the *Bach Gesellschaft* for 50 Marks.[7] The bookshop became one of Dent's regular haunts and its proprietor, the publisher Oswald Klemm, a kindred spirit. Dent dropped in almost daily to browse, chat and be shown gems Klemm had accumulated, such as a copy of the Bach Partitas 'engraved by Bach himself 1731'.[8] On 25 November he bought an autograph letter of Schumann's for 40 Marks.

> The Schumann interests me because he speaks of his first symphony being published … ein Freudentag für den Componisten … & later of its being "behind him" – he has other objects in view – and there is a kind word of encouragement to Kossmaly … about his compositions.[9]

4 LH 12/10/1899.

5 She would teach several generations of young Englishmen: J.B. Trend, Rupert Brooke, Francis Birrell, and others all went to her.

6 Diary 17/10/1899.

7 About 160 pounds. Binding was separate.

8 Diary 04/11/1899.

9 Diary 25/11/1899. The letter is now in the Fitzwilliam Museum.

Although he felt himself 'desperately hard up for a companion', the time spent on his own proved fruitful, time to reflect on what he was doing and to consider his future, seen in the long, ruminative letters to Lawrence. He was finding composition very frustrating:

> pianoplaying & strict counterpoint are useless & distasteful – whereas the organ might bring me an addition to my income – the drums are useful – & composition I need say no more about. In the useless & distasteful category I will also put Scripture knowledge & advanced mathematics.[10]

Prewar Dresden's English colony was an extended version of the upper-middle classes back in England, but international as well; following up the letters of introduction was tedious but necessary. The Scarborough aunts had given him introductions to a 'Miss Sitwell',[11] and Sayle had provided the formidable Frau von Brodorotti, 'whom I found most charming', doyenne of Dresden musical circles. In small measured doses Dent quite enjoyed her and her family; at one point he even playfully asked Lawrence which of her two daughters he might marry, while actually fancying the son, the painter Hermann. By December she considered him a good enough friend to show off some of her 'treasures': a card-case and cigar-case which had belonged to Liszt, and a thank-you note to her signed 'your devoted servant F. Liszt'. But she had also known Berlioz well, and Dent was far more interested to hear her read Berlioz's song 'Vive l'enfer où nous allons' from an autograph manuscript Berlioz himself had given her.

Another introduction was to a widowed Mrs Jane Spottiswoode,[12] living in the leafy suburb of Pillnitz with her spoilt little dog Ecki.[13] Dent came to love her, and escaping out to Pillnitz by foot, train or steamer was always a pleasure. She introduced him to many Dresden-based musicians and invited him to the exquisite concerts in her house or garden; the house became a refuge for him and several of his friends. Another old Etonian acquaintance trying to make a career at the opera there was E.F.C. 'Frank' Buckley,[14] beside young Rowan Hamilton,[15] composing and playing, and Dent smoothly assumed the role of teacher rather than friend, appearing older than his years. Sayle had also provided useful notes for meeting suitable young men at the Café König, but Dent found its chocolate too sweet and the company non-existent. He was making his own way.

The musical introductions so quickly multiplying were important at this stage, and Dent was being taken up as a serious musician by the people who mattered. Klemm got him into the King's Library, where he spent long hours reading through

10 LH 14/10/1899.

11 Who turned out to be a Mrs Sitwell and her daughter, connected to the larger, famous Sitwell clan who had a place near Scarborough. The three younger Sitwells later became close friends.

12 She was the widow of one of the founders of the Musical Association, William Spottiswoode, FRS.

13 Dent's nickname for him.

14 Edward Francis Cressy Buckley (1874–1943), Eton and Exeter College, Oxford.

15 Grandson of the Irish mathematician.

the scores of forgotten operas, and Grützmacher, the cellist, 'the most important musician in Dresden',[16] gave him a card to attend the Tonkünstlerverein meetings. On 24 October he met Dr Benndorf, the young music librarian, whom he liked immediately. But the real distraction was the sheer amount of excellent music-making.

To Dent, Dresden's musical life was astonishing and stimulating. At first he found sitting in the cheap seats at concerts and the opera very trying, too concerned about other people 'snorting into my back hair', too loud, too fat and wheezing, but the music itself soon obliterated any sense of his periphery. Having spent mornings fruitlessly trying to compose 'children's dances', possibly inspired by his young cousin Rhoda, aka the 'Elephant', who had entertained him at Ribston that August, Dent went out every evening and sometimes afternoons to concerts, opera and theatre. He was open to everything on offer: Egon Petri playing at a chamber concert on a Steinway from Klemm's – 'he played a few wrong notes – but had the true chamber music spirit & was intellectual';[17] an 'Historisches concert at Musenhaus; interesting items & some good old instruments'.[18] He heard the Venezuelan pianist Teresa Carreño[19] playing Tchaikovsky's B flat minor concerto, making no comments on her playing, being far more intrigued by the piece itself: 'very fine & strange music – Tschaikowsky has a wonderful way of writing waltz rhythms everywhere with most powerful emotional effects'.[20]

'These wretched people think that Dresden is the only place of education in the world & that education is the only business of Dresden!'[21] But he could not deny that Dresden's music was of a very high standard. In December he heard the recently composed *Ein Heldenleben*, conducted by Strauss himself, only twelve years older than Dent and already enjoying a successful career, grounds enough for some simple jealousy. Dent had 'wrestled with' the score beforehand ('it was awful'), and the performance did nothing to make it any better for him. He wrote sniffily to Lawrence:

> The Hero is R. Strauss himself, I imagine, as in the movement which represents the hero's works of peace he quotes motives from all his previous symphonic poems. You could not believe how perfectly hideous some of it is. When he is intelligible he becomes Humperdincky ... very German, very stodgy – very heavy & sentimental – But the work was immensely applauded.[22]

The Königliches Hoftheater gave daily performances, while the Residenz-Theater presented comic opera and plays. Using his newly purchased opera-glasses, Dent

16 Friedrich Wilhelm Grützmacher (1832–1903), principal cellist of the Dresden Court Orchestra, editor and composer.

17 Diary 06/11/1899.

18 Diary 03/11/1899.

19 Teresa Carreño (1853–1917), also a well-known opera singer, who had been living with the singer Tagliapietri, whom Dent got to know later, and later married the pianist–composer Eugen d'Albert, also performing in Dresden at this time.

20 LH 30/10/1899. The concerto, composed in 1875, was exactly the kind of music which startled and intrigued Dent, as it had its earliest critics.

21 LH 30/10/1899.

22 LH 29/12/1899.

particularly sought out operas seldom seen in England, like Weber's *Oberon* and Auber's *Fra Diavolo*, which he loved, while wickedly quoting in his diary Ebenezer Prout's remark that 'no composer has written for the triangle so happily as Auber'. He went to the first performance in Dresden of Smetana's *Die verkaufte Braut*: 'The orchestration is curious: Smetana evidently had a feeling for new effects – but his score does not always hold together very well'.[23] When he could, he went to several performances, carefully studying the scores. The Wagner operas Dent felt were less good here than in Bayreuth, while overall, the repertoire was broad: *L'Africaine*, *Lucrezia Borgia*, *Die Fledermaus*, *Pelléas et Mélisande*, *Les Huguenots* and *Il barbiere di Siviglia*. 'I did waste Money & time on Goldmark's The Queen of Sheba, millions of notes … terribly dull & ineffective'.[24]

Operatic productions then were often performed in several languages at once, the principals singing one with the chorus in another, but audiences rarely noticed. If translated versions of libretti were being used, they were often travesties of the original. Dent saw *Il barbiere* performed in German and declared:

> all the romance and Italian gaiety of it was gone. To sing flourishes in German words is silly … Les Huguenots is pretty good rubbish in French – but in German it is awful. Meyerbeer's rhythms & feeling (such as he has) are utterly incompatible with German words. The theatrically polite inanities & pomposities of the libretto come out heavy & stilted in German.[25]

Moreover, the relationship between sound and sense, music and words was obscured by the adulation of the celebrity performer, Dent felt; this became conviction. 'I am beginning to grasp the operatic system – but only just beginning', he wrote to Lawrence. What he thought he meant was an understanding of opera with a view to composing one of his own, 'living music' he called it, which he could triumphantly submit as a piece for his Fellowship or doctorate. It was, of course, terribly high-minded:

> my opera must be thoroughly English – on Shakespeare if possible … Opera must depend on human passions & human interests – so that the audience can get worked up to a real sympathy with the people on the stage. That is what you get in Fidelio. I must say that in Wagner … (with some exceptions) I don't get it. I feel that the people are not real, they are merely there to sing interesting music or to serve a a foreground to interesting stage effects. I don't despise stage effects any more than I despise music – but they must both be of such a kind as to stimulate your emotions & help on the drama.[26]

Dent never would compose his opera, but he was beginning to understand how the operatic medium should function as a whole. Far more important than composition was the use he made of the operatic ideas he was considering, based on

23 Diary 18/10/1899. These were among the odder operas he would try to introduce thirty years later at Sadler's Wells.

24 LH 30/10/1899.

25 *Ibid.*

26 *Ibid.*

his growing appreciation of production styles and standards, foundations for all his subsequent writings on opera beside his influential and radical views on how opera should be produced.

> for moments of awful tension let us have the speaking voice – But I reserve that for very rare moments indeed – The locus classicus is Fidelio – where Jaquino calls out in the prison scene that the Minister has arrived. There is also the commonplace element ... the Lancelot Gobbo & his ilk ... Mozart hinted in Don Giovanni that they were amenable to treatment.

By the second week in December he had only finished scoring the first movement of his new Serenade: 'I am afraid that you will think it a very small result of 2 months' work – & I suppose it is: but I have had so many other things to do.'[27] He was trying to incorporate ideas picked up through his constant listening: 'I made an attempt at a scherzo for my serenade in hornpipe style – but it is harder than it looks'. But Dent's 'work' was almost always done in a very sociable context, fitted in between coffees and concerts, drifting with each new influence. Having seen Verdi's *Falstaff*, he warmed to Boïto as a scholar and poet, then Swinburne's 'glorious effects of rhythm & colour', 'Paolo & Francesca' from Dante's *Inferno*, but 'some of the prose scenes are quite absurdly after the style of W.S. Gilbert!'. The conspicuous lack of progress vexed him, and that same December probably pushed him into postponing any elusive doctoral musical composition, instead to try for a Fellowship at King's, on his own terms. The attraction of such a step was dual: no college Fellowship had ever been awarded for Music, and if he actually succeeded, beside the official status, it would buy him more time for his Mus D. 'You see', he wrote to Lawrence,

> I want to send in something to the College council next December, which something will probably be a longer Serenade or Symphony. This of course will merely be a 'balon d'essai' – a forlorn hope – or whatever you like to call it – to pave the way for my last chance in December 1901 – After that, I shall feel more settled – one way or another: till then – i.e. till March 1902 – I shall do myself best by continuing to wander & pick up impressions – it seems.[28]

In the meantime, he set himself out to enjoy a Christmas of his own devising. First, the 'childish delight' in the Christmas tree his landlords the Gerickes had put up for him, with lighted candles: 'I mean to spend all my Christmases abroad in future. My relations are so much more agreeable at a distance'.[29] Then, after Christmas, his little fantasy materialised when both Cham and young Robert Vansittart[30] arrived to study German, 'C's fraudulent German lesson'. They went to the opera – to *Tannhäuser, Lohengrin, Fra Diavolo* – and at Vansittart's insistence to the Schauspielhaus for lighter entertainment. But their relationship had changed;

27 LH 17/12/1899.

28 *Ibid.*

29 LH 29/12/1899.

30 The Old Etonian and future diplomat, son of his brother Jack's friends who had visited Ribston the year before, when Dent had befriended him with illicit cigarettes in the gun room.

it sounds more like having an amiable but rather smelly dog around: 'I am secretly fearing Cham will be a nuisance'. He allowed himself to relax even more in the New Year, the turn of the century, going out to Mrs Spottiswoode's at Pillnitz, where the local pianist Bachmann played regularly, to Frederick Lamond's Beethoven recitals, to hear Eugen d'Albert play his own concerto, to more operas – *Werther* 'not very interesting & lamentably devoid of action – but the music is delicate & poetical'[31] – then to performances of *Manfred* and the play *Egmont*.

Really, he was putting off even his King's Fellowship proposal, his test of both college and himself, what he termed 'ringing the doorbell and running away'. At the time it was an unprecedented application, but if accepted, he would be forced to step up to the mark, which terrified him. His deliberate submission of a composition was also an implicit challenge to the status quo and therefore risky; such a public humiliation was for Dent of all things the worst that could happen. Not until halfway through February did he grasp the nettle:

> last night I got as far as writing a note to the Provost on the subject of my sending in a musical composition as a fellowship dissertation. I left it open on my table to give me time to change my mind … it was owing to my finding that I was really getting on with my 3rd movement that I decided to write. I put off writing a long time: I always had Sayle's words gnawing at my innards … 'Perhaps when you get to Dresden you will find that you want to give up music altogether.' & I had 2 or 3 spells of absolute incapacity & consequent rage.[32]

At the same time he mobilised Lawrence to sniff out what support he might have amongst the Fellows. In fact, King's was doing its best to accommodate this novelty, a musical composition instead of a dissertation, but the application had thrown them into confusion.[33] The Provost, Augustus Austen Leigh, listened to the only musical voices at hand, Mann's, Browning's and Nixon's, beside the other, more conservative views which strongly felt that academic standards had to be maintained and would somehow be undermined by Music. Dent knew his own worth, that he was a fit candidate for a Fellowship at King's, but how to demonstrate this via his music to 'Augustin the Cor Anglais' and the more conservative elements in college? When it came, he completely misunderstood College's clumsy attempt to accommodate him, afraid that because of their ignorance and in the absence of any precedent, the bar would be set so low as to be insulting.

> The PROVOST [written in Greek letters] … wrote that my case was referred to the Election triumvirate – which is one step. I can't see though why they should accept a composition & go through the expense of having it criticized & not reward it with a fellowship – I mean supposing it to be good enough. Of course I don't expect & I don't want a fellowship for stuff that isn't worth looking at. The

31 Diary 24/02/1900.

32 LH 13/02/1900.

33 In Florence that April he pumped Browning about it: 'OB was very full of my fellowship business, & gave me to understand that the council would have tossed my proposal into the wastepaperbasket without more ado if he had not stood up & fought for me.' LH 06/04/1900.

> Provost [Greek letters again] brought up the picture argument. But the University does teach free composition … and the new Mus. D. is to be given for free composition alone – & composition forms an important part of the Mus. Bac. exam. The University does not teach & makes no attempt to teach aesthetics as a branch of music. And although it examines us in musical history it doesn't teach it.[34]

He was already settled in Munich and sliding into the artistic and homosexual crowd around the Heck restaurant when he received a stiff letter from the Provost, 'saying that the electors wd accept a musical composition if it conformed to the regulations for the Mus M exercise. It gave me a horrid shock.'[35] What he felt to be 'worse than refusal' had happened: Music as an accepted academic discipline was to be strangled by outdated regulations. He immediately fired off a long letter to Lawrence.

> They would not waste time, sensible people, over trying to make out whether a musical composition was a dissertation or not – but fools-fools-fools – they passed a resolution compared with which the Lex Heinze[36] is a Habeas Corpus – namely that they wd accept a composition from me 'in support of my claim to a fellowship (sweet irony) provided that it conform to the conditions of the Exercise for the degree in Master in Music' … It means, I fancy, a party of pigs … influenced by such as Willy Leigh & Daddy Mann. It means stiff academic form – fugue–canon – it means choral music, which I can't write … things wch I would be ashamed to have performed or printed. A sacred work I will not write – unless I can make blasphemous & that might lead to awkward results … If a member of the council had popped up through a trap I should have strangled him.[37]

By the next morning he was feeling more rational about it all: 'The beastly exercise will at any rate be good practice. If I am an artist I ought to be able to triumph over the difficulties … the only horror of it is – if I fail: there is a year and a half almost lost'. He asked Lawrence to dig out the requirements for the Mus M and send them. When Lawrence ventured to make a few constructive suggestions, Dent bridled:

> Don't throw Bach's organ works at me: I'm not Bach: & fugue is not the normal, natural means of expression in the year 1900 … yes, I must do the hogwash business … I want the material advantages of a fellowship – if I can get them – & besides my duty to myself it is my duty to my art – to Eton & to Lloyd – to my greatgrandfather & his friend dear old Billy Shield – to Stanford & Cambridge music (bar of music) to make the attack.[38]

What was to have been Dent's year of consolidation was turning into procrastination and vacillation. His whole perception of himself was being overturned, first by the drab expectations of the Fellowship committee, then by his own failure to

34 LH February, 1900.

35 Diary 09/03/1900.

36 See below.

37 LH March 1900 (n.d.).

38 LH March 1900 (n.d.).

recognise the truest abilities in himself. But he persevered, plunging into the cultural unknown, and the prolonged struggle would bring out the best in him, forcing him to come to terms with his limitations as well as to recognise more clearly his strengths and his future path.

Dent was in Munich at a remarkable time in its history, on the cusp between the old and the outrageously new in art, music and culture. Most of his things had been left behind in Dresden at the Gerickes, and he settled into the Hotel Roth, near to the theatres in the centre, and for the first few days worked diligently on his variations, taking long walks around the city, along the nearby river, strolling into the Pinakothek, only gradually realising how different from Dresden it all was. At first he wrote to Lawrence, begging him: 'Will you take any bribe to come out here by the next available train? – even if I have to halve my income with you for life!' There was so much that was new: Strauss was there, conducting his *Macbeth* and *Also Sprach Zarathustra*: 'They were very finely played – far better than at Dresden: & both are clearer & more musical than the Heldenleben.'[39] He went to Cornelius' *Barbier von Bagdad*, to *Tannhäuser* and *Lohengrin*, *Die Walküre* again and *Die Zauberflöte*, which he described to Lawrence as 'the most perfect opera ever written' even though in this performance the singers 'hurried'.[40] He dismissed Siegfried Wagner's *Die Bärenhäuter* as 'fearful rubbish'. At the Hofkirche he heard masses by Victoria, Orlando di Lasso and a Rheinberger *Offertorium*, then d'Albert's *Die Abreise*, 'a most delightful little opera – very fresh & delicate: with unexpected reminiscences of Parry & Sullivan!'[41]

Although he had the fourteen volumes of the *Bach Gesellschaft* with him, there is little evidence that he spent much time studying them. He was too preoccupied, spending day and night at the arty little Kneipe or bar he had found on his previous trip, the Café Heck,[42] where the denizens exposed him to the alternative cultural life of Munich, far more avant-garde than Dresden, coupled with a much more open homosexual society. Suddenly, here was an open door to Dent's own hidden self; he was at once drawn to it and repelled by it. Beside his old acquaintance the oculist Jacobsen, who had known Brahms and fulminated against Wagner, another resident musician there was a young 'Behr-Waltrunn' who showed him his compositions and asked him out to his parents' country place.[43] This was the easy, clearly defined relationship Dent most liked. He 'liked' Behr-Waltrunn's work, 'except that he seems to be curiously awkward over modulation & over form'. They were joined by several other artistic types, and stayed there talking, smoking and drinking until the small hours: Franz von Schultze, a portrait-painter called Cantstellar and another artist, Hans Roth: 'attracted by a pleasant appearance & made an imaginary draught an

39 Diary 16/03/1900.

40 LH 19/03/1900.

41 Diary 24/03/1900.

42 By the Hofgarten. Unfortunately, it later became one of Hitler's favourite places.

43 I cannot find this composer: a Munich composer Anton Beer-Walbrunn (1864–1929) only took his wife's name in 1904.

excuse for moving my cup of coffee to his table'.[44] He saw quite a lot of Roth, but Dent still held back:

> I should like him better if he wasn't so amatorily inclined – not that I am a strict moralist – but because it raises up that same sort of ungetoverable. The barrier between me & him that I experience e.g. with men who are ardently religious. I am narrow-minded, I suppose & can't appreciate anything outside my own stupid little art-world. But 'Philadelphia e tolerana, ec'e solamente un passo dalla toleranza al perdono?' as Coyle Drummele [sic] says in La Seconda Moglie – otherwise Mrs T in which I saw the great Eleonora Duse on Saturday.[45]

His new circles were buzzing about the 'Lex Heinze', a law then being tested and much satirised in the contemporary magazines Dent was beginning to read, *Jugend* and *Simplicissimus*.[46] The law had originally been brought in with reference to notorious brothel keepers in Berlin, but 'certain sections apply to art: & against these artistic Germany is protesting'.[47] The acceptable boundaries were certainly being tested in Munich, and Dent always liked to see what was new, battling his own naturally conservative tastes. Paul Klee and Wassily Kandinsky were both students here at this time, Klee also studying the violin with Joseph Joachim.[48] Dent explored galleries and exhibitions, including the Secession exhibition with 'many startling pictures & a few good ones'; on impulse, he bought three, a Hans Thoma, a Max Klinger and a Böcklin.[49] His last night there he met another serious artist, Max Slevogt,[50] and his last evening in Munich was pleasantly passed at the Café Heck, arguing with Slevogt about the importance of Wagner, now for Dent superseded by Mozart.

❧ ❧ ❧

Dent had already been grumbling to Lawrence about the adverse effect of research on his 'work', i.e., his composition: 'I don't much want to research & I am indeed scarcely competent to do so. My work is at the devil', so it was fortuitous that Louis Paul's death in May cut short his time in Italy. As Louis' executor, he had to return to England after after barely handing over his introduction to the Marciana librarian Malagola – 'a sort of Italian Sayle' – in Venice, travelling back on 13 May. As it turned out, he needed the break, having allowed the newly discovered social aspects

44 Diary 14/03/1900.

45 LH 19/03/1900. 'Brotherhood and tolerance, and it's only a step from tolerance to forgiveness.' Quotation from Arthur Wing Pinero's play *The Second Mrs Tanqueray*, which he had seen in Italian.

46 The satirical magazine *Simplicissimus* was founded in 1896. *Jugend* is possibly best known for *Jugendstil*, the German Art Nouveau style.

47 LH 07/03/1900.

48 Klee's diaries show that he went to some of the same concerts as Dent. At one point he thought about becoming a cartoonist for *Simplicissimus*.

49 Hans Thoma (1839–1924); Max Klinger (1857–1920); Arnold Böcklin (1826–1901).

50 Max Slevogt (1868–1932), German Impressionist painter, who later designed a famous production of *Don Giovanni*.

of his travels to take over, even research taking a back seat. On arrival that April in Florence, to his dismay, the first people he had encountered at the Pension Bonciani were Browning and his secretary Fred, and for the rest of his stay, instead of any 'work', Dent let himself be hauled around Browning's Florence, to outlying villas and churches, visiting his celebrity acquaintances like Cosima and Siegfried Wagner, and finally, at the end of each trying day dragged and patted up to Browning's opulent rooms 'gorgeously decorated in crimson & gold', to play duets on his Blüthner grand, feeling tired and headachy, his usual symptom when he was unhappy.[51]

About the only thing Dent got out of Browning's vexatious company was an introduction to Robert Hobart Cust, brother of the art historian Lionel Cust. 'I thought he would do nicely for my garden (I have a garden in several places now – & I look out for new plants when I can, & water them diligently)', Dent wrote archly to Lawrence. By now Dent was automatically on the lookout for suitable young men, his plant-collecting a distracting habit: 'I think I shall probably find a young man or two here.' Cust would become an awkward acquaintance, but on the surface he was an urbane and civilised man, knowledgeable about Italian art and fond of decorating his rooms with 'viewy' young men.[52]

For a few weeks, Dent slid easily back into Cambridge life, going to Roger Fry's lectures on Masaccio, reading the new King's magazine *Basileon*, catching up with King's friends Haward, Hugh Meredith, [53] Will Mollison,[54] Jack Pollock, Waterlow and Forster, working with Rottenburg and Rubens on more Footlights music, sitting with Forster and his companion Spencer 'under the quince tree reading Emerson's curiously rhapsodic essay on Friendship'. He met Bernard Sickert, the painter Walter's younger brother, who sang in Mann's choir concert of *Judas Maccabeus*, and played bowls with him and Nixon. At Forster's invitation, he went to Milton Bryant to see his cousin, Miss Synnot. He spent a weekend at Eton, visiting Miss Hackett, and catching up with more old Old Etonian friends, Hugo Bell, Francis 'Timmy' Jekyll and Oliffe Richmond, but mostly to show his Serenade to Sir Walter Parratt and to Charles Lloyd. He even 'discussed the idea with S.[ayle] of making myself a permanent home in Cambridge. S. was very favourable.'[55]. Pleasant rooms were found at 10 King's Parade, just across from the college gatehouse, over Severs the printer.[56]

Otherwise, he tinkered with his music, anxiously writing to Stanford and begging a meeting, the Fellowship application heavy on his mind. Dent knew that the stated requirement, a dull piece of prescribed composition, even done to his own exacting standards, would help neither his application nor his long-term prospects, and he thought he needed something more, a dissertation, but time was running out: he was due to go out to Italy again on 2 August. On 28 July he finally bearded Stanford at the

51 Diary, April 1900.

52 Robert Henry Hobart Cust (1861–1940), art historian.'Viewy' is Forster's apt term.

53 Hugh Owen Meredith (1878–1964), economist, academic.

54 William Mayhew Mollison (1878–1967) became an eminent doctor.

55 Diary 08/06/1900.

56 The rooms are now part of Primavera art gallery.

Royal College of Music: 'He was tired & out of sorts & seemed to take no interest in my work at all. On the subject of my dissertation he was more interested – & suggested that I should work on the lesser Italian composers of which Leo is the chief.'[57]

Stanford had himself been editing Leonardo Leo's *Dixit Dominus* in C for performance, and the current lack of scholarly work on Leo must have made such a task difficult, but at the time Dent simply did not recognise what was a major turning-point in his career. 'I went in to Haward & received consolation.' The next day he consulted Grove's, then rummaged around in catalogues to get some idea of what lay in store for him. 'I am appalled at the quantity of material I must read.' Decades later, Dent commented on the state of musical research which had still not progressed, least of all in the teaching and support:

> As far as I know there is no University school of music in England where students are systematically trained for research. Researchers mostly have to train themselves. When I began work on Alessandro Scarlatti at the age of 24, I knew very little German and hardly a word of Italian; I had read a certain amount of musical history in the standard English books of that time, but I had no knowledge whatever of current foreign research. I had never even heard of the *Vierteljahrschrift für Musikwissenschaft*, although it was in our library at Cambridge; the only people who gave me any sort of direction as to how to set about my work were people quite outside the world of music who happened to have a general knowledge of library methods.[58]

So with very mixed feelings, Dent set out again in August, hoping that such an agreeable companion as Sydney Waterlow might mitigate the uncertainties of Venetian archives. They met in Lugano to sample the spectacular Italian lakes before making their way across to Venice, Sydney making it clear from the outset that no expense was to be spared and insisting on putting up at the Hotel Splendide: 'fearful extravagance', Dent groaned. 'The art of economy is one which I have to instruct Sydney in, but I prefer his tending to extravagance to Armstrong's … parsimony'.[59] But he allowed himself to enjoy the unaccustomed luxury, and to be coaxed into swimming again, in clear, cold lake waters surrounded by mountains. 'I had not bathed for 7 years or so', he wrote to Lawrence, 'mainly owing to a hatred of appearing in public without my spectacles – but at Lugano we had the place practically to ourselves'.[60] Regular bathing became one of the most liberating and joyful parts of his Italian experience; that, and long walks in the hills. It crossed his mind, he told Lawrence, to abandon everything, simply 'chucking the work' and retreating back up into the hills for the rest of his life.

But despite his impressive appearance, his excellent connections and intellectual brilliance, anxiety ran deep in Sydney, and with good wine and a sympathetic listener ('my priestly appearance'), he gushed about his 'devotion' to a young lady.

57 Diary 28/07/1900.

58 'Music and Musical Research', *Acta Musicologica*, vol. 3 (1931), p. 5.

59 LH 05/08/1900.

60 *Ibid.*

Dent was appalled; not only had he completely deceived himself in their relationship, but now found Sydney repulsive.

> It was horrible to me to see the self abasement with which he spoke of her … This is the second friend I lose in this way … how much more I had hoped to have from him! – I thought this was only the beginning – & find it the end – or almost that.[61]

The happy dynamic abruptly changed; now, if he was not to be a sweet distraction, Dent rationalised, Sydney was now an irritating one. 'I despair of doing any serious work as long as S. is here: at least at present … it takes all I can do to restrain his extravagance'.[62]

Once in Venice, installed at the modest Albergo Cappello Nero, Sydney fretted, so Dent went out alone, climbing up the tower of San Giorgio Maggiore, sitting in the cool interior of San Marco, taking pleasure in discovering a little 'curiosity shop' offering autograph scores of Porpora and Marcello, and even more pleasure in beating the price down from 200 to 80 francs for three Marcello cantatas. The music made its way back to Cambridge. They bathed at the 'glorious' Lido, but all the time Dent felt Sydney's less than wholehearted enjoyment, doubtless a response to Dent's grumpiness. Even encountering Dent's delightful friends, the Comptons, Sydney retreated, with the excuse that Lady Alwyne talked too much. When Sydney left on 24 August, Dent found that he missed him 'dreadfully – in spite of having work to do'.[63] The episode made him rethink any fantasies about travelling companions, but soon Dent was discovering distractions of quite a different kind.

For about a week he worked hard in the cold and 'horribly draughty' Sansovino Marciana library, reading manuscripts for hours on end.[64] Possibly helped by his excellent connections, he had got permission from the consulate to borrow books to take back to his more comfortable rooms, at first still resentful of all this unwanted research taking him away from his composing. On 6 September, Lawrence received an extraordinary letter, bursting with excitement:

> This afternoon I began reading some cantatas by A. Scarlatti, in the most delightful little MS book that belonged to the Contarini family – oblong: about as long as the extreme width of this sheet & about as high as this line from the top of the page. It take 4 staves a page – bound very elegantly – neatly if not always accurately written … The cantatas are interesting, & some beautiful. There is a lot to read here – I may have to come back again later. There are 8 operas of Perez in MS. wch he wrote for Lisbon: & some 200 operas of all kinds between 1659 & 1790

61 Diary 05/08/1900.

62 LH 18/08/1900.

63 LH 31/08/1900.

64 This does sound odd in August. The Marciana is dark and cool, lit mostly by the many windows, and reading MSS there must have been taxing.

– wch will include a good many of my people: but I am not sure whether there are libretti only or scores.[65]

Besides the Perez, Dent was thrilled to find some more autograph scores of Marcello and Porpora, and many more, less well known. 'My dissertation work is becoming a monstrosity. It grows & grows – & I begin to think it will take a lifetime to collect materials for & the whole University Library to hold it when written.' At this time, Dent gradually and it must be said, gleefully recognised, very few scholars knew much about early opera, and most of those were in Germany; the British scholars seriously working on early music known to Dent were Fuller Maitland and Barclay Squire, who in 1899 had published an edition of the *Fitzwilliam Virginal Book*. The mixed motives for testing the Cambridge system with his Fellowship submission were now driving this new passion for primary research: 'by the way', he added to Lawrence, 'I am going to give Fuller Maitland some bits of my mind in my dissertation. His inaccuracies & ignorances in the Fitz. Cat. are extraordinary: & one is quite funny.'.[66]

At last Dent had found something that was all his own. All the practical knowledge he had been building up to help him understand how to compose music was now being diverted to another purpose, while the necessity of copying scores accurately helped him to study the music more closely. Although enchanted by the Alessandro Scarlatti he was discovering, he found the Perez 'dull', and however exciting it may have been to uncover these operas and cantatas, he was not going to let the simple fact of obscurity overwhelm his excellent taste.

> I found the loveliest bits of vocal chamber music of A. Scarlatti – & copied out some which I will show you … the text is corrupt & requires a lot of emendation: some times quite obvious, & at other times most puzzling. Moreover as I copy them straight out with their soprano clefs & prepared basses I think you wd find them rather troublesome reading.[67]

Evenings, he relaxed again and listened to military bands playing Puccini, Bellini and Ponchielli's *I promessi sposi*, 'wch I rather liked', better than the Puccini, which he spent a lifetime trying to learn to like: 'Puccini seems to have no other ideas except successions of hideous 5th & endless sticky stuff'.

When at last he returned to Dresden via Munich on the 28 September, it was as an old hand, with specific work to do, now hot on the track of early opera manuscripts. Lawrence arrived on 3 October to learn German, and plunged into Dent's new world, first, to the opera, to *Der Freischütz*, to the premiere of d'Albert's *Kain* and to his *Die Abreise*, with Frank Wedekind acting.[68] He was introduced to Frau von

65 LH 06/09/1900. In his diary Dent records reading Perez's *Dido, L'Eroe Cinese, Ipermestra, Alessandro, Artaserse* (as well as Vinci's), besides *Pasquele Cafaras*, not in Grove's.

66 LH 06/09/1900.

67 *Ibid.*

68 Benjamin Franklin 'Frank' Wedekind (1864–1918), German playwright, actor, satirist, whose radical plays were later used for operas, most notably Berg's *Lulu*. Dent met him later, having seen him in plays and in the Munich cabaret *Die elf Scharfrichter*, and read his pieces in *Simplicissimus*.

Brodorotti, to the Sitwells, to Mrs Spottiswoode. 'I took Haward to see Klemm about 12 & naturally there was no getting him out of the shop.' Dent left him happily there while while he nipped into the library to transcribe the Wolfenbüttel catalogue.[69]

Back in Cambridge, armed with his exciting new knowledge and purpose, Dent rekindled his old enthusiasm and drive. He met and liked the new editor of the *Cambridge Review*, Hilton Young, who became one of his growing circle of friends.[70] In his new rooms hung his newly framed German pictures, his copies of Canalettos, his furniture arranged for the visitors he knew would come: Forster and Hugh Meredith came up straight away, followed by Nixon carrying scores of Piccinni,[71] and even Mann, with some autograph manuscripts of Marcello. 10 King's Parade quickly became a mecca for early music and Italian thoughts; Dent's friends both enjoyed and mocked his freshly acquired Italian affectations. Apart from their intrinsic interest, the operas and libretti he had been studying for the past month were beginning to give him ideas about his own composition: he was considering English poetry anyway, having developed a liking for Metastasio's libretti, so began to look at big, dramatic poems: Byron, perhaps. 'This is the result of Schumann's *Manfred* & D'Albert's *Kain*!'

'I have fairly well decided on Hellas (Shelley) for the composition,' he wrote to Lawrence in Dresden on 28 October, 'it pleases me greatly, & will go to music grandly. Read it.' 'We strew these opiate flowers' reflects Dent's deep appreciation of poetry and the natural rhythms of English verse. For a week or so he tried out settings on his piano, and decided it would 'do', evolving into a massive undertaking for full orchestra and chorus, almost unperformable, but now he put it aside. 'Furniture occupies my mind greatly', he told Lawrence:

> Do I take music seriously? I get more & more interested in A. Scarlatti & C. Leo's S. Elma al Calvario is very great. Mann remarks cynically to my outpourings of enthusiasm that 'the worst of these subjects is that they are so fascinating, that one can't take notice of anything else.'[72]

Completely engrossed, he spent most days at the Fitzwilliam reading Scarlatti cantatas, or going down to London to the British Museum to consult Barclay Squire, or in his absence, R.A. Streatfeild, who became a close friend.[73] There was a vast amount of work involved, transcriptions to be done of catalogues, manuscript

69 The Landesbibliothek (Herzog August) at Wolfenbüttel in Lower Saxony was and is one of the great collections, and has a large collection of Vinci MSS *et al.*

70 Edward Hilton Young, 1st Baron Kennett (1879–1960), writer and politician.

71 Niccolò Piccinni (1728–1800), popular Neapolitan opera composer. He went to look up *Atys* in the Pendlebury.

72 LH 28/10/1900.

73 Richard Alexander Streatfeild (1866–1919), musicologist, became Keeper of Printed Books at the BM. Like a number of his colleagues he was homosexual. He contributed to Grove's and wrote several seminal music books, especially one on Handel which greatly influenced Dent's own thought. His *Masters of Italian Music* (1895) was more about modern composers. Dent held him in high esteem, and he revised Streatfeild's standard work on *The Opera* (1896, 1925).

scores and parts. On 2 November he wrote to Lawrence in Dresden, 'I had the idea & Barclay Squire jumped at it of making a complete thematic catalogue (thematisches Verzeichniss) of the 400 or more cantatas of Alessandro Scarlatti.' He asked Lawrence to consult Benndorf for some idea of how to design the slips he was planning to use to keep his notes in order.

With his project now under way, Dent could settle down to enjoying himself. A passion for early keyboard instruments was taking off in Cambridge;[74] his harpsichord, now retrieved from Francis Jenkinson and installed in his new rooms, was a particular point of interest:

> had a pleasant harpsichord party on Friday; Miss Stewart, her brother, Jenkinson, Brewster & Crace ... Mrs Gaskoin was so fascinated with the harpsichord that she took off her gloves & played – which I had never heard her do before. She played pianoforte music of the very early period & of a rather watery type. It sounded very odd, especially as it was not at all suited to the harpsichord.[75]

After Mrs Gaskoin's attempts, Dent began to dig out more appropriate music, mostly from the Fitzwilliam. He did not like the Handel he found there (possibly the sonatas), but was enjoying the 'Italian cantatas' which he could play with Mrs Archbold, one of the excellent local musicians, and Jenkinson brought him an 'Elizabethan MS song' to transcribe.

Once again, playing tympani in CUMS, going to the Ladies Musical Club at Mrs Archer Hind's in Newnham, playing 'strange things for Alan Gray's lectures', Cambridge music drew Dent back in. There were musical evenings with the Corbetts and Mrs Archbold singing: 'not pretty but French with a good voice & is a musician ... won my heart by singing Alessandro Scarlatti'.[76] Such gatherings also made it possible for him to hear properly some of the music he had collected and stimulated his natural gift for inspiring enthusiasm. The Greek Play this year had Parry exuberantly conducting his own music: 'Parry amused us very much after Wood had concluded the rehearsal with God save the Queen (transposing in different sections) by playing it with each hand in a separate key.'[77] With it a stream of more visitors, largely Etonians. Morgan Forster was now coming round almost daily and soaking up all Dent's Italian anecdotes: the English travellers clinging to their Baedekers, the small absurdities of pension life at the Bonciani, all recounted in Dent's lofty acerbic style, mitigated by the underlying warmth he felt for the life-force there. 'I wish', Dent wrote to Lawrence in Dresden, 'I could stay on here the whole year instead of going to Naples. Shall I chuck the damned fellowship business?'[78]

74 Not only the Gaskoins, but Daisy Stewart (soon Mrs Jenkinson) had Mozart evenings at home; her niece Katharine inherited her harpsichord; the Bulloughs had an Italian harpsichord inherited from Mrs Bullough's aunt, Eleonora Duse, now in the Fitzwilliam. There was a burgeoning 'restoration' industry, one result of which was Sayle's ersatz clavichord, but also Harding's book *The Piano-Forte*.

75 Diary 13/12/1900.

76 LH 14/01/1901.

77 Diary 02/11/1900.

78 LH 10/11/1900.

Dent's obvious attachment to Cambridge continued to vex his family.[79] A variety of conciliatory gestures, invitations to Cambridge, promises to visit Uncle Ted and the aunts, now installed in their villa near Nice,[80] cut no ice. Under the weight of such disapprobation, Christmas at Ribston was a trial, and with so many duty visits spread out over the holiday, he couldn't get any work done. 'How can I', he moaned to Lawrence, 'get inspiration when I look up from my writing table to a vision of W.P. Frith's Road to Ruin on a hard green wall met by a slab of wood grained in imitation of alternate stripes of 2 light & one dark?'[81]

❧ ❧ ❧

He was due to leave England on 18 February, not expecting to return until the autumn, working up to the last minute. As he pored over the catalogues at the Fitzwilliam, Dent began to realise that there were serious mistakes not only in the catalogues, but in the current editions. 'I am now reading La Rosaura (A. Scarlatti) in the edition of the Gesellschaft für Musikforschung', Dent wrote to Lawrence:

> it is rather spoilt by the editing of Dr Robert Eitner[82] – who seems from his editing to be an ignoramus & from his preface to be a crass idiot. He has published 2 acts without the third; he has printed them from MSS in the British Museum which he has never seen & I fancy only sketchily has collated – His Italian is fatuous: that is, he has no idea of how words ought to be distributed to music … Wretched Herren Professoren! … He fills up his figured bass regardless of the figures & without the least feeling for Scarlatti's style which is plain enough to see from Scarlatti's own string parts.[83]

After more sessions in the Fitzwilliam he uncovered scholarly mistakes closer to home:

> Fuller Maitland is a perfect idiot. He finds a MS score of A-Scarlattis concertos (printed in parts by B. Cooke of London abt 1740: these at the Brit Mus: also 21 movts therof sent in a letter by B. Cooke to his brother 1740) at the Fitzwilliam & catalogues them as 'Scarlatti (probably Pietro)'. Pietro Scarlatti is '<u>probably</u>' a musical Mrs Harris.[84]

But Dent was right; it quickly became clear that even distinguished scholars were making mistakes when confronted with the unfamiliar, especially in manuscripts. Copies had to be painstakingly, laboriously, accurately made of each musical

79 Diary 31/10/1900.

80 This was La Selva, Brancolar, with spectacular views of the Mediterranean Sea. Dent often stopped off there, even though it meant a big shift in his behaviour and habits. They didn't approve of smoking.

81 LH 23/12/1900.

82 Robert Eitner (1832–1905), one of the pioneering musicologists, who published several reference books still in use.

83 LH 30/01/1901.

84 LH 16/02/1901. See also Diary 16/02/1901 and Dent, *Alessandro Scarlatti* (London, 1905), appendix, p. 205.

example, and this was where most of Dent's time was spent, while through the meticulous copying process he gained understanding of the texts and the musical styles. Although later in Rome he did bump into Maclean[85] and Brooke working at the Vatican Library, few scholars could afford the time or money to travel as extensively as Dent was prepared to do, and Dent was now a seasoned traveller who knew about the trains and the local transport, while his languages facilitated both his research needs and his personal wants. But the projected dissertation project was still by no means clear, and Dent had to improvise as obstacles presented themselves: the closed libraries, obstructive librarians, sloppy or non-existent catalogues, the wrong opinions given as fact, not to mention the fleas, the cockroaches, the damp and dingy working conditions, sticky covers and mouldy pages. He throve on it all. His enthusiastic, entertaining letters to friends like Haward, Lubbock and Forster encouraged them to travel as well. All eventually had careers which fed in some measure upon their European experiences.

Although desperate to get to Florence, first Dent had to 'dance attendance on the aunts' for a fortnight in Nice, at the Hotel Cuniez where his sister Isabel and his mother were staying for most of the winter. Even a concert with Paderewski playing Chopin made him squirm, he declared, but he turned it to some purpose: the cult of the performer was the subject of his later talk with Alessandro Kraus at Fiesole, who astonishingly could remember Paganini playing in Frankfurt in 1828.[86] 'He never played the same thing twice but was always trying to find out something new.' Such raw encounters stimulated wider ideas about Scarlatti, his musical world and about music history itself.

From this point on, Dent's new and separate life takes shape; the scholar, the new breed of musician, the man who can explore his sexuality freely, all became parts of his new persona, blossoming under an Italian sun. The voice in his letters becomes more mature, more assured, reflecting his pleasure in hectic daily life in Florence, then in quick succession, Rome, Monte Cassino, Naples, Sicily, Bologna, Modena, Venice and Munich.

Kraus's collection and Fiesole were the starting-point for Dent's subsequent travels and research. Besides some fatherly advice about not marrying – which amused Dent – Kraus produced a collection of 'Sistine Chapel music (copied for Stanislaus King of Poland & later in the collection of Prince Poniatowski)', containing some early Scarlatti, which Dent duly catalogued. Within the first week Dent was working at the 'Bib Nat' and the Real Istituto Musicale, looking at Scarlatti's opera *La Teodora*, and discussing others with its librarian, Riccardo Gandolfi. In Gandolfi's circle he

85 Charles Donald Maclean (1843–1916), British Secretary of the International Musical Society, who organised the International Congress at London, 1911; taught Director of Music at Eton before Dent's time.

86 Diary 09/03/1901. Kraus also told Dent: 'He wanted to marry my sister, but my mother would not hear of it – I am very glad he did not marry her. He used to play the fiddle from morning till night, walking up & down with no coat on & his waistcoat unbuttoned & a flannel shirt.'

met Professor Antonio Scontrino, a native of of Trapani, Sicily[87] and a composer himself, extremely interested in Dent's Scarlatti research, and so impressed with his work and ideas that he immediately offered Dent crucial introductions at Trapani, Palermo and Naples, and at the Accademia Santa Cecilia in Rome, an entrée to these enclosed academic societies. 'At last I feel started on my work: that is I ought to feel so: but at this moment I am chiefly conscious of having a good deal more Chianti on board than I am supposed to hold.'[88]

After that first hectic week in Florence, he wrote to Lawrence in Dresden, asking him to consult Benndorf about some of the Scarlatti trails he had uncovered so far, his tone far from confident: 'I am going to Sicily to grub for birth registers and Kraus … thinks it quite likely that I shall find something.' By then he was beginning to recognise his own points of ignorance; for example, that the libraries in Rome were closed from Thursday to Monday, that the Accademia S. Cecilia library was 'in confusion' and that there was no Scarlatti at all in the Biblioteca Vittorio Emmanuele. Even his precious introductions didn't guarantee success: through the voluble Conte Dandini he was given an introduction to the influential Prince Chigi,[89] but that great library was currently shut, 'I suppose some MSS got stolen or damaged', and the prince himself out of town.[90] From both the Prefetto della musica at S. Maria Maggiore, Monsignore Azzocchi, or Maestro G. Moriconi, he got little joy, only discovering by chance and dogged pursuit that he was looking in too many wrong places, finally finding Scarlatti's 'Amsterdam motets' at the Biblioteca Casanatense.[91] Sayle's friend H.D. Grissell helped him track down manuscripts in some of the more obscure libraries, but Dent was a quick learner, and learning on the hoof like this suited him, keeping his faculties alert.

At the same time he began to do more serious plant-collecting for his 'gardens'. Dent was enjoying the casual pursuit in these warmer, safer regions, and, inexperienced though he was, managed to score quite a few hits, discovering the Pincian Hill as a hopeful place of assignation, initially picking up several Germans, including a Schnorr von Carolsfeld. The names of Dent's young plants float past insubstantially for the most part, and over the years there would be quite a few, as Dent became ever more confident about approaching them in public. There were two clearly defined types: the regular, more substantial friendships with substantial men, then, later, the more fragile creatures Dent liked to nurse. Definitely in the first category was

87 Antonio Scontrino (1850–1922), composer and professor of composition at Palermo and in Florence. The music conservatory at Trapani bears his name.

88 LH 03/03/1901.

89 Count Guido Chigi Saracini (1880–1965), one of the vast Roman Chigi family, great patron of music, originally from Siena, where the family palazzo was turned by him into the Accademia Chigiana in 1932. Dent had many dealings with him and later tried to involve him with the ISCM.

90 LH 11/04/1901. Prince Chigi wrote to him later.

91 Eventually he uncovered material at the Bib. Casanatense, the Bib. S. Cecilia, the Vatican and the Bib. Barberini.

'Claudio', Cav. Claudio di Seyssel d'Aix, the Marchese di Sommariva,[92] a dashing cavalry officer about Dent's own age, whose English 'mother was a Craven' and whose acquaintance he made in the Caffé alla Loggia in Montagnana that August, in a conversation about pictures. 'He attracted me being one of those people who do everything – a character only tolerable among Italians.'[93] For years they kept up a regular correspondence and met from time to time, mostly when Dent was passing through Milan, where Claudio was quartered. In Vicenza there was another officer, Alfredo Zanello; while in Rome Emilio Bacchia, employed at the Casanatense, became for years a regular uncomplicated companion and lover, appearing in the diaries as 'EB'. In this matter at least, Dent could discriminate and control; he found the exotic Florentine scene that Browning wallowed in not really to his taste. Cust, with his ostentatiously 'men's tea-parties', was one such, but he was also a serious art historian, and Dent met his lifelong friend George Weston, 'a student of medieval Italian literature & an enthusiast of a certain sort of music',[94] at Cust's. At the same time, the complications which could arise from some 'friendships' were also being made clear to Dent, as when his former flame Johnson applied to him for money again. Dent's natural generosity was often taxed like this, but as he was beginning to realise, it was a very fine line between generosity and outright blackmail.

> I was suddenly called upon the other day to help a man whom I help when I can – he wanted more than I cd afford to send him so I feel that I must economize & scrape to send him the rest. It is not blackmail, nor has he any claim upon me except the best claim of all – viz friendship.

'It is a nuisance', he adds, rather less piously, 'but can't be helped, and I daresay Scarlatti will be the better for it.'[95]

In his little spare time there were concerts and the opera, also good places for assignation. In Rome, Verdi's *Requiem* 'with a chorus of about 200 … I have never heard such singing (in the Italian style) – it was very sentimental, but it was the right stuff';[96] Ponchielli's *I promessi sposi*, and the new opera by Umberto Giordano, *Fedora*, at the Teatro Costanzi, which Dent went to mostly to hear Gemma Bellincioni[97] sing.

After three weeks in Rome, on 17 April Dent arrived at the great monastery of Monte Cassino with its vast library and archives,[98] spending a week in its austere but

92 He became the Marchese di Sommariva in 1911 and was a war hero. Dent referred to him as 'Claudio' or 'Claudio di Seyssel'.

93 Diary 20/08/1902.

94 Diary 05/03/1901. Weston became Professor of Italian Art History at Harvard, and later tried to persuade Dent to come to Harvard, which he did in 1936, giving a lecture on the occasion of his honorary doctorate.

95 LH 03/03/1901.

96 LH 06/04/1901.

97 Gemma Bellincioni, aka Matilda Cesira (1864–1950), soprano, created the role of Santuzza in *Cavalleria rusticana*.

98 Although the collections were moved for safety during WWII, the monastery was flattened in one of the fiercest battles of the war, and much that Dent saw was lost.

flea-free accommodation and sketching the sea views in the evenings. It became an important source for Dent, its librarian Dom Ambrogio Amelli another friend and contact, but now he stayed only a few days before moving down the coast to Naples. First impressions of Naples were mixed; although he was moved by the beauty of the bay, and found the libraries better organised and more comfortable, 'there is a ... spirit of hostility to strangers in some Italian libraries, particularly at Naples'.[99] But his charm melted most antagonism; he took a tram to the Royal Conservatorio di Musica, where he sat each day from 9.30 am to 6.00 pm, 'far beyond the regular public hours ... I sit by myself in the Sala Scarlatti with a section of the catalogue at my elbow – lots of room: an armchair & an attendant close by to fetch anything I want'.[100] When the library closed, he wandered out to Pompeii and enjoyed walking among the ruins with his sketchbook, once meeting up with a Cambridge friend, Leonard Doncaster, walking along the sea cliffs to Scarlatti's tombstone at Monte Santo, but mostly he was lonely there.

On the fifth day at the library, the librarian Pagliara informed him that Hermann Kretzschmar, the German musicologist, 'was doing my work & had read AS at Naples 6 months ago'.[101] It was the scholar's nightmare, yet this was part of the overall experience Dent was accumulating about the vicissitudes that constitute 'research'. Kretzschmar was an established figure, well known in England. In fact, Kretzschmar seems only to have been working on Scarlatti in the context of his history of opera, not published until 1919.[102]

But Dent was upset, and the isolation and the constant hard work began to tell on him; his throat irritated him and he went down with a fever, bad enough to be stuck in bed for a few days, miserable and for escape reading the Italian novels of Maurice Hewlett.[103] All the things which had first charmed him about Naples were being translated by his bad temper, with too many guitars and mandolines going all the time. Sicily was a disappointment; Dent took a long steamer trip in hopes of finding solid evidence of the Scarlatti family at Trapani; fruitless, apart from making more contacts. But his warm reception from the librarian Giovanni Morello at the Casa de Musica in Palermo paved the way for his return.

Bologna was far more comfortable, the month there both productive and congenial. Every day he went to the Liceo Musicale to work and talk with academic contacts there, Luigi Torchi[104] and the librarian, Martucci, making a solid start on the dissertation, completing the bibliographical chapter on 16 June. With an ancient

99 LH 26/04/1901.

100 *Ibid.*

101 Diary 30/04/1901.

102 Pagliara was always an awkward creature to work with, and seems to have enjoyed making life difficult for any scholars forced to use his library.

103 Hewlett (1861–1923) wrote dozens of trashy historical novels, many set in Italy. Dent must have been desperate, learning which novels set in Italy were good and which to be avoided.

104 Luigi Torchi (1858–1920), besides teaching composition and music history at Bologna, he edited the *Rivista musicale italiana,* which Dent thought at the time far the best of the musical journals, and wrote articles on early instruments. He became a close colleague.

university at its heart, Bologna was exactly the kind of musical centre Dent eventually hoped to see at Cambridge, and he quickly found what he called 'the right set', comprising the best musicians, composers, intellects, including another visiting musicologist, a Finnish professor Martin Wegelius,[105] and a 22-year-old pupil of Torchi's, Ottorino Respighi.[106] Already a prolific composer, the darling of the Liceo, the multi-talented Respighi played 'all instruments', besides being 'the wit of the place', possessing the confidence of the acknowledged rising star. He was also lively company and very attractive; Dent was torn between jealousy and attraction. Dent liked Wegelius, aka 'Silenus', since he liked his wine and knew how to relax after long rehearsals. 'I am afraid we did not get through much musical criticism: but a good deal of Chianti. Just as we had finished, Wegelius attached himself to us & stood a bottle of Asti wch rather went to my head: but improved my Italian.'[107]

Wegelius proved yet another useful friend and contact: 'He has given me various delightful introductions – including one to Busoni at Weimar, whom I shall see if I get there as I hope in August'.[108] On 17 June, they heard Respighi's new Prelude Chorale and Fugue, *Il Giudizio Universale*, with four trumpets, which Dent called 'marvellously clever', but it was a reminder of what Dent himself yet had to produce; *Hellas* was stuck. 'Hellas does not progress much', was the sad refrain all that year. 'I find that I cannot write anything except bad Parry ... Hellas doesn't get on much: but I have written a lovely Italian tune that wd make Verdi turn green with envy.'[109] But when Lawrence sent back any detailed criticisms, Dent's hackles went up, his response rebarbative:

> I can't follow all yr criticisms: though I appreciate those I do follow. I am afraid my ear doesn't mind A sharp & A natural together. It is the result of those studies in Wagner & Bach & the older people, who wrote melodically rather than harmonically ... the A sharp is not a harmony note at all, but an embellishment of the melody: you observe that it fell on the weakest note of the triplet. And to make it A sharp wd spoil it melodically: & the bass can't be altered.[110]

He continued to tinker with *Hellas* right up to his return to Cambridge in the autumn, finishing it at the last minute.

'I consider my Bologna gardens well planted', he told Lawrence smugly:

> I told you I think about the Italian boys at Bologna. I wish I cd have seen more of them. They were a great joy – & living alone there you can understand that it was an acute pleasure even just to pass in the street & exchange greetings[111]

105 Martin Wegelius (1846–1906), composer, Director of the Helsingfors Musikinstitut, Helsinki, teacher of Sibelius.

106 Respighi (1879–1936).

107 Diary 15/06/1901, 22/06/1901.

108 LH 03/07/1901.

109 LH 14/01/1901, 11/05/1901.

110 LH 03/07/1901.

111 *Ibid.*

Bologna, rather than Venice or Florence, was where Dent really felt most comfortable; lazy, even; the 'Cambridgeness of the place making me slack', its noisy, bustling piazza society more to his taste. Bologna had no self-conscious ex-pat community living *la bella vita* – the beautiful life – on the fringes, nor grotesque sexual tourists; young Dent, tall, thin, self-possessed, a tan setting off his grey eyes, was utterly content to sit and listen to the citizen's band pumping out Massenet with enthusiasm if not accuracy, eyeing the clusters of sociable young men who promenaded in the evenings. Beside regular Liceo concerts and rehearsals, a visiting Venetian company in the Arena del Sole performed Goldoni in a Venetian dialect Dent found almost impenetrable, but he persevered, going to *La serva amorosa* and reading more Goldoni. On 7 July after 'the usual filthy journey' he was back in Munich, dining at the Heck.

This would be the pattern to Dent's European forays for some years: long days working in the libraries, followed by well-charted meals at familiar restaurants like the Heck, drinking wine with familiar acquaintances like Dr Jacobsen and the artists there, the small, cultivated homosocial circles as opposed to the open expansive piazzas of Italy. He missed Italy and Italian food, trying to address the constipation given him courtesy of meaty German cooking by going to vegetarian restaurants. But Dent's anxieties tended to overlap; work, diet, company, and by this stage, his finances – each had its effect on the whole, and 'Dear Leporello', with his fussiness, his solid understanding, his value as an equal, was on the receiving end of it all.

> Scarlatti is in a most jumpy stage: I have turned up a pupil or copyist who shows his admiration by trying to imitate his handwriting. For my dissertation he will give no trouble but when it comes to honest work & no bluff he will give me much. I am getting rather anxious abt my examiner as I have to bluff a good deal.[112]

Dr von Schultze at the Royal Library gave him more valuable introductions, to Mantovani in Vienna and most importantly, to Alfred Wotquenne in Brussels, also working in early opera. The company in the evenings was improved by a cheerful Austrian about his own age, Hermann Torggler, a painter of what Dent dismissed as 'Künstlerpostkarten … mostly pretty girls on bicycles but quite respectable'.[113] There was also Sedley Taylor's painter friend Alois Hierl-Deronco and his brother Otto, who was exhibiting at the Secession,[114] both part of the growing artistic homosocial circles which became another family for Dent, stimulating and congenial, whose ideas Dent could draw upon as he framed his own, parts of his unique construct.

By contrast, 'Vienna does not attract one at all … horribly, inconceivably, expensive'.[115] Dent never really warmed to Vienna, that cultured, elegant city of coffee-houses and fiakers, the Musikverein, Staatsoper and Theater an der Wien, Mozart, Beethoven and – presently – Schoenberg; the Imperial Library in the Hofburg is one

[112] LH 19/07/1901.

[113] Torggler (1878–1939) has since become very popular, judging by the current prices on eBay.

[114] Otto became another well-known artist, whose work is still in demand and in many collections. See also EJD to CC, 28/06/1906.

[115] LH 24/07/1901.

of the most stunning in the world. But Dent perversely found it all too expensive, too stuffy and worse, self-satisfied culturally, and this initial impression did not change much with time and circumstances. Later battles with the Viennese musical establishment began in 1901. But Dent's grumpy attitude, like his coughs and colds, was often displacement for not getting his own way. He had uncovered the autograph score to Scarlatti's *Telemaco* here, a real find, but there was little company to his taste.

A month in Dresden brought him round again. Going out to Pillnitz, Dent was amused to find Lawrence already there, completely at home, 'stretched out on a deck chair in the garden & enjoying himself hugely'. They both adored Mrs 'Spricklespots' and she them, one evening telling them 'ghost stories with a dramatically cracky voice'.[116] The company now included the ebullient, exasperating Francis 'Timmy' Jekyll[117] who, like Lawrence, was learning his German from 'The Gottschald' and came along to the opera,[118] arguing amicably about the music, the productions, the famous singers. They went for chocolate at Winkler's and called on Frau von Brodorotti. When the library was closed, Dent returned home or to Pillnitz to relax and grapple with his neglected *Hellas*, while Lawrence sat nearby in a chair reading scores.

His friend the helpful librarian Benndorf was on holiday, his assistant, the obstructive Bertling, now in charge. But Dent was now far more fly with the byzantine bureaucracies some libraries construct around their collections to protect them from being read, and he knew his stuff, kindly pointing out what was an autograph score of *La Maddalena* under Bertling's nose, then dismissing some of the treasures of the collection, a volume of Scarlatti cantatas, as 'not autograph'. A glance at the completed catalogue of Alessandro Scarlatti's manuscripts shows the scope of his undertaking.[119]

On 22 September he was in Brussels, consulting Alfred Wotquenne, 'whom I found young, pleasant & quite appallingly learned', working on complementary and useful subjects.[120] Brussels was hard if rewarding work, but Dent managed to finish the first chapter of Scarlatti in spite of a less than satisfactory catalogue at the Royal Library, and odd opening hours at the Royal Conservatoire. He 'hated' Brussels, all his work done with a bad cold and his arm in pain from all the frantic copying he had felt obliged to do, not trusting to any copyists. He was probably quite right: all the

116 Diary 01/10/1901.

117 Francis Jekyll (1882–1965), Newcastle Scholar at Eton, homosexual, musical, librarian at the British Museum, nephew and biographer of gardener Gertrude Jekyll. After her death she left him Munstead Wood, possibly because he had been so badly treated by his own close family.

118 They heard, *inter alia*, Chavanne sing Dalila in *Samson et Dalila*, and Rubenstein's *Der Dämon* (which Dent disliked), as well as Ernestine Schumann-Heink 'magnificent' as Azucena in *Il trovatore*, 'though very fat & occasionally rather too Bayreuthish in her gestures: the rest was Dresden of the very worst'.

119 pages of extant MSS. He doesn't include printed versions.

120 Alfred Wotquenne (1867–1939), Belgian bibliographer and musicologist, specialising in the 18th century. He became one of Dent's first important contacts in the field of early opera. Dent helped him with his catalogues on Gluck and C.P.E. Bach. Wotquenne soon moved to Paris and the Bibliothèque Nationale.

experiences of the past year had only confirmed to him how unreliable established scholarship could be, from catalogues to copies.

Once back in Cambridge, the chapter on Scarlatti operas was finished by 31 October, sacred music on 5 November, and overtures the following day.[121] 'Hellas is not very visible yet', he wrote to Lawrence, 'but there's more than meets the eye'. The Scarlatti work was being produced at a terrific rate, even though Dent was finding it impossible to work on both catalogue and dissertation at the same time; at least having so thoroughly done all the research, he knew exactly what he was going to write. On 8 November, 'I finished Scarlatti altogether & took the last lot to Miss Pate. I also wrote in the Italian to as many illustrations as Mimms had sent, so that I had a free evening & got all my letters, bills & miscellaneous papers tided up: a great relief.'[122]

With that out of the way, apart from the '47 small' manuscript illustrations which would have to be inserted by hand, on 10 November Dent began scoring *Hellas*, no light undertaking. Even though Dent had felt obliged – as with the Scarlatti – to cut a few corners now with the intention of returning to it later, the manuscript volume consists of ninety foolscap pages in Dent's meticulous hand.[123] On 3 December Dent played the *Hellas* chorus on his piano, timing it at seventeen and a half minutes. 'It is horribly noisy.'[124] *Hellas* was submitted on 10 December, the Provost asking rather after the fact if another copy might be produced. They had to get by with the one copy, three 'bulky' volumes circulated among the Provost Austen-Leigh, the Vice Provost Tilley, Mr Macaulay, Mr Berry, Dr James and Mr Dickinson: all the electors at King's.[125] In fact, the whole of Dent's Fellowship submission was a vast enterprise. By 11 and 13 December, Parry and Gray respectively had received the three volumes of Dent's dissertation. By February they were able to give enthusiastic reviews of every part.

While staying at the Hotel Marienbad in Munich, Lawrence received a postcard dated 15 March 1902:

121 Diary entries.

122 Diary 08/11/1901. Miss Pate was his typist.

123 Although there are constant disparaging remarks made by his correspondents about his handwriting, Dent's fair copy is exquisite: tiny, but perfectly clear.

124 Many big late-Victorian choral works are difficult to perform from the logistical perspective alone, and this one, with its full orchestra and chorus, is no exception. It is scored for two flutes, two oboes, two clarinets in B flat, two bassoons, four horns in F (I & II, III & IV), two trumpets in A, trombones and tuba, drums in C & G, cymbals, harp, violins I & II, violas, 'violon-cellos' and double bass. After an introduction of 100 bars the chorus comes in on an andante, followed by the soprano solo: 'Away! unlovely dreams, Avaunt! false shapes of sleep'. The andante first movement becomes a 'Largo e sostenuto: non troppo lento' with a baritone solo: 'Life may change, but it may fly not', then chorus. It is a rich, traditional, excellent summer pudding of a piece.

125 Although Dent writes to LH 10/12/1901: 'Between ourselves I rather hope he will ask for a second copy as then I shd be able to go through the first & see that the accidentals were all there! but I flatter myself I am generally very accurate.'

> Freedom so to what of Greece remaineth now returns. EQUES ALEXANDER SCARLACTVS REGIBUS OPTIMATIBUSQUE APPRIME CARVS.'[126]

Dent followed it up on 24 March with a full letter. 'Many thanks for your kind congratulations, or congralutions as Forster prefers to write the word.' He had seen Gray's warm report but not Parry's:

> Gray's was very good: well written & just the right thing though he said very little about Hellas. Indeed Hellas is very much in the shade. Parry's I want to see as it is said to be very short & inadequate so much so that it lost me a vote. Filon was the next candidate & there was only 1 vote between us: Harmer was the unexpected science man who voted for me ... People seem very much pleased on the whole – especially the Etonians as there has been no Eton fellow since Hurst 6 years ago.[127]

Although it never has been performed, *Hellas* is an impressive, substantial piece, far beyond the usual canons and fugues required for the M. Mus though using both. Dent's original intention had been tentatively to test the system, so perhaps his over-compensation is understandable, and it is doubtful whether any of Dent's electors apart from Nixon were able to read *Hellas*. In any event, *Hellas* was sidelined by the impressive piece of research on Alessandro Scarlatti.

Parry's report was a short letter to the Provost. Parry had always held a very high opinion of Dent and he evidently didn't see any need to overstate the case.

> Dent's treatise shows a wonderful amount of patient research, and I think, a judicious use of his materials. It will add greatly to our knowledge of Alessandro Scarlatti and enlightens us on many points where information has hitherto been scanty. The literary style might be improved upon, but I suppose that doesn't matter much ... As to his composition, that is also a high class performance – poetical and showing considerable command of resources. Unconventional also and interesting in detail and scheme.[128]

Gray wrote six sides of careful discussion, essentially in a similar laudatory vein, but with several acute observations of his own.[129] 'Mr Dent has shewn that biographer after biographer has been content to take facts from previous histories, & has not made an thorough examination of the works of the composer whose life he was supposed to be writing.' He pointed out that although Alessandro Scarlatti may have been well known, his works were not, and that Dent had more than addressed this gap. Although he felt that Dent 'suffers sometimes slightly from the "Lues Boswelliana"',[130] this was 'only to be expected ... Mr Dent shows clearly to what an extent Handel & even Mozart were indebted

126 'Sir Alexander Scarlatti, especially dear to kings and aristocrats / the best people.' As Dent later would explain himself, the references are from Shelley's *Hellas* and from Scarlatti's tombstone inscription, with an arch little pun on 'regibus'.

127 Dent had 8 votes, coming 3rd behind William. E. Johnson and Arthur Pigou, who had 15 votes each. KCGB/6/14/1.

128 KCA C/4/11/2/4.

129 Parry was paid 2 guineas for his report, Gray 3 for his six-page effort.

130 A biographer's tendency to magnify his or her subject.

to him ... I can hardly imagine a stronger claim for that novelty – a Musical Fellowship – than Mr Dent's work establishes'.[131]

Dent knew that however suitable his work may have been for an experimental fellowship dissertation, it was not yet complete. He wanted to take more time to track down the Scarlatti family and to satisfy himself on the quality and quantity of the manuscripts he had not yet seen, in e.g., the Santini Library at Münster in Westphalen, and now that his Fellowship undertaking had succeeded, he could do that supported with proper credentials and more of an income.

> historians of music take rather incorrect views of Scarlatti owing to the small proportion of his entire works that they have been able to study ... The magnitude of the task has resulted in superficial and incomplete work; but it seemed better to put forth something which might serve as a reliable foundation for others to build upon, than to write a more showy but less useful work by treating less of Scarlatti and more of his predecessors and followers.[132]

He categorises the manuscripts into three groups: autographs 'very rare indeed and non-existent before 1700. The present writer believes that many more exist'; contemporary manuscripts 'most common: there being three or four copyists whose work appears very frequently'; and modern manuscripts:

> Of these the most important are the numerous copies made for collectors by Santini, generally from autographs in his own possession, or from Italian church libraries ... Santini was not always very accurate in the notes themselves ... although he probably knew more about A. Scarlatti than any of his contemporaries, he was not infallible, as his catalogue at Vienna will show; classing unidentified opera airs as Cantatas, and including overtures which are obviously by Lully.

Citing Wotquenne's recent work on the subject, Dent also points out his shortcomings, and all in all presents what is an impeccable foundation for anyone undertaking research into the subject.

First in the queue was Dent himself.

131 No one had ever before applied for a Fellowship in Music, much less been awarded one – this is the 'novelty' to which Gray refers.

132 E.J. Dent, 'The Life and Work of Alessandro Scarlatti', dissertation MS 1902, KCAC/4/11/1/Dent, p. iv.

CHAPTER 4

The Travelling Fellow 1902–1906

I should get no good out of my holiday if I did not deliberately shake off my normal self. That is the real change that does me good.[1]

1902–1904

For the next five years from Michaelmas term 1902, Dent's Fellowship gave him a base and official status. His Fellow's perks included college rooms and dining rights at High Table; the money he saved went on books, music, entertaining and travel, while the vast quantities of new and unusual music he had collected, manuscripts or original Scarlatti pieces like *Volo Pater* he had copied himself, were brought to life again, sung at Nixon's or donated to the CUMC library or the Pendlebury. His rooms in Gibbs G3 were still unfinished when he returned, his instruments – the harpsichord and square piano beside most of his books and music – still being stored with Lawrence.[2] Even so, with so much in his daily life taken care of he could spend the day working on music at the British Museum, lunching with Ted, and catch the train back in time to take formal dinner in Hall, with excellent food and wine and the ponderous High Table humour about the Proctor's 'fine chases across Parker's Piece'.[3]

College provided routine stimulation of his intellectual life as well; Goldie wanted Dent at his weekly discussion club, where many were also Apostles, like Forster and G.E. Moore,[4] who read a paper on hedonism. 'Most of us … thought we were hedonists: Moore however insisted that I was not. He was very metaphysical and algebraical & I felt that he got a long way away from practical ethics.'[5] With Meredith and Barger[6] and other likeminded younger Fellows, Dent dabbled in college politics, proposing a 'secular scheme' for the college, setting themselves up in

1 CC 22/06/1905.

2 LH 23/07/1902.

3 Diary 21/10/1902.

4 George Edward Moore (1873–1958): 'An intellectual titan of his time, a pole star in the Cambridge firmament.' Paul Levy, *G.E. Moore and the Cambridge Apostles* (London, 1979).

5 Diary 21/10/1902.

6 George Barger (1878–1939), Fellow of King's, later Professor of Chemistry at Edinburgh. His wife Florence became one of Forster's closest friends.

opposition to what Dent called the 'clerics': advocating greater freedom from official religious activity, abolishing compulsory chapel for a start.[7] King's was divided on the subject, and its religious nature, the 'anti-clerics' felt, masked deeper debates on freedom in education.

For several years Dent continued to construct his own circles around younger university men like Mollison, Meredith, Greenwood,[8] Barger, and those who envied his comfortable Cambridge life, like Haward and Forster, still floundering in the outside world, unable to find solid employment or occupation. They came up for weekends, with Ted Haynes or Jack Pollock, meeting up with Trinity men Clive Bell and Thoby Stephen, whom Dent found 'very charming'.[9] Clive Carey,[10] the talented young singer and organ scholar at Clare College joined the little musical discussion group Dent had initiated,[11] quickly becoming one of many musicians dropping into Dent's rooms, along with Brewster and Reddaway, Jenkinson and Sayle, playing music, planning the CUMC concerts, and Rottenberg, Rubens and the Footlights crowd. As for breakfast parties:

> the one who comes first will have to call the host. I came towards 9 & found Greenwood only. Forster appeared about 9.15 & we waited for Haward. 'Just think,' said F. 'if we were a party of ladies, all late like this: how angry we shd be! & we don't mind it a bit.'[12]

Dent engaged with every aspect of Cambridge music: the CUMC concerts; the regular Guildhall concerts with Ysäye, Harry Plunkett-Greene ('Pea-Greene') and Leonard Borwick; the music-making at local families the Bendalls, the Gaskoins, the Jenkinsons – von Holst's new 'Ave Maria'; Dohnanyi's recital; besides all the music departmental gossip and squabbles, jockeying onto the Musical Board, the kind of internal politics Dent throve on. All very pleasant, and just a tiny bit dull.

Lawrence continued to lecture him on his 'idleness & unproductiveness',[13] but for a while Dent simply neglected composition. He had several important commissions in train,[14] while his election to the Musical Association was only a matter of time. Visits to Eton and Oxford became more calculated, helping Parry lecture on

7 Compulsory chapel was eventually officially abolished only after the Great War, but in typical King's style it was for years compulsory more in the breach than the observance.

8 L.H.G. Greenwood (1880–1965), Classicist, Fellow of Emmanuel College.

9 Arthur Clive Heward Bell (1881–1964), art critic, married Stephen's sister Vanessa. Another sister was Virginia, later Woolf. Like most of his contemporaries, Dent liked and fancied Thoby Stephen, who died tragically young.

10 For Clive Carey, see 'Dramatis Personae'.

11 Diary 25/11/1901: 'Tea with Brewster: GB Smith came – we discussed my long cherished project of a sort of Musical Association among us younger members of the University, to read papers & discuss them.'

12 Diary 04/12/1902.

13 Diary 06/12/1902.

14 A Scarlatti article for the *Sammelbände der Internationalen Musikgesellschaft*, reviewing two volumes of the recent *Oxford History of Music* and two articles for the MMR, edited by J.S. Shedlock.

early opera ('very erratic') and consulting F.S. Kelly: 'quite extraordinarily charming & delightful. He played his violin sonata & I made a rough dash at the 1st Hellas chorus: but a discussion on opera was more interesting'.[15] Cosmopolitan friends like George Weston from Harvard could now be invited into college.

Dent's second shot across the academic bows was – significantly – an article in an international journal rather than a domestic one, the *Sammelbände der Internationalen Musikgesellschaft*, edited by Johannes Wolf of Berlin,[16] being published alongside many of the great 'musical historians' of the early twentieth century, mostly German, but with a few British: Fuller-Maitland, J.C. Squire, Rosa Newmarch, Henry Hadow. Many of the names found in the *Sammelbände* are those who became Dent's closest colleagues – Écorcheville, Einstein, Chilesotti – and members of his growing international networks.

> Considering the celebrity which Alessandro Scarlatti enjoyed during his lifetime, he has met with scant justice at the hands of musical historians ... All catalogues of Scarlatti's compositions that have hitherto appeared are very inadequate, and the criticisms of historians of music have suffered from being founded on a more or less incomplete acquaintance with the music criticised.[17]

It is an impressive, confident piece. In refreshingly crisp prose, Dent provides a solid platform for his argument, giving a sense of occasion while leaving open a number of intriguing questions about the dissemination of Scarlatti's work. For example, *Il Mitridate Eupatore*: score in Berlin, Königliche Bibliothek, with a copy of that in the Paris Conservatoire; libretto in Bologna and Venice, with more fragments found in Brussels; produced in Venice at S. Giovanni Crisostomo 1707.[18] This brief entry implicitly demonstrates extraordinary scholarship; he had seen *and* carefully assessed such a wide range of sources, while the whole promised a solid foundation for future research into early opera. To Dent's irritation, other scholars thought so, too, that occupational hazard of the successful academic: 'The thing that is making me a bit savage is that Hugo Goldschmidt has been on to all these places a fortnight ahead of me, working at Scarlatti.'[19]

For the next three years Dent spent more than half his time abroad, officially to finish off what became his seminal book on Alessandro Scarlatti,[20] but also expanding

15 Diary 12/11/1902: 'They played the overtures to Rosaura & Griselda, & I had to rewrite horn parts to suit F horn.'

16 Johannes Wolf (1869–1947), German music scholar and teacher; university lecturer in music at Berlin when Dent first knew him; he became a lifelong friend and colleague.

17 E.J. Dent, 'The operas of Alessandro Scarlatti' in *Sammelbände der Internationalen Musikgesellschaft*, vol. 4 (November 1902), pp. 143–56, here p. 143.

18 As Dent knew, this theatre next to the church of the same name later became the Teatro Malibran, after the singer.

19 CC 15/05/1903. Goldschmidt's Scarlatti work never appeared.

20 Just in 1902, May: Milan, Venice, Paris; June: Paris, then Brussels; July: Münster in Westphalen, Antwerp, Innsbruck with Forster; August: Verona, Mantua, Montagnana, Padua, Cremona, Venice with Ted; September: three weeks learning Hungarian in Budapest, then home via Vienna, Prague, Pillnitz, Dresden with Percy Lubbock, Weimar, with George Weston in Bonn.

his personal frontiers while improvising his career path, his music and his sexuality developing in tandem. Although more prepared for navigating the waters muddied by his predecessors, some absurdities still took him by surprise. During one frustrating stint in Paris in May 1902, Dent could find no Scarlatti manuscripts at all, even with specific references in Wotquenne's catalogue. A frantic note to Wotquenne prompted the odd but perfectly accurate reply: 'Les Manuscrits (de musique) se trouvent á la Bibl. Nationale, au Départment des Imprimés!!!!!'.[21]

In July Dent arrived at the Santini Library[22] at Münster in Westphalen, stunned. Although there was indeed a treasure trove of Scarlatti and other gems there, it was all stashed up near the attics, under decades of dirt and neglect. The person in charge, Deputy Director of the local cathedral choir, Niessen, had never even heard of Santini's library and made it clear to Dent that he was not welcome to investigate. Before he could read a note of all that music Dent had first to spend days actually re-stacking, dusting and cleaning the volumes and the shelves:

> the caretaker provides me with a dustbrush, a towel & water: I provide soap & energy. I have had 6 hours today & 4 yesterday with the result that out of 51 shelf compartments of confusion I have got at least an alphabetical arrangement started besides a variety of mountains – & the mountains are A. Scarlatti (about 30 vols), Handel in English scores (Arnold), Liturgical, & misc. printed, also a long shelf full of theoretical works & general literature.[23]

'I enjoy it hugely', he told Lawrence, 'except the dust is perfectly awful & the windows do not open: so I am suffocated'. What he found under all that grime was of great significance,[24] – even Niessen was eventually excited enough to lend a hand – but the episode shows how deep and singular had become Dent's own knowledge and understanding of the music of that period. To be able to recognise the treasure buried under the most unprepossessing conditions gave him enormous satisfaction.

'The whole Scarlatti business is getting horribly complicated', he wrote to Lawrence from Naples eighteen months later, 'and I suppose I shall have to chuck composition for life if I am ever to unravel the history of Italian music 1650–1750'.[25]

21 'The (music) Manuscripts are in the Bibl. Nationale, in the Department of Printed Matter!!!!' Diary and LH 05/06/1902. Alfred Wotquenne, *Catalogue des livrets italiens du xviie siècle* (Brussels, 1901).

22 Fortunato Santini (1778–1861) collected and copied, not always accurately, much of Scarlatti's work, together with other manuscripts and printed music of the 16–18th centuries. The 1906 edition of Grove's includes an entry on the Santini Library by Dent: 'library of the Abbate Santini (of Rome) ... at present lodged in very inadequate quarters in the Episcopal Museum of Christian Antiquities. It has recently been roughly put in order by Mr. E.J. Dent, of Cambridge.'

23 LH 04/07/1902.

24 Besides 'music in huge quantities scored by Santini from the original printed parts' there were MSS of Caldara, 'Handel's Italian period', Palestrina, Pitoni, Longroscino and Vinci. *Ibid.*

25 LH 18/12/1903.

The composing all but disappeared;[26] replacing it already was letter-writing on a vast scale, but the whole process was a more complicated excursion into self-discovery. Writing letters to maintain widely scattered friendships kept essential contact with intimate friends alive, and allowed Dent's writing to develop a dimension beyond the scholarly; stimulating while both intimate and safe.

By summer 1902 he possessed enough linguistic and cultural confidence to sit happily in cafés and trattorias and strike up conversations with anyone, but especially the right sort of young man, the right sort having been established by social signals Dent was now so quick to pick up. His Italian life had become the means by which he could give rein to his other self and do a bit of exploring impossible in England. In Sirmione, for example:

> After dinner I went with Signor Bottone to the Café Concerto Scaglieri where we were much amused by 3 variety singers – 2 sopranos & a good baritone ending with a brilliant farsa in wch appeared certain 'signori dilettanti che hanno gentilmente prestato il loro concorso' [gentlemen amateurs who have kindly leant their contribution] i.e. the cook from the Alb. Catullo & 2 waiters from the Promessi Sposi.[27]

So when he returned to Cambridge, it was as the seasoned traveller, full of exotic music, ideas and stories, an object of envy to his friends and colleagues, who flocked to his rooms to be entertained in his sharp, gossipy style: how he had been struck by the *Lachtauben* (lit., laughing doves) at the Münster zoo, their noise exactly like the well-known 'heugh, heugh, heugh' of the Provost. Or the 'Hungarian glass engraver who had fled precipitately from Brussels owing to a love-affair with the Brazilian minister.'[28] Or 'a little jew[ish] lawyer from Turin who was most charming & I was very pleased to find that Italy regards Jews as men & brethren though perhaps not to the extent we do.'[29] Dent's first real contact with cultured European Jewish society came that September on a research trip to Budapest, and banished his condescending attitude.

He was following up one of his many introductions, to Dr Kohlbach, who taught at the Liszt Conservatory, and immediately invited Dent out to Kaposvár[30] to meet his big, warm extended family, all very musical. It was Dent's first view of Budapest, too, now prosperous and blossoming, having marked its millennium in 1896 with a new underground system, many elegant new buildings on the Pest side of the river, galleries, museums, a massive opera house and concert halls, all marking a lively and optimistic cultural paradise. Dent moved into Pest, staying at the Metropole[31] while

26 Between *Hellas* and 'The Willow-Tree Bough' (1918) there was one song, 'Good-night' (1904), the incidental music to two children's plays by Netta Syrett, *The Christening of Rosalys* and *Princess Fragoletta* (1905, 1906) and one movement of a string quartet (1908).

27 Diary 12/08/1902.

28 Diary 29/07/1902

29 LH 07/09/1902.

30 A small, pretty town about 50 miles (80 km) south-west of Budapest, 34 miles (55 km) south of Lake Balaton, on the Kapos river.

31 Still there, in VII Rákóczi út.

taking daily lessons in Hungarian with Professor Révai. In between, he looked at the pictures in the academy,[32] especially enjoying the 'modern' pictures, and had excellent coffee and the unspeakably delicious cream cakes at the New York Kávelkáy. He made the acquaintance of Kohlbach's lively niece, Fräulein Franciska Schwimmer,[33] who took him to the Kossuth celebrations, where he was captivated by the dancing and met another uncle, who wrote for *The Athenaeum* and knew Lowes Dickinson.

These might not have been the friendships he was looking for at the time, but they were important, part of the serious European networks he was beginning to build up, and a product of his better self. Relaxing and enjoying the life, he was surprised at his own perspicacity in recognising that the real roots of culture are to be found in such ordinary life. Music, especially opera, was not an added extra, but part of the fabric of everyday living. This discovery soon became a conviction.

❧ ❧ ❧

The stimulation often worked both ways, and Dent's cultural influence already extended beyond music. His uneven but lifelong friendship with Morgan Forster is brought to life in Forster's letters at this time – Dent's have disappeared[34] – and in his early novels. As an undergraduate at King's Forster had become a quietly persistent part of Dent's circles, largely through his musical interests, initially the CUMC Saturday concerts.[35] Eventually Dent came to appreciate Forster's exquisitely sharp sense of humour, his mild but stubborn integrity, his loving and terrible ties with formidable female relatives, and through Forster's fiction was brought to recognise some less pleasant aspects of himself.

Far less self-confident than Dent, Forster was at this stage that most gratifying kind of friend who listens avidly and then actually takes advice. In 1901, with a second-class degree which made any further academic pursuits unlikely, he took his small income and his mother to the continent for a year, mostly to Italy, where they could live cheaply yet in some style. He followed Dent's precise instructions about where to stay, what to see, what to eat, and how to deal with the pervasive fleas, his letters full of dry, distantly comic observations later recognisable in his novels:

> Hotel Europe, Milan, L. Bertolini prop. This is comfortable and costly. I hate it. The waiters hand the dishes in white cotton gloves and the bread comes in a silver spoon.[36]

32 The huge National Gallery was not finished until 1906, so what Dent must have seen was in the old Academy of Fine Art in Andrássy út, not far from it.

33 Franciska Schwimmer (1880–1963), one of a number of intelligent women who got under his defences; her correspondence with Dent is in KCA. With most of the family, she later emigrated to the USA, where she became a political activist.

34 Writing to Dent in 1950, Forster said that he had been going through all his correspondence and the only things worth keeping were 'yours'. But there is so far no trace of them.

35 CUMC XVI.1. 2 Visitors Book. Forster came first on 15 October 1897, as a guest of C.M. Mathews.

36 EMF 27/10/1901. The letters are in KCA.

Albergo Bonciani, Firenze: We have been here three days, and very comfortable, but my mother hankers after an Arno view and a South aspect, so we are not stopping … The people here beam greatly at the sound of your name, but I regret to say that at the O.B.s they stare blankly, and my Italian is insufficient to describe his appearance'.[37]

Everything about the Pension Simi seems nice except the lady who keeps it, who scatters her Hs like morsels and calls me 'the young gentleman' … The Bonciani pen is rather bad. Their piano though is very good.[38]

Yesterday I went to St Lorenzo. I had got ready all the appropriate sentiments for the New Sacristy, and they answered very well. More spontaneous perhaps were my feelings at seeing the cloisterful of starved and maimed cats … I was also much struck by there being a forth on the roof [of the cathedral]: I don't know whether I am more impressed by the number of the forths in Italy or by their fig leaf character. Talking of fig leaves, how flagrantly indecent are the statues in the Uffizi with their little brown paper bathing drawers. I almost feel that the permanent plaster article of the Catholic reaction is preferable. It did know its own mind.[39]

Dent introduced him to some of his young Italian friends beside a few odd characters. Although Forster never found the sexual liberation Dent had done – his mother's presence must have been damping – he did find inspiration fundamental to his creative development, and the perfect balance for his characters who are torn between the limiting ties of England and the more uninhibited emotional life of the Italians. In the early spring months of 1902 Forster began notes for *A Room With a View,*[40] and quickly drafted 'The Story of a Panic'.[41]

The Forsters followed in Dent's footsteps, even to Monte Cassino, where at Dent's introduction Forster was shown the library by Dom Ambrogio Amelli. His letters to Dent give amusing little vignettes he knew would be appreciated, about the scenes at the dinner table in his pension, with the 'amusing but wearisome fat Italian … learning English apparently for amorous purposes … "your face has pierced my heart" … He suffers from lumbago, and his remark "my heart is sad because my flank is sore" caught the well-bred dinner table off its guard and convulsed it.'[42]

'We are in a state of great agitation', Forster wrote from Naples:

The day after our arrival here, when I went up to bed my Mother met me with an ashy face saying, 'Mr Dent advised us not to come here, but we disobeyed him, and we have been terribly punished.' There, in the soap bowl was lying dead a [drawing of a cockroach on its back]. My childhood has been so pure that it was the first I had ever seen, and as it is I cannot draw it very well … Our gratitude & admiration for the extent & accuracy of your knowledge have always been

37 EMF 30/10/1901.

38 *Ibid.*

39 *Ibid.* 'Forth' was Cambridge slang for a lavatory of any kind.

40 Then referred to as 'Lucy'.

41 Furbank, *E.M. Forster: A Life. Volume One*, p. 92.

42 EMF 30/10/1901, Rome, n.d., but probably 25/01/02.

immense, but now they are mingled with awe. We speak of you in the words of the hymn: 'and soon the people all were dead who did not do as he had said'.[43]

Dent had planned to meet up with Forster and his mother in Venice, but the Campanile collapsed, sending the Forsters and their plans into a flutter. Dent was scornful: 'I can't think why as he cd hardly have intended to sleep in it'.[44] When in September 1902, Forster continued doggedly to follow Dent's advice, it had become something of a private joke between them. With only a shaky command of German, Forster had ventured up into Germany, staying in Nuremberg.

> I offended Nature on Monday by going to the Starnberger See, & Providence by going to Die Zauberflöte on Sunday, and between the two I have got a colossal cold. I enjoyed the Opera very much, & as I sat right at the side I had a splendid view of the machinery. But I am as yet too inexperienced a goer to listen properly to the music & singing. I will try to analyse the plot & the motives of the characters, for which I ought to be shot. As it was, I understood little except the tragic death of the boa constrictor in the first few bars.[45]

During their next Italian trip in 1903 the Forsters did meet up in Florence with Dent, whose open contempt for the other guests upset Mrs Forster.[46] But for Forster the travelling now had a sharper focus; the novel begun nearly two years before simply as a list of characters was firming up, and when 12 May, Dent took them to *Lucia di Lammermoor*, with the 'excellent' Luisa Tetrazzini singing Lucia to a noisy yet enraptured audience 'being mostly platea & loggione' – stalls and gallery – the scene would appear in what became *Where Angels Fear to Tread*.[47] Evenings spent in the company of Dent's lively young Bolognese friends Cavanna and Ferratini certainly helped Forster with their fictional counterparts.[48] By the time Forster returned home to West Hackhurst, he was asking Dent more particular questions of detail:

> Do you happen to know the kind of salary received by an octroi offician in Italy – the kind of man who prods the hay carts with a rapier? … And what corresponds in Italy to being married by a bishop's license? … These questions are due neither to insanity nor personal dilemmas.[49]

In those early years, especially 1901–04, when Forster was finding his creative voice, Dent was one of the trusted friends Forster turned to, and even if he didn't realise it at the time, Dent was also providing Forster with a mass of raw material. Although both were in their different ways well versed in obfuscation, how to express what is essential without giving away what is unacceptable, it needs quite

43 EMF 11/05/1902.

44 LH 23/07/1902.

45 EMF 19/09/1902.

46 Furbank, *E.M. Forster: A Life. Volume One*, p. 103. Forster used this as well: see below.

47 *Ibid.*, pp. 103–4. Tetrazzini was then unknown outside Italy.

48 See below.

49 EMF 28/08/03.

a refining process. From early on Forster had learned a creative circumspection, picking up on one unexceptionable aspect while leaving any subtext ambiguous, not unlike Dent's serpentine style. Forster's habits of observation came out of natural timidity combined with sharp perception; natural curiosity and a desire to understand human nature with the need to write about it. The motives behind Dent's detached observation were at least as complex as Forster's, and more mixed, but he only began to recognise these traits in himself when he later saw them in Forster's novels. An entry in Forster's (unpublished) diary for 1903[50] is the germ of an idea for a very Dentish character, although female: 'One of those difficult people who have developed through Music ... Properly conventional except when she forgets herself.' Forster could re-invent the world in his fiction, and fill it with versions of real people he had known or seen, while Dent increasingly would create scenarios and sit back to watch from a distance what he had stirred up. Forster had no illusions about Dent's complex character: attractive, civilised and yet capable of mischief. In 1901, Dent introduced him to Robert Cust, a man caught between his own pretensions and a genuine love of art.

Brother-in-law of George Wherry,[51] Cust was an established art historian, an aesthete, who, as seen in Chapter 3, liked to surround himself in his beautiful flat on the Via dei Bardi with 'viewy' young men. In 1897 he had published Plütschow's 'artistic' nude photographs of even younger men,[52] yet later felt obliged to provide himself with a wife to demonstrate the purity of his intentions. Where Dent was increasingly giving his sense of sexuality a freer rein, a chance to breathe, Cust was a man at war with himself, and one of Dent's least attractive traits was his enjoyment of stirring, disdainfully observing any weaknesses while encouraging the friendship.[53] Never suspecting any darker motives, Cust always considered Dent to be a close friend, consulting him when writing his book on Carpaccio, and generally seeking his company and his opinions. Like Dent, Forster enjoyed some of what Cust had to offer, the 'refreshing and luxurious ... *man's* tea-party',[54] but he kept his writer's perspective, and Cust and his 'viewy' young men would appear in early versions of *A Room With a View*, toned down, to 'illustrate futile aestheticism'.[55] Later versions of the novel abandon that thread and the ambivalent sexuality on display around Florence; instead, through the Reverend Cuthbert Eager and the more complex and interesting character of Cecil Vyse, Forster would hint more strongly at Dent's own dark side.

50 Part of his notes for the 'Lucy' draft which would eventually become *A Room With A View*. KCA.

51 George Wherry (1852–1928), F.R.C.S. had married Cust's sister, Albinia Lucy. He founded the CUMC library and donated much of its original collection. Their daughter was the ebullient Bee Wherry.

52 Koymasky, Matt and Andrej, Website: 'Gugliemo Plüschow – von Gloeden's cousin'.

53 'Cust is apt to be fussy and querulous at times – but he is well worth a little patience, as I have seldom known a man with so real a sense of friendship.' CC 24/11/1908.

54 Furbank, *E.M. Forster: A Life. Volume One*, pp. 84–5.

55 *Ibid.*

Where Angels Fear to Tread appeared in 1905, incorporating many of the Italian scenes provided by Dent, via Forster's refining imagination. The scenes in the piazza of Monteriano with Gino and his friends are strongly reminiscent of Bologna in May and September 1903, with the young Italians he had introduced to Forster. Dent himself also appears, or at least 'two-thirds' of him,[56] as Philip Herriton, and he did not mind in the least. The title was also Dent's idea, a typical double-edged reference to 'angels',[57] when Forster's publisher Blackwood's refused his initial title *Monteriano*. Dent loved the book, and said so to Forster: this in spite of knowing that the character, in some measure his *own* character, depicted through his friend's prism, is that of a 'Laodicean': 'you're without passion; you look on life as a spectacle; you don't enter it; you only find it funny or beautiful'.

When *A Room With A View* was published in 1908, much remains of Forster's Florentine experiences in the years 1901–03.[58] When he finally read it, Dent was shaken. Barely mentioning it in his diary, he fired off a letter to Forster, one of his more supercilious efforts, to judge from the vigorous defence put up by Forster in reply. Both Dent and Cust had provided Forster with the raw materials to create Cecil Vyse, the aesthete with Italian pretensions who is clearly fooling himself when asking the young heroine Lucy to marry him. Cust himself would continue to deny his sexuality, and his own unhappy marriage is a possible vision of what might have happened to Forster's Lucy Honeychurch and Cecil Vyse had not George Emerson come along. And George appearing at the right moment is a plot device Forster has turn upon a Dent-like piece of snobbish machination from Cecil: exaggerated, but close enough to sting. Over that six-year span when both Italy and Cambridge were common experience, their roles had shifted in ways Dent had not even considered. Cecil Vyse, a young man whose 'futile aestheticism', snobbery, self-delusion and pettiness are presented in a character so clearly modelled from aspects of his own younger self, 'irritated' an older Dent. Being 'without passion' was one thing; 'never to know anyone intimately' pulled him up as much as it did his fictional alter ego. He went into denial, disingenuously claiming as he so often did with some music he disliked that it was 'difficult to read', that 'if he is too young to realise that he can know no one intimately, he does not seem worth bringing in'.[59]

Their close friendship survived, although it would never again be at the same intensity as during these travelling years. They were both at this stage in their lives

56 Quoted in Oliver Stalleybrass' introduction to the Penguin edition, p. 10. 'Forster told me that I was Philip Herriton' (diary). But Forster also used bits of Hugh Meredith, or so he told Dent, although Forster denied it (diary 09/03/1905). Forster dedicated *A Room With A View* to Meredith.

57 Forster was a member of the Conversazione Society, aka the Apostles; 'angels' are Apostles who have left Cambridge. Dent also suggested as an alternative title, *From a Sense of Duty*. Forster didn't really like either.

58 Other small details probably through Dent were the name 'Eager', from some nice Americans he had just met, and the maxim 'mistrust all enterprises that require new clothes'.

59 The letter has been lost, but Furbank construed its contents from Forster's reply. *E.M. Forster: A Life. Volume One*, pp. 170–71.

working out what kind of relationship with other men was possible, something physically and emotionally satisfying; both strongly attracted to Hugh Meredith, after his return from Italy Forster appears to have had a mild fling with him, while Dent enjoyed just looking at him.[60] When eventually in 1913 what had been unthinkable took artistic form as Forster's (then unpublishable) novel of homosexual love, *Maurice*, Dent was one of its first readers. After reading *Monteriano*, Dent had been staggered by Forster's genius. And Forster had got it partly right: Dent's natural caution and dislike of putting himself in the public eye or in any way making a fool of himself were as inhibiting as Forster's own diffidence and cloaked desires.

❧ ❧ ❧

At the age of twenty-six Dent had already achieved more than most and could so easily have settled in Cambridge for life. But Dent was not an Oscar Browning, or a Cyril Rootham or even a Charles Wood, and much as he loved Cambridge, Dent spent half his life escaping its perceived confines in the same way he had escaped Ribston, and the long academic holidays perfectly suited his restless nature. At the end of Michaelmas term 1902, Dent was off, after a token few days at Ribston, spending Christmas and New Year in Munich. Officially, he needed to visit the Grand Ducal Library at Darmstadt, but really, it was the alternative Munich life he was seeking.

> At the Heck in the evening I sat down at a table with a charming young man who was very friendly; a painter by name Rolf Niczy – He took me on to a queer little restaurant zur Dichterlei, in Türkenstr. where we sat till 12: he was very charming & I congratulated myself on having found the right man.[61]

Niczy was part of a Munich circle of artists which included Wassily Kandinsky, known as the Phalanx group, whose contributions to the Secession exhibitions were opening the way to a new age in painting, abstraction and the birth a few years later of Die Blaue Reiter. Though intrigued, Dent found the new style not immediately to his taste, 'there was very little finished', but he was thrilled to be taken into such avant-garde circles. At the Dichterlei Dent was introduced to Ludwig Thoma, editor of his favourite satirical magazine *Simplicissimus*,[62] and to its principal artist,

60 Diary December 1903: 'I am bored by feasts & wonder why I go: the only redeeming feature to-night was the sound of "Sweete Flowers" & "There is beauty in the mountain" … & the sight of HOM [Meredith] nearly opposite to me … HOM who became delightfully sleepy and affectionate.'

61 Diary 29/12/1902. Niczy (1881–1950) eventually became a fashionable illustrator for magazines in the 1920s.

62 Thoma (1867–1921) was known mainly for comic descriptions of Bavarian life. His later writings were pointedly anti-Semitic. Based in Munich, *Simplicissimus* was one of the main satirical magazines of its time, and it published racy cartoons, Thomas Mann, Rainer Maria Rilke and Frank Wedekind. It was constantly under attack from the establishment, fined, its editor Thoma imprisoned at one point. Later, George Grosz and Käthe Kollwitz would contribute. It died down during WWI, but revived afterwards, lampooning the Nazis but somehow surviving until 1944.

Eduard Thöny. 'We looked at a lot of Thöny's sketches, wch are far better than the Simplicissimus reproductions: & I bought a very good portrait of the late Prince Hohenlohe.'[63] But Niczy, although good-natured enough to invite Dent along to the Dichterlei again, was not really interested; Dent was left to play Hungarian songs on its piano while the others talked.

At 5.30 pm on Monday 2 February 1903, a nervous Dent stood up before an audience of ten to deliver his first lecture in a series called simply 'Six lectures on the early history of Musical Drama'. Since Music had as yet no clearly defined faculty, the lectures took place in King's College,[64] and the audience included Lawrence, Forster, Ollife Richmond, Clive Carey, Mrs Adam, Mrs Mollison, Mrs Bendall and 'an unknown with a beard'. But it marked a real change in style and content from the usual music lectures: Sterndale Bennett lectured on acoustics, Charles Wood on harmony and counterpoint, while Stanford's Easter term lectures were on such specific topics as late Beethoven string quartets, or 'Four lectures on Advanced Practical Composition'. From now on, Dent and Edward Naylor undertook to give a careful, well-produced series of lectures, which gradually built up larger, enthusiastic audiences drawn from a broader local base. Since most needed live illustrations, these were in effect concerts, and became the focus for a new Cambridge music.

Another extended period abroad was planned for spring and summer 1903 to work on his Scarlatti book, and that April, Dent's first professional step into the international musical world, the first Congress of the Internationale Musikgesellschaft (IMG), or International Musical Society (IMS),[65] in Rome, where he was to be the sole English-speaking delegate. He was terrified, opting for a week in Florence beforehand to consult Scontrino and Gandolfi and visit the Real Istituto Musicale to brush up on Scarlatti's *Stabat Mater*, also visiting Kraus. He lunched at the hospitable Cantagallis and was shown over the family ceramic factory by Lorenzo.[66]

Using the excuse of a bad 'cold' caught in Florence – more likely a rare panic attack – Dent skipped the first day of the congress, yet managed to 'loaf' around the Palatine and later, to Boïto's *Mefistofele*, with Bellincioni singing 'superbly' and Vitale conducting a 'fine performance'. The second day, 3 April, he slid into the 'musical section', mostly concerts, where he spotted his old friends Torchi, Amelli, Schultze and Benndorf. 'We elect a fresh president daily & international courtesy insists on electing foreigners. So we had Max Friedlander [sic] … a great friend of Stanford's on Friday, Humperdinck on Saturday … & I suppose my turn will come later!'[67]

63 Diary 29/12/1902.

64 It is not clear exactly where, but Dent sometimes lectured in college rooms when there were only a few people.

65 The IMG/IMS had been founded in Germany in 1899, and had congresses every three years or so. It published a regular journal and a quarterly magazine, the *Sammelbände* in which Dent had published his article. The 1911 Congress was held in London. The (Royal) Musical Association became an affiliate. Dent was involved pretty much from the outset.

66 The Cantagalli family, which seems to have included Prince Chigi, always made him welcome, the son Lorenzo was at Trinity. Dent is unjustifiably dismissive of them in his letter to Lawrence.

67 LH 05/04/1903.

Dent was introduced to Max Friedlaender,[68] flattered to find that he knew all about his work on Scarlatti. He should have felt comfortable and enthusiastic; he did not.

> Our congress meetings are most depressing. We are all very unpunctual: the room is bare & cold with a brick floor: the chairs 'church chairs' are of the plainest. But I hope for a good discussion tomorrow from Villami of Turin on musical studies at Universities etc. ... & the same on Tuesday from Luigi Rasi[69] the actor & professor of acting at Florence, on the desirability of founding a museum of Italian dramatic art. I want to meet him: he read from Manfred at Florence once 5 or 6 years ago & it was splendid.. Torchi of Bologna (a great friend of mine) talks here too ... I might have said much but lay low.[70]

Dent's obligatory stint as president left him feeling raw and exposed: 'my speeches [in French] were not good & received with amusement especially by the Rasi Maddalena party'.[71] Mortified, he fled to Palermo, where at the Casa de Musica, Morello showed him a cutting from the *Giornale di Sicilia* with an account of Favara's paper on Sicilian folk songs at the congress, '& a caricature of various people there, including me – under the name of Prof. Pears il fin dotto storogia ... della musica'.[72] But Palermo was 'more or less a failure', Dent decided, having been unable to follow up on the puzzle of Scarlatti's antecedents,[73] and frustrated by the absence of his important contact D'Ali, and his pursuit of a young student, Guido Orlandi, while being obliged to pursue the introductions to rich bankers, the Whitakers, and 'the smart Anglo-Italian society ... princes and counts galore', their box at the opera with the Queen of Portugal, etc. etc. 'Failure' is too strong, the word revealing more of Dent's impossibly high standards as much as his touchy self-esteem. So back in Florence, although he was delighted to see Forster there, he was in his worst kind of temper: 'The Forsters are here but at the other end of Florence ... as I enjoy seeing F & even Mrs F but I don't care about going to their pension wch is full of old women.'[74]

In this trip Dent was discovering his personal cultural boundaries, and the process was often irritating, occasionally painful, with an unaccustomed sense of failure never far away. His Damascene moment came that May in Florence, when there was an interruption of his pleasant routines with the Scontrinos, 'where I feel I am on the

68 Max Friedlaender (1852–1934), German singer, writer and music historian specialising in Schubert's songs. He made his London début in 1880, and in 1903 became professor at the University of Berlin. Both he and his wife became warm friends.

69 Luigi Rasi (1852–1918), writer, and from 1882 Director of the Scuola di Recitazione in Florence. His ideas about a more natural style of acting would influence Dent, as did his work on Italian comedy.

70 LH 05/04/1903.

71 Edgardo Maddalena (1867–1929), theatre historian, specialist on Goldoni. Diary 08/04/1903. He left this out in his letters to Lawrence. In fact, Dent had impressed a lot of people there, even Rasi and Maddalena, who both became important friends.

72 Diary 15/04/1903: most learned historian ... of music. The cutting shows him with Maddalena and the acoustician Zambiani.

73 LH 05/04/1903.

74 LH 15/05/1903.

FIGURE 5. Cartoon of Dent ('Prof Pears') at the 1903 Rome IGM Congress from the *Giornale di Sicilia*.

surest of footings, since the poodle laid his nose on my leg after 2 minutes acquaintance: a thing he never does to strangers!'[75] and with Cust 'charming' at the moment, who had his sister Mrs Wherry and her daughter, the 'overwhelming' Bee staying.

❧ ❧ ❧

'I go to the Berensons tomorrow', Dent wrote to Lawrence, 'with fear & trembling as F. [Forster] says they ask you subtle culture questions: and I have got to a state of mind in wch Italy means music 1659–1750 and 1830–, and humanity 1903. I find that like Du Maurier's man I prefer Chianti to Botticelli'.[76]

It was to be one of the defining moments of his life. Ted Haynes, himself exactly the sophisticated kind of young man Mary Berenson liked to encourage,[77] had given Dent this introduction into the exalted Berenson circle. Perched in the hills outside

75 *Ibid.*

76 LH 15/05/1903. By 1903 Bernard Berenson had established himself as the oracle in the provenance of Italian Renaissance art. Dent may cynically have recognised his rather less purely aesthetic aims.

77 These young men she chose to invite and introduce to her daughters were mostly homosexual; it is not clear how deliberate a policy this was. Ted knew her gay brother, Logan Pearsall Smith.

the city, Berenson's Villa I Tatti was even by that time a centre for a certain kind of cultural hegemony, another world from what Dent had seen so far, where art and money were becoming inseparable and high culture could be bought and sold. Berenson himself had already made a fortune as well as an international reputation out of Italian art, thanks mostly to rich Americans like Isabella Stewart Gardner.

As mentioned before, Dent sat there in exquisite surroundings, dusty and sweating from his long walk up the hill, desperately nervous again, 'awkward and embarrassed' in the 'select' company, so glib and certain in their stated ideals to live beautifully, being grilled politely, remorselessly on his ideal: 'the teaspoon jingled on the pavement of the terrace, and my hostess watched her priceless china with anxious eyes'. Dent took a deep breath and collected himself, blurting out, 'to understand all the music that ever had been, or ever would be, written'. 'All music?' His host turned pale: the company shuddered. '"Both good and bad? ... But what would become of Taste?"' But Dent held his ground and in so doing, found himself: 'Taste? We might get some new ideas about it.' All the self-doubts raised by the congress dissolved in that bold moment of sudden perception, when Dent felt able to take issue with a monumental figure like Berenson and to recognise the difference between taste and understanding. The episode stayed with him all his life, and seventeen years later he used it to anchor his essay on musical aesthetic, 'Revaluations'.[78]

The Berensons and the expensive, self-conscious culture they accrued up in fortress I Tatti were not at all in Dent's style, and he did not like being made to feel intimidated by such people. He preferred to think that he was above all that, and he hated to be patronised, especially when he sniffed pretentiousness. But the experience was a defining moment, though emerging only gradually as he later tried himself to establish the foundations for 'national' theatre and opera through the Old Vic and Sadler's Wells, the opposite of everything he saw that day at I Tatti. Culture was not something to be distributed 'de haut en bas', but to be built up from the grassroots, through ordinary people. He saw himself choosing the homosocial, the masculine, the lively life of the piazza over that of the drawing-room; the noisy, visceral response to high culture over the studied refinement of the Fiesole villas.

He was glad to escape to earthier Bologna and Modena:

> I work under the most comfortable conditions: the place is open 9.30 to 12 & 1.30 to 6 – & the MS room is nearly empty & very comfortable. I find very little of the people I am doing for FM:[79] but I am scoring a Te Deum of Terradellas from the parts & I shall get in some work at Stradella, Legrenzi & Cesti for my lectures next winter.[80]

78 'Revaluations' in LM (September 1920) p. 619. He did meet the Berensons again often, but never intimately.

79 John Alexander Fuller Maitland (1856–1936), music critic of *The Times* 1889–1911, edited the *Fitzwilliam Virginal Book*, Grove's 2nd edn (which is most likely what Dent is referring to here), contributed to the *Oxford History of Music*.

80 LH 28/05/1903. Domingo Terradellas (Dent's friend and protégé Roberto Gerhard would edit Terradellas' *La Merope* in 1951).

The upper-class young men studying at Bologna had embraced Dent, and carried him along with them on their lively, noisy evening excursions into piazza life. Fifty years later he was still speaking the impeccably old-fashioned, aristocratic Italian he had picked up here.[81] He peeled Forster away from his mother, and out into the bustling piazza with Cavanna and Ferratini and their other friends Rossi and Guido Mimbelli, winding up at the Caffé San Pietro, where they ate and drank and argued, 'a very cheerful evening'. Dent even allowed himself to be swept along to an Irredentist demonstration in the Piazza Garibaldi, 'wch began ferociously but fizzled out after about half an hour',[82] and to prowl with them along the Via Armaroli, where the local working girls hung out: 'the women horrible to me: & I did not quite get over the feeling of nausea the whole evening'.[83] They had accepted him without question but also without knowledge, while he felt safe because they were mostly of his own class. Such relationships kept their charm because Dent never put his true self to the test, and felt free to escape while enjoying the illusory sense of belonging. For years he kept in touch with the Mimbelli family,[84] especially Guido, and that September went back to visit them at their lively, noisy family pile near Vergaiolo and drank their Chianti back in Cambridge. But it was fantasy; Dent was never going to be a real part of their lives.

The uncertainty of where his work was taking him, the constant travelling and uneven success in the libraries made him fretful and restless most of that summer, while his visit to Venice that year only confirmed in him the need to make sure that the next time he was going to see more of the 'inner life' of Venice, through his contact, Horatio Brown.[85] His musical research and his sexual exploration appear at this point to be inseparable to him, and he determined to get both under control.

> Venice seems to have no attraction for me whatever, except the Banda Cittadina [citizen's band] is the best wind band I have ever heard ... I don't see why I shd be beaten by Venice when I do so well in Florence or Bologna. But I believe the only way to do it will be to take a room somewhere for 2 months, & a private gondola.[86]

Next came Budapest, Vienna and Dresden, until finally in Berlin that July Dent had several breakthroughs: 'I found that Berlin music was rather a hornet's nest: but with my usual luck I dropped into the right lot.'[87] The 'right lot' included some top musicologists he had met at Rome, and after the doubts of the Rome IMG/IMS, his warm reception by Max Friedlaender could hardly fail to gratify him: 'an effusive hospitality wch Benndorf shakes his head over as being very Semitic: but wch I, accustomed to the ways of Italians, Hungarians and that still queerer race the

81 Christopher Raeburn, himself a later Dent protégé, told me this.

82 Diary 24/05/1903.

83 Diary 29/05/1903.

84 None of the correspondence has survived, apart from a piece of music Guido sent him.

85 Horatio Robert Forbes Brown (1854–1926), Venetian historian, Uranian poet, biographer of John Addington Symonds. Brown would have known all about homosexual Venice.

86 LH 13/06/1903.

87 LH 13/07/1903.

English, found a pleasant relief from the average German indifference'.[88] He was being taken seriously as a colleague by the German establishment, no mean feat. Friedlaender showed Dent his considerable collection of monographs and invited him to his seminar on Beethoven and Schubert. 'Professorial hospitality consists in inviting your guests to hear lectures', Dent remarked to Lawrence, with a typical sting in the praise: 'I managed to hear him hold forth on a very varied [sic] material: Orazio Vecchi & Caccini, Bellini, Chopin & Brahms. He is a good lecturer, and knows his history pretty well: but I suspect that in some cases he read history books & not scores'.[89]

Then one day in early July, he encountered the celebrity pianist–composer Ferruccio Busoni.[90] Their meeting, the first in a lifelong friendship, was largely accidental: 'I had for about 2 years carried about a letter to him, but had never been able to present it: & just by chance I heard he was in Berlin'.[91] Both were apparently on particularly good form, Dent chatting away easily in Italian, and they struck up an instant understanding: 'as I did not ask him to play or to hear me play (!) we made friends at once'. Four nights later they accidentally met again, at one of the Italian restaurants Busoni liked to frequent, complete with his Swedish wife, 'Mrs Bew … not pretty … very charming', and some of his entourage, that night including a young Australian, Percy Grainger[92] and a young and pretty American, 'Maude Durrant', who became better known as 'Maud Allan'.[93] Busoni's, Dent quickly learnt, was a large and gregarious personality; he loved always to be in company, surrounded by his pupils and some very odd, arty company. Dent was ripe for such experience, and in Busoni he saw the embodiment of everything a 'musician' could be. He coveted what Busoni had achieved, and however critical of Busoni's playing, Dent quickly fell for the man himself, handsome, cosmopolitan, sophisticated and a brilliant musician, both composer and performer. When Busoni gave a recital in London that November, Dent took him to dinner and the friendship was sealed.[94]

Dent had deadlines for articles, so rushed to Münster in Westphalen, to the stuffy Santini library where he managed to copy a toccata of Scarlatti's, and a finale of Longroscino from *Il Governatore*: 'The whole opera pleased me very much; it is almost as good as Rossini, but the Neapolitan baffled me', then a quick stop in Cambridge to finish off his article on Leo, only to discover a note from Fuller Maitland putting it off for a year. Dent had no real need now to stay in Cambridge for the summer, so, having submitted his article on Scarlattti's quartets for Shedlock's

88 *Ibid.*

89 *Ibid.*

90 See 'Dramatis Personae'.

91 *Ibid.* and Diary 05/07/1903.

92 George Percy Grainger aka Percy Aldridge Grainger (1882–1961), Australian composer, pianist, eventually moved to the USA. His piano music was used in the film of *Howard's End*.

93 Maud Allan (1873–1956) became notorious for her 'Salome' dance; see Chapter 8 on her failed lawsuit. Busoni often stayed with her in London.

94 Diary 18/11/1903.

Monthly Musical Record,[95] he was off again via Lucerne for another six weeks in Italy, starting this time at Venice, determined that this trip was to be very different from the last.

'Human society is my holiday, you know', Dent would loftily remark to Lawrence later, 'and I have had one of the best I ever had. I have been very lucky in my acquaintances as well as quite unscrupulous in my ways of making them'.[96] On the train to Venice, in between reading D'Annunzio and *The Portrait of Dorian Gray* ('much impressed … too tragic for the British public'[97]) Dent had spotted Sir Thomas Wright and an elegant young man (his 'Anonimo') arguing in a nearby first-class compartment. Within days he had snatched the Anonimo, Henry Holland, away, and was bathing at the Lido and dining in his company. At the same time he was meeting 'some of the most elegant and doubtful people in Venice', including George Magray and his lover James Baird, who shared an apartment in the Palazzo Barbaro, complete with grand piano, Italian valet and 'beautiful' gondolier. Imagining with unholy glee how envious Browning would have been at such a set-up, Dent wallowed in it, fussed over by Baird and Magray, who 'gave me a great blowing up for becoming a mouldy don and historian instead of writing songs, etc.'[98]

But Dent was never a sexual tourist like Frederick Rolfe in Venice or the men who haunted Taormina on the prowl for beautiful youths to photograph in the nude and for a small fee to take to bed.[99] He was too fastidious: such transactions degraded any high-minded notions of Greek love, he felt, and undermined friendship. Possibly he was too frightened, not only of rejection which could so easily be compounded by scandal, but of his own response. Dent liked to be in control.

In Florence again, Dent went to visit Cust and met Henry Somerset for the first time, one of the older homosexual exiles. Dent found him 'very agreeable' but his house 'all scarlet & gold with endless Beaufort roses & lilies I found oppressive'.[100] Ted Haynes joined him in Bologna and they went out with poet and photographer Max Arici. At this stage Dent was still trying to wed his two sets of experience, drawing in his old friends; it had worked well with Forster, with his unquenchable curiosity, but Ted was another matter.

> On the whole he is an admirable companion – we have a similar taste in the fine arts, and an infinity of subtle jests that go back any number of years – & good memories. On the other hand … he naturally doesn't see why he shd go out of his way to make friends with casual Italians whom he is not likely to meet again.[101]

95 'The Earliest String Quartets' (November 1903).

96 LH 05/10/1903.

97 Diary 19/08/1903.

98 Diary 28/08/1903.

99 See Robert Aldrich, *The Seduction of the Mediterranean: Writing, Art and Homosexual Fantasy* (London, 1993), pp. 99ff.

100 Diary 21/09/1903.

101 LH 30/09/1903.

After the lively, intense experiences in Venice, Florence and a week that September at Vergaiolo with the Mimbelli family, 'all laughing and shouting at once ... The charm of the life is its perfect simplicity', back in Cambridge, Italy never really receded. Forster up for the weekend, 'using it as a playground', playing duets with Carey, walks with Lawrence Haward and his shy brother Tristram. In one typical day Dent had Forster, Jack Sheppard[102] and Percy Lubbock[103] to lunch, then that evening, Lytton Strachey and his brother Oliver to dinner. He called on Sayle, on Leonard Woolf at Trinity, had Goldie and Hugh Meredith to dinner, when they were allowed to sample some of Dent's Vitali Chianti while trying to talk him into taking on the editorship of the *Cambridge Review*. Dent's own views were by now less parochial; he had seen how in Italy and Germany the high arts were more a part of everyday life, and he wanted to make that more the case in Cambridge, starting with the music.

His friends had begun to call him 'Il Signior'; there were jokes in circulation about his pedantic pronunciation of 'Scar-láttty' or 'Pull-aír-mou'[104] and his love of Chianti, beside other, rather bitchier remarks on how affected it all was. A.C. Benson, just re-establishing himself in Cambridge around this time, was dismissive: 'odd, quirky, frozen Dent, who spends his time in disinterring fragments of Scarlatti'.[105] But for the younger men, what Dent was doing – the travelling, the original research, the escape from stuffy England – was intellectually glamorous. There was late-night music and talk in his rooms peppered with books, music, pictures and stories picked up on his recent travels beside comic, down-to-earth accounts of darning his underwear and coping with the Italian fleas. His close friends found the combination irresistible, while Dent of course loved being the one in the know, the oracle, the fount of all such wisdom, and the chef d'équipe.

In fact, Dent was listening carefully to everything going, but what he heard even in London made him feel that for real inspiration he needed to be abroad. This dim view was only confirmed later that year when a visit to the Leeds Festival after he returned from Italy that September was all too painfully British, parochial and unsatisfactory.[106] He still found the time to read Otto Jahn's book on Mozart, or go to Mrs Frazer's French play, or play Schumann and Schubert quintets with the Grays and Miss Beard, but for much of Lent term he worked on the lecture he was to give at

102 (Sir) John Tressider Sheppard (1881–1968), Classicist, Fellow from 1908, held Sunday At Homes; first non-Etonian Provost of King's, generous, a gifted teacher in the spirit of his mentor OB. Annan, *The Dons*, pp. 111ff.

103 Percy Lubbock (1879–1965), Old Etonian, man of letters, became Pepys Librarian at Magdalene College. He was almost the opposite of Dent, and took up with many of the people and circles Dent rejected, like the Berensons. Elegant, handsome and rich, frustrated in his own career, would soon assume the role of pilot-fish to various literary sharks – Henry James, Edith Wharton and A.C. Benson. Right now he was cultivating a close romantic friendship with young Clive Carey, and it was irritating to find Dent, slightly older, talented, established, and a real musician where Percy was limited, attracted to Clive as well. Percy took any opportunity to poke holes in the fabric of Clive's worship, but with a carefully light and frivolous touch.

104 LHaward to CC 08/12/1903.

105 A.C. Benson, unpublished diaries, 24/41. Pepys Library, Magdalene College, Cambridge.

106 LH 27/09/1903.

the Musical Association[107] on 8 March. C.H. Lloyd put him up for the Savile Club, and nearly every week he went down to London concerts, the Elgar Festival or to the Queen's Hall with Charles Wood to hear a typically mixed programme, Haydn's 'Salomon [sic] symphony':

> Wood rather uncertain whether to treat it as 'quaint old stuff' or as a precursor of Tschaikowsky – the result was not very satisfactory: a Concerto of Mozart (A major), played indifferently by the band & to perfection by Raoul Pugno, an old gentleman with a patriarchal beard who played from his book. It was the best Mozart playing I ever heard … & Strauss' Don Juan wch I did not understand much of, though it was good stuff.[108]

That Lent term 1904, Dent was elected to the Musical Board,[109] so now in a better official position to determine the course of academic music. His Scarlatti book was accepted by Edward Arnold, subject to some serious negotiation on its size.[110] His ambitious series of lectures that term on Vecchi's *Amfiparnaso* needed good musicians and singers, and included many from Nixon's glees and from the CUMS chorus. Expansiveness and inclusion were part of Dent's tactics to shift Cambridge musical life into a wider sphere, and, in spite of his misogynist reputation, Dent went out of his way to include women.

> Miss Gunn being rather amazed at not being able to play the Schumann 5t at the Musical Club … wrote the following epigram wch she sent me on Wednesday:
> With respectful compliments to the C.U.M.C.
> See Apollo bars the door
> To the Muses nine:
> Saint Cecilia leads no more
> Harmony divine:
> For Orpheus no Euridice
> (Whom even Pluto pitied),
> For the Club has passed device –
> 'Ladies not admitted.'[111]

And Dent always felt obliged to look after his flock. Through his ongoing work at the British Museum with Streatfeild and Binyon, he encouraged Lawrence Haward to apply there for a job (it failed). Eventually he helped Lawrence to find his way as a music critic at *The Times*, offering introductions, and when his old friend Johnson, in financial straits again, sent begging letters, Dent responded with generosity, but he had yet to recognise how people on the receiving end of charity could come to hate that position.

107 The (Royal) Musical Association was founded in 1874 'for the study of the art and science of music … the object of the meeting will be to read original papers and to discuss all matters relating to the art.' Mrs Spottiswoode's late husband William was one of its founders. Parry was the current president.

108 Diary 27/02/1904.

109 Diary 24/01/1904. Charles Wood called by to tell him.

110 Diary 05/02/1904. Also LH 28/03/1904.

111 Diary 03/03/1904.

Now at Cambridge, even though so often away, he was constructing some comfortable homosocial circles, including Theo Bartholomew, a young librarian friend of Sayle's who initially loathed Dent, and the outrageous Noel Barwell,[112] yet another curious creature Dent decided to befriend. He was fascinated by uncompromisingly camp men like Barwell, flouncing around Cambridge on his raft of wicked anecdotes about mutual acquaintances, knowing he could never let himself go like that, while wondering if he really wanted to. Forster didn't like him, 'very much disgusted not by the subject but by the mind that arranged it'.[113] Dent knew that in Cambridge, such egregious public display would rebound, and helped to pick up the pieces: 'the fall of Barwell wch has at last taken place. Later I had to go & see Sedley in order to definitely suppress an unnecessary scandal about B. The Bankruptcy court will be enough without worse things.'[114]

Dent's hopes for the future of Cambridge music and his own personal future were becoming vested in Clive Carey, the young organ scholar at Clare. With his good looks, his fine voice, his musical and theatrical talents, Clive[115] was the most completely attractive man to enter Dent's orbit. He was only seventeen when he first came up, and Dent often condescendingly referred to him as 'the child', while taking him seriously as a musician:

> [Carey] showed me his [Robert] Bridges song this morning; it is really very masterly but too Parry/Stanford to be great. And at his age you cd not expect him to be anything but rather cold. But the workmanship is perfect. He really is a wonderful child.[116]

Like many of Dent's friends, Clive had a domineering, fond mother at home, and he was painfully diffident, except on the stage. He had already produced a successful *Trial by Jury* at Cambridge the previous March, and was being groomed as a student conductor of CUMS. He loved theatre and especially dancing, becoming closely involved with Cecil Sharpe and the English Folk Dance Society and the triennial Greek Play. That November 1903, in Aristophanes' *The Birds,* he played the part of the Owl and led the Chorus, with music by Parry, who wrote a new Parabasis especially for him and came up to conduct it himself. Clive was a star: he spoke the Greek beautifully, sang and danced beautifully, his natural charm and modesty very quickly attracting friends and admirers across all boundaries. He was also religious. These last two personal qualities Dent would never understand, and when Clive struck up genuine friendships with 'clerics' like Monty James, in opposing camps to Dent, or went to chapel,

112 For A.T. 'Theo' Bartholomew, see 'Dramatis Personae'. Noel F. Barwell (1878–1953) was a cousin of Sedley Taylor's, which probably gave him his entrée. He had a chequered career as a journalist, wrote a scurrilous novel, then in WWI was in the 5th Battalion Oxford & Bucks Light Infantry, eventually going to India. According to Scott's biographer R.M. Dunn, Barwell had an affair with Geoffrey Scott, spending time at I Tatti with him.

113 Diary 03/12/1903.

114 Diary 28/03/1904.

115 Dent quickly called him 'Clive', like 'Lawrence' or 'Ted', while Forster was always 'Forster'.

116 LH 16/10/1903.

Dent found it vexatious. Clive became devoted to Dent, as Dent had made certain that he would, but it was probably far less predatory than it sounds, although Dent was strongly attracted. The politics of small, self-contained communities had become almost second nature to Dent, and were based on personal allegiances, personal power bases. But for much of 1902–04 Dent was away from Cambridge, and each time he returned Clive was already engaged in a number of projects with friends of his own, and the older wing under which he nestled was Percy Lubbock's.

From Michaelmas term 1903, Clive was very much present in Dent's social and musical activities, singing to illustrate Dent's lectures and being consulted about musical matters. Dent's letters from abroad, which Clive kept all his life,[117] are self-consciously entertaining and lighthearted, and above all, inclusive, constantly engaging Clive's attention, making him feel that he was an important part of Dent's life. 'I wish you were here. There is my dear friend Alessandro Scarlatti, it is true, & I see a great deal of him: but it is not the same thing – although he reminds me of you perpetually – I think he wd have liked your stuff'. He included little musical illustrations he knew Clive would appreciate, of a Scarlatti tune 'Sarei troppo': 'I found this on Wednesday & it has haunted me ever since – I think Scarlatti loved it too, for he repeats it four or five times in the course of the cantata'. On a Brahms concert conducted by Niessen, a huge programme, with the 'Tragic' Overture and the *Requiem,* an 'almost Cambridge programme … they evidently thought it very difficult music & they never dared let themselves go at all … soprano solo wch the lady sang in tune, but with reechings & screechings like a pussy-cat on a channel steamer'. Even the sound of bells, he said reminded him of Clive's Parabasis: 'I've forgotten the words, but I can never forget the sound of your voice in them'.[118] With Clive, he assumes an almost avuncular air, even though he is only seven years the elder, revealing none of the misery or anxiety, much less his 'gardens' in his letters to Lawrence at the same time.

All that year, in spite of all his other distractions and obligations, Dent always made time for Clive and his needs (as Dent saw them); his diary is full of almost daily references to 'Clive'. He was determined that Clive should have some official recognition and status appropriate to his talents, and began with a campaign to keep Clive on as conductor of CUMS, writing to members of the orchestra, pressuring anyone with any influence, especially Gray: 'by dint of hard talking got Gray round to let Clive keep the orchestra: but it was hard work'.[119] They played a lot of music together; it was Cham revisited.[120] That May Week, Clive was playing Lady Bracknell to Alwyn Scholfield's[121] Chasuble at the Amateur Dramatic Club, so Dent took a party along, including Meredith, Waterlow and Haward. 'Clive was magnificent: Scholfield ridiculously

117 The whole collection was given to KCA, and became the basis for Hugh Carey's biography, *Duet for Two Voices,* which gives a personal but limited view of Dent.

118 CC 25/03/1904.

119 Diary 05/06/1904.

120 Diary 06/06/1904.

121 Alwyn Scholfield 'Scho' (1889–1969), very much part of Dent's Cambridge circles, being gay, musical and keen on acting and production. He was later University Librarian and worked with Dent on building up the music collections.

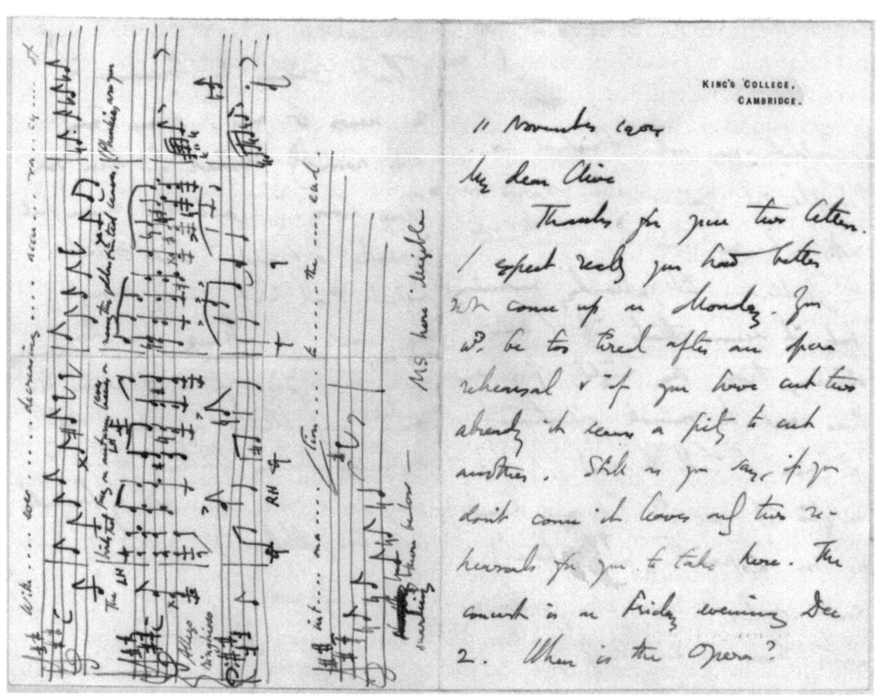

KING'S COLLEGE, CAMBRIDGE.

11 November 1904

My dear Clive

Thanks for your two letters. I expect really you had better not come up on Monday. You wd. be too tired after an opera rehearsal & if you have cut two already it seems a pity to cut another. Still as you say, if you don't come it leaves only two rehearsals for you to take here. The concert is on Friday evening Dec 2. When is the Opera?

That Greene is tiresome is no news to me. Alan Gray was horribly worried by him over "Glen Lora." Can't the man put "Awake o heart" last? but I suspect that isn't rusty [?] enough. He wants something like this:— (see next page for a specimen hitherto unpublished, by Ernest Little & Maude Valerie Walker, revised & fingered or rather thumbed by Samuel (and Tom) Walker.)

Yours

EJDent

Couldn't you ask Stanford or Temple if you can be spared or not? I can leave the Opera with the Jenkinsons till Monday morning: but it seems that if I am dining there the night you come there won't be much opportunity for me to talk to you. I shd. be glad if you wd. let me know as soon as possible, as naturally I don't want to leave Mrs Jenkinson later than I can help.

FIGURE 6. Letter from Dent to Clive Carey, illustrated with music. By kind permission of the Provost and Fellows of King's College, Cambridge.

convincing as Dr. Chasuble: HOM [Meredith] & I roared with laughter especially in places where the other people were too shocked to laugh'.[122]

The drama unfolded throughout the summer of 1904. Clive had been thinking about going to Dresden that summer to study German and go to the opera there, but he had no money. Percy Lubbock, thrilled at the idea of travel, investigated the opera season, finding it closed in July, not opening until mid-August. Then Dent picked up the thread; it seemed to him perfect that Clive should travel to Italy with *him*, and he began to apply gentle but very persistent pressure. But Clive had already begun to feel a little uncomfortable at Dent's increasing attentions, the gentle, relentless pressure: 'Why did you sport your door? Otherwise I might have had a look at you when I brought the peonies on Sunday morning – though I would not have waked you'.[123]

> It is so delightful to be in a decent hot climate & I enjoy myself so thoroughly that I can't do anything without wanting you to enjoy it with me ... If you would rather go to Munich I might arrange to meet you there – but I think Italy would be better for both of us. However I suppose if Percy says 'Dresden', to Dresden you go.[124]

A week later he was writing again: 'I want you so badly that I write for my own pleasure more than yours'.

Lubbock was applying his own kind of pressure, making Clive giggle. 'I was pleased to find Dent at Munich', he wrote to Clive in a letter set a fictitious three years in the future:

> I hadn't seen him for ages. He enjoys his work at Coomassie very much, & is delighted with the simplicity & force of the native Ashanti music. The complete absence both of harmony & of melody is so refreshing, he says. He has written a rattle concerto – & means to start a movement for freeing European music from its slavish adherence to Couperin & Vinci.[125]

They kept up the schoolboy jokes while planning their trip, but underneath it was determination – at least on Lubbock's part – not to let Dent have it all his own way, writing that, having just read Murray's *Northern Italy,* he was 'aching to go'.[126] He turned the trip into a naughty conspiracy of two against a Dent of his own fantasy:

> If you find you can, don't tell Dent anything as to dates, till we have settled more or less where we are going to. I am wild to have a night or two at Venice, (just to get a general sensation, not to sight-see) – I can't have Dent there, I am afraid ... but not a word to Dent about this. I won't have Venice shewn off to me by any living soul.[127]

They all met up in Verona on 11 September: a disaster. 'I believe I was very disagreeable', Dent wrote in his diary, meaning temper tantrums, 'headaches', jealousy

122 Diary 10/06/1904.

123 CC 15/06/1904. Written from Florence.

124 *Ibid.*

125 PL to CC 07/07/1904.

126 PL to CC 23/07/1904.

127 *Ibid.*

and complete misunderstandings. Lubbock would dine out on it for years, sticking to his own amusingly bitchy versions.[128] Clive was puzzled. 'We had much looked forward to his arrival', Clive wrote in his diary:

> but when he came he disappointed us – I think our British appearance and behaviour were too much for him. At any rate, he was not good tempered, that is to say, at times he wasn't – one could never be certain what he would be like the next minute … It was really rather pathetic after the pleasure Percy and I had been feeling at the idea of seeing 'our Dent'.[129]

Dent's own disingenuous explanation is both slick and false:

> I am learning by experience that life like the pianoforte is not big enough for three people to play at once in comfort. Frankly, Italy à trois is sometimes rather purgatory: and when I say this in the company of two such agreeable people as Percy & Clive, you will understand that it is a general principle … We don't quarrel at all: but I feel that I might just as well be with two people I had never seen in my life before if I am not to get any more out of them than I do. But they are inseparable.[130]

The reasons behind this contretemps were more complex than the gooseberry dynamic. Dent knew himself well enough to recognise that he had either to be in charge or completely retiring, nothing in between, and such limitations militated against his more generous and expansive impulses to bring those he loved into the other cultures he loved, become as liberated as he felt he was, the bumpy beginnings of his internationalist outlook. 'I sigh to think how much more deeply he might have penetrated into Italy with a less English atmosphere around him.' Dent failed to recognise that each in his different way, Clive, Percy and Ted would never wish to belong to Italy in the way he did himself.

Even as he wrote a long, self-exculpatory letter to Lawrence, Dent was not being entirely honest with himself or with his friends. The obsessive streak which propelled his intensive work habits and meticulous scholarship unfortunately extended to his personal relationships. As his obsession with Clive cooled, their friendship actually strengthened, a solid mutual trust established in matters of music and theatre. But all that year Dent had been in hot pursuit of another young man, the younger brother of his Sicilian friend Guido Orlandi, Valentino. Valentino was Dent's little secret; he didn't come clean even with Lawrence.

> I am not working here, except that it is hard work looking after an Italian convalescent whose ups & downs are inexplicable. He has had family troubles & a nervous breakdown – Yesterday he got bad news of his sister's health & I had to do all I could to prevent him committing suicide: I could not let him go to the post office even, alone.[131]

128 A.C. Benson recorded in his diary February–March 1907 that Percy had told him 'when he travelled with D. & Dent had dear friends & dependents in every town, those dear friends could never be found at home, & were always called away by sudden & unexpected business on finding Dent's card in their rooms'.

129 Quoted in Carey, *Duet for Two Voices*, p. 19.

130 LH 14/09/1904.

131 LH 07/08/1904.

The reality of the 'Italian convalescent' was very different. Having met him the year before and been strongly attracted – Valentino appears to have sent out strong signals of his own – Dent arranged to meet up for dinner and theatre on Christmas Eve, hoping for the perfect Sicilian Christmas, but something happened in Palermo which frightened him enough to take the first available boat straight back to Naples.[132] This curious episode marked the beginning of a curious relationship. In one sense it was a fulfilment of Dent's Paterian fantasy, being in sole charge of a needy and dependent younger man, and it was probably his first full relationship.

Over the next few years Dent had several holidays in Valentino's company, paying for everything, and continuing for some time to give money to his family, with the faintest hint of blackmail, from the family and over the next few years, from Valentino himself. At first, in Rome that August, Dent was happy to flutter endlessly over Valentino's every whim: 'we went to the Villa Borghese where milk refreshed him … then after the Pincio dined at the Toscana in the Pza Colonna. We went back to the Pincio for the Banda Communale wch played a good programme with a lot of Le Prophete'.[133] The next day at St Peter's, Dent was interested in the service music going on, but because Valentino took exception to the 'not very polite manners' of the Swiss Guard, they could not stay. Then Valentino was feverish and not sleeping well, Dent noted with concern, so made certain of a quiet day before taking the train to Fano on the Adriatic. All Dent could afford was the 'unpretending' Albergo Moro, with its crude sanitary arrangements, 'a most unattractive forth', 'a daily maelstrom', stinking and full of flies in the hot weather. Valentino was not impressed by Fano, either, calling it a town full of 'malfattoni' or crooks; while a bat in their room gave him an attack of 'nerves', as did the fireworks display one night and the music outside in the piazza. Valentino got headaches. A letter from Clive to Dent sent Valentino up into the boughs. Even the regular bathing which Dent had come to enjoy did not always soothe Valentino's frayed nerves: 'unfortunately an unknown lady made overtures to him in the water wch gave him a bad shock – He came back in a fearful state & insisted on lunching at home'. Unsurprisingly Dent too began to get headaches and suffer some sleepless nights of his own, with constipation as well; after two weeks, they parted in some relief. Only one letter of Valentino's to Dent has survived, an effusive expression of affection and gratitude, thanking Dent for being 'il mio dottore sei stato tu', from your Valentino 'che tanto ti ama!'.[134]

Back in Dent's other life, Arnold were being difficult about the length of *Alessandro Scarlatti*, about the German rights and about what to include. Dent was forced to do

132 According to Dent's diary, it was was something Valentino told Dent about another man he had recently met, Salvatore Padolfo: 'he gave me revelations about SP's character that made it desirable that I shd leave Palermo. I wanted to go to Girganti, but V. insisted on my going to Naples: so I got my ticket & went that evening.'

133 Diary 30/07/1904.

134 'My doctor was you', from your Valentino 'who loves you so much!' Before their trip, on 4 March 1904, Dent was startled to receive a 'letter from V.O.'s mother wch amazed me being a begging-letter of the worst type & not very literate.' Whether or not the Orlandi family were actually blackmailing him or simply playing on his generosity is never clear, but the begging letters did not stop for some time to come.

some rewriting and more cataloguing,[135] when he felt he really needed to get down to composition for his doctorate. He consulted Martucci and Pagliara on Vinci's *Le Zite u Galera*, and Pergolesi's *Frate unamorato*, but the most important meeting that spring was with Alessandro Longo.[136] It was a genuine meeting of hearts and souls; Longo had just begun his own Scarlatti research, although coming at it from another angle, since he was working on Alessandro's son, Domenico. Still, he was able to give to Dent 'interesting information about the Scarlatti family' which had so far eluded Dent's attempts to find out more, a subject on which they would continue to correspond for years. They also shared an interest in early keyboard instruments: 'He has an Adam Beyer square piano, 1784, not so playable as mine but beautifully inlaid & a Stein of about the same date'. Possibly on Longo's advice, Dent was working in the Biblioteca Nazionale reading Niccolo Conforto's diary.[137]

The English friendships were retrieved back in Cambridge, and in the autumn Clive would go off to Germany, bristling with Dent's introductions and advice. But from now on Dent kept his private life and any sexual activities separate, well away from Cambridge and any scrutiny. Increasingly the British music world appeared desperately limited compared with the musical cultures he experienced on the continent, not limited to nor defined by a class system or even scholarly hierarchies.

1905–1906

> I have come clearly to understand that I can do nothing here towards Cambridge musical education unless I take a higher musical degree … At present I am neither professional nor amateur & somewhat looked down on for my youth & ignorance. I never get a free hand anywhere.[138]

Alessandro Scarlatti: His Life and Work was published in February 1905, and 'gratefully and affectionately dedicated by one of his earliest Eton pupils' to 'Charles Harford Lloyd'. In spite of 'magnificent' reviews, it did not sell well,[139] but it remains a standard work. Frank Walker, editor of the second edition of 1960, remarked, 'After more than half a century the value of the book has hardly diminished at all. The discussion of the music needs no revision.'

It deserved better at the time, with dozens of little gems scattered throughout which show Dent's complete command of his subject, and an easy written style far

135 LH 28/03/1904 from Münster, where he was laboriously going through 'about 20 vols of miscellaneous things'.

136 Alessandro Longo (1864–1945), keyboard player, chamber musician, composer and musicologist, whose edition of Domenico Scarlatti's keyboard works (1906–13) was the standard for years, until Ralph Kirkpatrick produced a major revision in 1952, and the 'Longo' denomination was replaced by 'Kirkpatrick'.

137 Niccolo Conforto (1727–65), Neapolitan composer of operas, set Metastasio's *Festa cinese* and *Siroe*, later went to Spain.

138 LH 21/05/1906.

139 Two years later, Arnold still had several hundred copies left. Diary 01/03/1907: 'Of wch 13 to America … one I sent to Vincent d'Indy'.

in advance of its time. Only Bernard Shaw (whom Dent admired) wrote seriously about music with as much wit and verve. It is not only a pioneering biography of Alessandro Scarlatti, but a running commentary on the historical significance of his musical achievements, and only Dent could have made such an easy, polished job of it; like his lectures, his book is both scholarly and accessible. He is not blind to his subject's faults, calling an early attempt at opera seria, *Pompeo*, 'stiff and tedious' and remarking on the general poverty of most contemporary librettos.

> The voice was the only instrument for which chamber-music of a really advanced type could be written; it was the only instrument which combined a finished technique with the greatest variety of beautiful tone-colour, and which in the majority of cases was governed by minds of a high order of intelligence (p. 11).
>
> There is no direct connection between the choruses and descriptive symphonies of Monteverdi and those of Weber, except by the circuitous route that traverses the stony asperities of French opera (p. 42).
>
> Scarlatti's work covers exactly the period when concerted instrumental music was beginning to be recognized as a possible rival to the voice, and it is interesting to trace the gradual development of instrumental music in the work of a composer whose natural sympathies were all with the singers, but who was quick to take advantage of any other means that facilitated the expression of his thought (p. 42).
>
> But with *La Caduta dei Decemviri* (1697) and *Il Prigioniero fortunato* (1698) there appears a new element. Here Scarlatti either languishes to cloying airs in 12/8 time, all charming, and all exactly alike, or else stamps across the boards to music of that straightforward, square-cut character that one would naturally describe as 'Handelian'. They remind one of nothing so much as Sullivan's famous parody in *Princess Ida* (p. 65).

As he had said to Lawrence the year before, Scarlatti had 'held him together', and after its publication, for quite some time Dent was at a loss how to replace that immediate sense of purpose; certainly not with composition. In 1905 his future renown as a writer would have been impossible to predict, yet for a man whose professional livelihood came to depend so much on his writing, Dent produced very little between 1903 and 1913,[140] his research channelled mostly into teaching, lectures and productions, his writing mostly confined to his diary and his growing correspondence. Only after he had decided on another prolonged period abroad did it occur to him to write formally about the music he was hearing: 'Letter from Germany', 'Music in Berlin', 'English Opera in Berlin', etc. But for the time being, despite his achievements, Dent struggled.

In Michaelmas term 1904 he had been 'struggling with Gluck for my lectures and with Galuppi for the new Grove as FM [Fuller Maitland] wants it at once'.[141] He toyed yet again with the idea of composing for a doctorate, casting about for possible subjects. Otherwise, the only projects immediately presenting themselves

140 Besides his articles on early opera for the second edition of Grove's (ed. Fuller Maitland), 2 articles/lectures for the Musical Association, 3 articles for the *Sammelbände*, 10 articles for the CR, 21 articles for Shedlock's MMR, to which he contributed regularly from 1906. His editing of Purcell began in 1906. Haward, *Edward J. Dent: A Bibliography.*

141 LH 14/10/1904.

were a paper for Goldie's discussion group, on *Simplicissimus,* and the Galuppi article for Fuller Maitland. Academic music of the order Dent had seen in Berlin, Bologna or Florence was a rarity, the Musical Association mostly tepid, while contemporary performance and composition were stuck in the kind of worthy programmes he had seen at Leeds two years before. Dent was enough of an insider now to recognise the built-in problems at Cambridge, from its disaffected and absentee Professor to its tenacious but conservative exponents, clinging to what they knew, while Dent himself was considered to be still too young and inexperienced to make an official difference.

The struggle – and struggle is the right word – to establish Music as an academic subject had been going on for at least twenty-five years, the most recent attempt having been at Oxford in 1898, which was thrown out by the university.[142] Although as far as most locals were concerned music was flourishing, and the town benefiting from the numerous concerts and opportunities provided by the university,[143] the focal point so necessary in producing consistency in excellence was simply not there. Stanford's dream had included a proper Faculty of Music, with all facilities in place, but before that could happen there had to be a perceived need. A chicken-or-egg paradox: facilities attract students but students need facilities, and Music needed a big presence to drive it forward and attract the students to fuel its engines. Dent possessed the necessary ego, energy and intelligence, and was conspicuously accumulating a wider, more cosmopolitan experience and understanding which he tried to harness. His Fellowship submission, the Scarlatti work alone, was far beyond in its scope, originality and scholarship what would normally have obtained for other people their doctorates of Music, yet the next steps eluded him. The current state of Cambridge music did not help.

In term-time his efforts were dogged more than anything else, addressing dreary but fundamental problems and treading on local toes. He had learnt to organise and muster the resources to hand, scores and parts for any concert still often had to be painstakingly copied, any previous mistakes spotted, while the science lecture theatres in Free School Lane used for rehearsals were hardly inspirational, with residual scents of Bunsen burners and a vast blackboard 'covered in beautiful coloured drawings & neatly written explanations of the placenta & the urinogenital organs'.[144] The pianos available for rehearsal were often bad and/or out of tune. Clive Carey, for one, found it all too much; his health, never very robust, was poor enough that Michaelmas term for him to give up conducting CUMS. Dent kept him posted and the picture he presents, though amusing, clearly shows the difficulties:

142 The Oxford debate would continue for years, until sorted out under the various benevolent supervisions of Sir Walter Parratt, Sir Hugh Allen and to some extent Sir Hubert Parry.

143 Knight, *Cambridge Music,* pp. 90ff. Mann retired from his Festival Choir in 1904, and it became reinvented as the Cambridge Choral Society, later the Cambridge Philharmonic. The town continued to play many active parts in making music with the university societies, the university families acting as a bridge, as the many references in Dent's diary testify.

144 Diary 26/10/1905.

> the piano was very much out of tune: Gray thumped it occasionally but never where it was wanted to make the harmony intelligible. We trudged through Dazu ist erschienen at the sort of pace one goes across a ploughed field in autumn at the end of a long and wet walk.[145]
>
> This evening I have been deputizing for you again and have shouted myself hoarse & feel completely finished: I cd not walk straight from Free School Lane to King's – not from fatigue of body but a sort of drunkenness: & that not of excitement – but because I felt I had no brain left at all. We at last tackled the Bach: but as Gray had copied some of the parts – & as Levett in his sweet innocence had begun by copying others from Gray instead of from the score the result was unspeakable. Letters never coincided: the first violins had 2 bars too many & the cellos 6 too few besides half bars, three quarter bars & all sorts of vagaries![146]

Even so, CUMS and CUMC were still probably the best way forward, as practical music and performance became more of an interface between undergraduate music-making and professionalism. Clive's departure furnished the excuse for Dent to take over more of the performance side of CUMS, although CUMS was still officially Gray's. 'I hope people will not think me guilty of a coup d'état', he wrote to Lawrence: 'I am the only person available who could without sacrifice of dignity do the work gratuitously and with the understanding of playing second fiddle to Gray. But' he added mischievously, 'in certain cases the second fiddle has been known to lead the quartet'.[147]

Dent's sense of tact was at best self-deluding; what he called having to 'assume an aggressive humility', combined with his usual zeal and musical self-righteousness, must have been hard to work with. At the end of November he received 'a stormy letter from Gray who considered that I had openly showed my contempt for his conducting abilities at the rehearsal last night'.[148] Dent was still learning how to exercise his gifts while taming the more insufferable aspects of his own sense of superiority.

For the rest of that academic year and the next, Dent simply carried on with his hectic Cambridge routines, taxing his energies more than his intellect, at the end of term escaping to Italy and Germany. Otherwise, music was the same frantic collection of regular events, with the informal playing Dent especially enjoyed attracting a number of undergraduates, including a sophisticated and worldly young Viennese Jew up at King's, Ernst Goldschmidt,[149] who later looked after Dent in Vienna and became a lifelong friend, and John Maynard Keynes, 'though he does not consider

145 CC 22/10/1904.

146 CC 01/11/1904.

147 LH 17/10/1904. It was a favourite refrain.

148 Diary 29/11/1904.

149 Ernst Philip Goldschmidt (1887–1954), born Vienna, died London. Rupert Brooke stayed with him in Vienna. Later he became a well-known bookseller. 'Bookselling', he said, 'would be an ideal existence if there were no customers.' Notes from Christie's catalogue. Goldschmidt had caused a stir when he came up to Cambridge in 1905, aged seventeen and a half, described by Maynard Keynes in a letter to Lytton Strachey as 'the head prostitute of Vienna'. Quoted in Skidelsky, *John Maynard Keynes: Hopes Betrayed*, p. 163. How he knew this is left to the imagination.

himself musical'.[150] Sunday breakfasts would include six or seven people – Lawrence, Horace Cole,[151] Hugh Meredith, Forster, Adrian Stephen (brother of Vanessa, Virginia and Thoby), Clive, besides old Etonian friends like Rickett, all crammed into Dent's rooms for buttered eggs and coffee. At one of these, on 30 November, Dent met Francis Toye, a modern linguist up at Trinity, destined for the Foreign Office.[152] Toye was an excellent natural linguist, musical, scholarly and anti-clerical in a way Dent found congenial, and thanks to his recent Foreign Office training, he had travelled, with some operatic experience in Germany and in Florence. Toye's shrewd, affectionate portrait of Dent in his autobiography speaks for itself:

> Dent's was a curious personality. A bachelor from passionate conviction, he gave the impression rather of prim old-maidishness; by nature the kindest of men, he was often at pains to indulge in acid comments on people and their motives calculated to wound deeply; in practice exceptionally beneficent and unselfish, he proclaimed with vigour his detestation of the Christian virtues – indeed, of Christians in general. It was primarily the A.M.D.G. [the dedication, Ad Majorem Dei Gloriam] on the score of *The Dream of Gerontius* that aroused his dislike of Elgar ... A subversive modernist in most of his opinions, he remained at heart a lover of tradition ... he imparted to his Cambridge surroundings a cosmopolitan flavour that was very pleasant ... He had something very like genius for teaching, and I think he was conscious of a kind of mission in this respect, to be carried out with every weapon of indirect influence as well as of direct instruction ... Dent's first care, having discovered me, was to produce some kind of order out of my musical chaos. He gave me lessons in counterpoint and composition; he introduced me to the treasures of the Mozart he knew so well ... above all, he talked to me.[153]

There was constant teaching, coaching, some work at the DTC, dining out at Magdalene, at Trinity with Sedley, at Sayle's. On 1 November he went to a production of Marlowe's *Dr Faustus* by the Elizabethan Stage Society at the Guildhall: 'I was glad to be introduced to so fine a piece of literature – but the performance was the most priggish & self conscious absurdity I ever saw: Dolmetsch's music ditto'.[154]

150 John Maynard Keynes (1883–1946), Eton, King's College, Apostle, Fellow of King's, celebrated economist. He and Dent became solid friends over the years; Keynes enjoyed music, and founded the Arts Theatre in Cambridge for local plays, opera and ballet. During WWII, when asked to establish postwar arts policies with public funding for the arts, he sought Dent's advice.

151 William Horace de Vere Cole (1881–1936), best known as the perpetrator of the Dreadnought Hoax in 1910. That year Cole invited Dent to hear about his dry run for the hoax, 'the Sultan of Zanzibar's uncle'. Diary 05/03/1905.

152 John Francis Toye (1883–1964), Winchester and Trinity (1904). His younger brother Geoffrey, a talented composer and conductor, studied with Stanford at the Royal College of Music and later worked with Dent at the Old Vic and Sadler's Wells. Toye was a great dabbler and bon vivant who nevertheless became a serious music critic for the *Morning Post*, wrote plays and composed operas, and, with Marcel Boulestin, wrote a novel and ran a famous restaurant. The brothers ran a music festival at their family home in Boxford.

153 Toye, *For What We Have Received*, pp. 65–6.

154 CC 01/11/1904. Also diary.

He kept an eye out for new talent, spotting an exceptional new singer, Fräulein Meta Diestel from Tübingen, who became a regular performer, setting new standards for the locals, in May Week, performing Brahms's Two Songs for Voice, Viola and Piano, op. 91, with the Joachim Quartet's violist, Emmanuel Wirth.

After a family visit at La Selva over the New Year 1905, Dent escaped to Rome, picking up his alternative life of far more congenial companions, strolling on the Pincio or the Borghese or with Emilio to performances at the Teatro Costanzi and others. He met the Wotquennes at the station on 11 January, bumped into Alessandro Longo, called on Lady Louisa Legge and on Falchi, the Director of the Accademia Santa Cecilia. Although he found some of the standard productions on offer – such as the bass Vittorio Arimondi in *Mefistofele* – passable, the more earthy productions to be found in various corners caught his fancy: Grasso's Sicilian company at the Teatro Niccolini doing a Capuana play, and *Il barbieri* at the Teatro Quirino, one of the smaller theatres. 'I never saw such horseplay', Dent wrote to Clive, 'or heard so much gagging – but I must say it was exceedingly funny – Bartolo & Basilio both had voices "come un colpo di cannone" [like a cannon-shot] – the row was deafening at times: but the whole opera went quick & full of life. I don't wonder at its holding the stage as it does.'[155]

While he was hoping for some creative inspiration, in fact all the opera he was seeing abroad, all the new plays – *Il re burdone* at Milan with Claudio, *Mathias Gollinger* by Oskar Blumenthal at Basel with Mantel[156] – was instead becoming the gradual accumulation of a vast knowledge of music theatre. The experience all fed back into his lectures in Michaelmas and Lent terms on Gluck and Mozart's *Cosi fan tutte,* where he took delight in making his small audience laugh, with Lawrence helping out at the piano. 'I lectured on Gluck at 5 to the usual sort of audience: OB & Allen of John's were there & both disagreed with me violently afterwards – so I felt encouraged.'[157] A flying visit to his aunt Ella and uncle Harry in Scarborough resulted in the purchase of a harpsichord by Haxby of York for 50 pounds: 1775, single manual, with two eight-foot stops and pedal,[158] yet another instrument for his overcrowded rooms.

Between the increasingly pressing need to find a compositional avenue for his doctorate and the self-imposed sexual deprivations of his Cambridge life, Dent was jittery and out of sorts most of that Lent term. He still lacked a real focus for his energies, which probably explains his fleeting obsession with Hugh Meredith, who had left Cambridge for a job at Manchester. 'I miss Hugh fearfully', he confided to Lawrence. 'But all I have here is my little following of disciples wch is agreeable but not the same thing.' Meredith was back for about two weeks at the end of February, for the election of the new Provost,[159] as well as being in the final stages of his court-

155 CC 10/01/1905.

156 Diary January 1905. Mantel was yet another of Dent's plants, based in Basel.

157 Diary 24/10/1904.

158 It is not known what became of this instrument.

159 This took place in several stages, the final stage on 13 May. A.C. Benson was put up by Monty James, and deluded himself into thinking it was more or less his for the asking. He

ship of a Miss Hutchinson, begging Dent to wait outside for hours while he dithered over his proposing.[160] Dent had always succumbed to his charm and good looks as much as his neediness, his fits of severe depression or uncertainty, but his behaviour to both Dent and Forster – his ambivalent sexuality together with his sympathetic and intelligent friendship – was always unsettling for either man.[161]

Such teasing was baffling to Dent, a contrast to his relatively straightforward Italian life. As Sydney Waterlow had pointed out to him, he responded to people who seemed to like him, but when the signals were confusing, he often found himself out of his depth. And there was the self-delusion, when initial enthusiasm faded with proximity or he had misread the signs. Besides preferring to be in control, his standards were very high, his irritation threshold very low. Ted Haynes, Morgan Forster and Lawrence Haward were his intellectual equals and knew him well enough not to be upset when he abruptly retreated, and there were very few people whose company he could tolerate for any length of time, yet in his friendships he yearned for something more substantial. Unlike Theo Bartholomew, who was sexually very active at Cambridge,[162] Dent now kept his sexual life abroad.

His lack of spirits that term were not helped by over-exertion, his days filled with concerts and rehearsals beside his lectures. He would go to London to hear a rehearsal – as he often did before attending the actual performance – of Strauss's 'new' (1903) *Symphonia domestica*, then have lunch with the Kekewiches, and go back to the Queen's Hall for a huge programme of Brahms's 'Tragic' Overture, Mozart, Liszt and the Strauss. 'The orchestra was vile', he wrote in his diary, but he was feeling unwell himself anyway, having 'nearly fainted'. At the same time he was discovering new, more receptive friends like George Barger. 'I discussed many things very openly with him', and was left in a state 'strangely excited and nervous',[163] feeling the need to retreat to Sayle's, 'the only person I was fit to call on', where the careful niceties would always be observed, no prying. Soon he discovered George's wife, Florence: 'I never realized before what a fine character Mrs Barger is – her openness & openmindedness was to me astonishing in a woman.'[164] Keynes, too, was becoming more of a friend and confidante; he had come round to sample the Mimbelli wine and he 'found it very good. It led me to speak rather more freely than I should otherwise have done – but I do not regret anything I said.'[165]

After an intense discussion over tea on 26 February, Meredith casually plopped down a manuscript copy of Forster's *Monteriano* for Dent to read, and 'told me that

never forgave King's for the humiliating two votes he got.

160 Diary 24/02/1905.

161 Forster later modelled the relationship of Maurice and Clive in *Maurice* on his own with Meredith. Furbank, *E.M. Forster: A Life. Volume One*, p. 258 and Wendy Moffatt, *E.M. Forster: A New Life* (London, 2011), pp. 65–6. Other biographers doubt that there was any real physical relationship.

162 His diaries in the CUL are very clear about this.

163 Diary 26/02/1905.

164 Diary 22/06/1905.

165 Diary 16/07/1905.

Philip was intended to be Forster & himself'. The completed novel appears to have come as a surprise to Dent; although for months Forster had been coming up on a regular basis, there had been no mention of the book, or perhaps Dent simply hadn't taken notice. He devoured it, and was left in wonder.

> I finished Monteriano & think that Philip has much of me. The book is wonderful & some chapters – esp. that on the operas moved me I think more than anything in literature. The whole work is to me an extraordinary revelation of Forster & I cursed my stupidity in not being able to understand him before.[166]

When Forster came up again on 9 March, they talked more about the book. Forster gave Dent one of his ghost stories, 'The Helping Hand',[167] and told him he had based Philip on 'himself & me, and that Hugh does not come in'. After this, Dent's Meredith obsession faded.

❧ ❧ ❧

When term finished in March 1905, marked by a dinner at Magdalene followed by music, Dent left 'with a scramble' to Paris, then on to Florence via Milan, another flying visit packed with activity and socialising. He met up with Guido Mimbelli – after dinner and listening to Caruso on Guido's new gramophone, they went to the Teatro Verdi for a huge programme, including Luigi Manzotti's Wagnerian take, the ballet *Sieba*, which Dent enjoyed.[168] The next day he was in Rome, calling on Joachim to discuss his quartet's May Week concerts, resulting in an invitation to the quartet's very exclusive concert at the Farnese Palace, the French Embassy, an enormous Beethoven programme: the string quartets in G major and A major op. 18, in C sharp minor op. 131, in E minor op. 59 and in B flat major op. 127. Dent bumped into the Berensons, who were 'very cordial' but nonetheless shook hands with him 'rather hurriedly as I was not wearing a frock coat'.[169] It struck him that this was now very familiar territory to him; he was known and recognised, and it tickled his fancy to have been asked to such a grand social event and have got away with his shabby clothes.

On 1 April Dent was met by Valentino on the pier at Palermo. He had jumped at the chance to take charge of Valentino while he was recovering from an operation 'with every prospect of its being too much for him',[170] again paying for everything. A risk, since Valentino was related to the Sicilian librarian Morello with whom Dent was working closely, and who had written a glowing review of the Scarlatti book for *L'Ora*. After a formal meeting with Valentino's father, they went to a cabaret with Fatima Miris,[171] which Dent loved, but Valentino was – predictably – poorly, so they

166 Diary 27/02/1905.

167 Never published.

168 Diary 25/03/1905.

169 CC 02/04/1905.

170 Diary 04/02/1905.

171 Fatima Miris (1882–1954), born Maria Frassinesi, actress, singer, cabaret artist who made a big impression on Dent.

had to leave early. Two days later they were in Palmi, on the straits of Messina, staying at an expensive, very English hotel, the Trinacira. For a week, everything went well, Dent happy to fuss, noting Valentino's every response in his diary, while Valentino certainly cultivated fuss. 'We had a very good dinner at the Centrale – after wch V. discovered that he was tired & became very difficile. I put him to bed & took his temperature, wch was normal – & persuaded him to sleep well wrapped up, with the window open.'[172] Then Dent's own stomach began to play up and, he lost his temper:

> I had rather a bad stomach-ache in the evening, and consequently was induced to tell V. rather more plainly than I would have done that he was a nuisance, & interfered with my work ... However, V. took it more amiably than I might reasonably have expected & I think he was the better for knowing it.[173]

What had been exciting had quickly become irritating, but Valentino was kept on as a kind of occasional treat and duly joined Dent the following year in Rome.

Returning to Cambridge via Rome, Padua, Milan and Basel, taking in opera and friends along the way, Dent found that Ted was engaged to 'Miss Oriana Waller, granddaughter of Huxley & descended from one of the Miss Gunnings'. He was devastated: 'I suppose that closes another chapter for me.'[174] Immediately he felt 'tired', and went off to CUMC that night. Lawrence, ever understanding, came back and played to him for some time.

So Dent began that hectic Easter term even more out of sorts than before, still looking for a solid project. His friends the Corbetts wanted to put on some kind of concert in aid of the lifeboats, which grew into the performance of an original masque, *The Christening of Rosalys,* by the Corbetts' friend Netta Syrett,[175] who had already written several books and plays for children. The music was composed specially by Dent and the ballets choreographed by Miss L'Épine, a local ballet teacher. The Corbetts must have been very persuasive; at tea one day Dent suddenly found himself landed in it: 'I found that I shall probably have to write all the music for Miss Syrett's masque. Clive says he will not act unless I write him a song.'[176]

For a month Dent slaved away at *Rosalys,* using every minute he could spare from the many other musical claims on his time and energy that term: the Joachim concert on 9 May, DTC exams and the Stewart of Rannoch exam,[177] the Musical Board meeting on the 24 May, organising the KCMS concert, conducting Parry's 'Lady

[172] Diary 05/04/1905.

[173] Diary 09/04/1905.

[174] Diary 29/04/1905.

[175] Netta (Janet) Syrett (1865–1943). She attended the Cambridge Training College, now Hughes Hall, where she met the Corbetts. Three of her short stories had already been published in *The Yellow Book,* and after one controversial play produced in 1902, she concentrated on writing novels with women protagonists.

[176] Diary 07/05/1905.

[177] The John Stewart of Rannoch exam was for a scholarship in 'sacred' music or several other subjects, and often made the difference for would-be music students to be able to study. Denis Browne was a Stewart of Rannoch scholar.

Radnor' suite for the Trinity College Musical Society concert, along with rehearsals for the big CUMS May Week concert, Walford Davies' *Everyman*, conducted by the composer – all distraction from Ted's wedding.

The Christening of Rosalys: A Faerie Masque was put on at the Guildhall on Tuesday 6 June 1905, 'in aid of RNLI Cambridge & District Life-boat Saturday fund'.[178] The cast included Mrs W.M. Fletcher[179] as the Lily Fairy, F.C.S. Carey as the hero Hugo, Kenneth Duffield as Prince Pompous and Miss Grace Corbett as the Queen, with assorted Roses, Will of the Wisps, Nightshades, Lilies, Zephyrs and Bats. The orchestra included Gwen Darwin[180] playing the flute, with a lovely theme Dent had composed specially for her. Princess Rosalys, who had been christened in the outdoors (Nurse: 'Sometimes the spirit of wild woodland things enter the baby's heart and then it never rests'), doesn't want to marry Prince Pompous, and finds happiness in arcadian style with her childhood friend Hugo, the young shepherd, their love and her longing for the free, out-of-doors life represented by the flute's music.

Netta Syrett suggested another joint venture, setting her *Princess Fragoletta*; she sent Dent the manuscript while he was travelling in Germany in late August. At the time, Dent was thinking again about his own opera, so immediately sat down to work on it, describing it as 'charming but very sketchy. It gives me an impression of a parody of *Parsifal* by Humperdinck & Aubrey Beardsley ... What I shd like wd be to make it a thorough going opera, for wch it wd do admirably.'[181] Six months later, he was 'struggling' with *Fragoletta*, and testily began to refer to its demanding author as 'Miss Syrup'. The whole project became a nagging symbol of his own inability to compose.

'I am simply dying to get out of this country, & shall get nothing useful done until I do.'[182] He decided to take two months off simply to travel around Germany, hopefully in congenial company. Guido Mimbelli asked him to Vergaiolo again. His aunt Edith sent him her cello, and Lady Alwyne Compton sent him forty-six volumes of Goldoni, 'light & pocketable' and perfect reading for travelling, besides giving him a list of what she considered to be the most picturesque towns in the part of Germany he was hoping to see, mostly in the south-east, a swathe from Berlin to Munich.

Forster was now working as a tutor at Nassenheide in Pomerania for the Gräfin von Arnim, a cousin of Sydney Waterlow's and author of the best-selling book *Elizabeth and her German Garden*. And Clive Carey was in Munich, trying to learn German, but too shy and diffident to take Dent's briskly proffered advice and

178 KCA EJD/1/3/28/1. Carey wrongly states in *Duet for Two Voices* that it was never performed.

179 Maisie Fletcher, née Cropper, was a good amateur singer, one of the first women on the executive committee of CUMS, and would play Pamina in Dent's 1911 production of *The Magic Flute*.

180 Gwen Darwin, later Raverat (1885–1954), artist daughter of George Darwin, granddaughter of Charles. Gwen and her musical family became good friends of Dent's. Dent commissioned and bought some of the first woodcuts she did. Her memoir *Period Piece* is the best picture of late-Victorian Cambridge.

181 LH 29/08/1905.

182 LH 30/06/1905.

introductions to the Hierl-Deroncos and the Brahmsian oculist Jakobsen, breezily described by Dent to Clive as 'rather too fond of his bottle. His conversation is at times obscene, but he is wonderfully well read and really musical', so was miserable for a time. Since there was no Percy Lubbock around, Dent had no hesitation in asking Clive to meet up for a week in August.

There was some work to be done at Münster, where up in the Santini library 'Gilling had got things a little straighter – but not much'. Otherwise Dent was really in window-shopping mode, more relaxed and optimistic then he had been for weeks, at the beginning of what became a pleasant six weeks simply travelling around Germany: Berlin, Brunswick, Würzburg, Karlstadt, Kitzingen, Zell and Veitshöcheim, with its 'fascinating' eighteenth-century gardens. He went on long walks, mostly out of Baedeker, and did a lot of sketching. He read *The Way of All Flesh*, quickly a favourite, and Ernst von Wolzogen's *Das Dritte Geschlecht* (1899), which he found 'amusing'.[183] He decided not to visit Forster at Nassenheide, excusing himself rather feebly in a letter to Lawrence, 'Forster asked me to go to Stettin & Rügen, but it was too late and I am here. I shd have found the northern climate and cooking atrocious.'[184] He wanted to go his own way, and after trips to Bamberg, Winterhausen, Sommerhausen and Wertheim, spent sketching, chatting up any likely prospects, and going to theatre and opera, he met up with Clive in Regensberg. It was raining and dismal, but for a day they could simply catch up and dine. On Sunday 20 August, they were travelling in the guards van of a special train taking peasants to the hop harvest, '22 carriages of them' to Kelheim, then on to Nuremberg, staying at the Wittelsbacher Hof, which had its own theatre. Dent insisted on Clive seeing the medieval Rothenberg, which he had always enjoyed visiting as a pre-Bayreuth treat. But 'Clive's digestion struck'; he left on the 25th from Steinach. Abandoned, Dent travelled down the Dalmatian coast, idly discussing politics and music, then by train to Vicenza, to Palladian villas, winding up at the Villa Pagello, where the hospitable count gave him a personal tour and sent him off in his own carriage.

A few hectic days at Vergaiolo with the extended Mimbelli family were enough; the chaotic household soon got on his nerves: 'the kindest of kind souls – but I don't think I can stand it more than 3 days ... I find the family rather fatiguing as they all have voices like peacocks and dine in a room with a coved roof & no curtains or carpets, so that the noise at meals is like an express train in a tunnel.'[185] In the evenings he entertained them all with 'old fashioned Italian operas', accompanying himself on the ancient Érard. Still, he enjoyed the picnics, the walks to Montecatini with Gaddo, who also drove him to see the family pile at Montevettolini.

It was with some relief that he departed for a few days in Florence, where he was 'meeting Haynes and his wife(!)', as he expressed it to Lawrence. Vernon Lee was away in Bavaria, but Dent managed to pay a call on Kraus; his last, since Kraus died later that year. The meetings with the Haynes' passed without much comment on

183 Ernst von Wolzogen (1855–1934), German novelist and playwright, librettist for Strauss's *Feuersnot*, established the first cabaret in Berlin, Überbrettl. Dent met him later in Italy.

184 LH 01/08/1905.

185 LH 20/09/1905.

Dent's part, only noting in his diary that Mrs Haynes was 'unwell' – possibly a diplomatic illness, since Mrs Haynes was no fool – which allowed Dent to have Ted to himself for two days. It was a start; Dent came to like her very much.

A 'cold, wet & windy' Michaelmas term was mitigated by some new arrivals, such changes always a welcome part of Dent's Cambridge life, especially when they chimed with his own ideas. The new Provost Monty James's replacement at the Fitzwilliam Museum was the energetic and purposeful Sydney Cockerell,[186] who lost no time in seeking out Dent to show him a Scarlatti manuscript he had bought from A.G. Hill. Cockerell would turn the Fitzwilliam and its neglected but important collections into a world-class institution; he wanted to build up the music, and he was just the sort of political animal who appealed to Dent. A new freshman at Trinity, 'a musical prodigy', Harry 'Hal' Goodhart-Rendel, stepson of Dent's old friend Wilbraham Villiers Cooper, and the nephew of his former Eton master, 'Goody' Goodhart, was the other significant arrival.[187] 'At present he is in a transition stage', Dent noted in his diary, 'doing composition au sérieux with Tovey, and for his pleasure writing Albumblätter for smart ladies and musical comedy. He said Tovey told him he was musically underfed: wch is pretty true.'[188] Hal, with Cosmo Gordon,[189] Clive and Harley Granville Barker[190] became more of the cultural troops Dent was beginning to assemble, even if he didn't quite recognise the fact.

Dent's summer travels had revitalised his lectures on opera – Cherubini, *Fidelio* and Méhul – and reinforced his grim determination to carve out some local cultural movement of his own. So beside the usual bustle of CUMS rehearsals, CUMC concerts, including Dent's own on 28 October, with Hylton Stewart singing Brahms and Purcell, he threw out the germ of a new professional orchestra, the 'Cambridge Symphony', hoping to be 'flooded with concerts'.[191] With some pleasure but little excitement he went to the local concerts – Mischa Elman, the Kruse Quartet with their new violist Lionel Tertis – and to London with Francis Toye to *Madame Butterfly*, and Queen's Hall with Old Etonians Lempfert, Spring-Rice and Frere, for a programme of Mozart, Bach, 'Elgar Variations' (i.e., the Enigma Variations), a 'fragment of Beethoven's Prometheus', and Strauss's *Symphonia domestica*. Elgar

[186] Diary 15/10/1905. Sir Sydney Carlyle Cockerell (1867–1962), Director of the Fitzwilliam Museum 1908–35. His wife, the illustrator Florence Kate Kingsford, designed costumes and scenery for Dent's productions.

[187] Harry Stuart Goodhart-Rendel, CBE (1887–1959), musician, architect, writer, Slade Professor at Oxford; lifelong friend of Dent's. Lived at Hatchlands, where Dent visited him, and now home to the square piano which sparked this biography. Dent later co-opted him onto the Sadler's Wells Board.

[188] Diary 05/10/1905.

[189] Cosmo Alexander Gordon (1885–1967) became involved with the Marlowe Dramatic Society.

[190] Dent's Etonian theatrical friend Jack Pollock introduced Dent; he was responsible for many of Dent's theatrical connections. In October 1912, Granville-Barker's fresh approach to Shakespearian production would be helped by a number of Dent's former students whose ideas were formed in these years at Cambridge.

[191] It doesn't appear to have materialised.

and Strauss still produced tangled, almost incoherent reactions. At this point Dent was feeling his limitations without seeing how to get beyond them, always trying to appreciate what he could not actually enjoy, especially where he felt greater understanding might automatically produce better appreciation:

> I do not like the Elgar any better, except the few bits that I have always liked. There are many ugly ones, several meaningless – & the finale is quite senseless: it has no real progression of development and is full of sound & fury signifying nothing. The Strauss was more intelligible to me than before, and I have some hope for his cacophony.[192]

But the work outside Cambridge was closer to his real sense of purpose. In November Barclay Squire asked him onto the committee of the Purcell Society, two days later asking him to join the English committee of the IMG/IMS, the Internationale Musikgesellschaft or International Musical Society. On the 22nd, Dent was down in London again, calling on his publisher Edward Arnold to discuss a proposed book on Mozart. Although this initial attempt did not succeed – astonishingly, Mozart's genius was still not generally recognised then – the book and the ideas prompting it remained very much on his mind.[193] The nudge from Squire encouraged Dent's natural affinity with Purcell; by May he was editing *The Indian Queen* for the society.[194]

Weeks later, on the train to Rome, where he was to meet Valentino again, he encountered Enrico Bossi, the Director of the Liceo Musicale, Bologna, once organist at Trinity. They gossiped about all their mutual acquaintances – 'tutti quanti', the whole lot – Dent noting with malicious glee that 'like everyone else' Bossi loathed Pagliara the librarian. Like Elgar or Strauss, Valentino was being tried out again in the hope of getting beyond the exasperation; Dent had been looking forward to this break, and the walks, the eating out, the nightly theatre and opera were all he had hoped for.[195] They behaved for the most part as a couple, lunching, walking on the Pincio and going to the theatre; for a time, Dent records every little movement as if Valentino were an indulged and pampered pet. He was still in the process of learning what it was he wanted from such a relationship, his observations detached and almost clinical, but after ten days of Valentino's mercurial company, Dent was fed up, and after giving him a decent meal, gave him his congé. 'I tried to discuss with V. the drawbacks of our present situation. He became rather tragic & rhetorical, but settled down.'[196] Valentino was not at all reconciled to being turfed out back to Palermo; he 'became hysterical, or pretended to'. A week later, back in Rome in the company of Emilio and a 'dazzling Swiss Guard', Dent was catching glimpses of him 'with friends of his own', while in February there was a pitiful letter to which Dent

192 Diary 04/11/1906.

193 After the success of his 1911 production of *The Magic Flute*, Dent persuaded Chatto & Windus to publish *Mozart's Operas: A Critical Study*.

194 'Purcell: *The Indian Queen*' and 'Purcell: *The Tempest*', Purcell Society edns, vols 19 and 32 (London, 1912).

195 He saw *Giulio Cesare*, Berlioz's *Faust*, *Il trovatore* 'on a grand scale', *La traviata*, besides another Rovetta play, a 'Neapolitan farce', *La nutriccia*, *Hamlet* (in Italian), *Maschere* by R. Bracco and Goldoni's *Il ventaglio*.

196 Diary 30/12/1905.

responded with 'a curt postcard'. He turned up again several years later, in England; there are even vague hints at blackmail.

With some relief Dent left Rome to stop with his uncle Ted and the aunts at La Selva for a few days of old-fashioned, brisk ex-pat Englishness, but the testing process had been useful. Except for a short holiday at Fano in August, for a while he chose not to return to Italy, instead to explore Austria and Germany.

Work quickly took over, and before term started again, Dent managed to consult a grumpy and increasingly deaf Weckerlin at the Paris Conservatoire while researching more Leo for his February lecture at the Musical Association, going to Lamoureux concerts and more Berlioz. As ever, his opera experiences abroad inspired his lectures that term, on *Der Freischütz,* beside several articles for the *Monthly Musical Record.*[197] Excellent local concerts like the Bohemian Quartet with Lionel Tertis and Fräulein Diestel performing Brahms *Zigeunerlieder* gave him great satisfaction, 'especially Suk, Dvorak's son-in-law'.[198] The Mozart evenings at Mrs Jenkinson's, though a bit precious for Dent's taste – she enjoyed dressing up in 18th-century rig to play Mozart – fostered serious consideration of Mozart with exploration of lesser-known works. He went to Goldie's excellent discussion groups and spent more time with Maynard Keynes, often nipping down to the Queen's Hall, but …? The self-imposed question mark remains a resonating overtone throughout the rest of that academic year, when so much about his everyday life should have been simple fulfilment, his teaching, research, writings; really, it was too unexceptionable.

His escapes that Easter only helped him to clarify his malaise at home. Dresden he labelled 'time wasted', despite seeing friends, meeting oddities like 'one Hans Hechel, son of the wind-instrument-maker who made Strauss' Hechelphons'[199] at Marchi's wine-shop, and an 'atrocious performance of Die Zauberflöte' which he later milked for serious reflection, finding from its absence what he was looking for in performance. 'I can't say I enjoyed it much', he wrote to Lawrence,

> but I learnt something … the sound of the orchestra, and I got into contact with Beethoven for a moment, in the final choruses of the last acts. I also understood for the first time why Germans think the Z. so German, & only superior persons think it so silly. It was an inconceivably vulgar & provincial performance – Abendroth sang the Königin – transposing both her songs down, & then cutting all the high notes – Wächter sang Sarastro, and went down to various low C's etc that are not in the score … I was glad to find that even here it still maintains its indescribable influence over me.[200]

By contrast, Vienna became an unexpected source of delight, mostly because the ebullient Maddalenas took Dent into their warm, lively household, introducing him to their musical friends like the brothers Thern,[201] who had studied with Liszt,

197 'The *Amfiparnaso* of Orazio Vecchi' (March and April 1906).

198 Diary 25/02/1906.

199 Diary 27/03/1906.

200 LH 26/04/1906.

201 Vílmos 'Willi' (1847–1911) and Lájos 'Louis' (1848–1920) Thern. Willi's most famous pupil was Erwin Schulhoff.

and their families, including 'young Viola Thern, a boyish girl of about 15 or 16 who played the Largo & Rondo of (Beethoven's) C-minor concerto with a great deal of understanding & quite masculine style'.[202] Edgardo Maddalena enjoyed photography, and the photos which have survived give some idea of the easy-going style, music, excellent food and conversation.[203] He saw Hermann von Brodorotti, and discovered Max Reger's music to bring back for the CUMC, went to concerts in the Prater and Musikverein and Augustinerkirche, 'what purported to be a Mass of Mozart's – mainly in E♭'.[204] Dent managed some research on Mantuani and Jomelli at the Musikverein, but the high point was a new production of *The Marriage of Figaro* with a new translation by Max Kalbech which brought out the comic and even ribald aspects. Dent was enchanted, his ideas about Mozart's comedy vindicated.

> Figaro has been got up afresh with a new translation & new scenery & dresses. I can't judge of the translation – but it struck me as being good in making it very clear to everybody that Marcellina had once had a child by Bartolo, and that she was very anxious to get married to somebody. She was the most awful fright imaginable: a delightful surprise after the usual Miss Bauermeister type. She was very red in the face, & fat, with ferocious black eyebrows, & a fine moustache![205]

Back in Cambridge, Dent picked up where he had left off, with his lectures, music, students, and more new acquaintances like L.T. Rowe, 'a middle-aged solicitor, interested in D Scarlatti & Italian renaissance literature – I think really "curiosa".[206] Yet beneath this apparently happy and purposeful activity the deep frustration was festering. The Mollisons spotted it instantly when they bumped into Dent at yet another seasonal garden party, and whisked him off to tea at their house.

His friend Will Mollison had just passed his medical exams, the youngest ever to do so with top honours, his father, the Master of Clare College, 'wild with delight'. The Mollisons, and especially Will, had been on the fringes of Dent's more intimate Cambridge acquaintances, and as so often the case in times of unrecognised distress, had exactly the right kind of intelligent, disinterested sympathy he most needed. All that afternoon and into the evening he talked with Dent in the garden, and Dent 'definitely decided to leave Cambridge in July for a whole year. The decision is a great relief', as he expressed it two days later to Lawrence:

> I have come clearly to understand that I can do nothing here towards Cambridge musical education unless I take a higher musical degree: Mus D. if I can write good enough stuff, and Mus M. if I can't. At present I am neither professional nor amateur & somewhat looked down on for my youth & ignorance. I never get a free hand anywhere.[207]

[202] Dairy 06/04/1906.

[203] Some are in KCA.

[204] There are none in E flat.

[205] CC 07/04/1906.

[206] Rowe's collection would eventually form the nucleus of the Rowe Music Library at King's; Dent kept in touch with him for years.

[207] LH 21/05/1906.

The subtext here is unnerving. Dent was nearly thirty years old, at a real crossroads in his life. He had found it difficult enough to compose his Fellowship piece, that massive setting of Shelley, while the current requirements for the Mus D were overwhelmingly geared towards composition of the most conservative type, so turning his own high standards on himself must have been terrifying, especially given his recent output. Equally, he knew that his recent academic work in the newer, untested field of music history was setting new standards. It was the eternal dilemma of the true pioneer. Another obstacle of the doctorate was the exorbitant cost of the then mandatory public performance of the exercise in composition, with the candidate having to pay for, *inter alia*, orchestra and chorus, soloists, hiring the hall, on top of the college and university fees and the cost of the elegant cream and gold gown.[208]

Having consulted both Sedley Taylor and Alan Gray, who felt that he was right to go abroad and did not 'think me a base deserter', he moved very quickly to tie up his loose ends. 'I think it will be rather good for those not behind the scenes to realize how much I do here.' He still felt responsible, to some extent abandoning those he had nurtured, especially Clive, who had just passed his B Mus, but he had done what he could for Clive's singing career, in which he had great confidence, with introductions to composers like Roger Quilter. About Clive's composing ability he had serious reservations, while continuing to give advice: 'try to conceive a whole movement in your head if you can before you write it down', and suggesting that he take up the Syrett play.

After the CUMS concert on 7 June, one of his last official duties was especially irksome:

> Mann came & sang: we are all magnanimous now! I went at 5 to see him presented with a testimonial (a silver salver and a cheque) to wch I had been obliged to subscribe – in recognition of his 30 years services to the chapel, the university & the town!!! I have seldom felt more humiliated.[209]

It is a rare ungenerous moment; Mann's own struggles as well as his many kindnesses over the years were conveniently forgotten; for a long time Dent had been unable to view him as anything other than the personification of all that was most backward and intractable about Cambridge music.

His rooms, which he had hoped to lend to Clive, were given to Will Spens[210] and Oliffe Richmond. All the instruments had gone, the harpsichord to Mrs Jenkinson, the Broadwood grand to Broadwood's, '& the other to G & L's'.[211]

208 Scholes, *The Mirror of Music*, vol. 2, p. 658. Even in 1825 it came to over 200 pounds.

209 Diary 07/06/1906.

210 (Sir) William Spens CBE (1882–1962), natural scientist, later Master of Corpus Christi College and Vice Chancellor of the University.

211 LH 15/08/1906. By 'the other' he probably meant his square piano.

CHAPTER 5

The Wanderer 1906–1907

The more music I hear, the less musical I feel myself to be: and then I wonder why on earth I have been doing music all my life.[1]

Berlin may have seemed to some of Dent's colleagues an odd choice for his musical sabbatical; Dent himself was uncertain about it at first. Going to Berlin meant facing up to the next impossible life task he had set himself, composing something good enough to submit for a Mus D or finding some other way forward, like the growing demand for his writings, but the next steps still eluded him.

He delayed his arrival for two months, stopping at Fano for a fortnight's holiday at 'this haven of rest' after the hectic but unsatisfactory years of Cambridge music, bathing and his usual wandering, as the mood took him, playing the piano in the local cafés, going to a bizarre local production of Gorky's *The Lower Depths* in Italian, even turning down a plea from Hermann Kretzschmar to give a Scarlatti paper to the prestigious IMG conference in Basel. In this idle vein, over the next month Dent's only work was a stop at Urbino on the way to Rome to inspect the Palazzo Albani library, 'three fine rooms full' of scores and libretti 'of about 1700–1730, including many of D.S.'[2] For most of September he was loosely based in Rome, where Emilio had found him lodgings at 6 Viaolo Cartari,[3] his only music the military bands in the Piazzo Colonna playing Massenet's *Érinnyes,* which Dent found 'dull … Massenet's furies all seemed to wear pink tights'.[4] All these open-air concerts gave Dent the idea for an article on the subject.[5] On 29 September he went on to Florence, where he found Cust in 'a great state of excitement, as after a series of troubles (all related in detail) he has got engaged to an American widow',[6] while his young man Harry Burton was leaving to set up in partnership as a photographer. 'I dined with Cust: Burton was out so I had many confidences outpoured & much scandal: also much talk about Edward Carpenter wch interested me deeply.'[7] Cust was apparently seizing the premarital time to relive past affairs, giving Dent personal introductions to gay circles in Berlin, especially Bernard Esmarch, begging for advice, and since with

1 LH 25/01/1907.

2 Diary 01/09/1906.

3 The place is actually in Fano; Dent may have recorded it wrongly in his diary.

4 Diary 04/09/1906.

5 Never followed up. Diary 20/09/1906.

6 Diary 30/09/1906.

7 Diary 02/10/1906.

Cust high art was joined at the hip with high drama, requesting help with his translation of a book on Carpaccio. The Wherrys and the Bargers were there for the wedding on 23 October, and brought Dent up to date on all the Cambridge gossip in a most gratifying way: 'Mrs Wherry says they are all at sixes & sevens without me'. Two days later he was in Munich, 'half inclined to abandon Berlin & stay here for the winter'.[8] Consciously or not, Dent was breaking from old ways – writing a book on Dr Burney with Vernon Lee – in search of something new.

'So here I am, bucked up with work again', he wrote to Lawrence when he finally arrived in October, 'Encyclopaedia articles to be finished by this year – Purcell opera to edit: book on popular musical aesthetics – book on Mozart's operas'.[9] Although the largest German city, Berlin in 1906 was not yet an acknowledged artistic centre: Vienna or Dresden or Munich might have seemed the more obvious Germanic place to pursue serious musical studies, especially composition. But it was a centre for scholarship, *Musikwissenschaft*, and Dent had scholarly musical acquaintances in Berlin: beside Hermann Kretzschmar,[10] there were Johannes Wolf and Max Friedlaender, both teaching at the Hochschule and running the Deutsche Musikgesellschaft. Once he had made contact with them – after two weeks – he was instantly invited to give a big talk on Scarlatti for the local society in December. He requested Leo instead, having been pressed by Hugh Chisholm to get on with his revised *Encyclopaedia Britannica* articles on Pergolesi, Leo and Domenico Scarlatti.[11]

But music was not the only thing on his agenda; the day after his arrival he was lunching at Bartolini's with pianist O'Neil Phillips, and for the next two months they were an item. The attractive Phillips had certainly been a factor in his decision, while the stories he had heard from Cust, Somerset and others in his gay networks about the flourishing 'Schwulen'[12] sub-culture in Berlin, and their introductions provoked his infinite curiosity. The possibility of living more fully his other, hidden life was extremely appealing to Dent, his musical and his sexual explorations for once going in tandem. He loved facing up to the unknown, testing aspects of himself, fighting his residual puritanical streak and the idea that anyone might even think him puritanical. His usual epithets, 'disgusting' or 'improper' were used automatically, and seldom as dismissive as they might appear out of context. Even if initially repulsed, Dent rarely if ever retreated intellectually, at the same time trying to understand what was going on and see if it might afford him any amusement – another form of his detachment. He was not naturally at ease with what his Victorian family background might label 'obscene'; all his life he would wrestle with such labels and his

8 LH 31/10/1906.

9 LH 19/10/1909. The book on 'popular musical aesthetics' came to nothing, but there were editions of Purcell's *The Tempest* and *The Indian Queen*, published by the Purcell Society, 1912; *Mozart's Operas: A Critical Study* was published by Chatto & Windus, 1913; the 'encyclopaedia' articles were for the 11th edn of the *Encylopaedia Britannica*.

10 Hermann Kretzschmar (1848–1924), from 1904 Professor at the University of Berlin; Director of the Hochschule from 1907.

11 The talk was later published in the *Sammelbände der Internationale Musikgesellschaft* (August 1907). Haward, *Edward J. Dent: A Bibliography*, 169.

12 Originally the Berlin dialect word for gay people.

own deeper responses to them, while preferring the sexually attractive to be in the same package as the artistically interesting. In England he had felt too much the constraints of class as well as sexual orientation; Berlin confronted him with its possibilities, affording him ample opportunity to explore sexuality, music and other unknown quantities. An outsider who was being welcomed into several exclusive circles, musical and sexual, at thirty Dent still had to find himself.

His most significant relationship here by far, professional and personal, was to be with that other foreigner and outsider, Ferruccio Busoni. At this point in his career, Busoni was evolving from pianist–composer to composer–pianist, moreover a musician actively working on a philosophy of 'universal' music,[13] his ideas stimulating Dent's own evolving attitudes at this crucial time in his life. Berlin, rather than Italy or Zurich, was Busoni's own choice, indicating a tacit rejection of the settled, the conservative and the smug, opting instead for what his biographer calls 'a maelstrom of the avantgarde and a breeding-ground for all that was excellent in theatre, literature and painting as well as music'.[14] The Busonis lived in one of the new suburbs built at the turn of the century, in 55 Augsburgerstrasse, large, comfortable houses on tree-lined streets, with a number of small Italian restaurants nearby, especially the congenial, arty one where the Busoni crowd would retire after concerts, run by a Florentine, Bartolini, who spoke 'the most exquisite Italian', and whose wife did the cooking. Having quickly found rooms on the Marburgerstrasse 'wch I liked so much that I took the rooms on the spot',[15] Dent was right round the corner from all this. Quickly settling into busy new routines, he worked at his articles and at Purcell, seeing the Busoni crowd almost on a daily basis, most of his time spent going to concerts, recitals, rehearsals, to the opera and theatre, his attention divided between the Busonis and the artistic, homosocial men he was cultivating. 'I do no composition', he wrote to Lawrence, who was nagging him, 'nor do I feel much inclined for it: however I may feel more musical when I have got the encyclopaedia & the Purcell off my hands.'[16]

Dent genuinely liked the Busonis, 'Mrs Bew', Swedish Frau Gerda, 'who looks like a princess in a Norse fairy tale' and dressed like a Swedish peasant, and the two pretty, spoilt little boys, Lello and Benni. Ferruccio collected people, and the complete internationalist Bohemian himself, loved to hold court to a rich variety of characters, the kinds Dent would normally avoid: 'he was fascinated by the sight of odd characters who might have stepped out of a novel of Dickens'.[17] These were not like the starchy lesbians and antique gay men of Florence whose company Dent found slightly constrained; rather a new generation. Busoni's current pupils included pianist Michael von Zadora,[18] 'a Polish American who dresses to look like

[13] His *Entwurf einer neuen Ästhetik der Tonkunst* (Outline of a New Aesthetic of Music) would be published by Breitkopf & Härtel in 1907.

[14] Antony Beaumont, *Busoni the Composer* (London, 1985), p. 23.

[15] Diary 04/11/1906.

[16] LH 18/11/1906.

[17] Edward J. Dent, *Ferruccio Busoni: A Biography* (London, 1933), p. 137.

[18] Michael von Zadora (1882–1946), Austrian pianist, later collaborated with Egon Petri on the score of *Doktor Faust* (Beaumont, *Busoni*, p. 80).

Chopin and talks like a Yank: plays virtuoso music with great skill & a fine tone, but no poetry or brains at all',[19] Gino Tagliapietra[20] who 'looks like a waiter & adores Phillips' and quite a few women (Dent's friend Ursula Creighton had studied with him). Although Dent liked most of Busoni's male friends and former pupils, Egon Petri[21] or Leo Kestenberg,[22] Busoni's partiality for women, especially odd or exotic females of a certain age vexed him; he was simply churlish about the 'dwarf' Rita Bötticher, Busoni's highly competent secretary, who would later translate Dent's biography and many of his articles. Or those who sensed his attitude and teased him, such as 'Tessie dear', Jessie Haring, who wrote for the New York *Musical Courier*: '"the critic in petticoats" as B called her in all languages. I sat next to her and was rather unmerciful: however she smoked 4 of my cigarettes'.[23] Three of the women especially close to the Master Dent sarcastically dubbed the 'three graces': Marga Behmer, incorrigibly cheerful, fond of her tipple, 'wd be a pianist but has a wooden leg and pianists' cramp', the dancer Irene Sander, who 'danced for a party at the Bews in Hindu costume and bare feet'[24] and Fräulein Malakoff 'who passes for a beauty, & teaches Phillips German'.[25]

'There are too many young women here ... I have met a lot of queer people,' he wrote to Lawrence:

> Did I tell you of a party to wch I was taken where I thought I had stepped into a page of Punch of the Du Maurier period? The dregs of the asthetic [sic] movement – my hostess the wreck of a beauty with a trailing Burne-Jones gown and a head of chestnut hair all floppy like a Japanese chrysanthemum.[26]

The 'wreck' was Adela Maddison, the composer,[27] 'of no merit, I believe', Dent sniffily recorded in his diary after his first encounter with her, 'one of those Du Maurier women who are always in the act of shaking hands'. Like it or not, he was forced to appreciate that these emancipated women were an important part of this Berlin society he had chosen, vigorously exercising a new-found equality in music

19 CC 06/11/1906.

20 Gino Tagliapietra (1887–1954); cf. Beaumont, *Busoni*, p. 80.

21 Egon Petri (1881–1962), pianist, studied with Ferruccio Busoni in Berlin, became a lifelong friend of and collaborator with him and a good friend of Dent's. Later escaped to the USA, possibly with Dent's help.

22 Leo Kestenberg (1882–1962), distinguished Slovakian-born music teacher, pedagogue and administrator with whom Dent would later work in the ISCM, and after WWII advise about setting up orchestras in Israel. He was in the infamous exhibition of 'degenerate music'.

23 CC 06/11/1906.

24 Dent later relented somewhat and actually enjoyed one of her performances: 'I found her dancing most interesting, and often full of charm, in spite of her very large feet and not beautiful face'. Diary 02/12/1906.

25 CC 06/11/1906.

26 LH 18/11/1906.

27 Adela Maddison (1866?–1929), Irish-born student and possibly lover of Gabriel Fauré, moved with her husband to Germany in 1904. Her chamber music is beginning to come back into the repertoire.

and the arts. He would from time to time continue to 'flee' their company, but this automatic allergic reaction faded, for example, as he got on 'quite nicely' at tea with the Behmer on her own. 'Tessie' continued to tease him, perhaps deliberately, by telling him how she simply smiled at men she didn't know to get them to dance with her. 'Sancta simplicitas! it is all said in perfect innocence', Dent exclaims to his diary, completely missing the point. But he was loving it all, the louche café society, gathering at any one of a number of watering-holes: La Locandiera, Die Traube, Kroll's or what he called the 'Teatro Comico Bartolini'. At the heart was Busoni.

Even in his own day Ferrucio Busoni was a monumental figure, and one who had constructed his own plinth. Pianist, composer, pedagogue: at the time Dent met him again in Berlin he was trying to put into practice his original and complex musical aesthetic, working simultaneously on an early version of what became *Turandot*[28] and his opera *Die Brautwahl*,[29] beside a stream of piano pieces dedicated to his various pupils. He had the punishing schedule of an internationally renowned musician, constantly travelling. From childhood his had been a whirlwind existence, so that his extended family circle, even if on the move, was the centre of his life; he loved always being in company. Together with his energetic and active intellect, he possessed a voracious appetite for reading, discussing his art in hundreds of letters to his closest friends and colleagues, especially Egon Petri and Emilio Anzoletti. The ideas behind his major compositions would simmer actively for years before being realised.

Dent could be ruthless enough in his own pursuit of people he found attractive, and was always alert to fresh possibilities. From their earliest meetings Dent and Busoni had recognised in each other qualities which would grow into great mutual admiration, not to say affection.[30] On Dent's part it grew into something much stronger; Busoni's huge presence was physical as much as mental, and he was a very attractive man with a strong sexual charge not unlike that of his old mentor Liszt. In 1919 Busoni wrote to Gerda how touched he was to read what Dent had written about him in *The Athenaeum*: 'it makes me realize at bottom that Dent loves me very much'. Yet Dent quickly assumed his usual lordly pleasure in being able to express his doubts or his disagreements, and to provoke a vigorous debate, good for both of them and consolidating the friendship. Like many who trade on their own personal charm, and especially

28 *Turandot-Suite*, 'originally a concert work suggested by Gozzi's play. In 1911 the music was 'rearranged for stage purposes to accompany a new adaptation of the play made by Karl Vollmoeller and produced by Max Reinhardt at the Deutsches Theater in Berlin'. Dent, *Busoni*, p. 153. Later, Busoni composed a full opera, *Turandot*, which premiered in Zurich in 1917.

29 Eventually performed at Hamburg, spring 1912.

30 Although Busoni's early impression of Dent, after his London concert in 1903, was not really encouraging: 'My playing there, too, was very good and fresh, but to-day I have reached the boundary line. I begged Marga to go to Cambridge with me. After the concert we were invited by Mr. Dent, who speaks Italian so well, to a little supper in his small, very tasteful bachelor quarters (in the University buildings) ... Dear Gerda, I hope you will sympathise a little with me over the exertion I have been through. I am glad I was able to do it. Mr. Dent's cheerful zeal to show hospitality and his naïve, agreeable modesty were quite touching'. Busoni to Gerda, 19/11/1903 from Cambridge, in Ferruccio Busoni, *Letters to his Wife*, trans. Rosamund Ley (London, 1938).

performing artists, Busoni liked to surround himself with adoring acolytes, furnished with constant and unqualified approbation, and he was very manipulative. He also, according to his biographer, showed different sides of himself to different people, and was perfectly happy to give out completely contradictory views.[31] Adverse criticism roused him to fury, but he would deliberately construct concert programmes designed to bait the critics. When writing his biography twenty years later – a real labour of love, according to a close friend[32] – Dent often allowed his infatuation too free a rein, uncritically recording many of Busoni's anecdotes.

They were opposites, each in his own way manipulative and charming, while each recognising the maverick in the other, the outsider who liked to make his own place and his own rules in a world rigid with rules. During his months in Berlin in 1906–07 Dent gradually discovered how the odd and outrageous domestic circles cultivated by Busoni actually fed his creativity and his self-awareness as a musician, and how to appreciate the complex and paradoxical elements in Busoni's make-up: his seething intellect, his gregarious, expansive side, his constant struggles with the warring elements in himself, what he himself viewed as the Italian and the German sides. Busoni worked hard and played hard, was a devoted family man with a roving eye: 'The volatile vapours of the love-god are no hinderance, at least not morally … but the flatulent filth of piano teaching most certainly is', he wrote to Egon Petri around this time.[33] Although he found the 'flatulent filth of piano teaching' irksome, Busoni needed the income it generated, and had to remind himself how his teaching kept him sane. 'Both as man and as artist I prefer to look forwards rather than backwards, and I suppose that is why I prefer to have younger people around me … And may it be so up to the end, for when that ceases, it brings depression.'[34] Dent might have said the same.

Busoni and his entourage provided Dent with some of the serious challenges he needed, and his first two months were spent exploring everything to hand, musical and sexual, ultimately accumulating an extraordinary range of experience from which to draw in future. He went to a 'bad' production of *Die Zauberflöte*, 'but Destinn sang Pamina … & the Queen was Frida Hempel from Schwerin … she is the best – no, the only Königin der Nacht [Queen of the Night] that I have ever seen … perfectly glorious. Once more I found that the Z. will soothe me in the worst of tempers, even a bad performance.'[35] Much of the music he was hearing was new to him, much of it French: d'Indy, Alkan, Fauré, besides Sibelius, Goldmark and a new piece by Bossi; the experience kept alive through his letters to Clive and Lawrence.

And there were the astonishing performers: that winter he heard Artur Schnabel, 'not a Busoni type, but a fine solid Brahms player, with admirable

31 Antony Beaumont told me this.

32 Dent's close friend and colleague Jack Gordon told George Dannatt that Dent had been in love with Busoni. Valerie Langfield told me this, and Antony Beaumont concurred.

33 08/10/1906, cited in Beaumont, *Busoni*, p. 80.

34 Dent, *Busoni*, p. 155.

35 LH 18/11/1906.

technique – his defect being a rather hard touch in forte & in forte cantabile'.[36] On Carl Flesch: 'Flesch played well, but being a visitor anxious to show that he cd play classical stuff too, played it rather too reverentially … It wd have been stodgy if he had not had such a good tone & fine technique'.[37] For Fritz Kreisler's recital Dent sat in the front row.

> [I] … had the full benefit of his enormous tone – He played a dull programme, except for Bach's suite in E minor and 2 caprices of Paganini. A group of pieces ostensibly by Paganini, Couperin, Tartini and another old Italian were I think Wardour street compositions by his accompanist Haddon Squire.[38]

The musicians Dent encountered gave him even wider experience of programming and technique, if little in the way of practical inspiration. He went along to hear d'Indy rehearse, having charmed him by singing themes from his symphony and discussing their mutual love of Scarlatti. Liking him, Dent decided that he actually preferred him to Strauss, an opinion which did not last; Dent's prejudice against Strauss at this time was too deeply imbedded and irrational. When he went to *Salome* on 17 February, he commented first on how 'hot' it was in the theatre.

> I was not much attracted by the opera … I find it unequal, often quite common: and the whole thing coarse & clumsy – utterly different to the delicacy & refinement of Wilde – as to its 'perversity' & 'immorality' – 'repulsiveness' – I was in a state of complete indifference. Susceptible as I am to opera, I watched the whole thing with mere curiosity & was never moved for a moment – only more or less irritated & tired by the continual music without anything good to get hold of.[39]

By contrast, Ruth St Denis dancing to 'vile sham American Hindu' music fascinated him. In January at Mrs Maddison's he met Frederick Delius, 'the Bradford composer, whose opera (*Romeo und Juliet auf den Dorfe*) is coming out at the Komisches Oper'. He found Delius himself a bit odd: 'The evening was not very attractive. Z. [Zadora] played Bach suites & Delius called it finger exercises: Z played Debussy & Delius called it Javanese music'.[40] He went to the premiere on 21 February, finding it 'strange stuff, but not without poetry. The scenery was remarkably beautiful.'[41] But Delius' music excited him, and Dent always responded to strong, intelligent opinions. By the end of January he felt enough at ease with Busoni to speak his mind about Busoni's love of Liszt, at least, while continuing to have reservations about his playing.

> He adores Liszt and plays with intense conviction: but I don't think he will convert me to it, though I cd always derive pleasure from hearing him play it. I am glad I was there, as I begin to see that it is a good thing to hear that sort of

36 Diary 09/12/1906.

37 Diary 27/01/1907.

38 Diary 19/01/1907. This was in Dresden.

39 Diary 17/02/1907.

40 Diary 09/01/1907.

41 Diary 21/02/1907.

> thing to help one's judgement of technique in Beethoven [Busoni had played the Waldstein, op. 53 and the op. 111 sonatas] and other good stuff, because we are often so concerned about the interpretation of Beethoven that we ignore the technique.[42]
>
> I believe I am in disfavour at the court of Busoni, as I have openly expressed my dislike of Liszt. He gave a recital last night wch was rather memorable … Technically it was miraculous: he got the most beautiful colour effects in all the Brahms. The Chopin preludes … lose much of their 'intimacy' when played in a string like that … seldom have I felt it such a strain to listen, in the way I want to listen to music. My impression is that B. played everything too fast, or at any rate with too little consideration of the people who did not know the music.[43]

Surrounded by successful composers like Busoni, Delius, d'Indy – even Donald Tovey was around for a concert in January, playing trios, including his own, with Joachim and Hausmann – Dent felt his own conspicuous lack of inspiration or application. 'The more music I hear, the less musical I feel myself to be', he wrote despondently to Lawrence, 'and then I wonder why on earth I have been doing music all my life'.[44] Any composing, he decided, could be put on hold until he got to Rome later in the year, but musical distractions were only part of the picture. Berlin presented unprecedented opportunity for Dent to explore his sexuality in ways both clinical and emotional.

Although homosexuality had been criminalised in Germany in 1869, there was at the same time a typically Germanic reaction, a scientific approach to understanding sexuality, with pioneering studies published by Johann Ludwig Casper and Karl Ulrichs, besides the later work of Magnus Hirschfeld,[45] who founded the Wissenschaftlich-humanitäres Komitee or Scientific-Humanitarian Committee (WhK) for the better understanding of homosexuality, based in Berlin. Dent's diaries show that he was more than simply aware of such work; he had already read widely around the subject, even books of peripheral interest. While in Berlin he attended at least one meeting of the WhK, on 18 February, with Cust's friend Bernard Esmarch,[46] where he had a chance to meet and talk with Magnus Hirschfeld himself, the first of many such meetings and talks. It is of course a commonplace, this distancing of oneself from the untidily emotional by scientifically dissecting it, but beside his natural inclinations, Dent possessed the natural scholar's infinite curiosity and

42 LH 16/02/1907.

43 LH 25/01/1907.

44 LH 25/01/1907.

45 Magnus Hirschfeld (1868–1935), now becoming better known for his pioneering work. His institute was later shut down by Hitler, Hirschfeld's books and papers burnt. See Manfred Baumgardt, 'Das Institut für Sexualwissenschaft und die Homosexuellenbewegung in der Weimarer Republik', *in Eldorado: Homosexuelle Frauen und Männer in Berlin 1850–1950: Geschichte, Alltag und Kultur* (Berlin, 1984), a catalogue and collection of essays for an exhibition held in Berlin, 1984, pp. 31–41.

46 Esmarch translated J.G. Nicholson's homoerotic poetry into German. M. Keilson-Lauritz, *Die Geschichte der eigenen Geschichte* (Berlin, 1997), p. 494.

need to know. He found the meeting itself mostly tedious, but Hirschfeld himself 'very agreeable'.

By the time he met Hirschfeld Dent had already broken with Phillips, his longest, most intense relationship so far. Valentino had made Dent more wary:

> I see a great deal of O'Neil and like him more and more. Apparently he likes me, since the other night when we were dining together ... he found me in a contemplative mood & mocked my solemnity, saying, 'I shd like to make you very drunk indeed, and then make the most violent love to you.' I said I thought he might find the game a little dangerous.[47]

Within weeks O'Neil was regularly staying with Dent well into the small hours. Though talented, with rare good looks and great charm – his patron Mrs Knatchbull was footing the bill for his time in Berlin – like many charming and fundamentally insecure people, Philips could also be moody and difficult, in need of constant reassurance. Valentino-like jealous dramas soon emerged, the downside of passion, while the dependency Dent enjoyed encouraging became irritating. It must have been difficult to maintain some self-respect when confronted with Dent's massive and manifest intellect and abilities, and his self-possession, while Philips himself was hampered by his inability to learn enough German to be able to keep company in a very multi-lingual crowd. For his part Dent noted both the jealous fits and the deliberate drawing of lines of demarcation, them or me, while failing to notice the self-destructive elements: 'He is one of those unfortunate people who can never adapt themselves to their surroundings.' Such games of emotional blackmail he was by now well acquainted with; whether or not he actually encouraged them is one of those terrible grey areas.

But Dent had met some far more robust, interesting people at Bartolini's, 'the other sort', artists on the fringes of the Busoni set: Frietti 'an Austro-Italian who draws horses etc for Lustige Blätter, Herzog, who is editing the works of Kleist, and v. Kardorff, a painter & disciple of Liebermann',[48] all of them exactly the artistic, intellectual types which attracted him. In fact, Dent was laying the foundations for his extensive artistic and theatrical connections decades later, when working with Sadler's Wells, while their extended Bohemian circles opened up more of artistic and 'Schwulen' Berlin. By March Dent had met the artist Tommy Höxter and Fritz Drach,[49] both outrageous in ways Dent found captivating; soon both were coming back to his rooms, and he commissioned bookplates from Höxter. They introduced him to more of the theatrical circles around the Deutsches Theater, actors and

47 LH 18/11/1906.

48 LH 03/01/1907. Diary 21/12/1906: 'Dr Wilhelm Herzog 'a habitué of Bartolini's – a young art-critic etc whom I found very agreeable'. Wilhelm Herzog (1884–1960) and Konrad von Kardorff (1877–1945) both became lifelong friends. Herzog was a socialist writer, a pacifist in WWI, who managed to survive the Nazis; von Kardorff an impressionist painter, also a portraitist, a member of the Berlin Secession.

49 Dent bought some of Höxter's drawings; Drach worked in films, became an editor on the French photojournal *Vu*, and was killed by the Nazis.

designers like the Sterns,[50] who went on to design radical postwar German films as well as theatre.

Beside Hirschfeld's scientific approach, Dent was discovering, there was generally a far more tolerant attitude in Berlin, where in a number of 'Lokale', restaurants and cafés, homosexual men could meet freely, and the sight of men openly embracing or holding hands was accepted.[51] His new friends took him to some of the better-known clandestine places, such the exotic 'Dresdener Kasino' in Dresdener Strasse, where there was dancing, and transvestites put on elaborate shows, 'peculiar entertainment', but this was for Dent a step too far. 'I found the affair & the company psychologically interesting, but not attractive'.[52] Mostly he threw himself into this new life, lovingly recording in his diary Drach's lively twentieth birthday party at Bartolini's: 'a merry party. I got a large sheet of paper & wrote about 16 bars of music on F.D. [Fritz Drach] – and oddly enough found that the F.D. came out 20 times.'[53]

These months in Berlin had been among the most stimulating, illuminating times for Dent, with his satisfying personal and his professional lives, his insider–outsider status working perfectly, every different strand in his complicated life for once harmonious. He was part of both the conservative and the avant-garde musical circles, giving lectures at the Hochschule and spending a great deal of time with Busoni, while his homosexual circles now included both the WhK and artists around the Berlin Secession who were also involved in the theatre, artists and musicians who took him into far more avant-garde subcultures than he had dared before. The weeks just before he returned to Cambridge were crammed with stimulating activity, when he met so many people who became important in later life, possibly because he was now so comfortable with the experience. And his new friends were very generous; Dent came home to Cambridge laden with pictures and music. Just before he left, von Kardorff 'insisted on painting me though I had asked him to make me a rough drawing of his own head', posing for six hours while young Drach lay snoring on the sofa.[54] Höxter gave him drawings; while at Linde-Walther's[55] studio, 'he also gave me two sketches, a chalk drawing of a child and a pen drawing of Segovia in Spain'.[56] Artist Frau Doktor Clara Ewald, whose son Paul had studied at Cambridge,

50 This was Ernst Stern (1876–1954) and his wife, who worked with Max Reinhardt at the Deutsches Theater and designed Strauss's *Ariadne auf Naxos* in 1912, though Strauss thought his designs too 'trashy' and 'dashed off quickly'. They later worked for German films and in London, moving there permanently after 1934 and working with Dent's colleagues at the Adelphi, the Savoy and the Aldwych. See Michael Kennedy, *Richard Strauss: Man, Musician, Enigma* (Cambridge, 1999), p. 181.

51 *Ibid.*, pp. 60–61.

52 Diary 08/02/1907.

53 Diary 28/03/1907.

54 Diary 29/03/1907. His portrait of Dent does not seem to have survived.

55 Heinrich Linde-Walther (1868–1939), photographer and painter, also illustrator of children's books, member of the Berlin Secession.

56 Diary 24/03/1907.

introduced Dent to the violinist Alessandro Certani and his wife Syrina.[57] At the Certanis, Dent met the Schulhoffs, 'fortunately too late for music';[58] he met Eric von Hornbostel;[59] Oskar Fried, the conductor friend of Mahler; and playwright–actor Frank Wedekind.

Back in London only a few days later, staying at his mother's, he was bemused; his recent glorious life seemed almost never to have happened. The experience had made him bolder, though; his mother, who all winter had accused him of selfishness, of living 'a dreadful life', was shocked to discover that he never went to church, and went into a prolonged and difficult sulk. She invited W.H. Inge, his wife and mother to tea in the hope of converting him: 'I fancy Mrs Inge was rather pleased to find somebody there eventually who did not talk bishops priests & deacons at her'.[60] Jack and Isabel had escaped on a cruise, while Catherine was in Paris, so Dent was left alone to endure his Uncle Lovelace's golden wedding anniversary celebrations. His brother Charles told him he thought he had shown 'a great deal of moral courage'.[61]

The rest of the month in London that May, Dent salvaged some of his Berlin experience, taking Lawrence to a Komische Oper performance of *Hoffmans Erzählungen*, and a week later to Laurence Housman and Granville Barker's *Prunella, or Love in a Dutch Garden.*

> The play was poetical & attractive, but spoiled by too much incidental music by Joseph Moorat, of whom I remember that Barker told me at Cambridge that ' he always composes at the piano, in five flats'. It was dreadful. Otherwise I thought the play wd do well for an opera.[62]

Theatre and music were stimulated by prolonged talks with his Old Etonian theatrical friend Jack Pollock: 'Jack was a delightful companion, full of new projects for a London theatre on the lines of the Kammerspiele, to one-act pieces as French as the censors will allow!'[63] Such talks with Jack together with his correspondence with Herzog and von Kardorff, 'who has much the same family rows as myself', kept the ideas alive. Dent began to be more adventurous, going with Lawrence to see *Votes for Women,* something he would never have done before Berlin. The Certanis were

57 Alessandro Certani, violinist based outside Bologna but with an international career, including Berlin and London. He became a good friend. Frau Doktor Clara Ewald, an artist Dent met that February (diary 01/02/1907), lifelong friend whose portrait of Rupert Brooke Dent brought back to the Combination Room at King's. Paul Peter Ewald (1888–1985), crystallographer, later a refugee from Hitler.

58 It was young Erwin playing, so Dent missed a rare opportunity. He later worked with Schulhoff in the ISCM.

59 Erich Moritz von Hornbostel (1877–1935), born in Austria, but moved to Berlin to work with Carl Stumpf on psychoacoustics, pioneer in ethnomusicology and in a system of classifying musical instruments. In 1933 he fled to Cambridge, helped by Dent.

60 Diary 02/05/1907. Inge became a bishop and gave the famous sermon after Rupert Brooke's death in 1915.

61 Diary 16/04/1907.

62 Diary 06/05/1907.

63 Diary 21/04/1907.

in London, too, for Alessandro's Queen's Hall Concert on the 12th, and invited Dent to meet Thomas Beecham and his current wife. He was seeing the Bargers, the Collinghams, Mrs Knatchbull, went for pleasant strolls with John Christie.[64] He bought Forster's latest novel, *The Longest Journey*, devouring it overnight: 'first-rate: and has a new point of view'. He went up to Manchester to stay with the Merediths: the Waterlows and Hilaire Belloc were staying as well, 'Belloc left in the morning, having exhausted us all with his unceasing conversation'.[65]

By 18 May he was staying at a vexatiously expensive hotel in Milan with his sister Catherine, having hoped to be in company with either George Weston or Wilhelm Herzog. But Dent used the next two and half months to travel around Italy, walking great distances, mostly on his own, between Florence and Siena, over the Appenines from Ancona, Loreto, Fermignano, to Florence, stopping off to visit various friends like the Mimbellis at Vergaiolo, or simply enjoying the solitude or the odd company he picked up along the way, at tiny country inns. 'Isonica the most beautiful and the one where I found most kindness in rough places: this last was remarkable for hospitality & intellectual society. At Fermigerano, at Mercatello, at S. Sepolchro I stayed a day & talked all day to people I had never seen before'.[66] At Bologna he caught up with Respighi and the Certanis, Mrs Certani urging him to take on a Bolognese housekeeper for his projected new house in Cambridge. He bought 'huge quantities' of antique furniture from a charming rogue, Rambaldi.[67] 'I am still wrestling with a 4tet', he wrote to Lawrence, 'but I don't get on very fast, as I had one or two more Prometheus days with a Roman eagle gnawing at my liver'.[68]

But really, Dent had not wasted his time at all. Without his realising it yet, he had made great strides in his intellectual attitudes, shrugging off more of his youthful priggishness and ready to make a big stand for himself. He had decided to take the drastic step of giving up his college Fellowship and to take a house, to try to think outside the academic box as to his uncertain future.

> What will happen next year I don't know. I shall possibly be so reduced with the loss of my fellowship; & the expenses of a house that I may pass my summer peacefully in Cambridge, with the Extensionist meeting as my most voluptuous dissipation! What I should like really another year wd be to take a cottage in Italy, with a couple of peasants to cook my macaroni: bury myself in the country & write.[69]

64 John Christie (1882–1962), Old Etonian, founder of Glyndebourne Opera at his country house.

65 Diary 12/05/1907. Joseph Hilaire Pierre René Belloc (1870–1953), Anglo-French writer. Dent often met him in Ted's company

66 LH 07/09/1907.

67 LH 22/09/1907. It turned out to be fake; Rambaldi also sold things to art dealer Joseph Duveen. He came to Cambridge that November and tried to sell King's College Chapel a crucifix of 1600.

68 LH 27/07/1907.

69 LH 07/09/1907.

CHAPTER 6

The New Spirit 1907–1910

> When I came back to Cambridge in the autumn of 1907, after a year's absence abroad, I soon became aware that a new spirit was making itself felt. The first notable result of it was the performance of Marlowe's *Faustus* by a number of men who afterwards constituted the Marlowe Dramatic Society. It was a queer performance. The older generation were scandalised almost before the play began: no scenery, only dingy green hangings, no music, no footlights, frequent 'black-outs', no names of the actors printed … No wonder they were upset by it all. 'Faustus isn't a play at all' – 'absurd for undergraduates to attempt tragedy' – 'why didn't they get somebody with experience to coach them?' – 'why do they act in the dark?' … But in spite of these things and many others the play had a new spirit of its own. The tragic moments were genuinely moving. Crude, awkward and amateurish … it all was, there was the spirit of true poetry about it. One felt that to these actors poetry was the greatest thing in life.[1]

1907–1908

Dent's obituary of Rupert Brooke, quoted above, is also a memorial to everything his generation had brought to Cambridge, wrecked by the Great War in which Brooke and so many of his contemporaries were killed. At the time, Dent needed the painful exercise of writing it to remind himself of the ideals which had so captivated him on his return from Germany that October 1907, and which fuelled his own ideas of turning scholarship into performance right up to the war and beyond.

It took him a while to recognise that 'new spirit'; he returned to Cambridge far too preoccupied with his own projects to see what others around him were doing. First, he felt duty bound to help and encourage friends and protégés, expanding their horizons, while loyalty, even to the most difficult, awkward friends like O'Neil Phillips, was fundamental. Dent always worked to bring together the eclectic strands of his own complex experience, so quickly made sure that celebrities like Busoni and excellent unknowns like Certani and Phillips came to Cambridge.

> He [Phillips] is keen to play well here – but I anticipate a funny day … I shall think twice before engaging him to play a concerto under me at the CUMS orchestra concert in May! A white velvet waistcoat is however his principal attraction; & he

1 Dent, 'Rupert Brooke', CM (15 May 1915), pp. 390–6.

appears to expect Perrier-Jouet in a mug after his concert – I have half a mind to provide him with a bottle of Perrier wch is equally fizzy & less exciting.[2]

Clive also needed a push, Dent felt, and took him to task:

seriously, ought you not to begin working for your Tripos or your 'General' soon, my dear Clive I never knew anybody whose second year lasted as long as yours is doing[3]

I can't help thinking that you will be happier and more vigorous mentally & physically for a term of compulsory independence.[4]

He urged Clive to go abroad to learn German and French properly, to travel to Italy to refresh his musical ideas, expand his repertoire and his experience, offering him the money to do so, and raising a fund to which his friends contributed.[5]

In fact, Clive was accidentally responsible that term for the seismic shift in Dent's Cambridge life, through his involvement with the new Marlowe Dramatic Society. Before he packed for foreign parts and largely through his acting and producing experience in the triennial Greek Plays, Clive was acting the Chorus in the new society's revival of Marlowe's *Dr Faustus*. On 12 November, Dent was carried along by an overexcited Sayle to see 'Marlowe's *Dr Faustus* given by the new Marlowe Society at the ADC'.[6]

The Marlowe Dramatic Society[7] was 'begotten by the spirit of the times on a very ordinary student failure', Hugh Wilson of King's.[8] Visiting his friend Cosmo Gordon, he had happened to pick up a copy of Marlowe's *Dr Faustus,* a remarkable coincidence in itself, since in 1907 *Faustus* was all but forgotten, an antique curiosity rather than literature. Idly reading the closing lines, expecting ridiculous bombast, Wilson 'found himself a sudden convert to its inexplicable merits'.[9] As Tim Cribb pointed out, it is one of those exquisite pieces of Cambridge serendipity that Wilson's friends should include Justin Brooke[10] and Geoffrey Keynes,[11] both

2 CC 20/10/1907. It was successful; O'Neil returned in March to play at CUMC, and to Hal Goodhart-Rendel.

3 CC 14/10/1907.

4 CC 20/10/1907.

5 Diary 02–03/12/1907.

6 Amateur Dramatic Club. Diary 12/11/1907.

7 The Marlowe Dramatic Society (MDS) remains one of the most important student drama groups ever, a nursery for some of the best acting and directing talent in this country: John Barton, Peter Hall, Trevor Nunn, Ian McKellen, Derek Jacobi, Tilda Swinton, and more recently, Tom Hollander, Dominic Dromgoole, Tom Hiddleston, Rebecca Hall, Dan Stevens and many more. For years, George 'Dadie' Rylands at King's continued to emphasise the importance of the words underlying any production; the MDS ideas led directly to the re-establishment of the Globe Theatre. See Cribb, *The Marlowe Story*.

8 Older brother of James Steuart Wilson (1889–1966), the singer who came up to King's in the next year, and who would become one of Dent's close circle.

9 Cribb, *The Marlowe Story*, p. 10.

10 Justin Brooke (1885–1963), Bedales and Emmanuel College, of the Brooke-Bond tea family, no relation to Rupert.

11 Geoffrey Langdon Keynes (1887–1982), younger brother of John Maynard Keynes, up at Pembroke College. A true polymath, he became distinguished as a surgeon and as a

already primed with enthusiasm for the recherché Elizabethan drama by Keynes's Old Rugbeian friend, Rupert Brooke. Wilson lamented the lack of any performance of *Faustus*, so Justin immediately suggested that they do it themselves, focusing on the poetry, with minimal lighting and scenery, closer to Shakespeare's theatre, then a revolutionary idea.

Here were undergraduates starting up something radical, intellectually exciting and a clear departure from the old Victorian ways. In 1907 Cambridge lacked a Faculty of English, while the English stage was in a state of some torpor, with actors who had no idea how to speak poetry, and over-elaborate sets replacing production ideas. The great body of Elizabethan and Jacobean drama was almost completely neglected, except by William Poel's Elizabethan Stage Society, who had visited Cambridge in 1904,[12] and the MDS was determined to change all that. Dent was among the first to see the real potential, the opportunity to exercise his own love of words and music, of connecting unapologetically with the original works, parallel to his work on early opera.

The obstacles to the new venture were enormous. Dent's friend Francis Cornford's satirical little tract, the classic *Microcosmographia Academica*, published in 1908, expressed the current state perfectly: only by doing nothing will you avoid any offence, pain and upset.

> My heart is full of pity for you, O young academic politician. If you will be a politician you have a painful path to follow, even though it be a short one, before you nestle down into a modest incompetence. While you are young you will be oppressed, and angry, and increasingly disagreeable. When you reach middle age, at five-and-thirty, you will become complacent and, in your turn, an oppressor; those whom you oppress will find you still disagreeable; and so will all the people whose toes you trod upon in youth.[13]

Cornford, together with other younger dons, Jane Harrison[14] and Andrew Gow,[15] lent their weight to the Marlowe project. In fact, quite a few involved with the most recent triennial Greek Play, *The Eumenides*, produced in 1906, became involved with the MDS and several years later, with Dent's benchmark *Magic Flute*. Rupert Brooke[16] had caused a mild sensation simply by putting on an appearance as the scantily clad Herald; Clive was a grave Athena, Alwyn Scholfield, Orestes, with Justin Brooke as the Pythoness. For young men (and young women too: another first) hungry to work with fresh, stimulating material, the choice between the cosy

literary editor of Blake and Rupert Brooke.

12 They had presented the *Dr Faustus* Dent had seen in the Guildhall, with the Dolmetsch music he hated.

13 Francis Cornford, *Microcomosgraphia Academica* (Cambridge, 1908).

14 Jane Harrison (1850–1928), pioneering academic, Classics don at Newnham College.

15 Andrew Sydenham Farrar Gow (1886–1978), supervised by Cornford at Trinity College, later became a Fellow and taught George Orwell at Eton.

16 Rupert Chawner Brooke (1887–1915), educated at Rugby School, where his father was a housemaster, and at King's College, where his uncle was dean, 'the handsomest young man in England', icon of the times. Dent always referred to him as 'Rupert'.

limitations of the Amateur Dramatic Club and Footlights or having to wait three years for another Greek Play was simply not enough. Music, theatre and English literature were poised to become academically acceptable and beyond.

Initially, Dent was dismissive, but everything about that *Faustus* production might have been designed to appeal to him, especially the revelation that scholarship could be put to such artistic use without egregious pedantry. He saw every performance, but was sceptical: 'the tragic parts very impressive: the farcical scenes bored me', remarking on the 'great' resemblance of the Pope to the Master of Pembroke. He also sarcastically noted the older generation's response: 'We had the M.[aster] of Magl [Magdalene] close to us at the 2nd performance: he kept us very much on the hop with questions'. Two nights after *Faustus* he was inviting 'Lechery G. le M. Barnes in a dress of Mrs Frazer's, appropriately enough!' to Buol's for a chat. On the 20th he invited 'Cornford, Sayle and some of the Faustus gang' back to his rooms.

It was no simple coincidence that the MDS became the vehicle Dent used to focus his intellectual and scholarly energies at home; it was another extension of the loose international networks already forming with theatre historians (Rasi, Maddalena), theatre designers (Stern, Craig) beside his composer friends (Busoni, Respighi, Vaughan Williams). Even though the details were still fuzzy to him, Dent's return to Cambridge was marked by a grittier resolution than resignation or residual anxiety about what exactly he was going to do next. The decision to remain in Cambridge without his doctorate had been taken long since, during his ruminative walks in the Italian hills and mountains, and discussed with friends: Busoni, Gordon Craig, Lawrence and others.

First, while Dent's supporters wanted him to stick with Cambridge, bringing his considerable cosmopolitan experience to work for change there, he knew he needed a base. And if he was going to build his own alternative power-base in Cambridge coupled with the freedom to travel abroad, a safe, private space was essential, one where he was in charge. Resigning his King's Fellowship meant a loss of some income, but the loss of status was not a thing to worry a man like Dent, a symptomatic, if dramatic expression of his self-imposed otherness. He could see how college life had compromised other gay men like Dickinson or Oliffe Richmond, while the gesture declared his independence from institutional constraints. By rejecting conventional routes to career success he was forced now to improvise other, more unconventional ways, while his relationships with the older generation, Stanford, Mackenzie[17] and Maclean, became less predictable and more volatile, but definitely challenging.

He began by looking for a bolt-hole, somewhere far enough away from college to be private, yet not so far that he couldn't easily walk home after late-night doings in town, and accessible for the railway station. On 7 November he found what he felt to be perfect, 4 Belvedere Terrace, a modest three-storey, end-of-terrace house

17 Sir Alexander Campbell Mackenzie (1847–1935), Principal of the Royal Academy of Music, composer, President of the International Musical Society 1908–1912, which was how Dent knew him.

on the corner of Panton Street and Bateman Street,[18] just across from the Botanical Gardens and halfway between King's and the station. The small garden at the back delighted him and more than balanced the necessary financial sacrifice of 'my continental holidays'.[19] 'I can take care of myself', Dent wrote to reassure Lawrence, 'and I think I may say I am glad to have shuffled off my fellowship, or shall be.'[20]

Dent had a genius for recognising good ideas and turning them into excellent ones. Charles Sayle's example had inspired him, his tiny house on Trumpington Street and his frequent At Homes the cosy focal point for a collection of select young men, the 'Swans', together with older regulars like Theo Bartholomew and Jack Sheppard. The atmosphere Sayle managed to create there was even more insulated and homosocial than college, and far less pressured than the more formal discussion groups around Cambridge, where one was expected to be brilliant all the time. His excellent food and drink and exquisitely laid table were exchanged for music-making and conversation, while his young men, exalted and extolled in his gushing journal entries to the status of 'great' men, gave him the company and attention he craved. It had begun with the sons of old friends, Hugh Wilson and Cosmo Gordon, and quickly expanded as they brought their friends along: Rupert Brooke and George Mallory, but *not* James Strachey.[21] The carefully constructed illusion to himself and to his guests was that he sought their conversation and their minds, but really, he was fooling no one but himself. The objects of his fancy didn't seem to mind; they loved escaping from college, being fussed over by 'Aunt Snayle', being mildly daring in their outlook, taken seriously by a man who for all his affectations was genuinely cosmopolitan and knowledgeable.

But Dent was younger than Sayle, his ideas of a personal salon much more ambitious, with elements of the Busoni circles, the Maddalena circles, the arty gay circles in Berlin, where talk and activity were strongly connected, while working through the very institutions whose outdated ideas were being undermined. Dent was experimenting with the kind of intellectual subversion so attractive to undergraduates which Sayle could never furnish, and Panton Street quickly became the alternative stockpot for new music and theatre, where the brightest and best gravitated naturally, a refuge for troubled souls. Dent was as susceptible as Sayle, his motives at least as mixed, but his experience abroad had taught him a great deal about the art of combining business with pleasure.

18 Later renamed 77 Panton Street, but the original 'Belvedere Terrace' is still to be seen on its façade.

19 CC 13/10/1907.

20 LH 26/11/1907.

21 Hugh Wilson (later killed in WWI), accidental co-founder of the MDS; his younger brother James Steuart Wilson (1889–1966) became one of Dent's 'gang': see 'Dramatis Personae'. George Herbert Leigh Mallory (1886–1924), Magdalene College, later a mountaineer, killed on Everest. James Strachey, younger brother of Lytton, was far too sharp for Sayle.

Thanks to the combined efforts of his sister Catherine and his new young housekeeper Hills,[22] Dent moved into his little house one freezing January day. Two weeks later he was writing to Lawrence, 'I am terribly full up already!! But it suits me, and I feel I can really work here – I don't get half so slack & stupid as I did in college'.[23] To Sayle's furious jealousy, the young men – including his Swans – were soon calling at Panton Street on a daily basis; the most important for Dent was William Denis Browne,[24] reading Classics at Clare and the most talented young musician in Cambridge, who came to be coached for the Stewart of Rannoch music scholarship. Dent saw in Denis the personification of the Pateresque ideal of his imagination, younger, attractive, sympathetic and – most importantly – more than responsive to Dent's influence. He carefully cultivated Denis' friendship and esteem, encouraging him and helping him in every practical way, from the music scholarship to providing him with an exceptional musical education.

> Denis Browne came for a last lesson, having written 2 violin parts to a bass of 'La Staccata' an old Italian dance wch I found among Gianinno Mimbelli's stuff. His parts were not of the style, but quite good Bach.[25]

In Clive's absence, Denis became the new recipient for Dent's musical finds, the man to discuss new music with, or an autograph full score of 'a sort of oratorio by Gordigiani' bought in Bologna for 5 francs. For his part, Denis found it impossible not to be dazzled by the attention, to being taken seriously as a musician, appreciating the sympathy Dent so clearly felt about family opposition to Denis' musical career.

Really, Dent fell in love with this entire new generation, and made it his business to help them develop identity and purpose – the 'new spirit' – especially as their aims dovetailed so neatly into his own, both the intellectual and the performative. But for his personal circle, Dent fine-tuned his criteria. He had quickly appreciated that the dynamo, with his extreme good looks, his clever mind, his elusive and ambiguous character, was the charismatic Rupert Brooke; on 11 February Dent finally managed to entice him to dinner at Panton Street.[26]

Like Dent, Rupert had a famously domineering Victorian mama, the 'Ranee',[27] from whom much of his life had to be kept secret. Unlike Dent, Rupert wanted to blaze at the heart of things, an Achilles, universally and publicly acknowledged as the best, whatever he was doing. He was elected to the Apostles, joined the Fabians,

22 I have not been able to find out anything about 'Mrs Hills'. With his local connections, Sayle had found her; she was not from Cambridge, probably from Ely, and youngish when she arrived. Initially Dent's mother was concerned that she was too young a female to be working in a young gentleman's household, Dent was amused to be told. Hills would often go to work for his sisters while Dent was abroad.

23 LH 31/01/1908.

24 William Denis Browne (1888–1915), Rugby and Clare College.

25 Diary 16/03/1908.

26 Diary & CC 11/02/1908.

27 Bestowed by her son when he found out that his own nickname was 'the Rajah'. His biographer refers to some possible family connection with the Rajah of Sarawak: Nigel Jones, *Rupert Brooke: Life, Death & Myth* (London, 1999), p. 32.

gave papers at Goldie's discussion groups, and with Hugh Dalton[28] established his own discussion group, the 'Carbonari'. His bisexual attractiveness generated some interesting side-effects, not least the drawing-in of women to the MDS projects. Jane Harrison became a friend, and of his own age, the Olivier sisters,[29] the Darwin cousins[30] and their Newnham friend Ka Cox.[31] Dent's dealings with Rupert were to be invariably circumspect, since Dent had recognised from the outset that any relationship would be a very tricky undertaking, and with too much competition. Fascinating and unsettling, Rupert was a chameleon, prone to extravagant fluctuations in behaviour and language; charming and delightful company when he felt like it, just on the right side of outrageousness. His other, darker side was capable of shocking language and behaviour; he could be foul to friends, and given to racist, sexist rants; his closest friends saw through him and loved him nevertheless. Dent was in many ways a close friend, but recognising the danger to himself, made sure to keep some distance. Rupert trusted him, and often when the black moods and headaches overcame him, he would retreat into Dent's Panton Street garden. Certainly they had a mutual recognition: two manipulative people who discovered that they could actually work well in harness.[32]

The first 'general' meeting of the new MDS took place in Francis Cornford's Trinity rooms on the 13 February 1908. The Master of Christ's had already approached Justin Brooke about the new society's performing Milton's masque *Comus* as part of the college's celebrations that summer for the 300th anniversary of Milton's birth, with the radical decision to make it a 'bisexual' production, for the first time with real women in the female parts. Jane Harrison would help recruit, if needed, from Newnham College.[33] Incredibly, they were going to be allowed to work from the Trinity College autograph manuscript of *Comus*, and the Bridgewater manuscript of Henry Lawes's original music for the first production in 1634, only recently discovered.[34] Rupert was to be producer and director, and it was entirely predictable that

28 Edward Hugh John Neale Dalton, later Baron Dalton (1887–1962), Labour politician, became Chancellor of the Exchequer. Another conflicted man, he became a lifelong friend of Dent's.

29 The four daughters of Sir Sydney Olivier, cousins of the actor Laurence. Margery, Daphne, Brynhild and Noel.

30 Gwen Darwin, Frances Darwin.

31 Katherine 'Ka' Cox (1887–1938), rich, independent and orphaned, loved by most who knew her. Dent liked and admired her and kept up a correspondence.

32 Rupert had his own reservations: 'wasn't he too hard on pink people, too intolerant? Mightn't he be doing more harm than good? I fancied those great spectacles dim'. To Geoffrey Keynes, March 1911.

33 In fact, the Vice Chancellor refused his permission for this, and a compromise was made that any such 'bisexual' productions had to take place out of term. This set the mode for future MDS productions: one in term, one out of term. Cribb, *The Marlowe Story*, p. 18.

34 'Then I ought to have gone to a party at the Horace Darwin's – but instead I went to Christ's library where I worked all afternoon at the newly discovered MS of Henry Lawes' songs wch has been lent to the exhibition.' LH 14/06/1908.

he and Cosmo Gordon should approach Dent about taking on the music, in this case as essential as the text.[35]

There was another attraction to the project. Musical research was in a great state of change, and Dent was currently at the forefront of research into early song and opera, so putting together a performing edition from an original seventeenth-century manuscript suited him perfectly, especially as it involved challenging the current style of editing early music, already out of date, which had meant altering the music to accommodate late-Victorian musical taste.

> Arkwright sent me the other day the Musical Society's edition of the music to Comus: I never saw anything so bad. Some wretched amateur has been floored by Lawes' basses wch certainly are difficult to harmonize, and has altered them in nearly every bar. The result is absurd.[36]

But Novello's had already decided on someone of the old school to edit the Lawes music, Sir Frederick Bridge.

> I spent most of the morning working at Christ's on the Lawes MS. and most of the afternoon ... the owner thereof turned up ... very proud of the thing. But the silly fool has let Bridge use the book and draw upon it. However he was so flattered at my learned appreciation of it that I think he will let me write anything I please about it. Still what I do will probably appear under Squire's name, as I think he has a prior claim upon it.[37]

That Lent term 1908, the MDS and its radical projects injected Dent with some much-needed enthusiasm and purpose, which he funnelled back into the society as it was forming itself. He got himself elected to its committee as 'honorary member' and made himself responsible for the music; eventually, this involvement led to his important production of *The Magic Flute* in 1911, with many MDS members involved, and well beyond.

❧ ❧ ❧

Otherwise, there was little around to focus his energies: a few pupils, work on his editions of Purcell and Haydn, Nixon's glees, Certani's concerts, beside trips to London where only the Nicholson exhibition at the New Gallery and Shaw's *Arms and the Man* caught his interest. Most of the music – Enesco, Backhaus, Joachim, and especially Tovey – disappointed in content and execution: 'Donald is dreadful'. Only the Bach Choir concert, with Allen conducting Vaughan Williams' new *Toward the Unknown Region*, in the congenial company of Ted, Hilaire Belloc, George Butterworth[38] and Timmy Jekyll, gave him some glimmer of possibility in

35 Diary 04/03/1908.

36 LH 01/06/1908.

37 LH 15/06/1908.

38 George Sainton Kaye Butterworth MC (1885-1916) Old Etonian, Oxford, composer, especially of songs. Killed in the Great War at Lozières, what became known as the

the current dismal scene. Edward Naylor's opera *The Angelus* winning the Ricordi Prize only elicited his scorn:

> I suppose Giulio Ricordi having offered the prize picked out those operas wch were vulgar enough to sell: Percy Pitt picked out of these those that cd possibly be put on the stage, & Stanford picked out of these the one that was least hopelessly bad as music.[39]

There was now less need than desire to get to Italy at the end of term, but with his current lecturing beside his MDS involvement, Dent wanted to explore the history of music in the theatre, and talking with Rasi, Maddalena and Craig in Florence was a congenial way to pick up some necessary perspective contemporary theatre and music, an edge few other music historians had.[40] He caught up with Sayle's swan Harry Garrett and dined with Henry Somerset:

> a dear creature … I suppose there is more scandal about him than about any of that gang in Florence: but the more I see of him the more I feel that he is the cleanest of the lot. I am rather sick of Florence, I think. I don't mind the immorality of the place – all female men and male women headed by Vernon Lee who is a dear creature – but the society is too damned 'arty'; and if I lived here I shd feel obliged to paper my flat with little girls and fox terriers from the illustrated Christmas numbers.[41]

A fleeting trip to Rome gave him the chance to see Gemma Bellincioni as Salome in Strauss's opera; he loved her performance, but still had strong reservations about the music.[42] More to his purpose was an invitation with Frank Buckley from Alessandro Longo to see his new villa at Posilippo and talk about Scarlatti. The first volumes of Longo's catalogue of Domenico Scarlatti had already been published, and Dent could not help but compare Longo's excellent, original work with Maitland's 'new' articles on Scarlatti in Grove's, cribbed from Gehring's earlier, now outdated work, especially since Maitland had used a lot of Dent's own material.[43]

Clive was now happily settled in Paris, and with Dent's continued financial help, able to prolong his studies. Back home, Lawrence had been prostrated by a bad case of pneumonia, unable to move for his aching joints and difficult breathing, and unable to write his music reviews for *The Times*. He tried to make light of it all to Dent: '2 physicians, 2 surgeons, 2 nurses, & a diet of strychnine, oxygen & champagne (very dry Pol Roger 1898, he is careful to inform me)'.[44] Almost every day for weeks that summer Dent sent Lawrence letters he knew would amuse and divert

'Butterworth Trench'. Dent championed his music.

39 CC 10/02/1908. Dent's masterpiece of serpentine style is a review for the CR (04/02/1909).

40 *Ibid.*

41 LH 04/03/1908

42 Diary 24/04/1908.

43 LH 04/06/1908.

44 CC 02/06/1908.

him, mostly to do with the offstage dramas being enacted around *Comus*, but also revealing unexpected sides of himself.

> There is a divinity in the shape of a toad, presented to me by Miss Corbett, to eat the slugs [in his garden]. However, as I have not seen him about lately, I fear he may have felt dull here and gone back to Grange Road.[45]
>
> Well, the pansies are flowering, the heliotrope has turned the corner, thanks to Oxygen & strychnine, the verbenas & daisies seem healthy, the zinnias are hopeful, considering that the poor little things are only half the height of this paper & as leggy as Bee Wherry was in short skirts.[46]
>
> Miss Neville tells me that Maitland is in a frightful stew and doesn't know how to get on without you: and really the Times review is very dull now.[47]

That April, Dent joined Hugh Allen and Vaughan Williams at Petersfield, where he adjudicated the first of several annual choral competitions, with Allen conducting in his vigorous way, and Vaughan Williams, fresh from his studies with Ravel in Paris which had revitalised his composition, hearing his own work performed. It was one of the rare times Dent could work with inspirational British contemporaries he liked and respected, who could also discuss his odd and uneven career, Allen upbeat and positive:

> He is always very encouraging to me & is one of the few people who seem to have a complete confidence in my musical work and encourages me to go on.[48]
>
> When I am faced with something new older people say 'That's a thing you want a great deal of experience for'. Allen says, 'No experience? Well, it's time you began'.[49]

After this, conducting a desultory CUMS and working with Alan Gray brought out everything he was battling; he was fed up with the rehearsals with incomplete sections or chorus, the halfhearted attitudes to the challenging new music, Vaughan Williams' *Toward the Unknown Region*, or what he saw as Gray's ineptitude in tackling anything 'modern'.

> We had professional leaders to the strings, so that everything went better than I expected … The Debussy was rather odd & Gray played it rather badly, and got a beat wrong for several bars. It was complicated by Inwards,[50] who cd see Gray's part and thought it safer to follow him than to follow me.[51]

Fortunately, Vaughan Williams conducted it himself for the CUMS May Week concert.

Worse, at the Musical Board meeting that term, where the next year's lectures and workload were discussed, he felt that Stanford 'cut' him, while his proposed

45 LH 21/05/1908.

46 LH 31/05/1908.

47 LH 25/05/1908.

48 LH 15/05/1908.

49 CC 06/05/1908.

50 Haydn Inwards, the professional leader of CUMS.

51 LH 21/05/1908.

lectures for the next term, '2 hours a week for 2 terms on Mus. History and 1 hr a week on Analysis – all gratuitous ... were received with coolness'.[52] But when George Weston invited him to lecture at Harvard the next academic year, although tempted, Dent demurred: 'a prolonged absence from Cambridge means the loss of much ground: it means resigning certain offices, wch may be filled by other people & not kept open for me'.[53] But he casually dropped the possibility as a bombshell on Alan Gray: 'I never saw him so taken aback, not even when conducting an orchestra ... the Harvard project startled him as much as Pigou's appointment to the chair of economics did the University'.[54] Dent knew his own worth, but needed some unconventional and effective edge to progress; even now, he was aiming at some post that existed only in his imagination.

So the rehearsals for *Comus* that May and later in June came as a light antidote to everything else, Dent writing it all down for the convalescent Lawrence to enjoy, from playing for Mrs Fletcher's dance rehearsals at The Maltings House to ongoing gossipy accounts of rehearsals, with rude remarks about the creaking corsets, etc. But his intense involvement with these lively mixed groups marked another shift in his automatic misogyny. If at all possible, he would have avoided the women, but his defences had been eroded lately by women like Florence Barger and Jane Harrison, whose frank intelligence had surprised him into a warmer response, seeing them as individuals rather than 'females'. He slowly began to appreciate how such new women, together with other radicals like his old friend Vernon Lee, were suffering from being marginalised, prevented by social dictat from pursuing a fuller life. These young women, the Bedalians[55] and Newnhamites, had been raised to be independent, to campaign for the vote, for social justice and were perfectly happy to dance on stage for the MDS, and their outlook influenced local girls like the Darwin cousins, Gwen and Frances. Dent had always enjoyed seeing beautiful women, had an aversion to ugliness, as his crass response to the Busoni followers shows, but now his ideas were being updated forcibly. And he hated to be thought Victorian or too rigid, so he gritted his teeth, composed his scabrous descriptions to Lawrence, and, in the event, enjoyed himself.

Dent's collaboration with Rupert became part of his wider aim to educate his flock obliquely, through production. When Rupert came to dinner on 2 June, Dent fed him Hills's experimental boiled 'risotto' and proceeded to lecture him in his most detached academic manner about his directorial shortcomings, probably one of the few people who could get away with such constructive criticism, appealing to Rupert's perfectionism as much as his cultural avarice.

52 LH 27/05/1908.

53 LH 09/06/1908. Weston had suggested '6 or 8' lectures, but added that there were 'no funds available, but that if I come, probably the necessary millionaire will step forward & present Harvard with me'. But Dent remained hopeful for months.

54 LH 16/06/1908.

55 Bedales was an independent co-ed boarding school founded in 1893 by two former pupils of Lowes Dickinson on liberal, progressive principles. Many of the close-knit 'neo-pagans' of the Rupert Brooke circle were Old Bedalians: Justin Brooke, Jacques Raverat, the Olivier sisters, Ka Cox. Dent later became friendly with Ka Cox and Daphne Olivier.

> He is very much a puritan in artistic matters, and the absurd thing is that he imagines Gordon Craig to be one too. I was suddenly pulled up for talking of 'stage effects' wch was a phrase that to his mind meant something dreadfully wicked. It was apropos of Sabrina & her music. He desires music to accompany her speech: as Milton heads it 'song' and Lawes never set it … to Rupert I said that 'melodrama' did not belong to the Anglo-Italian atmosphere of Comus in 1634: that it was a purely German idea, and that it did not come in there till about 1770 etc, etc, etc. However, he thought it wd add mystery and so forth: and I asked if Sabrina was to come up through a trap, with lights down, or if she was merely to walk on and moo like the angel in Faustus.[56]

Dent had decided from the outset to gain Rupert's trust more than his affection in order to work with him effectively. 'Prince Rupert' was defensive about a number of points, especially his own inadequate voice, which has been variously described as harsh, squeaky and monotonous; apparently a family trait. He was not musical, and although he found it very hard to swallow criticism of his ideas and methods, he brought to the Marlowe a love and greater understanding of the plays as literature.[57] And he was conscientious: for *Comus* he studied verse and text with Sayle and Walter Headlam; and when Clive returned that summer, Rupert asked him for some basic lessons in singing and voice production. His promising career was encouraged by the introductions Dent gave him to Florentine theatre circles.

Rehearsals continued in intense, uneven bursts, after May Week for the performance in July, Dent in constant consultation with Rupert and with Albert Rothenstein,[58] who was being paid 15 pounds to design the sets. But everything was interrupted by Walter Headlam's sudden death. Headlam had been one of those rare teachers, influential beyond his subject and revered by both Lawrence Haward and Forster, amongst others.[59] There was a memorial service, but Dent did not go, thinking it 'absurd' to attend a High Anglican funeral when he had his own thoughts about Headlam, 'venerating' him together with Goldie, lamenting that 'the present generation do not find them clever enough'.[60]

When rehearsals resumed, beside playing piano, Dent was at The Maltings House, painting sets with Rothenstein and the Darwin girls, helping to sew innumerable spangles on the costumes, all the time entertaining various cast members to tea, dinner or lunch. All Sunday 5 July he worked on the Lawes manuscript for the exhibition at Christ's, then went to Sayle's, where he was forced to entertain George

56 LH 16/06/1908.

57 Cribb, *The Marlowe Story*, p. 20.

58 Albert Daniel Rothenstein (1881–1953), born in Bradford, went to the Slade, during WWI changed his name to the less Germanic 'Rutherstone'. A painter, he became involved with set and costume design. His brother William was the better-known painter; his nephew John became Director of the Tate Gallery.

59 Lawrence wrote a bibliography of all his works, while Forster wrote a biography. Dent found out some of his books, pictures and furniture and managed to buy some for himself, including a 1630 John Florio, a picture and a number of French books (LH 05/11/1908).

60 LH 23/06/1908. This was unfair, since Headlam had inspired a great love of Greek in many of his pupils, including Rupert Brooke, who was devastated by his death.

Mallory by playing the Schumann F sharp minor Sonata and three *Nachtstücke*. Dent obliged, more as a point of honour: 'Being in the last stage of exhaustion I played them with some sort of inspiration, as if I was drunk'.[61] In between rehearsals, he had also to nip down to London on Wednesday 8 July for a meeting of the Church Music Society, but typically, managed to seize the chance to dine at the Savile Club with Rupert and Albert Rothenstein before going on to see Isadora Duncan in performance with her protégées. Dance was just becoming all the rage; Dent was fascinated, as he had been in Berlin, and this time her act was followed by Busoni's former pupil, Maud Allan, who had found a more satisfying career dancing scantily clad as Salome.

❧ ❧ ❧

Comus was performed at the New Theatre on 10 July, to a distinguished invited audience which included Robert Bridges, Thomas Hardy and Edmund Gosse, a huge success. The younger members of the cast celebrated in style: after the two performances on the Saturday there was an exuberant party at the George Darwins, spilling out into the gardens by the river, with all the cast still in their costumes, spangles, beast-heads and all, dancing their pavanes and 'all sorts – it was a most uproarious finish to the whole affair'. For the first time Dent had been drawn into the production side of theatre, discovering through the process one of his fundamental principles, how museum pieces can be brought to life, and the differences between studying a piece and actively understanding it, beside that very Cambridge principle: in order to understand something fully, you have to go through the explanation or exposition to someone else. This principle became the centrepiece of his life's work, an antidote to what he later called 'musical archaeology'.[62]

The rest of Dent's summer was pleasant enough: trips to London for Certani's Bechstein Hall concert, meeting up with Parry, Vaughan Williams and Butterworth, now reviewing for *The Times* in Lawrence's absence. He saw Melba, Scotti and Zenatello in *Otello* before going off to stay at Highclere with the Arkwrights[63] for the Toyes' Boxford Festival there on 29 July. A quick visit with his brother Frank in Essex primed him for another duty trip to Ribston in October, to view the 'incredible pink tombstone wch Aunt L. has put up to Uncle Joe'.

Dent planned to spend the next two months in Italy, walking the Appenines between Florence and Ancona, starting from Bologna to the Certanis' family villa at Castel di Britti, and meeting up with various friends on the way: Respighi, described to Lawrence as 'a young composer in Bologna who arranges C[ertani]'s violin sonatas etc for him'; Harry Burton; the Conte Castracane at Cagni; even Forster and Woolley at Verona.[64]

61 Diary 05/07/1908.

62 The phrase was Busoni's.

63 G.E.P. Arkwright (1864–1944), musical writer and editor; edited the *Musical Antiquary* and several volumes for the Purcell Society.

64 LH 25/08/1908.

After months of such freedom, a flying visit to Ribston in October came as a real shock; his distance from his old family home could not have been more complete: 'the silence was oppressive, & I always felt my tail between my legs … The … real delight in shaving with rain-water, wch as always is the colour of black coffee when it comes out of the boiler. Also as usual, I am constipated'.[65] As soon as he decently could, he escaped to Aysgarth, where he went on long walks with Lawrence, convalescing there, up to Hardraw Force, to Leyburn, around the Dales, talking about music and books, even resuming work on his quartet. On the 15th, he was back in Cambridge, reading Forster's *A Room With A View*, just published, and having seen Forster so recently, it shook him completely. He tried to distance himself, writing to Lawrence: 'It is like Domenico Scarlatti – very hard & brilliant, clever & successful, but to me rather unsympathetic. However this is merely personal: as technique it is very good, & always amusing, with characteristic Forsterian touches of poetry'.[66] That new term his 'gang' expanded: Sayle graciously invited him to dine to meet his latest swans, James Steuart Wilson,[67] C. Armstrong Gibbs,[68] and J.B. Trend,[69] who was not only invited to play violin in CUMS, but asked to tea. Trend was smitten, while Gibbs, one of Dent's keenest pupils, began to take counterpoint lessons and constantly to present Dent with his numerous compositions, which Dent privately called 'poetical and logical, though quite schoolboy stuff'.[70] He caught up with Francis Cornford and Frances Darwin, who had fallen in love during *Comus*, and to his mild dismay were now engaged. Goldschmidt was coming to lunch often. Another new face was Ronald Firbank[71] of Trinity Hall, an eccentric, aristocratic and extremely effeminate young man. Dent does not often make such an obvious effort, but for Firbank his curiosity was piqued: 'I dined with Firbank – alone: it was a very elegant dinner, & I made myself as agreeable as I could, I even played Madame Butterfly in my most succulent manner, on a pianoforte that was thick with dust & out of tune'.[72] For his part, Firbank was struck by Dent, eventually using him (he said) as the model for several characters in his quirky, camp novels. They kept in touch. Perhaps his Italian experiences had made him more susceptible at home that term; beside Firbank's obvious flirting, Dent was smitten by a young Russian baritone, Reinhold von Warlich,[73] who sang *Die schöne Müllerin.*

65 LH 02/10/1908.

66 LH 19/10/1908.

67 See 'Dramatis Personae'.

68 Cecil Armstrong Gibbs (1889–1960) became a prolific composer, especially of songs.

69 John Brande Trend (1887–1958), 'JB', later first Professor of Spanish at Cambridge, the man who would most completely share Dent's life.

70 Diary 04/11/1908.

71 Arthur Annesley Ronald Firbank (1886–1926) presented Dent with signed copies of his novels, e.g., *Caprice*.

72 Diary 17/11/1908.

73 Reinhold von Warlich (1879–1939), born in St Petersberg into a musical family, became a lieder singer, specialising in Schubert, later helped found the American Schubert Society. See Gerald Moore, *Am I Too Loud?* (London, 1962) p. 74. Dent kept in touch.

> it was rather a case of Kardorff over again – like Kardorff he was surprisingly responsive at the first meeting ... It is quite pleasing to have a little excitement of this kind, as I thought I had got quite mouldy & was never going to have any more.[74]

The arrival that summer of the new Director of the Fitzwilliam Museum, Sydney Cockerell, was another cultural marker: 'a good sort, and very learned', Dent wrote in his most condescending manner, 'sufficiently keen on music to have bought a MS Scarlatti cantata for himself once: but not an autograph, as he believed it'.[75] Dent had thought of Sayle for the post, but Cockerell quickly showed how spectacularly right the appointment had been. 'The stupid man is married', Dent remarked glumly, but Kate Cockerell, a talented illustrator, became a friend and colleague, designing costumes for Dent's later productions. Under Monty James's tenure the Fitzwilliam had been allowed gently to decay, its collections hidden under dust and impenetrable bureaucracy. Straight away Cockerell began to reorganise the galleries to be more like rooms, with pictures, furniture and sculpture carefully chosen to complement; he determined that the music collections should be put in better order. Since at the time the Fitzwilliam held the bulk of the Cambridge music collections, having a sympathetic director meant that all the music Dent collected went to a safe home.[76] 'I found it a pigsty and I turned it into a palace', was his later comment on his achievement. The changes taking place in theatre and music, the shift from Victorian to Edwardian or even modernist aesthetics, were reflected in what happened to the Fitzwilliam Museum as soon as Cockerell took over. He started up the Friends of the Fitzwilliam Museum; Dent lent his support to the move to have the museum open on Sundays, a calculated hit at the old-fashioned 'clerical' faction while opening it up to more locals. And Cockerell was indefatigable in his pursuit of donations or legacies,[77] treating potential donors with personal tours, prescient in his aggressive approach to arts funding and collections.

> Vaughan Williams called about 10 & stayed most of the morning, looking at my compositions etc. I showed him Rosalys & the dances for Princess Fragoletta wch he liked very much, & he encouraged me to write for the stage.[78]

Vaughan Williams, now spending more time in Cambridge, asked Dent to join his Musical League, 'to found a local branch in Cambridge', and after consulting Fuller Maitland, who 'watered at the mouth' at the prospect, Dent decided to go ahead with it after another talk with Vaughan Williams in December. While he was up in Cambridge, he was 'invited by the Committee to write new music to *The Wasps*, tho'

74 LH 23/11/1908.

75 LH 04/06/1908. This was the one Cockerell had shown Dent the year before.

76 Items collected in these years include Scarlatti MSS, one of which was used for a recent recording by Cecilia Bartoli.

77 If that's Cockerell, the saying went, 'I must be dead'. Stella Panayotova, *I Turned it into a Palace: Sydney Cockerell and the Fitzwilliam Museum* (Cambridge, 2008), p. 64.

78 Diary 14/06/1908.

this is not officially published. The suggestion at the committee meeting was made by J.W. Clark himself – but it originated entirely with Sayle, though I backed it up.'[79]

His own musical composition now channelled into MDS productions, Dent continued to take a lateral approach to his long-term academic career. For several years now he had thought seriously of writing something substantial on Mozart, either *Don Giovanni* or *The Magic Flute,* to re-establish Mozart's diminished reputation. The articles on Mozart's operas in the second edition of Grove's show clearly the limitations of the then state of scholarship, with opinions set in concrete dismissing Mozart as a 'slight' composer. So when Hugh Allen invited him to give a paper to the Oriana Society ('an Oxford musical discussion club') on 4 December, Dent instantly accepted, seeing it as the perfect opportunity to air his fresh thoughts. 'I imagine they will mostly be clever, & not of the choral scholar type', he wrote to Lawrence, 'certainly you will say I am sailing very near the void if I read a paper on *Don Giovanni.* I thought first of the *Zauberflöte* – but am afraid it wd result in my preaching a sermon.'[80] In the event it was *Don Giovanni,* 'a step towards the Mozart book', but the audience was disappointing, the turnout very small.

❧ ❧ ❧

In these years, Dent's constant experimenting with ways in which he could draw together the complicated strands of his life – his music, his sexuality, his internationalist leanings, his hopes for Cambridge – began to bear fruit. His safe, private space at Panton Street was essential, and by now he had cultivated a strong public persona as a screen, employing his natural Old Etonian, landed gentry background, with a charming, rather old-fashioned polish designed to put people at their ease. But Dent seldom felt completely at home anywhere, 'among them but not of them', and sexuality was only one factor in his sense of otherness. This outsider–insider paradox was at the heart of everything Dent did, and right now he was constructing the foundations of his later life: his home and the institutions in his life were anchors, while his restless needs stipulated a back door half open to escape. So he built up the personal trusted networks, 'our gang', as he called the MDS people in 1908, with the long view of eventually establishing not just a music faculty, but something even bigger. Later, refined versions of this same impulse were channelled into forming national and international music institutions, creating the dynamic tension between solid institutions and networks of like-minded people testing the boundaries.

Dent's own personal traits were put to work as well, his ego and his battles with his natural prepossessions; *noblesse oblige* is a complicated albatross. His deepest, most personal feelings were almost always kept under wraps, and had been since prep school, only allowed to come out through music, while his homosexuality only exacerbated the need for control over the public persona, with the need for absolute trust and loyalty in his personal relationships. The ego fed a strong, subtle, competitive streak which fuelled his scholarly work but sometimes tainted or confused

79 Diary 18/12/1908

80 LH 25/10/1908.

personal relationships. And Dent was also a deeply political animal, always aware of group dynamics or of group versus group, enjoying the role of outsider while knowing himself to be at the heart of things; he was only half joking when he declared that he only stayed on the IMG committee to watch how Hugh Allen irritated the stuffy Maclean. In college, he played the college politics, often viewing that world in crude terms of them and us, the dynamics of his working personal relationships extremely delicately balanced; apparently minor episodes could be powder-kegs. The jealous exclusivity revealed with Percy and Clive that disastrous time re-emerged when Clive stayed at the Provost's Lodge with Monty James rather than with Dent. It blew up again the summer of 1908 when Clive unthinkingly wafted Dent's own 'swan', Denis Browne, off to the Provost's Lodge. Dent was furious; he felt betrayed, and fired off a long letter to Lawrence, the only person who could take him to task, trying to keep calm, to avoid the issue, even, but in the end letting rip.

> But it is too bad: as you know, Denis is my very particular swan just at present, mainly because of his extraordinary musical capacity (at present he is only the prospective favourite disciple & no more) – and I was keeping him even from Sayle. And now Clive comes & hands him over to the Lodge! ... you may say I ought to have personality enough to hold my friends myself – I lost Clive when Percy handed him over to James. I did not lose his friendship, but I lost him as a disciple ... And though people say Sayle spoils his undergraduate friends & makes them prigs – he does make them see that they have got to be leaders. He made me see it, I think more than anybody, except perhaps Allen – and naturally I don't bring you into these comparisons. James hates leaders as he hates philosophers ... I want to combine the two, and bring it about that the leaders shd be civilized people, but leaders none the less.[81]

Like most gay men of his time, Dent lived in some fear of exposure, and his generosity was in part driven by fear. He could never feel confident enough to lose his temper in public; instead, letting it out on a lead through writing or waspish expressions of spleen or vexation. While in Cambridge he needed the safe circles of men like Sayle and Bartholomew; they all needed each other, men they could trust who knew who they were. That trust was now being extended into his MDS circles, where many young men uncertain of their sexuality needed mentors, and Dent assumed yet another new role.

1909–1910

1909 was one of the filthiest winters Dent could remember, with the temperature getting down to 18°F (c. – 8 °C) and a spate of freezing fogs exacerbated by coal fires. Plagued by colds and sore throats, and lamenting about what the frosts were doing to his little garden, Dent resolved to cut down on his smoking; difficult, when he was socialising so much, and Panton Street in a constant fug with the streams of visitors. But Dent's mood was always worsened by bad weather, now combined with his continuing sense of frustration with the Music Faculty. A few months before, he had

81 LH 12/07/1908.

described his frustration to Lawrence as 'a desperate attempt to assert one's personality', comparing it to being forced to share a railway carriage with a screaming baby, and realising that the baby's screams were like his own threat to leave for Harvard. 'The points in favour of it, from purely selfish consideration were, that it was like the screams, an assertion of my personality in the face of people who ignore me'.[82]

The contrast with his fuller intellectual and social life abroad could not have been more marked, and as Dent increasingly turned to his embryonic professional writing as an outlet for his ideas,[83] any inspiration came from outside the faculty: the MDS, Vaughan Williams and Berlin circles,[84] especially Busoni's core work *Outline of a New Aesthetic of Music*, which he reviewed for the *Monthly Musical Record*.[85] Ideas which became part of Dent's own credo had first been aired in Busoni's drawing room and at Bartolini's before winding up on the page: 'Music, a bird on the wing, if it remains in German regions, is in danger of ending up in a cage. And the Germans will become museum janitors.'[86] Busoni's highmindedness stirred Dent to view music from different angles, raising provocative questions on the nature of musical composition and on the attendant roles of musicians: 'How far is the executant to be the slave, how far the interpreter, of the composer?'[87]

The burgeoning research on early opera, his professional writing, and the cultural worlds beyond Britain, with some music to support MDS productions, were dovetailing into a tacit credo about the place of music beyond the pages.[88] He had spent his New Year 1909 in London, combining duty by being on parade at his mother's new house in Rutland Gate, with some more research at the British Museum, digging out and copying more early music for the MDS and Mrs Jenkinson, including a pavane by Orlando Gibbons. By this time he had got to know well many of the staff there and they him – Streatfeild, Squire, *et al.* – and he could visit a convalescent Lawrence, now rebuilding his own career in journalism, to catch up on the latest publishing gossip and talk about the new production at Covent Garden, the first performance in English of the complete *Ring* cycle, with Hans Richter conducting.

82 LH 15/09/1908.

83 In the *MMR* from 1906 to 1911 there were 16 Dent articles with titles like 'Letter from Italy', 'French Music in Berlin', 'Music in Berlin', 'English Opera in Berlin', 'The new *Language of Music*', 'Jacopo Calascione and the band of Venice', etc.

84 Beaumont, *Busoni*, p. 91 describes 'the Radical Years' meaning 'the decade immediately preceding the First World War' as 'a general progression in all the arts – and particularly in music – to remove the last remaining constraints of the nineteenth century'.

85 *Entwurf einer neuen Ästhetik der Tonkunst*, published 1907, rev. edn 1916; English edition *Sketch of a New Esthetic of Music*, tr. Theodore Baker (New York, 1911); reviewed by Ernest Newman, Dent (MMR September 1909) and Paul Bekker.

86 Busoni to Egon Petri 06/09/1905, quoted in Beaumont, *Busoni*, p. 95.

87 Dent, MMR (September 1909), p. 198.

88 For the CR: *The Knight of the Burning Pestle* (1911), *The Wasps* (1909 & 1910) and *The Magic Flute* (1911).

Long talk w Sayle about Marlowe Soc & its fate: rather anxious lest the old set (Rupert, Geoffrey, Cosmo etc.) shd be supplanted by Pole and the Corpus Emmanuel semi-footlights set wch (it must be admitted) made Epicoene a great success.[89]

The latest MDS production, Ben Jonson's *Epicoene* (or *The Silent Woman*), was directed by a former King's choral scholar, Reginald Pole, whose nickname 'Arabella, Duchess of Poland' hints at both his drama-queen style and the thinly veiled contempt of the older MDS gang, but he had recruited the best undergraduate actors, including Miles Malleson[90] and Dennis Arundell,[91] and his efforts held the society together at a difficult time. The dress rehearsal was a mess – 'Only half band there ... hopeless' Dent groaned in his diary – but by the last performance in the Victoria Assembly Rooms[92] on Saturday 20 February, it was clearly a success: 'a full house that roared with laughter', including Sydney Cockerell and May Morris. Against the MDS committee's wishes, Pole took the production to London, with decent reviews but not enough finance. The 'old set' were already fired up to put on Beaumont and Fletcher's *The Knight of the Burning Pestle* in July, with a 'bisexual' cast, since it was out of term. All the old hands would be back – Justin Brooke, Rupert, Geoffrey Keynes, Cosmo – and they were determined to do it in the 'old' style, so throughout April Dent wrote long letters from Berlin to Denis Browne with detailed instructions about orchestration and the use of his square pianoforte.

In February 1909, Dent was asked to write a review in the *Cambridge Review* of his colleague Edward Naylor's opera, *The Angelus*, which had won the Ricordi Prize but was loathed by Dent. It was being produced at Covent Garden. In a masterpiece of serpentine writing, Dent focused on the preposterous libretto, comparing it to W.S. Gilbert 'in sentimental mood' or Longfellow at his worst: 'does Dr Naylor really believe in these monks and village maidens?', side-stepping direct criticism of the music. In deliberately eschewing a 'modern idiom', Dr Naylor 'has renounced the temptation of set purpose', with the rider, 'it leaves the composer with so very few resources at his disposal ... one often feels that he is giving us property music instead of the real thing'.[93] The review finishes up with what might be construed as a positive suggestion, that *The Angelus* belonged not beside the *Ring* at Covent Garden, but in the repertory of small travelling opera companies, with far 'more tolerant' audiences.

In April, Johannes Wolf asked Dent to contribute an article for the *Festschrift* being assembled in honour of Hugo Riemann's sixtieth birthday.[94] 'Being the first time I was ever asked to contribute to a Festschrift for anybody, and now for the

89 Diary 23/02/1909.

90 William Miles Malleson (1888–1969), actor in stage and film, translator, screenwriter, playwright.

91 Dennis Arundell (1898–1988), actor, director, writer, composer, scholar. Later worked with Dent at Sadler's Wells.

92 Now a Marks & Spencer.

93 CR (4 February 1909); Haward, *Edward J. Dent: A Bibliography*, 216iii.

94 Karl Wilhelm Julius Hugo Riemann (1849–1919), one of the first great musicologists and scholars of music, author of Riemann's *Musiklexicon*, a forerunner of *Grove's*. Dent loved to point out the mistakes he found in it.

most learned of learned Germans, of course I want to send something good.'[95] It was going to be difficult; he had already planned to be away that May for the IMG conference and the Haydn centenary in Vienna, and to offset his travelling expenses, had arranged to let his house to Forster's friends the Woolleys, who needed a temporary foothold in Cambridge.[96] Now he faced the challenge of writing a first-class piece for a prestigious Festschrift before the first of June, with the International Congress in between, on the hoof.

> My only possibility is to send extracts from my little Jesuit book – the supposed autobiography of a young Italian gentleman in 1680 who went to the opera & 'carried on' with a prima donna ... And as the essay is for a German public I need not translate the Italian, tho' I shall write an introduction & notes in English.[97]

The piece was 'A Jesuit at the Opera in 1687'; the opera, *La Verita Mascherata*.[98]

'We went to supper at Hugh's – Forster read a new story of his "The Machine Stops" – a vision of the future. It was very clever & interesting – but Lawrence slept through it, as unconscious of its beauties as Harold Barger was of the ugliness of a Simplicissimus-Album.'[99] Forster's prescient story and the arrival of Maynard Keynes to take up his Fellowship at King's were the high points that April. Hugh Allen invited Dent to another choral competition at Moreton-in-the-Marsh, but it was a far cry from Petersfield, Dent grumbling at having to conduct a Bach chorale on a wobbling platform and with no rehearsals.[100] A visit to the Sydney Waterlows at Rye did little to break his winter gloom, Dent disappointed by Sydney, 'very much absorbed in his garden & dogs and rather corpulent in mind as well as body'.[101] But on the 18th, 'motoring' to Hatchlands with the Coopers, Dent's old Etonian friend who had married Hal Goodhart-Rendel's mother, gave him a much-needed boost. Still occupied by Hal's uncle, Lord Rendel, 'the house was as Hal said rather like a mausoleum, being Georgian and gorgeous, & all swathed in brown holland'.[102] He stayed for three days, and enjoyed himself completely, talking about architecture

95 CC 17/04/1909.

96 Typically, though rather short of money himself then, he was still helping to support Clive financially.

97 CC 17/04/1909.

98 *Riemann-Festschrift: Gesammelte Studien* (Leipzig, 1909), pp. 381–93. Haward, *Edward J. Dent: A Bibliography*, 83. It was later reworked and expanded for a bigger piece on 'The Baroque Opera' in G.E.P. Arkwright's short-lived journal *The Musical Antiquary*.

99 Diary 04/04/1909.

100 CC 17/04/1909.

101 Diary 16/04/1909. Two years later, his marriage in shreds, he would propose to Virginia Stephen, later Woolf, who wrote scathingly of his 'immense soft pink stomach ... bellowing like a walrus' (Lee, *Virginia Woolf*, pp. 247–8).

102 Diary 18/04/1909. Hatchlands is now a National Trust property, with an important picture collection and the Cobbe Collection of keyboard instruments that had belonged to composers, including the instrument which inspired this biography. Concerts are still being given in the Music Room there.

and music with Hal and walking around the extensive grounds, investigating its stunning Music Room.

'I don't know how I survived the last month in England', he wrote to Denis from Berlin,

> as I really had to clear off my Purcell opera, & then go gadding around to festivals & visits – the only bright moment of wch was three days with Hal Goodhart Rendel – that was really refreshing, and I felt much the better for it. But I think I mean to fight shy of competition festivals in future.[103]

As ever, there was a strong element of escape. He had impulsively decided to go to Berlin rather than Munich because both Kardorff and Herzog would be there; such company for 'a fortnight or 3 weeks' was just the thing to revive his flagging spirits and his other self. With that in mind, after checking into the Central Hotel, Dent went straight to Bartolini's, immediately at home. For a week he simply let go. His visit to the Secession was rewarded by 'some good pictures by Kardorff & Rhein' and a collection of friends and acquaintances, including Thornely Gibson, now settled in his singing career there.[104] With the music and contemporary art, Bartolini's, Kardorff painting still lifes at his new studio in Polidamstrasse, Dent revived. With Kardorff he went to Café Sezession, to the Traube, to an Old Master exhibition, enjoying the fact of Kardorff's being 'very sniffy' about the pictures, which were, he declared, more 'the work of Hauser the restorer'. There was a timely call on Bernard Esmarch, depressed that his lover Eddi had just left him; he called on Respighi, and met more painter friends of Kardorff's, including Max Pechstein.[105] He went to *Faust*, to d'Albert's *Tiefland* ('dull'), but was enchanted by a 'private' performance at the Kroll of the 'Russian Court Ballet' put on for the Secession: *Swan Lake* and a a new ballet set to Liszt's music, 'horribly exciting ... marvellous dancing ... The performance was wonderful, and Liszt's 2nd rhapsody danced by half a dozen men & women in peasant costumes, almost without make up, was most exciting'.[106]

Sitting with Herzog and his sister, dining later with the Sterns at 'Dete', the Deutsches Theater, gossiping about Wedekind and Thoma, Dent was content, his mood far more receptive. He went again to the Russian Ballet, and on 8 April 'as a matter of duty', to one of the first performances of Strauss's new opera, *Elektra*: 'to my great surprise enjoyed it: it is almost noble, & at any rate very sincere, with a great deal of beauty – much more natural & vocal than Salome & much clearer, though I think it is a progress & not a retrogression'.[107] Berlin was refreshing but it was not Dent's home, nor could it be.

103 DB 30/04/1909.

104 Gibson's career choice was unusual for the time, probably down to the 'Schwulen' culture there.

105 Max Pechstein (1881–1955), member of Die Brücke; Dent first called him 'Hans'.

106 Diary 04/05/1909. This was Anna Pavlova's own tour prefacing the big tour of the Diaghilev company, when it took Paris by storm that May. Afraid that Diaghilev might flop, Pavlova wanted to keep her own reputation intact, so had her own tour. Sjeng Scheijen, *Diaghilev: A Life* (London, 2010), pp. 180ff.

107 Diary 08/05/1909.

> I feel like the grocer's boy turned loose among the almonds & raisins – they cease to have any serious attraction for me ... I can't quite make up my mind whether I am having a good time or not. I am very glad to have got away, at moments have a strange hankering for home.[108]

He was supposed to go on to the Handel festivals in Mainz and Nürnberg[109] before Vienna and the congress at the end of May, writing up the congress for Bruce Richardson at *The Times*, his first such assignment. After Berlin, he was in combative mood.

> I think I should shirk the congress part of it if it was not for the prospect of quarrelling and intriguing. I hope to bring off a fight with Maclean soon: my article for Reimann's Festschrift ... is full of inflammatory remarks about Jesuits and sexual morality. It is I think rather important ... Consequently it may possibly be reprinted in the IMG thing: if so Maclean is sure to boggle at my profanities & improprieties. This will give me the chance of threatening to leave the English section, in wch case I should apply to Wolf at Berlin & join either the Berlin or the Florence section, probably the latter, and send frequent contributions in Italian.[110]

Ten days in Dresden balanced him again, slowing him down, working on *La Verita Mascherata*,[111] enjoying the miniature dramas around Mrs Spottiswoode and Ecki, with relaxed summer evening parties at Pillnitz, readings in the garden, and Bachmann playing Schumann, even managing to meet up with Fritz Drach on the sly.

> The best bedroom is of course occupied by Ecki, now more generally known as Moloch. Moloch got kicked by a casual Italian at Venice, and as a result got a paralytic stroke 4 weeks ago ... Of course the anxiety has been fearful.[112]

If he had hoped, as he insisted to Lawrence, to write his string quartet in Mrs Spottiswoode's garden, he failed, but he refused to repent:

> although I had got as far as getting tickets for Mainz sent me as a representative of old Sheddy's rag [the MMR] and in addition one invitation to a banquet in Anwesenheit seiner königlichen Hoheit des Grossherzogs Ernst Ludwig von Hessen und zu Rhein, finally this wicked old lady whom I now call the Konigen der Nacht persuaded me to stay here and read The Opium Eater aloud in the evenings.[113]

Days later, miserable and sick from the steamer and train, and finding the Hotel Wandtl 'horribly expensive', Dent was again dreading the prospect of public, stuffy congress meetings and teas. Officially it was the Haydn centenary, with 'genial' Sir Alexander Mackenzie presiding over the proceedings, and every important music

108 LH 06/05/1909.

109 An article for MMR that June.

110 LH 18/05/1909.

111 Diary 13/05/1909.

112 LH 18/05/1909.

113 *Ibid.*

scholar in the world there, many of Dent's acquaintance: Friedlaender, Wolf, Guido Adler (with whom he had tea),[114] Amelli, Kretschzmar, *et al.*, and a number of Americans he met for the first time, especially Oscar Sonneck.[115] He went to Haydn's 'Mariazeller' Mass in the Hofburg Kapelle and a massive concert in the Musikverein: 'almost mad with excitement of Haydn & exhaustion. I am quite incapable of going to any more meetings ... horrible' parties. The self-satisfied, effusive account in the *Musical Times*[116] shows the general style of the congress which so irritated Dent, but being forced to sit through it all and having to write it up for *The Times* was a 'nightmare ... never again'.[117] Listening even to interesting lectures became a chore: Peter Wagner lecturing on music printing, 'but understood little, as I was writing & the reverberation was fearful'.[118]

> Mackenzie made a good chairman when in the chair, but generally talked to Adler in the window. Maclean as sec. had Sonneck to interpret for him wch was awkward, as Sonneck's ideas were very opposed to Maclean's. I sat it out as the situation amused me.[119]

On the 29th, together with Johannes Wolf, he 'presided over lutes & tablature, Wolf taking most of the words out of my mouth'.

But the Haydn experience was another matter: Dent loved the excursion to Eisenstadt, to the Esterhazy Palace where Haydn had spent most of his life as court composer, for a performance of the Nelson Mass and a choral concert there: 'It was very like Hovingham or Petersfield, choirs from neighbouring places, all amateurs & rather rough but very Hungarian & delightful ... I felt that it gave me new life & could have stayed a week there.'[120] Then there was his discovery of Wanda Landowska,[121] at the beginning of her career when she was reintroducing the harpsichord into chamber music, playing at several of the concerts; Dent drew a little cartoon of her hat like a huge mushroom, overwhelmed by her 'miraculous' playing.[122] A 'great stimulus', he wrote to Lawrence, getting back to his music history work and some music for the MDS.

114 Guido Adler (1855–1941), pupil of Bruckner, Professor of Music History at Vienna, pioneering musicologist.

115 Oscar Sonneck (1873–1928), Head of Music at the Library of Congress, had studied in Germany; later editor of the MQ, to which Dent contributed, and was involved with the ISCM.

116 'The Haydn Festival and International Music Congress at Vienna', MT (1 July 1909), pp. 432–5.

117 LH 01/06/1909.

118 Diary 28/05/1909.

119 Diary 25/05/1909.

120 Diary 27/05/1909.

121 Wanda Landowska (1879–1959), Polish-born pianist who reintroduced the harpsichord into concerts. Her own harpsichord was a specially commissioned monster built by Pleyel. Dent's later dealings with her included the Falla harpsichord concerto for one of the ISCM festivals.

122 LH 01/06/1909.

'I was bored by the congress, but had my vanity very much gratified: I started a placid friendship with an unpronounceable young man from Cracow who is sending me polonaises of 1600 for the "Knight of the Burning Pestle".'[123] The 'unpronounceable young man' was a Polish academic, Jachimecki,[124] who kept him company at the Burgtheater to see *Julius Caesar* and on other occasions. A visit to the Maddalenas included their new cat, 'white with limp hair like mine, and a huge persian-tabby tail ... a powdered squirrel'. Dent returned home via Breslau, Liegnitz to look up some Dowland dances there, and Berlin in order to see Busoni, whom he met in the street 'very unshaven & disreputable', but who affably asked him in to talk about the congress ('sneering at Haydn & Wanda Landowska') and about the *Verkaufte Braut* he had just seen.

Back in London that June, Dent faced up to the current family dramas at Rutland Gate before escaping to the British Museum where Barclay Squire had received a postcard sent from Vienna with 42 signatures on it. Touched at Dent's gesture, Squire was much friendlier, helping him to root through Scarlatti manuscripts at the British Museum and getting him drunk on forty-year-old port. In Cambridge, staying at the Jenkinsons, playing 'drums' under Stanford's baton for the CUMS concert, Dent relaxed a bit. Afterwards, at the Jenkinsons' dinner party with the Stewarts, Stanford was in top form – and he was an excellent raconteur – entertaining them with anecdotes and insider gossip, all recorded in Dent's diary. But behind the amusing stories laid out at the dinner table that evening, the current state of opera, the politics and finances behind it, which Stanford knew so well, was laid bare.

Contemporary music was in a state of flux, poised between the Edwardian and the new, and Dent was consciously witnessing the shift, striving to make musical sense of new or unfamiliar works, his first impressions reflected in his own uneven, often odd responses. In July, besides his ongoing work at the British Museum, he went with Clive to Ethel Smyth's opera *The Wreckers* at His Majesty's Theatre, conducted by Thomas Beecham, a friend of Smyth's and a champion of her music, with his own, hand-picked orchestra. Dent was predisposed to dislike it; his friend Streatfeild had already labelled it 'very masculine, or rather mannish', voicing the kind of unthinking prejudice Smyth generally had to put up with. Dent found himself impressed, especially comparing it with *The Angelus*: 'Miss Smyth at any rate is not banal. But it is always striving after powerful dramatic effects, and it is very choppy and discontinuous ... too much screaming and not enough symphonic development'.[125] They later became friends and colleagues. Astonishingly, after *The Wreckers*, Dent immediately went on to see the last three acts of the British premiere of Charpentier's *Louise* (1900) at Covent Garden, loving what he later called its 'great courage' for setting 'the slums of modern Paris on the stage with picturesque theatrical effect', even though the music 'often has very little bearing on the play'.[126]

[123] *Ibid.*

[124] Zdzislaw Jachimecki, who in 1920 wrote an article for the MQ on the composer Adam Jarjembski.

[125] Diary 22/06/1909.

[126] E.J. Dent, *Opera* (London, 1940), p. 94.

At the same time Dent's protégés were finding the transition into professional life difficult, placing Dent in a personal dilemma he found almost impossible. He could organise concerts, but emotional dependency confused him, and when faced with the complicated bundle of anxieties that was his ex-lover O'Neil, he distanced himself behind the practical support he could easily give – concerts, reviews, some financing. O'Neil's London debut should have been counted a success, with its excellent programme, including some Bartók, but his defensive, prickly attitude towards his audience and his long-suffering patron Dora Knatchbull militated against connection. Dent retreated, saying to Clive, 'but the real stuff is there: I feel clear about that now: and the only way to make a great pianist of him is to be systematically kind and gentle with him (wch is rather hard) until he can think that he comes onto his platform to play to a room full of real friends, not unknown critics'.[127] Within a year, O'Neil had shot himself in Montreal.

Clive finished his continental studies, composing some 'charming, delicate, and well finished' music for a marionette play and music to 'Love's Comedy', but was unsure what to do next. When He asked Dent's advice about taking some much-needed paid employment as organist at Guy's Hospital, offered to him by Will Mollison, he was given a tart answer: 'You must settle your affairs for yourself':

> How shd I know if £75 a year is an adequate remuneration for the work Will Mollison is offering you? ... Well, I don't advise you to describe yourself in your advertisements as Mr Clive Carey F.R.C.O. (organist of Guy's Hospital) – Baritone for opera & oratorio – Repertoire: – Parsifal, Pagliacci, Penitence, Pardon & Peace.[128]

He may have been more testy than usual; at Cambridge, the production of the *The Knight of the Burning Pestle* had collapsed, under more confusion in the grey areas between personal and professional lives. Rupert had written to him about the drama: 'I'm awfully sorry about this. I've spent the day at a telephone, with alternately Justin swearing, and Gwen Darwin weeping, at the other end ... Well, it's fairly rough on a few people, Justin indeed, and you, of course, most of all.[129] It could so easily have been a major setback for the whole fragile MDS enterprise, but it wasn't; the *Knight* was eventually put on in February 1911, with all the music Dent had gleaned from the remotest corners of half a dozen European libraries, besides all the notes and ideas on the production design. They were all learning how the arts are run at the margins.

Instead, that hot summer Dent enjoyed the luxury of some leisure time in his garden, reading a lot of French (Maupassant and Jean Christophe, *La Foire sur la Place*), entertaining Ted and the Marlovians still around, 'Justin in a great state of dramatic enthusiasm, wch I much enjoyed.'[130] Rupert was attracting an extraordinary range of visitors to his new retreat at the Old Vicarage, Grantchester, including the

127 CC 05/06/1909.

128 CC 17/07/1909.

129 Brooke to Dent, 29/06/1909. CUL Add MS 7973/B/105.

130 Diary 10/07/1909.

Augustus John family, who camped nearby in their caravan while their father was painting his portrait of Jane Harrison down the river at Newnham. In mid-July after returning from another Oxford 'Bachfest', Dent walked out there to meet Eddie Marsh[131] for the first time: 'I found him fairly amusing, but a little disappointing after all I had heard from Lawrence.'[132] That summer was indeed idyllic, with its 'neo-paganism', nude bathing in the Cam, picnics, camping, the easy camaraderie, the prewar golden period they would all remember best. Dent enjoyed it up to a point, but when invited to join the gang at Lulworth, 'I ... declined, not wishing to imperil friendship in that quarter.'[133] Cowardly or shrewd? Rupert's was an odd, fragile but important friendship, and Dent kept it in a special place. Others of Rupert's extended circle – like Hugh Dalton and J.B. Trend – perhaps lacked his special, stellar qualities, but were more constant and durable as friends. That summer Dent began to encourage Trend's attentions, but he was taken by surprise one day when Trend obliquely revealed how serious his music was, taking Dent to:

> a shop beyond Magdalen to look at some old music wch had belonged to Dr Hagen. I bought a score of Haydn's Stabat Mater: T. bought a lot of old violin music, including a MS volume of 10 sonatas by Pieter Hellendaal, with curious cadenzas – Sayle told me that he had a quantity of notes of Cambridge concerts in the 18th cent at wch Hellendaal performed.[134]

After that, Trend became one of Dent's most regular, devoted visitors, for some of the reasons that Rupert came, the need for a safe personal space and discussion. But after safe Cambridge, what was out there for all these talented, thwarted young men? One August day, just before Dent left for Italy, Hugh Dalton read out Rupert's new poem 'Some day I shall rise & leave my friends', which 'touched me strangely'.

All the time he continued to work on Scarlatti, the Jarzembcski Tamburetta and on Bononcini songs, often going up to London to the British Museum and meeting Ronald Firbank. Oliffe Richmond graciously offered to help Dent compose a 'silly piece of facetiousness' for Nixon's birthday, 'his jubilee', in the King's garden.[135] George Weston came to stay; Lawrence came up for the weekend of 24 July, and read his 'Memoir' of Walter Headlam after dinner to Sydney Waterlow and Hugh Meredith. He tried to interest Hadow in using next year's London IMG Congress in connection with the Church Music Society.[136] After Vienna, he wanted to stir, noting how the advent of his friend Arkwright's journal the *Musical Antiquary* had put

131 Edward Marsh (1872–1953), son of the Master of Downing College, secretary to Austen Chamberlain and to Winston Churchill, became the patron of *Georgian Poetry* and the main proponent of the Rupert Brooke mythology after his death.

132 Diary 18/07/1909.

133 DB 10/08/1909.

134 Diary 03/08/1909.

135 DB 10/08/1909.

136 Diary 09/07/1909.

Maclean's nose out of joint, seeing it as a 'dangerous rival to the IMG *Sammelbände*, of wch he is the "English Editor".'[137]

But Dent was pushing instinctively in several purposeful directions, his real preoccupation shown in the long, critical diary entry after seeing *Don Giovanni* at Covent Garden that July, with Percy Pitt conducting.[138] Even before his Oxford lecture in December, Mozart had been on Dent's mind, his growing scholarly understanding of early opera affecting the way he saw any production. He noted 'Percy Pitt's impossibly quick tempo', the arias constantly interrupted by applause, the general lack of understanding and some inappropriate voices.

> The scenery was good, and the stage management fairly so: but D.G. did not go with the necessary sense of hurry & excitement, and all the 'struggles' were very tame. At the end we had the cemetery & 4 'sheeted dead' arising from their graves: no devils & no sextet.

August and September, Dent escaped again to Italy via Pillnitz, Prague and Fiume, walking in the hills around Aquila, tinkering with his quartet, in spite of 'hammering' from the nearby blacksmiths, eventually meeting Ted in Florence, then, packs on their backs, tramping the hills to Arezzo, staying in rough accommodation not at all to Ted's taste: 'In the W.C. I found the covers of the G.F.S. Associates Journal – wch summed up the whole situation – though after that I was surprised to find that the sheets on my bed were damp.'[139] He returned to spend the last week of his escape in Florence, going to the theatre, calling on Cust, discussing theatre work with Gordon Craig and secretly visiting Henry Somerset with his current flame, Robert Condamine.[140]

❧ ❧ ❧

Dent had been hopeful of a resurrected festival in Newcastle that October, with Busoni conducting the London Symphony Orchestra and Egon Petri in his piano concerto. The programme included a number of big contemporary works: Elgar's *The Kingdom*, Rutland Boughton's *The Invisible Armada*, Granville Bantock's *Omar Khayyám* part II, and Adam Carse's Symphony in G minor, each conducted by the composer. Dent diligently attended rehearsals for Haydn's *The Return of Tobias*, conducted by Henry Coward, who had brought a massive 360-strong choir up from Sheffield. Dent found it 'disastrous … I never saw so incompetent a conductor'. Even after intense discussions with music critics Herbert Thompson (*Yorkshire Post*), R.H. Legge, besides the Busonis and Petri, most of the music brought up his bile. The Elgar's religious underpinning 'disgusted me', while the Bantock 'bored

137 Diary 23/07/1909. Dent wrote for both.

138 Diary 02/07/1909.

139 Diary 21/09/1909. 'G.F.S' is the Girls' Friendly Society.

140 Diary 05/10/1909. This may be the actor Robert de la Condamine aka Farquharson (1877–1966).

me to death, except the "camels crossing the desert"',[141] and, as for the Carse, he was 'ashamed to be seen there listening' to it. Expensive and lavish, the festival was never repeated.

The IMG committee was no better, in Dent's view: 'Maclean more tiresome than ever ... No business done except that I found out that M. cannot stand Allen: so I intend to get Allen on the committee at all costs'.[142] Only in Cambridge did he see fresh things emerging: 'Trend came to dinner and brought me some old Italian song-books that had belonged to his grandfather RJS Stevens'.[143] And even if there were only three pupils right now, Dent knew that he was making a difference: 'I went in to tea with Denis, who is very unhappy as his father will not let him take up music as a profession, and being over 70 and stone deaf is not to be argued with'.[144]

Even while Dent was finding contemporary music and opera style disappointing, his writing became more focused, incorporating his wider experience. 'I read a good deal of Symonds with a view to my opera paper & lecture'. His use of John Addington Symonds[145] for a major piece on 'Baroque Opera' for the *Musical Antiquary* is both radical gesture and conscious undertaking to harness both his scholarly and his personal driving forces. Symonds was an acknowledged authority on Italian drama, especially Gozzi,[146] but as important, he was also more openly homosexual, and had probably coined the term. He was certainly a role model for Dent himself, who had been introduced to his unpublished work through Horatio Brown, Symonds' close friend, who kept his manuscripts, including his unexpurgated autobiography. Symonds boldly blended the emotional life with the life of the mind, his work and his life together, exemplifying what Dent was struggling with; not simply defining who he was, but connecting that with the new frontiers of understanding he was establishing.

The resulting article[147] is one of Dent's early pieces of first-class scholarly writing, incorporating material he had used for his piece, 'A Jesuit at the Opera', beside his recent extensive research. By publishing it in Arkwright's new journal, he was in the kind of company he respected: Streatfeild on Handel, Ernest Walker, Robert Bridges, Naylor.

> The study of musical history, although less entirely neglected at the present day than it was a generation ago, still suffers from the fact that few historians attempt to trace the development of the art as a living emotional force ... the mere presentation of documents is not enough; to form a reasonable judgement on the music of a past age we must not be content with a mere exposition of technical

141 Diary 22/10/1909.

142 Diary 18/10/1909.

143 Diary 25/10/1909.

144 Diary 28/10/1909.

145 J.A. Symonds (1840–1893), cultural historian, especially on Italian and Greek culture, but also on early English drama, pioneering writer on gay history. His 7-volume *Renaissance in Italy* was still a useful source for Dent forty years later.

146 *Essays on Italian Impromptu Comedy* (1890).

147 'The Baroque Opera', *Musical Antiquary* (January 1910), pp. 93–107.

> processes. For the language of music is the most subtle of all artistic languages … it is therefore the language which is most susceptible to change.[148]

Dent's sensitivity to the basic nature of the opera experience, the audience's emotional response to an alternative world of music and words, pervades the scholarly historical background, even while he acknowledges how absurd the conventions can be. As an introduction to early opera, his article is difficult to beat, even now. The next logical step was to show how it actually worked on the stage, what the MDS was doing for obscure early drama, bringing it back to life.

Dent could turn with real pleasure to the most exciting event that term, the return of the triennial Greek Play, *The Wasps* of Aristophanes, its music specially composed by Ralph Vaughan Williams, who was staying with his local Darwin relatives for the rehearsals and performance. Most of the MDS people were involved, Steuart Wilson dropping in, exhausted by the intense rehearsals; working out any new piece takes time and patience, especially when the composer is present, but this was something more. In the weeks running up to the production, opinion was sharply divided over the 'modern' music; it was too unusual, too 'new'. Vaughan Williams' own local relatives had supported him, but his cousin Gwen (later Raverat) wrote about 'overhearing scraps of conversation about "that foolish young man, Ralph Vaughan Williams", who would go on working at music when "he was so hopelessly bad at it".'[149] Dent had backed Vaughan Williams from the beginning, attracted by the general subversion as much as the radical music, so different from anything else he had been hearing.

> I … wonder if I have interpreted it and V.W. right: apparently the tiresome old men of the chorus are symbolized by Stanford & Parry – the 'men who fought for Athens in the good old days' and now get in the way of the younger men, hostile to any new movement. When Philocles tries to be modern and gets drunk, he sings the march from the Birds with Joseph Holbrooke harmonies or worse.[150]

He was quite correct; the 'tiresome old men' were very exercised indeed, but without being quite able to express why.[151] His sympathies were fired even more when Steuart and Denis told him how shabbily Vaughan Williams was being treated by Charles Wood and Walter Durnford, trying to take liberties with his music without consulting him, cutting the Nocturne and one of the dances (later reversed, owing to pressure from the chorus) and messing with his tempi. Dent was outraged, and was so rude to Wood and to Durnford that neither would speak to him for some time. But the younger generation found it completely exciting and stimulating, with a great deal of animated discussion: Francis Toye over lunch with Rupert and JB,

148 *Ibid.*, p. 193.

149 *Period Piece: A Cambridge Childhood* (London, 1952), p. 273. Her Aunt Etty was similarly scathing of Forster's writing.

150 CC 08/11/1909.

151 Dent records several of these in letters to CC, e.g., 10/12/1909 tells how the Vice Provost was 'very angry' with Dent over *The Wasps*, but when pressed about his particular objections, apart from the usage of one Greek word by one of the slaves, he could not say why.

proposing 'great plans for a season of good plays & operas at Cambridge',[152] playing through *The Wasps* music on Sayle's piano.

The dress rehearsal did not go well. The musicians stumbled over this odd new music, and many parts needed correcting, while 'Wood (who was conducting) smelt very strong [sic] of whisky'.[153] In spite of this Dent could barely contain his excitement; everything about this provocative production appealed to him, the opposite of the Newcastle Festival.

> The music is extraordinary and will make a stir. I think it is wonderfully good on the whole. It has a great deal of folksong & quasi-folksong in it, wch gives it a definite character, and makes it intelligible – popular without being banal ... The music is appallingly hard to grasp: and I think it is intended to be a wild nightmare opera, but as far as I can see it is good, and new.[154]

Vaughan Williams was certainly a close and respected colleague; his views on music being a part of everyday life for everyone echoed Dent's own,[155] his mystical atheism also appealing. Cambridge provided exactly the right atmosphere and platform for such new music, beside radical ideas about the place of music in society. The Fabian socialists in Cambridge, young and old – Dalton, Rupert Brooke, their Olivier friends – had always promoted wider access to the high arts, with grassroots education to support that. So before the performance, Dent spent the morning at the George Darwins' house, Newnham Grange, helping Vaughan Williams correct all the parts over a hasty lunch, excited as the music unfolded itself.

The performance itself was another Cambridge landmark, the young cast throwing themselves into the broad comic scenes, fuelled by the wonderful music. The march of the kitchen utensils evoked laughter and applause; the rousing finale had everyone stamping their feet. Dent sat in his reviewer's seat in the New Theatre, almost in tears: 'The music is really great, and I was quite moved by it ... The harsh effects melt completely in the orchestra'. On the second night, word had got out: 'the audience was livelier and stamped their feet to the dances'.

Thanks to Dent, the *Cambridge Review* gave the occasion an unprecedented amount of space, with three reviews: Adam Sidgwick and Rupert (anonymously) on the drama, and Dent on the music. Dent's piece is rather more than a simple half column review; it is a credo, an exploration of what he felt contemporary English music should be, original and refreshingly free of any 'old-fashioned' references.

> Dr Vaughan Williams' consecutive fifths and sevenths have no real French spirit. Nor is this because the main tunes of the work are obviously based upon English folksongs ... Everybody uses folksongs nowadays; but nobody has come as near digesting them as Dr Vaughan Williams ... It is the stronger force at the back, that

152 Diary 22/11/1909.

153 Diary 25/11/1909.

154 CC 04/11/1909.

155 Vaughan Williams was on the Musical Board for years. As President of the International Society for Contemporary Music, Dent would oversee Vaughan Williams' music being programmed as part of five of the annual festivals.

> guiding power which is the essential thing in all music, that makes The Wasps a land-mark in our musical history.[156]

Dent had also spotted how the music worked with the text: 'The really new feature of The Wasps is that Dr Vaughan Williams has made it into an opera'. In his diary he gleefully pounced upon the ignorance of the mainstream critics:

> Maitland in the Times made an absurd mistake: after abusing VW for writing in the modern Parisian Style, he complimented him on the excellent joke of introducing a quotation from Richard Strauss in the Parabasis – the quotation in question being the first subject of 'L'Après-midi d'un faun'![157]

The attendant parties went on for days afterwards, an explosion of optimistic exuberance, at Steuart's rooms, at the Darwins' with bull-roarers in the garden, at Panton Street. Everyone who had seen it was full of *The Wasps;* fired by its success, the MDS committee fell to discussing what to do next. Dent had always liked and respected Vaughan Williams, but this music had revealed him on a different plane entirely, and now Dent could see that making a place for this radical scholar, composer, musician and philosopher in Cambridge was a real step towards realising his nebulous plans for Music beyond the current Faculty limitations.

First, Dent wanted to put on a chamber concert entirely devoted to Vaughan Williams' music; *The Wasps* had hooked his Cambridge audience, and a chamber concert was relatively easy to stage. In those days before recordings became the main vehicle for new composers, performance was essential, and Vaughan Williams had endured real problems getting his music an audience. Dent had already steered the CUMC into becoming the vehicle for new and contemporary music as much as classical chamber music, a place where Browne, Gibbs, Clive and the others had their new pieces played and discussed, but this was another step entirely.

From late December onwards, they talked and wrote at length on the subject, Dent visiting Vaughan Williams at Cheyne Walk on the 5 January and being shown 'the Shropshire Lad songs and the new 4tet, certainly rather startling'. His initial response shows the diffidence of a genuinely modest man accustomed to adverse criticism:

> Your letter fills me with intense pleasure – coupled with considerable alarm – it is nice of you all to think of such an idea – and it quite overwhelms me – but the idea of a one man show (except of course when the 'one man' gives it himself when there is a kind of 'don't shoot the composer he's doing his best' feeling about it) does alarm me ... Now as regards programme – you say 'of course the quartet' – but I must confess that hardly anyone but me likes it – and I don't want to put off people who were so nice about 'The Wasps' and all you who are (encouraging) this by producing something ... most people (apparently) loathe

156 E.J Dent, 'The Music of the Wasps', CR (2 December 1909); also connected: 'Greek Plays' (12 May 1910); reply to an open letter, 'Music without Tears', from O.L. Richmond (4 November 1910), who had lambasted the music.

157 Diary 27/11/1909.

> ...are you keen on having my new 'Shropshire lad' cycle – which I consider my best recent work.[158]

Dent drew in Denis Browne, already working with Vaughan Williams and Steuart Wilson on lecture–recitals of his music, another struggling composer who would benefit from observing the process.

> I wrote to Vaughan Williams about a chamber concert devoted to his music: and I can't do better than send you his letters. I am writing to Mr Horace Darwin, and shall go round to any likely entertainments that I can find in residence. Of course we must have the new 4tet as it is a challenge to the lukewarm.[159]

They quickly settled on a programme of Vaughan Williams' double-bass Piano Quintet in C minor (1903–05), *On Wenlock Edge* (his setting of Housman's 'A Shropshire Lad' cycle, with tenor and string quartet), and his G minor String Quartet (1908), with a few songs, to be performed at the Guildhall in May, with Gervase Elwes[160] and the Schwiller Quartet. Dent was to run the show, but he was also underwriting the whole thing, putting up 30 pounds of his own.

The wider consequences included a collaborative friendship that lasted a lifetime, with Vaughan Williams a solid, active presence in Cambridge throughout the years up to the Great War, while Dent's real and eloquent appreciation of his music proved important for both of them. That winter Vaughan Williams sent Dent the manuscript scores of the Sea Symphony, with its impressive opening bars, 'I hope my magnum opus – it has taken me about 6 years to do', and his cantata 'Willow Wood', a setting of Rossetti. His first lecture–recital with Browne and Wilson was on 14 February 1910, Dent mortified to discover that the MDS with Reginald Pole had decided to put on *Richard II* that same day. But good will prevailed, and Vaughan Williams managed both, dining with Steuart and Denis, and coming late to *Richard II* in time to hear Dent's arrangements of Purcell.

At the same time Dent was battling to incorporate this new music, his characteristic writing style was developing in these years, mostly in his articles for the *Monthly Musical Record*, provocative by design. Dent was a master of double meanings, yet his message was always clear. The openings of almost any of his articles are classics of their kind, the arguments peppered with contentious, erudite details. To Dent, there was no reason why education should not be entertaining, as these three different examples demonstrate, with a prescient nod to his own future career.

> In the days of classical antiquity, there was little or no distinction between the poet and the musician ... The Greeks could not conceive of a poet who was not a musician; nowadays it is rather the exception than the rule to find a poet who even cares to listen to music.
>
> The tendency to the simplification of rhythm had already set in well before the end of the seventeenth century, through the Ballets, which brought the influence

158 RVW to EJD n.d. (probably mid-December 1909), KCA/EJD/4/456.

159 DB 15/12/1909.

160 VW had agreed with Dent's suggestion that Clive Carey sing, but felt he owed Elwes a favour for singing before 'for practically nothing'.

> of the dance into vocal music ... At the beginning of the seventeenth century, therefore, the typical form for vocal music in England was not the madrigal of Weelkes or Wilbye, but the Ayre of Dowland, Camion and Rosseter.
>
> Of the International Congress there is no need to speak in detail. The deliberations suffered considerably from the attempt to combine a congress of musical savants with a festival on so large a scale ... If friendly co-operation is substituted for mutual jealousy in musical research, we may expect a rapid increase in the output of valuable work.[161]

He loved to shake up the Church Music Committee: 'I scandalized them rather by suggesting that we shd get modern composers to write music for us when we cd find nothing suitable among the old. Allen supported me and the idea was accepted.'[162]

In another shift of emphasis, which shows that they must have discussed it, Hugh Allen persuaded Dent to do a translation of *Fidelio* for Petersfield in April, Dent's first such undertaking, and he found it very hard going, 'owing to the awkward style of German'. But it was something he discovered that he very much wanted to persevere with, and he was far better placed than many to undertake such projects; beside his linguistic facilities, his scholarly approach to the text combining with his love of poetry and appreciation of what constitutes a *singable* libretto. That January 1910, he took the translation with him to Oxford, where he was staying for Allen's 'Bachfest', together with F.B. Ellis and George Butterworth. They were joined by even more Old Etonians, Timmy Jekyll and F.S. Kelly, managing to sing through fifteen Bach cantatas, two–three Palestrina masses and motets, Haydn, Schubert, Parry, Brahms. History does not relate the state of their voices afterwards.

When Dent returned, exhausted, to Cambridge, Magnus Hirschfeld came to stay in Panton Street while in the country to promote his work on sexuality, his visit eventually resulting in the establishment three years later of the British Society for the Study of Sexual Psychology.[163] Although the Wilde trial still resonated, Edward Carpenter[164] in *The Intermediate Sex* had begun to push at the boundaries, living at Millthorpe with another man, George Merrill. His friend E. Bertram Lloyd had met Hirschfeld in Berlin, and, like Dent, was astonished at the apparent openness of his life and research there. But as Dent's diaries amply show, Hirschfeld had begun to set up in Britain the kind of discreet networks he had already started in Germany, to address the needs of desperate men.

At King's, Dent arranged for him to meet with Lowes Dickinson, whose work he had admired, and Maynard Keynes, largely because they both spoke German, but more for discussion of topics close to all of them.[165] The following day he invited some

161 'Milton and Music', MMR, vol. 38 (August 1908), pp. 170–72. 'The Haydn Centenary at Vienna' MMR, vol. 39 (July 1909), pp. 148–50.

162 Diary 14/12/1909.

163 See Sheila Rowbotham, *Edward Carpenter: A Life of Liberty and Love* (London, 2008), pp. 332ff.

164 Edward Carpenter (1844–1929), poet, philosopher, writer, pioneer of gay rights. His partner George Merrill famously inspired E.M. Forster to write his novel of homosexual love, *Maurice*.

165 His visit escaped the notice of many scholars. Dent certainly kept it very quiet.

of the younger generation: Hugh Dalton and Gerald Shove. Ernst Goldschmidt was asked to dinner, a disaster:

> he & Hirschfeld were like two hostile cats: G perched on the end of the sofa, H walking up & down the room talking hard at each other & hating each other more & more. G said afterwards that 'he was a horrid dirty Jew' & H said afterwards that G was a typical Austrian Jew – schnoddrig – a word I don't know the meaning of: but I have always heard it applied to Jews, generally by Jews![166]

Otherwise, Hirschfeld's visit was a success, a real stimulus and focal point for Dent's circles, and in those few days he met a range of Dent's friends. Theo Bartholomew especially took to him and asked him around one evening, and Ted Haynes was very keen to meet him, since reform towards something like the Code Napoléon was one of his pet long-term projects. The ideas for Ted's many later books and pamphlets on social and legal reform,[167] especially on the nature of individual liberty, had some origins in the company he kept in Cambridge and London, especially exotics like Hirschfeld. Hirschfeld's cheerful, boundless curiosity was a source of delight and exhaustion; a Sunday visit to King's College Chapel was punctuated by Hirschfeld abruptly taking from his pocket a copy of *The Sunday Times* and reading it during the service, which, Dent happily recorded, 'scandalized the congregation'.

As one of Hirschfeld's named contacts himself, Dent was often called upon to correspond or talk at length with men in need, an extension of what he was already doing, helping men like Chester Purves to talk 'about his indiscretions'.[168] Chester was one of Dent's inner circle, close to Theo as well, who was making the common mistake of believing himself safe in this close, friendly environment. It wasn't that he behaved badly, but that he was too indiscreet; according to Denis Browne and Hugh Dalton, he had stepped over the extremely fine line between being amusing fodder for local gossip and putting everyone at risk of scandal. Chester took it all with good grace, 'rather frightened'.

After a patchwork Lent term, brightened only by a Drawing Society exhibition, where Gwen Darwin showed 'several good things, including a very original set of woodcuts'[169] next to some miniatures and 'beautiful' cat studies by Kate Cockerell, Dent escaped to Italy, meeting up with Nicholas Gatty for another walking tour in the Tuscan hills between Bologna and Florence, looking at the frescoed churches of Piero della Francesca. For once, Dent makes no complaints about anything, except having to share a bed in Montagione, 'not very comfortable'. In Florence, Gatty

166 Diary 29/01/1910. Goldschmidt, though an excellent companion, intellectually and socially, was a terrible snob; he had also sneered at another of Dent's new acquaintances, a diffident Trinity librarian, A.C. Landsberg.

167 *The Decline of Liberty in England, The Case for Liberty, et al.* Some have recently been reprinted.

168 Patrick John Chester Jervis Laidlaw Purves (1890–1960), official in the secretariat of the League of Nations.

169 According to her biographer, Gwen Darwin's (later Raverat) first woodcut was to be the tickets for *The Knight of the Burning Pestle,* so perhaps she had already done them for the aborted production that previous summer. Frances Spalding, *Gwen Raverat: Friends, Family and Affections* (London, 2004), p. 218.

introduced Dent to Geoffrey Scott[170] who, together with Cecil Pinsent,[171] was setting up as an architect, spending a lot of time at the Berensons' up at I Tatti, designing the gardens for Mary Berenson. While Gatty was being whisked off up to view the growing splendours of I Tatti, Dent took in a production of *La Vestale* at the Teatro Verdi, which he left after the first act, finding it 'dull, vulgar & noisy in its exaggeratedly clerical manners … all the faults of Aïda & none of its merits'.[172] But he did see his usual friends, preferring them to the 'colossally vulgar' Americans at I Tatti.

Back in Cambridge, Dent's main preoccupations were performances, Vaughan Williams' chamber concert in the first week in May, besides the big CUMS Busoni concert in June. But something even more distracting came up, as Dent expressed it in his diary: 'Lawrence & his father called for a moment in the morning with a Miss Courvoisier from Neuchatel … L bringing also a terrific amount of mud on to the carpets'.[173] 'Mud on the carpets' was Dentspeak for his revulsion at his closest friend's engagement, especially coming as it did after von Kardorff's to Ina Bruhn. Lawrence had tried to introduce Dent gently to the idea in April, without actually coming clean, but not until September, while Dent was away in Rome, did he dare to mention their actual engagement. Lawrence's instincts were right; Dent ripped off such a letter[174] that he immediately regretted it, and quickly wrote again in a far more conciliatory mode:

> I am sorry to have written so brusquely. Your news startled me so much that I thought at first it was meant for a joke … Don't be worried: confirmed misogynists are apt to forget that other people are not like themselves. I always thought you were the sort of person of whom women & married men wd say 'he ought to get married – it wd be very good for his character' – while I felt that you were very wise to do nothing of the sort … You are not the first of my friends to get married: and as I say I hope that Mrs Lawrence will belong to the category of the Mrs Bargers, Mrs Haynes' and Mrs Cornfords.[175]

For some years, the flow of Dent's letters to Lawrence slowed down and almost stopped altogether, but the friendship survived, and Lawrence's family became Dent's surrogate family; Lawrence's doctor son treated Dent in his final illness.

But now, after a desultory CUMS committee meeting to discuss the May Week arrangements and a very unpromising CUMS orchestra rehearsal, with 'few people' turning up, the Vaughan Williams concert on 8 May was a 'great success'.

170 Geoffrey Scott (1884–1929), actor, novelist, author of *The Architecture of Humanism*. He was very good-looking, was fancied by Mary Berenson and Edith Wharton, had affairs with both men and women, including Vita Sackville-West. He later married Lady Sybil Cutting, who later married yet another unlikely husband candidate, Percy Lubbock.

171 Cecil Ross Pinsent (1884–1963).

172 Diary 27/03/1910.

173 Diary 24/04/1910.

174 It has not survived; Lawrence must have torn it up.

175 LH 11/09/1910.

The audience was musical enough to hear the 5tet through & the 4tet without applauding between the movements ... and young enough to applaud & shout lustily for VW. We were all very pleased both with the music & its reception: I am more than ever convinced that VW is our coming great composer, and I have seldom enjoyed a concert so much.[176]

They had taken over 30 pounds in tickets, but still lost about 11 pounds, Dent reckoned, having shouldered the loss himself. Beside producing the kind of music Dent had been fantasising about, Vaughan Williams provided Dent a lifelong collaborative friendship with an equal. In another piece of serendipity days later, Dent went to the New Theatre to see a series of short plays by then barely-known Irish playwrights, Lady Gregory, William Butler Yeats and John M. Synge. *Riders to the Sea*[177] stunned him. He sat there and nearly wept, overwhelmed by the beauty of the language and the simplicity of the tragedy. Synge's fascination for the natural rhythms of the vernacular and his ability to use the expressive and musical qualities of dialogue was a revelation which Dent passed on to Vaughan Williams, who later set *Riders to the Sea* as an opera.

In mid-May his brother Frank came up for a visit to Cambridge, and Dent introduced him to the Fletchers, and to Jane Harrison, in the hope that Frank's daughter Molly might think about going to Newnham College. Dent was glad to see him and allowed himself to be taken around the less familiar parts of the university that Frank was keen to see, the 'new agricultural building & museum of science'. There was a MDS committee meeting on 13 May in Steuart Wilson's rooms, but the next fruitful idea would come during a dinner at Dent's on 31 May, when the Cornfords and Denis Robertson were joined by Chester Purves, Steuart Wilson and Pole, and 'hit on the idea of acting *Faustus* again for the German students'. Almost immediately the idea became a source of friction, with Pole demanding the part of Faustus instead of Cornford, and a whole new style of MDS revealing itself which made Dent uneasy.

Cosmo made the sage remark that Steuart was content to remodel orthodoxy to his own ideas, while Rupert wanted to make everything new. I am regretting the decline of the Rupert movement, and the rise of a new one around Steuart wch I fear has resemblances to the old type of M. James' days: a 'pink' type, not a 'blue' one, to use Mrs Cornford's expression.[178]

But that June Dent was constantly exploring other musical avenues: 'In the morning I went to the Psychological Laboratory & was tested by Myers with tuning forks – as to associations, ideas suggested by sounds, relative pleasantness or unpleasantness of intervals.'[179] In between such local diversions, and ongoing MDS disputes, Dent went across to Oxford for *Fidelio*,'astonishingly good – Not one of the

176 Diary 08/05/1910.

177 J.M. Synge (1871–1909). *Riders to the Sea* had been written in 1903.

178 Diary 22/06/1910.

179 Diary 08/06/1910. Dent continued to work with Myers, experimenting with the effects of sounds; Myers' work later re-emerged in WWI, on the after-effects on soldiers.

singers had ever sung opera before, but the performance went with spirit, and was always opera.'[180] Then *Pelléas et Mélisande* in London: 'I saw various friends in the amphitheatre – Lloyd, Colin Taylor, Ingram, Adrian Stephen, Trend, VW, Ellis … I thought the opera disappointing at a first hearing'. The very next day the Busonis arrived, and Dent was plunged again into rehearsals for the ambitious May Week CUMS concert of Beethoven, Wagner, Schumann and Busoni. He found little pleasure in it: from his sketchy diary entries, it would appear that the orchestra was underprepared, the chorus ditto, and there really was nothing to say:

> The chorus was very feeble. Busoni played the Beethoven E♭. Gray was very nervous & useless – so that I made a mess of the coda to the rondo … 'well, it would be very difficult if any of us played all the notes' said the canon [Pemberton].

After this, casually, Dent remarked: 'I went to tea with the Woods & discussed Zauberflöte: CW jumped at the idea of conducting it – so I think we shall see it through.'[181]

This monumental decision had not come out of nowhere, but out of recent events and a lot of peripheral ruminating around the subject: the current MDS state of excited flux, music and words working together, out of *The Wasps* and *Fidelio*, conversations with Vaughan Williams and Busoni, Beecham's 'clumsy' Mozart productions in London and Dent's growing vision of what a university could contribute to music and theatre, a marriage of the scholarly and the performative. It was driven by Dent's impulse to draw together all the different elements of his life and focus his frustrated energy on a project of importance, something only he could recognise as such. Dent had found his future.

[180] Diary 09/06/1910.

[181] Diary 19/06/1910.

CHAPTER 7

The Impresario 1910–1914

The voice of music will not fail us
When sorrow's waters rise in flood.

Cambridge in all its artistic pursuits ought to aim not at imitation London, but at presenting just those things wch London can't present.[1]

When shall we see you here? Rootham & I have had much talk over Z. We found we had to make up our minds at once about the Theatre, and it has been reserved for us for November 30 to Dec 2. 1911.[2]

1910–1911

With the big decision to produce *The Magic Flute*, opera became the focus and unifying element of Dent's life, this amateur Cambridge production only the first skirmish in his lifelong battle for opera in Britain. Producing an opera to his exacting standards would be a statement of defiance to the musical establishment, and in choosing Mozart's last opera, Dent was being even more radical in his approach. He knew that for an ambitious scholar to take what appeared to be such a massive diversion from his scholarly pursuits might appear academic suicide, especially when he ought to have been working on his doctorate. Colleagues like Edward Naylor were highly critical of the whole enterprise. But Dent was deliberately taking a course very different from the usual routes, and far more important in the long run than another *Hellas* would have been. In his teaching, increasingly in his writing, and now through performance and production, Dent was finding a working vehicle for his high standards of scholarship.

In 1910 'most of Mozart's operas were almost completely unknown in this country';[3] Mozart was somewhat in the shadow of late nineteenth-century opera,[4] while

1 CC 21/10/1910.

2 *Ibid.*

3 E.J. Dent, *Mozart's Operas: A Critical Study* (2nd edn, Oxford, 1947), Preface to the Second Edition, p. ix.

4 Dent's friends Oscar Browning and George Bernard Shaw were both notable exceptions. Dent later wrote an appreciation of Shaw's musical criticism, 'Corno di Bassetto': 'he was well in advance of his time, for hardly anyone in England, at that date, understood the ethical significance of *Die Zauberflöte*'. In Hugh Taylor, ed., *Edward J. Dent: Selected Essays* (Cambridge, 1979), pp. 248–9.

The Magic Flute was generally held in low esteem. Although *The Marriage of Figaro* and *Don Giovanni* were well established in the repertory – usually in heavily compromised versions – Mozart's other operas were largely ignored. Dent wanted to give Mozart and *The Magic Flute* a leg up into the twentieth century. '*Idomeneo* had never been performed here at all; *Die Entführung* had been revived by Sir Thomas Beecham for a few performances in 1910',[5] *Cosi fan tutte* had one performance in English in 1890, *La clemenza di Tito* abandoned after 1840 as being hopelessly old-fashioned. As for *The Magic Flute*, it had been performed in Italian, German and English, mostly in Italian, the last time in 1892, all in incomplete or otherwise tampered versions. Scholars had already noticed the references to Freemasonry in the libretto,[6] but none of this filtered down into productions, so an apparent lack of coherence coupled with its obvious musical vitality vexed many. C. Ferdinand Pohl in the first edition of Grove's expressed the received view: the 'patchwork' libretto, full of 'contradictions, improbabilities and even vulgarity, is undeniably adapted for the stage'. Or, as Dent put it, 'the libretto of *Die Zauberflöte* has generally been considered to be one of the most absurd specimens of that form of literature in which absurdity is regarded as a matter of course'.[7]

The Magic Flute was probably Dent's favourite opera; he had seen productions of it in Germany and Vienna, and was confident enough that Cambridge could produce a fresh, uncompromised version, faithful to the original but in English. The challenge for Dent himself was to provide a clear vision of the work for everyone involved, singers, musicians, designers and audience; theories discussed with friends like Rasi now put to a practical test. His gamble extended to relations with colleagues: having double-booked Charles Wood and Cyril Rootham to conduct, Dent had decided that he preferred Rootham, more pliable than Wood, a move both calculated and offensive.[8] Wood could barely speak to him for years.

> I can't help laughing at R. and his knowledge … of the Z … do you know he actually admitted (to me, strictly unter vier Augen) that he had never conducted an opera in his life. 'Well Rootham,' I said, 'I may as well tell you that I have never stage-managed one!'[9]

In spite of its shortcomings, Hugh Allen's *Fidelio* in his translation had delighted Dent, while the Oxford *Der Freischütz* in June 1911 only confirmed his resolve, especially seeing how well Allen worked in rehearsal with the young director, William

5 *Ibid.* Dent himself only heard (and played) *Idomeneo* for the first time at the Jenkinsons' in 1911.

6 Dent mentions that Otto Jahn in his monumental study of Mozart had noted a masonic interpretation in 1794, three years after the premiere. Dent, *Mozart's Operas,* p. 223, also J.S. Shedlock, 'Mozart's "Magic Flute"', MMR (July 1909), p. 150.

7 Dent, *Mozart's Operas,* p. 218. Dent had kept this part of his introduction from his booklet written for the 1911 production, *Mozart's Opera The Magic Flute: Its History and Interpretation* (Cambridge, 1911), p. 12.

8 DB 14/07/1910.

9 CC 21/10/1910; 'unter vier Augen': between you and me.

Bridges-Adams.[10] But the *Flute* production was punctuated by Dent's other commitments, his lectures, his writings, and the IMG Congress in London, beside *Faustus* again in August 1910 for a group of visiting German students, then the MDS *Knight of the Burning Pestle* in February 1911, and *Comus* at Southwell, a joint production with Clive, Bridges-Adams and Bob Maltby.[11]

Casting of the parts began in November 1910. Clive found the most difficult casting – the Queen of the Night – a student at the Royal College, Victoria Hopper.[12] Otherwise, it was a point of principle to use local singers: Maisie Fletcher, who had sung in *Rosalys* and at the Jenkinson Mozart evenings, eventually took over as Pamina, her sister Sybil Cropper initially Papagena. With his acting and dancing skills beside his fine voice Clive was an obvious choice for Papageno, and Steuart Wilson made a very handsome Tamino. Even in these early stages, what emerged was a clearer understanding of the opera's dynamics, how the music of the various parts reflected character and Mozart's genius at achieving this, all lacking in most productions Dent had seen.

> R.[ootham] tells me that Hubrecht's voice is too small for Monostatos: but I shd like him to be tried. Monostatos hardly ever takes part in a real ensemble where his voice has to balance others in the first terzetto, more in the last scene of all with the Q & ladies: not at all in the 1st finale, where he generally has a grotesque parody of the beautiful phrases of Tamino & Pamina.[13]

The standard English translation was that of Lady Macfarren, who had chosen to use rhyming couplets in flowery Victorian language difficult to get the tongue around, often masking the original meaning;[14] Dent wanted a completely new translation, which could easily be sung while being clear to the audience, with meaning and style for a twentieth-century audience unfamiliar with the original work. But for most of January 1911, Dent was away in Berlin at the request of Johannes Wolf to give a lecture–recital to the Berlin branch of the IMG, on Orazio Vecchio's early oddity, the *Amfiparnaso*: 'a series of fourteen madrigals illustrating the Comedy of

10 William Bridges-Adams (1889-1965), part of Dent's wider 'gang', worked with Clive Carey and Denis Browne before the war and later became a well-known director for D'Oyly Carte and for the Royal Shakespeare Company.

11 Charles Robert Crighton 'Bob' Maltby (1891–1916), was at Oxford with Bridges-Adams and loved dance. A photograph in Carey, *Duet for Two Voices*, p. 75, shows Bob dancing in Denis Browne's *The Spirit of the Future.*

12 She later changed her name to 'Sylvia Nelis' and performed the same role for Beecham's later production in 1915. See below. Another RCM student, Hilda Marchand, was Papagena.

13 CC 30/04/1911.

14 For example, in the standard editions of Mozart she did for Novello's, Donna Elvira's vengeful 'Ah che mi dici mai quel barbaro dov'e' (Who can tell me where the rotten villain is) comes out as 'Where shall I find a token to guide my steps to thee / My heart is nearly broken, the world is dark to me', which rather understates the case. Cherubino's 'Non si cosa fa cosi faccio' come out as 'And I blush when I meet any maiden'. Dent changed it to 'At the sight of a woman I tremble'.

Masks'.[15] Serious work on the translation only began when he returned in February, but the German immersion actually helped him with the idiom, while rehearsals for the Vecchio performance underlined historical struggles to create dramatic music:

> it is difficult to translate bad Italian into anything but worse English, and the result has been that opera in English is to most people a lamentably ridiculous affair … The first duty of a translator is to make the story of the opera clear, and to write words simple enough to be intelligible when sung.[16]
>
> The first librettos were written by real poets; in fact the words were often better than the music … It was not until Verdi – from about 1840 onwards – that the word libretto became a byword for nonsense and doggerel.[17]

Dent sent chunks of the translation to Clive: 'Of course the most essential test of a translation is to sing it through', he urged Clive. 'You will find it a long way from the German in places, but I believe I have brought out the really vital points, and have occasionally put in a few that were not there.'[18] He had the parts privately printed for the cast and musicians to try out, and by 14 April had sent Clive the entire draft translation; reassembling the libretto had brought up some dramatic conundrums as well.

> It seemed a favourable point at wch to bring out the symbolism. Also, do you approve of the symbolism in the fire & water scene – 'passion's fires' & 'sorrow's waters'? That is all me, you know! I shd be grateful for criticism on the words from a literary point of view, as this instalment contains much that is important.[19]

This is the point in Act II where Pamina and Tamino must walk through fire and water:

> Then take the magic flute and play;
> Its note gives light on danger's way.
> That flute from mystic tree was carven,
> And round it mighty spells were woven;
> The sacred bough my father tore,
> Nor fear'd the lightnings' thunderous roar.
> Then take the magic flute and play;
> Its note gives light on danger's way.

Dent quickly discovered that he was going to have to research Freemasonry. The symbolism which had vexed so many commentators, especially the masonic symbolism at the heart of Act II, had to be clearly understood and reflected in the language, not least because the staging and costume were also affected. What he found piqued his curiosity, 'some very queer things', he wrote to Clive:

15 Dent, *Opera*, pp. 30–31.

16 E.J. Dent, *The Magic Flute* (Oxford, 1937, rev. 1959), Preface, p. vi.

17 *Ibid.*, p. v.

18 CC 15/02/1911.

19 CC 14/04/1911.

> among others that the Duet of the Armed Men is practically word for word the same as the inscription on the Sarcophagus of Hiram the builder of Solomon's temple, wch is apparently still part of Masonic ritual, or was in Germany in 1836: and that there is a definite reason for the men being in armour. I fear that I shall have to revise the translation again, and that it may be desirable to consider certain details very carefully with regard to stage-management.[20]

The process itself was expanding Dent's own understanding, what he had been doing in his lectures but on a bigger scale, while he felt himself becoming a Sarastro figure behind the scenes, directing and guiding. His well-received but unorthodox lectures on *Don Giovanni* together with the *Flute* material were developing into a general work on Mozart's operas, explorations of the 'dramma giocoso' revealing aspects of the opera most often lost in current productions. 'I played & sang half of Don G yesterday with them & drove them wild with ribald delight, especially on "Madamina"'.[21] Shedlock's short, apposite piece in the *Monthly Music Record* on the *Magic Flute* had supported Dent's views but made no real mark;[22] production was an active, public statement.

As Dent later acknowledged,[23] Thomas Beecham's hugely successful Mozart operas that summer at His Majesty's Theatre showed that there was certainly public appetite for a Mozart revival, but Beecham's vision was very different from Dent's. At outrageous expense, backed by his rich father Joseph and the family pill business,[24] he had exploded onto the staid British concert and opera scene, grandly hiring Covent Garden the winter of 1910, employing his own hand-picked orchestra and soloists, putting on an extraordinary programme of the new, the unfamiliar and the British.[25] Their ambition was the establishment of a national opera house financed by Joseph, with Thomas in charge of the music and a permanent company and orchestra.[26] Both Beechams brought to the established musical world a novel edge of commercial PR very different from the gentlemanly world of Edwardian classical concerts, and the heavily subsidised Beecham season at Covent Garden, with its wide range of ticket prices, attracted the broader audience base both Beecham and Dent separately agreed was necessary for any 'national' opera.

But Beecham's prime interest was in conducting, not scholarship or production, and he wanted to run his own show. They had met in Berlin in 1907, through Dent's friends the Certanis, and again in 1909 at Mrs Bax's Hampstead soirée to

20 CC 25/04/1911.

21 CC 23/02/1909.

22 Shedlock, 'Mozart's "Magic Flute"'.

23 'Music in Berlin', MMR (February 1911), p. 1.

24 'Beecham's Powders' are still on sale, although not in the original formula of powdered aloes, soap and ginger.

25 The first performance in England of Strauss's *Salome*, Delius' *A Village Romeo and Juliet*, Debussy's *L'enfant prodigue*, together with *Carmen* and *Hansel and Gretel* in English, *Tristan und Isolde* and new productions of Ethel Smyth's *The Wreckers* and Sullivan's *Ivanhoe*.

26 John Lucas, *Thomas Beecham: An Obsession with Music* (Woodbridge, 2008), pp. 48, 55.

hear young Arnold's music.[27] Only three years apart in age, both with musical gifts recognised from an early age, both were fired with confidence in these talents and a love of music, and engaged in lifelong campaigns to lift musical standards. Other traits militated against any rapport: sexuality, and – more importantly – class. Joseph Beecham's ambition was to establish Thomas firmly in the upper classes of society, while Dent's intimidating Old Etonian self-assurance was entirely natural. Both had egos which drove their need to lead, Beecham from the podium, Dent from behind the scenes, and made them contemptuous of dissent. While Dent was building up grassroots musical standards gradually through education and performance, Beecham cherry-picked his excellent musicians, making it clear what was expected of them and for which they would be exceptionally well paid. Both saw themselves as working to make things better, and both had benefited from continental travels; from the way he dug up recherché pieces to perform, it is clear that Beecham possessed good scholarly instincts and abilities.[28] He championed new music, Frederick Delius and Ethel Smyth; as Dent acknowledged, 'the enthusiastic recognition accorded to Delius shortly before his death was almost entirely due to the energies of Beecham'.[29] But where Beecham was arrogant in a dictatorial, occasionally highly entertaining way ('gentlemen, do your *worst!*'), Dent's arrogance was subdued and mostly channelled into his subtle diplomatic methods, founded on a natural *noblesse oblige.* Dent found Beecham too unpredictable. His writing on Beecham – and there is a lot – is often particularly serpentine, but he gives Beecham credit for keeping opera alive:

> It was entirely owing to Beecham that opera was carried on at all during the four years of the war; and as most foreigners had left the country, the operas had to be in English. The result was that the public began to become much more 'opera-conscious' than it had ever been before, and it also got into the habit of regarding English as the natural language for opera.[30]

Eventually the two egos clashed, with an animosity which did not help the common cause.

In June 1910, on the point of deciding to produce the *Flute,* Dent had gone to Beecham's performances of *Die Entführung, The Marriage of Figaro* and *Cosi fan tutte,* finding the first 'a bit rough & rather odd' and the second 'a pleasant performance on the whole', but which demonstrated what he felt to be most at fault in current approaches to production, a sloppy, high-handed attitude to the integrity of the opera, with bits from other works stuck in. 'The orchestra was too heavy – & the sforzandos quite painful – Beecham cut a lot of Acts III & IV, and instead played a long selection from a divertimento with a minuet for 4 horns'.[31]

27 LH 12/03/1909. Beecham premiered one of Bax's pieces that April.

28 Lucas, *Thomas Beecham,* p. 28.

29 Dent, *Opera,* pp. 160–61.

30 *Ibid,* p. 161.

31 *Ibid.*

Each in his different way was addressing an artistic issue still not entirely resolved today, the different problems for both English opera and opera in English, then paradoxically connected: 'whereas the French, German and Italian singers all normally appeared in routine opera in their own countries', Dent wrote later, 'the English and Americans had no such advantages ... There was no permanent opera in English in any country'.[32] In *The Rise of English Opera*, Eric Walter White notes around two hundred first performances of English opera during the nineteenth century:[33]

> England's case is similar to that of many countries; there was a fair amount of operatic activity, and more native effort than is commonly supposed, but, if we except Sullivan and his comic operas, no talent comparable with the best in the international scene.[34]

That there should be an opera house of national status and importance was not in doubt: the British returning from the opera houses of Germany and Italy always felt the lack, apart from Covent Garden, and there had been a number of attempts to address this.[35] But Covent Garden's brief was to perform operas in the original languages, and its aim to attract audiences who weren't too bothered by their own linguistic deficiencies; listening to Italian or German was part of the appeal to those who had paid rather a lot for their seats and for whom the occasion was more social than musical. It remained the main opera house in this country, where no expense was spared to attract the best foreign singers and conductors, while lavish costumes and sets fed the simple expectations of most of the well-heeled audience: 'frankly exotic, a flower carefully nurtured to capture the fancy of a few rich people ... it were idle to pretend that Covent Garden is primarily concerned with opera as an art. The audience demands first-rate singers, and cares very little what they sing'.[36] While in 1912 the secretary to the Covent Garden Syndicate stated that he 'could point out with pardonable pride that Covent Garden is practically the only Opera House in Europe that pays its way unaided and unsubsidised',[37] in 1940 Dent could still comment that 'the history of opera in England ... is a record of dogged perseverance on the part of a few enthusiasts, amateurs and visionaries.'[38]

Since the eighteenth century the British had been in the habit of importing their musicians and their music, mostly from Italy and Germany; only in the late nineteenth century did the British really begin to train home-grown musicians in purpose-built academies.[39] In Italy, Dent himself had noted the popularity of opera even

32 Dent, *Opera*, p. 168.

33 In Leslie Orrey and Rodney Milnes, *Opera, A Concise History* (London, 1987), p. 171.

34 *Ibid.*

35 From Mapleson's 'National Opera House' c.1876 to Oscar Hammerstein's 'London Opera House' c.1911: Scholes, *The Mirror of Music*, vol. 1, pp. 262–4.

36 Francis Toye, 'Opera in England', *The English Review* (December 1910), p. 159.

37 Scholes, *The Mirror of Music*, vol. 1, p. 11.

38 Dent, *Opera*, pp. 14, 166.

39 The most notable surviving ones are the Royal Academy of Music (1822), Trinity College of Music (1874), Guildhall School of Music (1880), Royal College of Music (1882), Royal

in the smallest towns, so clearly dramatised in Forster's *Where Angels Fear to Tread*. He always took the cheapest seats at the opera, partly to sit among the grassroots music-lovers and observe their response. Why did Britain lack such grassroots? Bernard Shaw raised the question publicly in 1907, while for years Stanford had been agitating for music and opera to be more like the German example, where every town of any size had a thriving opera house, more than four dozen around the country. Stanford continued to compose his 'English operas', but many received their premieres in Germany.

Opera was on a number of contemporary agendas, for a variety of reasons. The Fabians of Dent's day, who included Bernard Shaw, Rupert Brooke and Hugh Dalton, concerned themselves with education as a social leveller. Dent's involvement with the Day Training College, like Forster's at the Working Men's College, arose out of a desire to address the needs of the culturally destitute, give them a helping hand out of mental poverty, through education; inspiring a love of the subject was not an optional extra, but the whole point of the exercise. An educated and demanding audience would lift the standards of performance, creating new standards of excellence, and his experience in these years only fed this belief, the first barrier overcome by workable translation into clear, singable English.

Within the next ten years both Beecham and Dent became involved with another, rather more modest venture at the Royal Victoria Coffee and Music Hall. Emma Cons, and from 1897 her niece Lilian Baylis, were social reformers who believed in trying to raise the tone of a neighbourhood – 'unwashed, sodden, unkempt, reckless humanity' – to one where entertainment was on offer cheaply, where a certain standard of behaviour was expected, laced with temperance meetings. From 1889, there were 'regular fortnightly presentations of opera sung in English'.[40] Money was always tight, and routine altercations with the regulating authorities made life precarious, but owing to the energy and determination of Miss Cons, it throve. After the Great War, this shaky, ramshackle temperance venture evolved into the Old Vic and Sadler's Wells, and eventually into the National Theatre and the English National Opera. But the ground for all this was being prepared in that prewar period, first by Beecham in London and later in Cambridge, where instead of composing one, Dent was about to direct an opera.

Although Dent's focus throughout most of 1910–11 was on the ever-evolving *Flute* production, the rest of his diary was heaving with other activities and little trace of the disgruntlement of the previous year. His Berlin trip in January 1911 to lecture the German branch of the IMG on the *Amfiparnaso* was a major event in the style of its time, with live musical examples involving a lot of rehearsal with full chorus and orchestra; the invitation in itself a reminder of Dent's international reputation, especially in Germany, the centre of *Musikwissenschaft*. There was no one comparable in England who possessed the combination of social and linguistic skills and academic standing. But Dent had been neglecting the *Amfiparnaso* recently; he only began writing up his lecture the day after he arrived, having planned other distractions,

Scottish Academy of Music (1890), Royal Manchester College of Music (1893).

40 Susie Gilbert, *Opera for Everybody* (London, 2009), p. 11.

meeting up with Francis Toye and singer Thornely Gibson (Gibby), travelling from England and Switzerland respectively.[41] Now, like Clive and Lawrence, Francis was both close friend and colleague; through his articles in *Vanity Fair* and *The English Review*, he disseminated many of Dent's ideas about opera and opera production, and they even collaborated informally.[42] Although he would be another of Dent's friends who eventually married, Francis was enough like Ted Haynes to go along happily with the homosexual subcultures Dent frequented when abroad. His close friend Marcel Boulestin openly indulged every aspect of his own many-faceted life, writing entertaining novels with gay protagonists (in French) beside serious articles for French magazines, including the *SIM* (the Parisian journal of the Société Internationale de la Musique).

Magnus Hirschfeld, effusively glad to see Dent, invited him to the current sexology lectures, but Dent refused politely, far too preoccupied. Instead, he called on the Friedlaenders, then the Certanis, who immediately put him to work sight-reading Respighi's 'concerto nello stilo antico', then on to Sigmund Klein, then on another plane, dining at the Como with Gibby, whose erstwhile lover Wladimir suddenly turned up, a loose cannon who appears to have needed some 'protection' from shady persons from his past tailing him. Dent loved playing between the different parts of his life, juggling such very different friends as Lance Cherry, on his way out to I Tatti to be secretary to Bernard Berenson, and murky Wladimir, earnest Hirschfeld, and friends like the Certanis and the von Kardorrfs, at their new house, 'all very charming ... Frau von K. much improved by matrimony – I enjoyed it all very much'.[43] In this busy, sociable period he met Eric von Hornbostel and his wife again, 'whom I like very much: they are different to the rest of that set & clever & alive'.[44] Francis was more of the musical companion; invariably one of any party to the theatre or opera, to Bartolini's afterwards, but when the company parted, he more often went home or with Dent while Gibby and Wladimir disappeared into the misty clubs.

Occasionally Dent himself seems to have been fairly enterprising: after tough rehearsals of the *Amfiparnaso*, and even after post-rehearsal suppers at Bartolini's, he would 'stroll' out in the cruising districts around the K'damm and the Tiergarten, in search of 'adventure'. Or to concerts with some demanding programmes – Nikisch conducting Delius and Mozart; Fried conducting Busoni's *Turandot* and Pfitzner's *Die Rose vom Liebesgarten* – or to the theatre.

> I liked B's suite enormously ... barbaric but amazingly clever & witty – everything comes off exactly right ... the most wonderful Italian clarity & logic, with every now & then a sense of real beauty. Pfitzner's stuff was good stage music at times, but very German and ultra romantic ... like a deliberate cari-

41 Dent had lost no time in soliciting Lawrence Haward's new fiancée, the well-connected Miss Courvoisier, to help Gibson in his Swiss career. Typical.

42 LH 08/02/1909. 'Read Francis on Tovey & Holbrooke this next number of Vanity Fair. We wrote the Tovey together – that is, he wrote it, and I touched it up. Holbrooke is his own.'

43 Diary 04/01/1911.

44 Diary 20/01/1911.

> cature of the Ring & the Versuchene Glocke … The audience naturally loved Pfitzner & hated Busoni.[45]

But there were limits:

> We went last night to see Anatol, a series of little plays by Arthur Schnitzler. It was admirably acted, and the plays are very clever and amusing: but it is very Wienerish, and to me incredibly repulsive, not because in one of them a ballet lady gets drunk in a chambre séparé and spits a mouthful of champagne over the shirt front of Anatol, but because the whole thing is nothing but a series of little liasons [sic] with balletgirls and other ladies of that style, rather as if it was the only thing to live for.[46]

It wasn't the fact of such plays being produced – Dent would never advocate censorship – but that behind the sexual daring the dramatisation celebrated an emptiness of mind and spirit which Dent loathed. Nevertheless, his curiosity on the subject was boundless; one evening he bumped into his artist friend Höxter,[47] who knew all the more louche places, and the next night allowed himself to be taken to the 'Nollendorf Bou … a hideously vulgar place'.[48] 'I spent the rest of the evening strolling but had no adventures'.

The lecture–performance of the *Amfiparnaso* was practically given a back seat, even though it had eaten up days of frustrating rehearsals, with Dent recopying parts, even standing in for conductor Hugo Leichtentritt, 'a tiresome little pedant & a bad conductor'. Although it marked Dent's establishment as a recognised expert in the field, the diary entries are curt; he knew his own worth.

> at 8 my lecture, in the alte Banahedheim. It went off very well & there were about 50 people there. The Amfiparnaso was sung very badly, & I think the chorus wd have broken down if I had not been singing alto & other parts from memory where necessary.[49]

'Music is at a low ebb here', he grumbled to Lawrence, which might seem an extraordinary remark given the sheer amount on offer.[50] 'The opera is very bad', he wrote to Denis: 'They have nothing to call a repertoire, & they never bring out anything new. If I was in Germany for the first time I doubt I shd be enraptured … The most attractive item is the marionette theatre from Munich, wch does old German

45 Diary 09/01/1911.

46 LH 06/01/1911; diary 05/01/1911.

47 Some of Höxter's drawings of productions have turned up among Dent's papers in CUL. Add MS 9197.

48 Diary 20/01/1911.

49 Diary 20/01/1911.

50 Besides the afore-mentioned events: a Dalcroze concert at the Hochschule 'dull'; at Adela Maddison's where Theodor Byard sang 'dull' songs by Strauss and Eric Wolff; Wühlner's Schubert recital at the Philharmonic only confirmed his dislike of the singer and what Dent called his lack of technique and his Germanic over-sensibility; Shakespeare in German at the Deutsches Theater, with lavish costumes by Luca Signorelli.

absurdities, and little operas.'[51] If judged by quantity, Dent wrote in his *Monthly Musical Record* article a few weeks later,[52] Berlin would be the top musical city in Europe, but the quality of all this 'artistic output' was inferior: Berlin 'has got into the habit of taking music for granted'. He goes on to criticise the architecture of the opera house in Unter den Linden, the poor quality of its singers, except for Hempel, and the conservative nature of a repertoire that 'sticks to the conventional classics'. Even the Komische Oper was 'at the end of its brilliant career … The forward movement, such as it is, is best represented by the "Gesellschaft der Musikfreunde", now in the fourth year of its existence', putting on Busoni and Pfitzner, the latter yearning after the past:

> romantic, not because romanticism is in the air, but because he has heard "Der Ring des Nibelungen", has read Hauptmann, and seen Böcklin's pictures … But Pfitzner seems to be dimly feeling for something, always hoping that it may come right eventually, never clear as to how it may be made to come right.[53]

This opinion reflects a personal checklist of what Dent was formulating as a standard for opera and music; at the top was his abhorrence of the '*reverence*' he saw for standard repertoire, a complacent attitude which effectively blocked new productions and thinking. When at last he saw his vehicle, as he did ten years later at the Old Vic, he was ready to bring this knowledge into play. Even the marionette theatre he saw then and at other times featured in years to come as a means for innovative production.

❧ ❧ ❧

Back in Cambridge, when casting was completed, Dent went to work on a second phase of *Flute* rehearsals throughout February, at the same time working on his articles for Wolf and the *Monthly Musical Record*, and music for the MDS *Knight of the Burning Pestle*, on the 24th. Another performance of early music, at the Coronet Theatre, only confirmed his current prepossessions:

> The Chaplin 4tet played Gibbons & Dowland in the style of late Beethoven, & Granville Bantock had arranged other pieces for them from the Virg. Bk. transferring literations to the strings the ornaments wch are only suited to the virginals.[54]

Most of the *Flute* rehearsals up to then had been of an exploratory nature, sorting out the dynamics and symbolism, while the short Cambridge terms made it important to get as much as possible done early on. But everyone he knew was being drawn in by Dent's energy and application. Hal Goodhart-Rendel had already made some initial set designs,[55] which Dent took together with his own ideas to Albert

51 DB 05/01/1911.

52 'Music in Berlin', MMR (1 February 1911), pp. 31–2.

53 *Ibid.*

54 Diary 13/02/1911.

55 DB 14/07/1910.

Rothenstein, and later, to Kate Cockerell, who designed the costumes. With his natural flair for design Marcel Boulestin was also consulted,[56] so by April Alwyn Scholfield helped Dent construct a model of the stage set. The only Cambridge friend not involved and not mentioned is Charles Sayle, who was taking the whole thing in bad part.

Dent and Clive rehearsed the principals throughout May, Clive taking over while Dent went down to the IMG conference in London at the end of May.[57]

> The Congress began with 'a symphony of horror & confusion' – 'una Babelle di voci d'ira, horribili parole' – Maclean behaving like a Prussian post office official, and complete confusion.[58]

The plus side was meeting Italian delegate Fausto Torrefranca for the first time,[59] having known his work from the *Rivista Musicale*, and seeing so many familiar foreign colleagues: Wolf, Kretzschmar, Adler, Kinkaldy, and so on. Dent took several of his foreign colleagues, including Torrefranca and the Écorchevilles, along to Rutland Gate, where they were entertained by his sister Catherine, a rare chance for his family to see his work-life. The actual proceedings opened the following day, with a 'fairly good speech' by Arthur Balfour and an evening of British music at the Queen's Hall, 'all of wch I heard for the first time': Vaughan Williams, Stanford and Parry beside Mackenzie's Tam O'Shanter,'which one might call a "Danse Mcabre": a dreadful & ridiculous scene from an Ossianic opera by Corder – a dull symphonic poem … an interminable tedious ditto by Holbrooke'.[60]

But as Vaughan Williams said, the 'old gang' came off very well: 'I was glad to find that several foreigners were impressed most by the Parry' and he enjoyed the chance to chat with Vaughan Williams and Donald Tovey: 'VW … said I went about like Cupid, introducing people to one another!'[61] It had been a useful break from the *Flute*; Torrefranca and several other delegates including Vaughan Williams came up to Cambridge afterwards, even helping out at some lively CUMS rehearsals. Vaughan Williams was right: Dent's great gift was the ability to bring all these people together, give them a sense of common purpose; twenty years later the revived IMG/IMS met at Cambridge.

Dent still found time to see how Allen's *Freischütz* was coming along in Oxford: 'I thought things rather backward considering the opera comes off next week: but

56 Boulestin later did caricatures of the cast, some of the few records of the production to have survived, reproduced in Carey, *Duet for Two Voices*, p. 63.

57 What is remarkable about the congress from Dent's current point of view is that although it was considered by all his British colleagues to be one of the musical highlights of the year, packed with unfamiliar people and ideas, Dent barely gives it a thought, he is so preoccupied. The MT did a special twelve-page report on it in July.

58 Diary 31/05/1911.

59 Fausto Torrefranca (1883–1955), Italian critic, librarian and 'music historian' equally at home with 18th-century or contemporary music.

60 Diary 30/05/1911.

61 Diary 31/05/1911.

A. likes to have things rushed.'.[62] All the careful 'buttering' of Redfern, the Manager of the New Theatre, seems to have given him a stake in the *Flute*'s success; from 10 to 22 July they were allowed to rehearse in the theatre all day, every day, the last real period of intensive rehearsal for several months.

> The rehearsals have been very strenuous & tiring. R. conducts, Clive directs, & I generally sit in the circle & criticise, or sometimes play, if Gibbs is not there … Steuart is shaky, but works hard. The 3 ladies … are now excellent; the 3 Genii Miss Hare, Miss Lock & Miss Bagnall very good. Hiller will be Sarastro & promises very well indeed. Miss Victoria Hopper (RCM) the queen comes today – a nice little person, who looks very tiny by the side of the 3 ladies, especially as she has a childish face, a stayless figure & very short skirts – but she sings very well indeed.

Everyone Dent knew was dropping in: Hugh Allen, Gibson, a heavily pregnant Kate Cockerell drifting in to observe how her beautiful costumes appeared – 'priestesses with cloaks like trellis, to show colours through'. Dent asked Gwen Darwin, now married to Jacques Raverat, to do a woodcut for 'Z', like the one she had done for *The Knight of the Burning Pestle*. Dent's booklet on *The Magic Flute* was finished finally on 18 August;[63] almost immediately he began work on Purcell's *The Indian Queen* and *The Tempest*.[64] On 2 September he was off to Italy for a complete break, walking around Tuscany and the Emilia Romagna for three weeks, then staying at Rutland Gate to show his sister Catherine the proofs of his *Magic Flute* book: 'she did not care much for it, I think'.

With the New Theatre unavailable that October, they rehearsed all over town, in some rooms over a shop, then a disused garage, or Rootham's rooms in college, not popular with his colleagues at St. John's.[65] King's came to the rescue; having bought up two houses in St Edward's Passage, they let the 'vacant ground floor premises in No 6 … to Dr Rootham and Mr Dent for rehearsals of the 'Magic Flute''.[66] In late October, Clive's father died, after what appears to have been a prolonged illness. Dent wrote a long sympathetic letter, and told him not to worry about his commitments for the *Flute*. By now Dent, Rootham, Scholfield and Clive had learnt to work as a team, so when Dent was lecturing or had to nip over to Hamburg, the rest could carry on.

Dent's 93-page 'booklet', *Mozart's Opera The Magic Flute, its History and Interpretation,* which he hoped would lead to a full study of Mozart's operas, was published by Heffer's in November 1911. Dent's intention was to ensure an informed audience, one primed to appreciate what was being presented, so it covers the history

62 Diary 08/06/1911.

63 Raverat's woodcut appears on the cover.

64 'Purcell: *The Indian Queen*' and 'Purcell: *The Tempest*', Purcell Society edns, vols 19 and 32 (London, 1912).

65 Diary 18/10/1911.

66 It was expensive: 5 pounds, 'together with any rates or other expenses which may arise in respect of their use of the premises'. King's College Estates Register, October, 1911. I am grateful to archivist Dr Patricia McGuire for finding this. The space was later incorporated into the Arts Theatre.

of performance of *Die Zauberflöte*, the background sources used by Schikaneder and Mozart for the libretto, and explores more fully the identity and role of the shadowy Carl Ludwig Giesecke,[67] who had claimed that he and not Emmanuel Schikaneder was the 'real author of *Die Zauberflöte*'. Dent's views on the importance of accurate and sympathetic translations were emphasised, with an impassioned appreciation of what kind of composer Mozart had been, how his apparently simple music was in fact expressing the deepest psychological truths.

> Music has suffered too much at the hands of commentators who try to translate every phrase into words. Poetry and music may once have been one and indivisible; we know that there have been times when poetry has utilized certain technical methods which we now consider to belong to music alone. But the tendency all along has been towards separation, and the reason of this has been that humanity has required the services of music to express not those ideas which other arts can express equally well, but precisely those ideas of which the expression in other media is utterly impossible.[68]
>
> To us who have been brought up on Wagner it may seem strange that, although 'The Magic Flute' was designed to show off scenic effects, there are, nevertheless, hardly any scenic effects in the music … Mozart prefers to concentrate our attention solely on the psychological aspect of the drama.[69]

As one who had himself been 'brought up on Wagner', Dent appreciated what Wagner had brought to opera, the relationship of words and music taken to its limits, the intense drama of the music, Wagner's desire to control all aspects of the production. Wagner was for many British opera-goers the model for all opera, and of all composers the one least likely but in fact most appropriate to be placed in comparison with Mozart, a point that Bernard Shaw had made years before. It was time for a shift in attitude.

The *Cambridge Evening News* asked Dent for notes on his lectures and on *The Magic Flute*, while Dent began putting up posters around town. All this time he was lecturing, taking time to go to productions at the Royal College in London and to see 'the Russians' at Covent Garden,[70] helping Cust with a translation of Alessandro Strozzi's letters, transcribing a Rossi manuscript for Henry Prunières, even taking time to listen to Gibbs's 'astonishingly good'[71] new trio, and travelling to Bilton Grange to hear the Bliss Trio, the three musical brothers who became his pupils.[72]

67 Giesecke, aka Johann Georg Metzler. Dent traced his extraordinary life from his time as an actor/singer/librettist to his later life as a distinguished scientist, Sir Charles Louis Giesecke, working and teaching in Dublin. Dent, *Mozart's Opera The Magic Flute*, pp. 33ff.; Dent, *Mozart's Operas*, pp. 234ff.; diary 29/06/1911, 01/08/1911; 11/08/1911.

68 Dent, *Mozart's Opera The Magic Flute*, p. 92.

69 *Ibid.*, pp. 67–8.

70 The Ballets Russes.

71 Dent often uses the epithet 'astonishing' when describing Gibbs's work. What it means is probably serpentine.

72 Diary 28/10/1911. Arthur was at Pembroke; Kennard a freshman at King's; Howard yet to appear.

Final rehearsals of Act I were on Monday 27 November, with Act II the following night and a further rehearsal on Wednesday, Dent bringing along newly made prop trumpets. On Thursday the scenery was put up for the first time in the theatre. 'It was the first time anybody even the painters had seen the scenery all up together, and we were delighted to find it far better than we had expected'. Ted had come up for a meeting of the Heretics, joined by his wife Oriana several days later for the performance. Dent's sister Catherine came for tea on Friday and immediately set to with gold paint, finishing off the last-minute details of Sarastro's 'golden emblem'. In his terse diary entry Dent says only: 'The performance went without a hitch, and everything was as successful as possible.' They took 171 pounds the first night;[73] half of Cambridge had come out into a filthy cold, foggy night to experience this odd, exciting new production.

The next day, for the matinée, disaster struck. Pamina lost her voice, and her part had to be sung from the wings by Papagena, Miss Marchand, which seems to have worked well, since Pamina and Papagena don't have to sing together.[74] When Dent appeared in front of the curtain to announce the change, a 'well-primed' child in the audience piped up, 'Is *that* the Serpent, Mummy?'.[75] A collective snort erupted, dissolving any residual tension.

It was by most accounts an enormous success. Not only did they make an astonishing 200 pounds profit, but in the audience were people whose opinions mattered. Forster had come up, Lawrence Haward, and Vaughan Williams, staying with his cousins; Robert Bridges, Barclay Squire and Streatfeild; all of Cambridge, including Maynard Keynes and many of the old gang. Percy Lubbock went to every performance, enchanted. He had dragged along A.C. Benson, his old housemaster at Eton, now at Magdalene, who expressed the older generation's view in his diary. 'I can't take the MF seriously,' Benson wrote:

> It was simply a bad comic opera with some pretty songs. The acting was not good, the play is beneath contempt & the singing was feeble … The whole seemed to me to have no relation to life beyond being a silly & pretty diversion … But there is nothing real about it. When I said after one of the interludes that it reminded me of one of my less successful improvisations, Percy looked simply sick.[76]

After the final curtain-call on Saturday, Dent fled home, unable in the euphoric aftermath to cope with what Catherine described as 'a lot of shouting and nonsense'. After *Faustus* in August, he had enjoyed being carried away by the post-production dancing in the streets, but now he was shattered, and with the sudden release of tension, his dream realised, he felt unable to cope with the success, overwhelmed by

73 This is nearly 1500 pounds in modern terms.

74 The problem seems to have been a recurring one, the real differences between amateur and professional voices, and the limitations of the former, not having been given enough consideration.

75 Dent's modus operandi had already by that time often been referred to as 'serpentine'; after this the nickname stuck, confirming what friends and enemies already had agreed upon.

76 A.C. Benson, Diaries, vol. 126, p. 35v. Pepys Library, Magdalene College.

THE MAGIC FLUTE

HINC LVCEM ET POCVLA SACRA

By

WOLFGANG AMADEUS MOZART

Performed in the New Theatre, Cambridge on Friday and Saturday, 1st and 2nd December 1911

THE CHARACTERS

(in the order of their appearance)

Tamino, an Egyptian Prince	Mr J. S. WILSON
Three ladies in attendance on the Queen of Night	Miss LILIAN GREENWOOD Miss M. A. GASKELL Miss SIBYL CROPPER
Papageno, a bird-catcher	Mr CLIVE CAREY
The Queen of Night	Miss VICTORIA HOPPER
Pamina, daughter of the Queen of Night	Mrs W. M. FLETCHER
Monostatos, a Moor in the service of Sarastro	Mr J. B. HUBRECHT
Three Genii	Miss D. C. HARE Miss DOROTHY LOCK Miss HILDA BAGNALL
The Orator of the Temple	Mr MAURICE GRAY
Sarastro, High Priest of Osiris and Isis	Mr H. G. HILLER
Second Priest	Mr C. G. B. STEVENS
Papagena	Miss HILDA MARCHAND
Armed men	Mr H. S. SHARP Mr J. R. EARP
Slaves Mr RUPERT BROOKE Mr J. R. EDEN Mr P. V. KEMP Mr R. M. KIRKPATRICK	Mr R. KNIGHT Mr D. G. ROUQUETTE Mr A. M. SAMSON Mr G. M. HERBERT-SMITH

The scene is laid in Egypt in the neighbourhood of a temple of Osiris and Isis.

FIGURE 7. Programme of *The Magic Flute*, December 1911. Clive Carey as Papageno. By kind permission of the Provost and Fellows of King's College, Cambridge.

what he had taken on and done. Rather than expose anyone to his lack of self-control, he left the party and retreated home. Later that same night he wrote to Clive:

> I expect you were rather annoyed with me for escaping ... at the end of the opera, but I was so tired that I should merely have been quarrelsome and obscene in language when everybody else was excited & happy – and I thought it less offensive to go away ... I am glad I was not there. Don't be offended with me – you sang & acted wonderfully ... I was hardly listening to the opera at all the whole evening except when I had to come in with a beat or something and I hope the whole thing will be a good thing for you with the public & engagements etc – also for the little Hopper & Marchand. As for me I wish I cd go to a hypnotizer & have the whole thing from July 1910 utterly effaced from my brain.[77]

He quickly recovered, but the episode haunted him. His closest friends had noticed the strain he was trying to conceal and kept quiet, knowing how Dent hated any fuss. The following morning Ted prised him from Panton Street and took him off for a brisk walk out to Grantchester to visit Rupert, and between the two Dent began to re-enter his world. 'The walk & Ted's conversation did me a lot of good.' The Horace Darwins asked him to dine that evening, and the company reassured him further. 'VW was at the Darwins, and had much to say about the Z. I was pleased that all my special points really had come home to him.'[78] And even later that evening he went to lose himself at Jack Sheppard's Sunday do, 'there was a great crowd & everybody very cordial to me: I think Z. has really deepened the sense of friendship to me in Maynard & Philip Bainbrigge – wch I value more than all the opinion of operagoers.'

Days later, he wrote a long letter in reply to Clive's careful enquiry about how he was.

> A stage-manager has no business to feel; and in order to do my work accurately I had to switch off the sense of music altogether ... So that when I was tired, I knew it; whereas you other people, who were just as tired as I was, really, did not know it, because you had the music to excite you and keep you going, like alcohol ... I knew I must keep my brain absolutely cool & clear to conduct those choruses.[79]

Then to Lawrence:

> If, as I hope, the whole thing is something remarkable & original as an operatic ensemble, don't worry about giving me any praise for it & put it all down to Clive, because he might get professional engagements as a result of it, and if you filled the whole Times with my praises I shd just go on writing disagreeable & learned pamphlet(s) about obscure Italian composers, with footnotes in bad taste.[80]

He hated that the press appeared to have taken far more notice of his role in it all than of anyone else – 'Mrs Rootham deserved as much as anyone, but what audience

77 CC 02/12/1911.

78 Diary 03/12/1911.

79 CC 07/12/1911.

80 LH 14/11/1911.

in the world wd have shouted for her?' – blaming himself for having deliberately put the book out beforehand as a kind of puff, but how else to lift public awareness for an obscure opera?

The reviews were very good, even those not actually primed by Dent. Marcel Boulestin wrote an amusing, glowing account for the Parisian *SIM* journal, with his own cartoons of the production, while Lawrence Haward in *The Times* managed to puff Dent's Mozart pamphlet.

> The usual dry pomposity of the English translation of old German and Italian operas has been avoided – an extremely difficult thing to do – and Mr. Dent's version breathes all the vitality of the music itself.
>
> Cambridge has shown us before what amateurs can do when skilfully organised and courageously led, but "The Magic Flute" beat all previous records ... It was a triumph of ensemble rather than of individuals.[81]

There were rave reviews for Dent's little booklet:

> The pity of it is that the reviews are practically useless to me. Heffer says that if I had written a novel, reviews like that wd have sold an edition of 5000 in three days. My book being a book about musical history, I may be thankful if I sell 500 in three months ... The enthusiasm of Vaughan Williams, Donald Tovey, Streatfeild, Robert Bridges and Charles Ricketts really does count ... the real results achieved – the best of which to my mind was that a lot of people came to the theatre thinking themselves unmusical & philistine, and found that their ears really were opened for them by Mozart.[82]

Dent never lost sight of what the opera meant to him. It, words and music, became his credo:

> But what is the magic flute itself, that mysterious instrument which makes Mozart almost become Wagner when Pamina describes how her father constructed it? And what is that chime of bells, assigned to Papageno, which has a magical power over everyone who hears them? The original author never tells us, and in my translation I have ventured to suggest my own idea of what they signify. The flute stands for music itself: the bells, for laughter. And after Papageno, in the first act, has used the bells to make authority, in the grotesque shape of Monostatos, thoroughly ridiculous, he turns to Pamina and they sing their duet in praise of those three things that are the most precious of all in human life: Music, friendship, and a sense of humour.[83]

81 *Daily Telegraph*, 4/12/11; *Daily Graphic*, 4/12/11.

82 LH 14/11/1911.

83 From an unpublished MS Dent wrote for a talk on *The Magic Flute*. KCA/EJD/2/3/1.

1912–1914

The years leading up to the Great War were a golden age for the arts: Diaghilev's Ballets Russes, Beecham's opera venture, the Balfour Gardiner[84] concert series throughout the winter of 1912–13, the Bevis Ellis concerts in March and June 1914, plays by Shaw, radical productions by Granville Barker, music unlike anything heard before, and exhibitions at the Alpine Club and Grafton Galleries in which the post-impressionists dazzled and bemused. New reviews – *Rhythm* and *Blue Review* – published new writing; radical new venues like Madame Strindberg's odd, arty 'Cave of the Golden Calf' off Regent Street[85] startled the public. In Cambridge *The Magic Flute* had given everyone involved new self-definition and purpose, and Dent's budding musicians, artists, producers and actors needed employment; for a few fleeting years it seemed that they might be in luck.

Clive was evolving into a talented producer and director who could sing, dance and act, but he still lacked necessary focus and drive, drifting into excellent but transient jobs with the Carl Rosa Opera in Bristol or with Granville Barker in 1912 on *The Winter's Tale*. Having been furnished by Dent with introductions to people in Florence, including Rasi and Gordon Craig, Rupert Brooke began to focus more on literature, working with 'the Tigers' John Middleton Murry and Katherine Mansfield on their short-lived journal, *Rhythm*, establishing his own short-lived journal *Blue Review* in 1913, all the while continuing to publish in Eddie Marsh's *Georgian Poetry*. Denis Browne worked as a tutor, an organist and second music master at Oundle, determined to produce Purcell's *King Arthur* while he was there. In 1912, he went for a few intensive weeks to Busoni in Berlin; in 1913 he was writing serious musical criticism, while composing longer pieces, but with little income. George Mallory was teaching; J.B. Trend was trying out the Civil Service; Alwyn Scholfield became a librarian in Calcutta. Armstrong Gibbs was

84 H. Balfour Gardiner (1877–1950), composer who sponsored orchestral concerts of contemporary British composers at the Queen's Hall in 1912–13, including Bax, Delius, Grainger, Vaughan Williams as well as Frederic Austin, W.H. Bell, Cyril Scott, Hamilton Harty, Holst, Norman O'Neill, *et al.* Scholes, *The Mirror of Music*, vol. 1, p. 483. The 'Bevis Ellis' concerts were similar, both chamber and orchestral: Dent's diary passim.

85 Frida Uhl Strindberg, former wife of the playwright, 'infuriating, sexually ravenous, unreliable with money yet magnificently fearless' founded the Cabaret Theatre Club in Heddon Street, with its basement room 'The Cave of the Golden Calf', decorated by the most avant-garde artists in London, designed by Spencer Gore and including paintings by Wyndham Lewis, sculpture by Eric Gill and Jacob Epstein 'astounded visitors were bombarded by incendiary images, assaulting them on every side'. There appears to have been some scheme to present opera there (Diary 15/08/1912, Cambridge: 'R Gatty to stay, to discuss plans for English opera in connexion with the Cabaret Theatre Club. Mrs Strindberg who runs it – a previous wife of the poet who still bears his name, though she divorced him'). This was why, interestingly, Clive Carey and Dent had been invited to come along. For a time Clive did sing there, but gave it up. Richard Cork, *Wild Thing* (London, 2009), pp. 53ff., Dent's Diary 17/12/1912. 'Clive dined here last night – very contemptuous of the Strindberg. The club seems to have become rather drunken now, and the serious music a great failure.' EJD–DB 13/05/1913. But it did host several attempts at opera.

trying to teach and compose, with mixed success; W.H. Kerridge managed to find a post as organist to the English Church in Paris, where he could keep up with contemporary music. Hugh Dalton tried to enter politics. But these ventures were characterised by their brevity as much as their excellence.

Still, these years were among the happiest and most optimistic of Dent's life. *The Magic Flute* had confirmed self-belief and direction, and harnessing his many cultural networks, Dent felt in a better position to help his old 'gang'. So he gave Denis Browne introductions to Busoni beside solid advice on producing Purcell, e.g., with the 'shivering' chorus, wrote for *Blue Review* and when the Carl Rosa Opera Company asked to use his *Flute* translation for their own revival, Dent recommended that they employ Clive to stage it.[86]

In January 1912, *Mozart's Operas* was taken up by Chatto & Windus, and while Dent was casting about for another project to follow the *Flute*, another offer came in the post:

> Letter from Friedlaender, offering me the post of professor of musical history – to organize a school on a large scale – at some 'midelle western' American University, not named [pencilled in: University of Illinois]. The president thereof, now in Berlin was apparently much impressed with what he heard of me – but I think Kinkeldy wd do better.[87]

Tempting, but having built up so much so recently, Dent preferred to remain in Cambridge, even though his position in the faculty – Stanford, Wood and Naylor, with Capstick teaching acoustics and Rootham teaching everything – was still makeshift, in spite of his devoted pupils and excellent lectures. So he kept his powder dry for months, until the Musical Board meeting in May, when it was abruptly decided to stop the popular public lectures. He dropped his 'little bomb … when they mentioned me, I said I shd not lecture any more, as I cd not be certain whether I shd be in Cambridge.'[88]

> It was received with complete indifference, so I think I was right. I don't mind Stanford & Wood ignoring me as a lecturer: but I now see, as I supposed, that they set no value on the subject, as they made no suggestion that anybody else shd continue it. Myself I am rather relieved to have given it all up. Except that Sedley wishes me to conduct a Brandenburg concerto for him at the Club on March 10, my organizing & conducting days are over & I retire into history & psychology.[89]

Of course he didn't 'retire'; he lectured to the Church Music Society, to Sedley Taylor's CUMC groups, on Purcell to the Ladies Musical Club, his old friends Mrs Fletcher, Miss Luard, who all enjoyed singing the illustrations, and Miss Hare. A new arrival, Ludwig Wittgenstein, 'a curious little man from Vienna', took him 'to the psychophysical laboratory to experiment on me for rhythms.'[90] But 'the Stanford

86 CC 14/01/1912.

87 Diary 18/02/1912.

88 DB 19/05/1912.

89 Diary 18/05/1912.

90 Diary 06/05/1912.

affair'[91] over style and content of lectures continued to fester for months: 'Some casual remark of mine about Stanford & Plunket Greene being very good friends got embroidered – whether by accident or malice I won't inquire.' An example of the trivial but vicious internal politics Dent knew how to sidestep: 'Stanford & I hardly ever see each other, so we may just as well remain good friends', he wrote to Lawrence. 'But there are certain people to whose interest it wd be to set the professor against me.'[92]

Now, performance was becoming far more interesting, his initial thoughts running to Berlioz – 'glorious – but utterly beyond us & hopeless for any small stage' or to Rameau:

> Les Troyens is of course quite out of the question: and I fear Cherubini's Faniska is disappointing. The arias & things are all too long & all in symphonic form. No, Hippolyte & Aricie, or else Castor & Pollux seem to me the most promising things.[93]

Dent loved the exploration of music that had been consigned to historical artefact: opera seria, Rameau's ballet and opera, extravagant Berlioz, the unexpected discovery of Mozart's opera seria, *Idomeneo* at the Jenkinsons', all revived through local amateur music-making. By May, after weeks of research on Mozart and his contemporaries in Vienna, Dent was reading *Idomeneo* more seriously, having sung through most of it with Maisie Fletcher at the Jenkinsons: 'it is just short of a masterpiece'.[94] As he later noted in *Mozart's Operas, Idomeneo* and *La clemenza di Tito* 'were museum pieces the moment that they were put on the stage', the genre itself intended for an aristocratic audience, 'exclusive and expensive',[95] requiring castrato parts, 'but M did rearrange the part for a tenor, later'.[96]

Vaughan Williams, fascinated by Dent's recent work on Purcell and early opera, felt that a production of *The Fairy Queen*, the first in two hundred years, would be a logical step.[97] An informal meeting that December in Francis Toye's rooms in Clement's Inn had Vaughan Williams, Clive, Geoffrey and Francis Toye and René Gatty discussing seriously what directions an 'English' opera might take, including composition and venues. Beside Purcell, 'The Cave of the Golden Calf' was mooted, while Dent had recently been tinkering with the idea of a 'Little Theatre' in Cambridge. Dent's talks with Busoni had always stimulated his ideas in ways as yet unimaginable to the current Cambridge academics; the complex ideas behind any of Busoni's productions, even Busoni's actual turns of phrase, often appear in

91 LH 27/02/1911 (sic: far more likely 1912).

92 *Ibid.*

93 CC 14/01/1912.

94 CC 31/05/1912.

95 Dent, *Mozart's Operas*, pp. 6–7.

96 CC 31/05/1912.

97 There had been 'a series of six performances at Cambridge in 1890'. Scholes, *The Mirror of Music*, vol. 2, p. 773.

Dent's own writings on music. In his later biography of Busoni, Dent quotes a letter in which Busoni defends his approach to the classics:

> You start from false premises in thinking that it is my *intention* to 'modernize' the works. On the contrary, by cleaning them of the dust of tradition, I try to restore their youth, to present them as they sounded to people at the moment when they first sprang from the head and pen of the composer.[98]

This aesthetic is a theme to which Dent often returns, that the aim of scholarship is performance which tests the ideas, and that each performance must present music as if for the first time, what he had felt was lacking in Berlin. That November Dent wrote his first article for the *Cambridge Magazine*, 'Cambridge Music: problems and possibilities'.[99]

The *Cambridge Magazine* was then in its infancy, started up by an idealistic and visionary young man, C.K. Ogden, a recent Classics graduate of Magdalene,[100]and providing a radical, alternative voice, continuing to do so throughout the war years, just what Dent needed. 'Is Cambridge a musical place?' he asks. 'Musical intelligence is a thing quite independent of skill on an instrument, or of such information as can be learnt and written down in examinations.'

> Here in Cambridge we rather pride ourselves on the logical and reasonable understanding which we bring to bear upon most of our intellectual activities. It ought to be our ideal to make Cambridge a really important centre, the most important centre perhaps, of English musical life ... Cambridge music has already suffered only to much from those whose 'reverence' and 'taste' prevents them from exercising any sound and healthy curiosity about the music of to-day. What we want is not reverence but enthusiasm, not taste but intelligence. If the music of the past can be made still to live, still to stir our emotions through its intellectual appeal, it does not matter in what century it was composed. The first reason for performing the music of the past is that we believe it (in certain cases) to be beautiful. ... Our policy should be not that Cambridge should hear, play, or compose as much good music as possible, but that it should <u>live musically</u>.

Beside these ideas, Dent never lost sight of the need for a solid financial platform in order for music to flourish, but felt that if only the right style could be found for Cambridge, a modest but excellent style, it would flourish. He urged the establishment of 'a powerful and wide-reaching central organization'.

> If we could show that our brains were more active, our imaginations more audacious, our enthusiasm for the arts more high-minded, more free from commercial considerations, we might make Cambridge a place of artistic pilgrimage – not a home of lost causes, but a real leading influence in the intellectual life of the country.

98 Dent, *Busoni*, p. 110.

99 CM (November 1912), pp. 107–9.

100 Charles Kay Ogden (1889–1957), polymath, linguistic philosopher and journalist; President of the Heretics. Became a close collaborator and friend.

This was only the first of Dent's penetrating articles on the subject, while his former students followed his example,[101] formulating the vision for music at Cambridge which he would spend the next forty years putting into practice, not only at Cambridge, but as eventual government policy and in the wider, international musical world. Stanford never really forgave him, seeing in the article an attack on himself – which it implicitly was – compounded by the publication of 'an admirable but cruel' caricature by Kapp in the *Cambridge Magazine*, a response to his 'offensive' remarks at a rehearsal of *Oedipus*. Stanford's disaffection – as he saw it – vexed Dent, and numerous diary entries on the subject throughout 1912–13 record many small examples of unease over his teaching: 'Stanford ... has a class of about 10, only half of wch got their stuff looked at'.[102] In December, at the five hundredth concert of CUMS, an almost interminable concert:

> Stanford pushed himself forward with a very egotistic speech ... Steuart's songs were rather spoilt by people tramping out, as it was on the stroke of 12 almost ... S.T. told Lindley later that he was very glad the concert lasted so long, as he feared he might be asked to sing King Priam.[103]

Another critical Musical Board meeting, on 17 February 1913, exploded:

> Musical Board meeting to discuss the ground covered by the public teaching of the faculty. Stanford was there – not at all pleased – & very disagreeable. He made himself most offensive to Rootham ... Stanford had shown himself thoroughly sordid & devoid of any idealism, devoid of any interest in Cambridge as a training ground for musicians.[104]

Although Dent continued to try to make peace with a man who had always been a source of personal inspiration, it really was no good, 'he turned away with some angry remark about "humiliation". I walked home with Rootham – rather sore.'[105]

> On Wednesday, to my surprise, I received a letter from Stanford, apologizing rather ungraciously for his disagreeableness on Monday. I wrote what I thought was a dignified and friendly reply: this morning I received a long and furious letter from him, boiling over. Fortunately he does not want me to answer it, and I think it is a good thing that he has got it all off his chest & told me what he thinks of me!

At the same time, all these future hopes involved a lot of socialising; Hills was run off her feet with teas, lunches, dinners, the weekend visitors up from London, the musical evenings. But she rarely complained,[106] and Dent made sure that she

101 These included Francis Toye writing in the *English Review*, Marcel Boulestin writing in the *SIM* and Denis Browne. Dent reviewed Toye's novel, *Diana and Two Symphonies*, which, curiously, laid down the outlines for a national musical organisation prefiguring the British Music Society.

102 Diary 28/04/1912. Apparently Arthur Bliss told him this.

103 Diary 07/12/1912.

104 Diary 17/02/1913.

105 Diary 27/02/1912

106 When she did it was made very clear. 'Hills says I entertain too much.'

had a holiday from time to time, even if it was only going to the Huntingdon Races or staying with his sisters. The wine was sparkling Moselle or Chianti from the Mimbelli vineyards: the food was school food, plentiful enough, but as Alban Berg later described it to his wife, 'a very fine lunch … except that the food had no taste at all. In this country a pheasant tastes exactly like a turkey or a chicken.'[107] The house was lively, the homosocial atmosphere poised to suit Dent's own delicate balance between prudery and subversive naughtiness. Philip Bainbrigge 'who delighted me beyond words' was becoming a close friend.[108] One evening he entertained Dent, Scho and Armstrong Gibbs with his spoof Greek Play, *Achilles in Scyros,*[109] in which a boy disguised as a girl finds himself fancying a girl disguised as a boy who had disguised herself in order to attract his interest. It was dedicated to Charles Scott-Moncrieff,[110] whom Dent also met for the first time that winter, later Philip's lover.

Here Aphrodite is not: Eros boy-like
Plays his boy's games among the leaves so green,
Bare-breeched; no decent tendril hides his toy (like
Some curious peach) that nestles warm between
His dainty rosy thighs – the toy that's been
A deadlier shaft to pierce the scholar's marrow
Than his more widely celebrated arrow.[111]

Beside Philip, there was a horde of amusing young things, William Oatfield, Robert Mackay 'The Lion',[112] Chester Purves (and his cat), Frank Birch, Iolo Williams, beside the actual pupils, Arthur Bliss and Armstrong Gibbs, and 'The Babies', Humphrey Noble and Kennard Bliss, with their kittens; Rupert's far naughtier and uninhibited little brother Alfred Brooke: 'Alfred, Gerald & Oatfield to dinner. Alfred got quite drunk & more charming than ever'.[113] Hugh Dalton often came up to stay, while jumping through the hoops of his embryonic political career; here he could meet up with old friends with whom he could be himself.[114] Timmy Jekyll frequently popped up, not always staying with Dent but visiting his numerous local acquaintance,

107 Alban Berg, *Letters to his Wife*, ed., translated and annotated by Bernard Grun (London, 1971), p. 376; diary 21/01/1931.

108 Philip Bainbrigge (1890–1918), Classicist, poet, taught at Shrewsbury. His letters to Dent show his later friendship with Wilfred Owen.

109 Diary 12/02/1912. Printed by the Cayme Press in 1927, ten years after Bainbrigge's death in the war. Ted Haynes had much to do with the Cayme Press was, if it was not actually owned by him. See also d'Arch Smith, *Love in Earnest,* pp. 148–50.

110 Charles K. Scott-Moncrieff (1889–1930), translator of Proust. In Dent's circle his nickname was 'Sco-Mo'.

111 Quoted in d'Arch Smith, *Love in Earnest,* p. 148.

112 The nickname owing to his mane of red-gold hair.

113 Diary 18/02/1912.

114 Dalton's biographer Ben Pimlott discussed at length the vexed question of Dalton's sexuality. I think there was no question but that he was sexually active in Cambridge, even if later, like many others of his generation, he married a very understanding woman.

the Cambridge and London circles by now completely entangled. A jealous Sayle banned Dent from his own salon for over a year.

> T [Theo Bartholomew] & I were amused at this outburst: but I was not very surprised: I think I have been getting on his nerves, and he thinks I take his friends away from him – so it is better to leave things to settle down quietly.[115]

But however cosy the domestic circumstances, Dent always needed his back door: later that March 1912 in Munich, he was very aware of his relief as he 'strolled' around familiar places, 'feeling very glad to be alone & out of England'. He had left London to do more research on his forthcoming book, *Mozart's Operas*, in Vienna, Salzburg and Prague, also to call on Busoni in Berlin and go to the Hamburg premiere of his opera *Die Brautwahl*. Right now, Busoni was formulating new ideas for opera, especially something serious on the *Doktor Faustus* story; of course Dent was interested. Travelling to Vienna via Munich, he called briefly on Frau Ewald at Holzhausen, then at Salzburg picked up copies from the Mozarteum of the Lange portraits of Mozart and his wife Constanze to use in the book.

In Vienna he was met at the station by Ernst Goldschmidt,[116] who invited him home the next day to meet his mother and his 'Onkel Max, Herr von Portheim who has a vast collection of books & prints of the Josef II period'; three of the illustrations for *Mozart's Operas* would come from Herr von Portheim's collection. Every day they went out, either to the opera, theatre or simply walking and taking coffee in the Café Central or a drive out to Edlach for dinner.

> I have had a good time here: I rather hate Vienna as it is so appallingly expensive. But Goldschmidt has got me into the way of not thinking about these things, and I manage to enjoy life pretty well. I have read several operas by M's contemporaries & rivals & have copied … the whole score of the duel & death of the Commendatore in Gazzaniga's Convitato di Pietra.[117]

They went to see *Die Zauberflöte* at the Hofoper: 'a thoroughly mediocre and provincial performance … no sense of style at all – the old Papageno gags, a chorus that seemed to belong to Parsifal, with holy German brown beards'.[118] Even so, it proved very useful to discuss this with the locals and gain some understanding of what lay behind such a production, to appreciate the idiosyncrasies of Viennese theatrical traditions, the broad local comedy Mozart had called upon.

Four nights later they went back to the Hofoper to see Strauss conducting his most recent opera, *Der Rosenkavalier*.[119] 'It is so extraordinarily well done', Dent wrote to Clive. 'The play is so clever, and the acting wonderful. I think I shd loathe the music if I heard it a second time … waltzes of the most banal type & other tunes

115 Diary 02/01/1912.

116 Not, as Carey, *Duet for Two Voices* says, Hugo Goldschmidt, but Ernst Philip, whom Dent had known since 1908.

117 CC 04/04/1912.

118 Diary 25/03/1912.

119 It had premiered in Dresden, January 1911.

of the usual Strauss kind. The mis-en-scene is miraculous'.[120] On Felix Weingartner taking a rehearsal of Bruckner's D minor symphony at the Musikvereinsaal: 'This time it impressed me very much.' But d'Albert's Beethoven G major concerto was played 'in a very Donald Toveyish style'. They saw Max Reinhardt's *Everyman* at the Circus Busch: 'very sensational & exaggerated & very vulgar German at times'. He loved the Good Deeds and a 'thoroughly German & delightful comic devil' but 'the music was abominable'.[121]

Even when he professed not to have enjoyed a performance, Dent always made sketchy references in his diary which would jog his memory. He was pushing his own ideas well beyond what he later called 'musical archaeology', and often at the core of his argument is an illustration from a performance or reference to a particular performance. *Mozart's Operas* is full of such experience, good and bad, and Dent's conclusions are often drawn from what he actually had seen. A case in point (one of many) is on pages 181–3, including a detailed, vivid discussion of the characters of Marcellina and Don Basilio in *The Marriage of Figaro*.

> They are both people to whom a certain artificiality of manner has become habitual, and we therefore hardly recognize them when they throw off their masks, because there is more individuality in the mask than in the face behind it. It is seldom that either of them is adequately presented on the stage. But I recall a performance at Vienna a few years ago (under Mahler's direction) in which Marcellina, instead of being a neat and unpretending general-utility actress, was brought on as a stout and vigorous woman of five-and-forty or so, glaringly overdressed, with a red face, thick black eyebrows meeting in the middle, and a very unmistakable moustache. Don Basilio too did let us forget that Beaumarchais described him as abbé and organist.

His point is that any understanding of the character affects how the music is sung. Or, having said that *Figaro* 'is not an opera that presents great difficulties in performance', Dent goes on to argue that '"Figaro" in Mozart's day was a play of contemporary life, and though it would be absurd to play it in any costumes later than 1786, it must yet present to the audience a sense of almost grim realism.' Such perception, raising questions through scholarship and through performance, was one of Dent's great contributions to twentieth-century appreciation and understanding, and ultimately, to staging.

In Vienna Dent worked mostly at the Gesellschaft der Musikfreunde, at the top of the Musikverein, which houses printed and manuscript music, only a 5-minute stroll from his hotel in Tegetthoffstrasse, enjoying a 'very amiable' session with its director, Eusebius Mandycyzki, and 'long conversations with Egon Wellesz & Dr Fehlber'. Dent's old friend Edgardo Maddalena had dug up something very interesting indeed, a translation of Goldoni's *Padre di famiglia* done by Carl Ludwig Giesecke, printed at Salzburg in 1787, firmly placing Giesecke in the theatrical circles he had claimed for himself. And the friendly von Portheims provided yet another illuminating avenue. When he left for Prague on 5 April, Dent had an introduction

120 CC 04/04/1912.

121 Diary 01/04/1912.

to another Goldschmidt cousin, Fräulein von Portheim, 'very charming', who took Dent to visit the Villa Bertramka, the small, charming house belonging to composer Franz (Frantisek) and Josefina Dussek where Mozart had stayed while in Prague in 1787. They walked in the nearby Kinsky gardens, and Dent was introduced to Dr Karl Horwitz, conductor of the German Opera there. A description of the Bertramka made its way into *Mozart's Operas*, beside impressions of the architecture of Prague, in order to convey some sense of a provincial society 'wealthy and artistic enough to encourage a local Italian opera, but not to maintain it on a very firm footing.'[122] Dent with his natural writer's instincts had hoovered up all these peripheral but lively materials to make *Mozart's Operas* into something extraordinary, scholarly and accessible.

After the very full two days in Prague, Dent made his way to Hamburg via Berlin, stopping off at Pillnitz to see how Mrs Spotty and 'Moloch' were getting on. 'I found her very well & cheerful.' Sadly, Klemm's bookshop had been sold on, he discovered. In Berlin he stayed only long enough to have lunch with Richter at Bartolini's and catch up on the Hirschfeld gossip, before taking the night train to Hamburg. The next morning, 11 April, he walked into a 'not very good' rehearsal for the premiere of Busoni's opera *Die Brautwahl.*

> It had a succès d'estime, but did not survive for more than three performances. The interpretation was hardly up to Busoni's standards. The orchestra was mediocre, some of the singers unequal to their parts, and the scenery too realistic – Busoni wanted it to be more in the style of a picture-book or a puppet-show. And the mechanism of the Hamburg theatre was inadequate for his effects of magic. It was hardly an opera for Hamburg, with its stiff and conventional audiences.[123]

Busoni himself was distraught that all the brilliant ideas he had so carefully nurtured for the past six years turned into such a damp squib: 'there was a good deal of hissing'. But he had surrounded himself with his friends and admirers, cushioning the blow, and the next day, after the actual premiere, and in spite of all the 'hissing', the mood was buoyant at the post-performance supper at the Esplanade. Dent found himself at a small table with other English, including Ursula and Basil Creighton and Miss Ley, while nearby were the Petris, Maud Allan and Irene Sanden. Dent knew it was no good even to think about talking with Busoni while he was immersed in his support crowd, especially after such a disappointing event when he needed support. On the train back, after making himself hoarse in a 'shouting' discussion with Artur Schnabel, Zadora, Buhlig and a Dr Wolfheimer, the lively party carried on into the Como, where the blind pianist played Bellini for them till late that night.

Dent went to the Secession, held in the wake of the travelling Blaue Reiter exhibition, 'more verrücht than ever with cubists and others. Liebermann, Kardorff & Conister are the best of the lot, tho' old fashioned. I suppose I can't get beyond

122 Dent, *Mozart's Operas*, p. 188. The Bertramka is now a museum and concert hall.

123 Dent, *Busoni*, p. 183. His source was Busoni's letter to Robert Freund, but it is likely that he discussed this with Busoni himself at the time.

Brahms'.[124] One important port of call was Max Friedlaender, to find out more about the Illinois job, and being shown his 'Beethoven-Mozart MSS' and a 'wax relief of M.[ozart] done in Paris, wch I did not know'.

But fully half of Dent's time was taken up with seeing the Busonis. He loved the family, while Busoni himself was the overwhelming attraction, with his huge physical and intellectual presence, one of the few men Dent knew who had this effect on him. That week the opportunities arose for several intimate conversations, a rare chance with Busoni, whose personal hordes were also a prophylactic against unwanted intimacy. One afternoon after a quiet family lunch, during an eclipse of the sun, Dent was moved to mention the last time he had seen a solar eclipse, on a train to Müryzuschlag. 'Müryzuschlag!' Busoni interrupted, 'it's so strange to hear that name again – all my childhood was spent in those parts!'. 'Busoni reduced us to a painful silence by his memories of Klagenfurt ... I forget what else he said, but it produced a horrible impression of poverty & suffering'.[125] When they happened to talk about Busoni's first violin sonata, Busoni sighed, 'das war mein erster gutes Werk' – that was my first good work – and Dent, smugly, 'rather startled him by whistling a good deal of the violin part'.

> Later a couple of 'futurists' called – Marinetti the poet and a painter Boccioni. The futurists are exhibiting now in Berlin, and Busoni bought one of their pictures – 3 1/2 yards wide, he said: but I did not see it. The futurists sat & talked very hard, and B. listened very patiently.[126]

It was probably then that Dent really fell in love with Busoni.[127] Much that week emerged years later in Dent's biography, and in the article Dent wrote later that year on music at Cambridge. They talked and argued amicably about music:

> He refused to see anything sacred and unalterable in the written words of a piece of music, or in the sounds produced by any one particular instrument. What interested him was the music itself, the music as it existed in the composer's imagination, before it had been written down on paper, even before it had been approximated into tones and semitones, a music as yet unheard by human ear. He sought to seize the unwritten conceptions of Bach or Mozart and to make them audible to his own generation.[128]

[124] Dent wryly echoing his own diary entry for 18 April, when he'd had lunch at the Kardorffs, with Oscar Fried and a Professor & Mrs Rosenheim, whom Dent liked and who self-confessedly 'can't get beyond Brahms' in her piano playing.

[125] Diary 17/04/1912.

[126] Diary 20/04/1912. Busoni was impressed, attracted by the movement's energy and its being Italian. In a 1916 letter to Egon Petri he said that Boccioni, 'who has become something of a genius, wants to paint my portrait'. *Ferruccio Busoni: Selected Letters*, ed. and trans. Antony Beaumont (New York, 1987), p. 236. Boccioni was killed in the war.

[127] See Chapter 5, note 32.

[128] Dent, *Busoni*, p. 111.

'About 4 I went to Busoni's & had a pleasant talk with him about Marlowe's Faustus, wch he is nibbling at as one opera subject'.[129] From this, Dent continued to bring Denis Browne's name to Busoni's attention, hoping for more.

Dent had begun his visit at Bartolini's and he would finish it there, in company with the young musician Richard Schade, who gossiped that Abert was to succeed Kretzschmar as Professor at Berlin, and later, Hirschfeld's friend Richter, the latter, 'depressed & nervous with living in Berlin'. His last encounter in Berlin, suitably bizarre, was with Guido Carreras, husband of pianist Maria, who revealed to Dent that he was the original 'Guido' who had been the constant companion of Frederick Rolfe, aka 'Baron Corvo', and the source of all his lurid stories, just the kind of mildly salacious piece of informed gossip Dent loved and would pass on to his Cambridge nestlings. But music and gossip were not the only exports Dent brought home with him; within a year a British Wissenschaftlich–humanitäres Komitee was launched.

❧ ❧ ❧

Dent spent most of the summer of 1912 finishing off his Mozart book, sending it off on 10 August. He then made a rare trip north for a week's walking around the North York moors with his sister Catherine, staying at the Mallyan Spout in the village of Goathland, seeing some of his relatives, Uncle Ted in Scarborough and his brother Charles at Snow Hall. By 2 September he was walking in the Veneto, exploring the small towns and villages and calling on Dr Oscar Chilesotti in Bassano, north of Vicenza.[130] Chilesotti, together with Fedeli and Fausto Torrefranca, was keen to establish 'a proper Italian section of their own … independent of the Assoc. dei Musicologi'. Dent instantly agreed to lend his support, another mental step in a musical life away from Cambridge. The next three days were spent 'loafing' around Padua and the hills and villas, casually mentioning his visit to Piazzola: 'I went over the palace, wch is being restored by Conti Paolo Contarini. There was a small but good collection of libretti & documents relating to the Contarini theatre, and a few good scores of operas still remaining.'[131] Such spectacular finds had become part of his routines.

At first Munich appeared to be exactly the kind of visit Dent had dreamt of ten years before, with Francis Toye, Trend, and Francis Birrell all there learning German. They went to the contemporary plays, concerts and revues, exhibitions: the Blaue Reiter, a Goya Exhibition at Galerie Heinemann and more Spanish pictures by Eugenio Lucas. To them, though, the most interesting thing was a production of Calderon's *Circe*, a 'fantastisches Festspiel', with lavish costumes 'à la Velasquez', the germ of an idea which Dent would later follow up. They saw a Maeterlinck play, *Mort de Tintagils*, with music by Debussy, and marionettes. What should have been the high point was a 'fair' production of *Rosenkavalier* with Bruno Walter conducting

129 Diary 19/04/1912.

130 Oscar Chilesotti (1848–1916), Italian musicologist, specialising in early music, especially the lute.

131 Diary 09/09/1912.

and Strauss sitting just in front of them, but Dent preferred Walter's conducting of *Cosi* two nights later, even with a lot of Act II cut: 'F.T. who did not know the opera except by Beecham's performance was much struck with its beauty, and with its admirable libretto'.

At this time, Dent's relationship with Denis Browne was probably one of the most intense of his life. Denis had got under Dent's guard; he was young, very talented and intelligent, responsive without being subservient, and also very good-looking, in a quiet, understated way, with dark brown hair and eyes, and a rare, infectious grin, who embodied his hopes for a musical future. In other recent relationships Dent had assumed the mentor–nursemaid role, but Denis managed to maintain a pleasing self-possession, possibly because he was himself in love with Rupert Brooke.[132] 'Denis' smile sent me into fits of laughter.'[133] 'Denis flourishes & is more adorably Dionysiac than ever. (Dionysiac from Dionysius + Denys: there is no other possible adjective.'[134] 'Denis is my swan!' For a time, Denis was practically living in Panton Street, his name cropping up in Dent's diary almost daily, playing, going to concerts, to the 'Irish' plays, with John Ireland to Leonard Borwick's recital in London, to drinks, dinners and teas, laced with music: 'starting Denis on the Tartini concertos in the Fitzm'. 'I began this letter by meaning to try and express some of my gratitude to you', Denis wrote him in 1912:

> But I find I can't do it at all. the last 4 1/2 years of education by you have been something that no later experience can ever equal, and that I shall value more and more all my life. I'm completely powerless to express all I feel, and all I owe to you – which is everything. You can't thank a person who has opened up vistas in every direction for you and influenced the trend of your whole life. If there is anything I can do in after life to serve music fitly, it will in the first instance be a thank-offering to you who have taught me all I know, and kept me straight when I have gone wrong.[135]

Back in London, Granville Barker's *The Winter's Tale* in November 1912 had engaged the talents and ideas of the old MDS gang and the attention of the newer critics.[136] The Busonis were in town for concerts with Fritz Kreisler in a programme of Busoni, Beethoven and Franck, then Mozart. Dent thought Kreisler's playing 'dull' the first time, improved in the second, but 'very much dwarfed by B[usoni]'. He threw a lunch party at Pagani's and took Gerda Busoni to see *The Winter's Tale* again with the Hawards.[137]

132 Having discussed this at length with Browne's relatives and one biographer, Dr Kate Kennedy, I agree with this point.

133 Diary 02/06/1910.

134 CC 22/03/1909. Browne's biographer, Philip Lancaster, thinks it unlikely that they went beyond the usual fondlings.

135 DB 25/03/1912.

136 William Barber was producing it, Albert Rothenstein designed the sets. Rupert fell in love with the young Cathleen Nesbitt, playing Perdita.

137 Diary 10/10/1912.

❧ ❧ ❧

> We intend to question things that have not been questioned before. We intend to enquire into them – to examine the authorities who have laid down the law about them – often, we believe, – always, it may be – on very insufficient grounds and we mean to push our enquiry on the basis of men and women working fearlessly and frankly together over territory that is really common to both, but which hitherto, has been ridiculously cut up, separated and divided.[138]

In 1914 the British Society for the Study of Sexual Psychology (BSSSP) was formed, largely down to Dent's friends Magnus Hirschfeld and Edward Carpenter, and supported by such liberal thinkers as George Ives, Havelock Ellis, E. Bertram Lloyd and Bernard Shaw beside Dent's old friends Timmy Jekyll and Ted Haynes, who was providing the necessary legal advice for the society[139] in what was otherwise a 'phalanx of respectability'.[140] The scientific-sounding name was for public perception, to play down what was mostly a homosexual agenda, the ideas largely drawn from Hirschfeld's Wissenschaftlich–humanitäres Komitee in Berlin, to change existing laws which discriminated against homosexuals and to change public understanding of homosexuality. Other proscribed topics were included in its brief, and explorations of such matters as women's sexuality were officially given equal weight. On the 19 May 1914, Dent was put up for membership by Edward Carpenter and Kains Jackson,[141] thus becoming a member before Forster, before Dickinson and even before D.H. Lawrence. None of this appears in his diary, nor in any of his extant letters; his diary entry for the 8 July 1914, the official launch date for the BSSSP, reading blandly: 'Society of Psychiatry at London Medical Society's Hall, Laurence Housman spoke inter alia. Lloyd on Prostitution, Carpenter on Inversion.' Carpenter introduced Dr Reddie of Abbottholme 'whom I liked'.

> Barwell was there … Cust, with a young clergyman: George Ives, who was very mysterious & anxious to get me to join some curious association. There were about 50 people in the audience – of wch a dozen or so were women: all middle aged or thereabouts & very serious!

Dent's membership of the BSSSP was a natural step; its anti-authoritarian stance alone would appeal, but Dent would rarely admit to any personal need. 'Convention must be no bar', its 'General Aims' stated:

138 BSSSP pamphlet no. 1 (written by Laurence Housman) 'Policy and principles, general aims' (London, 1914), p. 7.

139 Ted, as Dent noted, was already known for writing articles on liberalisation of a number of public–private subjects for the Cayme Press.

140 Rowbotham, *Edward Carpenter*, p. 334.

141 I am indebted to E.M. Forster's biographer Wendy Moffatt for this piece of information, who discovered it at the Ransom Center in Austin Texas, which houses the membership book. Less clear is the nature of the society that May: its 'inaugural meeting' was on 8 July 1914. cf. Rowbotham, *Edward Carpenter*, p. 333.

> for behind all conventions lie germinal forces infinitely older, infinitely more venerable, which conventions, formed on narrow and incomplete premises, tend only to hide. Because sex-questions are pornographically attractive, are they therefore to be neglected by those who have a clean-minded longing for their solution?

It went on to advocate sex education in schools and an entire rethinking of what was private and what public: 'We are a note of interrogation.'

Edward Carpenter and his writings had long been central to Dent's personal explorations.[142] As recently as October 1913 he had visited Carpenter and his partner George Merrill at Millthorpe, his remote place at the edge of the Peak, near Sheffield, a place of pilgrimage. 'It was 4 miles walk from Dore station, mostly in rain: but fine country & I enjoyed seeing him & George who is a good soul'.[143] Later, in August 1914, after war had broken out, Dent expressed the need to visit Carpenter again: 'a man like that is a source of real human feeling'.[144] During his own pilgrimage to Millthorpe only a month before Dent's visit, Morgan Forster had had his famous epiphany when George touched his bottom: 'It seemed to go straight through the small of my back into my ideas, without involving my thoughts.'[145] Forster went home, sat down and wrote *Maurice*, his novel of homosexual love, which was circulated in manuscript around his friends, including Dent, over the next few years. Lowes Dickinson had long been an admirer of Carpenter's work and philosophy, and kept a complete collection of his writings; when Magnus Hirschfeld stayed with Dent in 1910, he had just come from visiting Carpenter. Carpenter's name frequently crops up in conversations, and on 30 January 1911, Dent had heard him lecture. 'As to music', Carpenter wrote in 1908, 'this is certainly the art which in its subtlety and tenderness – and perhaps in a certain inclination to *indulge* in emotion – lies nearest to the Urning nature. There are few in fact of this nature who have not some gift in the direction of music.'[146]

For years, well before he met Carpenter and Hirschfeld, Dent had been keeping up with all the current literature on sexuality in English and German: John Addington Symonds, Havelock Ellis, Kraft-Ebbing, Karl Ulrichs. It was in his nature to want to understand who and what he was, and the new scientific objectification of homosexuality, the new definitions and boundaries of the human condition had intrigued him for some time. As Philip Brett has discussed,[147] Dent's position raises the historiographical question of comparing the then relatively new disciplines of

142 In 1906, he was quite keen to hear what Cust had to say about him, for example.

143 Diary 05/10/1913.

144 LH 21/08/1914.

145 Furbank, *E.M. Forster: A Life. Volume One*, p. 257.

146 Edward Carpenter, *The Intermediate Sex* (London, 1908), quoted in Philip Brett, 'Musicology and Sexuality: The Example of Edward J. Dent' in *Proceedings of the SIM* (London, 1997), p. 420.

147 *Ibid.*, pp. 418–27; also Joe Law, 'The Precariously Homosexual Art: Music and Homoerotic Desire in *The Picture of Dorian Gray* and Other Fin-de-Siècle Fiction', in *The Idea of Music in Victorian Fiction*, ed. Sophie Fuller and Nicky Losseff (Farnham, 2004), pp. 173–96.

musicology and sexology, the early undertakings to have them recognised as rigorous *academic* subjects, open to rigorous *academic* scrutiny.

> And though it would be unwise to press the parallels beyond a certain point except out of pure mischief, those mechanisms bear a distinct family resemblance to the procedures brought to bear on music. For – let us be clear about this – unregulated music is potentially as dangerous as unregulated sex to the concept of order in capitalist society.[148]

'Are you musical?' was coded language for homosexuality.[149]

Dent was never uncritical or earnest, recording his reluctance to go along with Hirschfeld's institute because the lectures bored him. Nevertheless, he always looked after the men sent to him by Hirschfeld: 'In the aftn I received a strange letter from a Dr T.H. Livingstone of Newcastle, to whom my name had been given by Hirschfeld.'[150] Mon 21 Aug: 'Another letter from Livingstone, extraordinarily frank.' By the 25th he had arranged a meeting with Livingstone at the Station Hotel in York, where they 'strolled … and talked matters over … I thought L. rather stupid, but comforted his soul a good deal, I think.' It was no mere coincidence that there were so many meetings with Hirschfeld's friend Richter in the years up to the foundation of the BSSSP. In May 1913 he came to stay at Panton Street 'for a few days' and only left after nearly three weeks.

❧ ❧ ❧

On 5 June 1913, Dent read through 'a good deal' of *The Fairy Queen* with Clive at the Roothams', and they decided to perform it in December 1914. For some time Dent had been working seriously on Purcell, most recently with the Purcell Society[151] to produce new editions of the operas, discussing the operas with Vaughan Williams. That June he talked with Alfred Littleton of Novello's 'about printing a cheap edition of the Fairy Queen. He could hardly have been more discouraging and contemptuous if I had wanted him to publish the full score of an opera of my own'.[152] Novello's eventually gave in, and by December Dent was producing a working copy, and had persuaded the Cambridge University Press to publish a 'proposed book on Purcell' which later became his *Foundations of English Opera* (1928).

He spent the rest of that June and into July in France, with research and opera in Paris, meeting with Jules Écorcheville and Mlle Pereyra, going to the Ballets Russes and to Notre Dame, where the choir 'sang intelligently, but the tone was harsh & they sank in pitch'.[153] Far more to his liking was *Khovantchina* at the Champs-Elysées,

148 Brett, 'Musicology and Sexuality', pp. 418–9.

149 *Ibid.* and Law, 'The Precariously Homosexual Art', pp. 173–96.

150 Diary 18/08/1911.

151 'Purcell: *The Indian Queen*' and 'Purcell: *The Tempest*', Purcell Society edns, vols 19 and 32 (London, 1912).

152 Diary 13/06/1913.

153 Diary 19/06/1913.

with the great Russian bass Chaliapin: 'quite wonderful. I was much impressed by the directness & simplicity of it all – especially the wonderful chorus treatment, & especially their singing of it: and the extraordinary silences, wch produce a thrilling effect.' Then a rainy but pleasant week around Beaume and Dijon, walking, making his way over the next month down to Provence, before moving on to Parma for an exhibition he was writing up for *The Times*, reading, composing a bit of counterpoint and generally looking at his surroundings. 'Yesterday I received notice that the Blue Review has ceased to exist. I am sorry, as it was a convenient outlet when I had ideas to express: but I am relieved at not having to write more articles just now.'[154]

Returning in time for the Leeds Festival, Dent heard Nikisch conduct Verdi and enjoyed hearing George Butterworth's 'Shropshire Lad Rhapsody' beside Bantock's 'Dante & Beatrice', 'dreadful ... like Liszt at his worst'. On 25 October, he saw 'the Magic Flute done by the Denhof Beecham Co. in my translation ... The orchestra was a good one, but noisy, & Beecham's tempi generally much too fast to get the words out ... On the whole the performance was good, though not at all original in its methods.[155] To Clive he was more forthcoming:

> Beecham made a horrid mess of the band: very rough & loud, and all the tempi of the ensembles much too fast. I suppose he was bored ... Altogether I enjoyed it very much. The words were very clear – even in difficult places – as a rule.[156]

What he had not realised at the time was Beecham's bland theft: no one had bothered to ask his permission.

Early in November he began working on *The Fairy Queen* quartos in the British Museum. On the 15th Clive came up for a few days and they discussed production ideas with Kate Cockerell; by 1 December, Clive was able to begin tentative rehearsals at the Maltings House. Clive was depressed at the time, and Dent tried to cheer him up with amusing letters and advice, saying how much good '3 months in the Cevennes' had done him:

> You always say you are afraid of being alone, and that you mope: but I wd risk the experiment, if you get the chance ever, of enduring it until you find that being alone is a real rest, and a rebuilding of one's soul ... Also let me recommend strict counterpoint, as a substitute for knitting, and as an addition to tobacco.[157]

Throughout those prewar years, as Dent saw, everything from the Ballets Russes to the short-lived literary magazines *Rhythm* and *Blue Review*, however excellent, needed solid financing to keep them alive. Desperation was the backcloth for most of these young men like Denis or Clive, Dent's talented gang who had lived so intensely while in the cushioned existence of Cambridge, now having to face the practical problems of how to get on in the world outside. The brief

154 Diary 22/06/1913.
155 Diary 25/10/1913.
156 CC 28/10/1913.
157 CC 13/10/1913.

cultural flowering that promised so much to their generation proved too fragile to survive wider events in the world.

Dent was himself even more blinkered than most; although he mentions the 'war scare' several times in his diary, he was far more concerned with opera, *The Fairy Queen*, and productions being staged by his friends. For a short time the cocoon held: that July Ted Haynes had a play on at the Little Theatre, Bob Maltby's *Enchanted Night* incorporated music by Clive and Denis, and it looked as if Clive was being asked to compose the music for *Starlight Express*. At the Darwins, Vaughan Williams had played through his new opera, *Hugh the Drover*.

> It was a warm evening and the sweat streamed down his face in rivers. It was a notable occasion, I think, for the opera is quite new in style, although built as a conventional ballad opera – The folksong idiom is kept up quite homogeneously, & it is really beautiful stuff. It ought to be a sort of Freischütz for us: but I hope nobody will scoff at it in 100 years as I do at Freischütz.[158]

Rootham was keen to start his new lectures on Busoni, Schoenberg and Bartók. It was all so hopeful at last. But then came a little local difficulty, when that June the assassination of the Archduke in Sarajevo threw the world into confusion and death. The quest for a national opera style would have to wait for a few years, but it was only on hold, really. Dent was about to fight this new war as he did everything else, in his own way.[159]

158 Diary 22/07/1914.

159 'Nearly six years – and a hundred letters – later the abandoned scenery was to become the province of Lionel Penrose, an undergraduate of King's, and Mrs Cockerell, with her sister Joan Kingsford (Wood).' Carey, *Duet for Two Voices*, p. 68.

CHAPTER 8

The Pacifist 1914–1918

The 1914 war destroyed everything. The 'music, friendship, laughter' of *The Magic Flute* could never be the same again.[1]

Whoever wins, it will be a victory for the stupid people.[2]

1914–1915

The day war was declared, 4 August 1914, Dent wrote in his diary: 'My work is getting rather disturbed by the war excitement but I generally manage to do some at home and read at the Library most days … We agreed that the best thing for ordinary people to do was to go on doing their ordinary things.' But it was the 'ordinary things' which would change first, and Dent found himself once again fighting elements beyond his control. It wasn't simply bland denial; he kept to the unpopular view that music should be kept alive *especially* in wartime. Nor was it simply that Dent hated war – he would later say that he hated '*this* war' – rather the blinkered, self-righteous attitude it fostered, too much like the unacceptable face of a self-righteous religion. A number of his friends and acquaintances like Bertrand Russell and Edward Carpenter immediately went to work organising anti-war movements, but Dent held back, declaring that music was his priority. The patriotism he saw emerging almost at once repulsed him, while its official vehicle, the Defence of the Realm Act (DORA), 'that all-purpose weapon against dissent' giving vague and enormous powers to government, fostered what historian Samuel Hynes called a 'conflict of values',[3] provoking strong reactions from a wide range of disparate groups.[4]

> Socialists, Bloomsbury aesthetes, radical women, trade unionists, Quakers, Christians, a few Cambridge dons … alike in one thing only … not a national but an international principle … a contradiction of the principle on which war … is fought … they conducted a war-against-the-war, often at considerable personal

1 J.B. Trend, 'Dent' obituary, quoting Dent, in *The Score*, no. 22 (1958), pp. 49–55.

2 From J.B. Trend's letter to Dent 26/01/1916, quoting Tom Buxton's 'bitter' remark. Dame Margaret Anstee used it in her biography of Trend. Margaret Anstee, *An Unlikely Spanish Don: the Life and Times of Professor John Brande Trend* (Eastbourne, 2013).

3 Samuel Hynes, *A War Imagined* (London, 1990), p. 57.

4 *Ibid.*, pp. 78ff.

cost. And the government fought back with the weapons that it commanded: suppression, prohibition, conscription, and imprisonment.[5]

Dent's own internationalism had begun years before, but the war would give it focus and purpose.

Immediately, Cambridge became a visible repository for almost every aspect of this new war. Only a week after war had been declared, Dent strolled out with Timmy Jekyll, observing the camps springing up on Midsummer Common and Coe Fen, the hospital being set up in Neville's Court at Trinity College. By 22 August he noted that there were some twenty thousand troops in Cambridge. In the university, opinion was divided between patriotic elation and a vein of intelligent dissent typified by Russell and some of the Bloomsbury Group. C.K. Ogden's *The Cambridge Magazine*, its tiny offices opposite King's, reinvented itself as a major alternative medium for Russell, Romain Rolland and other dissidents; beside these activists ran the deep pessimism of scholars like Sedley Taylor, who simply wanted to keep the old ways quietly rumbling along, gloomily prophesying ten years of war, 'until the whole of Europe is reduced to poverty and barbarism'.[6] The Grays, 'cheerful and energetic, Alan very jingo', talked politics with Dent over tea, but Dent knew himself to be 'too much of a pacifist and internationalist' to match their optimistic patriotism. Rootham, whose Fellowship at St. John's was confirmed that November, continued to plan his lectures on contemporary music, Bartók and Busoni, while Dent clung to the possibility of putting on *The Fairy Queen*. But attitudes had hardened against perceived frivolity, including music: 'We felt obliged to abandon the chamber concerts for the October term.'[7]

In fact, the war had already changed much more than Dent's daily routines; his confident relationships with many of the old gang were being shattered. While Dent continued to occupy himself with work on his 'Purcell' book, many friends and former pupils had their eyes on Belgium and France, inflamed by the new clarity of thought brought by war, and the cheerful haste with which they were abandoning the old life and its values took him completely by surprise. He failed to recognise that war provided a perfect excuse not to continue struggling with elusive and unsatisfactory careers, besides giving his younger friends a glimpse of the glory they had read about as schoolboys. As early as July, while Dent had enthused about a French holiday together, Denis Browne prevaricated. In a letter he must have known Dent would find hurtful, Denis talked about an alternative future for himself, with his delight at spending time with F.S. Kelly at Bisham, and his own deep frustrations.

> I get less & less able to criticise technically what I hear – I never could do much. But to hear a thing for the first time & to try & get hold of anything except its emotion & its line seems to me hopeless & impossible. I do want someday to write something and the more I criticise other people's music the more impos-

5 *Ibid.*, pp. 86–7.

6 Diary 24/08/1914.

7 Diary 14/08/1914.

> sible it becomes … But writing about other people's music, how deadening it is & how hopeless.[8]

In August, Rupert Brooke was up for a week, in high spirits, bouncing in and out of Panton Street, cadging lunch or a bath or quiet time in the garden, like the old days. The war had energised him; having taken the decision to enlist, he was keen to get himself a commission as soon as possible, and he knew how to pull the right strings. He entertained Dent with all the War Office gossip about Kitchener, 'the King of Chaos', and about their mutual friends who were settling in there for the duration. Dent watched the animation with some dismay, listening without comment to Rupert's confident speculations that it would take about a year and a half to beat Germany, then another year and a half for the combined forces to beat Russia. Discarded were the poet, the actor, the Fabian socialist and the scholar; Rupert had thrown himself into this latest new role, the soldier, and as always his enthusiasm was infectious; within a month both he and Denis were out at Antwerp. By Christmas Eddie Marsh had personally intervened with his boss at the Admiralty, Winston Churchill, to make sure that all his favourites, including Rupert and Denis with F.S. Kelly, were placed in the elite Hood Battalion and shipped out to the Mediterranean, towards Gallipoli. He thought he was doing them a big favour.

There is more than a hint of condescension in their letters to Dent at this time; Dent is no longer leading them into the future, but already a figure from their past. After three weeks of 'drilling' with the Inns of Court Officers' Training Corps alongside Frank Birch and Alfred Brooke, Denis was frankly dismissive. He hadn't been able to finish Dent's Mozart book: 'to tell the truth I was too unsettled to have understood it'. 'I'm happy now, or happier', his letter continues in a cruelly exuberant vein which epitomises the general mood:

> There are worse things than war! … Butterworth, Morris & Ellis have enlisted in Kitchener's Army. Steuart as you probably know, is at Sheerness. Eddie beams with joy at the Admiralty. Bob Crighton[9] is in the Public Schools Battalion … Goodbye my dear, & good luck. Make your book a big thing. If you do that it wont matter if German Kultur goes under.[10]

Vaughan Williams was out in Belgium as a non-combatant; only Clive held out until the New Year, joining the Royal Army Medical Corps in February. Throughout that autumn and winter Dent had to watch from a distance as they all peeled off into a world he had no part of.

Even though going abroad was now out of the question, Dent had decided to seize what holiday he could in September, with Theo Bartholomew, the first of several such wartime escapes. The Raverats recommended the walking around Sedburgh, in North Yorkshire: they decided to stay at, of all unlikely things, a temperance hotel, the Cross Keys, under Cautley Spout.[11] The Hawards were staying nearby,

8 DB to EJD 24/07/1914.

9 Bob Maltby.

10 DB to EJD 06/09/1914.

11 It is still there, now a National Trust hotel.

at Aysgarth, and a quick side-trip to Ribston was also easy. The young husband of Dent's niece Ruth had just been killed, an early casualty of the war, and the family was in shock.

Theo was one of many men worried about being called up once the initial confident jingoism receded, feeling that conscription was never far off. Like other gay men in Cambridge, Theo had been cocooned for years from most outside threats, while recent greater openness via the BSSSP had offered hope. No more. The war on dissent included sexual dissent, and this would get much worse as the war ground on. For the time being, though, he and Dent enjoyed their brisk walks on the moors; evenings, Dent occupied himself with the laborious task of scoring Vaughan Williams' 'London' Symphony. Having lent the manuscript score to Fritz Busch, Vaughan Williams had been forced to leave Belgium precipitately, so with George Butterworth and Geoffrey Toye, Dent had volunteered to score the whole thing from the remaining parts.[12] Such mental exercise took his mind off events in the wider world, and combined with the exercise, suited him well.

That autumn back in Cambridge the first waves of wounded soldiers and Belgian refugees had already settled in when the Canadians burst on the scene, 'the tag rag & bobtail of the wild west … a sort of modern equivalent of medieval mercenaries – Cambridge ought to be lively!', beside increasing numbers of young men at the local Officers' Training Corps, run largely by Old Etonians. Dent's 'foreign' friends the Parmas and young Fritz von Sonnenkamp, whose father was in the German war cabinet, had been stuck in Cambridge and were now rounded up and sent to a detention camp near Wakefield with others Dent knew.

Florence Keynes[13] headed the local Belgian relief operations, mustering everyone she knew, even Jack Sheppard, then still at a loose end, living in college and unable to make up his mind what to do. Under her brisk and efficient leadership, the flood of refugees was quickly dispersed around town, while activities were being devised to take their minds off what they had so recently lost and raise a bit of much-needed relief money: informal concerts and entertainments, just the kind of activity in fact that Dent had advocated, only now since it was all in aid of 'plucky little Belgium', everyone helped. Mrs Jenkinson and Mrs Stewart organised a 'Fête des Alliés' on 1 December in the Guildhall,[14] Dent grumbling, 'This should have been the first night of the *Fairy Queen*', but he helped to produce a CUMS concert on 5 December. To Hills's delight, Dent had an artillery sergeant billeted on him at Panton Street, company for her when Dent was down in London.

It took only about a month before the warm, charitable feelings faded, and the Cambridge ladies who had rushed to take in Belgians were now quarrelling with their guests, gratitude eroded by the frustrations of refugees unable to do anything but read and wait. Miss Darwin and Miss Luard brought in all the latest news and gossip, even from the War Office, now staffed by many ex-Cambridge people, and

12 Diary 09/09/1914 and Michael Kennedy, *The Works of Ralph Vaughan Williams* (Oxford, 1964), p. 464. Also Dent's correspondence with VW at the time, CUL Add MS 7973/V.

13 Mother of John Maynard, later Mayor of Cambridge.

14 Knight, *Cambridge Music*, p. 99. Diary.

rumours began to circulate around the tea-parties: nuns and abbés were spies after information on any refugees; six Germans had been discovered at Morley's Hotel, by the Admiralty Arch, with six rifles and a thousand rounds of ammunition, arrested and taken to the Tower. At lunch with the Allens in Oxford Dent heard the startling news that Scarborough had been bombarded, but stopping off at Rutland Gate on the way home found that the aunts had suffered nothing more than some broken glass.[15]

Dent listened to the gossip, engaged in endless French and German conversations mostly about the war, invited Belgians to dine and to play music.[16] He helped with the informal music being played most nights in various drawing-rooms around town and invited the Belgians to the CUMC. On 9 November the Parmas were released: 'very amusing about it'.

Music had also fallen victim to the war. That staple of the British concert stage, German music, was now 'enemy music', and this official attitude presented the organisers of public concerts with a dilemma, since the most popular programmes by far were of the standard German composers, Beethoven, Wagner, Brahms, while German musicians who formed the bedrock of British orchestras were being forced out of work by such outfits as the 'National Association for the Protection of British Interests in Music'. Most of the current British musical establishment, from Stanford to Delius, had trained in Germany under German musicians, while great German conductors like Richter or Nikisch had been taken to the public heart: 'No other art was so dominated by another nation's artists.'[17] In a brief panic, the August 1914 Proms programmes had hastily been wiped of any 'enemy music', a move so unpopular with audiences that a prim notice was inserted into the programme:

> [The management] take this opportunity of emphatically contradicting the statements that German music will be boycotted during the present season. The greatest examples of Music and Art are world possessions and unassailable even by the prejudices and passions of the hour.[18]

'German' music continued to be programmed, especially by Henry Wood and Thomas Beecham, to the relief of critics and pacifists alike, Bernard Shaw, Ernest Newman and Bertrand Russell, while the 'War Emergency Entertainments', sponsored by Isidore de Lara, beside the 'Music in Wartime' committee chaired by Sir Hubert Parry nurtured native talent and sponsored many concerts.[19]

But music cannot be doled out like pills – one of Dent's sayings – and the fact remained that German music and musicians had set very high standards which were proving difficult to meet. A local sample of 'Music in War-Times' left Dent less than impressed. Miss Mary Maud Paget haranguing 'very volubly and very foolishly' her

15 All this information is from Dent's diary entries at the time.

16 Including one who later became involved with the ISCM, Désiré Defauw, and composer Joseph Jongen (1873–1953).

17 Hynes, *A War Imagined*, p. 74.

18 *Ibid.*, p. 75.

19 Scholes, *The Mirror of Music*, vol. 2, p. 888.

audience about their patriotic duties was bad enough; 'a specimen concert was given by a baritone, a violinist, and Miss Sibyl Cropper … was so bad as to make me go hot all over.'[20] The movement did not make much headway in Cambridge. Initially, though, such dismal utilitarianism ruled, with even the *Musical Times* piously advocating the retention of musical activities to assuage 'the craving for music as a wholesome distraction and a solace'.[21] One of Dent's Cambridge friends, Mrs Perkins, wryly commented on ladies expressing shock that people seemed to be *enjoying* themselves at concerts. Some positive musical developments emerged, with more opportunities for British composers to have their music played, and, because so many male musicians were being called up, the emergence of women musicians.

Dent was irritated by general uncertainty as much as the dreary music and looked for diversion: 'I read 2 or 3 chapters of Stanford's autobiography & was bored: too many distinguished relations, & too many funny stories, some of wch are Sedley Taylor's, not his own'.[22] At Theo's behest he went along to the Heretics, the informal society for agnostic debate, founded in 1909 by C.K. Ogden and supported by a number of Dent's friends, including Ted Haynes. Because of its generally anti-authoritarian stance it was one of the more homosocial clubs, too, as well as being open to 'new' women like Jane Harrison, with speakers like George Santayana on transcendentalism. Dent liked Santayana, and the anti-war sentiments being voiced there and around Cambridge generally were of great interest to him.

> [Ogden &] Maynard have got some project preparing for urging peace proposals at the psychological moment … the idea being that we must then have the courage to trust Germany to learn the lesson of war by meditating on it, rather than crush them completely and thereby perpetuate too great a legacy of hatred.[23]

The ideas emerging from these Heretics discussions appeared later in Keynes' famous pamphlet *The Economic Consequences of the Peace* and Ogden's wartime *Cambridge Magazine*, but, lacking real personal energy and purpose, it was months before Dent could find ways to get more actively involved. Some tentative stirrings against his lack of purpose showed when Dent applied to his former MDS friends for money to send 'Arabella, Duchess of Poland' (Reginald Pole) to California for his crippling asthma and also to get him out of harm's way, knowing how unfit he was for service. Rupert alone balked.

> In ordinary times, I'd be very glad to help him to Los Angeles … But these aren't ordinary times. – I wouldn't for a minute have it inferred that I don't admire your great goodness of heart … I feel that if there's a ghost of a chance of Pole doing some good by giving his life, he should try to give it. Also, that if anyone has any spare money, he should be trying to assist with it some of the outcast Belgian widows & children.[24]

20 Diary 29/05/1915.

21 Scholes, *The Mirror of Music*, vol. 2, p. 887.

22 Diary 13/11/1914.

23 Diary 15/11/1914

24 RB–EJD 05/11/1914. CUL Add MS 7973/B.

The style of refusal hurt, not far off from what Dent was getting daily from his mother. But he persevered, and as the war ground on and on, he gradually, painfully regained for himself the position of cultural and moral anchor for those dispersed around the world.

Throughout that glum autumn and winter he helped with concerts for the wounded in hospital, with glees at Nixon's and helping Nixon through his last lecture at Gresham College. The first real distraction from such routines came just before Christmas, when the bubbly J.B. Trend showed up at Panton Street 'just back from Ypres & Hazebrouck … He looked very well & very military with a thick brown moustache'.[25] Although Trend had always been one of the Panton Street acolytes and often called in, Dent invariably implied surprise at how much he enjoyed his lively company, and now 'JB' brought real news of old friends and some connection with those gone away: at Hazebrouck he had been hailed by Steuart Wilson in German, and had seen a few other familiar faces. This fleeting visit marked one of the first important changes in Dent's new, rather directionless life; a correspondence with Trend was struck up which would last the war and beyond. For years Trend's devotion had been overshadowed in Dent's life by Denis, Clive, Rupert and latterly, Bob Maltby, but his energising appearance and his engaging letters that winter eventually helped to prise Dent out of his self-absorbed torpor and back into his own kind of fight, harnessing his intellect, his pacifist–internationalist beliefs and his subversive methods. He began to write more purposeful letters to his friends at the various fronts: Trend, Clive Carey, Denis and Rupert, Bob Maltby, Charles Harman, Chester Purves, Philip Bainbrigge and others, bringing to them alternative views of the war laced with entertaining gossip and ideas. Although for months he continued to be uncharacteristically sluggish, his usual sense of purpose undermined, Dent had clung to the hope that the war and its mindset must eventually pass, so through his letters, he continued to express the thoughts and ideas he felt were important regardless of the war. His friends would come back to a world ready to receive them, kept alive for them in letters, an imagined world of music and civilisation, especially important for men alienated by their sexuality as much as their ideas.[26]

He also – daringly – sent copies of the *Cambridge Magazine*, with pacifist articles by Gilbert Cannan and Dickinson, all devoured by Trend.

> I have sent – or tried to send – my copy home, to someone who will read it, and pass it on – You can imagine how these things stir one out here, in the middle of routine orders, & nations, & mud, & all the rest of the revolting business. I should like to write to Dickinson; but I am interrupted every other minute: and don't like to put my name to anything just now… Dickinson's main point seems to me very good; & if only we could really get a public opinion to believe in it, the three things he puts at the end might be reached too, & another (& shorter) book written called 'It never can happen again'.[27]

25 Diary 27/12/1914.

26 For a more detailed discussion of Dent's wartime correspondence, see below.

27 JBT–EJD 15/02/1915.

Anti-war voices were being silenced by the DORA, while the popular press sold papers through jingoism, so the *Cambridge Magazine* quickly assumed a sharper purpose and eventually, a wide readership. For most of the war its was pretty much a solitary voice, employing the traditional British intellectual weapons of intelligent satire and sarcasm to point out mainstream absurdities, both petty and horrific, as well as attempting to bring in writing from a much wider intellectual field, including the enemy's. Otherwise the choice of reading material in Britain concerning the war was limited and dismal, ranging between the 'toxic vulgarities' of Horatio Bottomley's poisonous rag *John Bull*, or the simply conservative *Westminster Gazette*, with the 'airy confidence' of Lord Northcliffe's *Times* somewhere in between. But soldiers increasingly felt alienated by what they were reading; the official literature bore no resemblance to what they were going through, so for Dent's friends, the *Cambridge Magazine* came as real relief and an outlet, with its informed and intelligent alternative points of view, largely pacifist, thought-provoking, and costing only a penny.[28] From October 1914, it announced that it would print letters from the front written by serving soldiers, many of them former student contributors, later including Bob Maltby and J.B. Trend.[29] Regular contributors included Bertrand Russell, Romain Rolland, Vernon Lee and Ogden's alter ego, 'Adelyne More', with recent lectures by Maynard Keynes and Goldsworthy Dickinson, beside poems, and articles entitled 'The Origins of the Present War', 'The Religious Aspects of War' and 'Women's Work in Wartime'. When the jingoistic mood was most volatile, the windows of its tiny offices were smashed by passing bricks. In the edition of 12 June 1915, Ogden cheerfully printed descriptions of his magazine overheard outside a local bookseller's:

> The pro-German rag; That peace at any price rat.; I prefer to buy 'Fags' with my penny rather than support such an emasculated creature; It is a paper produced by a backboneless clique for a crew of knock-kneed readers; he [Ogden] and a few others I could name should be tied in a sack, and for their and our good, be placed in the river till the war is over.

There were shilling drives to raise money for Belgian refugees in Cambridge, and drives to get the refugees jobs and places to live. Dent's contribution from summer 1915 was a section devoted to the foreign press, edited by Mrs Buxton, translating and editing articles to give a broader view of current events, which quickly became so popular that by late 1915, regular supplements were being produced out of term. In 1916, when conscription became a burning issue, the *Cambridge Magazine* printed transcripts of the tribunals. It printed hostile correspondence, for example Col C.H. Gardiner: 'Sir John Simon and these 100,000 unwilling young men are at this present moment our domestic enemies, who wish to remain at home instead of joining the grand élite who are fighting with such bravery, blood and brains'.[30]

28 Apart from the magnificent *Wipers Times*, started in February 1916, written and published at the front, and Bruce Bairnsfather's cartoons. See below.

29 The idea was very likely Dent's; he was soliciting letters from various correspondents at the time.

30 CM 05/02/1916, p. 283.

But Dent hated the increasingly heightened atmosphere and began to escape to London more and more, where even a visit to Robert Cust was a diversion. Cust was now nearly demented, writing venomous letters to his former protégé Harry Burton and his wife.[31] Dent pitied him, and gave him time and attention, taking him out to the Alhambra rather than the Brahms *Requiem* in the hope of lifting his gloomy and destructive spirits. As these escapes became routine, Dent began to think seriously about finding himself a pied-à-terre in London. There were still quite a few of his older friends about – Ted Haynes, Maurice Ingram,[32] Albert Rothenstein, the British Museum crowd, a few other Old Etonians besides Timmy Jekyll. Military duty was still officially voluntary, conscription still only a possibility, so for the time being those men with no inclination to fight had some freedom of choice. With Ted, Dent could be himself, drink too much Chianti and discuss Ted's contentious writings on sexuality, divorce, and later, some strong criticism of the DORA, while civilised dining with Maurice Ingram at the Cavendish was larded with Foreign Office gossip. Dent even felt brave enough to call in from time to time at Rutland Gate, where the hints dropped over the tea-things about his 'war-work' were often leavened by encounters with his more sympathetic brothers Charles or Frank.

On another plane, Alfred Brooke, William Barber ('The Saint'), Charles Harman, Chester Purves, Geoffrey Fry and others on leave were frequently to be found at Timmy Jekyll's comfortable flat in Half Moon Street, or out at the Café Royal or one of Dent's favoured restaurants in Soho, the Isola Bella or Pagani's, seeing serious plays like *The Dynasts* and Conan Doyle's 'stupid' *A Story of Waterloo* or some 'Ruritanian melodrama' or the less complicated delights of the Gaiety or the Alhambra. Timmy was another divided man, who enjoyed both high and low art, with sexual tastes to match; yet another friend Dent felt he had to keep an eye on, but unlike Cust, Timmy had a clear idea of his needs and desires, a generous and sociable soul. Dent loved his louche but stylish company, and in his wake, making the acquaintance of a number of dancers; Dent would always have a soft spot for dancers. Then Chester Purves took him along to meet Robert Ross,[33] also in Half Moon Street, the centre of intellectual gay London, and they became instant friends. This alternative London life gave Dent – as it did for soldiers on leave – the chance to loosen up, give rein to the side of himself he had largely to suppress.

Music remained mostly in the background, but for a while Dent continued to work on his Purcell book at the British Museum, looking at early, obscure operas, researching Playford's *Harmonia Sacra*: 'I found therein many strange & interesting things by Purcell & others wch I did not know.'[34] If a production of *The Fairy Queen* was impossible, at least a book on the subject could fill the gap and kept him occupied. He finished it in May and submitted it to Cambridge University Press,

[31] Dent included some of Cust's own letters besides letters from Harry Burton discussing the whole sordid affair, in the collection he gave to the CUL in 1938.

[32] Edward Maurice Berkeley Ingram (1890–1941), Old Etonian, part of Dent's circles at King's College; later a diplomat.

[33] Robert Ross (1869–1918), Canadian-born, Cambridge-educated friend of Oscar Wilde.

[34] Diary 23/10/1914.

but the press said it was 'not desirable, either in your interests or in ours to publish it this year', citing the war.[35] Such flat, unreasonable rejection seemed to obviate any similar efforts, and until the last year of the war Dent wrote very little on music. But Dent could never be idle. His lecture for the Cambridge Antiquarian Society on 1 March furnished the excuse to research Locke's masque *Cupid & Death*, copying it out, rehearsing throughout February, scheduled around the performers' duties at the local Red Cross, finally performing it on 1 March, prefaced by his lecture.[36] But throughout that first year of war it was hard going. The International Music Society had been dissolved in February. Dent was older – thirty-eight in July 1914 – his eyes were poor; he knew that he would be less than useless as a soldier, and wasted as a medical orderly, the kind of thing Vaughan Williams (and from late 1915, Forster in Egypt) was doing. His Cambridge teaching now was all but suspended, with only a handful of students, including the Siamese Prince Chudadhij and Humphrey Procter-Gregg,[37] between him and Rootham.

Dent and Rootham now rubbed along quite well, possibly because Rootham's recent Fellowship at St John's had made him feel more settled and happy, less defensive. In February, he finished what became probably his best-known piece, a setting of Laurence Binyon's poem 'For the Fallen', and gave it to Dent for comment, although at the time Dent appears far more interested in young Jasper Rootham's use of his father's discarded music manuscript paper to make Dreadnoughts: 'I didn't know you could put music paper to such good use'.[38] But they remained colleagues rather than friends.

The BSSSP was still active but keeping a very low profile; Dent continued to attend the few formal meetings. Some of its members were talking excitedly about a welcome diversion in discreet circulation that winter, Forster's manuscript, *Maurice Hill*, which Dent read 'straight through'. He loved it, 'it is a wonderful piece of poetry and psychology',[39] and could barely wait to discuss it with their mutual friend, Greenwood. He wrote Forster a glowing letter Forster found especially gratifying, and they finally met up on 26 March at the National Gallery where he was working, occupying a tiny room dominated by Michelangelo's *Leda*, considered 'too improper' to display in the Gallery. *Maurice* is Forster's own personal credo, written at speed after that visit to Edward Carpenter at Millthorpe, less clever and amusing than his other work, more innocent; but it came as the breath of fresh spring air to men stifling in their closets. This was the novel of *romantic* homosexual love he really wanted to write, but at a time when D.H. Lawrence's work was being censored, there was no possibility of publication.

35 Diary 11/06/1915.

36 CC 07/02/1915. Jack Sheppard helped with the directing, taking the part of the Host himself.

37 Humphrey Procter-Gregg (1895–1980), later first Professor of Music at Manchester, biographer of Thomas Beecham. Dent's relations with 'P-G' were always edgy, for various reasons, the most obvious being his devotion to Beecham.

38 Diary 09/02/1915.

39 Diary 20/02/1915. It was not published until 1971, as *Maurice*.

> You have given me the greatest comfort and pleasure. I wrote it neither for my friends nor the public, but because it was weighing on me: and my previous training made me write it as literature ... now, backed by you and some others, [I] do feel that I have created something absolutely new, even to the Greeks.[40]

Regular letters from Denis, Clive and JB throughout that winter 1915 kept Dent informed, but his matter-of-fact diary entries reflect a deliberate detachment, even when recording that Steuart Wilson and Frank Yeatman had both been badly wounded. When Steuart suffered a relapse later in the month, with subsequent depression, Dent was glad to be able to offer him a refuge in Panton Street. He needed activity, and continued to crave the society of men who were otherwise in transit, escaping to London, where he could meet up with his comfortable circles, transient and otherwise, go with Kennard Bliss to the Queen's Hall to hear Beecham conduct Berlioz and Debussy, laugh at Kennard's latest self-deprecating stories, about playing Berlioz on his gramophone in the trenches.

Denis' letters had gradually resumed the old, comfortable style, mostly cheerful: 'Shells burst all round but none on top of us', he wrote after seeing action at Antwerp:

> Taken altogether it was an extraordinarily pleasant time mainly because most of us saw the humour of a perfectly incompetent force without any guns trying to stem the advance of a trained enemy with splendid artillery ... some special power looks after fools.[41]

Since joining the Hood Battalion in December, Denis had been sent out on the *Grantully Castle*, together with Rupert, 'Oc' Asquith, the Prime Minister's son, F.S. 'Clegg' Kelly, Patrick Shaw-Stewart and American Johnny Dodge,[42] going to Gallipoli via Egypt and the Greek islands, and the mood all that winter was high. Denis had taken time to reflect more; the period of complete musical and intellectual deprivation had done its work, what he called 'a great clearing going on', and more ready to think about his future.

> Its [sic] all very well for you to say that you want to hear Brahms again: think of me, fed on Tipperary & Gilbert the Filbert until they are bitten into my feet & my brain, & I begin to think of music as divided into two parts, comic songs & classical music, represented by Lehar's musical comedies ... inside ... I'm becoming quite clear as to which of the new people we need to explore so keenly are pedants & which musicians ... V.W. Moussorgsky, French & the old Germans on one side – Holbrooke & Co, Strauss, Schmitt, & Steinberg & his lot on the other. On a back shelf and useless except for the study of technique & form, Stanford, D'Indy, Ravel, & I daresay Stravinsky & Schönberg ... What a burst they will all have when the war is over.[43]

40 EMF to EJD 06/03/1915.

41 DB to EJD 14/10/1914.

42 Astonishingly, during the next war, Dodge would take part in the Great Escape.

43 DB to EJD 13/12/1914.

'I am glad you have got Kelly to play with', Dent carefully wrote back, ever concentrating on the music: 'He will keep you in touch with music – though I am glad I am not within earshot of your duets for I suppose you have acquired the Balliol touch by now.'[44] The ideas of musical activity, composing and of some possible future career were gently, constantly pressed. 'If only Mann wd die & you cd get appointed to that job. I cd leave Cambridge in peace & go to live somewhere else while you 4 people ran new Cambridge.' Dent's letters continued in that same vein, showing Denis that he had a future, throwing out reminders of familiar people, places and the language of a world not in war. Around the Gallipoli campaign that April and May, the letters are even longer, more detailed, with, e.g., a visit to Allen at Oxford, or going to one of the CUMC concerts:

> Jongen & Defauw, the Belgians came, Jongen played some very rubbishy pieces for pianoforte of his own: and then … they played Jongen's Pfte 4tet wch I had heard at the Omega shop in the winter. It is too long, but on the whole very good … Defauw is a very good fiddler: & indeed they all played it remarkably well & Chetham Strode as usual snorting like a steam engine.[45]
>
> Last Thursday I went over to Saffron Walden to see Vaughan Williams – who is there with the RAMC [Royal Army Medical Corps]. He was in a very depressed state … He has nothing to do, & thinks everything very badly managed. Secretly, I'm rather glad, for the dreariness of it has thrown him back on his real self, and he has begun composing again … There will be a lot for you to do when you come back.[46]

For his own part Denis appeared more willing to respond to Dent's approaches about postwar music and ideas, the 'real self' of Dent's fantasy. But he was naturally more concerned with his immediate surroundings and playing duets with Kelly.

Reassured, Dent allowed himself some more pleasant and focused activities: 'I am reading two volumes of Liszt's symphonic poems, to clear my ideas about him … also Rossini's Semiramide, wch fills me with delight.'[47] Lawrence Haward was down from Manchester looking out for exhibition material for his gallery,[48] taking Dent along to the Goupil Gallery, currently showing the 'London Group', Nevinson and Epstein. Trend came for a few days early in April, with his infectious delight at being on leave and in Dent's company again. In any event, after spending a few pleasant days up in Manchester with the Hawards, Dent stopped off at Millthorpe to visit Carpenter and to catch up with a young musical protégé, Fred Bentoft: 'I thought C. rather tired & depressed – it is the result of winter & the war. But he was very delightful & I was glad to see him. George walked back with me & we dined together & saw the Follies at the Empire.'[49] On the way home he encountered a very young John

44 DB 21/03/1915.

45 DB 21/05/1915.

46 DB 01/06/1915.

47 Diary 01/04/1915.

48 He had just taken the job of running Manchester City Art Galleries.

49 Diary 15/04/1915.

Dover Wilson in the restaurant car, 'who interested me very much'. Ronald Firbank sent him his latest novel, *Vainglory*, which he read aloud to Theo one evening: 'It was very post impressionist Peacockery – & made us laugh hugely'.[50] In this more expansive, positive mood, Dent began again to write on music.

'Academic Teaching: A Defence and a Criticism'[51] was written as a response to current debate in the *Musical Times* and at Musical Association meetings, and continues the ideas Dent had aired two years before in the *Cambridge Magazine* on the real purpose of teaching music history.

> I want to experience all the music that I can reach, and when I find something that interests me me I want to share it with other musicians, whether it belongs to the 10th century or the 20th. The price that I have to pay for this is the boredom of wading through large quantities of rubbish of all periods. So far as I can see, musicians wrote as much bad music in the past as in the present, and therefore it seems reasonable to suppose that the musicians of the present and future will write as much good music as those of the past.

Dent tackled head-on the tricky questions involved when teaching music, citing Jules Combarieu, 'La musique est l'art de penser avec les sons' (music is the art of thinking through sounds):

> Music, like philosophy and mathematics, is an attitude of mind. We express it in sounds, but the sounds are merely the means by which we communicate our thought to others … The so-called 'rules' are neither objects of worship nor cities of refuge. They are simply attempts to codify the habits of leading composers.

Like Busoni, Dent hated any fossilisation of what is a fluid and transient art. Contemporary music is really only the latest in a continuation of the past, and should be taught as such, he argues, yet the problem remains of finding new ways to communicate musical ideas without resorting to what he calls musical 'halfpenny journalism', the reproduction of 'all the latest clichés … but when these are reproduced without any particular idea behind them, we only see how old-fashioned they have already become.' He argues for the validity of all musical endeavour, with the caveat that it might provide not a living for a musician, but 'habits of mind that will make him a useful member of musical society in other capacities'. Dent is really talking about himself, his own early experience of failure at composition beside his own battles to become that 'useful member of musical society', the strong implication being that there are more ways to be a 'musician' than are currently recognised. 'The new semi-modal tonality of the present day will inevitably find its own new forms; it is the duty of the teacher to help these to birth.' 'Let us not forget', he says in his closing remarks, 'that it is largely these men, rather than the real composers, who have the musical future of this country in their hands.'

As if to illustrate these other types of musician, at the same time Dent was writing an article for Oscar Sonneck's American journal the *Musical Quarterly*, 'The

[50] Diary 17/04/1915.

[51] MT, vol. 56 (May 1915), pp. 269–71.

Pianoforte and its Influence on Modern Music'.[52] Its dull title notwithstanding, Dent's is a virtuoso piece, prefaced with a mischievous quote from Orlando Furioso, beginning 'O cursed, abominable device, constructed by the fiend Beelzebub … Go back to Hell from which you came'. He continues in the same iconoclastic vein, presenting the piano and its antecedents as a kind of orchestral tart, used for imitating every other musical instrument, including the human voice. Such versatility, he argues, imposes a kind of 'tyranny': 'Bellini was accused of treating the orchestra as an overgrown guitar; is it not the tendency of modern composers to turn the orchestra into a monstrous pianoforte?' Rather, he argues, the best, most natural instrument for conveying to the audience the music of any time, is in fact the human voice. It was last piece of serious musical writing he would do for some time to come.

❧ ❧ ❧

On 24 April 1915, the news of Rupert Brooke's death filtered through to Cambridge and London. Dent was devastated; he doesn't expressly mention Rupert's death in his diary entry, but the effects are all too clear. Desperate for distraction, he went out with the usual crowd, all people who had known Rupert well, to the Café Royal: 'a thoroughly bad place – with loud music, bad food, bad wine & bad service. I was in the lowest depths of despair'. Later, in King's, he sought more familiar company, hearing for the first time how Rupert had actually died, before moving on to Sayle's, listening only abstractedly to the piano playing. Finally he wound up at Sheppard's rooms, where Maynard and a few others were sitting in desultory silence. 'Nothing was said of Rupert … M[aynard] & I walked round the court together for a little time afterwards – and came much nearer to each other than in the last 12 years.'[53]

Four days later, Denis Browne's letter reached Dent. After his initial apparently minor illness, Rupert had been laid up 'with a touch of the sun' and stayed in his cabin, recovering enough to explore the enchanting Greek island of Scyros, but back in bed by the 20th, apparently 'overtired' from exercises. The doctors pronounced 'a case of acute bloodpoisoning' and transferred him to the French hospital ship, the *Dougay Trouin*, where he died the following day. Denis and Asquith impulsively decided to give him a 'wildly romantic' funeral that same evening on Scyros. Denis' letter hit Dent very hard, but the shock of Rupert's death soon turned to anger when it became clear that Rupert Brooke was being used as poster-boy for the Glorious Dead. A sermon preached by Dean Inge at St Paul's earlier in the month had elicited scorn and mirth, when Rupert's poem 'The Soldier' was being held up as the shining example of the 'pure and elevated patriotism' so acceptable to establishment thinking. But Winston Churchill's emotive piece published in *The Times* on 26 April established in the public consciousness a version of Rupert wholly unrecognisable to anyone who knew him. The next day Dent sent a long letter to Denis:

52 MQ, vol. 2 (April 1916), pp. 271–94. It was actually written March–April 1915.

53 Diary 25/04/1915.

> It isn't just the loss of the individuals we knew & cared about – it's the uselessness, the destruction of what we felt was our work, just started on its way for you to go on & do 'better': and the filthy romanticism of the business, and the bloody nonsense that the older people write about it … I wanted to see his realities.

It is difficult to understand now the almost overwhelming grief his old friends felt at Rupert's death, the intense sense of loss; Dent's silent communing with Maynard says as much as his outburst about the 'uselessness, the destruction'. Rupert's was a character that possessed that indefinable lode-star quality of attraction, nothing to do with sex but often confused with it, while his energy and enthusiasm had been at the heart of prewar Cambridge. He epitomised everything that had been most hopeful and positive about his generation – the 'New Spirit' – even while his friends entertained no illusions about his faults. His was also one of the first high-profile casualties of the war, eliciting an early example of mass 'recreational grief'. But among his old friends it was heartfelt and pervasive; for Dent, it marked a turning-point in his own passive attitude.

The day that *The Times* piece was published, Sayle phoned Dent to ask him to write an obituary for the *Cambridge Review*.

> I think it was the first time he had ever used the telephone in his life … I refused. Ogden & Theo have half persuaded me to write something for the Magazine. (That wd be better. One can't submit Rupert to a committee of Foakes-Jacksons: & Ogden will print any thing.) Yet I hesitated, for if I wrote what I know it wd hurt so many feelings … But as Ogden said, if somebody doesn't write better the slosh will go on & be collected into a book.[54]

He spent the next week re-reading Rupert's letters and articles, then over the first days of May writing it all up. The memorial piece appeared in the *Cambridge Magazine* on 8 May, causing quite a stir. The 'Ranee' (Rupert's mother) hated it and, rumour had it, was threatening to sue. But Dent's is a very gentle account of Rupert, drawn largely from letters to himself, presenting the Rupert who keenly absorbed ideas, who responded to travel, to people, to literature, who was above all, vibrantly alive, inspirational:

> however much his personal beauty might count for, it was his passionate devotion to the spirit of poetry that really gave *Comus* its peculiar and indescribable atmosphere … *Comus* deepened his sense of poetry, of drama and of music; it made him develop an ideal continually present in his mind, even in later years, which gave solidity to his group, the ideal of Cambridge, of young Cambridge, as the source from which the most vital movements in literature, art and drama were to spring.[55]

Ogden was delighted, and invited Dent to the magazine offices off King's Parade. Initially, Dent helped to translate the popular foreign press section, only gradually assuming more of an editorial role.

54 DB 27/04/1915.

55 'Rupert Brooke', CM (8 May 1915), pp. 390–96.

But that was in the near future; for now, after he had written his therapeutic piece, Dent brooded:

> I spent a lazy but depressing morning loafing & reading Denis [sic] letter of last night describing Rupert's death & burial – a very remarkable & painful document: painful because so romantic. I was rather depressed by it all last night.[56]

He had sent JB a copy of Denis' description of the funeral. 'It's a pathetic thing', JB wrote back,

> such mixture of pure beauty and pure ordinariness – the last sheet especially. Drill seems to have fettered his soul into a sort of official way of expressing things. 'His brother officers' indeed! Yet, what he says at the end is inimitable; I mean 'the poise of his mind was so exquisite' and 'he had that capacity for being perfectly happy' ... Your theory of the whole ceremony being a form of artistic self-expression is most certainly right. I wish Denis & Steuart could convalesce together I don't think Steuart ever went into this with a subdued kind of holy joy, like [deleted] as Denis did, but as a tiresome necessity which might, all the same, lead to some new adventures and now that the adventures are all made & known, & he is disillusioned quite, he probably looks upon it as a more damnable affair than ever.[57]

Clive took issue.

> I'm afraid I don't agree with you about Rupert. I admit his nervous breakdowns, but I never feel that they affected his balance ... Your profession of all that appertains to the intellect as <u>opposed</u> to emotionalism always amuses me! Anyhow his last sonnets seem to me to be amazingly good – & of course promised much more. Also, my dear sir, we aren't <u>all</u> mad who have found pleasure in giving ourselves up to this beastly war, though I know you like to think so – not all quite sentimental & unbalanced – & degenerate![58]

Another letter arrived from Denis dated 12 May, describing the fighting in the Dardenelles, 'bullets everywhere – maxims especially – and shrapnel', and how he had been 'plumbed through the neck by a bloody sniper'. By 1 June, Dent began to worry: 'I hope my letters have reached you?' Then, on 11 June, Dent read in *The Times* that Denis Browne was 'wounded & missing'. His last letter to Dent was dated 23 May.

> My dear Dent
>
> If anyone is to sift my MS music, will you? Its all rubbish except Gratiana, (perhaps) Salathiel Pavey, & the Comic Spirit. It lies at 6 Sawfield St Chelsea. Mrs Ridler will tell you where it is.
>
> Its a pity there's no more. There would have been if there had been time. But [scratched out] Everything else except what I've mentioned must be destroyed.

56 Diary 19/05/1915.

57 JBT–EJD 29/05/1915.

58 CC–EJD 29/05/1915.

> Its odd being dead. Rupert's gone too, so there's no reason why I should mind; and at any rate I've had a run for my money [parenthesis obliterated] & he was stolen unfairly before a shot was fired. There'll be noone to give me such a jolly funeral as I gave him, which is a pity.
>
> Think of me sometimes. W.D.B.

Steuart Wilson was still convalescing in Cambridge at Dent's, and had begun to sing again ('his voice is better than ever'), and gradually emerge from his long depression.[59] He was with Dent when the news of Denis' death came through; there was still a college dinner and a concert to sit through, before going on to Sheppard's. 'We kept it to ourselves till afterwards', Dent told Clive:

> it wd have upset Rootham too much to tell him just before conducting. And I feared that if the news got about that dreadful old Canon wd have made a speech – 'or perhaps Rootham would have' said Steuart ... I hardly listened to the Beethoven concert

A day later, after Steuart left, Dent sat down and wrote a long letter to Clive: 'It was a great blow to Steuart, who was already rather depressed with Cambridge. We had always expected so much from the collaboration of these two.'[60] With a terrible matter-of-factness he discusses the concert takings, the 'CUMS matters for next year', an amusing account of singing part-songs to patients at the hospital, the concert party, then abruptly:

> Denis' death makes me more than ever convinced of the necessity of going on with as much musical life & academic survival life as we can. It makes me feel horribly lonely – for he was the only person who cd educate me ... If I only knew how to do for other people what I did for Denis – but one grows old, and 40 isn't the same as 30. Stanford still lives, still lives – and I feel a horrible lethargy creeping over us all ... I feel as if I wanted to retire into a library and do research work in the driest German manner – for I am utterly sick of the music I was brought up upon, and there is nobody to give me the new.

It was one of the worst times of his life. The devastating *personal* loss is only expressed obliquely; for Dent, who set such store by clarity of thought and expression, it was after all, quite beyond words; such a mass of emotional incoherence was incomprehensible, especially tied up as it was with his own sense of mortality and frustration. Beside those men he had loved Dent was mourning the death of promise, bleakly confronting the possibility that the old gang and with them all his prewar hopes might not survive.

His relations with Eddie Marsh, although cordial, had always been tinged with jealousy, not least because now Eddie had official possession of Rupert's and Denis' papers, and Denis' music. Eddie, staying with Denis' mother and sifting all his manuscripts, was able to tell Dent how Denis had died neither quickly nor painlessly.

59 Steuart's is the forgotten personal tragedy, whose initial trauma was compounded by a later wound and emerged much later in violent mood-swings, beating his wife and making public complaints about the domination of the arts, especially music, by homosexuals.

60 CC 13/06/1915.

> Denis was in very great pain, but quite conscious, and not weakening – & that in the judgement of the man the wound was such as could have been healed if D. had been got back to the British lines. All this only adds to his heroism in insisting, as it appears he did, on the man leaving him – but it makes the whole thing ten times more painful & terrible for us.[61]

He wrote again months later, 'I hear one new point in the story of Denis' death which is a little comforting – that he had some morphia with him, & injected it into himself before he was left alone.'[62]

After Denis, other deaths came.

> The Times announces the death of Alfred Brooke, and Ted also telephoned it. Trend came in in the morning – for a very short call – & was too much broken to talk: we cd only laugh over an absurd death-notice in the Times of a young lady of 19, ending 'Violet loved Jesus, Jesus loved Violet' – & then sat almost silent.[63]

Everyone had loved Alfred; Ted Haynes in particular was desolated by Alfred's death:

> I hear that Alfred was blown to bits instantaneously by a shell & I am glad to think that his beautiful body is preserved from slow decay ... My affectionate intimacy with him I owe to you & although I am still suffering acutely I am glad to thank you for one of the few things that has made my life to me worth living.[64]

The next night was Charles Harman's dinner party in Sheppard's rooms, with half a dozen, including Timmy Jekyll, to see Harman off to the front: 'Sheppard was in good form & very amusing: but there were grim silences, and we were very conscious of ghosts.' A few days later, after dinner at the Wilsons', Dent chatted with Eddie Marsh, Eddie already planning a 'ludicrously sentimental' memoir in the 'glorious dead' mode.[65]

Concerts, music, theatre parties, late-night gatherings at Timmy's were a useful block to other feelings, keeping fear and grief at bay, and all that June Dent was going to concerts nearly every day, to madrigals, listening to Lekeu at the Henschels' together with Arthur Bliss's recent piano quartet, going out to Grantchester for tea with Ogden and Theo to meet up with Vernon Lee and historian Eileen Power: 'both looking very charming – Miss Power in the height of fashion, extremely effective ... Later we "did" the Old Vicarage, & I cd see that VL was making mental notes for an article all the time'.[66]

61 EM to EJD 06/08/1915. CUL Add MS 7973/M.

62 *Ibid.*, 16/03/1916.

63 Diary 18/06/1915.

64 ESPH to EJD 18/06/1915.

65 His biographer Christopher Hassall showed how close Eddie had become to both men in the prewar years, which is probably why Dent was so prickly. But he did copy out Rupert's letters for Eddie. 'In the morning I went to see Eddie Marsh & looked at his memoir of Rupert – wch is not bad & has some admirable letters of R's in it'. Diary October 1915.

66 Diary 05/06/1915.

That summer opera returned to Dent's agenda, new projects to pull him out of his 'lethargy'. 'I dined with Albert Rothenstein at the Café Royal Grill & had a long talk about Barker & English opera,'[67] at the same time, with Steuart Wilson, he was seeing T.C. Fairbairn[68] at his embryonic London School of Opera,[69] before going on to dine at the Vaughan Williams' in Chelsea, with critic R.O. Morris, where to his disgust, the conversation was mostly military. Another proposal, the previous March, had appeared in a letter from William Foss, one of the old MDS gang, who together with critic Edwin Evans:

> had been approached to start in London a permanent English opera & English ballet theatre not on the scale of Covent Garden … The main basis of the scheme is (i) to give the younger coming men a chance to develop their individuality & not write for the caprice of modern requirements in the theatre of commerce – (ii) to obtain from such persons as yourself valuable works like 'the Magic Flute' which have not been performed before in England & (iii) the development of English ballet dancing & singing.[70]

The proposal involved 'purchasing' the entire repertoire of the defunct Théâtre des Arts, with Jacques Rouché[71] and Ravel lending a hand, and Geoffrey Toye conducting; Evans had already enlisted support from the main daily papers. Dent knew Evans,[72] music critic for the *Pall Mall Gazette* and a champion of contemporary French and Russian music, a fairly sympathetic, jovial soul. Months later, Dent took Foss to lunch at the Savile Club to discuss the 'scheme', writing about it to an interested Keynes:

> It is only an experiment at present. But I want to be more in touch with London now that things are so broken up. I shall have to try to do a lot of things that I left the younger people to do, when there were some! I make a great effort to be 30 again: but the process of rejuvenation rather suggests Medea's methods.[73]

On 3 July Dent moved into rooms at Frank Buckley's house, 22 Balcombe Street, a street of Georgian terraced houses in Dorset Square, a far more convenient base. 'I am not giving up Cambridge', he explained to Clive:

67 Diary 22/06/1915.

68 Thomas Fairbairn, mostly a theatrical impresario, one of the younger generation, who also promoted music, most notably Coleridge-Taylor's *Hiawatha*; he tried and failed to get Dent to join him.

69 There is no mention of such a place in the MT, which seems to have had an editorial policy of blanking out any such alternative ventures. It does mention one production, of Holst's *Savitri*, which premiered there in 1916.

70 Foss to EJD 17/03/1915. KCA.

71 Jacques Rouché, hugely successful Director of the Paris Opèra 1914–44, who lifted that institution into the 20th century. He knew and worked with Diaghilev and some of his artists.

72 Edwin Evans (1874–1945), music critic. After the war he worked closely with Dent on internationalist projects, eventually on the establishment of the International Society for Contemporary Music, succeeding Dent as President in 1938.

73 JMK 15/06/1915. KCA.

> least of all after all the kind things you say: but I want to have more of a root in London, especially with all this break up. And I want to get work in London – possibly at the L. School of Opera, possibly teaching counterpoint etc, as I think VW will send people to me if I have a regular day once a week.[74]

For Dent, that indefatigable walker, Buckley's house was within easy distance of the various Kensington palaces of music and handy for his favourite Soho watering holes. Once installed, his daily life quickly became far more centred around his London activities: a meeting of the BSSSP with Ted, where George Ives read a paper. On the 8th Stanford chaired a dinner of the English Singers, with the Toyes, critic Michel Dimitri Calvocoressi and Donald Baylis beside a resolutely silent Thomas Beecham.[75] Soon, he was busy translating Mozart's *Marriage of Figaro* for production, far more challenging than *The Magic Flute* had been: Da Ponte was a librettist of genius, while Italian lent itself far more naturally than English to certain emotions: 'dolce contento' (sweet contentment) or 'fiero tormento' (fierce torment).[76]

On 5 August, Clive was back for a week's leave, and together with Timmy, Eddie Hamilton and Geoffrey Fry, Dent went along to the box Timmy had taken for 'Tonight's the Night' at the Gaiety and supper at the Savoy afterwards: 'rather bored – Still it was a relief that it was all energetic & not sentimental & some of the dancing was very good indeed.' What he had really wanted was to discuss Figaro with Clive, recovering what he felt to be slipping away.

> I woke up still tired, & depressed – cussing this fearful fervent life when it's impossible ever to see one's friends alone in peace – I believe they all hate it too & are hopelessly tired & nervy – but they are frightened of being alone or talking of things that matter – because one must inevitably come upon the realities – and they hate facing them. And I suppose it is worse for them than for me, because I'm middleaged, & they have lost their own contemporaries. I've lost no contemporaries, & have hardly any that I care anything about.[77]

Now approaching forty, Dent knew how much he needed the stimulus of younger men, missing Denis especially in this time of grief and uncertainty; that summer, if not a replacement, Denis' friend Bob Maltby was admitted more into Dent's confidence, helping to fill those terrible gaps. Then on the 14 August Cecil Idell came to dinner at Panton Street, bringing with him another officer cadet currently training at Pembroke, Siegfried Sassoon.[78] 'We got on very well', Dent records. The next day, he eagerly went round to tea at the Cockerells' in the hopes of meeting Sassoon again, only to find that at the same time Sassoon had called round to Panton Street with a

74 CC 22/07/1915.

75 Diary 08/07/1915.

76 Carey, *Duet for Two Voices*, pp. 84ff., discusses this point well.

77 Diary 08/08/1915.

78 Siegfried Loraine Sassoon (1886–1967), writer, whose *Complete Memoirs of George Sherston* became one of the classics of WWI, and whose war poetry (see below) was the first published in the new style.

book of his own poems. This was the first and possibly the most important of many encounters with the new order, the officer cadets who for the rest of the war would become another set of young men to enjoy the food, drink, music and conversation on offer at Panton Street.

Together with his former pupil Bernard Jones and Frank Buckley, Dent went down to Rutland Boughton's Glastonbury Festival[79] which featured Boughton's 'Festival of Music Drama', with an ambitious programme including Purcell's *Dido and Aeneas* beside Boughton's own *Birth of Arthur* and *The Immortal Hour*. Dent found *Dido* 'not good. Boughton evidently took very little interest in it, & had not rehearsed it at all thoroughly: nor did they seem to understand it at all'.[80] Boughton's 'The Birth of Arthur was like extemporizations on Elgar & Wagner – very baseless & tedious – but I was interested in the "choral scenery'. *The Immortal Hour*, he conceded, 'might be a good opera', and he would later encourage Boughton to produce it.

Later that month Sassoon dined at Panton Street, and the friendship was sealed; when he left Cambridge, it was with the promise of more. Nearly ten years before, Sassoon had come up to Clare College as an undergraduate, leaving after only a year. He was another divided young man, a sportsman and aspiring poet, a man who rode fiercely to hounds and loved music, an unresolved homosexual, his background exotic and wealthy. His parents were descended from Sephardic Jews and upper-middle-class, artistic Catholics,[81] and he had been brought up in comfort and security, already a published poet. Sidney Cockerell, that pragmatic artist always ready to cultivate rich, civilised people who might contribute to his museum work, had picked him up instantly. But with Dent, Sassoon discovered that he could let loose that other, hidden and unresolved side of himself, and over the next year this encounter would be an important part of great changes in Sassoon's life. He had already met Edward Carpenter and Edmund Gosse, who introduced him to Robbie Ross.[82] All that autumn and winter, Dent and Sassoon kept in touch, their letters affectionate and easy; before long Sassoon began sending some of his poems to Dent, and their friendship grew into something more fruitful for them both.

That September 1915, Dent went on another spartan holiday with Theo, this time to Devon. Theo needed a break: his lover Harry Garrett had been killed, and Theo had only found out by chance: 'Harry's death has been a very severe shock to him: the first bad one that he has had, I think'. By then Dent needed a holiday as well, space to work on the new translation of *The Marriage of Figaro* for Fairbairn's opera

79 According to the MT, the festivals took place between 1914 and 1916, then after the war, from 1919 to 1927, 'and had as their major object the production of choral dramas and other works of their promoter, Rutland Boughton, though the works of other composers were also included in the programmes. They were held in the Assembly Room of that small town, with a pianoforte instead of an orchestra, and there was necessarily a good deal of makeshift about them.' Scholes, *The Mirror of Music*, vol. 1, p. 169. Boughton (1878–1960) was primarily a composer of choral works, including several operas.

80 Diary 18/08/1915.

81 Jean Moorcroft Wilson, *Siegfried Sassoon: The Making of a War Poet* (London, 1999), pp. 7ff.

82 Max Egremont, *Siegfried Sassoon: A Biography* (London, 2005), pp. 53–6.

school. When he returned, that opportunity turned into a nightmare of ridiculous proportions.

> I am still wrestling with Figaro recitatives, as Fairbairn now tells me that Beecham wants to see them – the Paul England version being unsatisfactory and the singers being unable to manage spoken dialogue. The Mozart opera has been put off – although they had originally intended to do the M.F. as their first show.[83]

Dent's diaries and correspondence with baritone Frederick Ranalow throughout autumn 1915 record his frustrated attempts to engage with Thomas Beecham over his translation,[84] but he had not reckoned on Beecham's obliviousness to anything or anyone outside of his own immediate requirements, that any collaboration was sheer fantasy. Beecham's deliberate ignorance was more than a slap in the face, and Dent felt the insult. When finally he had Ted Haynes send a formal solicitor's letter about the translation rights, Beecham simply walked out of the production at the last minute, leaving his singers high and dry.[85] So a minor squabble over Dent's new translations of two Mozart operas exploded into a major incident with long-term consequences for British opera movements.

> I'm very sorry to say that in spite of the very sporting way in which you have acted since the upset, Beecham has given up all personal interest in the season, and will not come near the theatre any more![86]

But Dent was not without influence himself, writing to his old friend H.C. Colles of *The Times*, who quickly responded:

> Many thanks for your illuminating letter which fills in many blanks in my information … It is a real misfortune that Beecham is not a bigger man than he is. He has such remarkable gifts and such unique opportunities for using them that he might do splendid and lasting work. But he seems to have an inveterate tendency to play the fool.[87]

By April 1916, a kind of uneasy, unofficial compromise had been struck. Dent was appreciated but not officially acknowledged or paid, the tacit lesson of how fickle and destructive patronage could be so clearly demonstrated by the dismal episode.

'Well', Dent had written to Clive in September 1914, 'we shall have to struggle along with Cambridge as best we can, and I mean to devote my energies to keeping music & Marlowe going. Other people will do refugees, relief and red cross, and we can't have the really important things neglected.' A year later Dent was still 'struggling along', turning down an appeal from Jack Sheppard to join him and Dilly Knox in translation work at the Foreign Office, having decided instead to stick with similar work for the *Cambridge Magazine*. As ever, his instincts were right even if

83 Diary 30/09/1915.

84 KCA EJD/2/6/2/1

85 Ranalow–Dent 09/11/1915.

86 Ranalow–Dent 11/11/1915.

87 Colles–Dent 25/11/1915. Dent kept all this correspondence filed together. There were others in this vein.

his optimism often misplaced, and in spite of constant frustrations and a number of false starts over the next few years, now he was improvising yet another side of his multi-faceted career.

1916–1917

Just how far Dent had come over that difficult year can be seen on the page taken from the *Cambridge Magazine* of 29 April 1916. Dominating the page is a poem, 'The Redeemer', deliberately signed by Siegfried Sassoon, the first example in print of the new war poetry. In the top left-hand column, there is part of a letter carried over from the previous page, while another 'from a young officer' is there in full. The poem still has the power to shock, a more graphic depiction of war at a time when many fighting men were still carrying Housman and Brooke in their pockets. As shocking were these letters from serving officers, expressing less publicised views. This page 'very nearly' got the magazine prosecuted.[88]

The first letter is from J.B. Trend, written at Dent's request.

> You don't hear anything about 'clean' fighting now. Everyone in the cavalry realizes at last that his only business is to kill as efficiently and extensively as possible … The war is so horrible that it must be finished as soon as possible. And you hear very little about war 'doing us good' or 'keeping us fit' except in Lord Northcliffe's dispatches from Verdun. War may bring out the best of some people, but it inevitably brings out the worst of most people.[89]

The second is from Charles 'Bob' Maltby, former collaborator of Denis Browne and Clive Carey. 'So we are all caught', Bob concludes, after presenting an elegant and impassioned argument against what he saw as 'a complete system of underground committees of more than doubtful legality' ignoring growing public doubts about the war effort while keeping the public voiceless and in the dark about what was really going on. Bob's letter was a protest in everything but name against the increasing powers of the DORA, his points about legality echoing what Bertrand Russell was currently writing in the *Cambridge Magazine* and elsewhere, especially his 'Justice in Wartime' pamphlet.

Ogden was taking a risk in printing such blatant anti-war statements at this time, only months before the Somme offensive, 'the Great Fuck-Up', that July. That June, Russell would be arrested under the DORA, convicted, stripped of his Trinity Fellowship, his goods confiscated in lieu of a fine. Yet printing these alternative views was imperative; by this time its considerable readership in the trenches would have understood if not sympathised, as Dent knew from his own correspondence. Only a few months before, the *The Wipers Times* had appeared (February 1916: 'Cloth Hall Ypres … Best Ventilated Hall in the Town' …'The Road to Ruin … 15,000 feet long / Every Foot a Thrill',[90]), produced by men in the trenches, using parody, black

88 CC 05/09/1916.

89 JBT-EJD 15/04/1916.

90 *The Wipers Times: The Complete Series of the Famous Wartime Trench Newspaper*, foreword by Ian Hislop, introduction by Malcolm Brown, notes by Patrick Beaver (London, 2006).

out the best of some people, but it inevitably brings out the worst of most people. I suppose I ought really to be a 'conscientious objector,' though my conscience, not being religious, may not be recognised by the Act or by Major Lionel de Rothschild. The fact that I have been out here for eighteen months doesn't alter it. Perhaps we have all sold our souls to unreason, as converts do to the Roman Catholic Church, to save themselves the trouble of thinking; or perhaps we thought we could be better advocates of peace by seeing with our own eyes the futility and ingloriousness of war. But the orthodox will not listen to us even now, for they know as well as we do that which ever side wins it will be a victory for the stupid people.

[The second is from a young officer about to rejoin his regiment in France, and is written from Folkestone.]

10 *April*, 1916. I came home on leave expecting to find that that large and growing body of intelligent pacifist opinion which I knew had been in existence for a long time had found its spokesmen, its leaders, its newspapers, and was successfully working for the only right and true course—the immediate cessation of this ghastly murder. But no. The right of free speech in England has entirely vanished. And instead I find that Mr. Lloyd George, Sir Edward Carson, Lord Northcliffe, and the rest, are working wonders indeed. There appears now to be a complete system of underground committees of more than doubtful legality, created to enforce obviously illegal laws; and most important of their duties is the immediate quashing of any contrary opinion. Soldiers and civilians alike, we are all entrapped. Surely never before can so large a body of public opinion have found itself so voiceless, so scattered, so apparently unable to make itself felt. Bullying tribunals reign supreme. One effort only to break the spell have I seen: a few bold women daring to demand the right of free speech in Trafalgar Square met with an organised resistance, and suffered the humours of our colonial intelligence (the resistance was obviously organised and chiefly carried out by colonial troops), the cruelties of our Star Chambers and the sarcasm of *The Times*.

Hence the silence at home. As for us soldiers, unfortunately, the politicians and military authorities know they can trust us. For one thing, an organised body of opinion in France is impossible. But they have a better reason than that to rely on our silence. We officers and men enlisted and took commissions in our genuine enthusiasm for a true fighting cause, and in that spirit accepted the army as it existed, and were proud to endeavour to emulate the old regular battalions in our discipline, smartness and obedience to rule. We responded in that spirit to start with, and they know we shall not go back on it, nor betray our oath. I shall return to my battalion, and shall be sufficiently a coward silently to assist in killing as I promised. My contribution to my cause will consist only in taking in *The Nation* and *The Labour Leader*.

That is how we soldiers are placed. So we are all caught. Is the reason for our continuing this war the same as the reason for which we agreed to fight? Of course not. "Without Belgium be violated, the nation will not countenance a declaration of war." So is the political excuse exploded and our hypocrisy becomes transparent.

You people at home are responsible for continuing this slaughter. Secretly you know it. Individually you mostly acknowledge it. But publicly there is but one cry: "War, war to the death, till we exterminate our foes; and after the war, more war. Economic, social war." Hateful, detestable cry. Not even expedient! And we enlisted to rescue Belgium!

That will go on as long as you speak as individuals, and so long as you do that, shall we continue to make war without hope of peace. And my letter is only to entreat for some organisation of this vast body of scattered opinion, in order that it may make itself felt, become powerful, recover our rights of speech and opinion, defeat our political immorality, and stop this slaughter. All this it may do.

THE REDEEMER.

Darkness: the rain sluiced down; the mire was deep;
It was past twelve on a mid-winter night,
When peaceful folk in beds lay snug asleep.
There, with much work to do before the light,
We lugged our clay-sucked boots as best we might
Along the trench; sometimes a bullet sang,
And droning shells burst with a hollow bang;
We were soaked and chilled and wretched, every one:
Darkness; the distant wink of a huge gun.

I turned in the black ditch, loathing the storm;
A rocket fizzed and burned with a steady flare,
And lit the face of what had been a form
Floundering in mirk. He stood before me there;
I say that it was Christ; stiff in the glare,
And leaning forward from his burdening task,
Both arms supporting it: his eyes on mine
Stared from the woeful head that seemed a mask
Of mortal pain in hell's unholy shine.

No thorny crown, only a woollen cap
He wore,—an English soldier, white and strong,
Who loved his time like any simple chap,—
Good days of work and sport and homely song
Now he has learned that nights are very long,
And dawns a watching of the windowed sky;
He has renounced all happiness and ease,
And dimly in his pain he hopes to die
That Brumagem be safe beyond the seas.

He faced me, reeling in his weariness,
Shouldering his load of planks, so hard to bear.
I say that it was Christ who wrought to bless
All groping things with freedom bright as air,
And with his mercy washed their spirits fair.
Then the flame died, and all grew black as pitch;
While we began to struggle along the ditch.
And someone flung his burden in the muck,
Mumbling, "O Christ Almighty, now I'm stuck!"

— SIEGFRIED SASSOON.

THE MAGIC FLUTE.

There was a large audience at the Aldwych Theatre on April 15th to hear The Magic Flute, with which Sir Thomas Beecham inaugurated his new season of opera in English. Several of those who took part in the Cambridge performance of 1911 were present, and some were even turned away from an overflowing pit. One member, indeed, of the Cambridge cast was on the stage in her original part, though under another name. We may heartily congratulate her on the progress which she has made, and have little doubt that she will soom be at the top of her profession. As all critics seem to be agreed that the story of the opera is of no consequence, Sir Thomas Beecham doubtless did well to abandon most, if not quite all, of Mr. Dent's rather *tendencieux* Cambridge translation. Mozart's dramatic short comings were supplemented, as at Drury Lane in 1914, by recitatives composed by Mr. Emil Kreuz, who in old days often appeared here as viola in the Gomperz Quartet and its successors; and the ineffective endings of several scenes were neatly masked by the presentation of copious and eminently well-deserved 'floral tributes.'

FIGURE 8. Page from the *Cambridge Magazine*, April 1916.
By kind permission of the Syndics of Cambridge University Library.

humour, absurdity and above all, 'the truth about the war'[91] to express the inexpressible. At the bottom of the same page is a very serpentine review of Beecham's *The Magic Flute*, a little in-joke filler.

This page marks how Dent had let the war in with all its absurdities petty and horrific, through the letters of men he cared for, the residual anger he had felt at the deaths of Rupert and Denis now channelled into enough intellectual energy to take on the war itself. As he well knew, a new language was necessary to counter the propaganda being churned out daily via the Northcliffe press, *John Bull* and later that year Noel Pemberton Billings' *The Imperialist*, early versions of what is now called 'fake news'. The men at the front needed and deserved something better which did not insult their intelligence, while those fighting 'the home-front wars', the conscientious objectors, artists and homosexuals being excluded from public debate, needed a voice. And in providing a voice for others, Dent was finding his own voice.[92]

A sense of urgency had arisen from his own vulnerability: on 27 January 1916, the Military Service Act was passed by a reluctant Parliament; now all men between the ages of eighteen and forty-one were liable for conscription; 'everybody is in a state of nerves owing to the conscription act', he wrote in his diary on 4 March. Dent was thirty-nine, and he immediately enlisted the help of sympathetic medics at Cambridge to get himself medical exemption on the grounds of poor eyesight.[93] 'All meetings now', he wrote after a meeting of the Heretics on the 12th, 'including Club concerts seem to resolve themselves ultimately into UDC or NCF meetings of an informal kind!'[94] A few days later, on the 15th at a Peterhouse smoker concert full of soldiers and subalterns, M.O. Marshall performed Beethoven after a rough day.

> MOM played the Moonlight sonata quite well – considering that he had been facing a tribunal. They began seeing University objectors today & Alderman Bester was singularly offensive. He asked MOM the usual 'deceased wife's sister' question – at wch the audience laughed, and after asking MOM if he wd go for the hypothetical German soldier with a revolver and a bludgeon finally asked if he wd go for him with a tea-spoon![95]

The *Cambridge Magazine* printed the tribunals in full, with Alderman Bester singled out for special attention. Over the next two years Dent would himself have to face the humiliations of a medical tribunal three times, leaving him shaken and feeling even more alienated. That winter, family disapprobation reappeared, with visits to Rutland Gate especially painful, marked by smiling, implacable pressure from his

---

The paper moved around, becoming The Somme-Times, The 'New Church' Times, etc. See also Paul Fussell, *The Great War and Modern Memory* (Oxford, 1975, rev. 2000), pp. 194–5.

91 The editor Fred Roberts' own words in 1930. *Ibid.*, p. xx.

92 See Fussell, *The Great War*, Chapter 5, 'Oh What a Literary War', for a full discussion.

93 Diary 16/02/1916. On the 26th, he was rejected, 'and did not have to take the military oath'. Dent, graded C3, would only be exempted finally in February 1918.

94 Diary 12/03/1916. UDC: the 'Union of Democratic Control'; NCF: the 'No-Conscription Fellowship' (Bertrand Russell), two of many such anti-conscription organisations.

95 Diary 15/03/1916.

mother to 'do something' for the war effort, and even Isabel telling him tartly that he 'was very ill spoken of in the north for not going into the army'.[96]

'I go up & down between Cambridge & London – talking, eating, wasting time', he wrote to Clive that January.[97] His teaching, such as it was, was edgy and unsatisfying; even his CUMS concert on 9 February was a half-hearted affair, the rehearsals forced into 'wet and dark' old lecture rooms since the army had co-opted everything else, with musicians imported from London, the Philharmonic Quartet. Before the *Cambridge Magazine* work, the only positive stimulation in his life was his growing correspondence with friends in the trenches, especially Sassoon, Trend, Carey and Kennard Bliss, which grounded him that miserable winter and kept him from sinking into despondency, eventually providing focus and direction.

Dent's correspondence with Sassoon had begun when they first met the previous August, 1915. The common ground which had been the first stage of attraction quickly developed through letters into an affectionate, almost flirtatious tone, Sassoon cloaking his earnest side in self-conscious facetiousness.

> Thank goodness I am with our best battn. the one that gets wiped out every few months … But I feel more my original self than I have done for months. The scenes of desolation & misery, the boom of heroic 15-inch.guns lead me to pleasant paths of introspection, & induce suitable & proper reflection on human vanities. Rich & sombre, like army rum, my imagination flows from metaphor to metaphor until I have mixed a suitable cocktail to bring me to a state of fiery fierceness … dear, dear! what tosh I write.[98]

When Sassoon's brother Hamo was killed in autumn 1915, Dent was able to condole, telling him that one lives for 'the affection [I] can inspire in others'. Sassoon was touched: 'Your letter did me a lot of good.' Dent sent him current poetry from Sidgwick & Jackson, and Sassoon sent Dent an Egyptian glass cup ('alas! broken later' Dent scribbled in the margin), writing, 'MY cup is thy cup'. He also sent a pot of ginger ('red roses are too lovely for the post, but these ginger pots look homely & I hope you don't hate ginger') – after which he addressed Dent as 'My Dear Gingerpot'. And he sent copies of his own poems. He asked Dent's views on current music: 'I always hated Liszt's music, & always shall. Give me the aqueous elegance of Debussy, the sweet shadows & crooked flittings of Ravel. Do you like Chausson?'[99] With Dent he could talk freely about his current love ('my blonde subaltern') Lt David Thomas, and later, when he was killed, let out his grief ('drowned in his own blood'). When Dent wrote about his shift from Bach to Handel, Sassoon teased him in verse.

> Fragment of an Ode written for the Anniversary of the discovery of
> counter-point
> Can it be true that you [deleted] we are tired of Bach?

96 Diary 19/02/1916.

97 CC 12/01/1916.

98 SS–EJD 28/11/1915.

99 *Ibid.*

Music's cathedral-builder, – spark
Of holy blaze on harmony's dim altar!
Vast presence in the shrine
Of Melody divine;
Can Dent be done with skilled Sebastian's stuff;
And has he had enough
Of Mozart
's art?
Perish the thought! It makes my style falter –[100]

At Sassoon's prompting Dent began to seek out Chausson ('I've been looking at more Shakespearean stuff by Chausson, wch is most remarkable'[101]) and to involve himself more closely with the literary circles in and around Harold Monro's Poetry Bookshop in Bloomsbury. They met for dinner while Sassoon stayed at Robert Ross's in Half Moon Street. Dent introduced him to Theo Bartholomew, who introduced him to his own literary mentor, Henry Festing-Jones.[102] His recent experience at the front had jolted Sassoon's poetic vocabulary; he now acknowledged that the old-fashioned, self-consciously literary language he had been using was out of step with the way he wanted to write about the war.

> Out on the ploughlands we see Bengal Lancers riding in great style – what would Walter Pater have thought of them in this country? … I hope you appreciate my literary phrases, faintly reminiscent of half-remembered authors, clouded with clichés, – redolent of a fitful apprenticeship to the second-rate & out of date. O shade of Eddie! when shall I become virile & repulsive; when will I paint a rainbow which shall be withdrawn by an outraged & too impulsive Methuen?[103]

Dent was entirely sympathetic, and Sassoon began to rebel against the more conservative of his mentors, Edmund Gosse and Eddie Marsh, still publishing *Georgian Poetry*. 'I'm jealous that Sassoon is being brought out by Heinemann', Monro later wrote to Dent, '& sorry it was impossible for me to publish some of his things'.[104] Eddie appears slightly ruffled but not unsympathetic: 'I never knew it was you who had snatched Siegfried from me that day':

> I had two very pleasant meetings with him in spite of you. I think his poetry is slowly getting better … but I don't want him throw away [sic] the gift of melody which occasionally shows itself in some of his more 'literary' pieces – the thing to hope for is that he may learn to use it in the service of his 'more direct & simple' manner.[105]

100 SS–EJD 18/12/1915.

101 CC 06/03/1916.

102 Henry Festing-Jones (1851–1928), solicitor, writer, biographer of Samuel Butler, edited Butler's works together with Theo Bartholomew. Started the annual Erewhon dinners, with others of Dent's circles: R.A. Streatfeild, Geoffrey Keynes, *et al.*

103 SS–EJD 18/12/1915.

104 Monro–EJD 29/09/1916. KCA.

105 EM–EJD 14/03/1916.

'I have done a few short poems lately, & wonder if you will like them', Sassoon wrote from the trenches in February. 'The mud here is beyond description … I am hungry, starved for music.' By March more poems were coming out of the Flanders mud and blood, and although Sassoon still left his work with Ross and Marsh, he now included Dent in that roster of readers. 'I wonder if you will like my Christ poem', he mused rather disingenuously on an early draft of 'The Redeemer'.

> Out here it is easy to conceive ideas for poetry, but the difficulty is finishing them; one never gets the silence or the long evenings with a favourable book, when the right word one has looked [deleted] waited for all day suddenly pops up.[106]

'The Redeemer' proved too strong for Eddie Marsh or the *Westminster Gazette*, so Dent arranged for its publication in the *Cambridge Magazine* that April, with the two related letters on the same page. More 'bloodthirsty' poems like 'The Kiss' appeared in the magazine.[107] At the same time, Dent gradually began to recognise how the *Cambridge Magazine* was becoming the vehicle for his own personal battles, through his shadowy editorial influence seen above, and later, through his articles, and like his letters, it became an important point of contact with those now dispersed in war-zones abroad, from France to Mesopotamia.

Even before the war, Dent had understood the necessity for such small, intersecting networks of trusted friends, to mitigate the sexual and creative frustration built into their daily lives. Now, he introduced Sassoon to E.M. Forster, off working for the Red Cross in Egypt for most of the war, and finding his own sexual liberation there; they hit it off immediately, striking up a friendship through letters. In 1917 at Craiglockhart hospital, Sassoon met Wilfred Owen, who had rented a room over the Poetry Bookshop, and through Sassoon, Owen met Ross. Dent bumped into Owen once when they were both visiting Sassoon in hospital, and later that year one of Dent's close friends Philip Bainbrigge befriended him in Scarborough. Bainbrigge was a close friend, probably lover, of another soldier–poet in Dent's circle, Charles Scott-Moncrieff, who had given a lukewarm review of Sassoon's collection *The Old Huntsman*. When Sassoon later published Owen's poems, Scott-Moncrieff wrote one of the few positive reviews. Later still, Sassoon got to know more of Dent's literary friends, the Sitwells.

But one of Sassoon's happiest contributions was to get Dent more involved with Harold Monro's Poetry Bookshop, the heart of an alternative culture running in tandem with the war.[108] Dent had known Monro since Cambridge days when he was in Footlights, and had met him again before the war through Rupert Brooke, who had often read his own poems at the bookshop in January 1913. Its homosocial atmosphere had if anything been heightened by the war, and in its own understated

[106] SS–EJD 20/03/1916.

[107] SS–EJD 05/06/1916.

[108] Monro was also a regular at 'The Cave of the Golden Calf', and was himself conscripted later that year and stationed near Manchester on anti-aircraft guns. Cf Joy Grant, *Harold Monro and the Poetry Bookshop* (London, 1967), pp. 75ff., and Dominic Hibbert, *Harold Monro: Poet of the New Age* ((London, 2001), p. 136.

way, fostered dissent. In the winter 1915–16, Dent found himself playing several parts in the bookshop rendition of Hardy's *The Dynasts*.

> I'm not much good as a disembodied spirit – except that Geoffrey Gwythen thought me wonderful at articulating such lines as 'Who shak'st the strong, who shield'st the frail' – but I seem to have given general satisfaction as George III – modelled on Canon Pemberton, at a committee meeting.[109]

The readings were a welcome light relief that winter; Dent enjoyed himself hugely, but Monro's 'deepest purpose' was the dynamic of live performance bringing the words off the page, which fed into Dent's translation work, both opera libretto translation, and later that year, his translation work for the *Cambridge Magazine*.

❧ ❧ ❧

> I am overjoyed at getting your letters –3 of them by now ... You can imagine how reviving they are out here, when one is entirely occupied with victuals & vegetables, forage, coal, & even 'débit de boissons'.[110]

In 1938 Dent gave the Cambridge University Library a collection of his correspondence, mostly from the war years 1914–18,[111] assembled after the war, in 1919. It is a deliberate selection of letters, including some of Dent's own, returned to him when the recipients had been killed, with pencilled annotations throughout in Dent's hand. Dent had been considering yet again leaving Cambridge and academic life, so shedding a substantial paper archive might logically have been part of that process. Throughout the correspondence runs an unexpectedly upbeat narrative, the subtext one of alienation and including homosexuality; taken altogether the collection presents some alternative views of the Great War.

Quite a few of Dent's correspondents were bright, inventive, frustrated young men, and far from being sordid or miserable, the tone and contents of their letters show how they found pleasure where they could as an antidote to everything else being out of control, pretty warm for the times, and often highly entertaining. In keeping with his BSSSP and personal beliefs, Dent wanted hidden matters to be placed in full public view, in an archive few would look at; he could hardly have failed to recognise its historical significance. Moreover, the act of writing the truth gave breathing space to the clandestine homosexual world most of these men knew but could not acknowledge in public, least of all in the trenches.

From 1915 to the end of the war, Dent was reading in his daily post intelligent, articulate grumblings very different from the 'unholy joy' expressed earlier by Brooke and Browne, more like those published in the *Cambridge Magazine*. By 1917, the year Siegfried Sassoon publicly declared his *non serviam* and threw his Military Cross into the Mersey, those serving at the front were beginning to believe that the war might

109 CC 21/01/1916.

110 Selling drinks. JBT–EJD 10/02/1915.

111 Add MS 7973. Hardly anyone had looked at it in 65 years when I first saw it in 2005.

rumble on forever,[112] one officer expressing the view that if the current rate of progress were preserved, they might just reach the Rhine in 180 years.[113] But the dissent had begun much earlier, and as the hidden powers of the DORA extended, stopping the publication of plays and putting eminent scholars into prison, it was both expedient and second nature for Dent both to keep his head beneath the parapet (one of many such expressions coined in this war) and yet somehow express his dissent while facilitating that of others. His subversion was entirely positive, keeping the idea of a saner world alive for himself and his correspondents.

One of Dent's earliest correspondents, J.B. Trend, responded at length, and his letters paved the way for their future life together. 'Your letters', he wrote in 1915, '& Cambridge Magazines keep one from getting as demoralized as one might; tho' as Rupert says in one of those letters to you, one decays in the absence of the stimulus of people one can argue with.' 'Do not fail to write to me', Hugh Dalton begged him in 1914, even after his recent plunge into matrimony, 'Dickinson ... said you went about Cambridge smiling & reminding people that there were other things than war, thereby helping to keep some joy in the world.'.[114] William Little, whose wartime drawing of Dent was for years in the Music Room at Eton, thanked Dent for his letters: 'It caught me in a very depressed state of mind ... not surprising ... there is no one one can talk to as one would really like to & one takes refuge in books'.[115] In other letters, Dent discussed current theatre with William Bridges-Adams, then working at Liverpool Rep with Muriel Pratt, offering to help out with a projected season of Restoration plays[116] and putting him in touch with Sassoon. Gordon Craig urged Dent to carry on with opera production.[117] There are letters from his Quaker and conscientious objector friends, Cyril Armstrong and Leonard Doncaster; from German POWs Richard Schade (to whom Dent sent music and an instrument) and Fritz von Sonnenkamp; from English POWs, especially Charles Harman; from C.L. Boulenger ('Bou') out in Mesopotamia, Chester Purves in Basra then Bangalore, Morgan Forster in Egypt. Some of the letters are a memorial to those close friends who died: Philip Bainbrigge, Rupert Brooke, Bob Maltby, Kennard Bliss. A number are single letters from bereaved parents, Arthur Gray and George Butterworth's father, Sir Alexander. Many are from musicians trying to keep up some connection with their music, whether composing or playing.

'Many thanks for your excellent letter – I like drawing a letter from you' Theo Bartholomew wrote to Dent in 1918. 'You have a very good letter technique – for you enter into details (this is, I think, the essence of a good letter) & yet avoid the common pitfall of producing a cross between Bradshaw & Who's Who.'[118] In a

[112] Fussell, *The Great War*, pp. 71ff.

[113] *Ibid.*

[114] Dalton–EJD 13/11/1914.

[115] Little–EJD 07/06/1918 and 18/08/1918.

[116] 28/11/1916.

[117] No date. Edward Henry Gordon Craig (1872–1966), director, was always trying to interest Dent in joining him in Florence to set up a school of opera and theatre there.

[118] ATB to EJD 31/03/1918.

golden age of letter-writing, Dent's general writing skills had been sharpened over the years by his regular diary entries and by the daily routine of composing innumerable cards, letters, and notes to friends and acquaintances. Telephoning was still considered – especially by someone as punctilious as Dent – less comme il faut than sending a card to express formal thanks or an invitation. Writing was second nature to Dent, his hand is fluid and confident, with very few corrections, the ideas and images fresh on the page, even if some of his correspondents complained of illegibility. He obviously thinks as he writes, quickly, yet with clarity and style.

With the letters Dent often sent copies of the *Cambridge Magazine*, cigarettes from Colin Lunn's on King's Parade, Tiptree jam, books, plays, and, if they asked for it, music. When in 1916 Arthur Bliss was looking for compositional inspiration, Dent sent him J.B. Trend's manuscript notes on Italian songs he had collected before the war. He gossiped about Timmy Jekyll's familiar outrageous doings, was able to confirm to his friends that Charles Harman was alive and a POW, about Chester Purves being hotly pursued by a widow in Bangalore. Beside music, the homosexual threads, implicit and explicit, running through the collection are one common bond, a continuation of the intimate conversations and table-talk Dent's friends had always enjoyed, now couched in terms which could pass the censor unremarked. As Dent must have known when he gave the collection to the university library, taken as a whole it presents a more uneven, complicated picture of the men in and around the war. These were the men on whom Dent pinned his hopes for postwar culture, music, theatre and opera, and the ones who survived became a kind of international brigade devoted to the arts, helping Dent to propagate all the elements of civilised society that had been suppressed for most of the war and taking them out onto an international stage. There is nothing of any anti-German, xenophobic or jingoist stance, even from the men fighting, only the desire for a more civilised world and a few ideas about how to achieve it.

Of all the letters that survive, JB's are the longest and the most responsive, replies of a man who has found relief and respite, an outlet for ideas bottled up most of the time beside conversation on mutual friends and a mutual past. Like most of the letters from the front, his are written mostly in pencil on all kinds of scrappy paper, nevertheless long and lovingly composed. 'Your letter gave me great joy, & your conversation was like being in Italy.'[119] His was an effervescent character, infinitely curious, and his letters from the front, where he was 'Requisition Officer to a cavalry brigade', express his ever-positive nature: during the 'Northern Campaign' in April 1915, he goes for a ride along a Roman road, loving the poplar avenues and comparing them with the 'green road' Goldie Dickinson had shown him by the Gog Magog Hills near Cambridge.

Dent's wartime correspondence grew out of his own inactivity and low spirits, when he began to perceive a need among men like Trend who had survived both the initial war-fever and the war itself and were in the process of moving onto another plane of understanding of what was going on. Like Sassoon, Trend was finding the language he had learnt so far, the traditional or conventional attitudes, inadequate.

[119] JBT–EJD 12/04/1915.

The act of writing helped him to articulate his distinction between the 'pathetic' and the simply 'brutal', groundwork for his future career as journalist and academic.

> Another of your letters has turned up – a puff of reason, where everything is unreason, & most people frantic. I feel I shall have to come to you, when this is over, to be civilized. While this 'great advance' is going on, I have fortunately been lent to the 6th Cav. Bde … But I feel I have shrivelled into myself most damnably … it has taken me all that time to come to look upon the state & consequences of this (but no other) war as a natural condition of things, and to accept them as one does other natural conditions of things. As to loneliness – it has come to be the feeling I have when I am least alone … In the afternoon I was on duty at a cross-roads near the dressing stations; and tried to write a brutally true account of it in my diary, to send to the Master of Christ's and any others who might still believe that there is any romance in a victory. But on reading it over, I find it not brutal at all; merely pathetic.[120]

From November 1915, Charles Harman,[121] one of the Marlovian gang and a good friend of Sheppard's, was a POW in Westphalia. In January 1916, he was thanking Dent for sending him not only Tiptree jam, but precious copies of Otway, Marlowe and *Tom Jones*, which made him 'shriek with laughter'. Dent also sent him all the latest gossip, carefully worded in the prescribed POW style.

> I'm also much amused the the photograph, and your comments thereon. I can assure you it shall not get into any paper; the public shall never know how fat and well-liking you are, or how baggy your trousers at the knees. I interviewed Colin Lunn and ordered your churchwardens; if there was any difficulty it is no doubt due to Littlechild having gone into the Army, leaving a young female in charge. Had she been alone there I should indeed have despaired, for I don't suppose she knows what a churchwarden is, even in the ecclesiastical sense: the stupidity of women is one of the things that are being painfully borne in upon us in these times … I like your young friend with the cigarette; and evidently the gallant ally does too.[122]

So Charles was able to hear about some of the naughty boys he used to know, through sly references Dent knew would both slide past the censor and be appreciated by Charles. 'I am sorry indeed if the curtain is really down on Timmy [Jekyll] but I suppose it is really a safety curtain and it will be safer to resume the play when the fire has burnt itself out – or is at least under control.'[123] That is, if the censor could read Dent's handwriting:

> I write by the request of the interpreter here who says he cant read your letters; and that I shant get any more unless they are written clearly and distinctly. They

[120] JBT–EJD 07/10/1915.

[121] Lord Chief Justice Sir Charles Eustace Harman (1894–1970), Old Etonian, KC 1913, left Cambridge to join the Middlesex Regiment, returned, took a first in Classics, married 1924.

[122] CH 03/16/1916.

[123] CH–EJD 24/07/1916.

> have been especially entertaining of late incidentally and I dont want to lose them so let me suggest that I should pay a typist agency to print them for you!

So Dent learnt how to type on the *Cambridge Magazine* typewriter, and what began as a joke became an extremely useful skill. Charles was learning a few skills himself, German and Italian, besides catching up on his serious reading. But by that November he was producing 'a sort of pantomime review at Christmas' and acting in the camp production of *The Importance of Being Earnest*, toying with the idea of adapting *Lysistrata* for performance, 'but cant really see my way': at 6 foot 4 inches (1.93 m), Harman certainly stood out in the POW photographs.

Philip Babington sent Dent a poem, 'The Memorial', about Sayle and the Swans.

> He spake and wrote and published: Let there be
> A Campo Santo for the University.
> There those who lived replete with youthful pride,
> Whose wounds and morals ne'er were bound with hide …
> The while my latest swan, with breast of snow,
> Prone on my hearthrug listens to the tale
> Of how (according to C— S—)
> Uncouthest lads can be made gentlemen
> Worthy of Campo Santo – and my den.

Marcel Boulestin, posted as a translator in the Dordogne, was glad to be in touch with his old life. 'What nonsense Debussy has been writing about music and the war!' he felt able to say to Dent: 'There is not one intelligent person to talk to, and not a good looking one to stare at!' He enjoyed a mutually satisfying relationship with his superior officer, Sullivan, and to amuse himself, produced and acted in plays in drag: 'Deceit Rewarded / A comedy in one act specially adapted from the French and produced by interpreter X.M. Boulestin … Ladies' Dresses and Hats by Paul Poiret, Paris'. Homosexuality in the armed forces had been made officially opprobrious, and Boulestin had been more or less openly gay for a long time. By 1916 severe measures were being taken publicly; prosecution was not an idle threat, and few men found it easy to keep up the pretence.

For others, like Kennard Bliss, brother of Arthur and Howard, even before he was sent out to France in 1916, life was more complicated. In his brothers' view Kennard was the most talented of the three, artist and musician, but he was neither composer like Arthur nor player and teacher like Howard; rather his musical abilities were more like Dent's own, scholarly and appreciative. He was also funny, articulate and self-deprecating, loving 'your chimerical scheme for refounding decent relations with Germany by getting Germans & Belgians to play at the same desk in the orchestra'.

> When my father heard of it, he was furious. 'How one of that unhappy people can play side by side with!' But my father is very excitable & irritable. He has called me a disgrace to the Army (I never thought I should give an opening for that insult!) for airing mildly pacifist views.[124]

124 All of these examples are drawn from CUL Add MS 7973.

Before he was killed at Thiepval in September 1916, Kennard wrote long, entertaining letters to Dent; with 'my dear Serpent' he could chat about all things he knew Dent would understand and appreciate. His first shock was at the childish company he was forced to keep, even before they were sent to France.

> I like the work on the whole very much, especially bayonet-fighting and digging trenches. And if I have not much idea of military smartness, I have at least the one quality that makes a soldier invincible! I adore my officer. You have no idea of what raptures he excites in me – a young, brown-eyed brown skinned subaltern with an amazing perfect figure & carriage & a large Adam's Apple. What more do you want? I follow him everywhere with my eyes. My squad is very much out of sympathy with such a sentiment, manly young suburban 'nuts' proud of their just-conscious puberty. But I am certain an amorous & jealous rage would be the best temper for our soldiers even in these Krupp-ridden days.[125]

For a time, Kennard was still able to get to concerts with Dent, and their friendship was far from being one-sided: Kennard was serious about music and about contemporary art, urging Dent to go the the Goupil Gallery to see the London Group there, especially the Paul Nash *The Orchard* he had just bought himself: 'It is now mine! I adore it'. With Kennard, Dent heard the Bliss Piano Quartet (which he liked) again, together with the unfinished Lekeu at the Henschels. At least as importantly, Kennard was able to be open about his sexual inclinations, his self-consciously amusing account of deciding to become an officer's servant (which outraged some back at King's)[126] in order 'to devote myself to preserving his physical perfection for the delight of my eyes ... Without him life would be insupportable.' But 'he is in reality a very dull young man'. He mischievously quoted the ending of 'an epoch making letter from the Snayle': 'All the life of your day seems now like a drama acted and gone away, as it is in fact.' After Kennard's death Dent sent all the letters to his brother Howard, to use his own discretion about showing them to their grieving father. Howard thanked him for 'these delightful letters – thank you so much for sending them all – it was really good of you – They tell me nothing fresh – but they would at least succeed in mystifying father if they did not upset him.'

Of all his former pupils, though, Dent was most hopeful of Kennard's brother Arthur, throughout the war encouraging his efforts to combine his soldiering with composing.

> Ever so many thanks for your two refreshing letters. It is very good of you to write, and an occasional breath from Cambridge cheers me enormously.
>
> Many thanks for your epithets about my music. I suppose a military march is just about my line. – isn't that it? One thing shell fire tells you – and that is the ruinous effect of anticipation. I believe it applies equally to music. Keep on making people notice the enormity of what is coming by the way you approach it.[127]

125 *Ibid.* No date.

126 Diary 07/03/1915.

127 A. Bliss–EJD 28/08/1915.

Although never as close to Dent as his brother Kennard, Bliss appears to have been fond of him, besides respecting his professional judgement. While recovering from having been shot in the ankle, that August Bliss was stuck in the Empire Hotel in Buxton:

> trying to work on a fiddle sonata – also scherzo-rondo for orchestra but what can one do in a hotel? Also, until the war is over, I shall never feel free or untrammelled enough to work really hard or well. Once the Army has me, it has me. It's easy to get in, but damned difficult to get out. And I saw sufficient at La Boiselle and Posnière to last me a lifetime.[128]

Other Cambridge pupils, Armstrong Gibbs, Bernard Jones and Philip Bainbrigge, had become teachers, teaching being a 'reserved occupation' for a while. Like Bainbrigge, Jones was called up in 1918; like them, Gibbs had been terrified of becoming a soldier, grasping at the chance to teach at his old prep school, Thring, near Brighton.

> No, I have not gone to out to the war. Partly because I have not got the physique for it – as you know damp & bad food are the root of all evil to me – & partly because I feel I may yet have work to do in the world which is more important than fighting & lastly because I am I suppose a physical coward.[129]

Gibbs was another musician keeping himself occupied with teaching and composing. After Denis's death he had written to Dent:

> I quite see what you mean by our little group at Cambridge. If only we could have all found jobs there & these damned Germans hadnt existed what a lot we might have done. But dont ever worry about not doing enough for me. You fixed my foundations & if ever chance arises I believe they will be still there under the debris for you to go on building. I ask nothing better.[130]

Although privately Dent saw Gibbs as one of his less talented pupils, he never stinted in his help and practical support, reading each new composition just as he had done at Cambridge, encouraging his natural talent for setting words to music, and judging the singing competitions Gibbs held for the boys. '[I was] also much amused by your account of the Gibbs ménage', Bainbrigge wrote to Dent, 'I think that when he was born the Fates decreed that his whole life should be bound up with slightly eccentric middle aged women with string bags.'[131] Unlike many, Gibbs managed to get his career launched during the war: in April 1917, the London String Quartet played his new G minor Quartet (dedicated to Dent) at the Aeolian Hall; the following year he began his collaboration with poet Walter de la Mare, *Crossings*.

From 1916 to the end of the war, death was the background drop for Dent's numerous activities; the prolonged Somme offensive and its terrible toll included the deaths of more friends, the hopes for the future: beside George Butterworth,

[128] *Ibid.*

[129] Gibbs–EJD 30/09/1914.

[130] Gibbs–EJD 16/06/1915.

[131] PB–EJD 10/09/1918.

Sayle's favourite swan, Archie Don, Bob Maltby and Kennard Bliss. Steuart Wilson had been badly wounded again.[132]

In early February 1916, J.E. Nixon died of a 'paralytic stroke', another death which hit Dent hard. 'I feel rather as if I ought to put on record something about his musical interests', Dent wrote to Clive about a possible obituary for the *Cambridge Magazine*, 'for as with OB I take Nixon's music quite seriously. His range was very limited, but he always liked the best and knew what was good. You never heard him praise a stupid song because the singer had a good voice.'[133] Nixon's passion for performance drove his music beyond its natural limitations; he had taught Dent lessons about the pure natural power of good music. Singing with Nixon, even through all the fa-la-las, had really helped him to get his B Mus and to understand the connections between madrigal and opera. His death marked for Dent the death of prewar Cambridge music, with its dottiness, its high spirits, its exuberance, but his music collection left to Dent was there for the future.

❧ ❧ ❧

By the end of 1915, having been insulted and stonewalled by Beecham, and finding no real place for himself in Fairbairn's opera school apart from his well-received Mozart translations, Dent began to think seriously about how he could run his own show with his own gang, some kind of MDS for opera, using all the ideas he had been gathering over the past few years. His growing correspondence with the dispersed gang energised him, made him recognise his own role as anchor for their future.

> I think your teaching idea is admirable, & I should follow it up. I don't see why we shouldn't do the thing together eventually – I could deal with people's production, & pass them to you for the other thing. That should be a sound grounding for operatic work, & might be a material help for our opera scheme. If only we could get money at the back.[134]

The episode with Beecham had revealed to him two musical camps with two very different methods of opera production. Dent was looking to build from the ground up, through teaching and performance, a new generation with fresh ideas, while Beecham took the high road, getting his funding from a besotted Lady Cunard and his audience mostly from the rich and fashionable. Sometimes the networks crossed, especially with singers and musicians, but the fundamental principles were too different: Beecham's expensive, erratic productions sprang from strong musical instincts and flamboyant personal style, while Dent's more careful, scholarly and holistic approach was tested through performance and took longer to establish. The tacit questions arising, not least that of the domination of the arts by a single figure in a position of financial and artistic power, continue down to this day.

132 CC 19/09/1916.

133 CC 08/02/1916.

134 CC–EJD 02/01/1916.

> We [Bob Maltby and Clive Carey] talked of projects, and English opera etc Something must be done by our group. He wants to live with you when the war is over – says that you are the only person that he could share a flat and that you bring all the best out of him.[135]

So throughout 1915–16, Dent continued to window-shop while discussing music and opera through his letters and in person over lunches at his various restaurants, the Isola Bella, the Spanish or Pagani's, with Vaughan Williams or Armstrong Gibbs, beside the men on leave. He tried to see everything on offer, from Boughton's Glastonbury 'Festival of Music Drama' mix of old and new, talking with Viola Tree and Ivor Novello about putting on Vernon Lee's *Ariadne in Mantua,* all the time taking mental notes on what made an opera work in this country. The wartime closure of Covent Garden and the departure of most foreign musicians meant that 'operas had to be in English',[136] so translation was on his mind anyway, musing how English, the language of so many great poets, might be harnessed properly. When Nicholas Gatty showed him his new English opera *The Tempest,* he was predisposed to like it: 'very good stuff'.

London's music and theatre was lively enough, some of it simply flighty, escapist stuff for men on leave, *Bric-à-Brac* and *Pell-Mell,* with their chorus dancers, either girls dressed as boys or 'elderly dandies', which Dent found 'singularly repulsive'. A year on from Rupert's death, he took his sister Catherine to a 'Georgian Matinée' at His Majesty's Theatre, a double bill with *King Lear's Wife*[137] and Brooke's play *Lithuania,* 'very repulsive … but a much better play than people thought', organised by Viola Tree and prefaced by Robert Ross's 'Tribute', 'a cautious & rather apologetic piece of criticism.'[138] Dent eventually wrote a review of it for the *Cambridge Magazine,* using the opportunity to put forward alternative views of Rupert, stressing his scholarship in Elizabethan drama and the promise shown in *Lithuania.*[139] 'The publication of his book on Webster ought to give the final blow to the popular sentimental view of his genius.'

But the music on offer Dent found mostly 'dull' or unsatisfactory, even Tertis and Ysäye playing Mozart duets at the Philharmonic. Thomas Dunhill's[140] concert at the Steinway Hall was dismissed;[141] Parry's Monteverdi lecture at the Musical Association 'told me very little that I did not know before – except as to the Ritorno d'Ulisse wch I have not seen'.[142] As for opera, the current high point was Stanford's *The Critic.* Although Dent's relations with Stanford were still strained – 'we met

135 CC 28/03/1916.

136 Dent, *Opera,* p. 169.

137 By Gordon Bottomley (1874–1948), another Yorkshireman, friend of Paul Nash and the Rothensteins.

138 Diary 19/04/1916.

139 CM 02/12/1916.

140 Thomas Dunhill (1877–1946), composer of songs and later, operas. The entry in DMMM describes his music as 'pleasant and optimistic, always scholarly'.

141 Diary 21/02/1916.

142 Diary 15/02/1916.

twice in the entrance hall & glared fishily at each other' – Dent wanted to see what constituted a successful production right now. 'I have now heard the Stanford opera twice', he wrote to Clive. 'It's quite [good] as a spectacle, for it wd delight you by its stage management & production'.

> All Stanford does is to set the tragedy to music. It has this justification as Colles said, that the conventions ridiculed in Sheridan's play no longer exist on the ordinary stage, but do persist in opera ... They added so many delightful little new touches the 2nd night that I expect the opera will grow & grow like any musical comedy, until it's all 'business' and Stanford's music will sink into nothing. For the music, my dear, is really paltry. ... One thing I am glad of concerning Stanford's opera – its success is entirely independent of Beecham, I gather. At any rate Beecham has had no hand in the production: and it was most noteworthy for good acting, production stagemanagement and clear enunciation – I think more might have been made of Mr Sneer – a part wch wd suit me![143]

But Dent himself continued restless, bouncing between Cambridge and London; he needed a base. He had suggested to Trend that they might share rooms, to which Trend replied: 'I do hope you will leave your offer open about rooms in town. – I mean that you and I can make some sharing arrangement. I feel at present that I wd make any sacrifice to do it short of desertion; and that may not be an impossibility if the bloody wars are going on for 3 or 4 years.'[144] A year later, it was not Dent but Trend who found the rooms in New Quebec Street which they kept for the next twenty-five years, a London base which became a refuge and common ground for their developing relationship. More than just good company, Trend could appreciate the *Goyescas* of Granados or discuss pacifism intelligently; they had a common language, a common background and sexuality, and Dent needed the solid prop and stimulus he only gradually recognised in Trend. Dent moved in on 20 March 1916. It was too small to share comfortably; they would gradually improve and expand the living and sleeping spaces, eventually acquiring a piano from Rutland Gate and a bed long enough for Dent. The landlady, Mrs Bennett ('La Bennettia'), was friendly and accommodating. Presently, JB was posted closer to home, and for the last two years of the war fitted in seamlessly with Dent's increasingly busy London life, going to concerts, restaurant parties, then along to Timmy's. The more devoted of the pair, JB had to take what he could from Dent, but it appears to have been a remarkably open and uncomplicated relationship.

Once he had his base at New Quebec Street, Dent's London circles expanded with men on leave or recovering, so he was often in company on the town, dining with Ross, Sassoon and Graves, with Theo and Festing-Jones and Desmond MacCarthy, with Frank Birch and 'the Lion' at the Café Royal, catching up with Hal Goodhart-Rendel and Edgar Mathews, even finding the time to visit his brother Frank, even discussing 'tribunals & conscientious objection'.[145] An expedition to Ridgehurst with

143 CC 16/01/1916.

144 JBT–EJD 29/05/1915.

145 Diary 18/09/1916.

Ferdy Speyer[146] and the Frank Bridges opened up some of Bridge's recent (1916) chamber music: 'extremely well written'. He was reading Sassoon's latest poems with 'Sco-Mo' (Scott-Moncrieff) and Philip Bainbrigge; in June going with Sassoon himself to hear more chamber music at the Aeolian Hall, including Chausson's 'Chanson Perpetuelle' and some 'well-made amusements by Frank Bridge' on 'Sally in our Alley'. Then, out of the blue, A.C. Benson sent him something astonishing just discovered in the Pepys Library at Magdalene College, five MSS volumes, 'instrumental part books c.1700, containing 60 suites of pieces, made up I think from theatre music. I identified about 20 bits of Purcell.'[147] It came as a pleasant shock to be consulted like this by Benson, who detested him, and that summer, got him back into serious scholarly music. The resulting ideas were passed on to his former pupil Bernard Jones, then still teaching at Radley. As with most of his former pupils Dent had kept in touch, lending a hand with the school concerts, especially Purcell's *King Arthur*, and included Jones in his trips to Boughton's Glastonbury Festivals. Such loose but important connections that summer kept Dent's mind on the unformed operatic visions he still entertained for a postwar future, so he persevered with Frank Bridge's recent music, or with Roger Quilter, 'who showed me his new pianoforte pieces … rather in the manner of Delius and extremely good'.

> I think he has come on a great deal. For years I had wanted to get to know him intimately, so as to be able to criticize his stuff, and point out his errors to him: and now that I am beginning to see something of him I find that he has done most of what I wanted himself … was very much interested and keen about our projects for an opera school and a new style of singing.[148]

The fantasy 'opera school and a new style of singing' continued to exercise Dent for the rest of the war and after, while little on offer caught his imagination. Even the current Proms he found only worth mentioning for chatting with Miles Malleson, about as close to the old stimulating, serendipitous Cambridge as one could get. 'The Promenades have been horribly dull: and I begin to think that I only go to them for the Promenade – the only one in London now, I gather! Anyway it seems to be the only place where I ever meet anybody I know.'[149]

> I heard from Chester the other day from near Basra … it seems a horrible place, and the only consolation is that the Arab singing reminds him of Stravinsky and Debussy: I almost envy him, for it seems impossible to hear modern music in London nowadays, owing partly to the expense of rehearsals, and partly to the fact that the present public takes music more than ever as a mere narcotic.[150]

He began tentatively to work with another discovery of his, the singer Gladys Moger, one of the English Singers.'The Moger is now going on tour with Sapellnikoff', he

146 Diary 21/04/1916. Ferdinand Speyer, son of Edward Speyer, banker and musical philanthropist, Old Etonian friend of F.S. Kelly and Frank Bridge.

147 Diary 15/06/1916.

148 CC 19/09/1916.

149 *Ibid.*

150 CC 03/09/1916.

wrote to Clive, who knew her well. 'and is to sing "Deh vieni" in English to my words. We did a lot of work at Susanna together, and she seemed to think I had given her a lot of new ideas.'[151] Later that year they were doing more, Scarlatti beside Mozart;[152] in Moger, Dent felt he had found a singer he could help to develop in the ways he was hoping for, his eventual school firming up.

> Parry wrote to say that he had put Eddie Marsh on to suggesting V.W.'s opera to Beecham; Beecham said he was too shy to ask V.W. for it. I hope V.W. will prefer to wait until we can produce it for him, with Steuart as the hero; I don't quite see any of Tommy's tenors in that part, except perhaps Webster Millar, who made a very pretty Cassio. I foresee [sic] that Fairbairn will never be any use to me.[153]

Later that same March, the current object of Dent's affections and hopes, Bob Maltby, was back on leave, 'very haggard & thin', his health and normal high spirits badly affected by having been through some of the worst of the trenches, north of Ypres, all that terrible winter.[154] Bob stayed at Panton Street for two days, quietly enjoying piano music and the company of Gordon Craig who came to dinner one evening, 'very large & cheerful'. Such contact was important for Dent, too; he was a sympathetic listener, but always an active one, his own anger at what was happening to these young men eventually sublimated into action. He wanted them to feel that they had a stake in the future, that evening conversations about theatre and music were not airy echoes of a former life, but real prospects. Throughout 1916, Dent's work for the *Cambridge Magazine* accelerated, with the translations from the Italian press: 'I little knew what slavery I was in for'.[155] By August, he was working there more or less full-time, squeezed in with his London life. 'My work has all got into hopeless disorder', he wrote to Clive:

> latterly I have been devoting most of my time to translating things for Mrs Buxton & the Cambridge Magazine. I have also promised to give Ogden regular help with editorial work, as he can't afford to pay a sub-editor. It would be a pity to let the Magazine disappear after all it has done.[156]

A fortnight's walking around Sedburgh with Theo in August 1916, 20 miles (32 km) a day, gave them both a break, Dent stopping to lecture on Mozart at a training college in Bingley. Theo was working on his index to Festing-Jones' *Life of Samuel Butler,* Dent reading, escaping the removal back in Cambridge into his new house at 77 Panton Street, supervised by a reluctant Hills, at the same rent but with a bit more space. 'The move was worth while if only for the pleasant dining

151 CC 18/08/1916.

152 CC 15/12/1916.

153 CC18/08/1916. The opera was *Hugh the Drover*.

154 CC 16/03/1916. But the diary records this as taking place on 27–28 March.

155 CC 13/04/1916.

156 CC 03/09/1916.

room at the back, wch gets the morning sun, my bedroom also: and the south window in the big room.'[157]

'I've got to conduct the CUMS while Rootham is away', Dent wrote Clive that Michaelmas term 1916, 'and feel rather unequal to it. Ten years ago – ! things have changed since then and I have settled down too hopelessly for antiquarianism. But perhaps when I get a stick in my hands I shall wake up.'[158] To his surprise, he found himself enjoying working again on Haydn, Mozart and especially Palestrina's *Iste Confessor*.[159]

Robert Ross wanted to propose Dent for the Reform Club, possibly since he had been claiming to avoid the Savile these days for fear of running into Stanford.[160] Philip Bainbrigge introduced him to Ronald Knox, whose flat Dent compared to 'a sort of ecclesiastical curiosity shop'. But the most important new encounter that autumn of 1916 was at William Barber's press in Watergate House, where Dent met the young conductor Adrian Boult.[161] The following day they were dining together at the Treviglio, Dent having given up the Isola Bella as attracting too many Colonel Blimp types. 'I like Boult very much', Dent enthused to Clive, 'he is now working with Sheppard – and we must rope him in to our schemes'. His current War Office work was similar to Dent's at the *Cambridge Magazine*, translating German. What tickled Dent's sense of the absurd was how Boult was juggling this with serious music-making, especially when his superior decided to co-opt him into becoming a government travelling sales rep. A year later Boult was still juggling: Dent had a letter from Arthur Bliss in Bath, doing a similar bit of juggling himself on a battered piano he had been allowed to use in whatever spare time he had.

> I ran across another friend of yours, Adrienne [sic] Bolt [del] Boult. He dashed in one evening with a small dispatch case in his hand, having travelled from Cardiff on business for the W.O. i.e. selling boots. In the case was two or three pamphlets about ladies' uppers & other Govtlike technicalities & score of V.W. London symphony, In the South, & Brandenberg, & an Arnold Bax MS. I have never seen anything so absurd in my life – absolutely Gilbertian.[162]

Bliss on a battered piano; Boult selling boots. Where was the future of music in all this?

When Dent moved into his new house next door, a new wave of officer cadets passing through Cambridge seized the opportunity for good food and wine and free, intelligent conversation. Word had got round about Dent, Bartholomew and Mansfield 'Manny' Forbes at Clare. Music and art were important, but probably the most important common factor was a subversive sense of humour. Several of the young cadets were artists, had studied at the Slade, many joining the Artists Rifles, and the old style of giving out nicknames, especially the archangel ones, returned:

157 Diary 28/08/1916.

158 CC 03/09/1916.

159 *Ibid.*

160 Diary 02/10/1916.

161 Sir Adrian Cedric Boult (1889–1983), knighted 1937, lifelong friend and colleague of Dent's, conducting for the ISCM concerts, ran the BBC Symphony Orchestra in its early days. He later married Steuart Wilson's rejected wife, a typical act of chivalry.

162 A. Bliss–EJD 12/01/1918.

John Wells, Harley Trott ('Harlequin') and William Atkin ('Gabriel'), W.H. Haslam ('Michael'), Beverley Nichols ('Nicolette') and W.J. Sprott ('Sebastian') echoed The Saint, The Little Wretch and The Lion. Their letters were often illustrated. Dent basked in it all, loving what sparkle these naughty boys, later the Bright Young Things of the twenties, brought into his life, especially towards end of the war. They joined him in London for lunches at Pagani's and evenings at the opera, begged him to visit: '... please come, & Ill really try hard to soothe you & make you forget about all meetings now & to come'.[163] He dispensed the wine and food, and they regaled him with their latest adventures; he looked after them, as mentor and friend.

But from 1916, public prosecutions of 'indecent' or 'lewd' behaviour were on the rise, under a broader DORA remit. That summer, Timmy Jekyll had been sent to a 'sanatorium' in Scotland, probably to keep him out of trouble: Dent often mentions steering Timmy away from imminent disasters and getting him safely back to his housekeeper Marguerite. From his incarceration Timmy wrote funny, desolate letters:

> Signor, I have been meaning to write to you, but I waited till I could adjust myself a little to the low visibility of the future – today I learn that I am to be released from this house of correction – Deo gratias – but only on condition that I abstain from the life of a Nibelung for the next 6 weeks etc after which vistas of agricultural usefulness might unfold themselves.[164]
>
> I am hungry for friends & music, & it seems so long since I enjoyed either of them. What was the Delius 4tet like I wonder? & the modern Spanish stuff? Ever your Tim Marguerite sends her salutations.[165]

Not all of the circle had fond memories. Sixty years later, journalist Beverley Nichols unkindly recalled Dent as 'a rather wicked old man in a withered sort of way' and 'naughty old gentleman'.[166] Dent was forty at the time, which may have seemed 'old' to someone of twenty, but perhaps the self-important Nichols had always resented being labelled 'Nicolette'.

The painter John Wells, on the other hand, loved having an indulgent audience for his entertainingly camp descriptions of work he had just done or his constant adventures on the edge. At one point Dent was recommending Ted Haynes to help him out of a possible disgrace – 'merely sordid but in no way scandalous'. One of the very reluctant soldiers, John made entertaining little dramas out of everything to hand, from the 'mint goddess blotting paper' battle dress he had been trying so hard to avoid, to his recent post.

> I have had a letter & a photo from a prisoner of war in Germany which looked very very optimistic for the first time ... he is dressed exquisitely with silk kerchief

163 Atkin–EJD, n.d. CUL Add MS 7973/A.

164 FJ–EJD 09/07/1916.

165 FJ–EJD 21/11/1916.

166 Beverley Nichols, *The Unforgiving Minute* (London, 1978), pp. 38–9. Nichols' attitude and stories were repeated in Egremont, *Siegfried Sassoon*, pp. 70–71, adding that 'Dent was often seen with rent boys' in London. See below.

> drooping from heart pocket & I believe intimately that the socks match – There were several in the photo & they look happier than anyone has ever looked in any place of amusement or funeral in London.[167]

Once installed at Hare Hall Camp, he managed to 'make the best of it':

> It was relieved last night by a funny little episode which is not suitable to pen & ink – As luck so often contrives it the boy in the bed (ie three wooden planks & three rough tickly blankets) next to me had a very good mouth & made eyes most susceptibly just before lights out. Intrigue is not very easy in a hut with 30 other men – but we made the best of the situation.[168]

Wells may have been amusingly flippant about it, but he was taking a real risk.[169]

Later in the war, William 'Gabriel' Atkin turned up on the doorstep, a young painter with a drink problem, charming, good-natured and easy-going to a fault; a man less likely to command other men could not be imagined, as his letters show. Theo Bartholomew often visited him at Margate where he was stationed, and after seeing what he was getting up to there, determined to introduce him to Henry 'Enrico' Festing-Jones as a seriously steadying influence. 'I do wish he could get some regular congenial society', Theo wrote to Dent, 'I talked to him seriously about poker & champagne & I think he will try to be a little more reasonable as I gather that others had hinted that he was becoming a little to conspicuous'.[170] 'We must use every effort to get Gabriel started upon some work as soon as possible … His nature is starved for it, though I daresay he does not know it! … he is very weak & easily led. He is much too good to be wasted.'[171] When later that year Siegfried Sassoon was discharged from Craiglockhart, Dent and Theo decided to introduce him to Gabriel; such an unlikely pairing might be to some useful mutual benefit, they felt, since Siegfried was now out of Craiglockhart and 'inclined to rush about too much'. 'It was a very good idea of yours to make those 2 meet. I told him about Gabriel & I think he will do G. a lot of good.'[172] It worked. 'Siegfried is the most amazing gorgeous person in the universe', Gabriel gushed a week later. 'He is the most wonderful thing that has ever happened. I'm not going to talk.' It didn't last, Gabriel's alcoholism too much even for Sassoon's monumental patience.

In the last eighteen months of war, from the winter of 1916, Timmy's friend Barwell was now up at Clare, with a Captain Evelyn Broadwood, scion of the piano-makers, and Albert Rothenstein or Rutherstone at Jesus. Men of all ages were being made to undergo the humiliating medical tribunals over and again, and with most of his former pupils now conscripted, Dent found Cambridge bleak. 'I can give

[167] JW–EJD, n.d.

[168] JW-EJD 19/09/1917.

[169] Hynes, *A War Imagined*, pp. 224ff. cites the *Manual of Military Law,* and a case described in Raymond Asquith's letters where a Guardsman was publicly humiliated and stripped of all his military honours.

[170] ATB–EJD 05/04/1918.

[171] ATB–EJD 09/09/1918.

[172] ATB–EJD 18/11/1918.

you no news of Kings – I hardly set foot in it – I can't bear dining in Hall now, nor can Sheppard when he comes for a rare week-end.'[173] Finally, he felt obliged to make a stand through his writings in the *Cambridge Magazine*; the 'Georgian Matinée' article he had written in May 1916 was the first in this more contentious vein.[174] The next, early in 1917, was the product of his recent reading on how other countries were responding to the endless war. Britain was not unique, only rather obtuse.

> Even now, when foreign politics ought to be more closely studied, and possibly are by some Englishmen not so utterly ignored as they were before the war, the general idea is that they are of secondary importance, because whatever changes of ministry may take place in any country, ally or enemy, we are always assured by our own press and theirs that 'it will make no difference to the conduct of the war'.[175]

In March, 1917, Dent and Ogden took on the Fight for Right movement,[176] which had now turned their attention specifically to the *Cambridge Magazine*, and the 'dangerous sophistry' it published. Dent was appalled that the movement had attracted a number of artists, people he knew, and that they had co-opted the Aeolian Hall for their meetings.

> During the last few weeks elaborate advertisements of the *Cambridge Magazine* have been prominent in many journals and reviews. These advertisements lay stress on the advantages of reading the extracts from the Foreign Press (edited by Mrs C.R. Buxton) which are a special feature of the paper; and suggest that those who do not thus acquaint themselves with foreign opinion cannot hope to see the war in true perspective ... On examining this paper one is struck by the fact that the view of the war put before us is remarkably free from any exhilarating belief in the victory of the Allied arms or predominating righteousness of their cause; also by the frequency of quotations from obscure and extremist papers, especially those which dwell on the possibility or desirability of immediate peace, the unlikelihood of an Allied victory in the field, the greed and hypocrisy of Great Britain, the brutality of Russia, and other themes beloved of the 'intellectual' type of Pacifist.[177]

Beside a robust defence of its principles, the *Cambridge Magazine* published a letter of support signed by Thomas Hardy, Arnold Bennett, J.C. Squire, Rebecca West, Jane Harrison, to name a few, calling for press freedom, especially in a time of war.

173 CC 01/05/1917.

174 'Georgian Drama' 27/05/1916; 'William Sterndale Bennett, 1816–1916' 25/11/2016; 'Italy and the War' 02/12/1916; 'Hungary and the War' 03/02/1917; 13 articles in 1917.

175 'Hungary and the War', CM (03/02/1917).

176 The movement was founded in December 1915, by Francis Younghusband, and included a number of musicians, such as Muriel Foster and Gervase Elwes. There was also a song by Elgar (one of the founders) in 1916, with words from William Morris' 'Sigurd the Volsung': e.g., 'Then loosen thy sword in the scabbard and settle the helm on thine head, / For men betrayed are mighty, and great are the wrongfully dead', a protest against the peace movements springing up. *Spectator* (18/12/1915), p. 14.

177 *Morning Post* (24/02/1917).

Along similar lines, in his article 'Novels and War Nerves', Dent reviewed three recent novels[178] 'which constitute valuable documents for the psychology of the civilian', presenting realistic descriptions of combat, of ordinary people being affected, the opposite of the inflated abstract heroic language used in the popular press. Dent went so far as to consider the current poetry being 'not poetry but versified journalism … There is no need to doubt the general veracity of their narratives; but anybody who has intimate friends at the front must know perfectly well by now that a great deal remains untold.'

In the winter of 1917, Clive was stationed in Italy, Ventimiglia, near Genoa, which Dent knew well, increasingly apprehensive about what might happen there. Dent, who had been reading the Italian papers for some time, was very clear on the subject.

> It is all very horrible, but I refuse to let myself echo the stuff people talk about the sacred soil of Italy. For one thing, Italy has been invaded more often than any other country, I should think; and no soil is more scared than any other. We shall regret the destruction of buildings and frescoes; but it is good for us to take Italy's own point of view, that Italy is not a mere museum; and I would gladly destroy all the museums in the world if that would stop the destruction of young life.[179]

'I am only just beginning to feel really alive again after the horrible winter', Dent wrote to Clive that May.[180] He never neglected the diaspora, always aware of where they were – Clive in Italy, Chester in Basra, Scho still out in Calcutta, Kerridge in Zurich, Hal Goodhart-Rendel spending six months in hospital recovering from what sounds like shell-shock.[181] Old friends who had been classed C3 were now classed A: M.O. Marshall and Cousens were called up, as was Philip Bainbrigge (whose sight was almost as bad as Dent's), Bernard Jones and other unlikely soldiers.

> nothing is ever certain now: anybody may be called up again at any time, so that one can never plan anything ahead … (I don't know whether we can open the Club next October.) It all depends on whether the war comes to an end: and if it doesn't come to an end before the winter, I can't see any reason for its ever coming to an end.[182]

The end of the year was marked by another ending: Madame died on the 10th of November.

> I had to go up to Yorkshire for the funeral on Thursday. She was 83, so we were all fully prepared for her death at any time, though she was extremely well, generally speaking. She had an attack of rheumatic neuralgia about 10 days before, but was getting over it, and there was no idea that her case was serious. She died in her sleep on Sunday morning – It was the best possible way for her life to end. Of

178 Wells's *Mr Britling Sees it Through*, Cicely Hamilton's *Dead Yesterday* and Rose Macaulay's *Non-Combatants and Others*.

179 CC 10/11/1917.

180 CC 11/05/1917.

181 The source for all of this is CUL Add MS 7973.

182 CC 10/11/1917.

> course we shall all miss her very much as a family centre, which she had been to all my grandfather's descendants, since she came to London.[183]

She had left Dent a small legacy of 200 pounds, money he badly needed; because most of his *Cambridge Magazine* work was unpaid, he had been living off his old trust fund. Dent had only stayed for the funeral lunch 'for politeness' sake', hurrying off to meet Greenwood in York. It was in some ways a relief; certainly a liberation.

1917–1918

The famous postwar parties had actually started around 1917, with a new breed of hostesses appearing in the social columns: 'lion hunters' like Sybil Colefax, who loved to have intelligent, famous people around her stylish dining-table in Chelsea, or Maud Cunard. Maud, who called herself 'Emerald', was terrifyingly solicitous about her guests,'a canary of prey', the 'Duchess of Covent Garden', whose long-term affair with Thomas Beecham dovetailed into her tireless efforts to make sure that he had a well-heeled audience for his operas. Osbert Sitwell, a guest at both Lady Colefax's and Lady Cunard's, later observed: 'there was no limit to the number of boxes she could fill. Her will-power was sufficient, her passion for music fervent enough, to make opera almost compulsory for those who wished to be fashionable'.[184] Unfortunately, as Sitwell goes on, it was 'necessary to rely on regular attendance by numskulls, nitwits and morons addicted to the mode'. This was hardly Dent's vision for opera in England.

Through one of his own networks, Dent had first met Osbert Sitwell[185] at a rather different style of party on 8 February 1918, given by Maurice Ingram[186] and James Baird[187] at Ingram's elegant house in Queen's Gate. The other guests beside Sitwell were Old Etonians, men from the War Office and the Foreign Office, well-connected, upper-class men who had no inclination to fight or who had been retired from active duty, useful to know. Dent and Sitwell shared a deep love of contemporary poetry and the arts; Siegfried Sassoon and Robbie Ross were only two of the friends they had in common. 'I felt rather uncomfortable & out of my element in so exquisite a house & so much F.O. but eventually settled to it: and Osbert Sitwell was fresh and amusing, full of enthusiasm for Siegfried.'[188] Osbert and his siblings 'Sachie' and Edith were setting themselves up against *Georgian Poetry* and its ilk with their

183 CC 16/11/1917.

184 Cited in Brian Masters, *Great Hostesses* (London, 1982), p. 120.

185 Francis Osbert Sacheverell Sitwell, 5th Baronet (1892–1969). Dent was probably the one who introduced him to his long-term lover, David Horner, one of Dent's coterie in Cambridge.

186 Edward Maurice Berkeley Ingram (1890–1941), Eton and King's College, part of Dent's homosocial circles there. When Dent met up with him again, he was still with the War Office, before becoming a diplomat. Dent later met him in Berlin and Oslo.

187 The same James Baird Dent had met in Venice years before.

188 Diary 08/02/1918.

own vehicle for contemporary poetry, *Wheels*.[189] The Sitwells were patrician–artists, visionaries, taking part in readings like the one at Sibyl Colefax's in December 1917, when some of the newer poets – T.S. Eliot and Robert Nichols – read their latest to shock and acclaim. They could be as outrageous as they liked and still be begged to dine at the most fashionable tables, straddling both worlds with a duplicitous ease Dent knew he lacked. But he liked the Sitwells, attracted by the combination he recognised in himself, of insider–outsider, and kept up the friendship over the years, warm but somewhat distant, with a pragmatic edge that solicited their patronage.

The public mood was hopeful, and well before the end of the war in November 1918, Dent's friends in Cambridge and London were disseminating fresh ideas about music and literature through lively formal and informal encounters, at parties or restaurants or concert halls, recorded in diaries and letters, and demonstrating the vibrant cultural life going on in some London drawing rooms, and including foreign musicians, refugees and rich Bohemians. Issues under discussion included the reconstruction of the British music scene, the re-integration of foreign music and musicians, the shortcomings of current musical teaching, and the setting up and financing of concerts and opera, including possible state support for opera. All of this was going on under an increasingly hostile DORA cloud, but London was very lively indeed, and Dent was finding some warm personal responses to the ideas he had been mooting now for several years.

One such private party, in March 1918, at the north London house of Australian pianist William Murdoch and his wife, was attended by Dent, who had recently been spending more and more time at New Quebec Street. Murdoch liked to play the latest music by his friends, especially John Ireland, and at these gatherings, new compositions were being played to an intelligent, discerning audience. Dent had been present the year before when Murdoch, Albert Sammons and Ireland 'were boiling down the Kreutzer and Ireland's sonata for gramophone records ... I was much interested in Ireland's music'.[190] The combination of Sammons and Murdoch playing his music would be Ireland's breakthrough; a week later, Murdoch gave a public recital including Ireland's 'Rhapsody', 'wch sounded very well'. This party drew together, in Dent's words, a 'half-smart, half artistic crowd',[191] with lively music being played by popular musicians like 'that amusing but rather horrid person Pedro de Zuloeta [sic]'.[192] There was dancing, which always attracted Dent, and he enjoyed watching Mrs Fraser Gange and Hilda Bailey dancing, together with the glamorous 'Cuban' [sic] Mme Gandarillas,[193] whom Dent thought quite the most beau-

[189] *Wheels* was partly funded by Nancy Cunard, always happy to rebel against her mother, Emerald.

[190] Diary 20/03/1917.

[191] CC March 1918.

[192] *Ibid.*

[193] Wife of the extraordinary Antonio de Gandarillas, a well-connected Chilean diplomat based in Paris, whose aunt was patron of Picasso. A friend of Diaghilev, he was the lover and patron of *inter alia*, a young Christopher Wood. 'A small, exquisite man, who looked like a spider monkey. He was exhaustingly, indefatigably social: after parties, he loved food, drink, opium, gambling, travel, art and young men. He had been educated

tiful woman he had ever seen. But he declared himself to be 'very incompetent socially', grumbling there were always 'too many women' at such affairs. 'Murdoch played John Ireland's "Chelsea reach" [sic] & "Ragamuffin" and a showy piece by Frank Bridge. I am still rather puzzled by Ireland. Chelsea reach suggests an English organist who has just discovered Granados.'[194]

But in spite of his grumbles, Dent was already becoming more receptive generally, with non-stop parties and concerts all that winter. In January he had delivered the manuscript of Forster's *Maurice* to another of Forster's friends, Sydney Lomer, part of a wider, more active gay network in and around London, the kind of friend Dent liked to have at hand but not too close. 'I liked him very much & was sorry to have to go away to-morrow.' Lomer was more of the old school homosexual, upper-class, completely pukka, his anti-war feelings stemming largely from his love of young masculine beauty.[195] 'We all curse the makers of war', he wrote to Dent, '& I wish for the return of the old Greek gods who at least loved beauty & did not pretend to be All- Merciful & Almighty.' The 'old Greek gods' were alive and well and currently operating in Chelsea, and Dent was given a cordial invitation to join him:

> & one or two others & with George & some of the golden hearted youths who come there would entertain you. I almost recapture my lost youth sometimes. The companionship of youth always seems to me to be the most wonderful stimulant in the world. And that I am still not regarded as an old fogey by some of them a great compliment.[196]

A few weeks later Dent was in London again, working with singer Gladys Moger on their Haileybury lecture, modern French songs, so the following day he wandered along to 58 Beaufort Street, Chelsea.

> 10.30 to Lomer's house in Chelsea where I met a new & amusing crowd: EF Benson, Charles Promp (?) the wine merchant: Maj-Gen. Ashmore ('Splash') and his exquisite ADC 'Collie' surname unknown – George Bradley – & others whose names I failed to catch. It was a most refreshing evening & I enjoyed it hugely.[197]

The 'exquisite ADC', 'Splash's joy-boy', as that source of all the best town gossip Noel Barwell ('The Little Wretch') was able to inform him, was Collie Knox, son of Vesey Knox, KC, who was having his portrait done ('à la Rupert') by Splash's formidable artist sister, the 'delightful' Sybil. The 'refreshing evening' was the first of

---

at Cambridge'. In Sebastian Faulks, *The Fatal Englishman* (London, 1996), pp. 10ff. Gandarillas was also a friend of Dent's later friend and colleague Jack Gordon.

194 Diary 24/03/1918.

195 He and his friend Philip Streatfeild took a very young Noël Coward on holiday to Cornwall and painted his portrait there. Philip Hoare, *Noel Coward: A Biography* (London, 1995), pp. 33ff.

196 Lomer–EJD 11/01/1918.

197 Diary 23/02/1918. Major-General Edward Bailey Ashmore (1872–1953), Old Etonian, CB, CMG, MVO. He later married. Both he and his sister were active in the Philharmonic Society.

many that year, and back in Cambridge Dent was taken to task by Theo, 'who was more severe than ever on my gadding about in London & making new friends'.[198]

'I hope you did not think Saturday evening too hilarious,' Lomer wrote to Dent after that first astonishing party, 'the flow of champagne was so steady that it was bound to be so'. The new friends included some senior officers, one a later friend of Forster's, General Leo Charlton,[199] beside 'Babe' Hartley, 'Dolly' Hewlett, several VCs, a number of ADCs and one very young Noël Coward 'acting at the Garrick & a successful song writer'.[200] The Chelsea parties were the other side of war, with that perfect combination of lively, elevated but uninhibited company, music and a lot of frolicking *au naturel* in the indoor swimming-pool (hence the nickname 'Splash'). 'The usual merry evening', Dent recorded in his diary, 'during wch I played Chopin while the dolphins gambolled.' John Wells especially seems to have fitted right in; by May, Dent was observing 'John is in high favour with Splash, and Splash having just sacked Collie Knox is considering John as a possible ADC in succession to him'.[201]

> Last night we had a merry time here – Splash Ashmore and a lot of others. G. & I gave a comic boxing display. Unfortunately my eye (since black) collided with his fist rather hard in the sham knockout blow & his hand is also 'part worn'. Splash presented him with the Lonsdale belt. Afterwards most of us bathed & then danced & sang & to bed about 3.30.[202]

But there is a sobering thread running through Lomer's letters to Dent all that year, up to the Armistice:

> Four out of five of my boys are under orders for France. Poor boys they are all so cheerful about it. By the end of next week as far as I see I shall practically have no Battalion at all to speak of … As far as I know I myself am permanently here to send boys abroad as they are ready to replace wastage at the Front.[203]

Lomer seems to have done what he could to rescue John Wells from being sent to France, but at the end of the war, anyone who could walk was being shipped across the Channel, including John that October 1918.[204]

'This term has been very crowded', Dent wrote to Clive:

> I am trying to lead a double life, half in Cambridge and half in London. I hoped it was going to be lucrative, but so far it is not … what little writing I do is also gratuitous, and I find myself so busy that I never write any papers of my own now.[205]

198 Diary 21/02/1918.

199 L.E.O. Charlton (1879–1958), later Air Commodore. See P.N. Furbank, *E.M. Forster: A Life. Volume Two: Polycrates' Ring (1914–1970)* (London, 1978), p. 136 & n.

200 Lomer–EJD 27/02/1918.

201 Diary 27/05/1918.

202 *Ibid.*

203 Lomer–EJD 26/03/1918.

204 Lomer–EJD 23/10/1918.

205 CC 21/02/1918.

His diary shows concerts and parties every day, meeting the people who were virtually running this artistic resurgence, with new ideas being mooted and the standards he had deplored for most of the war appreciably rising, Dent finding himself back at the cutting-edge, where he liked to be. At the Murdochs' he talked amiably with Pedro Morales,[206] the poet and composer friend of Mañuel de Falla whom he had met two years before, who had run a concert of contemporary Spanish music at the Wigmore Hall, and who piqued his interest that June with a new 'international conservatoire' of music. Adrian Boult and Lalla Vandervelde, daughter of the musical philanthropist Edgar Speyer liked William Foss's old idea of reviving the Théâtre des Arts: 'I went to see Nicholas Gatty about it: but his mind is full of air-raids', Dent wrote to Clive. 'But I hope we shall collect a few kindred spirits to discuss'.[207]

In February, Dent endured his third, final medical tribunal, with a Dr Young, 'who talked to me of Brahms & Babies … at 12-30 left the place finally & permanently discharged, with 2/9 – a day's pay!'[208] Otherwise, 'Cambridge has been depressing & irritating: we struggle along with music, and are always on the verge of quarrelling with each other.'[209] Elected Chairman of the Musical Board, Dent now found such work dreary: 'Rootham & I roused the lion in Plunket Greene by standing up for young composers and suggesting more or less openly that Stanford & Arthur Somervell were back numbers.'[210] He toyed with the idea of giving up the time-consuming *Cambridge Magazine* work while continuing to write some of his most provocative, insightful articles, six that year, reviews and translations beside 'The Future of British Music' (16 November), 'Nationalism and Internationalism in Music' (30 November), and 'The Leaders' (18 January 1919).

But London held his real interest right now. On 18 February, after dining with Lawrence at Pagani's, they were joined by Francis and Geoffrey Toye, Vaughan Williams and his wife, all going on to the Queen's Hall for the second of Adrian Boult's orchestral concerts. The programme, for which Dent had done the notes, was Vaughan Williams' 'London' Symphony, Elgar's *In the South*, Ravel. The concert had to be abandoned because of an air-raid, when they were bundled down into the basement, but the audience had been enthused. 'It was a good way of seeing friends, as there were plenty there. I was amused to be complimented on my programme entry by Mrs Frank Bridge! I did not know she was so literary. L. introduced me to Fox Strangways – & I rather liked him.'[211] Although the hall was half empty that night and others, the concerts were noticed by people who mattered. Elsewhere

206 Pedro Garcia Morales (born 1874), studied at Seville and the RCM. 'Of a non-prolific, over-critical artistic disposition, he devotes his activities as a musician to the creation of the Span. art-song, the least cultivated type of composition in his country' (DMMM). His prewar violin pieces were premiered in London by Fritz Kreisler. Although extremely influential, he is little known, not mentioned in the MT.

207 CC March 1918.

208 Diary 07/02/1918.

209 CC March, 1918.

210 Diary 15/02/1918.

211 W.H. Fox Strangways (1859–1948), then music critic for *The Times* and the *Observer*, later founded and edited *Music & Letters*, to which Dent would contribute regular articles.

in the series Boult was conducting more contemporary music, Vaughan Williams, Benjamin Dale, Richard Woodman and Gustav Holst, George Butterworth, John Ireland, Arnold Bax, Oliver Gotch – more of what Dent had been hoping for.[212]

Vaughan Williams put Dent in touch with his brother-in-law, H.A.L. Fisher, now Minister of Education, 'to get my ideas about musical education and English Opera. I liked him very much – an open & honest man, with no pomposity'.[213] Fisher was sympathetic, saying that there was no money right now, but the idea had been aired. At yet another dinner party that April, in company with Lalla Vandervelde, Henry Hadow, Boult, the Toyes and the Gattys, the promotion and future funding of music was the main topic of conversation.

> We had a great talk about English opera & such things. Hadow has been appointed by the Carnegie Trust to make a report on the state of English musical education etc. Geoffrey rather took command of the evening – very tactfully & very well … he seems to be developing into a perpetual chairman of committees.[214]

Dent spent most of that spring in New Quebec Street, since Panton Street had suffered from water-damage that winter and was still drying out. He had been thinking about letting it anyway, eventually to the Daltons, whom he often saw in London. He liked Hugh's wife, Ruth, and Hills was fond of Hugh, who was about to try for a Parliamentary seat in Cambridge. Really, the water-damage was an excuse; Dent was always out to concerts, French songs at the Wigmore, recitals at the Queen's Hall, to see the *Playboy of the Western World* at the Court, to the Stage Society, to the Friday Club, where John Wells had an exhibition, meeting Marion Scott to discuss a concert of women musicians of songs by composers killed on active service, dining out every night. The Spanish and Pagani's were now practically second homes, where he knew he would meet the Toyes, Baird, Ingram, Sitwell, Haynes and John Fothergill, whose own restaurant, the Spread Eagle, became another legendary cultural watering-hole. His regular work with Moger gave him great pleasure, promoting Denis' songs whenever possible, in London and Cambridge, and taking satisfaction from the fact that Denis' music at least, was alive. He even felt inspired to compose himself, setting Scott-Moncrieff's poem 'The Willow-Tree Bough', 'rather in the manner of a Purcell hornpipe – perhaps more like the Mass in B minor … begun as a joke & finished as a bore: and I am now quite tired of it'.[215]

So Dent continued to spread his nets in these fruitful seas, with some long-term consequences. Having put in a bid for a Scarlatti autograph manuscript at Sotheby's, he met L.T. Rowe on the Cambridge train, who 'presented' him with Bassani's *Harmonia Festiva*[216] for the King's College library. Then, after a lunch with

212 Scholes, *The Mirror of Music*, vol. 1, p. 399. The full programmes, from 4 February to the 18 March, are listed in Michael Kennedy, *Adrian Boult* (London, 1987), pp. 320–22.

213 Diary 05/04/1918. There is also a letter on the subject from Fisher in KCA.

214 Diary 10/04/1918.

215 Diary 07/05/1918.

216 Diary 11/05/1918. L.T. Rowe (died 1927), solicitor, collector of rare music, friend of Dent's. *Harmonia Festiva* is still in the Rowe Library, which had come to King's via Rowe's friend, Arthur Cole (1883–1968), when Rowe was killed in a traffic accident in

FIGURE 9. 'The Willow-Tree Bough', by Dent, to words by Charles Scott-Moncrieff. By kind permission of the Provost and Fellows of King's College, Cambridge.

Boult, Arthur Hill and Laurence Tanner at the Savile, where Dent told Hill about the Scarlatti manuscript, Hill responded by sending round Scarlatti's *St Cecilia*, which Moger sang from the manuscript score.[217] His lessons extended to Hal Goodhart-Rendel, now playing Turina, Granados and Alkan, and to Mme Vandervelde. When dining with Evelyn Broadwood one day, he met the rich patron of the arts, Lord Howard de Walden:[218] 'I got on very well & liked him'.[219] Howard de Walden was himself a musician who had written librettos for Holbrooke, and gave lavish musical parties at his country house, Chirk, where musicians and guests mixed: Lionel Tertis, Desiré Defauw and Sylvia Sparrow.

And, in spite of the war, Dent's musical influences extended beyond England. His former pupil W.H. Kerridge had taken up a post before the war as organist to the American Church in Paris. Once there, using introductions provided by Dent to Vincent d'Indy and to Mme Pereyra,[220] he became quickly absorbed into the wartime Paris music scene, working at history and theory with d'Indy. Kerridge was ambitious, while enjoying a sideline playing piano accompaniment to a 'conjurer/ knife-thrower'.

> A misunderstanding brought me to Zürich; but my vexation at the misunderstanding was eventually turned into joy, for the theatre was in need of an assistant. I am doing practically what I did with Beecham, only the repertoire is infinite.[221]

Kerridge could not have found a better place to spend the rest of the war and launch his own career in opera production. Neutral Zurich had attracted colonies of displaced artists: Busoni was there (Dent had given Kerridge an introduction), and Strauss, conducting his own works. There was a thriving theatre whose director, Dr Reucker, had worked with Gordon Craig, and in the middle of so much militant nationalism, it had an internationalist outlook: 'he is determined to keep the Zürich Theatre free from the flag-wavers, from which ever point of the compass they threaten to wave' and, Kerridge told Dent, he was 'greatly attracted by four of the works you have so kindly suggested'. He also joined an active 'English Stage Society' made up of more refugees: 'This society, two-thirds of which is of a pleasantly amateur amateur [sic] nature – has been called into life by one Joyce, an Irish author of

October 1927, 'leaving under his will the option of buying his music books to his friend … Arthur at once handed the library over to King's.' King's College Report, 1968. The collection comprises 18th-century printed music and 16th- and 17th-century part-books.

[217] Hill of the family firm of A.E. Hill and Sons, violin makers and dealers in London. A.E. Hill had written a standard work on Stradivarius, and Dent would write the introduction to *The Violin-Makers of the Guarnieri Family (1626–1762)*, by W.H. and A.F. Hill (London, 1931). Haward, *Edward J. Dent: A Bibliography*, 126.

[218] Howard de Walden, Thomas Evelyn Scott-Ellis, 8th Baron (1880–1946). The family had owned a lot of property since Elizabethan times, including Audley End House and quite a bit of London.

[219] Diary 11/05/1918.

[220] WHK–EJD 04/06/1915.

[221] WHK–EJD 12/05/1918.

daring books,[222] it seems, and is managed by a man Sykes, who was formerly at His Majesty's.' The repertoire at the opera was 'immense', with festivals of French or Italian opera beside contemporary works: *Pelléas* beside *Rosenkavalier* and Busoni's *Turandot.*

> The director of our theatre, an enlightened man, realising the unique position of Zürich just now, and the fact that, for some time to come it will be the most 'universal' town artistically & musically in all Europe, is anxious to have as catholic a repertoire as possible. He told me he would be glad to give some performances of English opera next year on if I thought it possible.[223]

Enthused, Dent sent Kerridge copies of *The Fairy Queen* and *Faustus,* suggesting also *Cupid & Death* and *Dido.* The productions ran into trouble, and after the war Kerridge reconsidered his career in Switzerland, but that is not really the point. Through Kerridge's dazzled eyes Dent had seen alternative possibilities, what opera and theatre were doing elsewhere in the world, but not far away, and in a country which had declared itself neutral.

❧ ❧ ❧

All that last year of war, the parties, concerts, socialising at Pagani's, at the Café Royal, the Spanish, were the intellectuals' and artists' response to what seemed interminable, not least because another war was emerging, a 'home front war'[224] against such artists, homosexuals and intellectuals, the hoary subtext being that 'effeminate aesthetes' had somehow caused the war in the first place. One case in point was Maud Allan's libel action that June against Noel Pemberton-Billing, 'a disgusting and disgraceful business', Dent wrote in his diary. Billing was a member of Parliament, homophobic, macho, he loved fast cars and planes and was publishing his own jingoistic journals, the *Imperialist* and in 1918, the *Vigilante.* According to Billing, the Germans had in their possession a Black Book containing the names of forty-seven thousand English perverts, which was being used to blackmail these into treasonous acts.[225] Beside the Asquiths, he almost certainly had in mind 'Splash' and his circles; class hatred came into the equation, and when Maud Allan decided to put on a private performance of her Salomé dance, the *Vigilante* published an inflammatory article entitled 'The Cult of the Clitoris', which averred that any audience for such a show would include several thousand of the forty-seven thousand. Maud sued – and lost.

222 James Joyce.

223 WHK–EJD 12/05/1918.

224 Hynes, *A War Imagined,* p. 64.

225 This Black Book might be related to the nearly contemporary Black Diary of Roger Casement, hanged for treason in 1916, the homosexual content of which shocked the public. Certainly the Casement case linked homosexuality and treason in the public mind.

An incompetent judge, Mr Justice Darling, allowed Billing free rein to rant and accuse, with crude attacks on 'decadence' which expanded publicly from Maud Allan to Robert Ross and the Asquiths.[226] Lady Cynthia Asquith recorded in her diary the kind of reaction felt by most liberals:

> Of course the Billing trial was discussed ... Lord Stamfordham said he understood the whole of the Royal Household were in the 'Book'. To my horror, Sir Charles said there was no chance of a conviction against Billing. It is monstrous that these maniacs should be vindicated in the eyes of the public ... He said the soil was prepared for the evil seed and that rumours of what came to us as fantastic shock had been rife in the public mind for years.[227]

In October, at another trial of decadence, Dent's acquaintance Rose Allatini – wife of pianist Cyril Scott – was charged under the DORA, her mild novel of homosexuality, *Despised and Rejected,* accused of including 'statements likely to prejudice the recruiting, training, and discipline of persons in His Majesty's forces'.[228] The resulting 'culture wars' had a terrible effect for years, with the populist view identifying all artists, intellectuals, pacifists and homosexuals, as outsiders and subversives, polarising popular opinion, which was played upon by the rising generation of right-wing politicians. Politically naïve Dent may have been, but he recognised the threats to his way of life and his belief in the importance of the arts at the most fundamental level; freedom and creativity go hand in hand. 'The public washing of Miss Allan's soiled tights did a great deal to keep up the spirits of the troops', Philip Bainbrigge wrote to him, adding in a more sombre tone, 'I can't see how that awful man managed to win his case; I suppose Ross is worried about it all.'[229] Dent's articles in the *Cambridge Magazine* throughout 1917 had mostly addressed the need for liberal thought and generosity of spirit, the appreciation of comedy, while at the same time Ted Haynes was writing about 'Private Morals':

> The attitude of the State to questions of private morals has never been at all clearly thought out or formulated either in this country or in any English-speaking community ... By private morals I mean such conduct as does not obviously disturb the King's Peace.[230]

For Dent, the Billings affair and the DORA business could not have been more unwelcome. For the first time since the war began he was close to enjoying himself

226 Hynes, in his excellent *A War Imagined,* p. 64: 'for many English critics, of many different critical persuasions, the war against Germany rapidly became a war against Modernism ... intended simply to eradicate from English life something that was undesirable, and especially in wartime – a sickness, a fraud, or a foolish triviality – and so leave England stronger and more English. What in fact they did was to diminish English culture, by declaring that everything that was lively and new in the arts to be alien and inimical to the English cause.'

227 Cynthia Asquith, *Diaries 1915–1918* (London, 1968), 3–4 June 1918, pp. 446–7.

228 Hynes, *A War Imagined,* p. 232.

229 Bainbrigge–EJD 09/06/1918.

230 E.S.P. Haynes, *The Case for Liberty* (London, 1919), p. 69.

again, finding a new and active role in the burgeoning London cultural world he chose to inhabit, welcomed at a wide, exciting variety of parties. The contact with Lomer and Splash had made him more openly comfortable with himself, and he could be seen about London all that spring and early summer in the company of 'viewy' young men like Beverley Nichols – 'Nicolette' – and Wells, probably the source of the later rumours about rent boys. But it was certainly spiced with some danger: at the end of May there was a curious episode when Nicolette and Wells had to be rushed out of the Savile Club because Nicolette seems to have committed some unspecified but socially damning indiscretion with a member.[231] Still Dent continued in this rhapsodic vein, with exhibitions like the Orpens at Agnew's, 'a rainbow fairyland of gay colour – wch makes the war the most ravishing affair on earth', lunches, dinners with Hal, a fruitful meeting with Herbert Howells, liking his songs and in turn showing Howells some of Denis' work; with the Sitwells to a big party at the Vanderveldes', where Ramsay Macdonald mixed with the Toyes and Sitwells, and Mme Vandervelde told Dent that she wanted him to write musical criticism for *The Nation*. But the Billing affair upset him more than he wanted to admit, while the renewed strain of having to keep up a public front only aggravated the sudden periodic depressions which came from underlying fear. Accompanying Moger in a recital of Denis' songs,

> I got the perpetual impression that Moger, Denis & I were interlopers. The programme was dreary in the extreme: Tovey & Walker played some variations by Kelly wch were ultra Toveyesque and strenuous ... I got a fit of nerves & played quite atrociously – Allen saying to me 'play louder' – it was the last straw.[232]

He came to feel that another self-defined set of musicians, 'the Frank Bridge set', were opposed to some of the music and musicians emerging at the war's end; any hidden agendas can only be guessed at. When Bridge's publisher Winthrop Rogers turned down Gibbs's songs, Dent felt had less to do with the music itself than a general prejudice against outsiders, the 'Cambridge Group'. Gossip at the Vanderveldes only confirmed this, as well as prejudice expressed from the same quarter against Adrian Boult as too 'amateur' to be considered as a serious conductor. 'Amateur' seems to have summed up the attitude towards former university musicians generally, a pejorative label Dent set himself to turn on its head.

In this time of transition, and however much he grumbled about it, Dent was now working more closely with women, very much 'new' women, as unlike his own family as possible; talented and purposeful, fun and not bothered by convention or respectability. Beside the wives of his old friends whom he actually, grudgingly liked, there was Jane Harrison, and latterly Mme Gandarillas, Mrs Mathews, Mme Vandervelde, and excellent women musicians like Sylvia Sparrow and Gladys Moger. Then at violinist Sylvia Sparrow's lively party in Pembroke Gardens, with Morales, the Alstons, Lionel Tertis, Lord Coke, Viola Tree, Beigel, the Ashmores, 'Miss A enthroned in a very conspicuous seat, looking very tragic & grand, with Ernest Thesiger at her feet',

[231] Diary 28/05/1918.

[232] Diary 03/06/1918.

he arrived to hear a quartet playing Dvorak, led by one of a trio of talented, aristocratic Hungarian sisters, Jelly d'Arányi.[233] He was stunned.

> The jelly [sic] played pieces by Paganini (including the A minor variations) in a marvellous style. It is a good deal to be able to play the notes: it is remarkable to be able to play them with ease: but she did more – for she played them with the most enormous dignity and nobility – After that the music degenerated.[234]

On 12 June, Morales took Dent to 188 Cromwell Road, right under the nose of the Royal College of Music, the shabby rented premises of the 'International Conservatoire of Music', founded that March by associates of Morales: Emile de Vlieger, a Belgian; Lea Isaacs, a Frenchwoman; and Ernest Cameron, described as a 'voice specialist', soon replaced by the telecommunications entrepreneur, Alfonso Marconi, 'Director of Spanish & General Wireless Trust Ltd'. After having heard Dent play one of his own songs one evening at the Murdochs, Morales invited him to join the Conservatoire teaching staff.[235] 'I was rather puzzled by the whole intrigue.' But he liked and respected Morales, and crucially, Dent saw the possibilities of an internationalist institution which could go beyond what was currently on offer at the colleges of music or at the universities, a school and a performance platform beyond the current parochial style. His uncertainly stemmed from distrust of the 'director', the Belgian de Vlieger, 'whom I rather dislike, as I think he has more genius for finance and publicity than for music', and he continued to ask questions about de Vlieger's background[236] while soliciting the best people he knew to teach there: Adrian Boult and Clive Carey, beside John Ireland. At a lunch on 29 September with Geoffrey Toye, Boult and Holst where they looked over the score for Holst's *The Planets*, which Boult was to conduct the next day, Dent showed them the new prospectus for the conservatoire, just printed. Toye laughed, saying it sounded more like a 'disorderly house'. In fact, the conservatoire was desperate to have Dent and his contacts: 'I have to name my price – & feel quite unable to do so.'[237]

By October 1918 Dent was showing signs of impatience with de Vlieger's evidently high-handed decisions over his teaching,[238] but he never had been a happy underling, and never joined any institution he didn't have an outside chance of running, behind the scenes or otherwise. After Sir Hubert Parry's death that October, when the question of his successor at the Royal College of Music was raised, Dent decided not to apply, although he was in the frame. An unsettling meeting with Barclay Squire probably tipped the balance.

233 Jelly d'Arányi (1895–1966), great-niece of Joseph Joachim, studied in Budapest with Hubay. She was the first to play Bartók's sonatas in England.

234 Diary 17/07/1918.

235 Diary 30/05/1918.

236 In September he discovered that his suspicions were well-founded: 'Rootham has been meeting De Vlieger, through his brother who is a City broker: & I heard accounts of the Conservatoire very different from what Morales told me.' Diary 23/09/1918.

237 Diary 15/07/1918.

238 Diary 01/11/1918.

> Squire talked of the RCM directorship & said 'of course if you hadn't got yourself mixed up with all those Jews – Marconi, Isaacs etc – your name would have been considered.' This certainly surprised me – for I never thought of myself as papabile [a potential Pope] and if I am papabile, why should the International make any difference?[239]

Although he was as guilty as anyone of his generation and background of using casual anti-Semitic language, this was another order of prejudice, and Dent did not like it. Hugh Allen became the Principal of the Royal College of Music, and their long friendship waned. But the episode had made Dent think about what exactly he was looking for. 'The Conservatoire is teaching me that there is not much fun to be got out of going concerns that are flourishing and in order', he wrote to Clive, 'I am only interested in Ishmael & Co. The Conservatoire has many enemies, and we have rather got our backs against the wall.'[240]

Within eighteen months the conservatoire was failing, in spite of attracting students and needing larger premises. Dent presciently wrote to Clive in April 1919:

> I don't know whether the negotiations about the other building (wch would have been the chance of our life) failed by reason of De Vlieger's curious personality, wch invites distrust, or whether (as is possible) influence from other institutions was brought to bear on the selling side, to prevent our getting it. Altogether I am worried about the Conservatoire, and can't help wondering whether it won't come to smash altogether. It would be a great pity if it did.[241]

The International Conservatoire was by no means the only experimental new venture to vex the current musical establishment. On 11 July 1918, Dent went to a 'new committee of Eaglefield Hull's new "British Music Society"' at 19 Berners Street, within walking distance of Soho restaurants, the Queen's Hall and the British Museum. Hull was another outsider, born the same year as Dent and in the same county, but from the other end of the social spectrum;[242] he had worked hard to get to Oxford, then via the organist–choirmaster route to establish himself as a musician, writer and educator. Others present beside Dent and Hull included W.W. Cobbett in the chair, H. Chadfield, Mrs Lee Mathews, Adrian Boult, Geoffrey Toye, an interesting collection of musical minds; Bernard Shaw had been invited but was 'too ill to come'.[243] Hugh Allen became Chairman, with several composers, including Arthur Bliss, co-opted onto the committee. It was decided to look outwards rather

239 Diary 05/11/1918.

240 CC 21/02/1919.

241 CC 18/04/1919. At some point his friend Morales had also fallen foul of de Vlieger, and sued for wrongful dismissal, and his outstanding claim delayed proceedings initiated in January 1920 to wind up the conservatoire. The books were only finally closed in 1927, by which point two of the three directors – de Vlieger and Marconi – had returned overseas.

242 Arthur Eaglefield Hull (1876–1928). In spite of his abilities, he never seems to have been accepted by the musical establishment, and was snubbed by influential critics like Percy Scholes, who doesn't even mention him in *The Mirror of Music*, and accused him of plagiarism. He was hit by a train; it was possibly suicide.

243 Diary 11/07/1918.

than inwards, a rejection in all but name of everything that had characterised the wartime constraints, to reshape 'British' music from the ground up, and concerts were not necessarily the end product. Hull summarised:

> The Society's activities are divided into three categories – organization, propaganda, and education. The work of the first department includes the establishment of common rooms with offices in all musical centres, the organization of an information bureau, the preparation of a catalogue of British music of permanent interest, and the formation of local centres in provincial towns for the giving of concerts of chamber music, lectures, causeries, discussions, &c., with schemes for the discovery and organization of local talent. Some of these meetings will be open to the public; others to members only.[244]

'The Society will be up against the two unforgivable things in art – provincialism and insularity.'[245] Francis Toye half jokingly claimed that the idea for the society had come from his only novel, *Diana and Two Symphonies* (1913),[246] which had expressed the need to 'advance the cause of music, especially English music, in every possible way', with concerts in London and the provinces, centrally supported, and bureaux of advice for foreign and domestic musicians and 'an independent musical paper corresponding to the French "S.I.M.", which should be an organ of musical thought'.[247]

That November, 1918, Dent wrote in the *Cambridge Magazine*:

> If we are to make our music known on the Continent, we must be prepared to meet our foreign audiences half-way, and we must also be rigorously critical of ourselves and see that we are represented by nothing short of the very best. The war has lowered all our standards, critical and artistic, as well as moral … The best thing that can be done for British music is to improve the quality of it, and to raise the intellectual and critical standards of our own audiences … After the earlier, wartime British Music Campaign, patriotic and somehow utilitarian, a British Music Society would have to be both domestic and outward-looking, encompassing and serving a British music in its broadest sense … This may seem but a small and humble beginning. But Dr. Hull and his fellow-workers are firmly convinced that the cause of art is not served by the methods of patent medicine vendors. It is better, in fact, to live healthily than to take pills.[248]

Dent's swipe at Beecham notwithstanding, the language of its public statements was expansive rather than censorious, the idea being to heal and build, carefully non-political in tone. Even though the musical establishment – the *Musical Times* – was largely dismissive, and in spite of the DORA setbacks that summer, artistic net-

244 A. Eaglefield Hull, 'A Few Words about the British Music Society', MT (1 February 1919), p. 71. I am grateful to Professor Rachel Cowgill for information about Hull and the British Music Society.

245 *Ibid.*

246 Toye, *For What We Have Received: An Autobiography*, p. 92.

247 Francis Toye, *Diana and Two Symphonies* (London, 1913), pp. 110ff.

248 'The Future of British Music' CM (16/11/1918), pp. 130–31.

works were generally optimistic. The British Music Society was aiming for the long term, with a more methodical, grassroots approach to music, building up a more broadly based, yet knowledgeable audience, one receptive to musical innovation. Twenty years later, Dent noted that in 1918 'there was a fairly wide-spread tendency throughout Europe, if not America as well, for *composers to take steps to organize the performance of contemporary music as well as to compose it individually* [my emphasis] and hope for the best, as was so often done in the past.'[249] In its first year it gave several successful concerts; initially, modest affairs, rather like the musical parties going on at the same time, at such private houses as Mrs Lee Mathews'; but with more backing they quickly graduated to larger, more public halls.

So that summer of 1918, there appeared to be real work to do for the future. The bleak moments still haunted him: going to see *Le Coq d'Or* that July he was suddenly, unexpectedly overcome: 'I was very tired, and the sound of Rimsky Korsakov took me back to 1914, and I began to feel as if that music meant nothing to me now when the people who were keen on it [were] all dead.' Kerridge's opera projects excited him, Theo introduced him to the 'charming Mr Sprott',[250] and some of the most painful memories were being healed. One day at lunch with Osbert Sitwell and the painter Paul Nash, Dent was able to talk at some length with Nash about Kennard, who had been a good friend and supporter of Nash and his work. That other great survivor Siegfried Sassoon had been wounded, now in hospital recovering rapidly.

> After lunch I walked across the Park (it was a very hot day) to see Siegfried & met him just leaving the hospital with a young officer whose name I forget – 'the Craiglockhart poet' – going to tea with Mrs Woodhouse.[251]

It was then, to help his recovery, that Dent introduced Sassoon to the flighty, funny 'Gabriel' Atkin, while later that summer, Wilfred Owen was getting to know Philip Bainbrigge. Another joyful point of cultural subversion that autumn was the return of the Ballets Russes, at the Coliseum rather than at Covent Garden, with Adrian Boult conducting the clever ballet adaptation from Scarlatti, *The Good-Humoured Ladies*, and the impish Lydia Lopokova and new man Leonide Massine dancing. Afterwards, Boult introduced Dent to Diaghilev, who discussed Italian opera and charmingly said he had read Dent's Scarlatti book. Dent went back several times to the 'Scarlatti ballet … wch delighted me more than ever',[252] and Boult invited him to lunch with Diaghilev and Mme Vandervelde.

> D. crossquestioned me a great deal about old Italian composers – He knows quite a lot about Paisello and Pergolesi – I trotted out Longroscino, Leo and Galuppi. Lunch was very exhausting as I had to talk French at great length in a very noisy restaurant. Diaghilev took Mme V & me in to the Coliseum to see 'La Princesse

249 E.J. Dent, 'Introduction', p. 1. Unpublished typescript. KCA EJD/1/1/1/2.

250 Walter John Herbert 'Sebastian' Sprott (1897–1971), later Fellow of King's, his saintly nickname bestowed on him by Dent and Theo, who said that 'Jack Sprott' simply would not do.

251 Diary 15/08/1918. The Craiglockhart poet was Wilfred Owen.

252 Diary 12/09/1918.

> Enchanté' a delicious pas de deux arranged by Marius Petipa to part of Tchai's Sleeping Beauty: and the Polovetsian scene from 'Prince Igor' – Massine was marvellous in it.[253]

It wasn't exactly friendship, but they had struck up an understanding. All that autumn members of the Ballets Russes were to be seen at exhibitions and parties around town, their heady, exotic, avant-garde style stimulating and disturbing. Dent tried to show Diaghilev some of Denis Browne's ballet music, but Diaghilev had caught a mild version of the killer Spanish influenza going round that autumn, and was laid up in bed, which had its compensations. 'I had a charming tête-a-tête with Massine, whom I like more & more – he is so clever & intelligent and so very modest & devoid of all vanity. "Dans le ballet russe il n'y a pas de soloistes" he said.'[254] They spent a very pleasant afternoon 'in a rather cold room facing the river' with Dent playing Denis' music and other pieces, but sadly, no further collaboration. After one of his reading sessions at the Poetry Bookshop, he went with JB to Massine's adaptation of *Snegurotschka,* a gathering of the most hopeful at the war's bitter end.

> The ballet was very Massine in conception & most delightful – it had a huge success. afterward JB & I had a kind of court in the foyer – everybody was there – Maynard, Sheppard & one Nelson a painter – Osbert, Lady O. Arthur Parry & wife, Beigel – Eddy & Siegfried – who said that Gabriel was 'the most glorious person' & is going down to Margate again on Tuesday to see him! Broadwood was there too with Navarro & one Pinnock a poet in khaki – Sheppard & Nelson took JB & myself to Adam Street for an entertainment at M. Shearmans rooms – but he was not entertaining, having influenza – and most of the others went to Mrs Mathews.[255]

'The signing of the Armistice was announced by bell ringing of a very unsuccessful kind about 11.30', was Dent's testy description of the official ending of the war. It was anything but joyful: Philip Bainbrigge and Wilfred Owen had both been killed in autumn 1918, the *Cambridge Magazine* was being threatened, Ogden fearful. 'Not with a bang but a whimper', the young poet Tom Eliot was writing in the new poetic language. The future was looking brighter, but the past horrors would take a long time to fade.

253 Diary 18/09/1918.

254 In the Ballets Russes, there are no soloists. Diary 17/11/1918.

255 Diary 21/11/1918.

CHAPTER 9

The Journalist 1919–1922

> It remains quite clear that, whatever else the war may have reformed, it has certainly not reformed music.[1]

1919–1920

It was 'the war to end all wars', and was supposed to have cleared the decks for a whole new cultural order to put on a sudden magical appearance. A hundred years on, received opinion on this postwar period in British music, so hopeful to its contemporaries, is that it was cripplingly parochial.[2] The full story is much more complex:[3] for one thing, they were experimenting, and much has not stood the test of time, although this attitude is changing as the music of that period re-emerges. Dent continued to do what he had always done, pushing at the boundaries through performance, through new institutions such as the British Music Society, and increasingly, through his writings. For a while his efforts were as chaotic as the cultural world around him, dispersed around theatre, music and opera, with a frantic social life to match; eventually through his writing he found his centre.

The journals coming into life after the war – *The Athenaeum*, the *London Mercury*, *The Nation*, *Truth*, *Music & Letters* – nurtured fresh literary and critical talent,

1 E.J. Dent, 'The Resurrection of Music', *The Athenaeum* (4 April 1919), p. 144.

2 Arthur Hutchings in the *New Oxford History of Music*, vol. 10: *The Modern Age 1890–1960* (London, 1974), pp. 503–04: 'During the years immediately after 1918 music in Great Britain passed through a tunnel rarely cheered by gleams of the light into which it was eventually to emerge'. He goes on, citing Constant Lambert in 1934, to blame 'the effect of war coinciding with the climax of a nationalist movement among artists who had little or no commerce with the *avant-garde* of other countries'. 'Native new music offered no technical advance upon Strauss's and did not approach the professional invention or design of even his poorest works.' Richard Taruskin in his *Music in the Early Twentieth Century* (Oxford, 2010) does not even mention British music. Also Erik Levi, 'Those Damn Foreigners: Xenophobia and British Musical Life during the First Half of the Twentieth Century', in *Twentieth Century Music and Politics: Essays in Memory of Neil Edmunds*, ed. P. Fairclough (Farnham, 2013) pp. 81–96.

3 The many diverse undertakings after the war to promote 'British' music included Sir Henry Wood in his Promenade concerts; the folk-music movements; and a number of attempts to use what was perceived as a native idiom; discussions in the MT, e.g., A.T. Froggatt 'The Concert Programme' (1 January 1919), pp. 35–6; Rutland Boughton's attempts to establish his British festival at Glastonbury and at the Old Vic; the British National Opera Company at Covent Garden.

providing many writers with necessary income, while the current London literary universe was made up of small tangential circles. Dent quickly became a part of this floating journalistic world, writing on music and theatre, with its cross-fertilisation beside the back-stabbing, bitchiness, professional jealousy and other such symptoms of a healthy culture, mostly expressed in elegant prose. Paul Fussell has commented on what he called 'The Persistent Enemy' in the postwar literary scene,[4] the adversary perceived by Osbert Sitwell and Percy Wyndham Lewis[5] as philistinism persisting in the shape of *Georgian Poetry* and other such relics of prewar 'high' culture; music was not much different.

'I do eternally miss you & Denis', Dent wrote to Clive, still out in Italy, 'not merely as friends but as types: the thoroughly competent musicians ... ready to take on any job that wanted brains and understanding'.[6] The ideas raised in William Foss's 1915 letter were now being realised in the new Drama League movement, headed by Dent's friend, Geoffrey Whitworth, and supported by Bernard Shaw and a number of Stage Society people. Its principles echoed those of the British Music Society, to educate a wider audience and provide the platform for new and unusual productions:[7] 'Drama was par excellence the art of the people, and the Theatre everyone's business.' Dent was in on it all from the outset, but his eclecticism made for a busy, complicated life.

In one day alone he went to the 'Berners Hotel where I corrected proofs of the BMS [British Music Society] bulletin with Hull', then off to lunch with Timmy Jekyll at Rinaldo's, before catching the train to Cambridge to discuss the formation there of a Dalcroze Society,[8] then back to London to Helena Matthias' house in Montague Square:

> preliminary meeting of the Drama League. King's was well represented – Roger Fry in the chair: Cannan, Charles Tennyson & self. Lena Ashwell & Fisher White represented the stage: W.J. Turner was there & Norman McDermott, and the Whitworths & social workers. I was put on a subcommittee to draft constitution.[9]

The day was rounded off by a committee meeting 'in the shape of a dinner at the Spanish': routine done in style.

A glance through the events columns of the *Musical Times* shows a great deal going on, new styles of production for old plays, a few new operas, new chamber

4 Fussell, *The Great War*, pp. 106ff.

5 The names of Lewis' publications were especially confrontational: *Blast*, *The Enemy*, *Tyro*. He asked Dent to write for *Blast* and later *Tyro*. JBT 13/04/1921.

6 CC 21/12/1918.

7 Dent's diary for 10 January records a meeting with Geoffrey Whitworth specifically to discuss 'a new Theatre league'. It was not officially launched until 22 June at the Theatre Royal, Haymarket.

8 Founded by Viennese composer Emile Jacques-Dalcroze (1865–1950), it was 'a system of musical and gymnastic movement' now known as eurythmics, which spread around Europe, based at several institutes in Hellerau, Geneva, Paris and London. Dent was an enthusiastic supporter and lectured to the Cambridge branch on music and rhythm.

9 Diary 19/01/1919.

music at the Wigmore Hall, while adverts from *The Athenaeum* give an idea of the chaotic mix, with e.g., The Old Vic advertising both Shakespeare and an opera, *Mignon*, or the Coliseum posting Ballets Russes star Tamara Karsavina and a corps de ballet on the same bill as 'Winston's Wonderful Water Lions'. The cultural drift, if that is what Dent was trying to catch, is neither clear nor straightforward at all, but with so many of his old friends being involved, Dent made an effort to take in as much as he could. He continued to seek out the more innovative or hopeful offerings: the new productions at Stratford under William Bridges-Adams, in London at the Gaiety under Granville Barker, and at the Lyric Hammersmith under Nigel Playfair, the latter doing a typical mix of new and old: *The Younger Generation* and Pergolesi's *La Serva padrona*. Dent thought the latter production 'very rough', the orchestra 'bad', even though conducted by Arthur Bliss who 'made the most of it'. He felt it important was that such productions were happening and that audiences were flocking to them, often taking a hand himself, advising and going to a lot of rehearsals, and he made sure always to support his extended 'gang': by 1921 Clive Carey would be producing and singing at the Lyric as well as at The Old Vic, in Cambridge and with Rutland Boughton at Glastonbury.

But Dent often appears to be slow to recognise real opportunity, and when on 4 February, he was handed it on a plate, he hardly noticed. 'Middleton Murry came to lunch with me at the Spanish to discuss the possibility of my writing for the new Athenaeum wch he is to edit.'[10] At the time, he was far more excited about the fact that composer Frederick Delius had just sent him a pupil 'to learn strict counterpoint',[11] adding, 'The Athenaeum has started under new management & I am writing a weekly article as well as doing as many concerts as I can.' Yet over the next two years Dent gradually carved out his place as one of the most respected and influential critics in London, writing regularly for *The Athenaeum*, then the *London Mercury*, the *Illustrated London News*, the *Daily Herald*, *Music & Letters*, the *Bulletin* of the British Music Society, the *Old Vic Magazine*, *Truth*, besides articles for *Musikblätter des Anbruch* and *Dresdner Woche*.

'The Conservatoire has many enemies, and we have rather got our backs against the wall. So has the Cambridge Magazine – and that is why I stick to them. The CUMC & CUMS can get on quite happily without me now.'[12] Dent still kept one foot in Cambridge, and in spite of often having declared his intention to abandon it, the *Cambridge Magazine* continued to be the main vehicle for his writing – more than sixteen articles from late 1918 to early 1919 – helping him to focus and anchor his current ideas: 'The Future of British Music', 'Nationalism and Internationalism in Music', 'Cambridge and the Theatre', 'The Spanish Chamber Concert', 'The Ideas of Monsieur Dalcroze', 'Glastonbury and Cambridge'. Really, its audience was gone with the war, and with *The Athenaeum* appointment Murry was offering Dent a source of income and a wider public platform, the perfect opportunity to move on. It was a great compliment; he would be in elevated company, most of whom were

10 Diary 04/02/1919.

11 CC 18/04/1919.

12 CC 21/02/1919.

old acquaintances: beside Murry's wife, Katherine Mansfield, there were Aldous Huxley, R.O. Morris, T.S. Eliot, Morgan Forster and many other members of the Bloomsbury Group.

The Athenaeum ('A Journal of English & foreign literature, Science, the Fine Arts, Music & Drama') had been founded in 1828, recently bought by philanthropist Arnold Rowntree, with the view to re-establishing it at the cutting edge of cultural affairs. John Middleton Murry – a controversial choice – was appointed its editor, given *carte blanche* to pick the best talent, and he spent Rowntree's money freely. Murry was disliked in some quarters, his elevation deeply resented in others: 'a galling event' to the Woolfs[13] since Leonard Woolf was editing a rival journal, *The International Review*. But Lytton Strachey was more positive: 'It is rather exciting that he's got the *Athenaeum*, isn't it? I really think it ought to give poor old English Kultur a leg up.'[14] 'Squire [editor of the LM] likes my stuff', Dent wrote to JB in October 1919:

> so that's satisfactory. There is a great row on, because Squire seems to have written a rather brutal article on Bernard Shaw in Land & Water: and the Nation has replied very hotly. People say musicians are quarrelsome: but I find these literary cliques just as bad: Murry & the Ath: Turner & the Owl: Squire & the Mercury: Monro & the PB: Osbert & Art & Letters. All <u>my</u> friends! I begin to think I am stuck not only between music & letters, but between the different members of the literary alphabet.

Even with so many new ideas and institutions cropping up, Dent was all too aware of how resolutely conservative the postwar musical scene remained, so while others fretted about where and how any new musical genius was going to manifest itself, through his fresh public platforms Dent made sure that new works would be given serious consideration. But from the outset, there were built-in Dentish caveats, e.g,. from his first *Athenaeum* article, 'The Resurrection of Music':

> There were plenty of young musicians in the first half of 1914 who never gave a thought to foreign politics, but who adored contemporary French and Russian music, and were sick to death of the music of Germany. The reaction against German music was not political, hardly even sentimental, but largely technical. Modern music was tending in the direction of plain song, of folk-song, of Oriental melody—that is, it was tending in the direction of free rhythms; and free rhythms are incompatible with that whole system of harmony on which the Italian music of the eighteenth century and the German music of the nineteenth were based.
>
> But these are mere diversions of the over-cultured classes. The war was to rescue Music from the stuffy atmosphere of theatres and concert-halls ... Yet the great heart of the people still remains loyal to its sentimental ballads and its sentimental hymns ...It is equally fatuous to suppose that the war would bring

13 Hermione Lee, *Virginia Woolf* (London, 1997), p. 394. Leonard would eventually edit *The Athenaeum* after Murry was sacked in 1921, having lost the proprietor a lot of money.

14 Cited in Anthony Alpers, *The Life of Katherine Mansfield* (Oxford, 1982), p. 291. Strachey himself wrote for *The Athenaeum*, and had hopes that his brother James might be 'sub-editor' when T.S. Eliot turned it down. *The Letters of Lytton Strachey*, p. 429.

> forth isolated compositions of outstanding greatness. In the first place, those of our composers who were still in the prime of life were for the most part absorbed by the war itself … Under the stress of war people had little time and little inclination to listen to music. They wanted either mere frivolities to distract them from thinking or those old favourite classics which required of them no conscious effort of thought.[15]

Besides building a broader audience base to counter any elitism, Dent advocated giving any new material a proper public airing, arguing that the real sign of a healthy cultural life came out of the *process* of making music, of understanding music, of enjoying music. This drive to instil a need and desire for excellence at every level had been with Dent for a long time now; excellence is never limited by class, age or nationality, he wrote; it is universal and lasting, if elusive, and bound up with the experience of artistic involvement, and his writing was giving new life to his old ideals.

He began one *Cambridge Magazine* article ('The Leaders' 18 January) by remarking on what was missing from all the obituaries he had read of a whole generation.

> But I never seem to read the things that stand out most vividly in my memory of them – that they were sensitive and accomplished musicians, skilful and daring draughtsmen and colourists, students of social problems, devoted workers amongst the poor, actors, poets, researchers into out-of-the-way subjects, witty and outrageous talkers … And while the idealist fought, suffered and perhaps died, vulgarity and commercialism have seized their advantage. A glance at the play-bills of London theatres is enough.

It wasn't that Dent was against commercial theatre or commercialism *per se*; during the war, he had enjoyed the Gaiety and the Alhambra as much as anyone. But he recognised the limitations of a wholly commercial attitude to the arts, and his *Athenaeum* articles often refer to various funding crises, from Covent Garden opera to Boughton's fading Glastonbury Festivals. Even Beecham's brand of higher commercialism was self-limiting, as Dent always enjoyed pointing out; new ventures could not be risked, while the old war-horses continued to be compromised versions of 'lasting' pieces. As an antidote to deadening commercialism he revived his arguments for the place of academic education in the arts:

> Academic training means, or should mean, the teaching of principles; commercial training teaches nothing but the reproduction of clichés. Academic principles are not in the least degree cramping or dangerous to art as long as they are thorough, and as long as we have no blind reverence for traditions, but keep our methods in working order by subjecting them to constant criticism and satire … No ideal is worth keeping until it has passed the test of being thoroughly well laughed at.

His writing apart, throughout 1919–20 Dent threw himself into various musical activities not necessarily mainstream, but important for establishing the grassroots, while continuing to help individuals, like Bruce Hylton Stewart and Steuart Wilson. He found audiences for Gibbs' new chamber music, which he had copied

15 *The Athenaeum* (14 April 1919).

out himself and 'corrected', before sending on to John Ireland. In spite of his badly damaged lungs, Steuart Wilson was determined to sing again, and Dent gave him support, financial and moral, as well as providing opportunities for him to sing and teach. He continued to coach and support Gladys Moger and Miss Ley, helping Moger prepare her lecture–recitals.[16] In spite of all the uncertainly surrounding the International Conservatoire Dent persevered on behalf of his female pupils there, knowing that they were 'not Beethovens' but 'real sloggers', delighting in their 'very accomplished and striking personalities'. He made sure that the younger musicians were supported and encouraged, taking especial pride in helping C.T. Smith to produce *The Magic Flute* with his schoolboys on the Isle of Dogs,[17] which became a kind of personal benchmark; he often referred to it when speaking or writing about opera production generally.

'Cambridge is tremendously alive', he wrote to Clive that same busy February 1919.

> I am quite possibly going to retire from the CUMS committee: not amicably! and I mean to give up lecturing as soon as I can. London engrosses me more & more: but I shall still keep on the house in Panton Street and Hills, and enter into the informal social life of Cambridge as far as I can.

That winter of 1919 Dent was only in Cambridge at the weekend for the odd Friday lecture or meeting. Returned old friends were glad to see him: Jack Sheppard, Andrew Gow, Frank Birch, 'Michael' Haslam, Charles Harman and his brother Eddy, Percy Lubbock and Manny Forbes. Birch, now a Fellow at King's, keen to revive the MDS, consulted Dent as to whether to stage an opera (*The Fairy Queen*) or simply return to the Greek Play.[18]

> I mean to stir people up about the Fairy Queen. I fear CBR [Rootham] wants to get his opera performed instead. If we ever did do a modern one, I want to do Nicholas Gatty's The Tempest wch has a wonderful Purcellian beauty about it. Gatty has got out of the W.O. [War Office] & is composing again. His stuff is dry & bony – but so bony that I like it – it has a queer individual character of nobility and austerity: modern feeling though with oldfashioned chords.[19]

Dent stood with the new lot, continuing to press publicly his own vision of a MDS that could produce the informed, intelligent, provocative performances which the commercial theatre was failing to do. 'Amateur' should no longer be a pejorative term.

> Cambridge is filling up again with new blood, and it is urgent that we should contribute our share to the new movements in art and letters. We want to see

16 Haward, *Edward J. Dent: A Bibliography*, 6: 'Musical Illustrations of History and Literature: Lecture Recitals for Schools and Colleges by Mr Edward Dent and Miss Gladys Moger', (Cambridge, 1918), privately printed.

17 'The Glengall Road Elementary School', *The Athenaeum* (30 January 1920). Dent commented on the production and on C.T. Smith, 'who manages to make his pupils imbibe music like a language as part of their usual routine – which is precisely what we all agree should be done, though few of us know how to set about it.'

18 Diary 16/03/1919.

19 CC 21/02/1919.

> Cambridge place of pilgrimage, a place where thought takes shape, where experiments can be tried and criticised both sympathetically and severely. We want Cambridge to be a place not only where people create, but to which other creators can come for their first audiences, where we may see the new plays and the new ideas in stage-craft, hear the new music, read the new poetry and look at the new pictures which London is not yet ready to face.[20]

When regular Marlowe readings were reinstated, Dent took part as Bosala in *The Duchess of Malfi,* and the first postwar production took place that June 1919, with *Henry IV, Part I,* produced by Jack Sheppard, with Percy Lubbock as Prince Hal and Charles Harman as Falstaff.[21] James Strachey's review in *The Athenaeum* picked up on all the positive points of such amateur production.[22]

> It is plain that what is needed is a new tradition, and the conclusion suggests itself that the best hope for a new tradition lies in the deliberate development of the instinctive style of the amateur ... it is his business, not to 'interpret' Shakespeare's words, but to speak them, that the first rule for acting Shakespeare is to trust him.

This became the template, soon picked up by George 'Dadie' Rylands and passed on to generations of British actors. *The Fairy Queen* was finally staged in February 1920, the Penrose sets and costumes reinstated, with a cast including Clive Carey's sister, Eila, as Titania, John Steegman, Eddie Harman and 'Sebastian' Sprott, with Rootham conducting.[23] But by that time Dent's attention, together with Clive's, was being diverted, producing Mozart at the Old Vic.

❧ ❧ ❧

When Clive came home on leave in March 1919, Dent took him to concerts, to the Drama League, to the International Conservatoire, eventually dropping in to see Muriel Gough in Donizetti's *The Daughter of the Regiment* being staged at an odd venue south of the river, a coffee-house-cum-theatrical venture, The Old Vic, run by Lilian Baylis: 'a jolly and amusing performance',[24] even if 'rather rough and uneven'.[25]

It took Dent a while to recognise that the Old Vic dovetailed perfectly into everything else he had been thinking about and doing, and how his interests might

20 'Cambridge and the Theatre', CM (25 January, 1919).

21 Cribb, *The Marlowe Story,* p. 39 also points out this ironic reversal of his later role in life as Lord Chief Justice.

22 As a close friend of Rupert Brooke and follower of all the earlier MDS ideas, and recently appointed theatre critic for the revived *Athenaeum,* James Strachey was particularly well placed to note and understand how such issues affected the current theatre. *Ibid.,* pp. 39 ff.

23 The programme and a number of photographs from the production are in Carey, *Duet for Two Voices,* pp. 100ff. The cast included Rootham's son Jasper alternating with H.F. Stewart's daughter Frideswide (Frida).

24 Diary 08/03/1919.

25 LH 15/02/1942.

complement those of 'Miss Baylis'. They were as opposite as two people could be, yet they put together a working relationship which lasted up to her death, while the institutions they built survive up to the present day. With Baylis, the need to keep costs low and the constant fear of financial disaster conflicted with the desire to give her audiences wonderful music. The decision to revive *The Marriage of Figaro* was based on the materials to hand, not least having in Muriel Gough a good Susannah. But Gough had no desire to produce it as well, and suggested Clive Carey, who agreed, on the condition that he sing Figaro himself and that they use Dent's recent translation. So Dent was finally going to have his translations used, his old friend employed in the production and a whole new prospect opened up for him and for 'English' opera. Since Dent had already left the conservatoire, that November they became involved more closely, and Dent's role soon became a far more active one.[26]

Twenty years later Dent wrote a history of the Old Vic and Sadler's Wells, a highly personal account of its early years drawn in the wider context of the history of English theatre, opera and ballet.[27] The Old Vic had been built in 1816 as the Royal Cobourg Theatre, its lease later purchased by Lilian Baylis' aunt, Emma Cons, and on Boxing Day 1880, it was reinvented as a 'coffee-palace', 'The Royal Victoria Hall – The People's Opera', an antidote to the more usual gin-palaces around that rough part of London south of Waterloo Station. Miss Cons, a friend of Octavia Hill,[28] and of a similar philanthropic and Christian Socialist disposition, was dishing up coffee and entertainment at a place where local families could enjoy themselves cheaply without the destructive influence of alcohol. It was popular from the outset, but with uncertain finances. In 1884, it was helped by another philanthropist, Samuel Morley, who donated 1,000 pounds on the condition that they include more lectures and educational events, which became The Morley Memorial College for Working Men and Women. Forty years later, the joint use of its premises would vex Dent, with its banging of hammers intruding into rehearsal space. Still, the co-existence was largely one of mutual benefit; broken sets could be sorted out more or less on the spot.

From its earliest days, the Royal Victoria Hall had put on music hall and platform performances of popular opera, the same kind of fare to be found in the travelling opera companies, Moody-Manners and Carl Rosa, but even more basic in execution. The 'Old Vic' audiences saw *The Bohemian Girl* beside Verdi and Gounod and popular nineteenth-century ballad operas, or parts of them: licensing laws did not allow them to present full performances of plays. When her aunt died in July 1912, Baylis took over completely and continued to run the Old Vic successfully throughout the war. After the law changed, allowing 'occasional full performances' of plays and operas,[29] she cut out the music hall and shoddy, loss-making concerts to focus on better-quality entertainment. She had studied violin at the Royal Academy, and

26 Diary 10/10/1919. 'We had a long talk with Miss Baylis about Figaro etc.'

27 *A Theatre for Everybody: The Story of the Old Vic and Sadler's Wells* (London, 1945), henceforth ATFE.

28 Philanthropist, founder of the National Trust.

29 ATFE, p. 21.

her love of music, especially opera, worked in harness with her aunt's Christian Socialist beliefs, and by the time Dent saw the Donizetti in 1919, the Vic was playing to audiences of around two thousand; 'The People's Opera' was firmly established.[30]

But Baylis was constantly begging from every possible source to keep her people's opera going; she had that at least in common with Sir Thomas Beecham.

> I have not much hope of Miss Baylis and the Old Vic, from what Steuart tells me; he said she wanted him to sing for her without fee and without rehearsal. That meant that everything would be done in the stock way, and that he would not get experience or learn anything at all, even the carl [sic] Rosiest of traditions![31]

Initially, Dent felt that their fundamental ideas were too divergent. His intentions always included the premise that the basics be done properly: that artists were paid and that enough time was taken for proper rehearsals; the performance must be as good as it could be. This was not quite what he saw at the Old Vic that summer, but he never could resist the siren call to his organisational skills.

> Miss Baylis hesitated about accepting a new translation. I do not think she ever read it, and I doubt whether Corri[32] ever did either; her immediate reaction to the suggestion was that it would be a great labour and expense to copy the new words into the old books, and that it would be most unfair to a voluntary chorus to ask them to learn new words, all the more since nobody ever heard the words that the chorus sang in any opera. The principal singers, too, would certainly very much resent having to learn a new version and, indeed, would probably say that to learn a new set of words was absolutely impossible in practice.[33]

Recognising that the source of Baylis' stated objections was her deep-seated financial anxiety, Dent copied everything out himself, often in a damp, dark backstage room at the Old Vic, and coached the chorus himself. Unpaid. That December he wrote of 'writing words into chorus parts while they rehearse Lohengrin in a dark & stuffy room – I got a horrid headache'[34] He also recognised that with Baylis, the production was more important than her ego: a real change from all that work with Fairbairn, with the International Conservatoire, the Beecham disasters, even with Cambridge. By then, though, Dent was nearly frantic with overwork: not only was he helping with the productions but writing it all up for *The Athenaeum*, with the aim of broadening its audience and its outlook.

'Opera at the "Old Vic"' ('The opera happened to be "Mignon"') is a dazzling explication of how despite its modest means the Old Vic was being remarkably audacious, ambitious, and *successful*. Dent anticipates any criticism – and incidentally harnesses his own initial scepticism – by comparing the Old Vic with a typical 'provincial touring company' in the way they both take the line of least resistance and opt for old favourites like the two well-known ditties from *Mignon*. But he turns that

30 *Ibid.*, p. 19.

31 CC 09/08/1919.

32 Charles Corri (1861–1941), conductor at the Old Vic and later at Sadler's Wells.

33 ATFE, p. 86.

34 Diary 20/12/1919.

point completely around, commenting on how tricky the rest of the opera is to bring to life on the stage – 'it is not an easy opera to perform, for, despite its conventionality, its workmanship is intricate and ingenious' – going on to show how successful the Vic have been, with this and with the rest of the repertoire.

> But whereas in the case of the provincial company one starts listening with a sense of anxiety at the outset, and wonders from scene to scene how they will ever get through the opera at all, the 'Old Vic' establishes at once a feeling of perfect confidence and security. They have no great singers, they have the shabbiest of scenery, their band consists of less than twenty players; but they do create that atmosphere in which one simply disregards inevitable shortcomings because one is compelled to enjoy the opera from start to finish.[35]

Like the production being reviewed, the article is a masterful exercise in making a virtue of necessity, demonstrating how apparent disadvantages are genuine opportunities. Dent moves on to speculate how these might be grounds for future development, for example, by joining up with Morley College to establish an opera school right there with the means of full production to hand. He focuses on how important the audience is, putting forward his radical view that its audience defines and is defined by the institution.

> The 'Old Vic' audience brings a valuable influence to bear on its performers and on its producers and stage manager, because it is unsophisticated and without operatic experience, and therefore insists on having everything made perfectly clear and intelligible. Thus common sense counts for more than tradition, and in most opera-houses common sense is the last motive to prevail with either a producer or a prima donna.

The Old Vic audience enchanted him; their spontaneous responses to what was on stage summed up Dent's own hopes about having here something solid to build upon, the whole experience reminding him of those exuberant provincial Italian audiences Forster had written about twenty years before.

> Miss Baylis and Mr Corri give it opera in the right spirit. The performances make no pretence of being perfect, but they are as good as the material at hand can provide. Indeed, they are a great deal better than one could ever expect from such material, for the simple reason that real brain-work is at the back of them and a determination to maintain a really high artistic standard.

Around the same time, at the opposite end of the operatic scale, for J.C. Squire's more conservative *London Mercury,* Dent was also reviewing Beecham's opera season.[36]

> As long as Sir Thomas Beecham was fighting the battle of English opera with dogged persistence and unstinted expenditure of material in the face of apathy and indifference, and possibly the hostility of vested interest as well, there was a very general feeling that his courage and high idealism should not be hampered

35 Dent, 'Opera at the "Old Vic"', *The Athenaeum* (7 November 1919), pp. 1159–60.

36 Which he thought excellent in principle. JBT 01/09/1919.

> by a too searching criticism of his performances. … The present season has so far been something of a disappointment … In the case of an absolutely new opera insufficiency of rehearsal may be pardoned; but it is not a sign of good management when the performance of stock classics is allowed to become slack and indifferent. Sir Thomas has not been seen very often at the conductor's desk, and this is the more to be regretted, since he has a most remarkable genius for pulling through a performance which in other hands would be always trembling on the verge of disintegration.[37]

It did not take long for the serpentine influence to appear in the reviews of other critics like R.O. Morris. But Dent never lost sight of the aim of public criticism: to enlighten and inform, and later critiques show that he never really forgot what Sir Thomas had done for opera.

> The Beecham opera did occasionally attain something like a worthy standard, but at a cost which made its permanent maintenance impossible. Yet the Beecham management did something more than just pour out money like water. It had what the Carl Rosa lacks – artistic direction.[38]

Besides, Dent was invariably entertaining, and his review of the Proms concerts around the same time shows the sense of humour supporting a less than wonderful concert:

> Sullivan's In Memoriam is one of those which might well be laid on the shelf; but like Walford Davies' Solemn Melody it brings in the organ, and to many English people of this kind would appear to offer all the spiritual advantages of church-going without its discomforts … all those desirable qualities of tune, rhythm, and a jolly noise. In one case Sir Henry Wood has managed to add the attractions both of organ and batterie de cuisine, thus combining mirth with devotion.[39]

The Athenaeum was changing his life, and being incorporated into everything else he was doing. The liberal internationalism driving its cultural engines suited Dent perfectly, and it became a platform for many of his ideas; he now had influence and a wider reputation. The editor, Murry, was nothing short of a genius at sensing cultural trends, and in July 1919 sent J.B. Trend off on assignment from *The Athenaeum* to Spain, to write about the music there. At the time Trend – later first Professor of Spanish at Cambridge – barely spoke any Spanish, had little formal musical background and had always intended to go back to Italy. Dent certainly had some hand in it,[40] from his own *Athenaeum* connection and the fact that JB went off furnished with an introduction to composer Mañuel de Falla, thanks to Pedro

37 Dent, 'The Beecham Opera', LM (November 1919), p. 248.

38 Dent, 'Opera in English at Covent Garden', *The Athenaeum* (12/11/1921). Compare the MT (January 1919).

39 Dent, 'The Promenade Concerts', LM (November 1919), p. 119. Batterie de cuisine, lit. kitchen artillery, i.e., kitchenware: a pun on the march of the kitchen utensils in Vaughan Williams' music for the triennial Greek Play, *The Wasps* of Aristophanes. See Chapter 6.

40 Diary 08/07/1919. After a performance at Covent Garden of Mascagni's *Iris*, Dent went off, 'leaving JB to talk to Mortimer about Spain'.

Morales. Spanish music had been on the cultural catwalk that spring, not only the concerts organised by Morales in London and Cambridge, but especially the dazzling new productions being staged by Diaghilev's Ballets Russes. This was much more the elusive style and standard Dent was hoping for to give conservative British music a jolt, and now Trend's new Spanish brief opened up more direct connections with Spain. The current inspiration from Diaghilev was multifold, in the adventurous production values as much as the way Diaghilev conjured up such excellence out of meagre and uncertain sources.

In the last years of the war, stateless and broke from the Russian Revolution, the Ballets Russes desperately toured Spain and Portugal, barely scraping a living, but all the time picking up fresh ideas and working relationships with Falla, Picasso and others of the current Spanish and French avant-garde, Joán Miró and Robert Delaunay, beside Jean Cocteau and Erik Satie, out of which came *Parade* and *The Three-cornered Hat*.[41] Initially, Diaghilev had pinned his hopes on Beecham's continuing support and an affluent Covent Garden audience, but Beecham took fright at the 'wild Spaniard Picasso'[42] and backed out, leaving Diaghilev to take the bold and terrible risk of booking the Coliseum, at the time hardly a substitute for Covent Garden. Built in 1904, as a 'people's palace of entertainment', the Coliseum was not only the biggest theatre in London but a genuinely populist one; the Ballet Russes' avant-garde productions were to be put on the same bill as talking dogs, comic turns and acrobats. Dent grumbled about having 'to sit through the whole dreadful entertainment, not knowing at what time the ballet came on'.[43] Later, he joked about it, quite enjoying the extras and expatiating on how the ballet had expanded its audience in such an odd way.

But Diaghilev had yet again worked one of his miracles, triumph out of disaster. The new audiences which Dent had been noting all along were at least as enthusiastic as those of the Ballet Russes' first prewar tour, and by the time of the long-anticipated first night of the *Three-Cornered Hat* in July, London had already been buzzing for months about Picasso's sets, Falla's extraordinary music and the Spanish dances incorporated into the ballet. Beside all this, the new seasons had opened up opportunities for younger conductors like Adrian Boult, Albert Coates and Ernest Ansermet. Dent loved being in the thick of such a mixed stew, reviewing *La Boutique Fantasque* and the *Hat* for *The Athenaeum*, enjoying the pastiche of Rossini by Respighi, capturing the lighthearted spirit of the piece.

> Moreover Bologna is the headquarters of the Italian antique furniture trade, and if any Italian composer could turn out Rossini sofas and dinner-tables as good as the originals, it would be Signor Respighi ... The virtue of M. Picasso's frankly unrealistic design ... is that it forces the theatregoer to be imaginative.

The various Spanish influences Diaghilev had tapped into so imaginatively were now being revealed to JB, just arrived in Spain, who – talented, musical, with his

41 Most of this information is in Scheijen, *Diaghilev*, pp. 333ff.

42 *Ibid.*, p. 338.

43 Diary 05/09/1918.

gift for languages and his curiosity – fell completely in love with the country, its language, culture and music. He was more than ready for such a love affair, and since his brief was to see as much of Spanish music and culture as possible, he fell upon it with real joy and pleasure: 'you are always coming across things which you've known before, only in delightful & surprizing forms. The most delightful thing … is the openness & friendliness of everybody.[44]

The experience turned him from an enthusiast into a writer; with a writer's eye, he conveyed the immediacy of his impressions in the cathedral at Burgos:

> At 5, they sang. there was no procession: the men in black & 4 choirboys in red 'hassocks'[45] strolled into their places, followed by an ascetic-looking individual with a bassoon. A large book with the four parts written out one after the other (not in score) was lifted up onto a lectern … The four little boys stood in front of it; & behind them the conductor with three other men; while in the background the reverend father in God played on his bassoon. The leader, when not actually conducting, laid a hand on the head of his favorite [sic] choir-boy, & another nestled close to him in their voices [del] divine rapture; but they sang abominably.

He noted everything: the 'exquisite diction' of ordinary people, the 'lightness of the houses', the ladies out of *Don Giovanni* with their mantillas and fans. But JB was never simply an observer of the scene; even more than Dent he had to become part of it, from his eager chats in halting Spanish on the train, to singing along in the churches. In Valladolid:

> The two most interesting things were my adventures in the cathedral & national dances. I arrived while they were singing; they were rather good, and had no need of a bassoon to keep them in tune. Afterwards I got the sacristan to show me their books, – the new 'Graduale Romanum'. Then an unshaven individual appeared, talked for a little, & suddenly lifted up his voice & sang an alleluja. He sang other things out of the Graduale; and as he stopped near the end of one, I couldn't help humming it to the end for him, which made a great impression.

Spain energised him. He went along to the street festivals, noting the different bands and what they were playing, the dances; to Avila, then to Zaragoza, 'strangely thrilled by the first sounds of tuning' in the midst of tantalising Spanish conversations he could not quite pick up.

The letters show more than JB's strong instinct for the important aspects of what he was seeing: these intense first impressions floated in the letters would be fine-tuned into his articles and later still, used in his books and actual productions. The subversive Robreño y Tort[46] and the 'shadow shows' which could, like marionette theatre, sidestep any censor (the DORA was still active in England) were being

44 All of this is taken from the letter to Dent 01/08/1919.

45 A private joke. The story was that when getting Royal approval for the King's choristers to wear their now-famous red cassocks, King George signed the chitty for red 'hassocks' instead.

46 José Robreño y Tort (1780–1838), actor and playwright. Trend discusses his influence at some length in his excellent *A Picture of Modern Spain, Men & Music* (London, 1921), pp. 133ff.

stored for future use. Like Diaghilev, JB quickly hooked up with all the sympathetic artists, subversives and homosexuals who were helping to create this Spanish renaissance, especially around the Residencia de Estudiantes in Madrid, and he soon began to appreciate Spain's historical battles between censorship and conformity, and the artistic Robreños involved. Within a month of his arrival in Spain, he had established himself with a number of useful and congenial people: the poet Eugenio d'Ors[47] and even the venerable Catalan musicologist and musician Felip Pedrell.[48] He was writing articles on such recherché subjects as the 'Elches', named after the Catalan town of Elx near Valencia, but which JB used to refer to the dancers in the cathedral performing to a medieval play.

By September he had found a pleasant pension in Granada and was settled down there to write his articles and to see the Alhambra, examining Catalan music and culture, beginning to cast about for evidence of Scarlatti in Spain. Then:

> Really the most extraordinary things happen. Falla has turned up at this identical pension with his sister, & the painter Vasquez-Diaz, who has a wife & a small boy, and a relation of hers who is partly or entirely German. Falla was a little the disappointed great man at first: but melted completely, when I talked about you, and Domenico Scarlatti, & the "Three Cornered Hat": and "La Vida Breve" … You must meet him.[49]

Under Falla's benevolent tutelage JB's Spanish improved exponentially, while his appreciation of Spanish culture was given the kind of boost most outsiders could barely dream of. In one of many evenings in Falla's company, he was taken up into the hills behind it to look down on the Alhambra: 'I realize now that it's the sort of architecture which is meant to be looked at by moonlight.' Dent was told 'how Falla took me about with him, listening to "Canto Flamenco" in the courtyards and inns'.[50] JB was in fact hearing some of the best music around: one 'Guitarrist', Angel Barrios, 'who is part composer of a Goyaesque opera "El Avapies"; the old man who sang was his father'.[51] He later wrote about hearing a young poet called Lorca at one of these sessions, reading his poetry in the moonlight while the guitars played softly.

> Last night we [Falla & Vasquez-Diaz] went to a small wine-shop, where a guitar (tuned in flats) was played with amazing technique and … a good deal of musicianship. I listened very carefully … one of the best had several neutral 6ths …

47 Eugenio d'Ors (1881–1954), Catalan writer and critic who later worked for the Franco regime.

48 Felip Pedrell (1841–1922), Catalan composer, musicologist, teacher, collector of folk music, credited with the regeneration of Spanish music (P. Morales in the DMMM).

49 JBT–EJD 14/09/1919.

50 JBT–EJD 27/09/1919.

51 In the 1924 DMMM, ed. Eaglefield Hull, Dent *et al.*, the entry for Ángel Barrios was written by Pedro Morales. Born in Granada in 1882 [DMMM says 1862], Barrios had been an orchestral violinist before turning to the guitar, playing, composing and transcribing Andalusian pieces, especially flamenco, founded Trio Iberia, died 1964. His father was known as 'El Polinario'.

the old man's intonation was very accurate, & they were out of tune with the guitar. Falla is writing some chamber music for Paris ... I hope he'll put in some of the innkeeper's tunes.

Falla introduced him to the composer Joaquim Turina,[52] and now he was asking Dent to send copies of his recent *Athenaeum* article, 'The Musician in the Theatre', to show to them. JB's scholarly drive resulted in the rediscovery of many lost manuscripts[53] and his excellent book, *The Music of Spanish History* (1926), while the articles led to more commissions from other magazines, more books, and constant travelling from now until the Spanish Civil War in 1936. One important result of this Spanish love affair was to expand Dent's own horizons, and soon bring Spanish music into a wider European framework through the ISCM; that November 1919 they were discussing how Falla's English publisher, Chester's, was not doing enough to promote his music.[54] Moreover JB's prolonged absence finally made Dent realise how keenly he missed him: 'I snatch the chance of writing to you when I can. I'm always wanting you, and missing you the more damnably because I'm not at Quebec Street – to which frankly I long to return.'[55] The relationship actually throve on absence, while JB's letters opened up new worlds for Dent, reviving all his latent internationalist instincts already stirred by the Ballets Russes.

In contrast to the cultural highs JB was enjoying, Dent continued doggedly to examine the mixed bag that was current British music, trying to sort the promising from the dross. His need to experience it all was apparently boundless, and he chose to expend his considerable energies without discrimination between the peripheral and the central: 'All music', he would declare in his final article for the *London Mercury,* and by then it must have felt like that.[56]

> we went to the Club concert in Caius Hall. Chausson 4tet & the rest by Elgar & Quilter: VW & I were horribly bored by nearly all the songs including Roger's – 'He has founded a school' said VW, in a voice of horror. The rest was very poor.[57]

52 Joaquim Turina (1882–1945). Like many Spanish composers of his generation, he studied in Paris, under Vincent d'Indy at the *Schola Cantorum.*

53 The Medinaceli MSS, a number of Victoria MSS, besides the music he was copying down and sending back to Cambridge. See Tess Atkin's articles on the subject, 'Perspectivas del hispanismo musical britanico en el siglo XX: el casa de John Brande Trend (1887–1958)'. Many of his transcriptions are still in the CUL. Vaughan Williams picked up his Galician carol 'Torches' for *The Oxford Book of Carols.*

54 Chester's was just reviving the new series of *The Chesterian,* edited by Georges Jean-Aubry, which was intended to address the needs of current music and composers. Falla, amongst other current distinguished composers, was asked to write for it. How much this revival might have been stimulated by Trend and Dent's work at this time is not clear.

55 1313JBT 16/06/1920.

56 Between November 1919 and September 1920, Dent wrote 29 articles for the LM, finishing aptly with 'Revaluations', his credo on music.

57 Diary May, 1919

Boughton's Glastonbury Festival was a chore, even with Clive joining him there to oversee rehearsals for Locke's *Cupid & Death*. 'I hope Boughton will take kindly to him', Dent wrote to JB:

> for he is going to stir up a little trouble over Cupid & Death in my interest ... The masque is far too literary for Boughton's understanding: far too consciously literary, which makes it worse still.. Boughton & I are poles apart in some ways; I felt that I wanted the whole thing to be very fragile and fine and formal, probably too much so.[58]

In spite of strong personal reservations about his over-ambitious projects, Dent respected Boughton and the effort he put into Glastonbury, and continued to offer him support and encouragement.[59]

He continued to be even-handed, though preferring the company of Arthur Bliss, or Ernest Ansermet or Edward Clark.[60] On Bliss: 'He's splendid, and to hear him talk for an hour does me more good than anything in the world. He goes ahead – I find dear old Gibbs & some of the others fearfully slowbrained and consequently tiring'.[61] But he supported Gibbs, whose important collaboration with the poet Walter de la Mare, *Crossings*, had to be postponed 'as none of us cd undertake the labour of the business arrangements'. The Promenade concerts took up a great deal of his time, only occasionally exciting his interest, some Malipiero *Impressioni dal vero* or 'Roger Quilter's "Children's Overture" wch delighted me greatly & really brought tears to my eyes.'[62] Ragtime was all the rage, having caught on during the war, its lively, different rhythms and exotic style a complete antidote to the older generation's tastes, so popular that soldiers officially could not be seen in uniform dancing in these clubs.[63] When the Southern Syncopated Orchestra came to town with the great Sydney Bechet, it was a big hit, some critics hailing the music of the future. Dent's piece on it was professional, but privately in his diary he is unusually vicious: 'I loathed [them] with a horrible race hatred, & hated them the more for their slick Americanism – but the whole thing was extraordinarily interesting.'[64] The coda is significant: Dent seldom allowed ancient prejudices to overcome his fundamental curiosity.

His growing reputation had its awkward side; he was alarmed to be told that Ronald Firbank was writing a novel 'not only to be dedicated to me (he told me that

58 JBT 06/08/1919.

59 Their correspondence in the BL shows this.

60 Thomas Edward Clark (1888–1962), conductor and proponent of contemporary music, supported the ISCM from its inception, succeeding Dent as President after his second stint in that office. Married (second) composer Elisabeth Lutyens. Dent had already been introduced to Clark by Clive Bell in August, fascinated to find that Clark knew about him and his work.

61 JBT 08/12/1919.

62 Diary 18/09/1919.

63 I am grateful to Professor Rachel Cowgill for this piece of information.

64 Diary 16/09/1919. His attitude changed completely when he visited Louisiana years later.

himself) but is also to have me for its hero'.[65] One of his daily working lunches with W.J. Turner and J.C. Squire concerned taking on the *London Mercury* job,[66] besides lunches with Goldschmidt, Turner and Evelyn Broadwood, being taken round the Broadwood factory at Old Ford. He could write to JB about his enjoyment of Ethel Smyth's 'amazing self-revelation' in her autobiography, 'I feel enormously drawn to the woman, even though rather against my will'; about meeting a young composer called William Walton, 'the little fair-haired Oxford boy … I don't know whether he is merely trying to say the right thing, but he seems to hold all the right views'.[67] Invitations to Spain or to Brussels had to be reluctantly turned down; Dent was simply too busy. That November, Busoni was back in town, and Dent took him and his entourage, including Alfred Cortot and Maud Allan, to lunch at the Spanish, even managing to get Busoni on his own for a few hours' precious conversation, 'a great joy'. Delighted with his reception and encouraged by Dent, Busoni returned to England the following year.

❧ ❧ ❧

> Rehearsals at the Old Vic and other occupations interrupted my diary, and finding it impossible to keep it up with any regularity, I abandoned it altogether.[68]

For the next year and beyond, Dent's main outlet for private thoughts became his correspondence with Trend, now partly living in Spain.

> I am too [enjoying life], I think, on the whole, in spite of the rush. People tell me that I get a great deal in … I see a lot of people & hear a lot of music – but hardly ever get a peaceful time & quiet conversation with real friends. And each piece of work seems to be more of an effort … and say to myself seriously over & over again – 'well, what is it that you really want?' and the trouble is that I never do know what I want. Not enough to act blindly on impulse: and not enough logic to live according to reason! Trotzdem is das leben nur ganz angenehm: so don't imagine that you will come home to find me a nervous wreck – anything but.[69]

In London all that autumn 1919, Dent kept up his punishing schedules, writing or proofing his *Athenaeum* articles, while going, for example, to Douglas Marshall's vocal recital, on to Dolmetsch's concert ('very bad'), then after a hasty Spanish dinner, on to Bathoni's Wigmore recital, the 'Chanson de Bilitis', which he enjoyed. Then Geoffrey Toye's Philharmonic rehearsal of Malipiero's *Pause del silenzio* ('rather chaotic but genuine stuff'), Meyerbeer's *Streuensee* overture, Mozart and Liszt. At supper with Miss Ley, Augustus Milner and Ursula Creighton, they played through Busoni's *Arlechinno*, until asked by the neighbours to please stop.

65 JBT 09/09/1919.

66 His first article, 'The Promenade Concerts' appeared in November 1919.

67 JBT 29/11/1919.

68 Diary 10/10/1920.

69 Nevertheless, life is simply delightful. JBT 01/11/1919.

There were Drama League meetings, dinner at the Sitwells' new place, then off to Bantock's new opera *Pierrot* ('dull'). Busoni's final recital on the 6th December – Bach, Beethoven, Chopin and Liszt ('I hated the Ballades less than I expected: and he played the C minor nocturne magnificently as an encore'). It was becoming clear to some of his colleagues, if not to himself, that he was spreading himself too thin:

> At this moment I am getting it hot all round. Murry complains that I send in my copy at the last minute, or later: Monro bitter over my neglect of the Chap-Book: Denis [sic] Browne fussing over the publication of his brother's songs: Clive & the Roothams very sick because 'I take no interest in the Fairy Queen'; Maud Allan rather hurt because I went to Cambridge yesterday to dine with the Brownes instead of coming up to see Busoni.[70]

After a relatively peaceful Christmas break with the Hawards, Dent met the Eugene Goossens and heard Arthur Rubenstein for the first time, greatly impressed. His sister Catherine moved into a new house in Neville Terrace, Chelsea; JB was back on 2 January. But after the New Year 1920, it was straight back to his frantic routines.

Beside Gibbs's *Crossings* and a new translation of *Cosi fan tutte*, Dent had committed himself to *The Magic Flute* on the Isle of Dogs, *The Fairy Queen* at Cambridge that February, then the Old Vic *The Magic Flute* in March. That January 1920, Clive urgently needed his active support for the Old Vic *Figaro* rehearsals: 'I went to the Old Vic yesterday & found that the chorus parts were only very partially done – mostly by someone not very bright.' So yet again, he did it himself, copying out the parts, constantly arguing over how things were being sung, determined in the teeth of uncertain finances, lack of time and space, tatty old costumes and cardboard sets, to make sure that the Old Vic kept up its growing reputation for the musical standards, supported by his articles in *The Athenaeum*. At the same time he was rushing on the train up to frustrating *Fairy Queen* rehearsals in Cambridge where people simply didn't turn up, then back to London for discussions about a new 'literary miscellany' with some of Sachie Sitwell's Oxford friends and local publisher Willliam Heffer. There was his regular critical work to keep up, much of it onerous rather than pleasurable; standard repertoire irritated him, while new pieces had to captivate. As it had so often before in times of stress, Dent's stomach began to play up, and he resorted to regular doses of quinine just to keep going.

'I am rather cussing Cambridge', he had written to JB in December 1919. 'In London people do things when you ask them, or refuse – In Cambridge you have to spend 3/4 of your time talking, cajoling, consoling, badgering, pestering & nagging to get anybody to do anything at all. That's what I'm sick of doing.' Dent enlisted John Wells's help with *The Fairy Queen* costumes, John already admiring Kate Cockerell and 'bubbling' with wicked ideas like bare-bottomed monkey attendants. In the event, the whole thing was a huge success: they made a profit, enjoyed themselves, enthused a new generation of students with the desire to put on odd opera. Dent should have been pleased; instead, conveniently forgetting how much his own frequent absences had contributed, he felt alienated from this new generation

70 JBT 19/12/1919.

of Cambridge musicians, unable to appreciate why Dennis Arundell was 'so completely devoted to Rootham', or why Charles Sayle rather than himself had been asked to write up a history of the production. *The Times* review, though, gave due credit, probably written by a friend: 'Mr E.J. Dent ... literary adviser and arch-inspirer in the background',[71] and Dent had been genuinely moved: 'to me the most wonderful experience of the F.Q. was to live in Purcell for a fortnight'.[72]

But it was difficult to let go of a role that had helped to define him, so for a time, up until he left for Germany in the autumn, Dent continued to cling obstinately to his Cambridge activities, including the opera syndicate that had produced *The Fairy Queen*, even though these were increasingly being taken over by the new crowd. That May 1920, he was writing to JB about all the 'intrigues' going on at Cambridge, the point being that while Dent wanted to produce *Idomeneo*, Rootham was on the spot and pushing for his own new operas.

> I expect Rootham means to spring it on me when I am in Germany, knowing that I shall resign from the syndicate. He will then get Arudel [sic] in to stage manage or produce, as Clive may also refuse to do it; and the object of this haste is that it may be done before Arundel [sic] goes down ... But I am sick of all this business, and sick of my own small-mindedness in letting myself be obsessed with it.[73]

The Old Vic productions compensated in some measure, with Clive assuming more of the producing responsibilities, *Figaro* followed by *The Magic Flute*, with an idea suggested by John Steegman for *Fidelio* later that year. So Dent was constantly buzzing around in various supporting roles, trying out singers, checking the scenery, finding ways to get around Lilian Baylis' penny-pinching: 'it is tiresome if we have got to send out special letters to all the critics on these occasions. Miss Baylis ought to do that sort of thing herself.'[74] She refused to advertise (too expensive[75]), but instead printed her own handouts which in 1919 had grudgingly evolved into 'The Old Vic Magazine'. Dent contributed articles to it on Mozart and 'Shakespeare in Germany'.

All that winter and spring of 1920 Dent had been busy as ever but frustrated by 'influenza' which dragged on for months, exacerbated by overwork. The diverse musical political skirmishes in Cambridge and London were too wearing:

> More intrigue – Arthuer [sic] Bliss called here on Sunday morning and told me with much amusement that Edwin Evans was preparing a great campaign against me, Clive, Allen, Boult, Colles and all the musicians connected with Oxford and Cambridge, who just at this moment are a very powerful gang ... It is mere jealousy, because we none of us take any notice of him, and he simply does not count.[76]

71 Cited in Carey, *Duet for Two Voices*, p. 107.

72 Diary 10/10/1920.

73 JBT 25/05/1920.

74 CC 29/03/1920.

75 In fact, *The Athenaeum* published notices of what was on at the Old Vic, paid for or not.

76 JBT 25/05/1920.

In public he resorted to composing 'serpentine' or simply 'bad-tempered' articles, one of the latter in Hugh Allen's Bach Festival Book, 'some people said it was the best thing in the book!'[77] His glum mood was not helped by the fact that Sedley Taylor, another old Cambridge friend, had died. Dent wrote a warm memorial the *Musical Times*: 'But behind the raconteur and the Bach enthusiast there stood another character, scrupulous almost to agony on the smallest question of right and wrong, endlessly and quietly generous of his private means to those who stood in need of help'.[78]

So, when the first week in May, the British Music Society, keen to make its mark on British music, was organising a congress, Dent didn't go: 'I pleaded ill-health and did very little for it, for it took me some time to recover my normal condition again.' This was a great shame, since its stated purpose was to discuss questions of interest to him, such as standard pitch,[79] 'The Needs of Music in Britain and how the British Music Society can best meet them', the 'Municipalisation of Music' (Bernard Shaw 'urging' the importance of subsidised music and opera in every 'centre of population'), the financing of music and 'social events', kicking off with a great banquet for two hundred hosted at the Great Central Hotel by Lord Howard de Walden. The tone, especially at the banquet, seems to have been upbeat, with de Walden teasing Beecham sitting not far away as a 'fine old reactionary' and that he 'frankly' preferred 'the Beecham of the old days, who was an ardent revolutionary and performed works at Queen's Hall that no one had ever heard before and that no one was ever likely to hear again.' More or less ignoring this, Sir Thomas spoke about what he saw as his own role, 'mentor to British composers of opera', but averred that British composers 'stayed away from the opera houses and thus had no real inner knowledge of the technique of operatic composition'; as for English municipalities, they could barely keep the streets clean, much less manage any music.[80] There were four concerts of mostly British music, and three concerts of chamber music at the Aeolian Hall and at the de Waldens' Seaford House. The programmes were certainly contemporary, if in fact 'very little was new': string quartets by Armstrong Gibbs, Holbrooke and Howells, piano music by John Ireland, Frank Bridge and William Baines, an oboe trio by Cyril Scott.

Otherwise, Dent continued doggedly to beat the drum, if increasingly grumpily, taking over over W.J. Turner's spot at the *Daily Herald*, so had twice the usual amount of work to do. Although he had done so much to support Glastonbury, when Boughton's productions came to London Dent felt they did not travel well, composing serpentine reviews with little reference to the actual performances,[81] while Fairbairn's productions at the Surrey, including Gatty's *The Tempest*, Dent

77 This article is not in Haward, *Edward J. Dent: A Bibliography*.

78 Dent, 'Sedley Taylor 1834–1920', MT (1 May 1920). Sayle left Dent the doctored square piano which was later passed on to Roberto Gerhard.

79 In London throughout the week of 3 May, reported in the MT by Alfred Kalisch. Current pitch was around 435 Hz, depending on the temperature of the hall. MT (01/06/1921), pp. 387ff.

80 In a letter to JB dated 25 May, Dent doesn't even refer to the congress.

81 LM (May 1920) and JBT 25/05/1920.

felt 'really bad, tho' there was good material … a beautiful thing even with a bad performance'.

> Last night I went to the Beggars Opera. I thought it perfectly dreadful, but as I'm a personal friend of Playfair, F. Austin and Lovat Fraser I had to be careful what I said. So I have executed a masterpiece of serpentism this morning[82] wch I hope will amuse you. … Austin's harmonizations & additions were atrocious and very badly scored. The music sounded dull & heavy & the harpsichord always wrong.[83]
>
> The Ballet is back at Cov. Gard. Pulcinella by Pergolesi & Stravinsky is dismal rot. Diaggers meant it originally to be an imitation of the Goodhumoured Ladies: but found in the end that it wd cause more sensation if it was an imitation of Parade … Altogether I am in a very bad temper, as you'll see from the Athenaeum.[84]

New Quebec Street had been uninhabitable since spring, with Mrs Bennett ill and some major repairs going on, while Panton Street had roof problems which would take months to repair, with the Daltons due to move in that September. With Francis Toye, Dent inspected some 'perfectly lovely 18th cent houses' in Ebury Square, then a run-down part of London. But JB liked New Quebec Street, and Dent's eventual decision to stay there came out of the recognition that in JB he had found a partner who understood him. So for the time being, that May 1920, Dent moved in again with Timmy Jekyll.

'I am very comfortable at Trevor Square', he wrote to JB. 'I like my big room and can sit and write there too.' He carried on using the Spanish restaurant as both dining room and office, Timmy's odd dining hours making it too difficult to rush off to 3 pm concerts at the 'Wigstein'.[85] Although Timmy had been very keen for Hills to come along too, Dent decided that she would be better off between Cambridge and his sisters, rather than being exposed to the odd company Timmy sometimes invited home: 'what we call the bodyguard wd be a little disturbing to her'.[86] Dent stayed at Trevor Square for several months that summer, and for the most part, he and Timmy rubbed along very well: 'I begin to think that I am really bringing a brightening influence to bear on him'.[87]

Cambridge was ticking along without him, even if Dent found the current productions trying and not entirely to his liking, for reasons he found difficult to express. He hated not being part of it:

> 10 June I went to Camb to see Comus. It was a queer show, very bad at times, but whenever I found it bad I tried to remember what ours was like, and came to the conclusion that ours was far worse … Lionel Penrose's costumes for the beasts were delightful. The performance was stiff & restless at the same time … Jack Squire as Comus was absurd. Too clerically clear a voice that when he gave

82 *The Athenaeum* (11 June 1920).

83 JBT 08/06/1920.

84 JBT 16/06/1920.

85 During the war, the Bechstein Hall had become the Wigmore Hall.

86 JBT 16/06/1920.

87 JBT 01/07/1920.

> the Lady the cup I expected him to say 'This do in remembrance of me' especially as the cup by some error had been covered up with a drapery, and poor Squire couldn't find it at all, at first![88]

Osbert Sitwell startled Dent by suggesting that he take control of a proposed Scarborough Festival. 'Osbert seems to think that I shd carry a great deal of weight there partly by my personal reputation & partly by my family connections.' He was flattered, but such a limiting role had little real appeal, and it forced him to reflect on what exactly he was working for. So, all the disparate, chaotic experience of the past two years was distilled that September into one short article in the London Mercury, very close to being a credo.

'Revaluations' addresses one thorny issue of the day, how to listen to new music, but moves to wider implications, questioning the role of critics and the general attitude of the listener, how an over-reverential attitude to the classical repertory actually hinders the understanding of music old and new; in Dent's view these are connected. It opens with the episode from seventeen years earlier, seared on his memory, when Dent's younger self was summoned into the presence of 'a distinguished art-critic',[89] and his own desire to understand 'all music', never to stamp his own personal taste on another. 'One derives from the practice an agreeably Olympian feeling of superiority to the wretched composer who has wrestled with his soul in blood and tears on the mere chance of being rewarded by … distinguished approval.' In none of his own critical articles did Dent ever damn outright; instead, he tried to follow his own precept as expressed in 'Revaluations', to *understand* all music, whether ragtime or Schoenberg, regardless of his own personal preferences. He addresses a dilemma confronting audiences generally: how the question of taste can interfere with the experience of listening to unfamiliar music, or even to 'classical' music. Yet again, one is reminded of Forster's poor Leonard Bast anxiously trying to listen to Beethoven, and Dent's ideas were being aimed at the Basts of this world as much as the critics. Dent says that it is not enough simply to know a piece through having listened to it over and again, citing his old friend Oscar Chilesotti, 'Studiamo l'antico per comprendere il presente' (I study the antique in order to understand the new):

> No music is new to us more than once. It may be wondered whether those who give up the riddle of modern music in despair have in reality a much more intelligent appreciation of the classics. The difficulty in the case of most of the classics is to warm them into real life, to put ourselves back into a period when they too were new and disturbing.[90]

'All art', Dent goes on, 'aspires to the condition of music':

> The condition of music which gives it an advantage over other arts is its transitoriness … The musician can forget or remember at will. He at least can be honest enough to admit that not even the acknowledged greatest works of music are

88 JBT 08/06/1920.

89 See Introduction and Chapter 4.

90 Dent, 'Revaluations', LM (September 1920), pp. 619–21, here p. 620.

> possessions for eternity. And it is for that reason that some of us begin to feel that it is impossible to pronounce the clear-cut judgements of the man of taste who divides music into good and bad, or, at any rate, that it is unimportant in comparison with the unceasingly fascinating occupation of trying to understand it.[91]

'Revaluations' is one of Dent's most important public statements, an inclusive credo to which he would often return.

JB's 'Letters from Spain' in *The Athenaeum* had proved so successful that a similar series was planned that spring for Germany and the current German cultural renaissance in the postwar Weimar Republic. And who better placed than Dent to scrutinise postwar German culture? The Daltons were installed in Panton Street, and Dent went off to Berlin. His initial brief was to spend three months there, starting in October, but being Dent, he spun something extraordinary out of the the experience and two years later he was driving the establishment of a whole new internationalist project, the International Society for Contemporary Music.

> So provided no new political complications arise I ought to have quite a good time. The only thing I am really frightened about is that I shall make a complete fool of myself when I try to write about literature and painting.[92]

1920–1921

> The first thing that a stranger noticed on revisiting Berlin after the war was its general grimness. There was only one building in Berlin which had a fresh coat of paint since 1914 – the British Embassy. The Friedrichstrasse, once the busiest street in the town, was a chaos of sand and wooden planks; some day there was to be an underground railway beneath it, but in 1920 Berlin was too depressed either to proceed with the railway or the remake the pavement. War had produced poverty and poverty crime.[93]

'The Berlin of 1920 was a changed city', Dent wrote ten years later. Arriving on 8 October, he found Weimar Berlin suffering from postwar depression, with rampaging inflation and acute shortages of food and fuel.[94] On that first morning Dent had to register with the police, who seemed 'quite amiable' when he said he was there to write about music, but to his amusement, sighed that of course these days there was no longer any 'good' music. Travelling was now far more complicated; since the 'British Nationality and Status of Aliens Act' of 1914, passports were necessary, while internal travel around Germany threw up many obstacles, especially for foreigners, and Dent wanted to get beyond Berlin. At one point, he thought he was not going to be allowed to travel from Berlin to Munich or even that he might not be allowed to

91 *Ibid.*, p. 621.

92 JBT 25/05/1920.

93 Dent, *Opera*, p. 137.

94 Dent, *Busoni*, p. 251.

stay at all.[95] Arranging for money, for German books or music to be sent to England – everything stalled.[96]

Exhausted from the trip, Dent immediately plunged into this 'grim' city to seek out old friends. Initially, he was disappointed: Busoni was out; Wilhelm Herzog was away in Hamburg most of the time, now editor of the *Hamburger Volksblatt* and married to a glamorous actress, Erna Morena. 'Frau H was very agreeable & knew more or less who I was.'[97] Dent feeling himself a stranger in this familiar but changed place, he automatically detached himself in order to apprehend the nature of the change, the journalistic side he had developed in the past few years taking over. Going to the theatre had always been an easy form of escape, and he loved to test his fundamentally conservative taste, so he tentatively went to the Kleines Schauspielhaus in Charlottenburg to see the comedy *Der Floh in Panzerhaus*,[98] which along with a revival of Wedekind's *Die Büchse der Pandora* at the Kammerspiele, gave him a shock of a different kind: behind its grimy exterior Berlin's theatre life was flourishing, and for a time diverted Dent's attention from music.

Berlin theatre, with Berlin film, was bold, sexy and contemporary, and instantly recognising its importance to his current work, Dent incorporated it into his first 'Letters from Germany'.

> To an English visitor the theatres in Berlin may well be a source of amazement and delight. There are two opera-houses, and any number of theatres at which one may see plays by dramatists almost unknown in London – Ibsen, Strindberg, Shakespeare, to say nothing of native authors such as Goethe, Hauptmann and Wedekind.[99]

But Dent's theatre-going motives were as mixed as ever, inspired by an encounter with a demobbed flying officer named Bowers, who became a regular companion, first to *The Importance of Being Earnest* at the Tribüne,[100] then to the new Likorstübe and some of the tea-rooms with music playing and same-sex couples dancing. Dent even went to Nelson's[101] on the Kurfürstendamm, 'supposed to be the smartest place in Berlin', where the mad cabaret, 'Total-Manoli' tickled every nerve: 'a very jolly show – not at all more bawdy than any English one'.

These smart borderline places attracted the arty types who also frequented the new, pared-down theatre, and there was, Dent noted, a new reverence generally for

95 Diary 03/12/1920

96 JBT 24/12/1920

97 Herzog was also writing for communist and pacifist papers, *Forum* and *Die Republik*.

98 *Der Floh in Panzerhaus: Schicksals Grotesque* by Robert Forster-Larrinaga (1916).

99 Dent, 'Letters from Germany I: First Impressions', *The Athenaeum* (5 November 1920), p. 628.

100 Diary 11/10/1920. 'Bowers' is a guess; Dent's handwriting is very blurred, the name might be 'Boness'.

101 Diary 12/10/1920. 'Nelson's is a smallish theatre with boxes in the German cabaret style – a very small stage. The show was a revue, quite clever & amusing, with very good music – No chorus, and only about half a dozen actors – rather on the scale of an "Ambassadors" or "Little Theatre" revue – accompanied by a pianoforte only.'

theatre, even for cabaret; where once German theatres had been raucous, now audiences were quiet, attentive.

> At the Kammerspiele the audience walked out in dead silence. It did not mean that the play was a failure; on the contrary, Wedekind's plays are performed oftener than those of any other author. It was partly the natural effect of a play so sordidly and repulsively tragic ... To that one may add the natural depression of people who have reduced their supper to a sandwich brought in a piece of paper and munched in the stalls.[102]

This exciting, innovative period was obliquely subsidised in these lean times by the flourishing new film industry: 'For the actors the situation is to some extent saved by the fact that many of them earn good salaries as cinema actors at the same time.' As Dent spotted from the outset, deprivation had its creative uses. Producers like Max Reinhardt were responding to the constraints by stripping down productions to the essentials and in the process, finding real breakthroughs in theatrical ideas. There was more artistic freedom to experiment, not least because there was less financial risk, while working without the trappings of production style brought the text back to centre stage, as the MDS had discovered, not so far removed from what was currently going on at the Old Vic.

> The German theatre sets out to produce the maximum number of plays at the minimum of cost; the English theatre aims at the maximum of profit with the minimum of plays. It is hardly surprising that ideas of production which are by now the commonplaces of the German stage should be almost unknown in England.[103]

The old German repertory system was dissolving, and beside the new plays, there were new versions of the classics, 'expressionist' performances of Richard III 'inspired by Simplicissimus, taken as a whole, it was a profoundly impressive performance'. Dent wrote a piece for Lilian Baylis' Old Vic magazine on the subject, arguing that Germans in fact revered Shakespeare as a dramatist, and had done so for years while the English had ignored him or produced Victorian travesties.[104] In one of his 'Letters' he attempts to explain the current place of German classical theatre and the 'heroic [acting] style of a hundred years ago ... perpetuated by the permanent stock companies and the repertory system ... the classical style lived on because the classical plays were continuously acted.'[105] Where England had rejected the old bombastic, declamatory style, the Germans kept it on, and as a result, even in these modern productions with minimal sets and a more 'natural' style of acting, the poetry of Goethe and Schiller was clearer than ever.

102 Dent, 'First Impressions', p. 628.

103 Dent, 'Letters from Germany VII: Reinhardt and the Theatre', *The Athenaeum* (4 February 1921).

104 Dent, 'Shakespeare in Germany', *The Old Vic Magazine*, vol. 2, no. 4 (January 1921), p. 3. Haward, *Edward J. Dent: A Bibliography*, 191.

105 Dent, 'Letters from Germany V: The Classical Stage' *The Athenaeum* (14 January 1921).

> The characters became men and women whose nobility of language expressed their nobility of character. The English theatre, weary of the heroic manner, cast it upon the dust-heap. The German theatre, which had preserved it with perhaps too deep a sense of pietas, has a groundwork upon which to build up the drama of the future.

He tried unsuccessfully for tickets to Strindberg's *Rausch* at the 'new' Königsgrätzer Theater, and went the next night to see Romain Rolland's *Danton* at the Grosses Schauspielhaus, an experimental production, very noisy, with the audience moving their seats about to accommodate the actors.

> I was not much thrilled by it as a play, and think the great arena stage is only half a success. Frankly I am one of those who do not like to feel that actors & audience are all mixed up: and I foresee that if other plays are given in the same manner the novelty of voices from the audience will become rather a bore.[106]

What really excited him was his discovery of Die Tribüne, a tiny, recently-opened venue, 'just a plain room with a platform approached by 5 steps moving across', where he saw Adele Sandrock as Lady Bracknell. There was barely any lighting, only drapes and hangings, no proscenium. The Wilde was not its usual fare, though; Die Tribüne was more a politically motivated theatre, part of the emerging experimental leftish arts movements eventually closed down by the Nazis. Dent approached its director Eugen Robert by letter, asking if he might come and take a closer look at the stage: 'he was very pleased & invited me to come to-morrow, and wants to publish my letter in the press! I feel rather embarrassed: but it can't hurt me if people do laugh & may help him, wch he certainly deserves'.[107]

'I love Berlin', he wrote to Clive in late November:

> people are infinitely kind ... and the hotel is well heated. I have hot water & the telephone in my room and only pay 55 M = 5/ a night. I feel rather a brute at times, living so magnificently – for the mark + penny, and my food is cheaper & better than in Soho – except that pepper is almost unobtainable! ... Berlin tries hard to be gay, but doesn't quite bring it off: mainly because the streets are ill-cleaned, & the places all ill-lighted ... In theatres etc you sit in semi-darkness between the acts & can hardly see to read your programme. Plays are very good indeed – I go to the theatre in preference to concerts.[108]

He described the Deutsches Theater performances, especially the way the productions – like the Old Vic's – were making such a virtue of necessity. There was no money: the stage was small and plain, with no sets and few props, one light, with a sense of intimacy and attention to the words, the new productions of classics and the new plays, definitely not the sort of thing on offer in London: 'the simplicity and style were delightful'. Theatre-going was quickly established as a staple of Dent's

106 Diary 13/10/1920.

107 *Ibid.*

108 CC 29/11/1920.

new life in Germany; he avoided the literary aspects of his *Athenaeum* brief, and it took him weeks to come to terms with the music.

In fact, Dent had arrived at an extraordinary time, both for himself and for Germany. Having left Cambridge with mixed feelings, after a few weeks in Berlin he finally sent in his resignation from the Cambridge opera syndicate, to Rootham's 'great relief'. His own future lay not with squabbles at Cambridge, but through engagement with a much wider cultural world, one that was unfolding to him daily. Through his writings – his letters and revived diary as much as his published work – he could scrutinise his first impressions and explore what lay behind them, continuing what he had begun back in England on a more cosmopolitan stage. Initially, though, it was all bewildering.

Dent's was a far more difficult brief than JB's had been in Spain; to many of his readership Germany was still the enemy, so he had to establish a tone which would not alienate his English readers, rather help them to understand the devastation caused to a former enemy and appreciate the new spirit emerging from the devastation. Diary-keeping was now reinstated; he had the time, and needed to record his immediate responses, as well as noting elements just beginning to reveal themselves, the German nationalists already publicly barracking anything 'non-Germanic' beside a remarkably liberal cultural flowering. His own internationalist leanings were stirred by the egregious political attitudes he could see from his own countrymen, when at fashionable Lauer's he bumped into Lowes Dickinson and the Malcolm Darlings, Malcolm there as part of an official commission.[109] 'I found him rather intolerable, taking a completely governmental view of Germany & asking me if I had found any signs of "repentance" – He seemed to think it odd when I said I always avoided discussing the war & especially its rights & wrongs.'[110]

His old friends at the library, Johannes Wolf, Springer and Altmann, 'all extremely cordial & friendly', informed him confidently that 'there was a great deal of music going on', but concert programmes revealed how conservative it really was.[111] 'I did not come to Berlin to hear Scriabin, Rachmaninoff and Prince Igor', he grumbled in his diary. 'I realise within the one week, – after 10 years absence from Germany – how deeply rooted in the German mind is the 19th cent romantic tradition – Weber is handled with tenderness and affection'.[112] Although the playing standards were generally high, the public was clinging to safe, familiar prewar music, so for a while, theatre replaced music.

And Dent was on a tight schedule, with the first of his eight 'Letters from Germany' due back to Murry only a fortnight after his arrival.[113] 'First Impressions' was written

109 Sir Malcolm Lyall Darling (1880–1963), writer and diplomat, friend of E.M. Forster, who spent much time with the Darlings in India. Forster mentioned and was upset by Darling's anti-German views. Furbank, *E.M. Forster: A Life. Volume Two*, pp. 1–2.

110 Diary 29/10/1920.

111 Diary 08/10/1920.

112 Diary 09/10/1920, 15/10/1920.

113 These were: 'First Impressions', 'The Tradition of German Music', 'The Return of Busoni', 'A Beethoven Commemoration', 'The Classical Stage', 'Knut Hamsen as Dramatist', Reinhardt and the Theatre', 'A School of Wisdom'. This last on 11 February 1921.

when he had barely scratched the surface of musical Berlin; by mid-November he had met more of the new blood in German music, but in that first month, he actually went to very few concerts.[114] On 15 October he walked through the Tiergarten to the Philharmonie, where Gustav Brecher was conducting Mahler's 1st Symphony and Strauss's *Don Quixote*.

> Mahler's symphony is almost indecently reminiscent. It seems incredible that in 1900 or thereabouts a man cd write symphonies with so many direct recollections of Beethoven & Schubert … The … themes are dreadful, in a way yet wonderfully developed – the symphony undoubtedly gave me the greatest pleasure to hear … full of rather Humperdinckish childish themes; then the last recalling Berlioz orgy of brigands, with a chorale – most un-Bachian – to end with. The return to D major at the end quite overwhelming. The whole (except for the Berlioz parts) incredibly Viennese – is Vienna still in 1820?[115]

Then a chamber concert on 20 October at the Sing-Akademie:

> players from the opera band. Bach sonata in G for Flute violin & pfte: a dull & fluent Clarinet Quintet by Ewald Strässer … a good trio for pfte oboe & horn in F by Max Laurichkus – rather Brahms & Humperdinck, with a delightful clever sense of fun in the treatment of the oboe. Lastly a pleasant divertimenti … of Haydn in F.
>
> One's first impression of music in Berlin is that it is fifty years behind London. Concert programmes confine themselves mainly to the classics … When I ventured to remark that I had hardly come to Berlin to hear the music which in London belonged to the repertory of promenade concerts, I was told that the promoters of modern music are obliged to go forward with tact and discretion.[116]

'First Impressions' had already been coloured by subtle but strong influences, apart from his own prepossession. The first was Busoni, for that first month Dent's prime source of musical information and opinion, especially that of the current avant-garde; second was his unexpected discovery that first day of the extraordinary theatre going on; as he had written to Clive, he went to every production on offer in preference to concerts or opera. Then third, the astonishing Weimar Berlin of Ludwig Kirchner, George Grosz and Max Beckmann, bursting with a postwar arts, film and cabaret and a lively 'Schwulen' scene. The contrast with late Romantic music could not have been greater, and Dent divided his time between the lectures and recitals with the old guard, the Friedlaenders and the Hochschule

114 In that first month Dent went to the Philharmonie concert, 'A Schumann-Pfitzner Abend', with Pfitzner accompanying, to the chamber concert at the Sing-Akademie, to a 'moderne Lieder Abend of Paul Bander' which he abandoned halfway through, to Michael Zadora's recital, and to the rehearsals and performance of Busoni's Piano Concerto given by Eduard Erdmann, and on 2 November to the *Anbruch* concert of modern chamber music at the Sing-Akademie. He went to two operas before seeing Pfitzner's *Palestrina* on 5 November.

115 Diary 15/10/1920. Gustav Brecher (1879–1940), Czech composer, conductor and opera director who also wrote a biography of Richard Strauss.

116 Dent, 'First Impressions', p. 628.

people, the afternoons with Busoni and his crowd, then the more arty friends – all kept quite separate.

On the serious side, he saw a great deal of Magnus Hirschfeld, sometimes accompanied by Lowes Dickinson. Myerfeld, the gossipy old thesp, friend of Wilde and Shaw, was delighted to see Dent again, and keen to show off his latest collections of erotica and some bizarre photographs taken by Robert Ross of Wilde's dead body. He became one of Dent's main contacts in Berlin and introduced him to Eugen d'Albert and his wife. The old artist friends were now all involved in theatre, film and contemporary design, that interesting borderland Dent liked so much to visit: the Sterns busy designing for theatre and film, including the notorious first production of Schnitzler's *Reigen*, while A.R. Meyer was still running his printing press and publishing 'ultra modern poets in little tracts & chapbooks'.[117] The Meyers took Dent to the studio of a poster-designer, 'where I met several pleasant people, a fat pastor, very worldy & agreeable, Uli Trotsch a young film actor from Königsberg – & Lindi-Walther whom I was delighted to see again'.[118] For the rest of Dent's time in Berlin, Uli often features in his diary entries; he certainly found Uli's film-star looks irresistible, and was soon watching out for him in the appropriate cafés and restaurants, often taking him back to his flat late of an evening. Uli later touched him for 3000 Marks.[119]

But in his usual way, Dent managed to weave a personal web of his various interests, with the young men he collected so easily fitting into the grey area between personal and professional. These actors and singers were part of the youthful cultural world he was exploring, and when it came down to understanding it all, their views mattered as much as those of his library friends. Kurt Schütt, a student of political economy at the University, 'with a very proper admiration for Maynard Keynes's book',[120] was also a singer with recent experience, asked to sing both Siegfried and operetta when he didn't feel ready for the one and didn't wish to do the other: 'This shows the sorry state of management'.[121] From Kurt, Dent heard 'a good deal about the state of operatic conditions in Germany. 40 opera houses have closed down, & another 40 will probably close down after this year' with hidden cutbacks affecting the standards. In Germany, Dent quickly discovered, dropping Maynard's name elicited a warm response, including from a young Graf from Freiburg who also admired Shaw and Keynes, 'wch latter enthusiasm increased when I told him what sort of a person M. was'.[122] Franz Konrad Hoefert; another young actor, who had worked with Max Reinhardt, had charmed Dent by his reading fairy tales 'very simply &

117 Diary 22/10/1920, 24/10/1920. Alfred Richard Meyer 'Munkepunke' (1882–1956), publisher, writer and polymath, who sponsored many avant-garde artists before turning to Hitler in 1933. Not to be confused with Dent's friend Anton Mayer, friend of Busoni, Dent's translator, editor.

118 Diary 24/10/1920.

119 Diary 20/01/1921.

120 *The Economic Consequences of the Peace* (1919). Keynes's book, arguing against reparations imposed on Germany, unsurprisingly became a bestseller.

121 Diary 16/11/1920.

122 Diary 14/12/1920.

attractively' to children, and became one of Dent's companions to the theatre, 'very agreeable & intelligent'.[123] Hans Rausch, 'the sort of person I have always wanted to meet in Germany', was another such companion, accompanying Dent to Max von Schillings' production of his opera *Mona Lisa.* But Dent knew where to draw the line, did not include him afterwards to be taken in to meet von Schillings, 'who was most friendly & asked us all to lunch to-morrow'.[124] Rausch was only placated by being taken to dinner at the expensive Hotel Bristol. By the end of the month Dent was suffering from sore throats and general exhaustion.

Dent's message was aimed at the audiences being cultivated at the Old Vic, but also beyond, where Bridges-Adams was busy establishing Stratford-on-Avon as a real centre for Shakespeare production and other, smaller societies like the Drama League were producing revivals of lost classics. So Dent wrote about how the younger Intendants at Darmstadt and Stuttgart, respectively Gustav Hartung[125] and Wilhelm von Scholz, were bringing fresh ideas to old plays, 'learning to act even the classics naturally', with young characters being played by young actors like Uli Trotsch and using 'simplified scenery' in such classics as *Egmont.*[126] To explore these ideas further, Dent went to the lectures on *Theaterwissenschaft* being given at the University by a pioneer of theatre studies, Max Herrmann.[127]

> He is a rather typical German professor, shut up in his own ideas – but his ideals of a theaterwissenschaft school were splendid and I quite made friends with him by my very cordial sympathy … Like many professors in Germany he seemed to know very little of what the students were doing … Apparently they do not give performances; he lectures to them on Regie & Dramaturgie.[128]

Altogether, Dent's view of current German theatre was a remarkably informed one, drawing as it did from such a variety of sources, many of which were unacknowledged, like Trotsch or the Sterns, Fritz Drach and Tommy Höxter, involved in the film industry, although Höxter's serious morphine habit did not help his career. But it was Magnus Hirschfeld who really showed Dent what cinema could do.

123 Max Reinhardt (1873–1943) was born Maximilian Goldmann, joined the Deutsches Theater; became one of the foremost producers, actors and directors in theatre and film. Invited Dent to join him.

124 Diary 18/11/1920. Max von Schillings (1868–1933), Intendant at the Staatsoper Unter den Linden, composer and director, became a friend of Dent's.

125 'Intendant': theatre manager. The younger opera house Intendants were often serious musicians as well, whereas before they had often been noblemen. 'The Revolution has swept away the old-fashioned notion that an Intendant should be a nobleman with an uncertain ear for music and a certain eye for ladies of the ballet.' Dent, 'The Classical Stage', p. 78. Gustav Hartung (1887–1946), real name Gustav Ludwig May, theatre director, studied with Max Reinhardt, was Intendant of several German theatres and associated with German Expressionism. Moved to Switzerland in 1933.

126 Dent, 'The Classical Stage'. Wilhelm von Scholz (1874–1967), dramatist and writer.

127 Max Herrmann (1865–1942) was one of the first to establish theatre history and theory as an academic subject. He became the first head of the Berlin Institute of Theatre Studies in 1923. When Hitler came to power in 1933, he lost his job and later died in Theresienstadt.

128 Diary 08/11/1920.

Hirschfeld saw this new medium as the perfect way to publicise his work to a growing audience of younger, more open minds. *Anders als die Andern* – Different from the Rest – was the first serious film about homosexuality, co-written by its director Max Fassbender and Hirschfeld, who played himself in it. Conrad Veidt[129] took the leading role, a violinist who falls in love with one of his male students and in the film is counselled by Hirschfeld. A few days before, Dent had gone with Lowes Dickinson to see another of Fassbender's recent films, a take on Wilde's book, *The Portrait of Dorian Gray,* but this other, more demanding film, he went to on his own. It cannot have helped that the electricity kept cutting out.

> I thought it horrible – the whole film system, and the actors vulgar & conventional to the last degree. The only really good seen [sic] was when the young man's parents interviewed Dr H. himself. Dr H. was a far better film actor than any of the professionals – it was the one moment when the thing seemed at all true & genuine … After the breakdown we were taken to the lecture room where Dr H. exhibited some cases of Transvestitism [sic] and lectured on them. There were two men there dressed as women, and another who wanted to be. 1 was apparently a middle-aged lady who admitted to being the parent of children, but declined to say whether 'she' had begotten them or borne them – In private life a detective. 2 was a sailor, who had from early childhood refused to wear breeches and was brought up a girl till 16, then entered the navy & had been on a submarine around the English coasts … 3 … a Swiss peasant, speaking only Swiss dialect, quite rough and ugly: had been a maidservant for 3 years, and saved up all his money to buy women's clothes. He was dressed as a man- sexually neuter, apparently: no desires at all, & wished to get rid of his testicles.[130]

What vexed him was that the film itself was such a dismal and unsatisfactory portrayal of homosexuality; apologetic, even. That he is fascinated is clear from the details he takes such trouble to record, but Dent had a horror of the Germanic way of publicly cataloguing and analysing his own preferred way of life even while acknowledging how significant a step forward this film was.

There was opportunity to talk with Hirschfeld about this, since Dent spent quite a bit of time at the institute, taking a fascinated Dickinson along and meeting Hirschfeld's new assistant Dr Kronfeldt several times. Dent's contact with Hirschfeld and his circle was both frequent and very discreet; he still barely mentions it in his diary, never in his letters, yet it was very important to him. Hirschfeld continued to give him a number of contacts, so when travelling to Weimar, he sought out a Dr Holbein ('a collateral descendant of the painter & has written a book on the Holbein family') and drank Tokay with him at his spartan bachelor house: Dent was reminded of Nixon, 'but an unsuccessful Nixon in very needy circumstances'.[131]

129 Hans Conrad Veidt (1893–1943), German film actor who later moved to England and Hollywood, appearing in *The Cabinet of Dr Caligari* and *Casablanca*. He loathed the Nazis but often played them in film.

130 Diary 08/11/1920. A full discussion of the film's significance can be found in Wolfgang Theis 'Verdrängung und Travestie: Das vage Bild der Homosexualität im deutschen Film (1917–1957)', in *Eldorado*, pp. 102 ff.

131 Diary 28/11/1920.

A Dr Doedrich in Stuttgart played Pfitzner's *Palestrina* to Dent on his harmonium and criticised Hirschfeld. Like himself, they felt alienated by their sexuality, yet very much a part of the active intelligentsia and wider cultural movements.

By the time he was writing the second 'Letter from Germany', 'The Tradition of German Music', Dent felt able to transform his initial scorn into an important point.

> it is the weakness of music in Germany that in Germany music is taken for granted; the fact that in England music is the perpetual struggle of a few artists against an apathetic majority gives us the best hope for English music. It is not likely that we shall ever make English music a national industry like hotel-keeping in Switzerland, but for that very reason we may possibly produce a small number of first-rate musicians … If Germans take a Chauvinistic view of music it is not by a direct act of will, but out of sheer inertia … new musical patriotism in England has at least driven us back to the refreshing sources of Purcell … it has also made the performance of works by young English composers a point of honour. In Germany patriotism has had exactly the opposite effect; it has settled Bach, Beethoven & Co. more firmly than ever on their pedestals, and it has very definitely slammed the doors of the concert-rooms in the face of all the young upstarts and revolutionaries.[132]

The narrative he is giving his *Athenaeum* readers is both sophisticated and simplistic, by no means telling the whole story. Dent knew that he had to be diplomatic and yet make several strong points, his agenda being not only to inform his readers, but to open them up to new ways of thinking about themselves and what was almost too familiar: if they could see how sophisticated Germans could evidently be so self-limiting, how would they see themselves? He had looked at the apparently lively, solid musical life in Berlin and seen it through Busoni's critical eyes as well as his own.

From the time he first arrived in Berlin, Dent's real musical anchor there was his old friend Ferruccio Busoni, one of the few people he could spar with easily and equally. Dent had found him relatively alone and melancholy at his old flat in Victoria Luise Platz, with 'a three days beard' but delighted to see Dent: 'he kissed me on both cheeks all'italiana'. In spite of going through a terrible 'inward crisis' Busoni was enjoying a surge of creativity, 'work was only an anodyne for anxiety'. The two boys Lello and Benni were artists working in Paris and Zurich, while his beloved St Bernard dog, Giotto, too big for a small urban flat, had been left behind in Zurich. Gerda had just arrived but could not stay long, with only his old pupils, Michael Zadora and Eduard Weiss, two publishers and one of the 'Caryatides' who had looked after things in Busoni's absence throughout the war. Soon, there would be Kurt Weill, Wladimir Vogel and Robert Blum, but now Busoni was depressed. He had returned to Berlin that September, the initial public reception galling to him, having built up so much there before the war. 'Today I read an article by P. Bekker attacking Berlin's Dr. Krebs', he wrote to his pupil Philipp Jarnach, 'who depicts me as the eyesore of the city's musical life. This is the kind of welcome I am

[132] Dent, 'Letters from Germany II: The Tradition of German Music', *The Athenaeum* (19 November 1920), p. 708.

enjoying here'.[133] The old cafés like Bartolini's had not recovered: no food, no wine, little socialising, but Busoni took advantage of the current lack of night-life to work hard. Beside compositions, there were recitals coming up in November and concerts of his orchestral works scheduled in January; he had been asked to teach at the Hochschule.

At his cluttered flat, over lunch, tea or informal drinks, there were discussions of 'pianoforte style', about current music and musicians, but they were not limited to music.[134] Always internationalist and expansive, Busoni was widely read in four languages and conversation was peppered with references to his current reading; his easy, eclectic, wandering yet purposeful style had always stimulated Dent's thinking, even when they disagreed, and a number of Dent's views about the place of music had been thrashed out in Busoni's company. Much of this, especially the views on performance, would be used later in Dent's biography, while Busoni's recitals that winter gave real substance to the ideas: 'Busoni's interpretations at this time gave the listener a strange sense of perilous adventure. He was no pianist for beginners in the art of listening ... Technique was for him merely the servant of expression'.[135]

His current preoccupations were of great interest to Dent, his love of marionette theatre, his concerns about new music, especially his opera *Doktor Faustus*, and he pressed a copy of the newly published libretto on Dent. With Busoni Dent could talk about Calderón and Spanish literature as easily as about *Doktor Faustus*; passion for literature was almost as important in their friendship as music, the connections between words and music a regular topic of their conversations. Their friendship deepened during this time, while his younger friends became Dent's, especially Philipp Jarnach, Egon Wellesz and Hermann Scherchen. Dr Otto Schneider, whom Dent met there that first day, editor of *Musikblätter des Anbruch*,[136] who was pro-

133 Busoni to Philipp Jarnach, 30/10/1920, in Beaumont, *Ferruccio Busoni: Selected Letters*, p. 326. Carl Krebs was one of the ferocious local music critics and secretary of the Akademie der Künste.

134 Cf, Dent, *Busoni*, pp. 258 ff. The diary entry for 25 October gives a good picture of their conversational style: 'He remarked that it was only in Vienna and Poland & Russia that there was the tradition of the great pianoforte style. There had been nothing in Italy since Clementi. I suggested Buonamici – but he said Buonamici was merely a "good German pianist" a copy of Hans v. Bülow: Sgambati more genuinely Latin. I suggested that Clementi's teaching had been more in London than in Italy – B. burst out laughing with the name of "Leonard Borwick" – so I said that at any rate he and Fanny Davies were good disciples of the Clara Schumann school. But in Berlin, B. said, they have no feeling for the pianoforte as an instrument: it is only for das Musikalische – in Paris merely elegant finger work and the lightning solfeggio "do re mi fa sol fa mi re" – this said prestissimo to an exercise on the table – He admired the Liszt pupils of the last generation – Reisenau, Sauer and even D'Albert. I said that in England we were still like the Germans & preferred chamber players – like Dohnanyi, whom B. regarded almost as an amateur with no technique – we liked the sense of intimacy – This did not seem to interest B. at all.'

135 *Ibid.*, pp. 258-9.

136 *Musikblätter des Anbruch* later simply *Anbruch* (Dawn) was founded in Vienna in 1919 as an antidote to the extremely conservative music cliques there and became one of the most important vehicles for contemporary music writing in the 1920s and 30s. Schneider

moting new music in Berlin through the Neue Musikgesellschaft des Anbruch, similar to Schoenberg's Verein für musikalische Privataufführungen in Vienna. On 2 November, Dent went to one of their concerts at the Sing-Akademie, the first real concert of contemporary music he had yet heard.

> A very academic pfte 4tet in E by Tanieiev. 5 Klavier grotesques by James Simon played by the composer – not at all grotesque: anxious to be modern, but like early Debussy – very timid and on the whole absurdly deutsch-sentimental. Some songs after Hafig by Szymanovski – more modern in feeling – and far less deutsch – a certain attempt at thinness of harmony & contrapuntal expression. Finally Ravel's 4tet –very indifferently played.[137]

But at least 'modern' music was being played, including some non-German composers. Busoni was himself 'sceptical' about the standard, but he recognised the need for such experimentation.[138] Not wishing to deprecate the efforts, Dent was careful about keeping his immediate negative responses to himself; these *Anbruch* concerts only appear obliquely in his articles. For a while, he found very little to excite his interest: e.g., Eugen d'Albert's popular new opera, *Revolutionshochzeit*: 'far worse than Tiefland. It tries to be modern, with whole tone scales & Straussian effects – foully noisy & hysterical: no real invention – and the style a mixture of Strauss and Puccini at their worst'.[139] The point was made publicly in 'First Impressions':

> His last opera, 'Revolutionshochzeit', which exaggerates the vulgar brutality of 'Tosca' without possessing any of the Italian composer's more attractive qualities, was given the other night at the Deutsches Opernhaus in Charlottenburg. The critics dismissed it unanimously with the contemptuous disgust which it certainly deserved; but it was quite clear that the public adored it.

But when he was put in contact with d'Albert[140] and went to tea with him and his wife, Dent liked them, having learnt from Myerfeld that 'D'Albert's wives are called

was director of the Neue Musikgesellschaft des Anbruch in Berlin, which gave the only formal concerts of contemporary music Dent saw while he was there. It featured early articles on Schoenberg, Schreker and Busoni himself; contributors included some who were later in on the founding of the ISCM with Dent, like Paul Pisk, while its ideas prepared the way. Dent's *Athenaeum* articles on Busoni as composer and theorist were translated by Busoni's secretary Rita Boetticher and appeared in *Musikblätter des Anbruch* in January 1921, 'very odd in the middle of all the solid German stuff. Frl. Boettecher [sic] has translated them very decently, but they lose most of the serpent's metallic lustre. It is sad to feel oneself turning from a serpent into a sausage.'

137 Diary 02/11/1920.

138 Dent, *Busoni*, pp. 254–5.

139 Diary 18/10/1920. This performance was before its official premiere at Leipzig on 26 October. It is possible that what Dent saw was not the finished product.

140 Eugen d'Albert (1864–1932), born in Glasgow, studied with Prout and Stainer, moved to Germany and studied with the elderly Liszt, making a career as pianist before turning to composition, his best-known opera being *Tiefland*. He was as famous for having married six times, including pianist Teresa Carreño.

after the Beethoven symphonies … this is the C minor'.[141] Even Busoni had good things to say about d'Albert's abilities as a pianist, and he was above all, a serious musician, and Dent was seeing everything on offer. On 30 October, after attending a rehearsal for Busoni's piano concerto, Dent had gone on to see *Der Ritter Blaubart* by Emil von Reznicek,[142] and later that same week, to Hans Pfitzner's *Palestrina* (1917) for the first time, having first read the libretto:

> rather boring. Its libretto is perfectly absurd even if one took Baini as historical fact. As a drama little happens … the popularity of the opera is due I suppose mainly to the 'süsses Kitsch' of visions of angels … more affinity with Humperdinck than with Strauss … I felt that the hero of the opera was Pfitzner himself: Palestrina was made up to look rather like him – and also der deutsche Kaiser (Ferdinand) who doesn't appear, but whenever he is mentioned there is a great to-do in the orchestra.[143]

Pfitzner was the current darling of conservative German musical circles, ardent German nationalist, champion of the conservative style, strongly influenced by Wagner; an important figure, and in opposition to everything Busoni was working for. Dent took Pfitzner's music and ideas seriously enough to devote a long article to him two years later in *Music & Letters*, and had actually enjoyed a recital with Pfitzner accompanying Tiny Debuser in Schumann and Pfitzner songs.[144] However much he disliked Pfitzner's politics and the way he applied politics to his creative output, Dent felt obliged to try to understand his qualities as a serious German composer, and he was forced to admire *Palestrina*. But Busoni's circle had 'laughed at me very much for my historical outlash on "Palestrina"'.[145]

> One reason why the young composer in Germany has such a poor chance is that people are all so terribly frightened of the critics. The critics know it, and delight in their tyranny … For us in England, who are obliged to earn our living by scribbling about music, it is a very good thing that no one attaches much weight to our opinions … The most influential are, as a matter of fact, the kindest, indeed, the most indiscriminately kind. Learning is tedious, patriotism ridiculous, and severity incompatible with good manners.[146]

141 Diary 10/11/1920. Apparently, d'Albert had approached Myerfeld on purpose to meet Dent in order to contact Granville Barker about composing an opera from Laurence Housman's play *Prunella, or Love in a Dutch Garden.*

142 Emil Nikolaus Freiherr von Reznicek (1860–1945), friend of Strauss, his music well known in Berlin. *Der Ritter Blaubart* was composed during the war. 'The music has a certain distinguished quality – but tends to get very noisy & ugly, especially in the intermezzi'. Dent liked the bit when the two thieves rob the grave but can't find the head.

143 Diary 05/11/1920.

144 E.J. Dent, 'Hans Pfitzner', M&L (April 1923), pp. 119–32.

145 Diary 08/11/1920.

146 Dent, 'Young England', N&A (26 February, 1921), p. 744.

Dent shared Busoni's view that German critics wielded far too much power; watching Busoni compose his monumental *Doktor Faustus* at this time must have coloured his wider perceptions, knowing how meticulous and conscientious a musician Busoni was. He had witnessed the debacle of *Die Brautwahl* in Hamburg years before, knowing what intellectual and creative effort Busoni had put into it. So witnessing the popularity of such lesser figures as d'Albert beside von Schillings' expressed joy at being able to perform *Götterdämmerung* with Wagner's original orchestration, he felt Busoni's reaction, 'as if the State Opera was to be a museum of musical archaeology!', his phrase summing up as it did most of what he felt was wrong with current attitudes to classical music, the lazy thinking that took excellence for granted. Busoni 'considered that it was much more important to perform contemporary music'[147] and was content publicly to applaud the 'enthusiasm and enterprise' of the younger generation.

Busoni's own music was being rapturously received in Berlin by a demonstrative audience; his massive piano concerto on 30 October played by nineteen-year-old Eduard Erdmann,[148] beside his two recitals in November. 'a triumph such as Busoni had never before experienced,' Dent recorded: 'The audience so far forgot itself as to applaud in the middle of La Campanella – a thing unheard of in a Berlin concert-room.'[149] The three concerts of his music in January had a more mixed success,[150] but Busoni remained a monumental figure for the younger musicians, as in these final years of his life, his teaching and influence took off again.

From the beginning of November, Dent's circles expanded further: he re-established contact with the former POW Richard Schade, taking him to Lauer's for dinner, while Hugo Leichtentritt became the source of many of his new contacts in the musical press, including an actor–journalist called Neruda, who wrote for the *Vossische Zeitung*.[151] Liking him, Dent went to watch him at the Neues Volkstheater in *Pericles, Prince of Tyre*: 'The performance was very Old Vic – simplified scenery a la M.D.S. but rather oldfashioned roaring acting.' Neruda and Leichtentritt shared a love of bawdy stories, which Dent recorded with some relish in his diary. Another of Leichtentritt's cronies, Oscar Bie, editor of the literary magazine *Die neue Rundschau*, Dent had already met in October, at a lecture he was giving on Respighi's new opera. Through Bie, whose own circles included Egon Wellesz[152] and Hermann

147 Diary 08/11/1920.

148 Eduard Erdmann (1896–1958), pianist, composer, part of Busoni's circle.

149 Dent, *Busoni*, p. 253.

150 'The audience was not very numerous & the programme hardly attractive to anyone outside the Gemeinde': JBT, January 1921.

151 The liberal *Vossische Zeitung*, known as *Tante Voss* – Auntie Voss – was the oldest newspaper in Berlin, published by Ullstein. Its editor, Georg Bernard, kept it going until it was closed down by the Nazis in 1934.

152 Egon Wellesz (1885–1974), studied in Vienna under Schoenberg and Guido Adler, became a composer and musicologist specialising in Byzantine music, fled to England after the *Anschluss* and was helped by Dent to settle at Oxford.

Scherchen,[153] the conductor and editor of *Melos*, the contemporary music magazine,[154] Dent began to penetrate the surface of the new music scene.

> In the aftn to Scherchen who lives in the wilds of Friedman – I arrived very late. Egon Wellesz was there & I was delighted to see him again … His opera has been accepted at Frankfurt. We were very much disturbed by perpetual telephoning, among others Leichtentritt who wanted me to go at 5 to a house near the Bayerische Platz to hear his new sonata rehearsal. I found Scherchen & Wellesz much more interesting. Wellesz played his Persian Ballet – wch I found very difficult to grasp … Windisch the assistant editor of Melos was also there: quiet & very pleasant. I felt that at last I had got into the sort of circle I wanted.[155]

Soon, Dent was lunching regularly with César Saerchinger,[156] Bie (now christened 'OB'), Wellesz, Leichtentritt and the Scherchens, and invited to Mannheim to see Franz Schreker's *Der Schatzgräber*. Other invitations soon followed, to meet music publishers, to listen to new music at Erdmann's, where he heard the Finnish Yrjö Kilpinen's recent piano works and Erdmann's symphony, 'very thick & congested … all sincere stuff with no padding'. Wellesz became a close lifelong friend, and through Wellesz that Dent was at last properly introduced to Max von Schillings, having gone to his opera *Mona Lisa* ('full of ideas & always very distinguished in style').[157] The next day they called on Schillings, where Wellesz played his opera *Prinzessin Girvana*: 'it has some very modern brutalities, but the mystical parts are beautiful. Schillings didn't say much, but evidently understood it very clearly, and liked it very much'.[158] Dent was fascinated by Schillings, who had known Armstrong Gibbs, and was amusingly rude about patriotic compositions in the recent war, and about some Germans' view of English music as 'analfabetisen' – for ignoramuses.

Nevertheless, he somehow managed to juggle his other, hidden life. In late November Dent went out to visit Dr Kronfeldt, Hirschfeld's second at the institute.

> I was rather surprised to find him married, and to a very odd woman, a Calvinist & a Huguenot, who was very delighted at my enthusiasm for the Huguenot Psalter. Kronfeldt is the most interesting talker that I have met in Germany – a most clear headed and stimulating brain.

Kronfeldt swept Dent off to a 'reception':

> a very odd person – a Pole named Malecky who runs a dressmaker's shop, I think. He is about 28, incredibly feminine, with a fairly normal sort of sister: the com-

153 Hermann Scherchen (1891–1966), became closely involved in the establishment and running of the ISCM, spent the war in Switzerland while his wife Gustel lived in Cambridge.

154 Diary 12/11/1920.

155 Diary 20/11/1920.

156 César Saerchinger (1884–1971), musicologist and musical journalist, had just written *The International Who's Who in Music and Musical Gazetteer*, the biographer of Artur Schnabel, emigrated to the USA.

157 Diary 25/11/1920.

158 Diary 26/11/1920.

> pany largely transvestiten, mainly normal – Some literary people there, one in the Vossisches [Zeitung]. Giese also came and Bachmann, all from the Institut: Dr H went on to a concert.[159]

Intrigued, Dent went off to a restaurant with the mixed transvestite and institute crowd, and even though he clearly enjoyed himself, he felt moved to record, 'I do not like transvestiten and Giese though quite a pleasant sort is too feminine for my taste'. Next day he wandered round to the offices of the *Vossische Zeitung* for a more sedate lunch with Neruda: 'he presented me to various colleagues on the literary & artistic side'.[160] Bristling with yet more introductions, Dent was ready to explore beyond Berlin.

❧ ❧ ❧

After some trouble organising the required travel permits, on 27 November Dent began a three-week trip to visit the opera houses in Weimar, Mannheim, Frankfurt, Darmstadt, Stuttgart and Munich. He already had the essential formal introductions to meet the various Intendants, but the company he kept meant that he often enjoyed the rare privilege of meeting them more intimately and informally. The Friedlaenders had introduced him to Fritz Busch,[161] the new Intendant at Stuttgart, and his wife, who after some gossip about Donald Tovey, warmly invited Dent to Stuttgart. He found Weimar 'so delightful that I am tempted to stay a week here', and managed to read the *Anbruch* Mahler issue, and saw Busoni's *Doktor Faustus*. Next was Mannheim ('hopelessly unattractive') via Frankfurt, greeted by a delighted Schreker, who over lunch introduced him to his friends the Eckhards' charming house, good pictures & very good food',[162] before going off to Schreker's opera, *Der Schatzgräber*:

> a splendid orchestra & the performance on the whole very good … The opera is a regular opera: Schreker has learnt a certain amount from Verdi – I do not find any Puccini influences. The style is very largely German and with … occasional outbursts of modernity alla Rosenkavalier. The book very strong & dramatic – and the great thing about it is that the characters develop psychologically.[163]

159 Diary 21/11/1920.

160 Diary 22/11/1920.

161 Diary 02/11/1920. Fritz Busch (1890–1951), conductor brother of violinist Adolf Busch of the Busch Quartet, studied with Fritz Steinbach. After Stuttgart, he went to Dresden, where he continued to produce outstanding operas, including premieres of Busoni's *Doktor Faust*, Hindemith's *Cadillac* and Strauss's *Intermezzo* and *Die ägyptische Helena*. In 1933 he moved to England, became musical director of Glyndebourne Opera and enjoyed an international career.

162 Franz Schreker (1878–1934), Austrian composer, conductor, very highly regarded in the early Weimar period.

163 Diary 02/12/1920.

Afterwards at the Eckhards' there was a party with the principal singers and the conductor Franz von Hoesslin.[164] After a few days in Darmstadt, Dent returned within the week to see *Die Schatzgräber* again.

> It is a good opera, but I cannot see that Schreker is the genius wch Bekker makes him out. The love scene & the erotic intermezzo are the weakest part of the opera, for just where musical form is wanted it breaks down--And the more erotic Schreker tries to be, the more he falls into reminiscences of Tristan.[165]

Dent's prejudice against 'eroticism' in music, fuelled by his recent talks with Busoni on the subject, was part of his opinion, but he remained unconvinced about Schreker, however much he liked him personally. He sat in on von Hoesslin's rehearsals for Pfitzner's *Käthchen von Heilbronn* Overture and Reger's *Prologue to a Tragedy*:

> I liked the Reger much the best – it is rather Brahmsish & severe, very definitely classical, but has great dignity – Reger understood the use of common chords in a quasi modal arrangement: most Germans have no conception of that and ruin their attempts to be austere by putting in dominant 7th.

In von Hoesslin Dent found a kindred spirit, whose ideas nicely coincided with his own.

> I find him clear & interesting – a pupil of Reger – age about 35 … military family … I shd have liked to ask him whether his family approved of his being a musician … He is sceptical about Schreker – thinks Bekker rather off the rails – sceptical also about Mahler – 'Mahler is at his best in his scherzos & satirical movements – It is the spirit of the present day to see everything in caricature – a sign of decadence.' For Bruckner he had a great admiration & thinks him a greater man than Wagner in his depth of real feeling. Parsifal he regards as a religious pose – I think he is right.[166]

As the colder weather set in, Dent went to Darmstadt to make contact with Intendant Gustav Hartung, where he saw Bernard Shaw's *You Never Can Tell,* which he enjoyed 'enormously' and Hartung's 'new & much discussed' production of Schiller's *Jungfrau von Orleans,* which Hartung was very keen to discuss. Dent had enjoyed the Schiller but told Hartung flatly that the inappropriate incidental music

> was quite appalling – a brass band behind playing stuff like bad Meyerbeer or very early Verdi … it utterly ruined his effect … But H evidently sees that with Schiller as with Weber one must keep the romanticism down, and never allow it to become ranting.[167]

164 Franz von Hoesslin (1885–1946). Dent spells it 'von Hoeslin'. A great conductor of Wagner at Bayreuth, he was married to a Jewish singer and was exiled in 1938 for refusing to conduct the Horst Wessel Lied. Killed in a plane crash.

165 Diary 05/12/1920.

166 Diary 06/12/1920.

167 Diary 04/12/1920.

More than anything else, this Darmstadt visit provided the intellectual materials for Dent's later *Athenaeum* pieces on theatre, thrashing out the ideas informally with his new acquaintances, the way he preferred, and casually setting up sympathetic internationalist networks. He sat in on a rehearsal of Knut Hamsen's *Königin Tamara,* and enjoyed lively suppers with Hartung and Cosimus Edschmidt, a publisher who knew Bernard Shaw.[168] The next day he trudged through the snow to find Otto Reichl, the publisher, with a message from the Chelsea Book Club,[169] before going in the evening to *Die Ehre,* 'an impossible play nowadays – almost as bad as Pinero'. The next day was spent in a session with the philosopher Hermann, Graf von Keyserling, who talked to Dent 'in very voluble English' about his 'Schule der Weisheit'.[170] Hartung was an excellent host, 'delightfully friendly: he seems really to have taken to me personally, as I have done to him'. Dent enjoyed the performance of *Die Frau ohne Schatten;* as the current insider gossip had it, Strauss was referring to it as 'FROSCH': 'a good performance, with much simpler and more formal scenery than in Berlin … 1840 setting quite absurd, but curiously attractive'.

There was another performance of *Palestrina* which Dent enjoyed far more than the one in Berlin, and afterwards an introduction to Paul Bekker, the critic and champion of new music.[171] Dent went on to Stuttgart, where an old-fashioned production of *König für einen Tag* was 'very agreeable & amusing'. The next day he went to see Wedekind's *König Nicolo oder So ist das Leben* and the following night to *Egmont* at the Landestheater, 'wch I enjoyed much more than I expected'. He was able to congratulate the 'dramaturg' Wilhelm von Scholz, whose play *Der Wettlauf mit dem Schatten,* 'a grandguignol triangle drama in terms of metaphysics … the characters seem to stand in a triangle of mirrors with endless reflections & counterreflections of personality. It was harrowing and intensely interesting.' But German nationalists demonstrated at Bekker's lecture on Beethoven and *Egmont,* shouting that he was a Jew who had spent too much time in England. Dent thought Bekker's lecture 'exactly right'; it was a long time before he could take such demonstrations seriously. Lunching with Busch and enjoying his 'amusing stories about Donald Tovey' was pleasant enough, but Dent found himself 'rather oppressed' by Stuttgart. The people whose opinions mattered to Dent, especially Busch and Busoni, had a generally dim view of music in England:

> Busch is more sympathetic than most Germans towards English music: but he is very conservative, though only 30. What he and all Germans say about English music – including Tovey's opera for wch he has an enormous admiration – is that it is 'primitiv'. Tovey will write accompaniment figures that might have come from Haydn … They find even Elgar 'primitiv' – It is true – just as Ouseley used

[168] In 1923 he would still be talking with Hartung about the possibility of the MDS visiting there.

[169] Dent continued to promote his scheme with publishers he met: 'Please talk to people of the right sort, who write, about my scheme for a library of modern English literature to be printed & published in English by a German publisher for German circulation.'

[170] Hermann, Graf von Keyserling (1880–1946). His anti-militarist views were attractive, but he doesn't seem to have had much time for Dent.

[171] Paul Bekker (1882–1937), music critic, correspondent of the *Musical Times.*

> to write quartets in the style of Mozart … No doubt that's why they like Cyril Scott, because he was not (in their sense) 'primitiv'. What are we to do about it? … I fancy it comes partly from the fact that the good composers in England are all incapable of playing the pianoforte. And the composers who can play the pianoforte never have the intellect or the great personality & character as men to become great composers. Even our pianists are considered primitiv. They are too … There is something very old-maidish about us all.[172]

That dismissive 'primitiv' vexed Dent and remained with him all that year, emerging in his articles. Otherwise, Dent's ideas were becoming clearer and more confident, more open as he understood the cultural contexts so much better. At Darmstadt he heard the Beethoven commemoration, was critical of Balking's slow tempi in the 1st and the 9th symphonies, but willing to allow that 'he gives the symphony great dignity'. Dr Hans Joachim Moser gave 'an oration … much too correct and pompous'.[173] Although Dent later enjoyed some remarkably cordial relations with Moser during his first Handel Festival at Halle, he never agreed with Moser over nationalistic principles guiding artistic decisions. In January he posed such questions to another new Berlin acquaintance, a Prussian government official, Osmund:

> We spoke of music & theatre and I mentioned the fact that the young composers were prevented from being heard because the classics still held the field … He said that the new Germany was very anxious to show that revolution did not mean barbarism, and that the Republic was still true to old ideals of culture: hence the emphasis on the classics. Also that people felt that at this time Germany required every incentive to unity of national feeling – The young people, individualistic, made for separation: the classics were the expression of unity.[174]

Dent stayed in Munich over Christmas, visiting a number of old friends there from before the war, especially the Ewalds. Paul with his wife and soon-to-be four children, and Dr Clara were still living at Annersee, by the lake, and Dent spent a happy Christmas Eve with them all, cheered to see the portraits of Rupert Brooke and Francis Birrell she had done in 1912, 'the Rupert all unfinished & rough, but all the better'.[175] 'We had a cheerful evening talking of old friends – Frau Clara, like Frau Friedlaender and other women of that age still feels very bitterly the starvation of

[172] JBT 24/12/1920.

[173] Hans Joachim Moser (1889–1967) was the son of violinist Andreas Moser and godson of Joseph Joachim, his academic career already advanced, a prolific writer on musicology, wrote one of the classic studies of German music. He was one of the strongest proponents of the idea that German music in this postwar period being corrupted by Americanisation, 'negro' music and foreign influences, hugely influential in expressing what conservative German musicologists feared most, the antithesis of what Dent was trying to achieve. Pamela Potter, *Most German of the Arts: Musicology and Society from the Weimar Republic to the End of Hitler's Reich* (New Haven, 1990), pp. 2ff.

[174] Diary 07/01/1921.

[175] This is the famous portrait of Rupert Dent had brought back to Cambridge, still hanging in the Combination Room at King's.

Germany'.[176] He saw a German production of Tirso de Molina at the Kammerspiele, went to the Residenz, to some cabaret, 'Und München Tanzt'. Wellesz had paved the way, with introductions to Alfred Einstein[177] and Baron Clemens von und zu Franckenstein,[178] who had been at the Frankfurt conservatory with Cyril Scott, Percy Grainger and F.S. Kelly. Christmas Day was spent with the Franckensteins, a jolly party with the kind of gossipy stories Dent loved, about Strauss and Beecham. Einstein warmly invited him to lunch – 'Frau Einstein a most charming & friendly person – a very good lunch too!'– and to hear Bruno Walter conducting Schreker and Wagner. He introduced Dent to a number of publishers including the famous Drei Masken Verlag, 'to discuss my writing a book for them on Shakespeare music: but none of the partners were there,'[179] and asked his views on several possible projects ('a Shakespeare book, additions to Riemann, etc etc.').[180] Although they had already corresponded, their long friendship really began with this visit. That same evening Dent went to hear Schreker's *Die Gezeichneten.*

> The orchestra was wonderful under Bruno Walter. It is often much too loud, and altogether too fat & heavy, in spite of great variety in orchestration & beautiful sounds. It is that all German music has the bad Wagnerian quality – the quality one finds in Scriabin too – the orchestra dominates the thought: the voices just swim or sink or struggle on great featherbed waves which heave regularly at the normal moderate rate ... scenery incredibly vulgar ... the island of vice like an old English provincial pantomime.[181]

Dent took Paul Ewald to Walter Braunfels' opera *Die Vögel,* an adaptation of Aristophanes, and at dinner afterwards met Hallmuth Wolfe, the co-repetiteur, who had brought along both Braunfels[182] and his wife and a conductor named Rudolf Siegel.[183] 'Braunfels enjoyed his wine & became very cheerful, wch pleased me', Dent wrote later, reminded of Timmy Jekyll. He pressed Braunfels to talk about his ideas for opera, his reaction against Schreker and the 'cinematographic style of opera'. He went to *Götterdämmerung* for the first time in years, with Walter conducting, a performance which stimulated thoughts about Wagner and his place in German music. After a lively conversation about music with the Wolfes over lunch: 'Wolfe is absurdly Deutsch, with a complete ignorance of all other music and also of older music, and a corresponding contempt for it. I left him La Revue Musicale with the

176 Diary 24/12/1920.

177 Alfred Einstein (1880–1952), musicologist, editor of the ISMR journal, *Acta Musicologica,* became a friend and close colleague of Dent's. Later moved to the USA.

178 Clemens Erwein Heinrich Karl Bonaventura Freiherr von und zu Franckenstein (1875–1942), composer, conductor, Intendant of the Bayerische Staatsoper, before being forced out by the government in 1934.

179 Diary 27/12/1921. The Drei Masken Verlag in Carolinenplatz was founded in 1910 to publish theatrical and music theatre books. It still exists.

180 Diary 05/01/1921.

181 Diary 27/12/1920.

182 Walter Braunfels (1882–1954).

183 Rudolf Siegel (1878–1948).

Tombeau de Debussy', there was a concert at the Tonhalle and a 'chopped about' production of *Zauberflöte*: 'The pleasantest thing about the Z. was the audience, mostly children, who vastly enjoyed Papageno's gags' and an excellent Tamino, Karl Erb. By his last week, Dent had made yet more friends and more contacts with Munich publishers, the Kurt Wolff Verlag.

> I began to imagine that I was gifted with a supernatural charm that made everybody fall in love with me – people begged me to come back and stay a long time ... The real fact is that people of the right kind are feeling horribly cut off from foreign literature & ideas, so that my visit meant a sudden gleam from the lost world ... we do feel when we meet each other that that common country of ours means more to us than mere England or Germany.[184]

Having encountered a number of Germans who were brittle and defensive about non-German ideas and people, Dent by now knew how to address this cultural blockade, his internationalist approach not limited to music. 'It's a great moment for making propaganda of reconciliation, and for infusing English ideas', he wrote to Maynard Keynes in December to persuade him to write something on the subject for the leftish German publishers.[185]

When he returned to Berlin on 6 January, he was welcomed as a friend by the Lauer family at the restaurant, with gossip about local politics, the hotel strike and general corruption. Going to the theatre was now real pleasure, Goethe's *Torquato Tasso*, 'a beautiful performance of a most beautiful play – I think the best work of art that I have come across in my visit to Germany.'[186] He went to the Deutsches Theater production of Shaw's *Caesar and Cleopatra*, which he had never seen before, 'hugely amused' with Werner Kraus 'perfectly delicious' as Caesar. Schnitzler's *Reigen* (*La Ronde*), had been produced for the first time that December at the Kleines Schauspielhaus, and 'excited a great scandal, even in Berlin ... 10 little scenes & a copulation in each! And this in the rooms where Donald Tovey used to play Brahms!'.[187]

Accompanied by Hans Rausch, Dent travelled to Dresden to see old friends, including the Gottschald – the last time he would see her – and to sort out some of Mrs Spottiswoode's complicated affairs. He returned to Berlin on 26 January, in time for the last of Busoni's concerts, and the most popular – 'a huge audience', since Busoni himself was playing his Konzertstück and his Concerto. The next day, after making his farewells at the library, he took the night train to Munich. His last day in Germany was full: lunch with Paul Ewald, tea with the Einsteins, in the evening to the opera, *Die Vögel* again.

Three days later he was in Nice, where a letter from Murry was waiting for him, informing him that '*The Athenaeum* is dead': 'I was tired & wretched and this on top of it was incredibly depressing'. But even if he was too exhausted to see it at the

184 JBT 08/01/1921.

185 JMK 16/12/1920. Dent mischievously threw out the lures of 'charming lad(s)' devoted to him and to Shaw.

186 Diary 19/01/1921.

187 JBT 16/01/1921.

time, Dent had achieved more than a series of articles, however significant. He had consolidated his internationalist credentials and understanding, widening his own networks and through his contacts, establishing his own place.

1921–1922

'I am getting some ideas to work out', Dent had written optimistically to JB that December, 'about the theatre in Germany – so I can go on writing "Letters from Germany" for a considerable time wherever I am'.[188] But the *Athenaeum* work had served a purpose well beyond hack journalism. In Germany Dent had hoovered up everything he could see of contemporary culture, even styles and subjects he found loathsome, but the drive to explore was coupled with a need to understand. His brief to inform British readers came at a time when the War Graves Commission was building its monuments in northern France and memories were still raw, but he recognised a public hunger in both Germany and Britain for a new postwar cultural expression, even if the new sat so uneasily beside the conservative clinging to the familiar. He spent the next eighteen months continuing to open up his public's perceptions of the foreign and the new, and even if he appeared for a time to be lacking in focus, everything he was doing in these years would serve his internationalist leanings, the credo expressed in 'Revaluations' emerging in the International Society for Contemporary Music. His *Music & Letters* article on Pfitzner is a case in point.[189]

Written two years after he had first heard Pfitzner's music in Berlin, it is a cultural study as much as a musical one, capturing much of the 'Bildung', the self-conscious connection to his 'German' roots Dent felt lay behind Pfitzner's music, allowing the reader to understand what makes a potentially unattractive artist like Pfitzner tick, and undermining the trumpeted Germanness of the music by mischievously finding in it strong elements of the French music Pfitzner professed to hate, e.g., whole-tone composition reminiscent of Fauré and Debussy. Dent could so easily have been dismissive; instead, he leads the reader through Pfitzner's early works, the songs: 'a song of undoubted beauty in itself', he says of a setting of Petrarch, 'I shudder to think of what the average German singer would make of an attempt to follow the composer's instruction' ('Sehr langsam, mit Wehmut und Überschwang' – Very slowly, with wistfulness and exuberance)

Pfitzner's highminded 'preoccupation' with Schopenhauer clouds any practical connection of ideas with real music: 'The papers on his own librettos explain the moral ideas that lie behind them; they do not enter into the really difficult problem of how to construct a libretto for musical setting.' Finally, having demolished through a reductio ad absurdum Pfitzner's recently published philosophy, *Die neue Aesthetik der musikalischen Impotenz*, Dent addresses the difficult question of how Pfitzner sees himself through his opera *Palestrina*:

[188] JBT 24/12/1920.

[189] Dent, 'Hans Pfitzner'.

> Poet and philosopher by temperament; somewhat narrow and pedantic by education ... what the world calls a man with a grievance. A German, intensely conscious of his Germanism, with that curious German idolatry of art, more especially of the art of music, and, as the result, with the German exaggeration of reverence for himself as der Künstler, as one of art's high priests ... It comes of an excessive reverence for the past, more especially for the great German past of music.

'He has come to be regarded as the musical representative of the extreme Nationalist party', with his expressed need for German unity through the classics: 'many Germans view modern art with apprehension at this particular moment, because they feel that the reckless individualism of it is disruptive in its influence just when Germany stands most in need of unity'. He finishes, however, on *Palestrina:*

> which belongs to the category of Festspiele, like Parsifal, and both performers and audience are expected to approach it in a spirit of special devotion. It is an intolerably boring work ... Yet in spite of its appalling tediousness I went four times to see it, and would never miss an opportunity of seeing it again.

Only Dent could arrive at such a paradoxical point; his German friends appreciated what he was attempting, and his articles were being translated into German.[190]

For most of 1921, Dent continued to explore contemporary ideas and impressions through his writing, and thanks mostly to the popularity of 'Letters from Germany', his talents were much in demand. *The Athenaeum* smoothly morphed into *The Nation & The Athenaeum,* under the financial nous of Maynard Keynes, with a new editor, W.H. Massingham. That April, Bruce Ingram asked Dent to write on drama for the *Illustrated London News,* while Geoffrey Whitworth of the Drama League[191] wanted him to do a seminal book on German 'Kultur' 'with music to be rather primus inter pares'. But he was startled when Wyndham Lewis approached him 'to write something for his new paper to be called the *Tyro*. I am amused that I shd be regarded as so up-to-date!'[192]

In one sense Dent picked up pretty much where he had left off, covering the current concert and theatre scene for various journals, connecting what he saw in Britain to ideas nurtured in Germany, especially anything to do with new music, but his observations were now far less forgiving; he wanted to be provocative. After one of the regular Patron's Fund concerts at the Royal College of Music, where Hugh Allen's students played their new works, Dent wrote in the *The Nation & The Athenaeum*: 'It is a matter of luck on these occasions whether one chances to hear anything of outstanding merit.'[193] He uses the 'nameless' example of one unmistakably English piece to ask if it had been selected simply because of its Englishness, moving into a comparison with German attitudes: 'Which, I wonder, is the worse

190 Haward, *Edward J. Dent: A Bibliography*, 194, 195, 222, 224.

191 Diary 19/01/1921: Tea w 'Dr Max Hochdorf, secretary of the Genossenschaft Deutscher Bühum [sic] Angehörigen – I arranged a treaty with the Drama League. Dr H. knew several friends of mine: Mrs Maddison & Martin Mundt: he also lived in Brussels & knew Mme Vandervelde well – "eine schöne und anmutige Frau" (!)'.

192 JBT 13/04/1921.

193 'Young England', N&A (26 February 1921), pp. 743–4.

– to hate music because it is foreign and strange, or, because it is one's own, to have to be ashamed of it as well?' But while never actually deploring the choice of piece, Dent compares the fact that in Britain at least it has been given public performance, while in Germany the combination of over-powerful conservative critics, a lack of funding, and an attitude to programming which obviated any mixture of the new with the classics, meant that such performance was a rarity. It is Dent at his disingenuous best. He knew that copies of the *The Nation & The Athenaeum* would be making their way to Germany.

He ends with a plea for more cross-fertilisation with Germany. 'English music is at this moment, a hundred years behind Germany because it is still essentially aristocratic, and basically amateur.' 'Primitiv': that epithet had stung. In another article, centred around Edward Clark's 'delightful' concerts of new French music,[194] Dent lightly compares the music of Les Six to the Impressionists' joyful spattering on canvas of everything they saw, the result an attractive 'Schlaraffenland'.[195]

> M. Poulenc's effusions are merely a gesture of impertinence directed at his old teacher, M. Vincent d'Indy, and when people take life and art as seriously as M. d'Indy does, it is very natural that their pupils should have moments of impertinence.

'It is an exceedingly self-conscious form of naughtiness' Dent continues; these entertaining new compositions are trying to give 'the outward impression of street music', but are really all style and little substance: 'it makes no appeal to those people who naturally take pleasure in the music of the streets … It represents a purely imaginary France'. But there is a place for such frivolous art: 'We do not wish to be taken for Germans … As long as the musical world was dominated by German influences people had to pretend to enjoy a great deal of music which was really very dull and tedious … The present generation revolts rightly against the hypocrisy of these spiritual exercises.'

Edward Clark's[196] concerts of contemporary music (Bliss, Schoenberg, Falla) that May certainly reflected Dent's own vague internationalist hopes, furnishing the opportunity for him to write on the music in his own inimitable way, and, whether he had indeed stimulated a new and wider interest in music or was simply reflecting the zeitgeist, Dent was no longer alone. The composer and critic Philip Heseltine was now writing for *Anbruch*, while in the *Chesterian*, Leigh Henry[197] was giving bland surveys of the musical life of London which, displayed over two pages, at least appears impressively healthy. Echoing Dent, Henry noted 'the increasing growth of chamber-music and of chamber-music players, which is probably due to the social

194 'Cinéma Nouvelle Muse', N&A (30 April 1921), pp. 177–8.

195 Land of milk and honey.

196 Thomas Edward Clark (1888–1962), conductor, BBC producer, studied with Schoenberg in Berlin, knew Busoni. Dent knew him well, often had lunch with him; Clark later succeeded Dent as President of the ISCM.

197 Leigh Vaughan Henry (1889–1958), composer and critic, worked with Gordon Craig in Florence, was interned during the war at Ruhleben camp.

impetus which music is receiving, and the attention which this form is receiving from our most individual younger composers'.[198]

After catching up with Boris Ord at Cambridge, that August Dent passed a pleasant two weeks with Clive in the Auvergne, working on the *Don Giovanni* translation[199] while Clive had his daily lessons (paid for by Dent) with Jean de Reszke.

> Clive liked Da Ponte's dialogue so much that he asked me to translate the whole of the secco syllabically, to use it as spoken dialogue if possible. I am amused to find it contains some terrible obscenities wch I never noticed before ... I was staying with Mrs Campbell ... near Woburn on Sunday & showed it to her: and before she had finished the first scene she said 'How you hate Donna Anna!'[200]

Between the walks through the hills, he could discuss a number of things with Clive at leisure, mostly about the translation, but also future Old Vic productions: *Fidelio* and *Norma* beside Nicholas Gatty's *Tempest* and a possible double bill of *Prince Ferelon* and *Dido and Aeneas*. Dent thought a German tour by the English Singers would serve a double purpose of the small-scale concert with little-known English madrigals.[201] JB was still in Spain, doing some research on Goya for a production style suitable for *Don Giovanni* that autumn. Dent had fastened onto the comic 'dramma giocoso' aspect, usually neglected; he wanted people to feel able to laugh, then a rarity at the opera.[202]

His writing in 1921, over sixty articles in the *The Nation & The Athenaeum* and in *Truth,* continued to support the various kinds of music being performed: Purcell, Falla, Schoenberg, Busoni, almost programme notes to the cultural shifts going on. 'The End of the Promenades', for example, is as much about Delius and Bliss as it is about the Proms' place in the musical world, while 'Opera in English at Covent Garden' was both 'squib' condemning 'the mephitic influence of old Covent Garden', the old-fashioned 'grand operatic manner', and an argument for the use of proper translations. The new audiences should not be forced to sit through productions made incomprehensible because they either couldn't understand a word being sung or were having to listen to entirely inappropriate words. 'We must accept the principle that an opera in English will have to differ from the original more or less in its whole vocal color-scheme [sic]'. Dent's position is not simply to puff his own translations, more to bring operatic production more into line with trends in the more radical theatre: a greater sensitivity in the production of music and poetry, the musicality of words, working together as an artistic whole.

'I wish to goodness you'd go & give my Glastonbury lectures for me!' he wrote to Lawrence: 'I hated it more than ever – Rutland Boughton (a good soul really, by

198 Leigh Henry, 'London Letter', *The Chesterian* (February 1921), pp. 402–3.

199 This was not published for the production; instead, Dent had laboriously to write his new words into the Old Vic copies of the old Novello edition. JBT 05/09/1921.

200 LH 18/08/1921.

201 The English Singers at that time consisted of Clive Carey, Cuthbert Kelly, Steuart Wilson, Winifred Whelan, Lillian Berger and Flora Mann.

202 LH 18/08/1921.

himself) "like a Turk, with his doxies around"'[203] But really, Dent had outgrown not only Glastonbury, but England. Although he continued to enjoy himself through the Old Vic and through his writing, making his serious points in an entertaining yet illuminating way, invariably contentious, there is an underlying and utterly characteristic restlessness. His letters to JB and to Lawrence that summer and autumn are full of castings about his future.

> I met Ogden the other night at the Spanish. I was glad to see him – he is one of the people who always make me feel that life is worth living. He tells me I ought to chuck journalism & write books: that if I wrote books steadily, I cd make just as good a living out of that. His latest idea is that I shd write a book to take the place of Dr Pole's 'Philosophy of Music' ... But I'm not attracted to the notion of writing a standard text-book of any kind. I can't resist the temptation to set off squibs.[204]
>
> There are all sorts of things abroad I want to go to – not the Mozart festival at Munich, for I think I shd only be annoyed by any Mozart performances except at the Old Vic – but there's a Handel festival at Göttingen with 2 Handel operas on the stage! I can't afford these things now: and Massingham has cut me down to 2 articles a month.[205]
>
> There is nothing to tell you – I am leading the dullest of lives – but it is refreshing in its way. I wish I cd chuck everything and go to Italy or Spain![206]

While he had been gnashing his teeth at Glastonbury, another music festival far more to Dent's taste was taking place in Donaueschingen in Germany, one dedicated entirely to new music. In two years it would furnish the platform for the new International Society for Contemporary Music,[207] with Dent as its first President; entirely characteristic that it took him so long to notice. But for the time being, Dent's attention on new music was focused more locally, returning to the book on early opera and mustering some support for Ivor Gurney, one of the younger composers whose music he admired: 'I must write to Eddie M. about Ivor Gurney. Clive knows him, & Steuart too. He's rather a genius'.[208]

All that autumn he continued to write articles on Schoenberg, on Falla, on Bartók besides the Proms programming: 'We have had too many pretentious symphonic poems, dependent for their construction upon a printed programme. No programme can ever make up for the lack of pure musical architecture.'[209] He wrote a review of Wanda Landowska's book on *Musique Ancienne*:

203 LH 01/09/1921.

204 JBT 05/09/1921.

205 LH 18/08/1921.

206 JBT 05/09/1921.

207 The best single source for the complete history of the International Society for Contemporary Music / Internationale Gesellschaft für neue Musik remains Anton Haefeli's monumental *IGNM: Die Internationale Gesellschaft für neue Musik: Ihre Geschichte von 1922 bis zur Gegenwart* (Zurich, 1982).

208 JBT 23/01/1922.

209 'The End of the Promenades', N&A (29 October 1921).

Her agreeable chatter conceals a vast amount of erudition ... It is the common failing of writers on music, even of the most learned, to suppose, that instrumental music, after it had once parted company with the singers in the early seventeenth century, developed exclusively on its own lines, and that all progress in the evolution of musical forms was confined to, or at least initiated by, the composers for instruments.[210]

One scathing article is an introduction to *Faust,* another new German journal, which had published Busoni's article on the theory of opera: 'Apparently there still exists in Germany the feeling that opera as a musical form is not quite respectable. Serious musicians compose symphonies. In England we have far fewer opportunities of hearing opera than the Germans enjoy, but we have no prejudice against it.'[211]

In January 1922, Dent managed another long trip to Prague, Germany and Vienna, to hear new music and to follow the progress of the English Singers' tour he had done so much to set up. 'I had a pleasant time in Berlin', he wrote to Lawrence from Dresden:

The most interesting music has been 2 Sunday evenings chez César Saerchinger, a funny little Yank who represents the N.Y. Musical Courier – one of the most appaling [sic] papers in the world – but he is a good little soul & though no very profound musician keen on getting modern stuff done. We had a Pizzetti evening, with the Budapest 4tet who are splendid. They must be got over to England ... Last Sunday week he asked people to play more modern German stuff: the evening was got up specially for me! Alma Moodie played Erdmann's solo violin sonata. She is a young Australian, who was studying violin at Brussels in 1914 & stayed there all the time, very well looked after by the Germans who recognized her talents & took her back under military protection to Berlin, where she is with Carl Flesch. She is about 17 or 18 and is a most remarkably fine player.[212]

He had just come from Prague, where Adrian Boult conducted a concert of English music on 5 January, Butterworth's two folk-song *Idylls,* Bliss's *Mêlée Fantasque* and Elgar's Symphony in E flat, with 'the addition of some madrigals and folksong arrangements sung by the "English Singers"',[213] making the point that although the concert was superbly played by the Czechs, 'critical minds in Prague had no illusions about it'.

As one (Bohemian) observed, the three English composers represented three tendencies which were little different from those of Central Europe – Butterworth making a conscious return to the simplicity of folksong, Bliss the modernist and 'masterly blender of orchestral colour,' and Elgar 'the Pope of music, the man of ripe experience, the conservative who has gone through the school of Liszt's technique, and there fixes, more or less, the boundaries of music'.

210 'La Muse Naissante', N&A (1 October 1921), pp. 25–6.

211 'Back to Cimarosa', N&A (3 December 1921), pp. 393–4.

212 LH 09/01/1922.

213 'English Music in Prague', N&A (21 January 1922).

As with his 'Letters from Germany', Dent was giving the British reader positive spin, an opportunity to appreciate the significance of what had happened, but without mentioning in the article the fact that the audience was small. Putting six a capella voices on the same programme was 'inappropriate', Dent says bluntly. But 'the English Singers completely captured the Czechs', he wrote to Lawrence: 'They had to sing another group of madrigals after the concert was supposed to be over, & were recalled & encored several times.' With this tour, 'English' music was being given an international airing, and in Berlin, Dent persuaded many of the library and Hochschule people to come, and even tried to get Max von Schillings to hear Clive. Dresden, he felt was 'a most wonderful success'. He wrote excitedly to JB, optimism possibly overriding judgement:

> here at last was English music that was absolutely first class both in itself and in their performance: and at the same time absolutely English and derived from English ancestral tradition – a thing that Germany had never heard before, and a thing that Germany cd not do.[214]

'I felt sure that that bloody fool Massingham would want an article on Strauss!'[215] Forced to write on Pfitzner for the *Music & Letters* article when he had hoped to write more on Busoni and new music, Dent was glad at least of the company in Berlin. Dorothy Moulton and Thornely Gibson were there, while Chester Purves, now working for the League of Nations, was coming over from Vienna. With his head so full of both composers, comparison with Pfitzner was inevitable, and Dent's Busoni article[216] manages to express how remarkable it was that an Italian had been appointed under an Austrian to teach Germans how to compose music (at the Berlin Hochschule, Busoni had attracted thirty students to the German Pfitzner's one), before describing what it was like to be taught by Busoni, whose pupils then included Kurt Weill, Robert Blum, Dimitri Mitropoulos and Wladimir Vogel, all sitting under the 'huge and chaotic canvas of Boccioni', while 'a huge golden Buddha looked down upon the group with a benign and enigmatic smile'. Dent skims the details, commenting that 'considering the work [was] exhibited merely as academic study, there could be no doubt as to the wonderful ability which they showed. It was not mere technical facility, but real intellectual ability, real constructive and reasoning power', implying that the future of music was in safe and familiar hands: Busoni had recently given more concerts in Britain and was a popular figure.

Dent's articles at this time on Bach and Handel, though different from his contemporary musical concerns, are in fact connected to his general point that through performance comes better understanding. His review of the Newcastle Bach Choir seems to be stating the obvious: 'Dr. Whittaker understands what few conductors of Bach have grasped – that Bach must be interpreted first and foremost as a musician.'[217]

214 JBT 05/04/1922.

215 JBT 23/01/1922.

216 'The School of Athens' (4 February 1922), translated into German by Lotte Dorman for the *Dresdner Woche*, 15 April 1922.

217 'The Newcastle Bach Choir', N&A (4 March 1922) pp. 838–9. But 'Bach-Worship' and 'Handel-Worship' came into other articles (29 October 1921), mostly to demonstrate

But this remark is being made in the context of a brief history of 'the Bach cult' in England, when in the previous century Bach had been made 'the scholar's composer … the starting-point of all that enthusiasm for old music which is so remarkable a factor of contemporary musical life in England', while his music was edited to suit late nineteenth-century taste: 'There was still a feeling that there was something not quite nice about florid singing – it might remind people of "La Traviata"'. Only performance could bring out this point. Dent's own shift to Handel began around this time, partly to support what currently unfashionable, but more, Dent could see a neglected great composer whose music deserved much more serious attention; Handel needed a champion in the way Mozart had needed one.

In May he was 'ordered' by *The Nation & The Athenaeum* editorial assistant with the amazing name of Vera Cruz to the new Handel Festival at Halle, Handel's birthplace, for four days of his music: *Semele* and *Susanna* 'to represent oratorio', a chamber concert and an orchestral concert, finally a performance of *Orlando furioso*. Dent was underwhelmed: 'curiously wooden and unintelligent. Few performers at the concerts seemed to have any sense of the rapturous beauty of the music before them.' Forty-five years later, Dent's pupil Winton Dean was less diplomatic about these early productions:

> The Hagen versions were heavily abridged and rewritten. The da capos were nearly all cut … the first parts of arias chopped up and sometimes reduced to a fragment of ritornello. Many were omitted altogether. The accompaniments … were rescored for a romantic orchestra … Handel's image in Europe, especially in Germany, is still saddled with a load of false tradition. This may well have contributed to the slowness with which his operas have won wider recognition, not because their texture has puzzled modern audiences, but because they have scarcely ever been allowed to hear it.[218]

But at the time Dent was more hopeful:

> It means that the musical researchers are coming out of their libraries and getting into direct contact with the public … In the first place it brings new ideas into the opera-houses … Handel demands, even more insistently than Mozart, a concentration of interest upon pure singing.[219]
>
> The spiritus rector of the Opera – translator & adapter & combiner of the functions of Clive & me is our old friend "Beethoven's Butler"! Dr Hans Joachim Moser.[220]

From Halle, Dent went to Frankfurt to see Bartók's opera, *Bluebeard's Castle* – exactly the kind of thing he wanted for the Old Vic[221] – then on to Darmstadt 'for Flecker's play', to Münster to look at Scarlatti manuscripts again, then to Düsseldorf

---

how audiences' 'devotion to Bach is a genuine devotion to pure music' and Sir Henry Wood's part in achieving this.

[218] Winton Dean, *Handel and the Opera Seria* (Berkeley, 1969), pp. 200–02, p. 210.

[219] 'Handel on the stage', N&A (29 April 1922).

[220] JBT 29/05/1922. Dent later changed his mind about Moser.

[221] CC 23/07/1922. Dent wanted the British National Opera Company to do it.

for the contemporary music festival, then Florence and Venice, before going on to Donaueschingen and Salzburg in August. Through all the travelling, his main concern was how to bring everything he was seeing back to stimulate British activities. 'I wish we cd get the Vic going properly', he lamented to Clive.

But mostly, Dent was enjoying himself. Out of the work Anton Mayer was doing on Dent's Mozart book – to be published in German by Erich Reiss – more Mozart collaboration was arising, with the possibility mooted of a Deutsches Theater production of *Il re pastore* at the Kammerspiele 'under the direction of ME! … I can't think that it will come off: but how amusing it wd be for you & me to run a Mozart show in Berlin!'[222] His letters that summer are full of entertaining detail, from the 'English demimonde' in Vienna, mostly louche friends of Chester Purves, now based there, to catching up with a range of old friends. 'I have had a pleasant & amusing time here: music very disappointing' he wrote from Vienna that May. 'The public doesn't mind whether it sees Die Rote Stadt or Cavalleria – as long as the Jeritza sings. I haven't heard her, as I can't waste time on Cav & Pag & such like'.[223] Even if he was not a great Mahler fan,[224] he loved hearing Helge Lindberg sing *Kindertotenlieder*: 'magnificent voice, and a wonderful legato & breath control … & Wellesz says a great boxer too!' He stayed on to hear Bruno Walter conduct Mahler's 2nd Symphony, having disliked Furtwängler's version: 'I may be converted.'

In Florence, ten days at the Villa Palmerino with Vernon Lee were lively but 'exhausting', Dent blaming 'the nervous effect of the perpetual inhibitions one has to be making when one is staying in a woman's house'.

> She looked an odder sight than ever, for she has had some sort of disease of the scalp wch has necessitated cutting off her hair: and dressed in a white coat & skirt, with very large white shoes (and black stockings) and a white skull cap on her head, she looked like the Pope.[225]

While staying with her, Dent walked over to a nearby villa to visit Fritz von Unruh,[226] whose plays he had recently seen in Berlin: 'then suddenly breaking the ice, which in his case led to a long lecture on the past, present & future of the relations between the sexes'.[227] Unruh's pacifist ideas were in accord with Dent's, while his love of scurrilous gossip past and present had Vernon Lee soon inviting him over to Palmerino: 'he is highly excitable – like Siegfried Sassoon at the moment of his shell shock'.

> I must be growing very old – for I no longer fall in love with every other person I meet. The standard of beauty seems to me to be much lower: and I don't like

[222] CC 09/05/1922.

[223] *Ibid.*

[224] 'I have a violent prejudice against Der Knaben Wunderhorn and all the oldfashioned nonsense about Blümlein blau. The Blue Flower of the Blue Bird are both a Blue Boar'. *Ibid.*

[225] JBT 28/06/1922.

[226] Fritz von Unruh (1885–1970), playwright and pacifist, his very public anti-Nazi stance forced him to leave Germany for decades.

[227] JBT 28/06/1922.

> the tendency to little whiskers, or the Quattrocento couffure, wonderful as it is at times, with waves that can hardly be natural! Some young men cut their hair very close on the neck, & fluff it out with their hands like a sort of Federbusch in German heraldry. It looks absurd with modern clothes.[228]

Dent continued his contact with the British Institute at Florence (which Francis Toye would soon be running), while making more musical contacts, with Castelnuovo-Tedescho, and Pizzetti, Respighi at Bologna. The Maddalenas were sadly now 'very badly off, I fear, and rather bored with life'. Italy was changed: 'I miss the open air music', he lamented to Clive, 'the Italian papers complain bitterly of the Government's economy in cutting down military bands'.[229]

Back in England JB was writing articles for the *The Nation & The Athenaeum* (or *The Athenasius* as Dent began to call it), *Music & Letters* and other journals. Dent's regular correspondence with JB now became even more of an extended conversation, expressing his thoughts, current ideas and fancies.

> I told Alfred Einstein that you were working at Spanish music, so he will probably send you a lot of Sonderhefte. I expect he wd be delighted if you'd ever write a learned article for the Zeitschrift für Musikwissenschaft: the sort of thing F-S [Fox Strangways] refuses to print! It wd be good for your international reputation.[230]

Spanish music was nearly as polarised as some German music, with little international scope and deeply conservative foundations. JB's contact with the more avant-garde elements centred around the Residencia de Estudiantes in Madrid and with Falla and his circles underpinned his efforts to make more and stronger cultural connections with Britain. They considered how to woo Alfonso Salazar, music critic for *El Sol,* away from Jean Aubry's *The Chesterian.*

But it did not take long for Dent's fundamental restlessness to reassert itself. 'I am wondering & wondering whether I cant give up musical criticism and live by writing books, as Ogden always told me I could', Dent wrote to Clive from Venice that July.

> I am sick of it all, and more & more annoyed with Massingham & the Nation. That life entirely prevents me from doing any solid work. But if I do give it up it means a financial loss, and an awkward period, even if my projected books did bring in money! So I suppose I am chained to it still. Italy & the heat have rather demoralized me.[231]

Even as he wrote this, Dent's attention was being redirected elsewhere, back to Germany. 'A Festival of Modern Music' presented an undertaking close to his heart: the annual festival of the Allgemeiner Deutscher Musikverein with an 'aggressively modern' programme was being held this year in the 'most notoriously conservative' town of Düsseldorf: 'it was quite touching to hear a violin sonata by one of Schönberg's younger pupils played by two grey-headed gentlemen with a refine-

228 JBT 28/06/1922.

229 CC 23/07/1922.

230 JBT 22/05/1922. JB did write for Einstein.

231 CC 23/07/1922.

ment that was positively Mendelssohnian. … The hissing and whistling party were pretty obviously from outside, for their censure was always directed against what was either old-fashioned or incompetent … It is hardly to be expected that every item in every programme should be a masterpiece'.[232] He gives an outline of the programmes, with Karl Horwitz, Ewald Strässer, Alois Hába, ending with a warm reception for chamber works by Reger, Schnabel and Philipp Jarnach, and 'by far the best work of the whole festival', Webern's *Passacaglia*. The programme was everything Dent had hoped to see for new music, a mix of the experimental, the accessible and the conservative, but it wasn't until the following month that the vision really began to take shape, at Donaueschingen, in Baden, where the wealthy Prince Max Egon zu Fürstenberg was sponsoring a music festival, run by his efficient librarian, Heinrich Burkhard.

Dent's article, 'At the Source', refers both to the source of the Danube springing from the prince's garden, but also a source of inspiration, the realisation of his own vision of what a contemporary music festival ought to be.

> About a year ago I wrote that the young composer in England had a much better chance of being heard, and when heard, a much more sympathetic and encouraging reception from the public and from the critics, than the young composer in Germany. I do not wish to withdraw this statement; but the Donaueschingen festival sets an example which England would do well to follow. Such an institution is an isolated and exceptional thing in Germany; it gives opportunities which many young composers may find nowhere else, as well as providing an occasion on which young composers, critics, and friends of music generally from Germany and outside may meet on pleasant and agreeable terms … a festival of this kind would be a very desirable thing in England, still more so if it bore an international character. Our only difficulty in England is to find the man who is willing to make himself financially responsible for it.[233]

Busoni, Strauss, Pfitzner and Schreker had chosen pieces by Krenek, Fidelio Finke, Hindemith, van Dieren, Max Butting and others. Ten out of thirteen were first performances. But what struck Dent's optimistically internationalist side was the 'peculiar charm and friendliness of atmosphere'. Shortly afterwards, that first week in August, Dent went to Salzburg and his life changed yet again.

232 'A Festival of Modern Music', N&A (1 July 1922), p. 482.

233 'At the Source', N&A (19 August 1922), p. 691.

CHAPTER 10

The International Musician 1922–1926

The name of the English Professor of musicology Edward J. Dent … the first President of the ISCM, is linked to memories of the 'heroic period of the ISCM' … Dent, without doubt, held the whole thing together.[1]

It was the first really international festival on a large scale devoted solely to contemporary music, and the first in which performers from countries recently at war sat down to play together in one and the same work.[2]

1922–1923

The history of the founding of the International Society for Contemporary Music (ISCM) / Internationale Gesellschaft für neue Musik (IGNM) has been well documented,[3] but its sudden burst into life in August 1922 was neither spontaneous nor entirely calculated; rather an opportunity recognised and seized to give contemporary music a forum and an internationalist outlook. Previous fragmented efforts included the various festivals which had captured Dent's attention that summer,[4] the high point being the festival of contemporary chamber music at Salzburg from 7 to 10 August, organised by the Schoenberg circles in Vienna, largely the brain-child of composer Rudolf Réti,[5] who had enlisted Dent's friend Egon Wellesz in a Vienna coffee-house the winter before. Réti was an idealist, an enthusiast, who wanted a 'celebration' (Feier) of contemporary music rather than simply another festival. His idea was to expand the Schoenberg circle by inviting like-minded contemporary musicians – 'composers, interpreters, critics, etc.'[6] – from all lands, even the USA, in an internationalist spirit, a contrast to the current strong nationalist tendencies Dent had been documenting. His gushing enthusiasm and verbosity were later unkindly

1 Haefeli, *IGNM*, pp. 295–6.

2 Dent, 'Introduction', p. 2. KCA.

3 Haefeli, 'Die Gründung der IGNM', *IGNM*, pp. 38 ff. Contemporary accounts include Edwin Evans' article for the MT (1 September 1922) and Dent's own article for the N&A. Other sources, most notably Réti's own and Dent's 'Looking Backwards' were written years after the fact.

4 Haefeli, *IGNM*, pp. 31ff. and notes.

5 Rudolf Réti (1885–1957), Serbian-born, friend of Kodály, pupil of Schoenberg.

6 Haefeli, *IGNM*, p. 42.

compared by Dent to 'a dribbling tap', but he carried the tricky project through. Having no money, and with inflation in Austria nearly as bad as in Germany, they persuaded Viennese bookseller-cum-concert agent Hugo Heller and Emil Hertzka of Universal Edition to underwrite the event, very much in their business interests as the main publishers of contemporary music.[7] Younger composers in Vienna had felt stifled; music was dominated by the conservative critics Joseph Marx and Julius Korngold – the latter, as Dent remarked, 'would recognize no modern composer except his own son',[8] a Dentish exaggeration, but close. The Schoenberg private contemporary concerts – *Privataufführungen* – had been set up in direct response to such local obstructions, but now the composers involved wanted to expand the remit of these. Financial constraints dictated a programme of chamber music, and holding the event in Salzburg, 'an important tourist centre, and it had a pleasant little theatre and a small concert hall … which was all that the organizers of the festival could afford',[9] dovetailed nicely with ordinary tourist events, with the Max Reinhart *Everyman*, and with the Mozart Festival. What they achieved was breathtaking: 'a series of chamber concerts at which as many composers as possible would be represented, rather larger than the organizers could comfortably manage', with seven concerts over four days and over fifty different composers represented.

Each concert was huge, a test of stamina as much as anything, demonstrating an enthusiastic rather than considered approach to programming the pieces. For example, the concert on 8 August began at 7 pm, not finishing until after midnight: Nielsen's Sonata for violin and piano, Rangstroem's *Four Songs*, Ravel's Gaspard de la nuit, Busoni's *Sonatina in diem nativitatis 1917*, Szymanowski's 'Tantris', from *Masks*, Wellesz's String Quartet, Finke's *Marionettes* for pianoforte, Webern's String Quartet, and finally Pijper's Sonata for violin and pianoforte. Relatively unknown British composers – Gibbs, Bliss, Ethel Smyth, Holst and Bax – were being performed beside Stravinsky, Strauss, Milhaud, Ravel, Webern, Szymanowski, Falla, Hindemith, Kodály, Bloch, Malipiero and Schoenberg. The performers, who mostly played for no fees, were equally breathtaking: Gieseking, Poulenc, Hindemith leading in his own string quartet; Jean Wiéner playing Poulenc and some startling Stravinsky 'ragtime'. Dorothy Moulton reprised Arthur's Bliss's *Rout*, a surprise favourite. 'Surprise' was perhaps the best word to describe it all.

'Looking Backward', Dent's own account of the early days of the ISCM, is a standard reference on the subject, even if it does glide over some awkward moments. Written nearly thirty years after the event, it is a generous and mostly warm-hearted sketch of how and why the ISCM came to life, and must be taken with a large pinch of salt. Though even-handed in his careful public way, Dent's narrative nevertheless emphasises a number of his own personal perspectives: that Germany's 'defeat had brought spiritual liberation

7 Haefeli, *IGNM*, p. 44, quoting Réti's retrospective 1957 article on the founding of the ISCM; Egon Wellesz, 'E.J. Dent and the International Society for Contemporary Music' in the *Music Review* (1946), pp. 205–8, here p. 205.

8 E.J. Dent, 'Looking Backward', in Taylor, *Edward J. Dent: Selected Essays*, p. 273. Originally published in *Music Today*, vol. 1 (1949), pp. 6–22. The son was Eric Korngold, who as a refugee later made a career composing music for Hollywood movies.

9 1500 *Ibid.*, p. 274.

... creative artists in every branch of culture became intoxicated with freedom';[10] that the ISCM had arisen out of Donaueschingen and the Salzburg festivals organised by the Schoenberg circles, frustrated in their own city of Vienna, 'entirely dominated by that most conservative of critics Dr Julius Korngold'; that Salzburg was ultimately unsatisfactory; that the atmosphere, though 'somewhat chaotic' was friendly and informal, and that the standard of performance was 'high', because enough time had been taken over rehearsals. Dent also stressed the inclusiveness:

> The Schönberg 'clique' ... were anything but narrow-minded; they cast their net over all Europe and America too. They even went so far as to include England, and that in itself was proof enough of their utter unmusicality.[11]
>
> As the festival went on, and as we all perpetually made new and interesting contacts, personal as well as musical, the idea gradually spread that in Salzburg a really new movement had been inaugurated, and that it was desirable to proceed with it by making these international meetings annual events.[12]

He describes the process as if it all had unfolded quite naturally from the grassroots throughout that week, but it stretches credulity that he himself had been passive the whole time. He had managed to circumvent Réti and get Wellesz onto his side; he manoeuvred Edwin Evans into an active but malleable role and established a consensus to make London, and the new British Music Society, the headquarters, a step that before the war would have been risible: London as the epicentre of contemporary music.

Most accounts agree on the surprise and delight at the quality and variety of the music on offer, the spirit of international co-operation, the general warmth.[13] For Edwin Evans, 'it seems almost incredible that one can have heard so much music in four days ... fifty-four composers of fifteen different nationalities!'[14] His voluble and partial account outlined the process of turning that sense of success into solid 'provision for the future': 'With general consent Mr. Edward J. Dent took the chair, and he displayed great tact in keeping the discussion on the international plane whenever there was a tendency to deviate into national channels.'[15]

The informal first meeting took place on 11 August, at the Café Bazar in Salzburg.[16]

> The two things which stood out in all our minds were that here was a great demonstration of music that looked forward to the future, and also a demonstration of international friendly co-operation ... A small group met for preliminary discus-

10 *Ibid.*, p. 272.

11 *Ibid.*, p. 274.

12 *Ibid.*, p. 275.

13 E.g., Réti in Haefeli, *IGNM*, p. 45. But Anton von Webern was far less enthusiastic, writing to Alban Berg that it had been 'verfehlt-elend' – misguided and wretched (Haefeli p. 49), probably still raw because of the initial reception of his own work (Dent 'Looking Backward', p. 275).

14 Edwin Evans, 'The Salzburg Festival', MT (1 September 1922), pp. 628–31.

15 *Ibid.*, pp. 629–30.

16 Haefeli, *IGNM*, p. 52.

> sions: Poulenc, Jean Wiéner … Wellesz, Pijper, Bliss, Evans and myself … The suggestion of London, I must insist, did not come from the English group. We had all taken for granted that the only centre could be Vienna, as the whole movement had started there. But we had reckoned entirely without the bitter jealousy between Vienna and Berlin … The Americans solved the problem by proposing London … Evans then clinched matters by stating … that as there was already a flourishing society for contemporary music in London, as a branch of the British Music Society (which) would be very happy to undertake all the responsibilities of the Central Office.[17]

'It was clear from the first', Egon Wellesz wrote years later, conflating Dent's chairing that meeting with his becoming the first president, 'that only one person had all the necessary qualities for this position: Edward Dent. Everybody liked him and had confidence in his impartial handling of affairs which required both competence and tact.'[18]

It probably did happen as smoothly as that, without anyone really seeing how. Although Dent credits Evans for the idea, they had impetuously committed the British Music Society to an extraordinary undertaking without the slightest remit to do so.[19] In fact, Dent had decided to use Evans, in spite of many personal reservations about him:[20] Evans spoke good German; he was ambitious and intoxicated by what he was seeing, especially keen to get British music involved. He was also biddable. 'I need hardly say how valuable Evans' wise counsels were', is the serpentine comment. Writing to JB, Dent was rather more frank about Evans:

> We had a meeting last Tuesday about the new International: and on the Monday I had Edwin Evans to lunch – All goes well – he made useful additions to my document & it was passed by the committee & will now be sent out … It's amusing to see how these people use me as a ladder. E.E. went to Salzburg knowing nobody & unknown to everybody. I introduced him to all the important people: and he now means to collar the International as his own.[21]

'Owing to the confusion of european currency at the moment, individual subscriptions were out of the question',[22] so they decided to base the society on a 'federation' of existing societies like the British Music Society, but with national sections, each responsible 'for its own local activities and finances, but [each] would pay an

17 Dent, 'Looking Backward', pp. 275–7.

18 Wellesz, 'E.J. Dent and the International Society for Contemporary Music'.

19 'We had no authority whatever from the B.M.S. to make such a promise, but, as we foresaw, it was ratified in due course with much satisfaction.' Dent, 'Looking Backward', p. 277.

20 E.g., diary 06/07/1917, on a talk at the Aeolian Hall during the war: 'I thought his talk mostly empty words – except the illuminating remark that certain moderns – e.g. Schönberg & Stravinsky deliberately uglified their melodies to show that they were intended contrapuntally & not harmonically, to concentrate the hearer's attention on the horizontal line … Evans speaks badly, with many er-ers'.

21 JBT 14/10/1922.

22 Dent, 'Looking Backward', p. 277.

annual contribution to the central funds'. But the most important principle – and it cannot be stressed enough that this was Dent's idea – was that the annual festivals would be programmed by an independent jury:

> elected solely as individuals of musical distinction, in no way associated with and still less under the authority of whatever national section they might happen to belong to. The absolute integrity and independence of the jury, elected annually by the delegates, is in fact the artistic conscience of the whole society.[23]

Throughout October and November 1922, while all of these proposals were being considered, Dent was busy writing letters to all the people he considered important to the cause. Such personal letter-writing became the foundation of his presidential style, appealing to the individual rather than to the section or country or affiliation, and although the effort nearly killed him, his letters often kept things together when everything else was fragile or explosive or both. He was also mustering his own troops: before the next meeting he had begun to gather in old friends like Chester Purves, C.L. Boulenger, J.B. Trend, Gerald Cooper, Scott Goddard; he was going to need such solid support, trusted personal assistants who knew him well, in an otherwise uncertain working environment. Most of his personal task force were gay.

The Viennese committee wanted another festival in Salzburg at the same time next year, 1923, and it was decided to have a conference of delegates that January in Vienna to organise the first stages. In October 1922, when he met with Evans to thrash out the constitution, Dent was beginning to doubt the wisdom of having given Evans so much of the official credit for work that he had done and to worry about what might come from Evans as representative; staying in the background, he realised, had its disadvantages when he needed to be conspicuously present.

> As January drew near it became evident that the financial situation of Central Europe would make it very difficult to carry out this plan, and the English Committee felt it their duty to invite the conference to London instead, and to ensure the presence of an adequate number of delegates by offering to pay their expenses and find them hospitality.[24]

The meeting for the Council of Delegates, as it was called, was held in London, 19–22 January 1923, out of the Contemporary Music Centre in Berners Street, with Lord Howard de Walden backing its new remit. Financial issues were always going to be a source of trouble: how to pay for musicians, even though many played for nothing, to pay for piano hire, room hire, travel expenses, and music critics who usually expected freebies and preferential treatment.

The first jury elected that January in London consisted of Ernest Ansermet, André Caplet, Eugène Goossens, Ildebrando Pizzetti, Hermann Scherchen, Oscar Sonneck and Alexander Zemlinsky. Dent's article in *The Nation & The Athenaeum* that February states the aims:

23 *Ibid*. See also Haefeli, *IGNM*, p. 53.

24 Dent, 'Plans for Salzburg', N&A (3 February 1923), p. 696.

> The most conspicuous activity of the International Society will be the festival of contemporary chamber music … The real work of the Society will be the performance of new music, various local branches, and the collection and distribution of information regarding it.[25]

Another aim of the society was reporting on 'interesting modern works that are performed for the first time', getting such new music into general circulation 'for the benefit of performers and organizers of concerts' rather than simply for the 'music trade'. This last was aimed at music publishers like the Universal Edition or Chester's, who had vested interests in what was performed. Performance, accessibility to new ideas and new music, information, free exchange: these were to underline this new society.

> The important fact about the Selection Committee is that its members have been chosen not as representatives of important countries, but wholly on their merits as musicians. One of the difficulties of the Conference was to hold the balance evenly between nationalism and internationalism … no country had any right to make special claims on account of its past history in music.

'We have no rights', he later said, and was often quoted, 'we have only duties.' Dent's accounts of all this early history are not always consistent, like his occasional relaxed interpretations of points of process, having stated one aim then not quite adhering to it.[26] But far from undermining the principles, such flexibility more often facilitated them, and determining the points of flexibility quickly became part of Dent's loosely defined presidential role. Dent recognised that the constitution at least had to be clear and simple, even if implementing it was never going to be either, and his own principles never really wavered. One case in point is his interference with the voting process to ensure that there was a French representative on the jury: 'a curiously troublesome matter' he called it, probably because he knew it contravened at least one of the stated principles. Although Ravel as French delegate had accepted the original vote which included no Frenchman on the jury, he was clearly unhappy about it. Dent interfered: 'I persuaded the delegates to go on voting until they did give a Frenchman the necessary number of votes … it was the general feeling of the meeting that the results of the first scrutiny were unsatisfactory.'[27] Such inconsistency on the part of the president was bound to be spotted and when it suited, criticised strongly.

> As the society grew larger and larger, it became quite obvious to us all that the first aim of every delegate was to get one of his own compatriots elected, and after that many delegates had such slender contacts with the musical world in general that they either followed the lead of the bigger countries, or put down the names best known to them. These names were, in most cases, German.[28]

25 *Ibid.*

26 Anton Haefeli calls it 'Wahlmanipulationen' (electoral manipulations).

27 Dent, 'Looking Backward', p. 278.

28 *Ibid.*

If Dent felt obliged to bend the rules from time to time, it was always in the service of the fundamental principles.

> It would be contrary to the whole spirit of the Society if the Salzburg festival were regarded as a sort of musical tournament in which different countries competed against each other for the championship of musical Europe. It is the desire of the Society that while the fullest liberty is allowed to individual expression, political frontiers should be disregarded.[29]

As high-minded as it all may sound in retrospect, from its inception every smallest action which helped to bring the ISCM into life was bristling with hidden politics, mostly because of its fundamentally democratic nature. Elected committees would decide everything, from the choice of music to the choice of venue; in such free and open debate with such adamant conclusions, friction was unavoidable. Eventually, important – and prickly – figures like Schoenberg would be offended enough to cut all ties with the ISCM.

Gradually, Dent put his considerable abilities behind the new society, including his unfailing instinct for finding and cultivating the right people to help out. One such was Werner Reinhart, 'our Swiss Howard de Walden', generously dispensing essential time, money and hospitality. Reinhart (1884–1951) was a music-loving philanthropist, one of three art-loving brothers from a wealthy Swiss family. The family firm Gebrüder Volkart was a worldwide import–export business based in Winterthur, an industrial town about half an hour from Zurich, dealing in tea, coffee, cocoa, cotton, silk and machines in the late nineteenth century when such concerns were flourishing. Young Reinhart had spent time abroad with the family business, in England besides China, Japan and India, and he spoke excellent English as well as French and German. His large, comfortable modern house surrounded by its gardens, up on the slopes of the Rychenberg, overlooked the pleasant town and valley, just around the corner from his brother Oscar's grander establishment.[30] The family also had a lakeside house at Greifensee, Flue, where Dent, JB and Mañuel de Falla stayed, 'Dans la Maison Ideale' as Falla put it.

Having met him at Salzburg, Dent had made sure that Reinhart was invited to the London conference that January. Reinhart was not simply a source of funding; he was a serious musician, a clarinettist and a good friend of musicians who regularly enjoyed his hospitality at Winterthur, including Paul Hindemith, who composed music for him and drew entertaining sketches in the Rychenberg guest-book. Dent ensured that he was appointed 'special representative of the Council on the Austrian sub-committee … to whom the practical organisation of the Salzburg Festival has been entrusted'.[31] Initially, Reinhart demurred, but allowed himself to be persuaded by Réti and Dent,[32] who wrote to Reinhart throughout that winter, always very care-

29 Dent, 'Plans for Salzburg', p. 698.

30 Both are still there. Werner's house is now the Music Conservatory and Oscar's now a museum, the Reinhart Collection.

31 WR 21/02/1923. Winterthur Kunstmuseum archive MK 352/40. All the Reinhart correspondence is here.

32 WR 22/02/1923 and 24/02/1923.

ful to observe the old-fashioned Swiss formalities, keeping a polite distance, all the time drawing him into the affairs of the society, in an inclusive, intimate vein, full of familiar names, building up trust by confiding in him a number of the current difficult issues going on.

> I have heard from other sources that the German Section is in a state of 'Krise' – and I think (this between ourselves and 'nicht amtlich') that the reason is that many people in Germany do not like Weissmann. However, it is their business, not ours, and if they don't like him they must get rid of him & send someone else. And there is obviously a good deal of jealousy between Weissmann & Bekker. Things might be just as bad in England – but I think we shall run our section more smoothly. We shall be delighted to have you as a member of the B.M.S. I will tell Mrs Balkwill to send you documents.
>
> with kindest regards yours sincerely Edward Dent[33]

Dent was doing the same with a reluctant Hermann Scherchen, mixing friendship with pragmatism to achieve the goals they shared. Reinhart appreciated what Dent was doing and played his own part with immense generosity of spirit; the big house at Rychenberg became a haven for musicians up to and including the next war. The guest-book records their appreciation, from Alma Moodie's expansive script to Paul Hindemith's cartoons; Alban Berg, de Falla; later, Rudolf Serkin and Adolph Busch; Sir Robert and Lady Mayer (Dorothy Moulton), younger Stewarts and Roothams from Cambridge, Lawrence Haward. Reinhart provided funding and the support most musicians appreciate, not just facilities for practising and relaxing, but genuine sympathy and understanding.

So the presidential persona was quickly established, an extension of Dent's natural unfailingly good manners, charm, diplomacy and wit. Years later, Heinz Tiessen wrote an appreciation of Dent's diplomatic skill and leadership qualities while conveying an internationalist outlook.[34]

❧ ❧ ❧

On another front, JB was kept busy all that winter and spring, liasing with the embryonic Spanish section in Madrid and Barcelona, bringing Falla into the fold beside Joaquin Turina and critic Alfonso Salazar. Dent, meanwhile, was writing to the efficient secretary of the British Music Society, Violet Balkwill, to Evans, to Reinhart, to Heller, to everyone involved with the Salzburg Festival, asking opinions, conveying information in an oblique way, but above all, making sure that everyone felt informed and part of the operation, a remarkable blend of the formal and informal.

33 WR 24/02/1923.

34 'Edward J. Dent, a born Prime Minister, slim and tall, really knew, by virtue of British understatement, how to lead the ISCM unobtrusively. Never did I hear him utter a loud word. With a diplomat's courtesy and a scholar's witty serenity, he stood above the fray at all times and pursued his policies, which at first could not assume tangible form owing to the ever-present threat of national rivalries.' Quoted in Haefeli, *IGNM*, p. 296.

> Saerchinger has written from Berlin asking urgently for information about the International, so that steps may be taken to organize for America & elsewhere. As the Contemporary Music Centre does not meet till October 10, don't you think it wd be very desirable that we shd get everything through at that meeting if possible, without having the matter referred to a sub-committee, then further considered at a later date?[35]
>
> I don't know how matters are going for the Ambassadors' Conference – but I told Miss Wadham to write to the Home Office about visas & permits for the 'enemy' delegates & hope that will go through … if you wd like to come & lunch at the Spanish … and talk over plans … I think we ought to consider very carefully the drawing up of our agenda paper, and a strict distinction (which some of our foreign delegates have not quite grasped) between what must be laid down & ratified formally as the constitution and rules of the society – and what we agree to as general principles of policy.[36]
>
> I was in London yesterday & saw Mrs Balkwill – wrote personally to 7 people asking for hospitality.[37]

'Germany is going to give trouble', Dent wrote to JB in February, 'internal quarrels are the reason: but they will throw the blame on me.'[38] In April, Dent was asking Clive, touring with the English Singers, to find out what people in Prague were saying about the ISCM.

> I rather fear the Czechs & Germans are quarrelling over the International in Prague – but I have had correspondence with Steinhard, and have written a little article specially for him. It is too tiresome this narrow nationalist egoism everywhere in the East! The Poles have just got a section going, and the secretary writes an absurd letter about national 'prestige'![39]

Letters of acceptance from Ansermet, Zemlinsky and Schoenberg all express their delight at being part of the society, but from the beginning, most of the really difficult decisions were thrown onto the president, and the first festival at Salzburg in 1923 amply demonstrated what could go wrong. Even before the actual festival, the Austrian Committee via Paul Stefan tried to touch Reinhart for yet more funding; Dent was angered, both at the fact that it had been done underhandedly, and that it imposed even more upon Reinhart's generosity, and he had to remonstrate. In that first year he was forced over and again to improvise his new and developing role as president, which included the need to be present far more than he had anticipated at the various functions. He hadn't expected that the Winterthur jury would require him, but his presence at any jury meeting quickly became an adopted principle: essential, in fact, as everyone quickly realised.

35 EE 28/09/1922. BL Add MS 7144.

36 EE 06/01/1923. BL Add MS 7144.

37 EE 10/01/1923. BL Add MS 7144.

38 JBT 24/02/1923.

39 CC 12/04/1923. The 'article' appeared in *Die Auftakt*.

> Reinhart is very anxious that I shd be there: and if I don't go Evans certainly will – and though he wd be quite reasonable, I think, I don't want the impression created that he is the real pivot of the Society! I have gone some way towards pacifying Paul Bekker: and now have to try to smooth the Czechs who are making trouble. I shall be represented after my martyrdom with an oil-can in my hand.[40]

At the same time, that winter of 1923, Dent was writing his 'Geschichte der englischen Musik seit 1880' for Guido Adler's book,[41] beside his usual articles for which he felt obliged to keep up with current concerts: Moger's, Vaughan Williams' Mass and Bantock's 'Vanity of Vanities' for which 'Ursula the Pig-Woman' Greville sang solos. Ogden had got him a contract to revise Streatfeild's standard book, *The Opera*; he was looking after Friedrich Perzynski[42] at Cambridge, and in his difficult company spotted many of the same problems he was finding with the International.

> he has a curiously German mind, wch comes out in various discussions: the German, especially when he is by way of being 'ein Gentleman' is always insisting on his rights, large or small. With them the emphasis is always on the 'noblesse': with us it is on the 'oblige' – They have no conception of duties towards their 'inferiors', only of the duties of the inferiors to them. We talked of museums and collections. P. hates museums and thinks they ought to be broken up & divided among the intellectual aristocrats capable of appreciating works of art ... 'when you possess a work of art', says P. 'you possess all that has gone to the making of it: you possess the artist; he is your slave; 'Sie beherrschen ihn'.[43]

In May, just before he was due to go off to Winterthur and feeling ill, he was desperately looking for a bit of calm.

> I think I had got into my usual state of overdoing things – too much work, too much alcohol, too much smoke – so I reduced all and am fairly straight again, especially with a warm sunny day! On the top of all this, endless worries with the International – I had to send out about a dozen telegrams abroad yesterday.[44]

Most of the jury so carefully, painstakingly assembled, had managed to find other pressing obligations to get in the way. 'I think the Zurich meeting will be postponed for a week', Dent wrote to JB:

> Goossens is captured by the BNOC: Ansermet by Diaghilev at Monte Carlo: Zemlinsky by the late Mr Mahler – curse his memory! and Scherchen by Paul Bekker. I have just got a letter from Weissmann – Bekker is 'halb Monomane, halb Primadonne' and apparently intriguing all he can against Weissmann and the Internat. Scherchen appears to be 'nationalist-communist' and a certain section

40 JBT 09/04/1923.

41 *Handbuch der Musikgeschichte*, vol. 2, *Die Moderne* (Berlin, 1924), pp. 1044–57; Haward, *Edward J. Dent: A Bibliography*, 90 (the 2nd edn). See below on the 'Elgar Hetz'.

42 Friedrich Perzynski (1877–1965), bookseller, specialist in Asian art; Dent corresponded with him for years.

43 JBT 09/04/1923.

44 JBT 02/05/1923.

attacks the Internat. as 'pacifist'. It is horribly annoying all this coming at the very last moment. The Czechs are making trouble too, I gather.[45]

That May the Alfred Einsteins were coming to England; Dent had hoped to see them but there was too little time. He had to go to Winterthur via Paris, where he met the French Committee, then took the night train on to Zurich; after that he intended to go on to Milan 'to see a friend of mine', then to Vienna. At the same time he was negotiating via JB to get the Spanish officially involved; with no official Spanish representative as yet, someone non-Spanish had to assume responsibility for presenting a Spanish work for consideration. He managed a few pleasant days at Geneva with Chester Purves, now based there, before going on to Italy to see various people in Milan and Turin – Farinelli and Gatti – about the fractious Italian section, before returning via Paris and the French section for his Cambridge lecture on 2 June. He and Purves had missed the last tram going back from the little opera at Ménières, so walked the 12 miles (19 km) back to Lausanne in the dark, to Reinhart's astonishment, but in fact, the peaceful walk had done him good.

Dent was sanguine about the jury: 'I think the Zurich committee will be extremely interesting to watch', he wrote to Clive:

If any English work passes their sieve at all I am inclined to put my money on an entirely dark horse. But as we have now 18 countries joined up and only 12 hours of music at Salzburg there will be a lot of disappointment.[46]

I reached Winterthur at 9.15 – Reinhart met me with the car & took me to his house – everything exquisite … a lovely bath! excellent lunch, & then the same aftn by car to Donaueschingen … The concerts on Thursday were most interesting. Scherchen was there & I straightened everything out with him … We had Hába's 4tet in 1/4 tones – a marvellous performance, but it sounded like an ordinary 4tet out of tune. The Prince was in great form & we had a very jolly evening at the hotel.

At Winterthur, the jury was inquorate because Zemlinsky was ill. Although in his article 'Plans for Salzburg', Dent had mentioned the need for back-up in such cases, it had been forgotten, but in the event, it doesn't seem to have mattered.

This villa is paradise – It is 8 miles from a station – on a lonely & lovely lake, with a distant view of snow mountains. Werner Reinhart & his brother Hans (poet) are here – both bachelors. Everything is perfect – the house so clean & white & polished that it seems a profanation to exist in it. I couldn't be more comfortable: and Reinhart being an East India merchant of colossal wealth is a connoisseur in coffee and pepper! Wellesz is in great form, and kept us in fits of laughter over his descriptions of Oxford & Cambridge. He is at present going rapidly through stacks of music – Tomorrow Caplet & Scherchen arrive: Ansermet Monday: Goossens Wednesday. Sonneck refuses altogether & I am pursuing Kramer by telegram. I thought it useless to try to get Salazar here at this short notice. I

45 *Ibid.*

46 CC 12/04/1923.

> feel optimistic on the whole & Wellesz is really very practical & understands everything.[47]
>
> We sat in Reinhart's warm and comfortable library and read scores of chamber music all day long. Suddenly Scherchen burst out excitedly, 'Who is this Walton?' ... Walton's First String Quartet was chosen unanimously.[48]

The Walton quartet was not yet published, the twenty-year-old William Walton then almost completely unknown, in spite of the notoriety of *Façade*, his collaboration with the Sitwells the previous year.[49]

> It was given a preliminary performance in London, where it called forth shrieks of horror from the conservative critics, who thought it quite 'unrepresentative' of British music, and asked why a work of Elgar had not been chosen instead ... Wellesz is here and we are very keen to get some Spanish work in: in the last instance we shall probably leave a space free and ask Goossens or Ansermet to choose a Spanish work.[50]

The Salzburg Festival the first week in August was to open with Schoenberg, Berg and Bartók in the Mozarteum, followed by days of new chamber music. Beside the Walton there was Prokofiev, Erdmann, Florent Schmitt, Janáček, Honegger, Milhaud, Malipiero, Poulenc, Kodály, Busoni, Ravel and Stravinsky. 'We got some good programmes chosen, and all went well', Dent wrote to JB from Venice, where he had retreated for a few days after the jury meetings.

> I expect there will be a great outcry in London, as nothing by Bax was chosen: Bliss rhapsody: no songs at all – though possibly Bliss clarinet songs may be added: and (as I foresaw, but didn't say a word about it) Willie Walton's quartet! ... Willie's 4tet will of course bring the Sitwells and I hope they will stir up all their friends to come.[51]
>
> I hope to goodness the London people will have done something about Salzburg in my absence: but Edw. Evans is very slack & Mrs Balkwill says nothing is done if I am away. But I felt I must have my holiday or I shd die.[52]

He needed that brief respite. For the next two months there was nothing but trouble coming his way, all from the ISCM. In spite of his efforts that May, his fears were vindicated about the lack of Italian works in the programme, and he spent the next year, up to the 1925 Venice ISCM Festival, trying to patch things up with the Italians. 'It had been curiously difficult from the first to get a section formed in Italy', he noted in retrospect:

47 JBT 12/05/1923.

48 Dent, 'Looking Backward', p. 279.

49 Haefeli is very sniffy about Dent's account, calling it 'one-sided and fragmented' – which it probably is – and arguing that such an important historical moment should have been more carefully documented. *IGNM*, p. 59.

50 JBT 12/05/1923.

51 JBT 24/05/1923.

52 JBT 24/05/1923.

> a French musician had even said that it would be utterly impossible, as the Italians were all much too jealous of each other ever to form a committee ... They refused to take part in the Festival to be held at Salzburg, and said they would withdraw such works as had been chosen.

The whole massive, ambitious, hopeful, fragile, infuriating enterprise kept all Dent's improvised diplomatic skills on constant alert.

> The International proceeds from worry to worry. The Italian section has retired altogether in a huff & will have nothing more to do with the society. Weissmann is in London & told me that Gatti had written to Busoni – I suppose to try & get his support for the move: but Busoni told Weissmann that if he was well enough (wch I very much doubt, from what W. says) he would be delighted to play the Fantasia with Petri at Salzburg – So I shall tell Gatti that we intend to keep the Italian stuff in the programmes, out of loyalty to the jury, and the invocheremo la cortesia di altre sezioni nazionali per incaricarsene .[53]

One attendant problem with this conciliatory approach was that each national section was supposed to pay for the performance of its own works, so if any Italian music was to be played, who would pay for it? 'I think the French singers will take on the Malipiero songs, and possibly Goossens would play the Castelnuovo. He has volunteered to play the Valses Bourgeoises of Berners with somebody.' But it took time and excruciating trouble to write the endless letters, make the expensive telephone calls. And now England was throwing up difficulties: since Bax had not been chosen, Eaglefield Hull was giving an alternative concert with Harriet Cohen playing the Bax concerto. The French were also heaving more demands Dent's way:

> having got 6 composers on the list (more than any other country) [the French] are now trying to insinuate a 7th (Erik Satie). Prunières told me in Paris that they had no money & suggested that England shd raise the £100 demanded by Fleury & the other 4 French wind players. Reinhart offered the Swiss wind for nothing so England accepted them, the more so as Wellesz wrote a confidential letter saying that they feared anti-French demonstrations at Salzburg. I saw the secretary of the Austrian Embassy about it & he said he wd write to Salzburg about the business. Of course we could not say a word about this to the French – please don't let it out – and now Prunières writes that the French have raised the money for Fleury & Co. Austria works well, I think: ditto Czechoslovakia, who also offered to play Florent Schmitt for the French. That is who we want.[54]

Then the Germans made a fuss, sending Dent 'verbose et grandis epistola [verbose and overblown letters] with all sorts of formal protests about the infraction of &&x&y of the Londoner Satzung etc etc, etc, but state quite definitely that they do not wish to repudiate the programmes, as to damage the Festival. So I have written a very friendly letter back explaining my difficulties, sympathising with their griev-

53 we shall invoke the courtesy of other national sections to take care of it. JBT 20/06/1923.

54 *Ibid.*

ances and thanking them for their loyal cooperation'.[55] Small wonder that he threw everything at an article he was writing for Prunières, on internationalism in music:

> I showed it to Weissmann, who was much tickled. I said that 'Internationalism' as a doctrine didn't exist: it was the normal state of educated minds. Nationalism was the perpetual enemy of pleasant human intercourse.[56]

Salzburg was a disaster only narrowly averted, no thanks to the mainly Viennese committee officially in charge. By July the London office was anxious about inertia at the other end. 'Things are in horrible confusion',[57] Dent wrote to JB from Vienna a week before the festival, staying at his old hotel, the Tegetthoff. He had found musical Vienna in confusion, a conspicuous absence of ISCM supporters owing to illness or whatever, and the rest quivering in terror at either the Universal Edition or local critics Korngold & Co.; Heller, responsible for the business of the concert-management, was away on holiday in Venice. 'Our local committee has collapsed entirely',[58] Dent wrote in desperation. The funding was in disarray, the musicians not sorted; there was a massive drama with a local diva, Mme Charles Cahier, about singing some Kilpenen songs. No pianos had been booked for Busoni's two-piano Fantasia: 'If I hadn't remembered the 2 pianos we probably should have had to do without them.'[59] Only Heller's assistant, Rudolf Bing, 'who fortunately combined both efficiency and elegance' was able to help ensure that the programme could go through, although he had been told nothing about what was supposed to happen. 'He is a very competent lad', Dent wrote to Clive, 'but he wants somebody to keep him straight and if I hadn't been here the programmes would have been the most complete hash!'[60]

> It was lucky I came here: the programme was in utter confusion. Wellesz went off to the country some time ago … Stefan is a broken reed, always balancing on the tight rope of the Universal Edition … they are all terrified of old Korngold & the other conservatives, because all these people like Stefan depend on Hertzka & the U.E for their daily bread. Damisch is hopelessly ill: Reti has had an operation & is only just out of hospital. There remains Pisk & Beckert: but both tied all day to the UE office … Pisk is a good soul & comes in occasionally to help. … We have had to make revisions of the programme, and alter things every day … the fall of the mark will make the German position more & more difficult. They are always telegraphing to say that some person can't play & that they have hopes of getting someone else. However 5/6 of the programme is quite safe.[61]

55 *Ibid.*

56 *Ibid.* I cannot find the article; it may not have been published.

57 JBT 17/07/1923.

58 CC 26/07/1923.

59 JBT 27/07/1923.

60 CC 26/07/1923. Bing later ran the Metropolitan Opera House in New York.

61 JBT 27/07/1923.

Then there were nationalist protests by pan-German anti-Semites to contend with: 'There are some fears of a Hakenkreuz [swastika] Antisemitic, anti-foreigner & particularly anti-French demonstration on the part of the local population: but I hope to have a talk with the Salzburg government representative on Tuesday.'[62] The protest – threatening stink-bombs if the Czech songs were performed – was stopped, simply because the Czech section compromised by having the songs sung in German. When Dent appealed to them, the local authorities did nothing, also earning another black mark from Dent with their mean refusal to let the German Hindemith Quartet off the extortionate visitors' tax.

> My only fear is that there may be no audience. For that the political situation is largely responsible. Even a year ago we should have had a lot of Germans & Austrians: it was just then that the Krone fell so badly to where it has stayed steady. I hear that yesterday the German Mark was at 2 millions to the £![63]

Werner Reinhart came to the rescue again, but, having undermined the festival in principle, the local forces were at work to set up alternatives. Korngold had published a 'scornful attack'[64] on the new ISCM, calling it a new 'Gunpowder Plot' on the part of the London office to take over German music, which threw the Austrian section into a panic.

> Our festival at Salzburg is to be followed by a counter festival, organized by that odious person Wilhelm Gross, and that idiot Korngold. The Universal Edition is behind them. I call it the festival of the Lokal-Grössen und Universal-Kleinigkeiten [local greats and Universal trivialities]. Our committee want me to make a speech at our first concert, or give a lecture, in order to take the wind out of the sails of Richard Specht who is going to lecture against us on 'Wien musikalische Gegenwart'.[65]

But Dent managed to score a few public points against Dr Korngold:

> Stefan insisted on my making a speech in reply to this article, and I was surprised to find the room completely full. I was much amused to observe Dr Korngold's sudden astonishment – he was a conspicuous figure in the audience – when I remarked incidentally that the whole-tone scale was nothing new and had been employed by English composers in the days of the Pulververschwörung [Gunpowder Plot].[66]

At the last minute before the opening concert, Dent walked through an 'empty hall' into an 'empty artists' room' and 'seriously wondered whether either artists or audience would arrive at all'. He wrote to JB:

62 *Ibid.*

63 CC 26/07/1923.

64 Dent, 'Looking Backward', p. 280.

65 CC 26/07/1923.

66 Dent, 'Looking Backward' p. 280. Korngold remembered this incident in his memoirs.

> Well, as Marcellina says, 'marriages have been broken off at the church door before now' and so it may be with the voluptuous nuptials of curiosity & originality! But I wish you were going to be at Salzburg – for I am badly in need of someone like you or Steuart who is a safe stand-by. These other people will do a good deal, but they so often let one down quite callously at the most critical moment.[67]

'I think Salzburg was quite a success,' Dent wrote to Clive when it was over:

> It was appallingly exhausting for me, and lasted on for me 2 or 3 days longer, as Dr Springer & I had to write up the minutes of the Conference. … I didn't listen to the music much, as I was too tired with the conference & general worries – but on the whole I enjoyed it more than I expected. I am coming round to Stravinsky! The Busoni Fantasia was great: Arthur Bliss's Rhapsody a great refreshment to tired ears, and Kodály's violoncello sonata exciting beyond description. The programmes improved as they went on – the 1st was good, the 2nd & 3rd – rather depressing: Sunday's the 4th put everybody in a good humour, even old Dr Korngold! … at 3 Casella got the Belgian 4tet to play Malipiero's Rispetti & Strambotti 4tet and his own.[68]
>
> I do feel that in spite of all troubles the International Society is now very firmly established. we practically made Casella withdraw his Italian protest & apologize. He had to admit that it was quite unjustified & that it was written dans un moment de mauvaise humeur [in a moment of ill humour]. And he wrote an apology to Scherchen, whom he had attacked in letters & who had been attacked in Italian papers. I thought it was something of an achievement on my part to make an Italian fascist apologize to a German Communist! like Papageno – I never knew I was so strong! … the idea has got about, even among responsible members of the Society, that I was its creator, wch I certainly was not: and among our enemies the idea that the Society is primarily English & dominated by London in English interests: which is also untrue. One reason why things were in such a muddle this year was because I refused to dominate.[69]

The Poles had said much the same, while the Germans had only implied it. 'I said to the delegates, and I have had to say it again at almost every meeting: "None of us has any rights – we have only duties."'

Salzburg gave Dent ideas about possible future festivals, which he and Wellesz were invited to discuss with a group of city fathers. Far more to his taste were invitations from Max Reinhardt to dine with him and Lady Diana Cooper, and to go to a private dress rehearsal of *Le Malade Imaginaire* at Schloss Leopoldskron. The Festspielhausgemeinde people, all very young, 'seem to swallow me whole', talking excitedly about future productions of Mozart he might do, their enthusiastic support in complete contrast with the Salzburg officialdom. At the official meeting, Dent threw out wonderful, rich ideas which included different theatre groups, marionette theatre, church services, peasant and costume shows, 'publish it in February and

67 JBT 27/07/1923. The 'voluptuous nuptials' is a reference to an article JB's Spanish friend d'Ors had written on Mozart.

68 CC 14/08/1923.

69 *Ibid.*

March and send it out to all the tourist agencies of Europe and America. My suggestion was received with howls of derision; it was absolutely impossible!'[70] The next festival was divided into two parts, taking advantage of the Czech centenary celebrations of Smetana to give three orchestral concerts at Prague at the end of May. Salzburg would host the ISCM chamber music again, but for the last time.

> I expect the festival of 1924 will be at Prague. It is a most worrying matter. If we have it at Salzburg people say it is too far to come: if we have it at Prague or Zurich the Austrians say it is prohibitively expensive on account of the exchange. I suppose I shall be re-elected as chairman: anyway I shall have learned something by this year's experience.[71]

Now, wherever, Dent was in a much better position to anticipate trouble. With infinite patience he had persuaded the Italians back into the fold; the new Italian section started up in September under the unlikely leadership of poet Gabriele d'Annunzio, with Casella 'the most loyal and helpful of co-operators. The three Italian festivals, which were perhaps the most generally successful of all our meetings, owed more to his energy and enthusiasm than I can adequately express.'[72]

The new ISCM changed Dent's life, giving it a new focus and purpose. It also changed the dynamics of Dent's friendships. Within two years Clive Carey was off to take a job in Australia – finally to get away from his mama, Dent joked with JB. Clive had always depended a great deal on Dent's support and friendship, with some financial help; perhaps he needed distance to find out what he really could do on his own. Dent had learned to exercise the public persona he had developed all his life which allowed him the freedom to do and say what he liked without attracting attention, always polite and accommodating, but increasingly at a terrible cost to himself.

1923–1926

> Few people realise what an immense amount of work was needed to set up an organization which finally comprised twenty-five countries. Dent had to deal with the local branches of all these countries. He had to settle difficulties which arose among their members. He had to prepare and attend the meetings of the members of the International Jury, which assembled each year somewhere in Europe to select works for performance from the compositions sent in by the local sections. He had to remain in touch with the rising generation of composers and, finally, he had to prevent a break-down of the Society when Germany and other countries refused any further co-operation with an internationally minded organization.[73]

Given its constant internal squabbles, the political climate, the raging inflation, and the rise of fascism, the ISCM festivals with their conspicuously high musical

70 Dent, 'Looking Backward', p. 281.

71 JBT 27/07/1923.

72 Dent, 'Looking Backward', p. 282.

73 Wellesz, 'E.J. Dent and the International Society for Contemporary Music', p. 207.

standards were nothing less than miraculous. The presidential job was accruing all kinds of responsibilities as the organisation itself gained momentum and confidence, and Dent became its lynchpin and diplomat; it was exhausting, and no coincidence that Dent's chronic health problems over the next thirty years began at Salzburg. Even apart from the ISCM, Dent was ferociously busy, still writing for 'Foxy's' *Music & Letters*, trying to drum up Italian interest in a centenary project on Scarlatti, and after Busoni's death that year, beginning the laborious research on a biography besides rewriting what became *The Foundations of English Opera* and his short study, *Terpander, or Music and the Future*, and collaborating on *A Dictionary of Modern Music & Musicians* (1924), writing its preface and a complicated article on 'Harmony'. He was also editing *Dido and Aeneas* and the Mozart *Requiem* for his new acquaintance, young Hubert Foss,[74] now establishing the music side of Oxford University Press.[75] While his active involvement with the Old Vic was on hold, he wrote two articles for *The Old Vic Magazine*[76] and helped launch other new opera projects, at Bristol and at Birmingham, besides a production of *Dido and Aeneas* at Münster. He was still on committees of the British Music Society, the Drama League, the Old Vic, while keeping an eye on the re-formed IMG. The ISCM was proving less an anchor than yet another self-induced responsibility to yearn to escape from.

After Salzburg, Dent joined Lawrence Haward in Vienna to lecture there at 'Mr F.S. Marvin's Summer School of Unity & Progress'[77] on 'Music in Relation to Human Progress and the Theatre as Synthesis of the Arts'.

> My suggestion at Vienna was that the dynamic arts have a higher value – and that the static arts constantly try to create an illusion of dynamism (?!) – to suggest motion, as in baroque architecture, perhaps in Gothic too: and critics perpetually talk of the 'rhythm' of a picture[78]

Although he disparaged it as being vague ('gasbag lecture'), the lecture marked a return to musical aesthetics and an excuse to travel with Lawrence again. 'I dream vaguely of … going out to Italy at the end of Sept', Dent had written to JB in July, 'and staying perhaps 3 or 4 months in Rome. But I doubt if my finances will stand the strain: the International will ruin me!'[79] Real income from his regular journalism was drying up, mostly because the ISCM, however promising and satisfying, was already eating into Dent's time and his purse. Ever generous with either, he continued to disburse, 10 pounds of his own money, together with 50 pounds from the

74 Hubert Foss (1899–1953), composer, editor, brother of William.

75 Haward, *Edward J. Dent: A Bibliography*, 26–46. p. 3 notes that these OUP editions included '(1) a preface on operas, librettos, and the nature of operatic translations … (2) an introduction dealing with the history and story of the particular opera and, in some cases, a brief life of the composer; (3) a list of characters; and (4) a note on first performances'.

76 *Ibid.*, 191: 'Mozart at Salzburg' (November 1922) and 'English Opera' (May 1926).

77 JBT 20/06/1923.

78 LH 19/10/1924.

79 JBT 17/07/1923.

BMS, to help shore up the struggling German section.[80] Another 50 pounds went into the fund for Steuart Wilson's ongoing lessons with Jean de Reszke.

But the vision of finding some solid theatre project to harness all his production ideas, translations and energies continued to exercise him; most came to nothing or dissolved after brief spells of success. Dent's initial hopes and enthusiasm of collaboration with Max Reinhardt had quickly faded: 'I don't think Reinhardt is interested in anything except his own ideas', the music to Reinhardt's productions he found to be 'badly arranged, badly scored & badly played.' Although new opera and theatre projects continued to heave into life back in England, Dent found most of these unsatisfactory for various reasons. From 1923 to 1926, Dent continued to collaborate loosely with producers like young Jack Gordon[81] or Philip Napier Miles,[82] hoping to revive the Carl Rosa Opera Company at Bristol, or Barry Jackson:[83]

> He has the money and the position in the theatrical world; he is very keen on just the same sort of scheme, and he is the kind of man that I like enormously and could work with; but I think all I should do with him would be what I have done at the Vic or at least might have done if Barry had been there instead of Lilian.[84]

His own thoughts on the subject are inconsistent and/or disingenuous: in one letter he will aver that he is 'incompetent to produce'; in another enthusing about producing *Zauberflöte* at Stollbrunn, enthusiasm always clashing with whatever limitations are uppermost in his mind.

'Venice in September', Dent wrote to JB, 'will be a hotbed of iniquity (wch will be amusing) and gossip (wch will be dangerous)'.[85] Eventually it would be a kind of King's on the Lido that September, but for the first week on his own Dent was grumpy and bored, complaining to JB about the heavy rain, the stench, the preponderance of English people and mosquitoes, not to mention the expense and stuffiness of 'correct' places like the Regina, the old quiet shattered by the new motorboats, the Goldoni and Gozzi theatre replaced by 'rather trifling and stupid plays in verse', the music largely absent. Then they all arrived: Eddy Harman and John Denman, Scho with one Griffiths of Trinity, Dennis Arundell 'with Mumma and Sheppy',[86] 'Michael' Haslam; Chester Purves with Roderick Meiklejohn. Timmy Jekyll arrived

80 Werner Reinhart 25/07/1923.

81 John Barrit Gordon 'Jack' (1898–1978), Repton and New College, Oxford. One of Dent's closest friends and correspondents; director at Sadler's Wells.

82 Philip Napier Miles (1865–1935), composer of several operas, including *Westward Ho!* and *Markheim*. The Bristol festival carried on for several years; a production of Falla's *Master Peter's Puppet Show* was put on there.

83 Barry Jackson (1879–1961), later knighted for services to the theatre. He founded the Birmingham Repertory Theatre, which involved Dent and many of his circle, and often worked with both the Royal Opera House and what became the Royal Shakespeare Company, Stratford-upon-Avon.

84 JSW 29/11/1923.

85 JBT 17/07/1923.

86 'Sheppy' was J.F. Shepherdson, music master at the Leys School in Cambridge, who ran the Cambridge Philharmonic.

FIGURE 10. Hotel Bucintoro, Venice. Author's photograph.

on the 15th 'looking 10 years younger & incredibly healthy', dividing his time, Dent noted with amusement, between his aged and correct aunt Eden and the House for Dissolute Sailors run by a Mr Bolt. Dent was transformed.

Settling into the Bucintoro, editing proofs JB had sent him of Denis Browne's songs,[87] Dent sank into his favourite amused detachment at all the little dramas going on. Suddenly – with the right company – the food was excellent, the theatre amusing. Timmy was in his usual ebullient form, chasing after everything in sight, from 'sullen and unattractive' little Antonio and his waxed rollups, to a Hungarian pianist whose compositions he insisted Dent hear. Nights at the 'vaudeville' theatre, restaurants, swimming on the Lido; holding an ISCM Festival in Venice became an attractive possibility. 'The other night as I was walking along the Procuratia a group of young Italians called out "Tutankamen!" at me. I was startled, but much amused.'[88]

All that relaxed time, thoughts of opera projects continued to exercise him: 'I am much interested in the Carl Rosa idea', he wrote to JB:

> but still sceptical, knowing more or less what opera managers are ... Hudson of the Vic is about the best I have struck so far: but I think I frighten all of them. Theatre people as far as I have known them in England are often anxious to get ideas from me, but they always expect to have something ready made.[89]

Even as Dent's toyed with the idea of running an opera company to his own standards, Cambridge began to make more specific appeals, throwing even more into the rich, uneven mix of his life.

> Boris & Henry Moule want me to start lecturing again at Cambridge ... Frank Birch is very keen that the Marlowe shd strike out a new line by doing La Vida es Sueño.[90]

JB's growing Spanish interests were becoming a source of inspiration for the Cambridge crew as much as to the ISCM. In Spain, he had gently drawn in Falla, Joachim Turina and Filipe Pedrell, even engaging some of the more conservative people like Alfonso Salazar, but only eventually forming a Spanish section. He hoped for Falla's friend Pedro Morales to be the Spanish representative, and persuaded critic Eugenio d'Ors[91] to come to Salzburg:

87 JBT 19/09/1923. 'I have been through the proofs of Gratiana and have noticed only a few mistakes – accidentals and [?] contradicted etc [sic]. I am suggesting that the beginning shd be marked sonore ed un poco forte: I think that really best expresses what Denis meant. I expect he first wrote f: then modified it with poco – which doesn't mean what he meant, un poco – and lastly amplified it with sonore. By the way, does the word sonore exist? shouldn't it be sonoro?'

88 JBT 22/09/1923.

89 *Ibid.*

90 JBT 27/07/1923.

91 Eugenio d'Ors (1881–1954), Catalan writer and critic.

> His friend Eugenio d'Ors is coming to Salzburg and has written a delightful article about it in wch he says that Mr Dent is preparing in the rococo alcove of Mozart the voluptuous nuptials of Curiosity and Originality![92]

JB's friendship with Falla had flourished from their first serendipitous meeting in 1919, and opened up for him much more than Spanish music. Throughout 1920 their long conversations had touched on many mutual pleasures besides music and poetry, particularly an interest in marionette theatre as a theatrical medium to express the odd or the unacceptable. All those conversations, ideas floated at leisure, a creative process as unlike the average committee meeting as it is possible to be, were bearing rich and exotic fruit. Falla's marionette idea became *El Retablo del Maestre Pedro* (*Master Peter's Puppet Show*) and was taken up eagerly, first in Madrid in March 1923, then later that same year in Paris at the Princesse de Polignac's salon, at Napier Miles's Bristol Opera Festival and later still, in conjunction with the 1926 ISCM Festival at Zurich.[93] Falla's music had been chosen by the jury, in spite of there being no official Spanish section yet, Falla himself coaxed out of his reclusive state to compose again on an international stage.

❧ ❧ ❧

> The most exciting piece of news is that Stanford has announced his intention of resigning the Professorship in April.[94]

Three of Stanford's former pupils were in the frame: Charles Wood, Vaughan Williams and Dent, beside the expectant Cyril Rootham. Dent had heard about it from Hugh Allen, although nothing was official until that December. Stanford had been ill, and Allen had spent weeks trying to convince him to stand down and take it easy. At the end of March 1924, he died.

It was the end of an era. Stanford had been an exciting and exacting if irascible teacher, 'but he was always right'.[95] In the 1890s, just before Dent came up to Cambridge, Stanford had begun the task of establishing music in the academic world; thirty years on, Stanford's visions of professional performance with a nationally funded opera were still remote. That he had clung to his Professorship for so long was almost entirely due to constant financial need, but without his physical presence the Music Faculty had stultified. In the meantime, as Dent observed, the Royal College of Music under Allen had assumed the role Dent had hoped for Cambridge, but things were already changing. In Lent term 1924, the University Senate moved to revise the professorial statutes which had allowed an absentee professor for so long, to the detriment of the subject: 'It was not the fault of the Professor; it was the fault of the system under which he had been elected, a system

92 CC 26/07/1923. 'Voluptuous nuptials' became a shared joke.

93 For a fuller discussion of these Spanish ideas, see Anstee, *An Unlikely Spanish Don*, pp. 113ff.

94 EJD–CC 09/11/1923.

95 Trend, 'Dent', quoting Dent.

which had been found to be unsatisfactory.'[96] When Charles Wood was eventually elected in 1924, the stipend was increased to 500 pounds, and the Professor was expected to give more lectures and to make himself available to his students for at least two hours a week.

For weeks that October 1923, Dent pondered the question, finally putting down his thoughts into a long letter to Clive after long talks with Boris Ord and Hugh Allen, chair of the Electors.

> The Board of Electors – the V.C. Bond, Hadow, Tom Marshall, Allen, H.F. Stewart & probably others … will in all probability vote as Allen tells them … The 4 obvious candidates, as he said, are V.W., Wood, Rootham and myself. Ten years ago VW told me that nothing wd induce him to be professor, or to teach at all … I said to Allen "If you want a distinguished composer who will always be a great inspiring force in Cambridge music, then V.W.; if you want a competent teacher of Mus B subjects, Wood: if you want a man who will be energetic and raise money to build a music-school and endow it, Rootham."[97]

He postulated what he felt most important in the appointment, that the Professor ought to 'reside' here and 'make Cambridge his first consideration', rather than serving as a 'nursery-ground' for the Royal College of Music. Of course, the contrarian in Dent had to have the last words, suggesting that they appoint Arthur Bliss:

> I don't at this moment want to be Professor at all. It wd have the advantage of relieving me from journalism, which I do very much against the collar. But I want to write books: and I want to concentrate on international things and to be a free lance: to feel that I can go to Prague & Vienna and Rome etc whenever I like … Seriously, I think VW will be elected, if he consents to stand. At any rate the wish is father to the thought.[98]

He wrote in a similar contradictory vein to Steuart Wilson, having discussed the various operatic ventures going on outside Cambridge: 'you will see that if they do elect me, it is hardly possible for me to go and live at Bristol and run an opera-house'.[99]

It was a question which unsettled him deeply, even though he had known it was coming. Dent badly wanted to be in a position to draw his friends back into his benevolent orbit, but equally, he was aware of his underlying restlessness, his constant need for an open back door, for control. So, keeping all options open, and making sure that his presence was felt and – more – wanted, Michaelmas term was spent in Cambridge, with the MDS Calderon, teaching, chatting with Boris Ord about programmes,[100] examining Dennis Arundell's Fellowship dissertation on Purcell, 'a very solid piece of research, and must have meant an enormous lot of

96 Report of the Council of the Senate on the Regulations for the Professorship of Music (25 February 1924), CUL 39.10.(1). Cited in Dibble, *Charles Villiers Stanford*, p. 462.

97 CC 09/11/1923

98 *Ibid.*

99 JSW 29/11/1923.

100 JBT 17/07/1923.

work'.[101] With the death of Francis Jenkinson, the post of University Librarian had gone to Dent's old friend Alwyn Scholfield, who immediately declared himself keen to build up the music sections of the library. 'Sayle tells me he gets £1200 a year. I gather that he intends to do all he can for the music department there, which is satisfactory.'[102] 'No further news about the Professorship', Dent wrote to Clive in December, 'except that I'm told that Boris is suggesting Adrian Boult as a solution of the domestic problem … But I'm sick of the whole business.'[103]

Although that winter Dent conscientiously kept up with current music in and around London, it was more out of loyalty than real desire. Clive had finally decided to emigrate to Australia, so there was less of a practical edge to Dent's listening. Besides, his musical standards had changed, his mind on the next ISCM 'Smetana show' at Prague in late May, so Royal College of Music performances of Woods's opera *Pecksniff* were 'too Wagnerian & solemn', and Gibbs's new opera *The Blue Peter*, with 'a most improper libretto' by Clifford Bax:

> too much like Sullivan: too beefy & hearty & Victorian … Gibbs' score was too filthy for words: badly composed, badly orchestrated and abominably played … The right stuff is undoubtedly there but I gave him the worst dressing down he has had in his life.[104]

After a leisurely trip via La Selva, checking in on Steuart and his growing family at Villefranche, Dent himself was in Rome that March to review the current music, but really to escape the cold, stuffy English winter, with warmer weather, better food and wine, and the more relaxed and open homosocial life; everything he did not wish to give up for the Professorship. It was very cheap to live well there; he was going out every night, in such congenial company as John Beavan with 'another cheerful young Englishman', and a young Spaniard who recited 'amorous Spanish poems to me', he wrote to JB; lunches with Raymond Lawford and writer Norman Douglas, 'most charming, and extremely friendly'.[105]

> I have not begun work at Scarlatti yet, nor have I called on Casella and Respighi … I feel very well and very lazy, as usual … Schönberg is here: I met him at a party which Casella gave, Malipiero also. I like Malipiero very much, and his wife, who is English; they insist on my going to see them at Asolo when I go to Venice.[106]

Jean Fleury playing in *Pierrot Lunaire*, Thornley Gibson, Geoffrey Scott: in such 'agreeable' company Dent relaxed, and in spite of 'wretched' weather, he could slip into the Vatican Library to copy a Morales Kyrie for JB, while planning a weekend in Spoleto, then on to Bologna to copy another MS and persuade Respighi to do a

101 CC 09/11/1923.

102 JSW 29/11/1923.

103 CC 13/12/1923.

104 *Ibid.*

105 Norman Douglas (1868–1952), writer of *South Wind*, bisexual hedonist, exactly the kind of louche character Dent loved to seek out.

106 JBT 26/03/1924.

Scarlatti bicentenary instead of celebrating 'that charlatan Palestrina' and Rootham to do some Scarlatti at Cambridge.

'The International gives me much trouble', Dent wrote to Clive that April.

> The French are the mutineers this time, and I had to go to Florence for a night last week, catching a filthy cold in pouring rain, to have a talk with Prunières. … I have cultivated the Germans, Austrians and Italians personally (the Italian section is now in good working order) but I have neglected the French rather hoping that Edwin Evans would look after that department.[107]

This begs a few questions on Dent's often awkward working relationship with Evans, who was putting forward his own performers without consultation, while neglecting other areas. A flying visit to Paris in mid-June for the meeting of the French section was now necessary for practical and political reasons, to get some decisions out of them. 'The French section is almost a fiction: a committee & nothing else.' Prunières was 'muddle-headed', Roussel 'intelligent' but absent, Florent Schmitt a 'decayed owl', Aubert 'a decayed vulture', Malherbe 'of a stupidity indescribable'; the only 'bright, clear-headed' one who could get things done was Roland Maussel.[108]

> The International, I see, can only be run on a basis of personal friendship; and I begin to wonder whether it is now my duty to devote myself to cultivating that in various countries. What I should prefer to do is to settle down quietly somewhere and write books![109]

Again and again Dent stresses the 'personal friendship' in his ISCM work, harnessing the trusted networks, not unlike the trusted homosexual networks, he could rely on for support in any crisis. Dent was arguably far more successful as a diplomat than as a politician; he inclined to that view himself. All that spring and early summer he was kept on the move, from Bologna to Venice, Milan, Paris, Vienna in May before going on to the Prague International Festival (31 May–2 June), making contact with various interested parties along the way, smoothing the path of the ISCM with his charm and the simple fact that he was seen to be taking such trouble.

The Prague Festival, in Dent's view, exemplified the ISCM spirit, providing not only a 'magnificent orchestra' but a great deal of 'music of all kinds'.

> At the Prague Festival, a very serious-minded German composer told me that he was astonished at the ease with which the Czech orchestra read his work at sight. 'well, naturally,' I replied, 'the Czechs are the best musicians in Europe.' He was – 'sprachlos' [speechless].[110]

Every concert was full to overflowing; the mostly Czech audiences couldn't get enough music, from ten in the morning to the small hours: concertos by Prokofiev

[107] CC 10/04/1924.

[108] JBT 19/06/1924.

[109] CC 10/04/1924

[110] Dent, 'Introduction', p. 6. Unpublished, in KCA.

and Szymanowski, Schoenberg's *Erwartung* and what Dent called 'the most interesting item', Satie's *Socrate*. 'Interesting' was often Dentspeak for contentious:

> this choice of the jury very nearly lost us the French section. They had not sent it in, and entirely refused to pay for the performance. By way of further protest, they organized a concert of French music on their own, after the official concerts were over.[111]

These these first orchestral concerts of the ISCM brought heavy criticism from some of the Germans, since one stated aim of the society had been specifically chamber music, but it opened up other avenues to find real alternatives to Salzburg.

> Salzburg, to tell the honest truth, was never very friendly to us, and I was glad when we abandoned it altogether, the local interest of Salzburg was purely commercial.[112]
>
> It is very desirable to take the festival away from the atmosphere of the German and Austrian set; I like them personally and bear no ill will even to old Korngold, whose attacks on me are always one of the delights of the festival; but as a body the German and Austrian critics easily get into the way of thinking that the whole festival exists for them, as one meets exactly the same crowd at Salzburg, at Prague, at Donaueschingen and at Frankfurt or wherever the annual Tonkünstler fest happens to be.[113]

❧ ❧ ❧

On 27 July 1924, just before the Salzburg Festival, Busoni died, aged fifty-eight. The last time Dent had seen him, in 1922, Busoni had entrusted him with the biography, and although he had known for some time that Busoni was not well, since he had not been able to play his Fantasia at Salzburg in 1923, it was still a shock.

> 'My dear Dent, how pleased you will be when I am dead and gone, for then you will be able to look at me from a historical point of view.' Needless to say, no answer was expected; after this disconcerting remark Busoni, as always, covered up his tracks with his characteristic roar and rumble of explosive laughter.[114]

Busoni had been a keen supporter of the ISCM, and with his death a major force in Dent's life for over twenty years was gone. He was both mentor and friend, without apparent emotional complications – astonishingly, since Dent had long been in love with him. Dent's desire to 'understand all music' had its source in Busoni and his own quest for musical perfection, while at the same time Dent had recognised the limitations of the perfectionist, his own limitations and his strengths reflected in Busoni. But it was years before Dent had time to do more than think about the

111 Dent, 'Looking Backward', p. 283. See also Haefeli, *IGNM*, p. 96.

112 Dent, 'Introduction', p. 6.

113 LH 28/08/1924.

114 Dent, *Busoni*, Preface, p. x.

biography, which became a labour of love culminating in a study of Busoni's unfinished opera *Doktor Faust*,[115] which Dent saw as Busoni's swan-song, expressing his perpetual search for perfection, the impossible ideal, so little understood: 'the will for knowledge and for impact, which vanquishes death and the Devil'.[116] Dent certainly understood all that.

❧ ❧ ❧

The Salzburg ISCM Festival that August was another success, even if 'the English contributions went badly'. Dent privately blamed Evans for interfering with the singers and for not getting the English section to provide any back-up. Thanks to Reinhart's secretary, H.W. Draber, the English songs – Heseltine's 'Curlew' and Vaughan Williams' 'On Wenlock Edge' for string quartet and tenor – were both done at short notice by 'an American singer from Vienna … I believe really in order that they might be sung badly, as the Austrian section were annoyed at their being chosen'.[117] Dent felt that the string quartet from Zurich played the piece well; in fact, the Swiss had made fundamental contributions to the overall success, Werner Reinhart playing his clarinet alongside Draber.[118] He thought the Stravinsky Octet the best thing at the festival, 'played by people from Frankfurt under Scherchen … a most brilliant end to the festival'. More of Evans' choices, Harriet Cohen[119] and Beatrice Harrison[120] went down very well, though Dent was less impressed by the fact that both Harrison and Lionel Tertis 'behaved abominably' to Harriet Cohen, refusing to play with her. 'The English contingent of performers caused amusement if nothing else', he wrote to Clive. 'Tertis played finely, but was very much the prima donna and took no part in the social side of the festival; Batrice [sic] Harrison the same.'[121] Wickedly, Dent enjoyed repeating Korngold's review in the *Neue Frei Presse*: 'die schöne Harrison sah aus wie eine heilige Cäcilie mit dem Cello, aber eine heilige Cäcilie die eine sehr anstrengende Saison im Himmel hinter sich hatte'.[122] A post-festival party organised by the English and American sections at the Münchner Hof was a spontaneous burst:

115 Completed by his pupil Philipp Jarnach and performed at Dresden in May 1925.

116 Beaumont, *Busoni*, p. 352, quoting Paul Stefan in *Anbruch*.

117 LH 28/08/1924. The singer was Charles Albert Case, a 'thoroughly bad singer to begin with, a fairly good musician', who had never heard of VW.

118 Hermann W. Draber (1878–1942), flautist, critic, translator, studied with Busoni.

119 Harriet Cohen (1895–1967), English pianist: many composers wrote or dedicated music to her, including Ralph Vaughan Williams, Edward Elgar and Belá Bartók. Spanish music was also a speciality.

120 Beatrice Harrison (1862–1965) later famously played her cello to the nightingales. Delius, Bax and Cyril Scott all wrote pieces for her.

121 CC 21/10/1924. Harrison often had played with Harriet Cohen, and it seems odd that both she and Tertis snubbed her like this.

122 The beautiful Harrison looked like a St Cecilia, but a St Cecilia who'd had a rough season in Heaven behind her. LH 28/08/1924 (also to CC).

FIGURE 11. Dent and J.B. Trend in Salzburg, 1924, taken by Sydney Loeb. Reproduced by kind permission of Jessica Loeb and Caroline Watts.

> Erwin Schulhoff was in great form playing jazz music with the Zika quartet, minus Czerny, the viola who did a danse des apaches with Harriet.[123]

It was here he first encountered young Hubert Foss, brother of William, just poised to make his mark as a music publisher.

Even though he had JB's company and competent assistance, throughout the festival Dent had been plagued by 'a nervous gastritis', compounded by 'a long-standing case of hydrocele – accumulation of fluid round one of the testicles, due I believe to a bruise about 15 years ago'.[124] But before he could have the necessary operation, he had to get fitter; impossible, with all the activity, stress and travelling. After the festival came the conference, 'less trying than I had anticipated'. Dent had to cope with the 'tiresome' Prunières, who 'always had some perfectly impracticable short cut to propose for business which I knew had to be done

[123] CC 21/10/1924.

[124] *Ibid.*

slowly and carefully'.[125] He later told the other delegates what a lot of trouble the French had given him this time, and expressed the hope that they might follow the example of the Italians – 'l'educatrice del mondo' (the world's educator) – in developing 'an active and energetic section'. Holding up the Italians as an example to the French was purest gall and wormwood.[126]

The withering sarcasm often expressed in letters to his closest friends shows what strain Dent put on himself by keeping up such a inscrutable public face. He was perpetually vexed and irritated by Evans and his unreliability, but never gave him the slightest hint of this in public. He was genuinely fond of Prunières, too, but had found it trying when the French section refused to pay for the Satie piece chosen by the jury, and musical politics had taken the day. 'Casella is as a matter of fact much the strongest personality in the International. I don't like him much nor do I trust him altogether; but he is very energetic at present, and does his work well'.[127] Casella himself would have been surprised at this view, since Dent went out of his way to be friendly and encouraging to him personally, always publicly praising him and his efforts.[128] But Dent appreciated Casella's efforts to keep the Italian section happy, and their bid to host the next festival at Venice in September 1925 went through more or less on the nod. 'The three Italian festivals, which were perhaps the most generally successful of all our meetings, owed more to his energy and enthusiasm than I can adequately express.'[129]

Still, this tricky Salzburg Festival marked several great strides forward in stabilising the society, not least in the president's firmer understanding of his own role. Dent had borne the constant criticism with dignity and humour, but the calm public stance was difficult to sustain, and his already poor health suffered even more: 'any sort of journey and sudden effort such as all these uncomfortable train journeys have involved brings on stomach pains and pains in the back, which sometimes wake me up in the middle of the night'.[130] Few knew about the hundreds of personal letters he wrote, the extra time he put in to make sure that everything went smoothly for performers and audience.

As a much-needed holiday, Dent and JB had planned a retreat to an island off the Istrian coast, going by sea via southern Germany, Dent's old haunts at Münster and Würzburg, where they dawdled over Tiepolos and a 'delicious little 18th century garden' at Veitshöchheim, making their leisurely way down to Trieste, the launching point for the Istrian islands. It rained hard, so they were forced to spend the night at 'what might have been a sailors' brothel', catching a steamer in the early morning that pottered all along the great bump of what is now Croatia, stopping at

125 *Ibid.*

126 CC 21/10/1924. This was written after his operation in early October.

127 LH 28/08/1924.

128 This is clear from their long and mostly friendly correspondence.

129 For an excellent full discussion of these politics, see Benjamin G. Martin, *The Nazi–Fascist New Order for European Culture* (Cambridge, MA, 2016), Chapter 3, 'The European Character of the German–Italian Axis', where Casella's ambivalent part is laid out.

130 LH 28/08/1924.

Parenzo, Revigno, Brioni and Pola, before arriving at Lussinpiccolo in the afternoon. At the suggestion of Viennese critic Paul Bechert they stayed at the Villa Mignon, at Lussingrande (now Veli Losinj), 3 miles further south. JB had to get back to London, while Dent hoped to stop in Venice before going on to Vienna, where he was to lecture, with a few days' leisure to see some exhibitions of theatre design, then on to Basel, where the IMG/IMS was beginning to reassemble itself, its first meeting since before the war.

Though still in some pain and discomfort, Dent enjoyed himself in Basel. Gerry Cooper and J.C. Squire were there, 'quite a delightful party': Torrefranca, Alfred Einstein, Johannes Wolf, Springer and old Friedlaender from Berlin, beside some of the new generation of musicologists. Peter Wagner was elected the new President.[131]

❧ ❧ ❧

> I can at any rate thank my testicles that I escaped having to attend a dinner organized by Daddy Mann to welcome Charles Wood as Professor.[132]

Charles Wood was already suffering from the cancer which would soon kill him, but his brief Professorship bought Dent more time to consider his own place. His two-month convalescence that autumn 1924 was Dent's first prolonged stay in Cambridge for years, and to his mild surprise, he found himself enjoying the time to read and reflect beside catching up with old friends, spending most of the day reading in bed, waited on by Hills, writing long letters to Lawrence, comforting widowed Mrs Jenkinson, 'fearfully absorbed in grief' for Francis. He still found Proust too 'trying', but was enjoying a return to Zola, whose old-fashioned style stimulated his biography ideas. By Christmas he was feeling much better, having gone at Steuart's suggestion to see the gastric specialist Conway Davies and being put on a diet avoiding alcohol and tea, living on milk, butter and eggs, which he kept up all that winter: 'it makes me very unsocial, but is a good excuse for refusing invitations'.[133]

After a relatively pleasant ISCM jury meeting at Winterthur and a few weeks with Uncle Ted, now living alone at La Selva, Dent returned to Cambridge in January. With Camille Prior,[134] the new force in local music, he went out to Girton Gate to see his old friends the Stewarts.

> Jean, her sisters, father and the parlour-maid acted a little play written by Jean herself. It had originally been got up to entertain the bricklayers, and was about a harassed country rector's wife preparing for a jumble sale … Frideswide and Margaret as her daughters were delicious, and the most absurd episode was

131 Peter Wagner (1865–1931), German musicologist, specialist in medieval music and Palestrina.

132 CC21/10/1924.

133 CC 25/03/1925.

134 'Vivacious and charming' widow of the Professor of French, she took over from Dennis Arundell as opera director. Vaughan Williams' *The Poisoned Kiss* at the new Arts Theatre in 1936 was done in collaboration with Gwen Raverat, who designed it.

> Katharine as 'Miss Vinegar' coming to reclaim a lost thimble, and giving the most obvious caricature of Auntie Daisy … I am invited for the 22nd, if still here, to a performance of 'The Fairy Queen' on the toy theatre.[135]

Dent had always liked Stewart, a most unorthodox clergyman, and he loved the three ferocious little girls, all talented and outgoing and very musical, especially Jean and Katharine 'Katten'; the third, Frideswide 'Frida' had been in *The Fairy Queen*, doubling up with Jasper Rootham; Jasper and Jean both stayed at Winterthur. They were some of the women in Dent's life who actually broke through his prepossession; wild and wilful and completely uninhibited. He could always talk easily with them, and his letters to them are easy, funny and intimate. The family gift for languages and love of foreign parts became refined into a committed internationalism and socialism interwoven with the arts,[136] Dent remaining a close friend and collaborator.

The production of *Dido and Aeneas* he had been working on for Schulz-Dornburg[137] at Münster in March was postponed, but his time in Cambridge afforded Dent opportunity to focus again on early opera, with several editions in the pipeline for Hubert Foss and the OUP, *Dido and Aeneas* and Mozart's *Requiem*:[138] 'he seems bent on making the Oxford Press run a music business that shall knock the bottom out of Peters, Breitkopf and Universal-Edition.'[139] Arundel del Re at Oxford was consulting Dent about a possible edition of Monteverdi's *Orfeo*, asking his views on Chester's Malipiero edition.

> I do not like it much, though it is the best available. Apart from the fact that Mal piero [sic] has to my thinking misunderstood the harmony at times, the Continuo part won't do for the stage as it stands, and there is any amount of work to do in working out the details of orchestration etc, to say nothing of planning cuts, stage setting and making a translation.[140]

Dent helped with Dennis Arundell's ambitious production of Handel's *Semele* (1744), that Lent term 1925, although their ideas about production differed.

135 CC 02/02/1925.

136 See below, Chapter 15. All three became very politically committed in the late 1930s, going out to the Spanish Civil War; Jean was interned in WWII. In 1936 she had helped to set up refugee links between Spain and Cambridge which resulted in some 300 Basque children coming over.

137 Rudolf Schulz-Dornburg, conductor, co-founder with Kurt Jooss of the Folkwang University, dedicated to a holistic approach to the arts. He worked with choreographer Jooss, who later founded the Ballet Jooss and became a close friend of Dent's as a refugee in Cambridge in the 1930s.

138 *Dido* included a substantial preface together with a German translation by Anton Mayer; the Mozart had a 'prefatory note on the history and interpretation', with Latin and English texts, in Dent's translation. OUP published Dent's Purcell 'Anacreon's defeat', 'Let the dreadful engines', 'My beloved spake' and 'Rejoice in the Lord', beside Locke, Church, Christopher Gibbons, Scarlatti and *The Beggar's Opera*, and Dent's own Motets.

139 CC 02/02/1925.

140 CC 25/03/1925.

Arundell's lavish sets and costumes masked the drama brought out by the music alone, Dent felt, but he was attracted by the novelty of assembling a working edition for performance to audiences who had no idea about early opera.

> To us who have been brought up on Wagner and Verdi, it is extraordinarily difficult to realize the adventurousness of those early composers who interpreted a complete drama in terms of music.[141]

More thorough breakthroughs in scholarship and understanding of Handel's operas would come later through Dent's pupils, especially Winton Dean, who found that Dent's work, though 'always stimulating and often penetrating, contains many odd judgements, governed perhaps by experience of the music on paper rather than in the theatre'.[142] Dent's Handel tinkerings for *Semele* may indeed now sound odd:

> my own surgical operation on most of the arias, which I invented a long time ago, but never had a chance of trying in practice – it consists of transplanting the middle section into the middle of the first section, thus avoiding the Da Capo but preserving the outline of its form … Original: Tonic to dominant, dominant to tonic; minor keys; tonic to dominant, dominant to tonic. My scheme: Tonic to dominant; minor keys; dominant to tonic. You will find that in nearly all the big arias of Handel this dodge will work quite happily, though it may want a chord or two altering at the joins.[143]

The eventual production prompted his most sarcastic tone, with Borzois and fantails on stage, the chorus in Venetian dominoes in the last act looking like 'dissipated parsons and nuns coming away from a night club … Barkworth said the front trees looked like green polar bears trying to climb the columns; I thought they looked more as if they were making water against them'.[144]

Dent was feeling well enough to return to London that winter, busy with articles and editions, listening with half an ear to the current rumblings about Charles Wood's health and viewing with satisfaction how JB Trend was becoming more than simply another link in his growing international networks, more recognised for his work on Spanish music and culture, a specialist internationalist. JB had been looking after the Spaniards visiting the King's Weston Opera Festival, then overseeing his Calderon collaboration with Frank Birch at Cambridge, *Life's a Dream*:

> with incidental music arranged by JB from Alessandro Scarlatti, whom he considers appropriately Gongoristic, though he deplores the way in which Frank will substitute 'service English' for his own elaborate Gongorisms in the translation.[145]

141 E.J. Dent, *Foundations of English Opera: A Study of Musical Drama in England During the Seventeenth Century* (Cambridge, 1928), p. 232.

142 Dean, *Handel and the Opera Seria*, p. x.

143 CC 20/02/1925.

144 *Ibid.*, also cited in Knight, *Cambridge Music*, pp. 105–6.

145 CC 02/02/1925. 'Gongorism' from the elaborate word-play of the Spanish poet Luis de Gongora y Argote.

JB's close friendship with Falla had become a working partnership, to their mutual benefit. Beside his already impressive collection of articles on Spain, these years saw *A Picture of Spain, Luís Milán and the Vihuelistas,* while he was also working on his collection *Alfonso the Sage & Other Spanish Essays,* building up to *The Music of Spanish History* and *Spanish Madrigals and Madrigal Texts.* Dent said only half jokingly that really, they should elect JB to the Music Chair.

London music was the usual mixed bag: Wood's *Pickwick* again at the Royal College of Music, besides Barkworth's *Fireflies* ('Old Barky's opera was dreadful'), Gavin Gordon Brown's ballet *Les Noces Imaginaires,* in contrast to Jelly d'Aranyi's Mozart at the Queen's Hall.

> I begin to think she is the finest violinist living. To JB and me it was beautiful and perfect beyond all conception or description from beginning to end; but none of the critics seem to have noticed anything about it … Well, well, these Hungarian women.[146]

He saw her again in late March, playing with Adila: 'Bach's concerto in C minor & a Spohr duet: it was glorious & Jelly in a gold dress looked rather like my statuette of Paganini'.[147] Steuart was singing some Vaughan Williams songs 'very well', Dent thought, 'fearfully difficult to understand. They baffled the critics completely: but I am sure they are great things'. Fifty copies of *Dido and Aeneas,* published by Novello's, were sent to Clive.

Now the British Music Society was in crisis, partly because the Carnegie Trust had backed off, 'but I hope we may yet save it … I suspect Eaglefield Hull has been doing something unpleasant', Dent wrote to Clive, 'the question for me is to save the Contemporary Music Centre and the London office of the International'.[148] The British Music Society had been founded by Hull, but feeling increasingly sidelined at home and abroad, he had somehow managed to offend a number of influential people. Moreover, the embryonic BBC was already superseding the British Music Society, its funding more secure and its remit far broader. Dent's rare genius lay in his ability to see how all these different bodies might work together and actually getting them to do so.

> The sad fact is that there are very few people in the world of music who have any sense of public duty and of statesmanship. Jerry [sic] Cooper has the first, to some extent, but though he is less explosive than he used to be he is still far from being statesmanlike.[149]

[146] CC 25/03/1925.

[147] CC 01/05/1925. This is the infamous statuette which some said looked like it had an erection, as apparently Dent enjoyed pointing out.

[148] CC 25/03/1925.

[149] CC 02/02/1925. 'Jerry' was Gerald Cooper, Secretary of the Purcell Society, who later became a close colleague and constant source of irritation at the Philharmonic Society and the ISCM.

In a move both ambitious and diplomatic, the ISCM had decided to give two big festivals that year, Prague in May and Venice in September, appeasing Czechs and Italians.[150] But the Prague Festival was again under threat from a German protest.

> The jury chose 2 works not sent in by the section, whereas they only have the right to choose one ... The fact was that the German parcel did not arrive till very late, & the jury had to make their programmes without it, choosing such German works as they knew & really taking endless trouble to give Germany a good place in the programmes.[151]

Evans, meanwhile, against the expressed wishes of composers and organisers, was running his own people to play at the festivals, part of what Dent called 'Evans's perpetual campaign against any musician who has been educated at a public school or university'.[152]

In May, Dent travelled to Prague via Berlin. Meeting him at the station, Anton Mayer told him how dismal the Busoni household was in the aftermath of Busoni's death, with both the sons only interested in the money and Rita Boetticher 'the little hunchback woman ... saying the most incredible & abominable things about Frau B.'[153] But Jarnach had finished *Doktor Faust*, to be produced at Dresden later in May; Dent determined to go to hear it, in spite of Mayer's gloomy opinion that it would 'certainly be a failure'. While in Berlin he also seized the chance to speak more formally with Gerda about carrying out Busoni's wish that he write the biography and that Foss and OUP should publish it,[154] arguing that there would be too much squabbling over the remains and if anything was to be done well, he was the one to do it. Mayer had advised him to keep all the letters he had, since it was highly unlikely that Berlin would get up any kind of archive or museum to Busoni. Before too long he was starting up a fund to help Gerda in her financial difficulties; now, he specially invited her to the Venice ISCM and while she was there, took great pains for her comfort and enjoyment.

The Prague ISCM Festival of orchestral music took place between 15 and 20 May and went astonishingly smoothly, without any dramas, a model of what good organisation could deliver, but 'far too much music. Our own concerts were ... too long'.[155] 'The Czechs' thirst for music is indeed unquenchable; they filled the hall even for our concerts and stayed to the end although many of them had to miss their last tram home.' The Czechs put on an extraordinary show, with a male-voice choir performing contemporary pieces and Janáček's *The Cunning Little Vixen*, which, oddly, Dent fails to mention, instead emphasising 'that profoundly moving and impressive work', the Vaughan Williams 'Pastoral' Symphony, probably because he felt moved to defend it from Paul Stefan and Artur Schnabel:

150 See Haefeli *IGNM*, pp. 110ff., 120ff., 142–3.

151 JG February 1925.

152 CC 02/02/1925.

153 JBT 07/05/1925.

154 JBT 13/09/1925.

155 JG 26/05/1925.

> He … said of the VW symphony that it was poetical, but he thought that all that 'orientalism' was rather vieux-jeu nowadays! … I explained that it was primitive Keltic – so he said that his ideas what were Scotch in music came from the Scotch Symphony of Mendelssohn! I said something about the absurdities of Beethoven's Scotch Songs.[156]

After it was all over, Dent enjoyed a leisurely drive back via Dresden with Gerald Cooper, whose presence at Prague, with his languid manner, fashionable fur coat, and expensive tastes, he had found less abrasive than Evans'. They spent ten days, seeing performances of Jarnach's finished version of *Doktor Faust*, just published by Breitkopf & Härtel. 'It was received with respect rather than enthusiasm', Dent later commented.[157] He wrote to Jack Gordon that it had been 'most exhausting – more so than usual', with too many people 'grinding' their particular axes: 'I am talking to people all day and most of the night, and yet feel most horribly lonely, because there is not a soul with whom I can discuss the Society's politics unreservedly'.[158]

His stomach was playing up again, and although he blamed the bad ('ersatz') food in Dresden, really, it was symptomatic of the unremitting stresses, uncertainties, and dramas he so enjoyed fussing about and which perversely seemed to keep him going. After his return from Prague, all that hot June he threw himself into work, finishing his edition of the Mozart *Requiem* for Foss, an article on madrigals for Colles and his article 'On the Composition of English Songs' for 'Foxy'.[159] But finances were still in poor shape; he had been forced to let Panton Street again with Hills into the bargain, while the lease for New Quebec Street was again uncertain. 'I hope the house business will be all right, for I am very hard up and considerably overdrawn', Dent wrote to JB in Spain.[160] Uncle Ted had asked him to come out to La Selva to stay for two months: 'Heaven knows what work I can do there', he wrote to JB, 'I can't write a book away from libraries, but I must hope that Foss can give me something else like the Requiem to edit'.[161] Going to concerts was out of the question now, unless he was given a comp, the only exception being the Fauré memorial concert on 9 June, where he splashed out a guinea to hear Murdoch, Sammons, Tertis and Sharpe playing the two piano quartets, and the songs, all of which Dent loved. His clothes, he finally noticed, were in tatters.

Fortunately, his alternative life presented some relief; Chester Purves was now back in London before being moved to Berlin, with his partner Roderick Meiklejohn, and as always, Chester's presence pulled Dent out of his self-imposed shell. They

156 JBT 07/05/1925. For once Dent was more brutal in print about the episode in 'Looking Backward', p. 284: 'all that *Jewish* style is quite played out now', he cites Schnabel as saying 'contemptuously'.

157 Dent, *Busoni* p. 296. Dent's final chapter is an appreciation of Busoni's treatment, using this last work as a comment on Busoni himself.

158 JG 26/05/1925.

159 The Mozart brought him fifty guineas, while Fox Strangways paid him five guineas per 5,000 words.

160 JBT 21/06/1925.

161 JBT 21/06/1925.

went up to Cambridge for May Week to catch new talent like the young Cecil Beaton[162]and current gossip, injecting Dent with some badly-needed light entertainment and a sense of belonging. 'Roderick gave me the happy idea that possibly Siegfried Sassoon might like to take my house here for the winter; he says he wants to escape from the Turner menage but does not quite know how to do it.'[163] He managed to recruit a number of these arty young men to come along to the Venice ISCM in September, some to lend a hand, supporting the festival and Dent by their presence. Many, like David Horner or John Beavan, could easily afford to travel.

> David flourishes marvellously, though he says he is doing 3 people's work at his book. He is particularly pleased because at some party Ernest Thesiger introduced him to his wife and said in a loud voice – 'You know all about David, don't you? The fact is I'm his father and his mother is the Duke of York!' John Wells has asked me to a party on the 18th – given for Chester, I understand. The company is to be of both sexes, so as to include Lesbians – d'après 'les Biches' Poulenc's ballet, now at the Coliseum under the title of 'The House Party'. – I am told we are all to come in shorts or pyjamas. I need hardly say I shall not go.[164]

If the Czech Festival had been outstanding for its music and organisation, the September Venice Festival was the one Dent remembered most vividly for ever after: 'No festival of ours ever produced such a series of embarrassing and comical situations.'[165] The Italians, led by Casella and Mario Labroca, had thrown themselves into its organisation with great enthusiasm, but when Dent carefully arrived three weeks before the official start, he found Labroca about to go on holiday, Casella in Aosta and H.W. Draber off on his honeymoon. The photographer Jan Mikota was already in place, learning his way around.[166]

'Venice is full and I am sure you would hate it', he wrote to JB, describing the sexual smorgasbord on parade, from Philip von Hessen to the 'exquisite' Alixis Ffrench; Diaghilev 'with his latest ballerino'. Soon, Dent was surrounded by his own team, C.L. Boulenger ('Bou'), who with his partner Fred Riley, were regulars by now, then Jack Gordon, Boris Ord, Evans, who at least knew the ropes, and Scott Goddard, whose writing had to be deciphered later.

Concerts were to be given in the Palazzo Pisani, but because of the overwhelming demand for tickets, these had to be transferred to the big opera house La Fenice, even though its steeply raked stage presented problems. It was a very congenial atmosphere with the Lee Mathews, Miss Lacey, Foss with his wife and sister-in-law, 'Arthur Somervell and wife (!)', the Princesse de Polignac. Critic Adolf Weissmann appeared, a vision in woollen mountaineering suit and heavy boots that

162 Cecil Walter Hardy Beaton (1904–1980), photographer, designer. At St John's College, Cambridge, he acted in stunning drag for 1925 Footlights *All the Vogue*.

163 JBT 21/06/1925.

164 JBT 10/06/1925. David Stuart Horner (1900–1983), crime novelist, long-time partner of Osbert Sitwell, probably introduced by Dent.

165 Dent, 'Looking Backward', p. 284.

166 His photographs survive in KCA. Copyright uncertainties prevented their publication here.

hot Venetian September, prompting Labroca to whisper in some awe, 'Si riconoscono subito i tedeschi dalla loro predilizione per il costume sport' (you can recognise the Germans by their predilection for sports clothes).

Labroca had efficiently allocated seats by nationality, but when the powerful Berlin critic Leopold Schmidt found the front seats of his allocated box occupied by his biggest rival Weissmann, he declared that he was returning to Berlin this instant. Labroca ran to Dent, who kindly asked Schmidt if he might call him a gondola, that so sorry! he didn't quite catch his name, helpfully pointing out that it was too late to catch the night express.[167] After Schmidt and wife had been ushered to their new seats, Casella told Dent that he had to make a speech. So, completely unprepared, Dent got up onto the Fenice stage to make a speech in Italian and German to two thousand people. Emma Lübbecke-Job was supposed to be playing a work dedicated to her, Hindemith's piano concerto (now Kammermusik No. 2, op. 36 no. 1), but cried off because of a swollen mosquito bite, offering instead to play some Schnabel not chosen by the jury. When Dent obligingly offered a Swiss pianist to replace her, she suddenly recovered:

> I watched them all walking up and down the Piazza that evening, arguing, cajoling, protesting and persuading; finally the husband, a man of massive proportions, plumped himself down at at the table where I was drinking my coffee alone, and said ... 'It's all settled. My wife plays. Kellner, ein Bier!' The waiter brought the beer, and by some strange and happy accident poured the whole of it over the gentleman's head.[168]

A piano had been sent by Bechstein for Artur Schnabel's piano sonata, but the Fenice stage had such a steep rake that it had to be propped on bricks. Eduard Erdmann sat himself down to play as if nothing was awry, and after a particularly difficult passage 'beyond Liszt', 'a high-pitched voice from the gallery screamed out "E ora BAS-TAAA!" Erdmann kept his face; I think that was his greatest achievement.'.[169]

Then there was the rehearsal time required by Schoenberg for his *Serenade*, achingly slow and painstaking, with no thought to other pieces needing the rehearsal time and space. Dent had the delicate and unpleasant task of asking the Master when he was going to finish, so that Gruenberg could rehearse his *Daniel Jazz*. After a lengthy and extremely careful exchange, in which Dent pointed out that the *Serenade* players had done it before as well as rehearsing it here, Schoenberg would have none of it. When Dent hinted that perhaps he ought to be more considerate of his 'colleagues', Schoenberg said 'I have always understood that at all musical festivals I am the only composer.' But he relented. As Gruenberg came in and set up his *Daniel Jazz*, Dent noted that there was only one percussion player, where they appeared to need four. Gruenberg shrugged: 'Of course one's enough; I thought he would have a jazz-machine.' The only jazz-machine in Venice was currently in use at the Caffé Orientale where the Harvard Boys were playing every night. So instead of a

167 The full story is in 'Looking Backward', p. 285. Dent took unholy joy in retelling it.

168 *Ibid.*, p. 286.

169 *Ibid.*, p. 288.

jazz-machine, Gruenberg conducted Dent and Boris Ord, who sight-read the whole thing. Dent loathed the piece, but made sure it was played properly, later skewering it in 'Looking Backward'. To Clive he wrote more frankly. On Schoenberg:

> To see him rehearse is like watching a small boy who has got hold of a live butterfly and is pulling off its legs and wings one by one ... Stravinsky was very cordial and friendly at Venice, as he well might be; for he got 5000 French francs fee, which Reinhart insisted on paying, and also a great ovation when he came on to the stage. Schönberg ostentatiously got up and left the theatre![170]

After Venice, Schoenberg gave up all connection with the ISCM. Dent wrote to JB: 'I regard the Venice festival as a huge success ... One of the agreeable functions of the presidency is that I can say the most horrible things – in my sweetest and politest manner – to people who consider themselves little tin gods.'[171]

Such financial, logistical and emotional strain – having to prop up the great and the mediocre alike, having to offend one of the greatest composers of his day then having to fork out 15 lire for a much-needed cup of coffee, not to mention rescuing the unfortunate Viennese Dr Felber from prison for 'oltraggio al pudore' (an affront to modesty) – was a constant drain on Dent, however cheerfully he absorbed each and every one of such problems. His real genius, as he knew, lay in his constant attention to such apparently trivial details, knowing how it held everything together even while he took mischievous pleasure in taking on the 'little tin gods' and dining out on it all later. But the concerts were delivering as promised, the standards high, even though throughout the whole long, fractious process, Dent was constantly barracked by outraged, insistent partisan interests.

❧ ❧ ❧

That autumn, Dent stayed at La Selva until the jury meeting at Winterthur on 3 January,[172] when he could be relieved by his sister or his cousin, Lady Dallas, and working on *Terpander, or Music and the Future*: 'It is horribly hard to write; and that is why I long to be in my own house with nothing else to think about.' Money was still an issue; he was aware how much he had spent on the last ISCM and desperately waiting for Foss's cheques to arrive: 'Writing books and editing Purcell is not lucrative.' JB was joining him in Zurich, having convinced Falla to come and to hear his *El Retablo*,[173] while Dent's edition of *Dido and Aeneas* was being performed in concert form on 27 January.

The Zurich Festival which followed from 18 to 23 June 1926 was a critical and popular success, Falla apparently very pleased with everything, from the Reinhart hospitality to the marionette performance of *El Retablo*. 'The music of the festival was far

170 CC 23/09/1925.

171 JBT 13/09/1925.

172 The jury was Arthur Bliss, Arthur Honegger, Hermann Scherchen, Walther Straram, Karol Szymanowsi. Haefeli, *IGNM*, p. 484.

173 CC 11/07/1926.

better than in previous years', Dent commented to Clive, months later. Because the next festival was to be at Frankfurt, Dent went there to meet 'the Oberbürgermeister' before going on to the Handel Festival at Göttingen as well as a new production of *Figaro* in Cologne 'all rather too pretty for my taste, but very well done in a quite modern style'.[174] At the same time he arranged for Boris Ord to go there to work with Jeno Szenkár.[175] As he wrote to Clive, most of that year was spent going to concerts, including Constant Lambert's new *Romeo and Juliet*: 'Lambert's stuff is all reminiscences of other people, but it is well made and very exhilarating', and Boult conducting the Russian Ballet. But now Charles Wood was dying, and the Professorship question alive again.

> As for me I feel rather bored by it all. I am not going to contest an election again. If I was elected unanimously I would accept it from a sense of duty; in any case I admit that £500 a year would be a great assistance to me; but I want another £500 a year and freedom to do all my various activities, not £500 a year and prison, which is what the Professorship would mean. I should have to give up a great many of my interesting activities and I doubt whether I should find much time for writing learned books. And I feel that I am now completely out of the world of lectures and examinations, and don't want to go back to it. I love teaching, but I am not competent to teach modern composition. I hate lecturing, and I have forgotten all I ever knew about harmony and counterpoint and fugue. And I simply loathe examining … I want to produce operas and work in a theatre with you and other people of the right sort. But I am growing old, and when I meet P-G [Procter-Gregg] I realize that I am regarded merely as an aged and incompetent amateur with a bee in his bonnet and several grievances as well. I think the best thing will be for me to recatalogue Scarlatti.[176]

Disingenuous? He badly needed the money, but as if to reinforce the point not just with Clive but with himself, in this long letter Dent listed the many different and interesting things engaging his time and efforts right now. He was just about to celebrate his fiftieth birthday, and besides the Bristol Opera Festival in October, he was poised to start on his demanding Busoni biography, planning to research in Berlin. There was the jury meeting in London in January, and La Selva duties. In late March the congress of the re-formed IMG/IMS was meeting in Vienna, coinciding with the centenary of Beethoven's death, with his edition of *Dido and Aeneas* being performed in the Hofburg. The Handel Festival in Breslau was in May; the Frankfurt ISCM Festival was in June. He was working on several books now: *Terpander, or Music and the Future*, and his chapter for the *New Oxford History of Music*, on the Middle Ages, a chapter for Hill's book on the Guarneris, the musical life of Cremona and Mantua 1650–1750,[177] an article for the *Musical Quarterly* which Sonneck had

174 CC 11/07/1926.

175 Jeno (Eugen) Szenkár (1891–1977), Hungarian-born conductor at the Frankfurt Opera, fled to Vienna when the Nazis rose to power, then to Moscow. He was a friend of Hindemith and Wellesz.

176 CC 11/07/1926.

177 See Chapter 8, note 217.

begged him to write on 'why the younger generation can't do with Beethoven any more'. He was also revising what became *The Foundations of English Opera*: 'Some of it is quite good, but a lot of it is badly written, and much of it is very much out of date. I am amazed to think what a lot I have learned in the last ten years about the art of writing.'[178]

Even with everything else to occupy him, the vexed question remained on his mind all that year: 'I am not particularly keen on becoming Professor', he wrote again to Clive that September, but it is clear that Dent is airing his many reservations while still entertaining the idea.

> I am fifty now, and haven't the driving power that I had 20 years ago ... The people who are now about 20–25 are painfully conscious that the previous generation has been practically wiped out ... I don't think the younger generation are wanting in idealism, but they don't look at things in the same way as mine did ... But it seems pretty certain that they will elect me, for V.W. absolutely refuses to stand and has written strongly to me about standing for it ... I find that I am received in Cambridge with marked cordiality – and both Gray and Mann make no secret of the fact that they want me to be Professor ... it seems to lie between me and Rootham, and everybody seems to view Rootham's election with dread and horror.[179]

178 CC 06/09/1926.

179 *Ibid.*

CHAPTER 11

The Professor 1926–1931

> I am determined that if I am elected professor I am not going to take on any odd jobs or committees, at any rate until I have had a couple of terms in which to survey the situation.[1]

Possibly because of his prevarication over the previous three years, by the time Dent came back to Cambridge as its new Professor of Music, it was on his own clearly defined terms. He needed the financial stability and had negotiated a decent stipend, but his own independence was always Dent's primary personal concern, the freedom to do things in his own way, his public life facilitating the private side. The short university terms marked some useful boundaries, and Dent was determined to devote term-times to his professorial duties. The actual election that October was a foregone conclusion, the result of long, careful negotiations.[2] Vaughan Williams, the only other serious candidate, flatly refused to stand, and Dent had made it clear to Hugh Allen as the unofficial chairman of Electors that he would only accept a unanimous decision. They knew what they were getting.

'The period between Wood's death and my election was very trying', he wrote to Lawrence from Berlin:

> for I never quite knew what I wanted, or what the electors were likely to want. It was a relief to have things settled, one way or the other. I dread 'settling down' at fifty – just when I want to learn a lot more, and enjoy life as long as I have the capacity to enjoy it.[3]

He had no illusions: 'I am distinctly amused to note what a lot of my congratulations seem to be moved principally by a sense of relief at the deliverance from horror', he wrote to JB.

> I have … taken the plunge, and written straight to Rootham (who has <u>not</u> written to congratulate me!) to ask his advice about it all. I fancy he wants to stick to all the composition & quasi-composition teaching – i.e. lecturing on form & etc –

1 CC 06/09/1926.

2 It took place in the Sidney Sussex Lodge on Friday 29 October, the result announced on the 30th. The Notice of Vacancy had only been advertised on 1 October: *Cambridge University Reporter 1926–27* (Cambridge, 1927), pp. 68 and 318. 'The Professor of Music be not bound to reside in the University further than may be necessary for discharging the duties hereinafter mentioned': *Ordinances of the University of Cambridge to the end of the Easter Term 1927* (Cambridge, 1927), p. 423.

3 LH 18/11/1926.

and that he is responsible for the Board's expressed hope that I will give a course on the General history of music. Just what I don't want to do.[4]

Dent knew himself to be a new kind of academic musician, one who had come to his post from the outside and was prepared to improvise his new position, mustering a remarkable set of skills: a linguist, an historian who knew theatre history as much as musical, a practical musician and director, a critical listener with extensive experience who connected performance with scholarship, a writer with cutting-edge publications on a wide range of musical subjects. Carefully easing his way in rather than abruptly taking charge, Dent began to shape his new academic role, one of the few British 'musicologists' with an international reputation, a scholar whose purview included both past and present. His self-imposed exile had been spent exploring and forming his ideas about what a music faculty both should and could be doing, most of them to be found in his extensive writings, most recently *Terpander,* and an article dedicated to his own teacher C.H. Lloyd:

> the up-to-date teacher who knows all the tricks of modern effect very soon becomes old-fashioned. His pupils only learn from him how to imitate the mannerisms of the music that is just out of date … All that a teacher can give him [a composer] is a method of self-criticism, a sense of style, a grasp of principle that will enable him to teach himself … another test of the good teacher, his power of illuminating such studies as strict counterpoint and fugue.[5]

'I hope it will make a stir in the musical world; it is a very concentrated piece of writing.' *Terpander* demonstrates Dent's facility at making elusive concepts accessible, utilising the good teacher's arsenal of paradox, rhetorical question and metaphor, beginning with some familiar cross-disciplinary ideas: Walter Pater's 'all art constantly aspires towards the condition of music', Goethe's description of architecture as 'frozen music' and Dent's favourite Combarieu: 'music is the art of thinking through sounds'.[6] The pages of this short book burst with ideas; Dent's style was always to stir his readers into thinking for themselves, his aim, to express for the ordinary reader the inexpressible, transitory nature of music, to give a listener a platform for intelligent receptivity. It is uneven. As Dent's pupil Winton Dean[7] observed, 'it also contains, as one might expect, a good deal of coat-trailing' and 'he can topple into silliness ("Sincerity is a virtue with which art has no concern")'.[8]

> Music expresses itself and nothing else … The real music is not that which is written down: it is the sounds which are made by those who perform it.[9]

4 JBT 25/11/1926.

5 Dent, 'The Personality of a Teacher'.

6 E.J. Dent, *Terpander, or Music and the Future* (London, n.d. [1926]), pp. 13 and 8.

7 Winton Dean (1916–2013), son of theatre producer Basil Dean, educated at Harrow and King's College, Cambridge, became one of the great Handel scholars.

8 Winton Dean, 'Edward J. Dent: A Centenary Tribute', M&L, vol. 57, no. 4 (October 1976), pp. 353–61.

9 Dent, *Terpander*, p. 20.

From the historian's point of view everything is worth preserving as a historical document; but if we judge works of art from a purely aesthetic standpoint can we honestly say that the art of the past has any value for us? … Is a work of art a complete and finite thing, beautiful when it left its maker's hand, beautiful now and for ever, or is it frankly transitory, a momentary expression of a momentary experience?[10]

This preoccupation with the 'story' … constantly distracts the attention from the fact that all the arts are in a perpetual state of change … The stability of material works gives us a false idea of aesthetic permanence … All art, after all, is an adventure.[11]

The mind very soon regularizes the new experiences, but the fascination of the arts is that they are always offering us the chance of further ones. … We do not enjoy music as an art until we have learned to appreciate it rationally; but at the same time it cannot give us a real aesthetic emotion unless it confronts us forcibly with a further irrational element.[12]

Where *Terpander* shows some of the ideas behind Dent's teaching, his introduction to medieval music for the *New Oxford History* demonstrates his breadth of knowledge, in spite of his routine disclaimers. Re-writing his 1914 book – which became the 1928 *Foundations of English Opera* – was interwoven all that year with everything else he was doing, especially teaching and preparing editions for production, and one of Dent's most significant maxims emerged: 'It is fundamentally important that the historian of opera should always study his documents with the eye of a producer'.[13] It is no coincidence that so many of Dent's pupils became what we today call directors, from Clive Carey to Boris Ord, or that production became a staple at Cambridge.

Before taking up his new duties, Dent was off to Berlin for two months, November and December 1926, with Jack Gordon, ostensibly to research the Busoni biography, but also to engage in some pre-emptive ISCM groundwork before the actual jury meeting in London. For two weeks Dent threw himself wholly into his double world, first staying with Jack Gordon at the 'very expensive' Hotel am Zoo while looking for cheaper lodgings, eventually winding up in Kalckreuthstrasse, going to concerts of music by people he knew played by people he knew, going out at night with the dancers, actors and men he had cultivated for the past seven years – especially Anton Mayer, who also straddled various social worlds – allowing himself to be smitten by one of the young dancers, Rupert Doone, who pirouetted in and out of his life for the next ten years.

We have been much amused by the company of a young English dancer who is at a music hall here: Rupert Doone. He is a charming child and was and is

10 *Ibid.*, pp. 21 and 23.

11 *Ibid.*, pp. 27 and 82.

12 *Ibid.*, p. 83.

13 Dent, *Foundations of English Opera*, p. vii.

> a great friend of Duncan Grant, Lytton Strachey, Arthur Bliss and all sorts of Bloomsburians.[14]
>
> Rupert Doone leaves to-night for Paris. He has been good fun, but a little tiring. But he introduced me to a most charming Baron Hans von Veltheim, whom I like immensely: and at his house to a very agreeable young actor – H.M. Ritter, who knows many of my friends ... though he may powder his face at times, his mind is quite free of powder.[15]

In these early days of their long friendship, Jack was not yet used to Dent's indefatigable style when abroad, and seems to have served as an unofficial secretary-cum-companion, in on each different aspect of Dent's complicated affairs. What Jack saw in Berlin was a master-class in how to run an unwieldy, chaotic international entity with time for personal research and a bit of fun, and he was also just the kind of intelligent, informed and trusted companion Dent liked to have around as a sounding-board for his initial impressions of new music or to discuss revised opinions.

> We went to Elektra last night – I was bored till Clytemnestra came on: and thought Kleiber was doing his usual trick of over-nuancing everything and never getting the broad ... rhythm: but after Cl. comes on ... everything woke up: and I suddenly found myself overwhelmed with emotion at the beauty of her [deleted] the appalling dissonances when Elektra recognizes Orestes. I must hear it again.[16]

Jack could see how all the informal meetings and concert-going were also serious preparation for the ISCM jury meeting in London months later, all concocted behind the scenes, at the personal level where Dent operated best.

> I was with the Jarnachs last night after a concert at wch Furtwängler conducted a new work by Jarnach – Morgenklangspiel – wch is most beautiful. Jarnach is delighted with the idea of going to London ... I will tell Jarnach about the Falla concerto: he says Bartók is writing a pianoforte concerto, but the difficulty is to get him to finish it in time for the Jury.[17]

Jarnach was on the jury; Frankfurt was going to produce Busoni's *Doktor Faust*, and Bartók would be playing. After Berlin, Dent was to go to Münster for the Handel Festival in December followed by Cassel for Krenek's new opera *Orpheus and Eurydike.*

So Dent made the tentative beginnings of assembling Busoni's rich life history while navigating the minefield of his exuberance, protecting Gerda from the most difficult revelations he was uncovering in interviews and in the documents laid out on the floor of his old flat. As Volkmar Andrae had told him, Gerda was already in financial trouble, and a fund was being set up for her by Busoni's old friends.[18]

14 LH 18/11/1926.

15 JBT 01/12/1926.

16 *Ibid.*

17 JBT 06/11/1926.

18 LH 06/01/1926. The fund was erratically kept going for years.

Altogether, a near-impossible task, Dent discovered, to assemble an acceptable narrative out of the difficult childhood, the oppressively devout and overbearing mother, and much more: 'there are episodes of wch Mme Busoni does not like to explain much. A woman of 50 fell violently in love with him: and he came into the Sacher-Masoch circle in Berlin. I think Mayer can tell me more'.[19]

On 29 January Dent was 'admitted' to his professorial fellowship in the Chapel at King's, with Mann playing Bach on the organ and old friends Dickinson, Keynes, Sheppard and Gerald Shove all in attendance. He made light of it all, 'a tiresome little nuisance', but he appreciated the warm feelings being expressed at his return, even if the considerable perks – free rooms in college, free food in Hall – meant nothing to him, he continued to aver, always independently minded if not quite accurate. But he was touched at the warm reception, not least the lavish college feast Mann organised and generously paid for, all six courses.

> I have got started at Cambridge and feel fairly comfortable. I lecture in an informal way to two classes each once a week and talk about all sorts of odd things ... I feel dreadfully ignorant. But I hear from other people that they like my lectures very much, so I hope it is all right. They also come to me singly and privately and bring me their compositions and exercises. Most of them are rather duds, but I hope to make something of them ... it looks as if I should have to take upon myself the work of teaching them to write plain straight four-part stuff, which I did not think was going to be the Professor's work. But I suppose the Professor's work is to teach them all that their other lecturers can't, won't or at any rate don't.[20]

His academic life quickly expanded, his strong sense of obligation driving him to take on much more than he needed to, as former pupils testify. Besides working on the Busoni biography, lecturing on Arundell's Greek Play music on 16 February, he was giving a lecture on opera at Oxford, and going to a 'book recommendation committee meeting' at Emmanuel College, for which he scribbled down some modern German books. Scho co-opted him onto the Library Syndicate. It was hard work.

> First, the May exams revealed a number of fundamental weaknesses which had to be sorted and addressed. I am just through with the Mus B. 12 ploughed out of 16 – They were a poor lot on the whole: but I have been much interested, and all this work (it really was very strenuous, especially the final discussion with Naylor & Rootham) has made me feel definitely settled to my Cambridge life & work – I know now – at last – what is wanted & can make plans for the future.[21]

He began to appreciate 'Naylor's musicianship', Dennis Arundell's 'excellent' lectures and how his more up-to-date composition teaching was better than Rootham's, 'though here I can't quite say how far the results were due to him or to Henry Moule'. Arundell published his book on Purcell in 1927, and they began to plan the next opera, Purcell's *King Arthur*, beside outlining plans for a 'Collegium

19 LH 18/11/1926.

20 LH 30/01/1927.

21 JBT 12/06/1927.

Musicum', 'for the playing and singing of old music',[22] Dent's first attempts to bring performance formally into the new regime. When Hubert Foss brought up some Boyce symphonies Constant Lambert had recently scored, Dent thought this perfect for the new 'Collegium'. But it was all taking up his time.

> Committees – committees! I avoid all I can in Cambridge: but there are too many notwithstanding. 'Don't let yourself become an administrator' says Scho. 'leave that to the people who are too stupid to do original work'.[23]

It needed all his diplomatic skills to open the windows at Cambridge, bring in some fresh ideas from the wider musical world and stimulate interest without offending the locals. He focused first on Rootham, drawing him into the Frankfurt ISCM Festival and encouraging him to invite Kodály and Vaughan Williams to come and conduct their own work. Rootham was soon working in harness, and at every committee, Dent kept pushing for all the facilities he considered necessary for an up-to-date Faculty of Music, but it took years.[24]

Dent, being Dent, was always yearning to do more, push well beyond his physical and mental limits – was it endless ego or a genuine desire to give? There is an element of self-righteousness in everything he did, but a healthy ego and self-confidence can be invaluable assets when running major institutions, while Dent's constant instinctive need for an escape route meant that he also needed to furnish the excuse. The Professorship grounded him, even as he kicked at its restrictions, and he used its status shamelessly in the ISCM and elsewhere; he always had worked through institutions while hating to be defined by any one of them, always retaining his secret identity, his private Otherness. He really had nothing to prove now, so if Dent was driven by any personal crusade, it was to establish music, 'all' music, in everyday life through the cultural institutions in his charge, and the effort involved nearly killed him. So when less than a year into his Professorship, Dent was formally asked to become a governor of the Old Vic, he jumped at it. Opera production was one way to connect everything Dent loved and was striving for; the Vic was outside the Cambridge confines, and had lacked outsider–insider direction.

> I went last week to my first meeting of the Old Vic governors ... They are a queer lot. I think when it comes to Sadlers Wells Geoffrey Toye & Aveling & I shall be able to do what we like. Miss Baylis was there and went off into wild hysterics over the telephone shortcomings – apropos of one estimate for electric lighting! Sir Wilmot Herringhouse just let her run on till she had exhausted herself.[25]

[22] CC 27/07/1927.

[23] CC 13/05/1927.

[24] In 1976, thanks mostly to the efforts of Dent's former pupil, Professor Robin Orr, a new concert hall was opened as an extension of the old faculty buildings extemporised from former houses on West Road. Since then, more facilities have been added. But c.1927, musical performance was mostly still spread around the town and colleges, then at Downing Place, where the CUMC concerts continued on Saturday evenings.

[25] CC 13/05/1927.

While Dent and Carey had been mostly absent, the Old Vic itself was badly in need of refurbishment, so in 1925, Sadler's Wells, a near-derelict eighteenth-century theatre in North London had been bought and was gradually being done up along the same lines, with alternating drama and opera. Lilian Baylis had made friends with a former Diaghilev ballet star, Ninette de Valois, who was starting up her own company; it was a natural step for de Valois to bring along both her ballet company and her expertise in coaching movement to singers and actors.[26] The projected opening of Sadler's Wells for 1931 meant that decisions had to be made now about the policies and running of the place, another challenge for Dent. In these turbulent years, Dent continued to undertake deliberate practical connections between the various elements in his own life and work: the IMS Congress, the ISCM, the Cambridge Faculty, the Old Vic and Sadler's Wells, and all his writing and editing, especially of Purcell.

Thanks to his travels and research, Dent now possessed a much clearer vision of what he considered the ways forward. In March 1927, the congress of the reformed International International Musical Society (IMS) in Vienna centred around Beethoven and a production of *Dido and Aeneas*, using Dent's recently published edition. Dent planned his extended trip around various other Purcell productions, only to be 'utterly exhausted with annoyance' at the Viennese production: 'I shall not even go so far as to call this show Dido mit Schlagobers', he wrote to JB.[27] '"Wiener Baroch" rather than English … sumptuous in the extreme … all produced in the style of a Lully opera, as stiff and inhuman as possible … The score is indescribable.'[28] He saw wilful ignorance of Purcell, beside massive arrogance arising from that ignorance, and scorn for his own scholarship. 'I am certainly not wanted in Vienna … one must be polite here. That is the only thing to do here: to be polite and never get annoyed with anything.' The Viennese complacency he had observed in ISCM wranglings had been revealed again; apart from the twelfth- to fifteenth-century music, 'the whole Festival seemed a huge fake got up to attract Americans, I have shaken hands with dozens of people & hadn't a notion who they were.'[29] Apart from a 'delightful evening' with Wellesz, the Einsteins and Ficker,[30] 'it is all dead. Vienna has no use for contemporary ideas at all'. In this relatively benevolent company he could return to ISCM gossip:

> Gruenberg had made an alliance with that half witted fool Hába and that absurd Dane Simonsen to outwit Straram. Szymanowski told me that Straram had said he had done his very best to get Szym's Stabat Mater accepted, but was prevented by Gruenberg: in Vienna Gruenberg told Szym. that <u>he</u> had done his best for the Stabat Mater but had been prevented by Straram.[31]

26 See Gilbert, *Opera for Everybody*, pp. 38ff., and Dent, ATFE, pp. 108ff.

27 With whipped cream: an obligatory topping for Viennese confectionery. JBT 04/04/1927.

28 JBT 25/03/1927.

29 JBT 04/04/1927.

30 Rudolf von Ficker (1886–1954), Austrian musicologist, specialising in early church music.

31 JBT 04/04/1927.

Still, Alfred Einstein had expressed great enthusiasm for JB's book on Frottole, and asked him to write for the *Acta Musicologica* which he edited, which would help JB's current bid for the Oxford Professorship.

A week later, in April, Dent was relieved to be enjoying the 'peace' of Mayer's comfortable Wilmersdorf flat again: 'very like being in Quebec St. and has the advantage of a wide view over unbuilt land.' Jack Gordon was not far away with friends and Gerry Cooper at the Adlon. But Dent was too busy for socialising this time, with a lot of work to do on Busoni, and after Vienna, another week of Gerry's company had been enough to put a strain on relations.

> Gerry became quite unbearable. I expect he wd say exactly the same of me. Alone, he was delightful: but a party always produced his explosiveness & uproariousness.[32]

Instead, he relaxed by going to the latest operas and plays, Kurt Weill's *Royal Palace* and Strindberg's *Traumspiel.*

> I was intensely moved by Strindberg's realistic plays, when I saw them here a few years ago, though the torture is almost unbearable: but here the torture became too symbolical and conventional, so that one couldn't be very much stirred by it.[33]

About the only real pleasure Dent had taken in the Vienna Congress was meeting the Paul Hirschs of Frankfurt, who warmly invited both Dent and JB to stay during the ISCM Festival there in June–July 1927. Dent was sorry to have to decline, since they were 'booked for the Consulate', but they became good friends. Hirsch was one of the benefactors of the Frankfurt Festival, an accomplished amateur musician, playing violin and viola, whose inherited wealth was poured into his Music Library in Neue Mainzerstrasse, one of the world's great collections, curated by Dr Kathi Meyer and open to the public.[34] Frankfurt itself was an important cultural centre, a rich industrial city with a major opera house and music conservatory, and a cosmopolitan audience.[35] Like Werner Reinhart, Hirsch generously opened up his house to the festival people, his children joining in, playing cowboys and Indians around groups of eminent musicologists and composers gathered in the Hirsch garden.

The Frankfurt ISCM Festival was one of the most successful and done on a lavish scale, opening with Busoni's *Doktor Faust,* completed by Phillipp Jarnach, produced by the Frankfurt Opera. The programme included Béla Bartók playing his First Piano Concerto, Carl Nielsen's Fifth Symphony and Alban Berg's Chamber Concerto, with Spanish music represented by Turina's piano trio. 'Frankfurt did us sumptuously', Dent wrote to Clive, telling him how he had given a speech, waiting 'a good 30 seconds' before they saw the joke and 'roared with laughter'. A heavyweight British contingent there included, besides Evans and Cooper, the Section Secretary Helen Wadham, Colles, Fox Strangways, critics Bonavia, Goss and Capell, Eaglefield Hull,

32 JBT 12/04/1927.

33 *Ibid.*

34 Paul Hirsch (1881–1951). I am indebted to Nicholas Bell, then of the British Library, for helping me with research about Hirsch and about the BL Hirsch Collection. It is still not clear how it was moved from Frankfurt to Cambridge.

35 Haefeli, *IGNM*, p. 152.

FIGURE 12. Frankfurt ISCM, 1927. Dent with his head in a noose in the Hirsch garden; from left to right, Gian-Francesco Malipiero, Paul Hirsch, Dent, Paul Pisk, Erwin Schulhoff, Max Butting. By kind permission of the Provost and Fellows of King's College, Cambridge.

Foss; Miss Ley had come with Frau Busoni; Boris Ord, Jack Gordon, and W.G. Whittaker[36] plus his daughter and his choir. Dent had hoped that Whittaker's choir might impress a German audience as much as the English critics, but Whittaker's Psalm CXXX 'was not quite the success I had hoped.' But critical success was not really the point.

> However, they [the British contigent] were stirred up in a way, and quite began to think that we ought to have a Festival in England, possibly at Cambridge … so far as they respect me, they think I am doing the wrong thing in being associated with such people as Evans, Willie Walton and Berners etc, and so far as they respect the International and English participation in it, they think the head man ought to be somebody more 'representative' than either myself or even Evans – someone like V.W. or Walford Davies or Elgar or possibly even Landon Ronald.[37]

Critical opinion on new works was always going to be divided, and Haefeli records less favourable reactions to the music played at Frankfurt, especially accusations that the jury had been guilty of choosing inferior music this time, 'such dreadful salon music' (citing Turina's piano trio and the piano piece by Castelnuovo-Tedesco)

36 William Giles Whittaker (1876–1944), composer and conductor of the Newcastle Bach Choir, which had given the first performance in c.300 years of Byrd's Great Service, recently re-discovered in Newcastle by Edmund Fellowes. The man himself had attracted the formidable Australian Louise Hanson Dyer, who went to Newcastle to hear him conduct it, resulting in her devotion to early music and the foundation of L'Oiseau-Lyre. Jim Davidson, *Lyrebird Rising: Louise Hanson-Dyer of L'Oiseau-Lyre 1884–1962* (Melbourne, 1994).

37 CC 23/07/1927.

played by musicians of the first rank.[38] But the Turina trio had been one of the pieces pushed forward to encourage the Spanish Section, as Dent had written to JB that June, 'Turina wrote that nobody had a peseta – so the Spanish Section is doing nothing: and he says that neither Madrid nor Barcelona have much use for the International.'[39] Frankfurt, with its strong local support and munificent funding, had been an exception, so Dent pushed for a smaller, more manageable festival in 1928.

> Neither Paris not [sic] London will take sufficient interest in it. Copenhagen and Amsterdam are not quite ready yet. New York talks a great deal and makes a great fuss; but I don't think it is capable of organising its own committee yet, and I won't go to America to be run by Salzedo and Varese and George Anthill! … So we are going to have a festival on a small and intimate scale at Siena, with Prince Chigi and Sir George Sitwell (I hope) to entertain us.[40]
>
> The Austrians want to have the 1928 Festival at Vienna: and the Americans are desperately keen to have it in the USA the following year or some time at any rate. I think it wd be a very good plan.[41]

Bringing in the Americans to escape European bickering was a possible side-step, with colleagues like Oscar Sonneck and Louis Gruenberg keen to make their mark on contemporary music. There was serious funding to be found in the USA, too, with active support from Mrs Elizabeth Coolidge, already making her presence felt at the festivals.[42] But the immediate future at least was clearly defined, with a small festival at Siena and Dent's aristocratic friends to support it.

After Frankfurt, that July Dent went to Homborg 'for some rest' before going on to Stuttgart to oversee some rehearsals for *Dido* being produced by Wilhelm Kempff,[43] far better known as a pianist but very 'keen'.

> Heaven knows what it would have been like if I had not been there! Kempff is … a remarkably fine pianist but no conductor. He loved the work, but what he really wanted to do was to extemporize variations for the pianoforte in the style of Max Reger on all the little dance tunes! … Erhardt pulled things through somehow, and I nagged at Kempff … until I got them to sing in something like time (tune was hopeless) and to run the numbers without pauses.[44]

Dent never could resist the impulse to cast his bread upon local waters, and he appears to have got on well with Erhardt, who encouraged him to come to

38 Haefeli, *IGNM*, p. 154.

39 JBT 02/06/1927.

40 CC 23/07/1927.

41 JBT 02/06/1927.

42 Elizabeth Sprague Coolidge (1864–1953), American pianist and musical philanthropist who sponsored or commissioned music, especially chamber music, from many 20th-century composers.

43 Wilhelm Kempff (1895–1991) had already composed a number of pieces for choirs, but was best known for his improvisations.

44 CC 23/07/1927.

Ludwigsburg 'to see the theatre in the palace where Jommelli used to produce operas. Erhardt gave a Handel opera there one day by candlelight; it must have been very dangerous ... there is a lot of old scenery there still'.[45]

> I long for Italy and wish I could spend my evenings in the Piazza at Venice; but I doubt if I shall have time to go there. I shall have to go to a meeting of musical researchers at Basle in September or early October to plan out the constitution of a new International Society for Musical Research. I shouldn't be surprised if they make me president.[46]

Now he needed to make a start on the Busoni biography that July and August, staying in Mayer's flat in Wegenerstrasse, not far from the Busonis'. Gerda Busoni had not wanted him to work every day at the flat as he had been used to doing, spreading out the great mass of material there, so he took time out to go to the Caspar Hauser museum, to a theatre exhibition at Magdeburg and wandering around Potsdam and its 'pleasant Anlagen [layout] and avenues', Sans Souci, with Voltaire's room and its 'parrots and other birds and flowers in rather high relief on the walls'. Gerda Busoni's tenant Alma Moodie had just left to get married, so Dent pressed Maurice Ingram to find a 'nice diplomat' bring in some much-needed income, but her fragile state made any collaboration difficult if not impossible.

> I have made extracts from a good deal of the stuff I took to England & brought back: but I see it is impossible to go on in this way owing to the gigantic mass of material. I am picking up a good deal of odd information from little Dr Schnapp, who was a pupil of Petri. He told me a great deal that I cannot possibly talk to Frau B. about.[47]

For the next three years, at odd times and in between his other commitments, Dent continued to check on Gerda and carefully consult about questions arising.

> It has been a wonderful experience soaking myself in these Busoni letters, – some of them are incredibly touching – and they are full of interesting ideas. But it wants the combination of a Lytton Strachey and a Romain Rolland to do it justice.[48]

It took him two years to appreciate fully how to write biography, how to devise a narrative for Busoni's complex life, and how to be truthful without upsetting Gerda or the reading public, besides the ongoing problem of finding a place where he could concentrate.

> I shall never get that book written until I can shut myself up somewhere in a place like Vicenza where I know nobody & have no distractions & can concentrate on the book all day long.[49]

45 *Ibid.*

46 *Ibid.*

47 JBT 12/09/1927.

48 *Ibid.*

49 LH 30/12/1928.

Eventually, in 1929, he discovered a routine which suited him perfectly, retiring completely to one or other remote hotels in the Dolomites, staying there for weeks, usually in the company of a young Italian called Carlo.[50] Busoni would have laughed.

En route back to Cambridge in late September, Dent stopped in Cologne for a week of opera, then to the 'Confédération Internationale de Musicologie' on the 28th with Gerry Cooper; a lecture on *Idomeneo* at Essen, then Paris, for a meeting with Ravel and Roland Manuel[51] to revive the fractious French Section.[52]

❧ ❧ ❧

> Life is very busy here, but I like it quite well & am generally well in health – I sometimes feel rather a prisoner, but it can't be helped.[53]

Only after a meeting of the Old Vic Board on 7 October could Dent finally drag himself back to Cambridge. He was to lecture one hour each week, beside 'arranged' afternoon lectures with 'illustrations', and he insisted on seeing his twelve students individually at least one hour a week. So began the long labour of building up new foundations in the faculty teaching style, besides the extra details – pushing the Council about Boris Ord's Fellowship, working with Arundell to fix *King Arthur* for February, with Frank Birch and the MDS, translating Goldoni's *Servant of Two Masters*, while building up the subtle outreach which brought international players – Falla, Andres Segovia, Elisabeth Schumann and more – to a Cambridge ready to receive them, whether at Mrs Hackforth's chamber concerts[54] or King's College Chapel.

> It is amusing to see how I have stirred people up to make a little social for our foreign musical celebrities! It is worth doing, as they get to feel that Cambridge is a different sort of place from Bradford or Wolverhampton … Elisabeth Schumann sang here on the 8th: I had a party for her & her husband, as I know them well.[55]

Such gestures were actually the small building-blocks in Dent's practical internationalism, bringing what had been foreign and exotic into more domestic circumstances, part of his constant drive to use every means that came his way.

50 This is probably Milanese Carlo Cavalli, who became part of Dent's wider gay Italian circles, later attaching himself to others in that circle. See below.

51 Roland Alexis Manuel Lévy (1891–1966), friend of Satie, studied with Ravel and Roussel, critic at Paris *Éclair*, wrote a book on Ravel.

52 CC 23/07/1927.

53 LH 18/11/1927.

54 Mrs Hackforth's weekly 'Informal Music Club' concerts became a Cambridge fixture from 1926, prefiguring Jim Ede's better known, later series at Kettle's Yard. She conducted the Perse Girls School orchestra and generally helped to lift standards. Knight, *Cambridge Music*, pp. 110-111, 126.

55 LH 18/11/1927

> Chester Purves writes to say that they propose putting me on to the L of N Int committee for the Arts in place of Weingartner (who is useless) … so I have written to accept.[56]

The League of Nations committee had been set up following the principles laid out by Guido Adler and others of Dent's close acquaintance.

> What art is better adapted to form an international connecting-link, than music? – especially instrumental music, which is in a manner an international language, an expression of the most intimate, the profoundest emotions of man.[57]

But from the outset and in spite of the interesting people involved – Paul Valéry and Hélène Vacaresco, *inter alia* – Dent found it disappointing, and although he persevered for another three years, his became simply another voice at a committee meeting.

> I have just come from the Geneva meetings – it was interesting to meet people, but the nonsense talked was terrible & I was very much bored. However I made friends with Weingartner & we got some resolutions through. And I think many people on the committee were genuinely pleased that music was being tackled seriously at last.[58]

Siena was taking shape, the jury – Alban Berg, Volkmar Andreae, Alfred Casella, Philipp Jarnach and Karel Jirák – having bent the rules (again) to include Falla's Harpsichord Concerto, encouraging the recalcitrant Spanish Section. Beside the Falla, there was Prokofiev's Wind Quintet, Martinu's Second String Quartet, Frank Bridge, Zemlinsky, Hindemith, Ravel, Webern's String Trio op. 20, and Stravinsky's *Les Noces*, the last included in a 'special' concert of the Italian Section, together with Walton's *Façade* and Casella's Sonata for Cello and Piano.

> The Jury have chosen Falla's Cembalo concerto – Andreae says that Wanda Landowska is bringing an action against Falla about it … I said I thought probably the English section wd have to push itself to a little trouble about it … as Spain will do nothing. The only Spanish music sent was a set of wretched pianoforte pieces by Mompou from Barcelona.[59]

Only half jokingly, Dent suggested that they give a concert of 'bad music'.

Dent was himself travelling all that summer, to Berlin, London for Old Vic and Philharmonic meetings, then Geneva, and Milan, often in company of Lawrence Haward or JB, winding up at Prince Chigi's opulent palazzo for the Siena Festival. Lawrence was bombarded with advice about finding Dent's own Italy, complete with introductions to Claudio, 'the Marchese Sommariva' and Torrefranca, 'also to a young man who does not move in those circles at all, but is a great friend of Enrico

56 JBT 18/10/1927.

57 Guido Adler, 1925, quoted in 'A Musical League of Nations'?: Music Institutions and the Politics of Internationalism, symposium at the Institute of Musical Research, London, 2018.

58 LH 21/07/1928.

59 JBT 30/03/1928.

Festing Jones, Malcolm Davidson & Sebastian Sprott. You will have to pay for his meals, but you will find him companionable and thoroughly sensible.'[60] He was also advised to be 'extremely careful'.[61]

Michaelmas term, and the most immediate problem was stabilising the faculty. Daddy Mann had suffered a heart attack, and was in poor health, so Dent ploughed straight in to get Boris Ord's Fellowship renewed, backed by Maynard Keynes and Sheppard. 'I need hardly say we are desperately tactful, and no one mentions (except in the strictest privacy) what they are all thinking about.'[62] But Dennis Arundell's Fellowship at St John's was probably not going to be renewed. In these years, some of his best new pupils began to come through the system: Robin Orr, Philip Radcliffe, and in the first wave of women, Rosamond Harding.

For the next few years, at least, the ISCM was relatively calm, the jury meetings assuming a less frantic, more familiar mode. The jury at Geneva on 10 December, was certainly less fraught than usual: Ansermet, Willem Pijper, Ravel, Bozidar Sirola and Heinz Tiessen.

> I think the Jury was very well balanced. Ansermet is of course much the best man. Ravel was not a very good worker: he flitted from one thing to another, and his voting paper was mostly ?'s. When we began to discuss any work he had no note of it, had completely forgotten it, or couldn't make head or tail of the score! But he is a distinguished personality: and I won't say that he was not a good juryman: for he stood out for finished workmanship ... Pijper was delightful.[63]

Ansermet, acting as host, saw to it that they had a bit of fun.

> One evening Ansermet took us all ... (to) the Fete de l'Escalade – an attempted attack on Geneva by the Burgundians in 1603 or thereabouts ... everybody in masquerade. We went to a 'foire' & had ourselves photographed in an aeroplane (painted on a backcloth) all together: wandered about among the swings & roundabouts in a good deal of slush & then went to a 'dancing' avec champagne obligatoire.[64]

'The English parcel was very good', Dent wrote with enthusiasm, even though they had been forced to drop younger composers Constant Lambert and Lennox Berkeley while choosing Vaughan Williams and John Ireland. As Dent knew by now and the individual national sections too often forgot, the question wasn't simply the quality of the music, but the balance and the logistics of putting on, e.g., a big choral piece of Lambert's. 'The most interesting thing, I think, will be Janáček's Glagolithic Mass (wch can only be given if Prague sends a chorus) and an 8-part motet by one Karl marx (!) of Munich, to words by Rilke. I want to

60 LH 20/06/1928.

61 LH 03/08/1928

62 JBT 30/10/1928.

63 JBT 15/12/1928.

64 *Ibid.*

FIGURE 13. Zurich ISCM jury in a Geneva funfair aeroplane, 1928: Willem Pijper, Heinz Tiessen, Bozidar Sirola, Ravel and Dent. © The British Library Board. Add. 71144, p. 33.

translate it and get it done at Cambridge.' There were about 15 'new names' for the next festival. But beside the built-in regrets, there was bound to be trouble.

> The terrible thing is that the Jury rejected the whole Italian parcel, and even a new violin concerto by Rieti wch Ansermet brought with him. Really I don't wonder: for Casella has now set the fashion of what I suppose if Musica fascista – back to Vivaldi & Co – It is all very cheerful & agreeable, & quite well made: but it is all rather sham stuff and at best merely 'Unterhaltungsmusik' … I suppose there will be trouble.[65]

He dealt with it by making sure that Casella was on the jury for the London–Oxford Festival of 1931.

❧ ❧ ❧

'I had rather a bad time with the cold weather in Cambridge; it got me at the stomach again', Dent wrote to Clive, touring in Saskatchewan that March. His stomach troubles reflect the constant underlying stress, since his current machinations were by no means confined to the ISCM, the League of Nations, Cambridge or even the Old Vic and the Philharmonic Society. The British arts world was rapidly changing, expanding via the relatively new and subsidised BBC, and by now Dent's work on these various domestic committees put him in a position to oversee and nudge any

65 Light music. *Ibid.*

changes. He was always very clear about what the arts could and should be doing, while the complex dynamics of working committees only stimulated his more subversive instincts. Keenly attuned to 'intrigue', especially on the part of people he disliked or distrusted, Dent worked to sort them before the issues came up officially, always preferring to avoid confrontation.

The history of the London orchestras at this time is unspeakably complicated, a minefield of cross-purposes, misunderstandings and underhand dealings, far too complex to go into detail here. In 1929, the Philharmonic Society committee was trying to assemble the means to support a new 'permanent orchestra' for its regular concerts, to define its role and to establish better standards. The London visit in 1927 of the Berlin Philharmonic had shown how poor current orchestral standards were compared to Germany's, and critics like W.J. Turner inveighed against the old system of deputising,[66] 'a sign of degenerate musical life'.[67] Thomas Beecham had wanted to improve orchestral standards since before the war, but his self-centred efforts depended on how much money he could raise and on retaining his own artistic control. Historically, the Philharmonic Society concerts had been collaborations with the London Symphony Orchestra, often with Beecham at the podium, and now Beecham was proposing a new arrangement, a rescue package for the Philharmonic, offering up a collaboration with himself at the helm of a 'new' orchestra, to be called the Royal Philharmonic Orchestra, which would double as orchestra for Beecham's other current enterprise, the 'League of Opera'. In an offer almost too good to be true, he guaranteed the orchestra an income of 10,000 pounds, with at least twenty of its annual concerts 'under the sole control of the society'.[68] Dent never trusted him for an instant.

> The negotiations about the permanent orchestra with Beecham and the B.B.C. etc go on and on and on, and I have more or less brought the Phil. Committee to see that we are the real controlling factor in the intrigue, and that our game is to … temporize as long as we possibly can; at the end of which Beechams scheme will be melted away in smoke as usual, and the Phil, in a much sounder position than before.
>
> I see that Beecham has suddenly got busy again with the League of Opera; I received 2 days ago a huge circular asking me to organize all sorts of 'snowball' devices. When I was in London the talk was all for the Permanent Orchestra scheme, and the League of Opera seemed to have been dropped and its funds appropriated for the Orchestra.[69]

At around the same time, the BBC through Adrian Boult, his own standards honed at the ISCM festivals, was also assembling a permanent orchestra for similar reasons, and with its stable funding and growing remit, it was at first seen as a threat

66 Orchestral players could 'deputise', arrange substitutes for themselves, even at the last minute, if something else cropped up, undermining any rehearsals or performance.

67 W.J. Turner, 'The New B.B.C. Orchestra' in *Facing the Music: Reflections of a Music Critic* (London, 1933), pp. 61–71.

68 Lucas, *Thomas Beecham*, p. 180.

69 CC 27/03/1929.

to established musical institutions like the Philharmonic Society. Formed in 1922, the BBC had taken several years to decide how its new technology could be used, and only very recently was beginning seriously to broadcast music, to a very mixed reception.[70] The fact that it was publicly funded caused consternation in ways still around a century later, with protests about the waste of public money and unfair advantages. Its broadcasts of live concerts provoked strong protests from such establishment figures as conductor Sir Hamilton Harty, who called them 'the amiable bandits of Savoy Hill', declaring that 'it was morally wrong and quite indefensible for it to enter into direct competition with private musical interests'.[71] The *Musical Times* applauded the BBC's efforts to broadcast unusual or lost pieces of music, while – oddly – condemning its attempts to broadcast contemporary music to a tiny audience.[72] Dent's old friend Percy Pitt,[73] who had worked with Beecham over the war years, was the BBC's Music Director from 1922 to 1930. By 1931, the BBC Symphony Orchestra under the BBC's new Music Director, Boult, was making its mark in contemporary music, providing the orchestral platform for the Oxford–London ISCM Festival beside its regular broadcasts of new music.

But where Dent found it easier to negotiate with the BBC in some matters, he found impossible the prospect of coming to any stable, long-term arrangement with Beecham. For two years more the Philharmonic dilemma drifted unresolved, the London Symphony Orchestra prevaricating about any new impositions on its established style, so Beecham, backed by the rich Elizabeth Courtauld (until her death in 1931), simply plucked the best musicians from its ranks, consolidated them with musicians from the Philharmonic Society, and formed the new London Philharmonic Orchestra, nearly destroying[74] the London Symphony Orchestra and the Philharmonic Society in the process. Besides being an inspiration, Beecham became a source of irritation, but like the grit in the oyster, the rivalries he set up were forcing the other orchestras and opera companies to rethink their own priorities and identities. By October 1931, Dent was writing to Lawrence:

> They have made me standing chairman of the Philh. and I anticipate very troubled times … We are on the verge of complete ruin, thanks to the BBC & Mrs Courtauld. But the real worst is that certain numbers of the Cttee simply don't

70 Although he famously later gave many broadcasts, Thomas Beecham, e.g., was against the idea of broadcasting music. In 1928 he said: 'Ever since the beginning of the present century there has been committed against the unfortunate art of music every imaginable sin. But all the previous crimes and stupidities pale before this latest attack on its fair name, the broadcasting of it by means of wireless … The performance of music through this or any other kindred contrivance cannot be other than a ludicrous caricature … If the wireless authorities are permitted to carry on with their devilish work, in ten years' time the concert halls will be deserted.' Scholes, *The Mirror of Music*, vol. 2, p. 798.

71 *Ibid.*

72 *Ibid.*, pp. 797ff. Scholes was personally against such broadcasts, calling them 'mistakes'.

73 Percy Pitt (1869–1932), conductor.

74 See Lucas, *Thomas Beecham*, pp. 205–11.

> seem to care a damn whether the Philh. goes on or winds up for ever. They have had too much experience of theatre work & English opera, I think![75]

As President of the Philharmonic Society, this mess was what Dent had to deal with, but he loved firefighting, confident in his own ability to sort out destructive and acrimonious internal squabbles; he believed that basically, all the competing parties were really struggling towards a common aim, the solid establishment of music and opera in Britain.

At the same time as these struggles to keep the Philharmonic Society going, the Old Vic governors were trying to launch their own opera project at Sadler's Wells, so for the next few years Dent's every spare moment was focused on this. Apart from the problems of competition with the BBC, with Beecham's orchestra, and with Beecham's proposed League of Opera, there was considerable confusion at the Old Vic and Sadler's Wells about the actual style of the new venture. Dent's own agendas were clear: that the best musicians available should be employed, with Clive Carey as a continental-style Intendant at the new Vic–Wells. Dent also wanted Percy Pitt onside, both for the Sadler's Wells development as it came into being and for possible future joint ventures with the BBC. 'I find Pitt much more friendly and approachable than I had expected', he wrote to Clive:

> After all, he is a good musician in his way and he sees through Miss B[aylis] easily enough. The difficulty is that one can't <u>discuss</u> these things properly with Miss B: and I can't go into plain words about Corri etc at the Governors' meeting although I am sure most of the Governors realize <u>his</u> situation.[76]
>
> It wd take a lot to stir up these unmusical Governors (especially against the wishes of Miss B) to put in an Intendant of the Opera, equal in power to Miss B. And at what salary?[77]

Throughout 1930, while the negotiations were still in progress for the opening of the renovated Sadler's Wells theatre on Boxing Day, Dent wanted to ensure that everything – Intendant, orchestra, solid production plans – was in place beforehand. His main opposition, as he saw it, was Lilian Baylis, who fought against bringing in anyone who might overrule her, while suggesting people who in Dent's view were simply not good enough to sustain the kind of quality operation he wanted for the Vic–Wells. First, she wanted to 'get along' with an all-purpose producer, her candidate being Sydney Russell, who had been with the British National Opera Company.

> I have had talks with P.P. [Pitt] and he seems to be completely in agreement with me … that you are the right man to be Intendant. He said quite frankly that Russell, although <u>most</u> competent as a stage manager & producer in the ordinary way, is <u>not</u> the type of man or musician to be <u>Intendant</u>.[78]

75 LH 14/10/1931.

76 CC 24/10/1930.

77 CC 16/11/1930.

78 *Ibid.*

But there was another obstacle to Dent's plans; Clive had got married in Australia. 'At least it might get him away from his mama', Dent commented to Lawrence. To Clive, he wrote:

> I hope you are having a successful honeymoon and everything points to marriage being a great success. And you will feel less difficulty as regards your mother now ... it is problem daily before me with the life of Busoni.[79]

Dent wrote this to Clive from San Candido, Italy, where he had retreated to get on with his Busoni biography in peace, convenient for Venice and Trieste, where he planned to meet up with singer Malcolm Davidson later in his stay. 'This place vaguely reminds me of Aysgarth, in spite of the Dolomites', he wrote to Lawrence, 'for it is a simple country place without even a cinema and I live a quiet life, working at Busoni and talking to nobody, wch is an immense relief after my usual sort of existence.'[80] Dent stayed there for a month, managing to draft most of the book. In Milan he had found a very congenial companion, young Carlo Cavalli, who came recommended, having made himself agreeable to a number of Dent's friends and acquaintances: Festing Jones, Malcolm Davidson and 'also Humphrey Procter-Gregg!'.[81] They appear to have had a trial run beforehand, a weekend at Arona, before they decided it might work.[82]

The Busoni biography was probably the most difficult and personal piece of writing Dent had ever undertaken. Positive feedback came from Anton Mayer and Egon Petri, who had seen the first two draft chapters on Busoni's early life, and approved the 'intimate' style. He realised that he needed to see Gerda again, beside Dr Melanie Praelinger, whose reminiscences had 'a wonderfully vivid way of putting essential things in a word or two', so another trip to Berlin late in September was shoehorned in before a committee meeting in Paris in early October.

Cambridge Michaelmas term brought nine composition pupils, including several future professors, and Philip Radcliffe's Fellowship dissertation, 'I think a very good piece of work'. The MDS were doing *Henry IV, Part I,* with Donald Beves as Falstaff and Dennis Robertson as Shallow: 'It is easy enough to do comic old men in Cambridge', while the Greek Play was using music Dennis Arundell had arranged from Handel, which Dent thought all wound up 'sounding like Stanford!'. Artur Schnabel was playing and stayed with Dent at Panton Street.

But the winter cold soon began to get to Dent; his stomach played up, and he was anxious to get to the jury meeting at Frankfurt that March while wishing he could be with JB in Marrakesh instead.

> Casella & his crowd have organized a rival Festival at Venice Sept 7–15. He only informed me of this 3 days ago (I had heard of it by roundabout ways from Berlin a month before!). It is obviously a sort of unfriendly act: but the only way to deal with it is to pretend that it is all very laudable, & we wish all the sections wd do the same.[83]

79 CC 22/08/1929.
80 LH 27/07/1929.
81 *Ibid.*
82 JBT 17/07/1929.
83 JBT 28/02/1930.

The 1930 ISCM Liège–Brussels Festival especially showed how Dent's vision of carefully mixed programming could work, being done in association with the first congress of the re-formed International Musical Society.[84] Alban Berg's opera *Wozzeck* in the Stadttheater Aachen, with Szymanowski's *Stabat Mater* beside a concert of a capella music, Josquin, Gesualdo, Lassus, Tomkins, *et al.* With that mixing in mind, the 1931 Festival was planned for Oxford and London, with evenings of ballet, of theatre and a concert of 'Old English' music, bringing in the BBC for the first time. But for various reasons, Dent himself would take a back seat.

JB was in Algeria for the first part of 1930; Dent sent him long letters and candied fruits from La Selva, where he stayed for a month over the New Year, looking after his elderly uncle, reading him Queen Victoria's letters, which amused them both. For once, Dent went to operas at Monte Carlo, Mozart's *Zaïde* and Mussorgsky's *Marriage*, and having enjoyed them more than he expected, planned to go to *Elektra* and *El Amor Brujo*. There was gossip about Carlo going off to Dublin to work, and about Dent's surprise at actually enjoying the Elgar night at the Philharmonic Society:

> it seems so remote now that one just accepts it as 'old music' and I began to see that Elgar had qualities wch I preferred to Strauss & much preferred to Mahler ... I had no chance of speaking to Elgar, who was in great spirits, and slightly tight, I think! ... he looked much older ... much less like the retired Du Maurier Colonel of old days, and now & then very obviously <u>not</u> quite the aristocrat he has always tried to be![85]

In London Dent was back with his comfortable gang: Jack Gordon, Roderick Meiklejohn, Bou and Fred, often with Malcolm Davidson or Gerry Cooper, who seems to have replaced Timmy Jekyll in Dent's London concert life as well as being his sidekick abroad. 'I have had a meal or two with Gerry – who is perfectly delightful tete-à-tete – but in company he is unbearable.'[86] Fred called him 'Miss Geraldine'.

It is sometimes difficult to tell from Dent's own expressed perceptions of his world what was happening in the wider picture, the events which have come down as momentous. The stock-market crash of October 1929 had a devastating effect; money coming from the USA in the form of Pilgrim Trust or other grants was now far less reliable a source. Money was even more scarce in Europe now, too, the cultural flowering of the Weimar Republic already well into decline. Rather too airily Dent wrote to JB from Berlin that June:

> The elections passed off nicely: but people are all horrified at the enormous gains of the Hitler party – I do not think they will be much of a danger: they have no programme at all. But they will probably be a nuisance and utterly irresponsible in the Reichstag.[87]

84 The pre-war Internationale Musikgesellschaft (IMG) / International Musical Society (IMS) / Société Internationale de la Musique (SIM) was re-formed in 1927 as the Internationale Gesellschaft für Musikwissenschaft (IGMW) / International Society for Musical Research (ISMR) / Société Internationale de la Musique (SIM). Henceforth it will be referred to as the ISMR.

85 JBT 31/01/1930.

86 JBT 18/04/1930.

87 JBT 16/09/1930.

CHAPTER 12

The Juggler 1931–1934

> I am already beginning to make plans for a Festival at Cambridge in 1933! Not a 'contemporary' one, but a Congress of the Research International, with a really first-rate festival of historical English music. Perhaps in 1934 (if not in 1932) we might have a 'contemporary' Festival here, but not an International one: I mean a Festival of the British Sections and branches, like the Pyrmont Festival of the German groups. It would be a great idea to have some sort of musical Festival at Cambridge every year, but each time different in character.[1]

1931–1933

The year 1931 marked the high point of Dent's optimism and enthusiasm, with the birth of Sadler's Wells, his election as President of the ISMR – the only person to have been President of both the ISMR and the ISCM – and as Chair of the Philharmonic Society standing committee, and the first ISCM festival to be held in England. In Cambridge, beside nurturing new generations of musicians at the university, he had been co-opted onto the Cambridgeshire committee to produce an important report on the teaching of music in schools. By the end of the year the Busoni biography was nearly drafted, mostly because any relaxation he managed to seize over the past five years had been centred around his Busoni work, in the Dolomites with Carlo and in Berlin. The only committee Dent gave up was the League of Nations music ('I am not sorry; it was a great waste of time, and on the whole, a bore'),[2] his internationalism and teaching now focused elsewhere.

1931 was also a year of 'intrigues', around the ISCM Festival in London and Oxford, the conflicting but purposeful interests of the BBC and the Philharmonic Society, Sadler's Wells and other operatic ventures, and quite separately, to get JB elected Professor of Spanish at Oxford: 'I am doing what I can about Oxford … which included letters and background talks between Sheppard and Stewart from Cambridge talking it up with Dawkins at Oxford'.[3] Behind all the intrigues lay Dent's continuing vision for the institutions developing in his care, outward-looking and inclusive. By 1933, he would find another purpose for all this groundwork, when the refugees began their desperate knocking at his door to seek help of a different kind.

1 LH 10/07/1931.

2 *Ibid.*

3 JBT May/June 1931.

Yet the one event from this eventful year to stick in the public mind is what Dent called the 'Elgar Hetz' – the Elgar agitation – against him.

❧ ❧ ❧

A second edition of the German book *Handbuch der Musikgeschichte,* first published in 1924 by Dent's old friend Guido Adler, was published in late 1930, and Dent's brief remarks on Elgar[4] brought self-righteous wrath down upon his head. By this time Elgar's reputation was in decline and opinion on his music polarised; moreover, his health was poor. There were outraged letters to *The Times* and other papers, all 'instigated' by Peter Warlock and signed by many musical great and good, Percy Scholes and Bernard Shaw, William Walton and even an old friend like Donald Tovey 'who in his young days had invented an adjective "velgar" and christened *The Dream of Gerontius* "Gerry's Nightmare"'. Taken out of context, the offending passage seems at most high-handed and flippant.

> He was a violinist by profession, and studied the works of Liszt, which were an abomination to conservative, academic musicians. He was, moreover, a Catholic, and more or less a self-taught man, who possessed little of the literary culture of Parry and Stanford … To English ears, Elgar's music is too emotional and not entirely free from vulgarity. His orchestral works, two symphonies, concertos for violin and cello, and several overtures, are vivid in colour, but pompous in style and of a too deliberate chivalrousness [Ritterlichkeit] of expression.

Initially, Dent thought that the rumpus had been caused by his more incendiary remarks in his contribution to *La musica contemporanea in Europe* in 1925.

> I refused to go to Percy Scholes' Conference at Lausanne the following week, as I knew I should be dead tired, and quite unfit to throw myself into all its activities. And since then I am glad I refused, as Percy Scholes has been curiously tiresome in joining the 'Elgar Hetz' and pointing out that I said severe things about Elgar's music in an Italian magazine some 5 years ago![5]

JB, working at Oxford, expressed the fear Dent might actually be attacked during the July ISCM festival: 'he is firmly convinced that Mr Robert Lorenz, who started the "Elgar Hetz" against me, will come to Oxford and assault me violently in public, or make some other sort of disturbance'.[6]

4 'Geschichte der englischen Musik seit 1880', *Handbuch der Musikgeschichte,* vol. 2, *Die Moderne,* ed. Guido Adler (Berlin, 1930); Haward, *Edward J. Dent: A Bibliography,* 90.

5 LH 10/07/1931. Scholes ran a collaborative course for British and American music teachers, chaired by Sir Henry Hadow, first in London, then in 1929, at Lausanne: 'The First Anglo-American Summer Holiday Music Conference', with 'hundreds of music teachers from both sides of the Atlantic'. Cf. Scholes, *The Mirror of Music,* vol. 2, p. 629.

6 LH 10/07/1931. Even in a recent (2012) book on music at Eton College, Dent's Professorship is mentioned, and while none of his other achievements is acknowledged a whole page is devoted to this episode. Philip Radcliffe, Brian Trowell and recently, Matthew Riley, have all spent more time discussing this than any of Dent's other achievements. The need to explain and/or apologise is very strong.

Philip Radcliffe, studying with Dent at this time, later took some trouble to provide context for Dent's remarks,[7] with sympathy and understanding of Dent's 'idiosyncrasies', his sometimes apparently contradictory stances, his dismissive phrases 'too emotional and not quite free from vulgarity', beside the 'chivalric rhetoric which badly covers up his intrinsic vulgarity'. Radcliffe personally remembers Dent 'inveighing against the English ultra-respectable fear of vulgarity' while appreciating – as he does in the offending article – Elgar's 'orchestral brilliance and glowing expressiveness'. The point, not picked up at the time but since aired, is that Dent's apparently casual use of an emotionally charged term like 'vulgar' is in fact part of his complex distinction, made over a long period of time, between what can be acceptable and what is pretentious or sentimental; populist. Dent's personal aversion to late Victorian piety made him suspicious of Elgar's undertakings of 'nobility', and he hated music to be used as crude emotional manipulation; film music irritated him, as did a lot of church music. But the episode shows what a great public reputation he had achieved by that time, in order to be attacked in the vigorous style the British have always enjoyed throwing at their public figures. Dent actually liked some of Elgar's music, although some newer pieces attracted his bile: 'the Elgar [cello] concerto is dreadful slop, only fit for Beatrice Harrison',[8] he grumbled to Lawrence Haward, 'slosh of Sibelius and Elgar'.

Although he appears to have made a joke of the whole thing to close friends like Lawrence, and he didn't bother to respond to the public demands for an apology, such an attack must have rattled Dent, raising the spectre of homophobia behind all the sound and fury.[9] He thought it an attack on himself rather than his views on Elgar and decided to ignore it, an attitude many gay men adopted to divert any unwanted attention to their personal selves, taking refuge in work and keeping out of the way.

Now, Dent was determined to enjoy his favourite escape, Berlin, with new productions like *Feuersnot* and new operas like Braunfels' *Galathea* (1929); Strauss and Klemperer were conducting an 'International Society' concert. Having found Gerda Busoni desperate, virtually insolvent and unable to pay the rent, Dent did what he could to get the fund actually working. Other ominous signs of the changing times were dismissed or rationalised: Max Friedlaender's son was already in London, now calling himself Franz Röhn, having 'changed his name because it was Jewish – a foolish thing, wch I expect he now regrets … working at some prints & drawings at the BM & at Windsor Castle'.[10] 'I am told that the reason the "Kroll" opera is to be closed is simply a hatred of modern music. Klemperer is too modern, although

7 Philip Radcliffe, *E.J. Dent: A Centenary Memoir* (Rickmansworth, 1976), pp. 17–18.

8 LH 20/05/1934.

9 In a recent study, Sarah Collins thought the episode part of a more complex, pervasive anti-intellectualism at the time. Sarah Collins, 'Anti-Intellectualism and the Rhetoric of "National Character" in Music: The Vulgarity of Over-Refinement', in Jeremy Dibble and Julian Horton, ed., *British Musical Criticism and Intellectual Thought 1850–1950* (Woodbridge, 2018), pp. 199–234.

10 JBT 27/01/1927.

Mayer says the Kroll opera pays far better than either of the other 2 houses'.[11] But its closure, on 3 July 1931, was part of a growing political agenda. Of the three opera houses in Berlin, the one that was shut was the one producing the most controversial and contemporary productions, perhaps the emblem of everything that had been most artistically exciting about the soon-to-be-defunct Weimar Republic. Ironically, its last performance was Mozart, *The Marriage of Figaro*.

Although he continued to take in his favoured Berlin treats, Dent was becoming more circumspect, refusing to take visitors to the notorious club Eldorado, 'I declined and said I really could not be seen there. It is a place run for foreigners who want to see the night life of Berlin, and they think it wonderful because the men are dressed up as women'.[12] Instead, what was really one of Dent's last uncomplicated Berlin nights out was spent at the Jockey with two of his congenial young men, Terpis and Rolf Arco:

> full of theatrical and literary people, with a remarkably good pianist, who played a piece of Bach extremely well, as soon as we came in; and a negro woman sang erotic songs in American and German … in a deep contralto like a bassoon with a cold … exquisitely clear in rhythm and diction … it was curiously attractive and fascinating, for that sort of thing is quite unique in music and is such a welcome relief from the traditional light or sentimental stuff of any European countries.[13]

❧ ❧ ❧

> Sadler's Wells is approaching completion, and I foresee endless worries over its future and the organization of opera there. I suppose Geoffrey Toye will really settle the matter: Aveling and I shall just have to fall in with things.[14]

Sadler's Wells had opened on a freezing, foggy January night in 1931, not with an opera but with Shakespeare: John Gielgud and Ralph Richardson in *Twelfth Night*. Dent wrote a glowing and optimistic account in the new *Old Vic and Sadler's Wells Magazine*, a puff to welcome the new home of English opera and a statement of intent.

> They suddenly accomplished what English musicians have been struggling and fighting for since Opera was first attempted in England nearly three hundred years ago … the establishment of a permanent English Opera House … musicians have long accustomed themselves to regard it as quite hopeless to expect Parliament to give any practical encouragement to either music or drama. … I should be very sorry to see the Old Vic become a dependency of either Covent Garden or the B.B.C. Independence is vital to us here. We have our own style, our own traditions and our own audiences … those gallery boys and girls … Opera every night for eight months. That means that you can engage a permanent

[11] JBT 07/04/ 1931.

[12] JBT 30/04/1931.

[13] *Ibid.*

[14] JG 29/12/1929.

> orchestra, always rehearsing and playing together. It will have to be a small one, but that is no great matter, when you have a great musician like Mr. Corri who is ready to take endless trouble in his holidays to arrange a big score for a small band, not as any hack might do it but with the sensitiveness of an artist ... Sense of espris de corps and devotion to the theatre ... Discerning musicians often said that for certain operas the 'People's Opera' gave very much more intelligent performances than the Court Opera.[15]

More hopeful than factual, Dent's article hides his personal aversion to Corri's cobbled-together efforts while praising the special audience – 'those gallery boys and girls' – they had worked so hard to attract and wished to keep. The Old Vic and Sadler's Wells company was more of a work in progress, divided, in the tart opinion of several of its governors, without due consideration between opera and drama, with ballet thrown in.

> Miss Baylis herself was utterly unprepared for the new developments which the opening of Sadler's Wells inevitably involved ... it had never occurred to her that the whole work of the opera department would from now onwards be doubled if not more.[16]

From its inception Sadler's Wells had to compete not only with Covent Garden and other opera venues, but its own, because its Old Vic audience refused to come north of the river, and any 'new' opera audience was thin, especially in this time of economic depression. But Lilian Baylis insisted on alternating opera and theatre, even though it meant endless logistical problems of shifting the scenery and costumes back and forth across London. North London, it soon became clear, had a different clientele on its doorstep, developing around ballet rather than opera.

> We have evolved a new system, by which Sadler's Wells gets a larger proportion of Opera, as that public seems to like Opera better than Shakespeare. What it does love is Ballet, but the Baylis can't be brought to see that she ought to put on more ballet nights.[17]

Under the direction of Ninette de Valois and Constant Lambert, the ballet had moved in and was an instant success, quickly developing its own programming style and its own audience.[18] The public hunger for ballet was initially fed by the Ballets Russes; then, after Diaghilev's death, the Camargo Society had stepped in, founded in 1930 by Maynard Keynes and his wife, the former Ballets Russes dancer, Lydia Lopokova, with Constant Lambert, who both as composer and as conductor had a natural affinity for ballet music. In its few years of existence, the Camargo Society staged some expensive, ambitious ballets, including Walton's *Façade* and Fredrick Ashton's *Pomona* as well as Vaughan Williams' *Job*, but in the end it was all too ambitious, and

15 E.J. Dent, *The Old Vic and Sadler's Wells Magazine* (January 1931), pp. 2–3.

16 Dent, ATFE, p. 96.

17 CC 17/12/1931.

18 Constant Lambert (1905–1951), composer, conductor, music critic. Dame Ninette de Valois (1890–2001), born Edris Stannus in Ireland, she danced with the Ballets Russes; her Sadler's Wells company became the Royal Ballet and she founded the Royal Ballet School.

the costs of hiring the Savoy, the musicians, the original sets, became too much; by 1933 it folded. But its sets and productions were handed over to the Old Vic and Sadler's Wells company, where de Valois was building up her company from six dancers to a full corps, performing in opera and ballet. For a time Sadler's Wells simply kept going, trying to fulfil its obligations to both opera and theatre, never quite succeeding with either, yet too good an idea to be allowed to fail, run at a deficit, subsidised by several benefactors, its ballet and the Old Vic takings, but still seen by its supporters to be the best hope yet for a permanent English opera company.

As Dent later pointed out, through its teething problems Sadler's Wells was trying to find its own style. The theatre itself was not very welcoming, 'built in a style of aggressive austerity and contrasted strangely with the picturesquely faded grandeurs of the Vic as it was in 1920',[19] while its stage was 'too near' for Wagnerian dramas and 'too far for the intimacies of Mozartian comedy'. Although the auditorium had a terrible acoustic, the general facilities were greatly improved, with a lot more space, so that rehearsals were less cramped and easier to schedule. Then there was the conflict between the artistic desire for excellent productions of old favourites beside the risky new productions, and Lilian Baylis 'with more anxiety than pride' concerned to keep only the full houses which would pay for it all. She would ruthlessly pull any production which failed to attract a full house in its first two or three performances, regarding it a 'hopeless failure'. As Dent later observed, even if the Wells had enjoyed a full house every night, it would have 'just kept its head above water'.[20] The later great successes at the Wells – including Lawrance Collingwood's Russian opera series, first English performances of *Snow Maiden* and *Tsar Saltan, Boris Godunov,* a 'sensitive and understanding production of Eugene Onegin', and various British operas – paradoxically seem to have been done as much in spite of Lilian Baylis as through her efforts.

For the next few years, as a governor, Dent kept in close touch with the Vic–Wells but was less active; from 1931–33 he was simply too busy elsewhere, travelling for the ISCM when not in Cambridge. 'I hope to get something sensible done about Sadler's Wells', he had written to Jack just before its opening, 'but not living in London I could not keep closely enough in touch with things, and I fear they will just go on in the usual Baylis-Corri style'.[21] He continued to find inspiration from the continental productions he was seeing, in touch with Kurt Joos at Essen and other young German directors. With several of the other Vic–Wells governors, Dent believed that for more stability the outfit needed a professional guiding hand like that of the Intendants in Germany, but for months Baylis would not admit the idea of an Intendant who might overrule her, least of all one backed by Dent and his supporters. Balked at every turn, Dent became suspicious of everything he saw as compromise, even Sydney Russell's tentative request for help with *Dido and Aeneas* at the Old Vic:

> he knows practically nothing about the opera, but in two lunches I have succeeded in winning his confidence … but what I rather suspect that he hopes to

[19] Dent, ATFE, p. 97.

[20] *Ibid.* p. 99.

[21] JG 24/12/1930.

get out of me is my pushing him in as complete artistic director of the Vic Opera. What a world of intrigue![22]

'Constant made quite a good show of "Dido" with Sydney Russell', Dent reported to Clive, still travelling. 'It wasn't as good as it ought to have been, but it was the best performance of "Dido" that I have yet seen.' Ethel Smyth was 'wild with enthusiasm' about it, Dent noted, adding with acerbity, 'I expect she had got the impression that Dido was the composer.' The central problem with every production of early opera – particularly *Dido* – Dent had seen in Germany had been the misunderstanding of the music, especially the differences between the big orchestras employed to play nineteenth-century opera, and the far smaller orchestras and limited musical language of the court orchestras of the eighteenth century and earlier.

> The trouble with practically all conductors in all countries is that they are very seldom interested in voices or in what is going on on the stage ... modern orchestral players are completely at their ease in Wagner and Strauss ... And even if some instruments do go astray, the chances are that very few members of an operatic audience will notice it, since their attention is a good deal distracted by the stage. On the other hand, operas by older composers, utilising a smaller orchestra and preferring in general a much thinner instrumental texture, are often very troublesome to rehearse, since an exact balance must be obtained in combinations of instruments that are now out of fashion and in many cases the music refuses to 'play itself' like Wagner and requires really imaginative interpretation.[23]

Smaller, cheaper, but excellent orchestras. By the time he wrote this in 1945, Dent had seen where the Vic–Wells and Cambridge could make a difference and set new standards, with productions requiring not so much money as intelligence and imagination, and at the heart of both these institutions he worked so hard to set up were Dent's ideas about the essential place of scholarship: theatre not just as spectacle but revelation. Throughout this teething time, Dent made sure that both Clive and Jack Gordon, with their broader continental experiences, were kept in touch with the Vic–Wells, and working on tangential projects with Geoffrey Toye, so that when the right moment came, as he was certain it would, they would be ready to step in. For the time being, both practised their craft directing operas at the Royal College of Music – not mainstream ones, but rather, the unusual or smaller operas Dent hoped eventually to see at the Vic–Wells. With Dent's help and advice, Jack had done his own translation of *La forza del destino* at the Vic in 1929.

But persuading Baylis, as suspicious as Dent of any intrigue, to open up was a laborious process. At the same time, the ISCM was holding its first festival in England.

❧ ❧ ❧

The jury had met in January 1931 at Cambridge, in Dent's rooms at King's: Alban Berg, Alfred Casella, Désiré Defauw, Gregor Fitelberg and Charles Koechlin. It

22 LH 10/07/1931.

23 Dent, ATFE, p. 99.

FIGURE 14. Oxford–London ISCM jury meeting in Dent's King's College rooms, Cambridge, 1931. Charles Koechlin, Alfredo Casella, Adrian Boult, Alban Berg, Dent, Gregor Fitelberg, Désiré Defauw. By kind permission of the Provost and Fellows of King's College, Cambridge.

was a congenial meeting, with far less friction than was often the case. 'Dent is like a kindly nanny to me, made a splendid tea in the afternoon', Berg famously wrote to his wife Helène about the trip, and about his pleasant meeting with Edward Clark in London before taking the train up to Cambridge, where he was met by Mrs Stewart 'in her car (a very ancient affair)'. He loved staying in the Stewarts' 'genuine old English country house' off the Huntingdon Road, with 'lovely meadows where sheep are grazing'.[24] 'Food good and plentiful', he said, adding that it had no taste whatever. It had been hard work, ten hours a day, four solid days of reading manuscript music and taking big decisions. Dinner at High Table in Trinity, with its ceremony and college silver 'really made an unforgettable impression'.

But the various sections of the ISCM, especially the Italians and Germans, continued to seethe in turn, and after the crash of 1929, finances were even more strained. The lack of a unifying factor in contemporary music pitted the Schoenbergians against the conservative Italians, whose traditions were more 'predominantly vocal',[25] and against those influenced by folk traditions and tonalities. Such constant minor frictions could also be seen as one of the signs of a healthy institution,

24 *Alban Berg: Letters to his Wife*, ed., trans. and annotated Bernard Grun (London, 1971), pp. 376–8. It was January, so the green countryside must have taken him by surprise. The Stewarts' house had only been built twenty years before.

25 Radcliffe, *E.J. Dent*, p. 15. Haefeli also points out that Berg and Webern played cox and box on the jury, making sure each had his best works voted for.

one constantly questioning its values and aims: this was Dent's optimistic view. In 1930 and 1931, some of the different 'Germanic' sections – German, Austrian, Czech and Swiss, together with the Scandinavians – decided to give smaller festivals along the lines of the ISCM.[26] Two festivals took place at Bad Pyrmont, a pretty spa town in the mountains between Hamelin and Münster, much of the music on offer reflecting the zeitgeist in the shape of *Gebrauchsmusik*, the 'music for use' which could be played by amateurs, and *Gemeinschaftsmusik*, community music. It all sounds very cosy and comforting, the kind of folk traditions Dent had supported Rolf Gardiner[27] and his group in years before, but in fact such music-making was becoming politically charged and in opposition to everything the ISCM stood for. At the time, though, Dent thought it encouraging.

In these few years, however illusory, Dent's optimism was sustained by his German interludes, especially seeing how his Handel and Purcell editions,[28] were being used in productions such as those at 'proletarian' Essen, where his friends Schultz-Dornburg and Kurt Joos were producing *The Fairy Queen*, having done *Dido* the year before. Dent thought the Joos *Fairy Queen*, with its music 'rather cut down … amateurish … but perhaps all the more amusing and spirited for *that*',[29] but he continued to encourage his protégés – Boris Ord, Jack Gordon, Clive – to work with their German counterparts – Joos, Szenkar *et al.* – to promote cross-fertilisation.

❧ ❧ ❧

> I had some talk with Foss & Kerridge about the Oxford Festival of 1931 – apparently Evans is doing his best to shift the centre of gravity (or levity) to London instead of Oxford … If this is carried through I shall resign the presidency definitely on grounds of health.[30]

Dent himself had wanted to keep the festival in Oxford, not only because he had the local support of Hubert Foss and the Oxford University Press – a counterweight to Universal Edition and its pervasive influence – but also to challenge the notion that only London was capable of staging such an event. But Evans had seized the opportunity to put on a big show, a 'top-hat festival'. Dent didn't 'resign', but it was probably just as well that Evans did take it over; Dent had to have another small operation, this time for a 'lump' on his forehead, which meant taking a week off in July just before the festival.[31]

26 Haefeli, *IGNM*, pp. 167ff.

27 Rolf Gardiner (1902–1971), Bedales and St John's College, Cambridge, English rural revivalist, nephew of Balfour Gardiner, father of conductor John Eliot Gardiner. Dent knew him through his touring folk-dance groups in Germany in the 1920s.

28 Dent's *Dido and Aeneas* had been translated by Anton Mayer, published by OUP in 1925.

29 JG 04/06/1931.

30 JBT 30/06/1930.

31 It is not clear what the lump was, but the operation seems to have been a simple one, with no mention of it later.

In spite of the extra expense and organisation it involved, the all-inclusive festival, with both chamber and orchestral pieces, was now an established ISCM aim, but for the 1931 Oxford–London festival of 24–28 July,[32] the main purpose was to bring a wide range of the most contemporary music to the British musical public, with an 'historical Prologue' given by combined college choirs on 22 July. Philip Radcliffe 'vividly recalls' the effect on his young self of hearing astonishing new works like Stravinsky's *Symphonies for Wind Instruments* and Berg's *Wozzeck*. Dent, staying at The Mitre, could see how it worked very well, with the chamber concerts and ballet in the smaller Oxford venues followed by the orchestral concerts in London, easy for people to get from one to the other.

The first chamber concerts were given in the Sheldonian Theatre, with a matinée on the 24th at the New Theatre of three modern ballets, by Vaughan Williams, Erwin Shulhoff and Constant Lambert. Lev Knipper, Józef Koffler, Jean Huré and Jan Malklakiewicz had been programmed with the better-known Sessions, Halffter and Wellesz, and Paul Hindemith's *Wir bauen eine Stadt* with schoolchildren in the small Holywell Music Room. English choral music was performed in Christ Church Cathedral, while the two big orchestral concerts at the Queen's Hall in London 'changed the character of the Festival'.[33] Although critic Paul Stefan said that here 'eines der Zukunftsländer der Musik erwächst', uneven programming exercised some: Webern's Symphony, op. 21, alongside Gershwin's *An American in Paris*, a 'bedenkliche Koppelung'.[34] But Webern had written to Berg, 'Dent schrieb mir auch ein paar liebe Worte über meine Symphonie und dass Scherchen sie gut gebracht hat (viel klarer, wie er sagt, als Klemperer in Berlin).'[35] 'London was one of the few places where they [Schönberg and Webern] were always received with the respect and admiration that was their due', wrote Dent.

The resources of the BBC Symphony Orchestra under Boult, with Scherchen, Knippers and Vogel, demonstrated the progress in orchestral playing, one of the better outcomes of the ongoing orchestral battles of recent years. Probably because of his ISCM connections, Scherchen liked working in the UK, while enjoying an international reputation for interpreting difficult contemporary music. Anton Haefeli credits Edward Clark, then with Boult transforming music at the BBC, with the open-mindedness (Aufgeschlossenheit) of the English public towards new music so evident at the 1931 festival. In fact this evident appetite for new music, on the concert platform, on the BBC, and being published, had been nourished by a growing number of younger British music critics with discernment and wider knowledge, such as Constant Lambert.

32 Haefeli, *IGNM*, p. 488, makes a rare mistake, giving June as the month.

33 E. Evans, 'The Oxford Festival', MT (1 September 1931), pp. 803–6, here p. 805.

34 'One of the future lands of music awakes'; it is possibly also a snide pun on 'Zukunftsmusik' or pie in the sky. Haefeli, *IGNM*, p. 173.

35 'Dent also wrote to me with a few kind words about my symphony, and that Scherchen performed it well (much clearer, as he says, than Klemperer in Berlin)'. Anton Webern to Alban Berg, 29/06/1931, quoted *ibid.*, p. 403 n. 422.

In his articles on the subject, Edwin Evans seized the opportunity to make several points,[36] especially the need for subsidising the arts to maintain the stability necessary for continuing high standards. He was able to say with authority how 'difficult', what a 'hazardous undertaking' this festival had been, and while stressing its many positive aspects, deplored the fact of having to make a virtue of necessity so much of the time. Where other countries had opera houses and concerts halls which were 'public property', ours had only an 'Entertainment Tax' which failed to address anything. Evans praised the efforts and the support of Oxford University, the Oxford University Press and the BBC. 'On the musical side', he went on, 'there is to be noted first of all the remarkably high level maintained throughout in performance. There was not a work presented that was not put in the most favourable light. As for the works themselves, they showed that the relative calm which set in at Geneva and prevailed at Liège has come to stay.'

> The notices of the Oxford Festival have been coming in. The people who seem to have enjoyed it most are the Italians. The Czechs and Austrians are rather sniffy; the French patronizing and the English merely idiotic. However Adrian Boult and the B.B.C. seem to be vastly pleased with the whole affair.[37]

It was probably a good thing that Evans had been so enthusiastic and effective in overseeing the London–Oxford Festival. Beside his ongoing illnesses, Dent was still juggling an insane number of major projects like the crisis-ridden Philharmonic Society committee and the 'Cambridge Report' on teaching music in schools, his life sharply divided into periods of extreme stress and exertion and those of complete relaxation. After the Oxford–London ISCM Festival, he spent a restful four days with Philip Steegman in Oxfordshire, before dashing off to the Dolomites again in August to work at Busoni, at Baie di Lagos.

But the mountain peace worked its magic; he drafted the difficult final chapter of his Busoni biography, using an analysis of *Doktor Faustus* to address aspects of Busoni's 'character and personality'.[38] He had at last settled on a style, and compared his efforts to the recent biography of another famously awkward subject:

> I hope I have succeeded in giving the book a certain musical form as a biography, planned rather differently from most. I rather fancy the model wch has influenced me most was Wortham's life of OB, wch I think is extraordinarily good both as a character study & as a work of literature.[39]

❧ ❧ ❧

> I am tackling the Cambridge report on music teaching in schools, which drives me to despair. I have got to edit the stuff generally – that is put it into decent English; it is a collection of short chapters and paragraphs written by all sorts of

36 Evans, 'The Oxford Festival'.

37 LH 03/09/1931.

38 *Ibid.*

39 H.E. Wortham, *Oscar Browning* (London, 1927). JBT 06/09/1931.

different people, whose outlook on life and literary style too is very variegated ... the general effect of the book will be appalling, I fear.[40]

Although at the time it gave him so much trouble, Dent was naturally drawn into the ideas he could see emerging behind the report, 'soundness' of principle, but 'I miss the spirit of missionary enthusiasm'.

There are long schemes for the teaching of musical history in schools; firstly, I can-t [sic] believe that anyone will carry them out, and secondly they are all based on standard books and invite teachers to 'get up' the subject out of some book which gives a conventional but not really valuable view of the subject ... One thing does strike me; the difference between the obvious keenness and detailed elaboration of the 'elementary' and 'secondary' types of teacher-contributor, and the slovenly indifference of those representing preparatory and public schools.[41]

His work for the Cambridge report enhanced his growing reputation as a pedagogue and inspired him later, when in 1935 he worked with Leo Kestenberg on an International Congress of Musical Education at Prague, where he hoped to 'revive on a more international basis the so-called "Lausanne" conferences ... started by Percy Scholes'.[42]

His Italian time also gave Dent necessary distance to think, so for the next few summers he continued to retreat to the Italian mountains, even without Carlo, essential for his health and sanity. Each time, he had taken care to go to a different hotel in a different part, feeling the need to avoid any possible scrutiny.

I have all sorts of schemes for Cambridge: a music research congress and festival of mediaeval music in 1933 and perhaps a festival (British Section of the International) of 'contemporary' music in 1934 or earlier. In any case I want to have some sort of really big show at Cambridge every year and make Cambridge into the most important English 'Festspielstadt': but in Cambridge (style), not Salzburg![43]

Musically, Cambridge was flourishing: throughout the new academic year the emerging new order, including the redoubtable Mrs Hackforth, with Camille Prior,[44] enthusiastically took up some of Dent's schemes. CUMS did the first of a series of Handel oratorios at the Guildhall, *Samson*, with Steuart Wilson singing

40 JBT 14/08/1931. The 'Cambridge Report' became Dent's important contribution, 'The Value of Music to the Community and the Place it Should Occupy in Education' and Preface, *Music and the Community: The Cambridgeshire Report on the Teaching of Music* (Cambridge, 1933), pp. 9–16 and xiii–xiv; Haward, *Edward J. Dent: A Bibliography*, 92. This report had come out of the radical reforms begun in the 1920s by King's College man Henry Morris, who set up the incomparable Village College system in Cambridgeshire. At the time, Morris was Secretary for Education in Cambridgeshire, then one of the poorest counties in the UK.

41 JBT 14/08/1931.

42 LH 04/08/1934.

43 LH 03/09/1931.

44 See Chapter 10, note 134.

Samson, conducted by Rootham and advised by Dent, with costumes by Gwen Raverat, the first of many such joint efforts. Dent was delighted to see her again: 'she is wonderfully rejuvenated and I could hardly believe it was her. I had not seen her since Raverat's death'.[45]

Dent exercised his office as President of the Musical Association to ask Johannes Wolf to reprise his Musical Association lecture on fourteenth-century Florentine music up in Cambridge at the end of Michaelmas term, persuading Boris Ord to 'get up the illustrations'. But Dent was playing a deeper game. With Peter Wagner's death, he knew he was in the frame for the presidency of the ISMR, the more conservative of the two societies, and wanted to be sure of Wolf's support when he broached the idea of a big ISMR Congress at Cambridge, his main objective. Cambridge obliged and put on a show. Wolf saw a thriving, lively cultural community, with the regular music in the college chapels and the two university societies beside informal concerts and recitals, jazz and classical. Wolf went to Boris' madrigal concert and Mrs Hackforth's extremely popular chamber concerts: the Pro Arte Quartet performing all of Beethoven's quartets over five nights, filling the Guildhall. In London, Dent took Wolf to dinner at the Étoile, inviting Boris, Gerry Cooper, beside Erlebach (the Musical Association secretary), Evelyn Broadwood, and Edmund Fellowes.

After the Musical Association lecture, Dent left with Wolf to Paris, where they both attended a meeting of the French Société Internationale de la Musique (SIM) at André Pirro's house, with Merian the secretary already there, before the main meeting, where in due course Dent was formally elected President of the ISMR. The committee:

> approved my scheme of a Congress to be held in July 1933 at Cambridge with a great festival of old English music … I got Cyril and Boris quite keen about this – though Boris kicks at my suggestion of music by Henry VI in his own chapel, and Milner-White [the Dean of King's] can't bear the thought of the John's choir being allowed to sing anything anywhere.[46]

This was something he had wanted badly, but it meant yet more hard work and correspondence when every day he was routinely responding to dozens of letters, and although they might irritate him, even the smallest, most trivial applications never failed to elicit a polite, considered response. The sense of obligation also hemmed him in, from requests to critique material, such as Ursula Creighton's manuscript 'popular history of music for the young', consultations about small festivals, or the first of many Rupert Brooke pilgrims, Richard Halliburton, pressing him for details.

> I can't make up my mind whether to give him everything – or to leave him to continue the 'Legend of Scyros' … The comic & pathetic thing is that I am in just the same situation: writing to total strangers to ask for intimate information about Busoni![47]

45 CC 17/12/1931.

46 *Ibid.*

47 JBT 12/09/1927.

After an 'exhausting' term at Cambridge, with ten composition pupils and more the following term, the pressures continued to mount. Lilian Baylis wanted him to do two new translations: *Un ballo in maschera* and *Carmen*, sending 'a wonderful Victorian translation' to tinker with. 'Dear Lilian always wants things in a hurry', the urgency not so much a tribute to his talents as a way of avoiding royalties, he knew.

> I have had voluminous correspondence with Ethel Smyth – who thinks I can stir up all Europe to demand the broadcasting of The Wreckers on the 'national' wave instead of the 'regional' – I told her to write to all the British Ambassadors & all the Intendants! She did!!![48]

❧ ❧ ❧

'Will all the new political developments in Spain affect your chances?' Dent wrote to JB about his application for the Oxford Professorship in September 1931. 'If Oxford had any sense they ought to seize on you as the one person who understands the psychology of the new Republic'[49] Although JB's application was passed over in favour of 'a rather dull Spanish scholar, William Entwhistle', from Glasgow,[50] it paved the way: in 1933 Cambridge finally decided to set up a Chair in Spanish Studies, and Dent sprang into action:

> I talked to Beves about the Spanish job at Cambridge. He says the University want to make it a full Professorship and are prepared to find the money. B. seemed to welcome you as Professor but wondered whether you wd be a good organizer? I said I felt sure you would & that I knew you were a very good lecturer ... I haven't seen Bullock but will tackle him. I fear Allison Peers might be a strong candidate. Praz sent me to-day a wonderful testimonial from Grierson ... There was also a letter from Lawrence Binyon saying that Rodd was in favour of Praz. Gardner is pushing Pellizzi, because (Praz thinks) G. fears that the anti-foreigner campaign may make Pellizzi's position in London insecure ... Piccoli was recognized as a great man: and I expect my own stock has gone up with those who know that I pushed him!.[51]

With his scanty official qualifications, Trend might have appeared to be a complete outsider for such a major academic position, especially up against such a strong academic field, including Mario Praz[52] and Allison Peers, who later became Professor at Liverpool.[53] But by now Trend had firmly established his Hispanist credentials

48 JBT 06/09/1931.

49 JBT 06/09/1931.

50 Anstee, *An Unlikely Spanish Don*, p. 142.

51 JBT 01/03/1933.

52 Mario Praz (1896–1982), born in Italy, came to England and was teaching at the University of Manchester at this time; distinguished literary critic, who also wrote about design history. His career was just taking off at this time.

53 JBT 01/03/1933. The election is discussed in full in Anstee, *An Unlikely Spanish Don*, pp. 142ff.

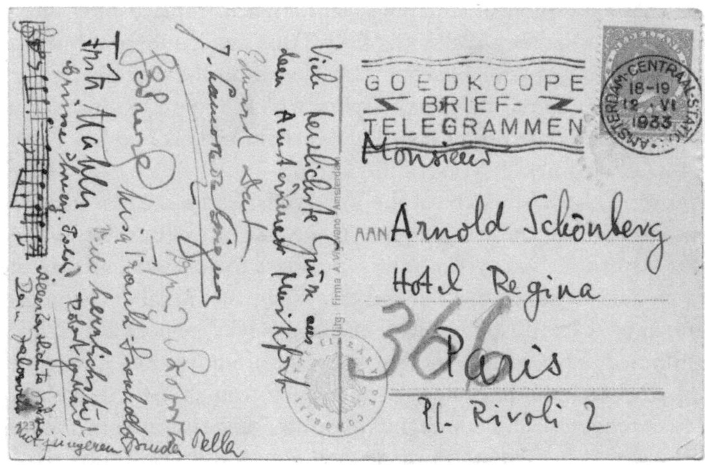

FIGURE 15. Postcard to Arnold Schönberg, signed by Dent, Roberto Gerhard, and others, 1933. By kind permission of the Provost and Fellows of King's College, Cambridge.

in much the same alternative ways as Dent had established his as a musicologist, through his published writings, contacts and his conspicuous knowledge of the current state of political and cultural affairs. And his was the same internationalist agenda: even before the Professorship, Trend had written to Dent from Barcelona, exploring plans for a major international festival at Barcelona with the dynamic new Catalan minister for music there, the composer Roberto Gerhard, continuing the cultural intercourse begun at the Residencia. Dent was delighted: 'What a marvellous diplomatist you are!' Their efforts would result in the 1936 joint Congress and Festival, one of the cultural high points before the slide into war.

But if Cambridge was ticking along nicely, with production of a German Ur-*Faust* and a 'marvellous' MDS *Hamlet* in Byronic costume, there were yet more ongoing troubles at the Philharmonic: 'the losses were so heavy that we have had to ask the trustees to let us use the whole of the foundation fund'. Relations with the BBC were currently good, probably down to Dent's own relations with Boult and Evans, beside the success of the 1931 ISCM, and he was more optimistic about the next season: 'but there is always the ghost of Beecham and the prospects of a new rival orchestra; and you know what negotiations with Beecham are'.[54] Beecham had formed his new breakaway orchestra, the London Philharmonic Orchestra, forcing the Philharmonic Society to steady itself and generate income by getting Henry Wood to conduct popular Rachmaninov and Beethoven concerts. Fed up with it all, Gerry Cooper had decided to 'chuck' his Philharmonic duties and 'devote himself entirely to the stage', even printing a card in the Daily Telegraph: 'Mr GERALD

54 JBT 24/02/1932.

COOPER – At Liberty'. Immediately, Dent tried to replace him with Howard Bliss. Meanwhile at Sadler's Wells, Geoffrey Toye was handing in his resignation, citing his commitments with Beecham; by November he was managing director of Beecham's new Imperial League of Opera, which 'sought to modernise Covent Garden and present opera seasons both of Beecham and his London Philharmonic and of visiting companies.'.[55] None of this lasted.

Finances were also a headache at the Vic–Wells, where the first-year deficit was three thousand pounds; the second year 'showed slightly better results'.[56] Although early on the governors had agreed it was 'madness to continue' alternating drama and opera divided between the Vic and the Wells, the initial decision for change took up much of 1932, mostly because of Lilian Baylis' opposition. While the old system continued, even with 'a modest measure of innovation and success',[57] the production side was sometimes sloppy and inept, too much so for its ambitions, with the old lack of rehearsal, and complaints about the singers not knowing their parts. Some improvement had begun in 1931, when Henry Robinson took over as stage manager, and conductor Lawrance Collingwood began to overlap with Charles Corri. Together with Baylis, Collingwood is credited with the formation of the permanent opera company, with regular rehearsals, but the ideas were Dent's.

But behind every fresh success in those formative years 1931–33 lay the spectre of that cultural predator Thomas Beecham, who now wanted to 'amalgamate' the Vic–Wells with Covent Garden, focusing on his own new orchestra and his 'Imperial League of Opera' based at a revived and refurbished Covent Garden, funded by subscription. The scheme was bold and entrepreneurial, with massive publicity, especially Beecham himself making speeches up and down the country, fortified with serious backing and serious money, but more significantly, the complete confidence of the massive ego. It helped him to raise a lot of money and had convinced Prime Minister Ramsey MacDonald to subsidise it to the tune of thirty thousand pounds,[58] which outraged many enduring the Great Depression and set MPs against the scheme. Still, Beecham's name behind a venture could conjure magic. His conducting thrilled: in his *Tristan* in May 1931, *The Times* critic declared that it was Beecham's spectacular conducting driving everything:

> even with a cast of Bayreuth singers Sir Thomas Beecham made the orchestra the most potent, expressive force; not that he ignored or slighted the singers' importance, but that the voices were incorporated into the instrumental texture.[59]

He had already co-opted Geoffrey Toye, who for months argued the case for amalgamation to the Vic–Wells Board, nearly tempting a wavering Baylis. The threat continued all that autumn of 1932 and well into the next year, especially keenly felt by

55 Gilbert, *Opera for Everybody*, p. 49.

56 Dent, ATFE, p. 96.

57 Gilbert, *Opera for Everybody*, p. 49.

58 Lucas, *Thomas Beecham*, pp. 190ff.

59 Quoted *ibid.*, p. 205.

Dent, who knew all too well how battles with Beecham at the Philharmonic Society had left two institutions tottering.

> Did you know that Lady Cunard & party came to the Wells last night & upset poor Miss B. dreadfully by saying that the orchestra was shocking & that Buesst had no idea of the opera ... so I did my best to console Miss B. & said that we all respected Buesst immensely and thought him an excellent conductor. I was very much annoyed about this invasion of Lady C. because we mustn't let Miss B. have her confidence shaken in the present lot of workers at the Vic. TB [Beecham] & Lady C. wed never have dreamt of putting their noses inside the Vic 12 years ago![60]

Dent could see in 'Tommy' the destructive and whimsical ego behind the unquestionable genius. 'T.B. thinks it [Sadler's Wells] wd suit him to play with as a toy', he wrote bitterly to Clive in October 1932, 'and we can't have him take it'.[61]

> [Beecham will] run the V–W company in the provinces under his own name, so as not to look like the Old Vic Company – G.T. [Geoffrey Toye] wants a new name, like 'The London Opera Co.' wch will suggest that it is entirely a new creation of TB's. LB [Baylis] naturally kicked violently & I supported her![62]

But Dent's other objections were more fundamental: Beecham's operatic style was very different from what was being developed at the Vic–Wells:

> It is tiresome having these things foisted on us just when we are beginning to build up our own style. T.B. has no understanding of that, I fear; he sees opera first as an orchestral conductor, and secondly as a 'grand opera' social affair, I think.[63]

The daily press supported the more modest enterprise and opposed any amalgamation with Covent Garden, *The Times* drawing the distinction between the two houses, with Covent Garden being the 'cosmopolitan company giving masterpieces sung by the world's greatest singers', while Sadler's Wells helped nurture 'home-grown talent'.[64] The *Radio Times* commented on the typical Sadler's Wells audience emerging from the performance, young, chatty, and comfortable. Fox Strangways in *Music & Letters* published two articles by 'Choragus' on the subject, and at the same time Reginald Rowe, one of the governors, wrote an impassioned and frank article on the current financial difficulties while stressing the importance of the Vic and Wells to the grassroots development of British music and drama, echoing Dent's ideas of the natural place of this centre of production at the heart of a creative nexus incorporating the music colleges.[65]

60 CC 07/10/1932. 'Buesst' was the Australian conductor Aylmer Buesst (1883–1970), who had trained in Germany and conducted with, *inter alia,* the Beecham opera in its various forms as well as the British National Opera Company, later with the BBC.

61 CC 07/10/1932.

62 CC 20/04/1933.

63 CC 12/05/1933.

64 Gilbert, *Opera for Everybody*, pp. 48–9.

65 P.R.R. Rowe, 'The Old Vic', M&L, vol. 12, no. 2 (April 1932), pp. 141–6.

As a governor, Dent continued to press for his own team at the Vic and Wells, still determined on an Intendant. In 1932, both Clive Carey and Jack Gordon were directing operas at the Vic–Wells, the fresh direction and focus on production values they brought with them helping to establish the company identity more firmly. Dent had by this time been writing to Jack for nearly ten years, nurturing a talent he had recognised but until now had not been able to help as much as he might have wished.

> I hope that … it will be an even stronger coalition of friends than I had originally hoped. I know now that Miss B. fully realises how valuable it will be to have Clive, Geoffrey Toye, you, Sumner Austin and Miss Gough all working together with me in the background, because we all have the same ideals and are all close personal friends who will enjoy working together and do things for each other which we might not do for people we had not great sympathy with … I feel sure that the Vic (if all this goes through) will give you a much freer hand and much more scope for your abilities than the R.C.M., though I don't want you to lose touch with that.[66]

In spite of all these promising signs, Lilian Baylis continued to be torn between her deep desire to keep control of her baby while Beecham was dangling financial security before her at a time when both companies were still so deeply in debt. 'I have always the fear', Dent wrote to Clive, 'that Lilian might any day throw us over completely, if it came to a choice between me and T.B. … She has a genuine personal affection for all of us, but no ability to estimate our artistic value to the theatre – and the great value of ourselves to the theatre is our corporate value as a group of personal friends with the same ideals, helping each other.'[67]

Dent's own misgivings had a large personal predisposition, which he only allowed himself to vent in private.[68] Beecham was having troubles of his own; the 1933 Covent Garden season was not well received, with poor production standards which Geoffrey Toye was addressing, enlisting the help of talent from abroad, not just the expensive singers, but now refugee producers. When a vacancy came up on the Old Vic Board in August 1933, Dent was writing to Clive that Baylis was 'getting very suspicious of G.T. [Geoffrey Toye]. She has begun to discover that he really knows very little about opera, and she does not trust his machinations with Tommy.'[69] He kept pressing his own candidates for the board, the 'personal friends' he knew he could work with, Muriel Gough, Thornely Gibson, or Hal Goodhart-Rendel, none of whom was acceptable to Baylis. 'GT has many merits', Dent wrote to Clive:

> but he has never seen Opera abroad or anywhere in larger quantities: he is quite out of touch with recent developments and has no knowledge of what goes on in other countries: & his knowledge of the general standard repertory is <u>very</u> small. On the other hand he is a good business man & a good conductor.[70]

66 JG 27/05/1932.

67 CC 2/05/1933.

68 CC 12/05/1931.

69 CC 22/08/1933.

70 CC 20/04/1933.

Toye is often credited with establishing the production standards at Sadler's Wells;[71] certainly he learned a lot while he was there, but one of the great strengths of the Vic–Wells was its team effort.

In the middle of all these ructions Dent mused on his own future, once again expressing his wish to 'chuck everything except the Vic Opera, and devote myself solely to that; but I couldn't live on it, so I fear I must go on with Cambridge; and that ties me to the other things, though you may not at first sight see the connection.'[72] His reluctance was not out of simple financial need; Dent knew that his current status as Professor gave him useful power and influence in the two big international societies, and how important such wider connections were to the musical health of his own country.

> I have had some long & curious conversations with Foxy – I sometimes thought he was going quite off his head, though his ideals are sound. It all came to this, that music in England is in a rotten state & that we want a 'leader' – He seemed to suggest that I ought to make myself a sort of musical Mussolini – but I don't see how to do it: and I prefer to pursue my plan of working quietly in the background – He also thought I ought to train you up systematically to become President of the ISCM in five years' time-[73]

The ISCM festival at Vienna in June 1932 coincided with a Schubert Jubilee, with the kinds of 'side-shows' Dent felt would add nothing to the main event. A *Schubertiade* in Vienna was hardly a radical idea, Dent sniffed; but really, the principle was not so very different from Oxford.

> Pisk wrote proposing all sorts of concerts including side-shows which I rather deprecated, and when it came to including 'Eine Schubertiade im Geburtshaus Schubert's' I wrote and asked if that meant a Gala Performance of 'Lilac Time' [*Das Dreimäderlhaus*, a pastiche Schubert operetta]. I am quite willing that they should be determined to be very 'radical' in their programmes, and I would not make any great resistance to an attempt to make the Festival practically a Schönberg Festival; but I won't have any truck with the traditional Vienna of Strauss and Suppé and so forth, or even with performances of the older classics – Haydn of course excepted.[74]

The jury meeting had been moved from Geneva to Berlin because Ansermet was conducting there, a 'concert of American music', including Sessions and Copland. Dent took the unprecedented move of travelling de luxe, 'a fearful extravagance in these days'. It was worth the expense; he was rested enough to fight his corner throughout the 'long and tiring' meetings:

> for Haba and Webern were determined to make the Festival exclusively their own, with as much music as possible by Schönberg and Zemlinsky and others …

71 Lucas, *Thomas Beecham*, pp. 216–17.

72 CC 10/09/1932.

73 JBT 12/03/1932.

74 JBT 14/08/1931.

> The split between East and West is most remarkable. The Schönbergians simply cannot bear any music that is agreeable and amusing to listen to; and the Germans are now reacting against all 'concert' music, and are going only for a primitive sort of choral music composed for proletarian choirs, with political words.[75]

❧ ❧ ❧

At a time when the wider world was beginning to fragment, the postwar optimism and culture all but spent, Dent was now probably at the peak of his power and influence, and exercising that influence at every opportunity to achieve his vision. While in Zurich in September 1932, he was meeting the secretary of the ISMR, Merian, to discuss the forthcoming congress at Cambridge, at the same time seeing opera there, visiting Winterthur, meeting Granville Barker to discuss Shakespearean music for his new book, inviting Wellesz to lecture at Cambridge. 'We all enjoyed your visit immensely and the lectures too. It is always a great stimulus to my young men to meet a distinguished foreign scholar in this way, and it helps to improve my reputation too!'[76]

After a jury meeting in Amsterdam in December, Dent went on to Coburg with the Malipieros to see his new opera, *The Mystery of Venice*, noting how these other opera companies were operating: 'about on a level with Sadler's Wells as regards resources, but with more ingenuity and sense of style than we have has yet attained'.[77] The same in Berlin a week later. He was now actively trying to persuade these companies to come and perform at Sadler's Wells. Wellesz had already been spreading the news, especially about the ballet, and Dent was hoping that Strohbach might be able to 'bring off his idea of an exchange week between the Vic company and the Darmstadt Company (opera)'.[78]

> To-day I lunch with His Serene Highness the Erbprinz Heinrich the Forty-fifth of Reuss … and go on to see a matinée of Hänsel und Gretel by his company at the Schiller-Theater … Geoffrey talks of doing Freischütz at the Vic, but I am more keen on doing Oberon with the original Planché libretto, which I found in the University Library.[79]

But he was tired: 'Berlin is rather depressed, but I manage to find it fairly amusing, though I am growing old and no longer want to be very energetic in the pursuit of amusement.'[80] This was to be his last visit to Weimar Berlin, and to the Weimar Republic. The wider world was catching up.

75 CC 17/12/1931. Haefeli is incorrect about the jury meeting: *IGNM*, p. 175.

76 EW 01/12/1932. ÖNB F13 Wellesz 1198.

77 JBT 21/12/1932.

78 *Ibid.*

79 *Ibid.*

80 *Ibid.*

1933–1934

> Musical life in England is rather depressed at present; financial crises, cold weather and universal influenza! Musically the general effect is a return to the classics; it is the musical equivalent of getting into bed with a hot [water] bottle.[81]

The July 1933 congress was the natural next step in the realisation of Dent's expressed vision for Cambridge as a 'Festspielstadt', an intellectual and cultural centre of international standing, where scholarship did not simply lie on the page, but was put on display daily, alive in the daily chapel services and in the CUMC performances as much as the lecture theatres. Unlike Salzburg, Cambridge had no touristic agenda in place (then!), but – as at the Oxford ISCM – its historical significance was there for all to see in its working attractions, so little known on the continent, its ancient colleges and chapels. It was Dent's idea to utilise everything – university, town and colleges – Cambridge had to offer to demonstrate his points about 'musical archaeology', connecting the subjects of their learned papers with living music, promoting Cambridge to foreigners still fixed on the 'primitiv' label. Dent was looking for fresh alternatives to the huge Vienna Congresses; the Cambridge Congress was to be on a far more modest scale, but that was no reason it should be less significant.

But even with its relatively modest scale, the practical problems included old financial and emerging political obstacles, especially for the Germans, and Dent had written to reassure Wellesz. Arrangements had been made with Hickson at the Board of Extra-Mural Studies to secure reduced fares on rail and the Channel ferries,[82] with inexpensive lodgings in college sets, while many – as Alban Berg had been – were being put up by university families, the Stewarts, the Burkitts and the Roothams. For those who could afford it, like Werner Reinhart or Louise Hanson Dyer, founder of *L'Oiseau-Lyre*, there was the comfortable University Arms Hotel. Hans Hammerschlag of Budapest requested original instruments to illustrate his talk. There were also the usual squabbles and misunderstandings – André Pirro was cross about the French representative, Mme Yvonne Rokseth – beside acrimonious debates about where the next congress should be held. Then the topical problems: Dent contacted his old friend Stephen Gaselee at the Foreign Office about securing visas for the German delegates.

> With regard to your fears concerning the difficulties which may be placed in the way of German members attending the Second Congress of the International Musical Research Society to be held at Cambridge next month, we shall certainly be pleased to do what we can through our Embassy in Berlin … to secure their attendance should the necessity arise.[83]

The 'difficulties' of course stemmed from the appointment of Adolf Hitler as German Chancellor in January, and the swift movements that winter to consolidate all political power into a central authority, the Third Reich. Germany's postwar

81 EW 04/02/1933. ÖNB F13 Wellesz 1198.

82 EW 01/12/1932.

83 Gaselee to Dent 10/06/1933. KCA ISMR bundle EJD/2/8/1.

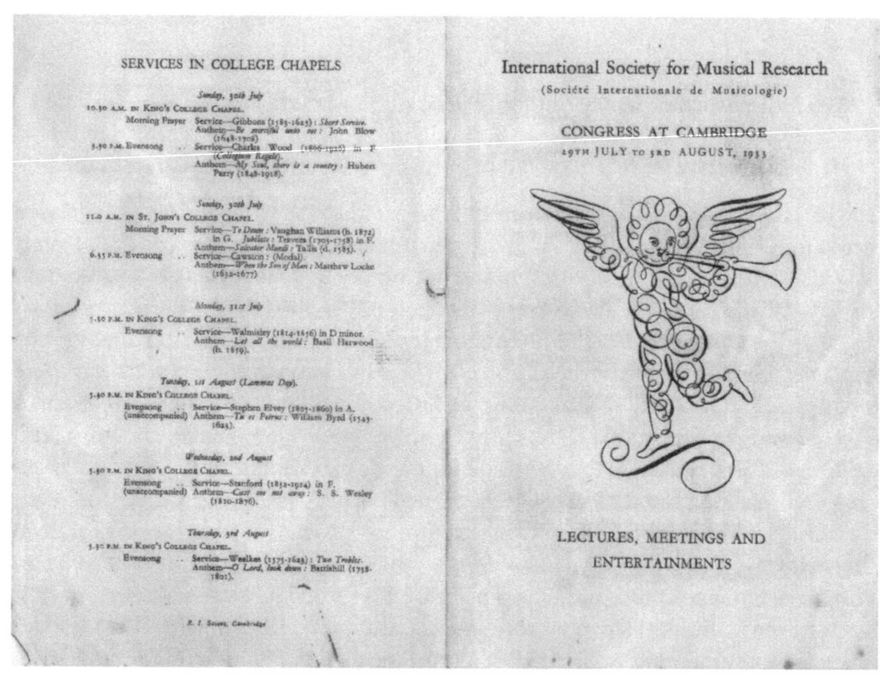

SERVICES IN COLLEGE CHAPELS

Sunday, 30th July

10.30 A.M. IN KING'S COLLEGE CHAPEL.
Morning Prayer Service—Gibbons (1583-1625): *Short Service.*
Anthem—*Be merciful unto me*: John Blow (1648-1708)
5.30 P.M. Evensong .. Service—Charles Wood (1866-1926) in F (*Collegium Regale*).
Anthem—*My Soul, there is a country*: Hubert Parry (1848-1918).

Sunday, 30th July

11.0 A.M. IN ST. JOHN'S COLLEGE CHAPEL.
Morning Prayer Service—*Te Deum*: Vaughan Williams (b. 1872) in G. *Jubilate*: Travers (1703-1758) in F.
Anthem—*Salvator Mundi*: Tallis (d. 1585).
6.35 P.M. Evensong .. Service—Cawston: (Modal).
Anthem—*When the Son of Man*: Matthew Locke (1632-1677)

Monday, 31st July

5.30 P.M. IN KING'S COLLEGE CHAPEL.
Evensong .. Service—Walmisley (1814-1856) in D minor.
Anthem—*Let all the world*: Basil Harwood (b. 1859).

Tuesday, 1st August (Lammas Day).

5.30 P.M. IN KING'S COLLEGE CHAPEL.
Evensong (unaccompanied) .. Service—Stephen Elvey (1805-1860) in A.
Anthem—*Tu es Petrus*: William Byrd (1543-1623).

Wednesday, 2nd August

5.30 P.M. IN KING'S COLLEGE CHAPEL.
Evensong (unaccompanied) .. Service—Stanford (1852-1924) in F.
Anthem—*Cast me not away*: S. S. Wesley (1810-1876).

Thursday, 3rd August

5.30 P.M. IN KING'S COLLEGE CHAPEL.
Evensong .. Service—Weelkes (1575-1623): *Two Trebles.*
Anthem—*O Lord, look down*: Battishill (1738-1801).

R. I. Severs, Cambridge

International Society for Musical Research
(Société Internationale de Musicologie)

CONGRESS AT CAMBRIDGE
29TH JULY TO 3RD AUGUST, 1933

LECTURES, MEETINGS AND ENTERTAINMENTS

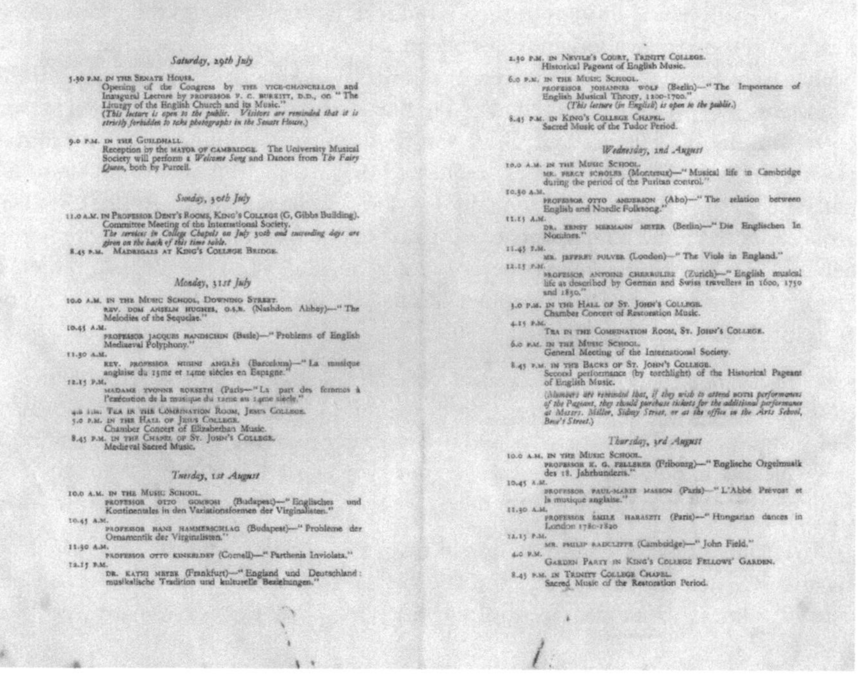

Saturday, 29th July

5.30 P.M. IN THE SENATE HOUSE.
Opening of the Congress by THE VICE-CHANCELLOR and Inaugural Lecture by PROFESSOR F. C. BURKITT, D.D., on "The Liturgy of the English Church and its Music."
(*This lecture is open to the public. Visitors are reminded that it is strictly forbidden to take photographs in the Senate House.*)

9.0 P.M. IN THE GUILDHALL.
Reception by the MAYOR OF CAMBRIDGE. The University Musical Society will perform a *Welcome Song* and Dances from *The Fairy Queen*, both by Purcell.

Sunday, 30th July

11.0 A.M. IN PROFESSOR DENT'S ROOMS, KING'S COLLEGE (G, Gibbs Building).
Committee Meeting of the International Society.
The services in College Chapels on July 30th and succeeding days are given on the back of this time table.
8.45 P.M. MADRIGALS AT KING'S COLLEGE BRIDGE.

Monday, 31st July

10.0 A.M. IN THE MUSIC SCHOOL, DOWNING STREET.
REV. DOM ANSELM HUGHES, O.S.B. (Nashdom Abbey)—"The Melodies of the Sequelae."
10.45 A.M.
PROFESSOR JACQUES HANDSCHIN (Basle)—"Problems of English Mediaeval Polyphony."
11.30 A.M.
REV. PROFESSOR HIGINI ANGLÈS (Barcelona)—"La musique anglaise du 13me et 14me siècles en Espagne."
12.15 P.M.
MADAME YVONNE ROKSETH (Paris—"La part des femmes à l'exécution de la musique du 12me au 14me siècle."
4.0 P.M. TEA IN THE COMBINATION ROOM, JESUS COLLEGE.
5.0 P.M. IN THE HALL OF JESUS COLLEGE.
Chamber Concert of Elizabethan Music.
8.45 P.M. IN THE CHAPEL OF ST. JOHN'S COLLEGE.
Medieval Sacred Music.

Tuesday, 1st August

10.0 A.M. IN THE MUSIC SCHOOL.
PROFESSOR OTTO GOMBOSI (Budapest)—"Englisches und Kontinentales in den Variationsformen der Virginalisten."
10.45 A.M.
PROFESSOR HANS HAMMERSCHLAG (Budapest)—"Probleme der Ornamentik der Virginalisten."
11.30 A.M.
PROFESSOR OTTO KINKELDEY (Cornell)—"Parthenia Inviolata."
12.15 P.M.
DR. KATHI MEYER (Frankfurt)—"England und Deutschland: musikalische Tradition und kulturelle Beziehungen."

2.30 P.M. IN NEVILE'S COURT, TRINITY COLLEGE.
Historical Pageant of English Music.
6.0 P.M. IN THE MUSIC SCHOOL.
PROFESSOR JOHANNES WOLF (Berlin)—"The Importance of English Musical Theory, 1200-1700."
(*This lecture (in English) is open to the public.*)
8.45 P.M. IN KING'S COLLEGE CHAPEL.
Sacred Music of the Tudor Period.

Wednesday, 2nd August

10.0 A.M. IN THE MUSIC SCHOOL.
MR. PERCY SCHOLES (Montreux)—"Musical life in Cambridge during the period of the Puritan control."
10.30 A.M.
PROFESSOR OTTO ANDERSON (Abo)—"The relation between English and Nordic Folksong."
11.15 A.M.
DR. ERNST HERMANN MEYER (Berlin)—"Die Englischen In Nomines."
11.45 P.M.
MR. JEFFREY PULVER (London)—"The Viols in England."
12.15 P.M.
PROFESSOR ANTOINE CHERBULIEZ (Zurich)—"English musical life as described by German and Swiss travellers in 1600, 1750 and 1850."
3.0 P.M. IN THE HALL OF ST. JOHN'S COLLEGE.
Chamber Concert of Restoration Music.
4.15 P.M.
TEA IN THE COMBINATION ROOM, ST. JOHN'S COLLEGE.
6.0 P.M. IN THE MUSIC SCHOOL.
General Meeting of the International Society.
8.45 P.M. IN THE BACKS OF ST. JOHN'S COLLEGE.
Second performance (by torchlight) of the Historical Pageant of English Music.
(*Members are reminded that, if they wish to attend* BOTH *performances of the Pageant, they should purchase tickets for the additional performance at Messrs. Miller, Sidney Street, or at the office in the Arts School, Bene't Street.*)

Thursday, 3rd August

10.0 A.M. IN THE MUSIC SCHOOL.
PROFESSOR K. G. FELLERER (Fribourg)—"Englische Orgelmusik des 18. Jahrhunderts."
10.45 A.M.
PROFESSOR PAUL-MARIE MASSON (Paris)—"L'Abbé Prévost et la musique anglaise."
11.30 A.M.
PROFESSOR ÉMILE HARASZTI (Paris)—"Hungarian dances in London 1780-1820
12.15 P.M.
MR. PHILIP RADCLIFFE (Cambridge)—"John Field."
4.0 P.M.
GARDEN PARTY IN KING'S COLLEGE FELLOWS' GARDEN.
8.45 P.M. IN TRINITY COLLEGE CHAPEL.
Sacred Music of the Restoration Period.

FIGURE 16. Programme of the Cambridge ISMR Congress, 1933. By kind permission of the Provost and Fellows of King's College, Cambridge.

uncertainties, the flowering of the arts under the Weimar Republic together with the terrible economic depression, the aggressive–defensive nationalism fuelled by fear of anything alien had been co-opted; people voted for certainty, 'Germanic' nationalism, what they thought familiar and safe, a political hot-water bottle. What they got was a highly centralised government dictating the conditions for employment, including the Reich Culture Chamber presided over by Joseph Goebbels, which soon controlled all propaganda and the arts.[84] The agenda pursued by the Culture Chamber was 'Gleichschaltung',[85] a kind of uniformity, driven by a nationalism which excluded any undesirables and/or aliens, including Jews, Communists and sexual deviants like many of Dent's friends. Its public manifestations were the infamous exhibitions of Degenerate Art in 1937 and Degenerate Music in 1938, which meant Paul Klee together with Stravinsky, Schoenberg and 'negro' jazz.

The Reich Culture Chamber had immediately taken control of the finances for all institutions of higher education and the arts. Central government was now in the position of being able to decide who could teach, who could play music, who could be employed. By April 1933, most Jewish academics and musicians suddenly found themselves without employment and without a livelihood. Moreover, music was being put to political use, all the trends in German music – *Volksmusik, Gebrauchsmusik, Gemeinschaftsmusik* – over the past decade sliding easily into Nazi purposes.

William Beveridge, sitting in a Viennese café in April, was told by Leo Szilard, who himself became both refugee and activist, about the dismissal on racial or political grounds of many academics from German universities and schools, and he instantly acted to form the AAC, the Academic Assistance Council. Within weeks Beveridge had enlisted the support of a number of prominent British academics, including many of Dent's friends and colleagues such as Maynard Keynes, Lord Lytton, A.V. Hill, W.H. Bragg and H.A.L. Fisher to help the already growing tide of displaced academics,[86] initially, scientists and social scientists. It seemed incredible that Germany should be shedding the cream of its intelligentsia, and yet there was strong British resistance domestically to take in even the Nobel prizewinners. Refugees were seen to be stealing jobs, but underlying anti-Semitism and homophobia played their parts.

Music had yet to be included in the official AAC lists, but Dent was already aware of trouble in store. In June, his old friend Alfred Einstein was removed as editor of the Deutsche Musikgesellschaft journal, *Zeitschrift für Musikwissenschaft*, having received his dismissal from an unhappy Johannes Wolf: 'conditions are stronger than we are and force us, in the interest of the DMG's future, to execute a change in the

84 The best source for a full history of all this background is Pamela Potter, *Most German of the Arts*. And more recently, Benjamin G. Martin, *The Nazi–Fascist New Order for European Culture*.

85 See Potter, *Most German of the Arts*, pp. 3 and 11ff, for a fuller discussion of the aims of the Reich Culture Chamber.

86 Academic Assistance Council founding statement letter, 22 May 1933, in Jeremy Seabrook, *The Refuge and the Fortress: Britain and the Flight from Tyranny* (London, 2008), pp. 238–9.

editorship of our journal by the end of the fiscal year'.[87] Over the next few years Wolf would have many more such apologies to make, as the Deutsche Musikgesellschaft changed its name to the Deutsche Gesellschaft für Musikwissenschaft and its purpose, severing its connections with the international societies. Initially the new society justified itself as focusing on 'German' music, which loose concept still included Germany, Austria-Hungary, Switzerland, Holland and Sweden.[88] By the time of the Cambridge Congress in July 1933, most Jewish musicians and musicologists were being forced to think about their futures; among those coming were Alfred Einstein, Kathi Meyer and Ernst Meyer, and Otto Gombosi. In October, Einstein's more famous distant cousin, Albert, would address ten thousand people in the Royal Albert Hall about the urgent need to tackle the impending crisis.[89] So in Cambridge Johannes Wolf was brought face-to-face with the man he had been forced to sack – a man he liked and respected – together with his wife and daughter.

It is both tragic and miraculous that this realisation of Dent's personal vision for a festival at Cambridge should have come when it did. Cambridge was ready to host such an international event, while many of the signatories to the AAC letter – such as Keynes and Thomson – lived and worked in Cambridge. Music and politics were now inextricably intertwined, however much Dent might hate the idea, and the atmosphere over those four warm summer days must at times have been bristling with hidden feelings, yet determination that the music should prevail. The Cambridge Congress went ahead in the full knowledge of what was really happening in Germany and in spite of it.

But the Cambridge Congress already had several points of internal contention in place, with German-trained conservative delegates like Higini Anglès,[90] the eminent Russian–Swiss musicologist Jacques Handschin,[91] and Karl Gustav Fellerer, a German living in Fribourg, who had recently published articles warmly praising the 'current political developments' and arguing that the Swiss might benefit from 'this strong German identity'.[92] He was due to speak on the relatively neutral subject of English organ music of the eighteenth century. Dent had asked Dom Anselm Hughes,[93] the medieval musicologist who had recently crossed swords with Handschin, to give a paper in the same session. Although they disagreed about many things, not least religion, Hughes and Dent had a similar, English style of approaching serious subjects with light humour, which irritated the more earnest scholars.

87 Quoted in Potter, *Most German of the Arts*, p. 66.

88 *Ibid.*, pp. 66 ff.

89 Seabrook, *The Refuge and the Fortress*, pp. 29–30 and Appendix.

90 See 'Dramatis Personae'.

91 Jacques Handschin (1886–1955), Russian–Swiss organist and music theorist, based in Basel. See Janna Knaizeva, *Jacques Handschin in Russland* (Basel, 2011) for his complicated life and influences.

92 Potter, *Most German of the Arts*, discusses Fellerer's role as willing handmaiden to Nazi music policies at length: pp. 51–2 and 128.

93 Dom Anselm Hughes (1889–1974), already a distinguished pioneer scholar of early liturgical music, contributed to the *New Oxford History* and other books.

> I am prepared to battle with Handschin if it is worth while; but I am really too busy for one of those German Erwiderung-auf-Handschin's-tatsächliche-Berechtigung [response-to-Handschin's-factual-justification] sort of things ... But to be serious, if his matter is important & he is ready to dispute in English, French or Latin, would you be so good as to ask him if he will give me warning, that I may get time off in order to prepare the defence?[94]

Of his own paper Hughes wrote in a similar vein:

> the 10th and 11th century free melody-composition shown in the terrific quantity of materials collected by H.M. Bannister. This being wholly unpublished is bound to be 'news' to the musicologs; being an emancipation from the liturgical bonds will be popular with yourself; and being a subject of which the importance is musical rather than bibliographical, should escape your condemnation so rightly meted out to those who produce Lists of Trumpeters at the court of Charles IV.[95]

Hughes's approach reflected what Dent was trying to promote both in his university teaching and in his professional societies, the kind of musical learning which is devoid of complacency or preciosity, and in which the music of the past is viewed on an equal footing with established classics, without 'reverence', something to be brought to life through intelligent understanding and ultimately tested through performance. Performance was part of the scholarly process. Equally to be avoided was the thoughtless and safe reiteration of 'classics', that 'musical equivalent of getting into bed with a hot [water] bottle'.

Most of the visitors had already enjoyed a lavish reception at the Royal Academy of Music in London, possibly to reassure them that they had not just come to a provincial backwater. The University Vice Chancellor, Will Spens, also invited three or four 'leading people' to dinner at Corpus Christi. High Table dining is invariably impressive, as Alban Berg had seen, with the conversation, the medieval hall setting, the ancient silver service and the general ceremony, and Dent took care that the 'ladies' involved might not be excluded from the masculine rooms. On the Saturday there was another lavish do at the Cambridge Guildhall, hosted by the female Mayor, the formidable mother of John Maynard Keynes, a fact which especially impressed the Germans. There were madrigals sung from King's College bridge over the River Cam against the backdrop of Clare College, King's College Chapel and Gibbs Building; daily services with music in several chapels with resident choirs, especially St John's and King's, and a lavish 'Historical Pageant of English Music' along the riverbank by the Bridge of Sighs and Wren Library, Purcell's 'Ye tuneful Muses' sung by the Cambridge University Musical Society chorus and orchestra, conducted by Cyril Rootham and Boris Ord. Every day that week, concerts of a particularly Cambridge kind were laid on in between the lectures and discussions. Much of this music being performed as part of regular services was relatively unknown to these eminent scholars: beside Byrd and Purcell, Gibbons, Locke, Tallis, Weelkes, Blow, and that of the contemporary locals, Charles Wood and Ralph Vaughan Williams.

94 Hughes to Dent 12/4/1933. KCA, EJD/2/8/1.

95 Hughes to Dent 4/7/1933.

And the setting of Tudor music being sung in Tudor buildings underlined the general English theme of the Cambridge Congress: 'English' music had been around for a long time.

'It will have a wonderful reverberation on the Continent and in America, I think', Dent wrote to Clive that August when the notices came through. Dent himself was delighted with everything, reception and performances, and at the way so much of what he had striven to convey had indeed been appreciated, especially, he thought, by the Germans. 'Really I was quite amazed at it myself. I never in all my life heard such technical excellence of singing and playing in Cambridge before.' Although critics Bonavia, Fox Strangways, Eric Blom and Herbert Thompson expressed their warm approval, 'English people more or less cold-shouldered us.'[96] The press reports were mixed, for example the local *Eastern Daily Press*, whose correspondent seems to have missed the point: 'England has modern composers whose works are infinitely more interesting than the works of composers who lived between 1200 and 1700 … museum pieces … pathetic'.[97] The big papers were mostly very positive, possibly because their critics were well-primed former students of Dent's. Thompson in the *Yorkshire Post* spoke of 'the opportunity of hearing the English music of five centuries performed in its own surroundings by those to whom it is a natural heritage', while the *Musical Times* gave more coverage to the Welsh Eisteddfodd going on in another part of the country. In the German press the congress was used as a platform to make a wider point, both Kathi Meyer's detailed and carefully phrased review in the *Frankfurter Zeitung* and the *Berliner Zeitung am Mittwoch* emphasising how music was a common bond, with no encumbrances.[98]

Probably the most sympathetic review was by Knud Jeppesen for *Acta Musicologica*, house publication of the ISMR, sending a message out to all the members who had not come to Cambridge.[99] He described how perfect was the setting for English music in this idyllic ancient university town, with Tudor colleges and old-fashioned style. But his final sentences make the common agenda clear:

> It was demonstrated that English music not only has a great past to praise itself for, but is also possessed of a cultural present, which can hold its own in any international sphere. It is to be hoped that future congresses of our society will be held in the same way as the Cambridge Congress, namely to have as its central purpose, to illuminate scientifically [wissenschaftlich] the musical history of the countries concerned, and in connection with – what is especially important – practical performances to make more immediate for foreigners the real treasures of all older national music. The Cambridge Congress has in any event shown that this is a happy way forward.[100]

96 CC 05/08/1933.

97 *Eastern Daily Press*, 03/08/1933.

98 02/08/1933.

99 Knud Jeppesen, in *Acta Musicologica*, vol. 5, no. 4 (October–December 1933), pp. 145–6.

100 *Ibid.*, author's translation.

But the Cambridge Congress captured more than simple musical zeitgeist. Two of the Germans who had managed to come, Kathi Meyer and Hermann Meyer, stayed on. Both had been recommended by Johannes Wolf, who himself gave the keynote lecture of the congress in English, while Dent already knew Kathi Meyer from the Hirsch Library in Frankfurt. As the Cambridge Congress was being held, that library was being removed from Frankfurt and gradually being transferred, together with the entire Hirsch family, via Paris to Cambridge.[101] Hermann Meyer sought refuge in England, where he taught at London University and at King's, Cambridge, throughout the war. By August the Einsteins were installed at 8 Oldbury Place, a mews in London, with 'no intention' of returning to Germany.[102] Even before the congress, Dent was being applied to for work from German musicians who saw which way the wind was blowing. 'I have now had 3 German Regisseurs asking me for jobs', he had written to Jack Gordon that June, 'Schoen (who is in London) – Erhardt of Dresden and Heyel who was at Essen and also with Strohbach – now in Vienna – I suppose there is no chance of giving them work at the Vic or R.C.M.?'[103]

Dent's apparently halfhearted appeal here masks a genuine concern and sense of frustration. He knew that far from being a threat, such refugees were a potential source of fresh ideas and talent which created more work, helping to transform the high arts in ways not yet achieved; the case he had been arguing for years now. But battling on the domestic musical front was already difficult enough, between the formidable financial problems being faced by the arts generally beside the more immediate threat to Sadler's Wells from Beecham. Dent could have done without even more demands on his time and resources, but he continued to negotiate on behalf of Otto Erhardt[104] and others all that summer and autumn, his genuinely altruistic efforts often sprinkled with sarcastic comments on the apparently high expectations and self-importance of the supplicants. From Italy he asked Clive to take a look at Erhardt, who really wanted to work with Beecham: 'a young assistant (from the Berlin opera) probably thinks that he & Beecham by their own little selves can create a Staatsoper in London by a mere wave of the bâton!' And after Clive had met with Erhardt:

> what do you think of him? Is there the remotest chance of employing him at the Vic? ... His reply sounds as if he though he had only to land in England to build up an English Staatsoper complete (or replete) ... in 24 hours. They all think that; and some of them put their foolish trust in 'doubtful Thomas'.[105]

101 For the next ten years the Library remained in Cambridge, and after the war, Dent had hoped for it to go into the University Collection, but the university refused to stump up the money for it. Instead, Maynard Keynes managed to find the money from the sympathetic American Pilgrim Trust and other sources, to save it as the cornerstone to the current national collection at the British Library. To this day no one knows for sure how exactly it all happened. Dent must have known, but breathed not a word about it.

102 JBT–EJD 26/08/1933.

103 JG 22/06/1933.

104 Otto Erhardt (1888–1963), stage director, friend of Kurt Weill, later worked at Chicago Opera.

105 CC 22/08/1933.

These were only the first wave.

> Have you come across Curt Prerauer, who was on the staff of the Berlin Opera under Blech as coach, organist and general assistant etc – turned out as being a Jew? … sent to me by Dr Kapp of the Berlin Opera with a cordial recommendation. In the summer he got a job with the 'Metropolitan' Co, but that has come to an abrupt end. At present he is coaching Ann Fletcher, and Lady F. seems very much pleased with him … He is now trying to get in to Vic–Wells, and Coates has recommended him strongly to Miss B[aylis].
>
> Miss B. appears to have told him that the Home Office won't allow her to engage him, but what she really thinks I don't know; I have only heard his side of the matter. On the face of it I should think he would be a most valuable addition to our staff, provided (as I very firmly wrote to Miss B.) that she thinks he would work harmoniously with the rest.[106]

Prerauer and Erhardt were only two of many experienced, talented people willing to work for nothing just to get round the current Home Office restrictions on their stay, but 2 pounds per week had to be found from some source, most likely one of the Jewish refugee organisations which were springing up out of such need. Dent offered to pay it himself in order to keep Prerauer at the Wells, since Prerauer was keen to produce Bizet's *The Pearl Fishers*, then practically unknown in Britain.

It was clear that Germany was deliberately shedding a great deal of its native talent in the arts as much as the sciences, and within two years, many distinguished refugees were active in British music and theatre under varying conditions and pay. Some, like Erhardt, quickly became part of the establishment; Kurt Joos started up his own Ballets Joos, partly based in Cambridge and performing at the new Arts Theatre, opened in 1936. Hans Strohbach worked for a brief period with Jack Gordon at the Wells, but returned to Dresden, miraculously surviving the war there. Erhardt shared Dent's love of Handel and Purcell; if as Dent wanted, he had come to the Wells, things might have been different.

In spite of having imported some spectacular singers – such as Lotte Lehmann and Alexander Kipnis in *Rosenkavalier* – and with imaginative, ambitious programming (*Don Carlos, La damnation de Faust, Tristan*), the quality of the current Covent Garden productions and even of the singing was heavily criticised.[107] The critical disaster was mitigated by a fresh undertaking by Philip Hill and a formidable board to rescue both the finances and the decrepit fabric of the opera house,[108] but all of this would be useless, as Toye with his Sadler's Wells background appreciated, without a complete rethink over the current dismal production standards, so he snaffled Erhardt. 'I shall be amused to hear Erhardt's impression of C.[ovent G.[arden] after a few weeks of work there. I can't think that even he will be able to effect much change.'[109] Dent was right about that, but in spite of the constraints, Erhardt seems to have made a conspicuous difference that season. He got the Berlin

[106] CC 30/10/1933.

[107] cf Lucas, *Thomas Beecham*, pp. 213 ff.

[108] *Ibid.*, pp. 216 ff.

[109] CC 05/12/1933.

sets for Weinberger's *Schwanda the Bagpiper*, rejected because of the composer's Jewishness, and hired Rex Whistler, who was also doing his famous sets for *The Marriage of Figaro* at Sadler's Wells, to design *Fidelio*.[110] At Glyndebourne, John Christie had invited Dent's old friend Rudolf Bing to run the company, together with Fritz Busch from Dresden and Carl Ebert from Berlin. Christie wanted the high standards they could bring and was prepared to pay. He was not disappointed; the Glyndebourne style began in that first season in 1934, with high production values and high musical standards.

But in 1933 it was all happening too quickly for any long-term decision-making. Although Dent was entirely sympathetic to the plight of increasing numbers of refugee musicians, many of whom were old friends and colleagues, there was little more he could do for most, apart from offering some immediate financial support and undertaking through his personal channels to sort out some immediate solutions, the support, position, and funding they needed to stay. Wearing his ISCM/ISMR hats, he continued to believe for a few years yet that so long as he could keep such channels open, without offending the new fascist governments too obviously, the international festivals could be kept going as a distinct and important public face for all music, where current issues could be debated in the open.

Dent has been accused of being 'blinkered' in his presidential style, for failing to acknowledge the political games being played with international music, even two years after the German section had left the ISCM.[111] Publicly Dent continued to adhere to his old view of the ISCM as an 'unpolitical' organisation, and some music historians have questioned this apparently wilfully naïve stance.[112] But Dent was neither naïve nor ignorant, and he was himself a very political animal. His methods of fighting the human brutality he loathed above all were subtle ones, honed throughout his life, especially during the Great War; whether or not they were effective is arguably another matter. At the time Dent was trying to play a deeper game, possibly unsuccessfully, but vindicated when after the war he was asked to return to head and rebuild both international societies. In 1933 he knew that there were refugees to protect and still many others unprotected back in Germany, especially Jews and homosexuals, so the public forum of the international societies had to appear as neutral as possible, he felt, at least to remain open as a means of expression and possibly, a route to safety. It was Dent's old homosexual ploy updated: to operate quietly, unobtrusively, unexceptionably.

Now, on top of his usual correspondence, he was writing dozens of personal letters, in Italian, German, French and English, to those still in positions of power, especially to composers and musicians involved with the ISCM and the ISMR being compromised by politics, holding everything together with words. One such letter to Gian Francesco Malipiero in late 1933,[113] is typical: Dent is at his most engaging, joking about Hitler, testing Malipiero's commitments to the fascist tide, reassuring

110 Lucas, *Thomas Beecham*, pp. 217–18.

111 Haefeli, *IGNM*, p. 196.

112 Haefeli in particular, but others as well.

113 01/12/1933. Fondazione Giorgio Cini, Venice.

him and his circle that standards would be maintained for the impending Florence Festival, asking his advice, all lightly and easily phrased, about how to deal with the German problems, as if it was of no consequence whatever. Malipiero was one of many musicians now in a cultural grey area, friendly with fascists like D'Annunzio and Mussolini, but his natural sympathies more with music than politics. Deftly, Dent drew him in on a friendly, personal level, casually mentioning how Max Butting was telling him how embarrassed ('si trova molto imbarrazzata') the German Section found itself by the political decisions having to be made, and asking his opinion on how best to proceed. There was urgent need for such diplomatic skill; if international music was to survive, the institutions it depended on had to be in good running order.

Still, many of Dent's letters in these years might be construed as 'blinkered', because there is so little in them of the more savage or portentous events. Dent tended to compartmentalise his life anyway, partly out of the simple necessity for a gay man to lie low and keep his own secrets, but also because he did not wish to see what was there in front of him, that many colleagues, many of his young men, the same young Germans who had given his life colour and fun, were caving in to prevailing modes and happily becoming Nazis: Wolfgang Frommel, Hans Raab, architect Friedl Friedrich and others.

> Wolfgang's friends are all in the thick of the 'new youth' – they have accepted Nazism, but seem to preserve their former idealism. I haven't seen Wolfgang for 3 or 4 years, but he writes as if he was the same sort of Rolf Gardiner idealist that he used to be: and although he is now in uniform as one of the Berlin Radio staff, he lodges with a completely Jewish family, the son of wch wrote to me the other day about getting a job in England![114]

It is a feeble piece of equivocation, demonstrating Dent's weakest side, his moral vulnerability to sexual loyalty, and it is difficult in hindsight not to deplore his deeply flawed judgement, his apparent failure to recognise the insidious way Nazism in the shape of attractive young men had slid under his personal moral radar. He continued to keep in touch with his young Nazis, choosing to travel with Friedl Friedrich several times in the next two years. 'Only connect', Forster had put it, and Dent seems to have failed.

There is another possible interpretation. In times of great stress, for good or ill, the familiar and the routine are anchors. Dent kept to the principles which had seen him through the last war, to do what he was good at, keeping music and high culture alive until the storm passed while looking after his friends, and as with the ISCM, thinking that it would do no good to alienate former friends over differing principles, while hoping to change their minds. In 1936 Hans Raab did eventually flee, and Dent was able to help him.

For a brief time that spring the old life reasserted itself around the April 1934 ISCM Festival at Florence. Between La Selva and Florence Dent had enjoyed a reviving two days at San Remo with Carlo, now making a success of his tailoring business, fashioning smart suits for Pizzetti and Malipiero: 'he did not come to

[114] LH 07/06/1934.

FIGURE 17. Dent and Wolfgang Frommel, Berlin, c.1932. By kind permission of the Provost and Fellows of King's College, Cambridge.

Florence, which was tactful of him, as I could not have taken him to all the state functions'.[115] After a brief visit to the Francis Toyes at Portofino, Dent finally made it to the Sitwells' Montegufoni, with only Sir George and Lady Ida and their grandson Reresby there.

> Lady Ida was laid up with a broken bone in her leg, but was wheeled in to lunch, and put down vast quantities of Valpolicella and cherry brandy, in quaint old Venetian glasses with Bible stories pictured on them. Her liqueur glass, I observed, had the story of Noah and the vine; the old English butler must have a malicious sense of humour.[116]

The 1934 ISCM Festival (2–7 April) was, on the face of it, an artistic success of no mean order and a reinstatement of the musical standards some had felt missing

[115] LH 18/05/1934.

[116] *Ibid.*

FIGURE 18. Hans Raab in his Nazi uniform. On the back written: 'A man who is dead – forever! 31/10/35'. By kind permission of the Provost and Fellows of King's College, Cambridge.

from the previous festivals. Mussolini had been relatively benevolent to musicians, and although taking place against a background of disturbing events and political interference, it was probably the last festival relatively uncluttered by internal politics, or even wider political movements. There had been the usual divisions in the jury meeting at San Remo, that is to say, accusations of partiality, recriminations and hissy fits galore, but these were minor. Nadia Boulanger had brought music by her own pupils along with her, pressing them on the jury with the excuse that they were 'independent' works, with no national section behind them, therefore worthy of consideration. The jury countered by selecting instead a Martelli piece chosen by the French Section, which she dismissed as 'unFrench', provoking Ernst

Krenek to growl 'she talks like the Nazis'.[117] But Alois Hába generously offered to give up his own chosen piece so that one by an unknown, the Czech Jaroslav Jezek, could be played.

With only a few Germans at Florence – Hindemith succumbing to the cancellation of his Trio for Violin, Viola and Heckelphone – there was nevertheless a rich mixture of unknowns like Knudåge Riisager, a very young Benjamin Britten's 'Phantasy' oboe quartet, and some items, new then but now established classics: Berg's *Lyric Suite*, Jean Françaix's *Sonata for String Trio*, Bartók's *Rhapsodie for Violin and Orchestra*, Ravel's *Piano Concerto for the Left Hand*. Performers included Joseph Szigeti, Paul Wittgenstein, the Griller Quartet; conductors: Vittorio Gui, Igor Markevich and Hermann Scherchen, whose teenage son Wulff became a close friend of Britten while they were there.

But the elephant in the room was German music. At the end of June Dent was in Berlin again, trying to sort out the depleted German Section of the ISCM, with only a few brave German composers and musicologists daring to defy the government. Then Dent witnessed the public shootings:

> Berlin was quite quiet during the week end; Göring ordered a raid on the queer places … I think myself that the most horrible part of the whole thing is the utter indifference with which the public seems to regard these political assassinations en masse; but after all, Röhm and Heines had murdered so many people themselves in the same way that it is no wonder Germany is quite accustomed to it.[118]

It was a great shock to Dent. His old, comfortable, cherished place of refuge no longer existed; homosexuals were among those now specified as undesirables. Although he must have felt afraid, Dent stayed on for a few more days in order to try to see what might be salvaged. He was stonewalled:

> Talk with Dr Beneke of the Reichsmusikkammer – and Havemann – to discuss the German Section of the International. Beneke is a good sort, I think, and I suspected that he was more liberal in his private opinions than he would officially admit; but he and Havemann (especially H. who is a thorough blockhead) were completely anti-semitic and crazy about 'the race' etc. … I was very glad to get away from Germany, and I have quite decided not to go to Berlin in the autumn.[119]

A month later, he told Lawrence 'although the streets were quite quiet and there was no danger whatever for me as a foreigner I felt very glad to get away and cross the frontier; and I do not want to go back to Germany until there is some considerable change'.[120]

By this stage, Dent had already been identified as an enemy to everything that was happening in German music, with the German Section about to break from the

117 Haefeli, *IGNM*, p. 234.

118 JG 04/07/1934. In the 'Night of the Long Knives', Hitler got rid of dissenters in his own party, including his former intimate friend Ernst Röhm, and blamed the revolt on Bolsheviks and pederasts.

119 *Ibid.*

120 LH 04/08/1934.

ISCM altogether. The Nazi government set up a 'Ständiger Rat für die internationale Zusammenarbeit der Komponisten' (Permanent Council for the International Cooperation of Composers), its President, composer Richard Strauss, was also President of the Reichsmusikkammer. André de Blonay was clear about its aims:

> Following upon the Florence Festival of the I.S.C.M. last year, the position of this Society had become very serious – not from the artistic point of view, but from the political, so to speak. Many years before, some of its section had started giving questions of prestige precedence over artistic questions, and insisting on being well represented at the Festivals at all costs. Then Germany withdrew from the Society, and now at Richard Strauss's instigation, a 'Permanent Council' has been formed in opposition to it, with the object of pursuing a throughly Hitlerian policy in music – Strauss being the 'Führer' who appoints the delegates of all countries; and of securing a triumph for the reactionary tendencies now rife in Germany.[121]

Germany was now closed to Dent, although he never ceased communicating with the German musicians and musicologists who remained his friends. At home, he continued his punishing schedules, his election to The Athenaeum Club on 27 February another public acknowledgement of his standing, beside the constant requests for him to write articles, lecture, examine, or help refugees. His presence on the Vic–Wells Board was now very active, while translating opera librettos into English for Sadler's Wells and for Erik Chisholm at Glasgow had become for him both an intellectual exercise he loved and a means of keeping himself closely involved with opera production. It was also escape: as the outside world was becoming unspeakable, translation, like strict counterpoint, kept Dent's mind otherwise occupied. Although he made some money from a few of his published translations, he donated it back into the Wells, or else allowed people to use his translations freely, if asked.

Dent's letters to Clive Carey and to Jack Gordon are particularly detailed in these years from 1932 up to the war. Both Gordon and Carey were now producing operas at Sadler's Wells and in other places, and Dent continued to take not just a keen interest in their work, but to offer genuine collaboration, the personal and the professional. His correspondence on these matters was also another intellectual exercise, not unlike Cambridge High Tables, going through the process of explaining for himself and for his recipients exactly what the operas in question were about, what was going on in a scene or with a character, getting the character's linguistic register right and the words singable. He loved proposing new repertoire, and since in term-time Dent was forced to be in Cambridge, the best way he could converse about such things was via letters.

> After seeing your Traviata I am convinced that the right policy for the Vic is not to rest content with traditional ways, but to show the public and the critics that the old-fashioned operas can be made much more dramatic and interesting … than they ever supposed.

121 *Schweizerische Musikzeitung* (15 October 1935), quoted in the MT (December 1935), p. 1099.

> I feel sure Rossini wrote the opera with a keen sense of the ridiculousness of all the operatic conventions and purposely exaggerated them. This is quite unmistakable in the trio (Rosina, Count, Figaro) in the last act.[122]
>
> I have just been considering Don Pasquale, … fascinating musically, I think, and should be much easier to produce (and possibly to sing) than Barber; on the other hand, the story … is so incredibly fatuously silly that Cosi fan tutte is Ibsen by the side of it! It would make a delightful opera for marionettes. If we did it at the Vic it would have to be staged in some peculiarly fantastic way and I wonder (1) if that could be carried out (2) if the audience would take it. But a serious 'straight' performance of it would be dreadful.[123]

He could ask Jack to lunch to discuss 'worried letters' from the other board members Sumner Austin and Muriel Gough about tackling Beecham's continuing attempts to take over, about a vacancy on the board, about the more or less constant financial crises (at one point Jack was not only director but 'anonymous donor', lending some of his own furniture for a scene in his production of *Tosca*), while keeping discussions open with Austin and Gough and Gordon about how to sing Dent's words for *The Barber of Seville*. The detailed letters rolled in from all over Europe, keeping everyone informed and involved; it grounded him.

> Since I have been working at Handel I have begun to wonder whether it would be worth while putting a Handel opera on. I never can make up my mind about Handel's operas. Those I saw in Germany I thought dull: but when I read Streatfeild I feel I want to make the attempt. I am quite sure Oskar Hagen's arrangements are bad, and should like to try arranging one myself from the score – but I haven't studied them carefully enough yet. At present my inclinations are towards Alcina, which is a romantic story from Ariosto, with all sorts of 'magical' episodes – Alcina is the same sort of lady as Circe and Armide. I know the opera has some very lovely songs and a lot of ballet, which would be an advantage. … It is the success of Orpheus which has rather turned my head in this matter – for Orpheus, in spite of its being supposed to be the starting point of modern opera, is really very like a Handel opera in many ways.[124]

In May 1934, Dent's little book on Handel was finished, significantly with only one German reference, to Hugo Leichtentritt's 1924 *Händel*.[125] It was the product not only of his connections with the German Handel revival of the 1920s, but his own current teaching; pupils included the future Handel scholar Winton Dean, then an undergraduate at King's and involved with the Handel oratorios being staged at Cambridge.[126] Like all the best teachers, Dent had discovered again how reciprocal

[122] JG 17/11/1933.

[123] CC 23/05/1933.

[124] JG 19/12/1933. Oskar Hagen (1888–1957), German art historian who helped to run the Handel festivals Dent saw at Göttingen, later fled to the USA.

[125] Joseph Müller-Blattau had published a biography in 1933. See Potter, *Most German of the Arts*, pp. 226 ff for fuller discussion of such issues.

[126] *Samson* (1932, with Steuart Wilson), *Jephtha* (1934), *Susanna* (1935), *Saul* (1937): Knight, *Cambridge Music*, pp 113–15. All were collaborations between Dennis Arundell, Gwen

good teaching can be; ideas put to students had to be clarified, while students' input was often refreshing and illuminating, and the productions at Cambridge and at the Vic–Wells gave Dent a practical dimension not afforded to many musicologists. Dent could teach Handel to his students at Cambridge, discuss, observe and advise on the productions done there, consider how they might be done at Sadler's Wells and brought into the public eye.[127] A month later when he was asked to the Handel festival at Krefeld, his book already written, Dent had prefaced the visit with some research at Münster, tracking down a 'lost' Handel cantata manuscript beside a fair copy by 'one of Scarlatti's copyists' and copying a 'long' Salve Regina by Domenico Scarlatti for mezzo and strings. Handel's Italian influences, both literary and musical, were very much on his mind, and in the book he had spent much of Chapter 5 on the operas inspired by Ariosto and Tasso.

> Orlando is one of Handel's most original operas; he seems always to have derived a peculiar inspiration from the poems of Tasso and Ariosto, as in the case of Rinaldo. Orlando is a thoroughly romantic opera – Chrysander even compares it with those of Weber – full of episodes of madness and magic; it is so far removed from the ordinary conventions of its time that we can well imagine it to have startled both its audiences and its singers.[128]

So at Krefeld, Dent was loftily unimpressed, writing to Clive: 'Handel's Orlando was completely misunderstood ... The Germans used to have no use for Handel ... Now he is being painted brown, and boosted as a great German, and as an inspirer of everything that is national and heroic. Little they know about Handel's English environment! or about Ariosto ... Musically they do not get there at all.'[129]

> The tradition of Italian culture had for generations been more firmly implanted in England than anywhere in Germany, except perhaps in Vienna, and, since those three years in Italy, Handel's musical outlook had become completely Italian, as his music shows.[130]

Dent loved the scholarly high ground, but this was especially apt in the current political climate infecting music. The deliberate point about the Italian influence was an important counterweight to what was happening in current German Handel studies, the way in which Handel was being co-opted as the model of a 'German' composer.

> My intention has been to concentrate on the Life only; and to state nothing but what are ascertained facts. This makes it rather dry, I fear, but I have allowed myself a few intermezzi which I think are honestly my own, and I think I have produced a new theory about Handel's borrowings.[131]

Raverat, Elizabeth Vellacott, Cyril Rootham and later, Boris Ord.

127 There was no production of Handel at the Wells in Dent's lifetime, which is a pity.

128 Dent, *Handel* (London, 1934), pp. 85–6.

129 CC 22/06/1934.

130 Dent, *Handel*, pp. 44–5.

131 LH 01/06/1934.

The reviews were very good: 'an outstanding example of short biography'.[132] Decades later, Winton Dean called it 'still the best of its kind … notable for a new theory to explain the wholesale borrowings from other composers in the years after 1737'.[133]

In 1934, beside his book on Handel, finished at the same time he was examining his 15 B Mus candidates, Dent was engaged to contribute to four other books and to correct proofs of his British Academy lecture. He churned out twenty-five thousand words for his 'awful section on Opera for Bacharach-Gollancz's mixed grill book', and Edmund Gardner's *Companion to Italian Studies*, a 'fritto misto', the section on Music in G.M. Trevelyan's *Early Victorian England*, and a section on 'Bellini in Inghilaterra' for Pizzetti's book on Bellini.[134] At least, the establishment that year of a more solid Covent Garden company meant that Beecham was off their backs at Sadler's Wells, something Dent was grateful for, even if not everyone agreed with him about Beecham. 'F.T. [Francis Toye] rather denied the intentions which I ascribed to T.B. and I suppose all the people who want to get something out of T.B. are inclined to think I am unjust towards him.'[135]

But while Dent was anxious to establish the Sadler's Wells style, as distinct from that of either Covent Garden or Glyndebourne, achieving it, taking the necessary risks, was proving difficult. One factor was Lilian Baylis and her deep fear of taking any risks at all. Dent sensed that she was desperate to trust the people she was working with, but always held back, preferring at the last to keep control.

> How characteristic of L.B. to say that Fra Diavolo was a failure! Poor dear, she has no imagination of what any opera might be, if only it was put on properly. I wonder what she really thought of Traviata. I'm sure she could never realize that that performance was really epoch-making … and the first time that Traviata has ever been done in England … from that point of view – as a serious and beautiful work, and a deeply moving play, instead of just a Melba night out and a hopelessly vulgar and ridiculous opera.[136]

He sympathised with her fears while finding them obstructive and frustrating. For her part, Baylis found Dent 'visionary' and at times overpowering.[137]

> She cannot make up her mind, and I never can make out who it is that she trusts. I thought it was Collingwood, and felt safe, for C. is an honest man and a good musician, and knows more about opera than any one else there. I could put up with G.T.'s [Geoffrey Toye's] ambitions and vanities, if he was not in with Beecham all the time. I feel sure that G.T. prevented Miss B. doing Fidelio because T.B. wanted to do it at Covent Garden. T.B., I think wants eventually to run C.G. [Covent Garden] on the grand scale as an English opera house, and to keep the V.W. [Vic–Wells] permanently under, as a nursery garden for himself,

132 HG in the MT (January 1935), p. 32.

133 Dean, 'Edward J. Dent: A Centenary Tribute', p. 358.

134 LH 20/05/1934. Haward, *Edward J. Dent: A Bibliography*, 94–8.

135 CC 12/05/1933.

136 *Ibid.*

137 CC 22/06/1934.

> and as a popular Opera Comique; on paper this sounds all right, but it means that we shall never be allowed to do anything original or interesting ... But I want to be able to do medium-sized operas at the V.W., such as Flute, Freischütz, Oberon, etc and of course Fidelio, which is opéra-comique, in spite of all the monumental nonsense and the Furtwänglering of it into a Helden-Oper. [Handwritten] I want the V-W to get the credit of doing operas that no one else has the courage to do.[138]

Geoffrey Toye's continued presence on the Vic–Wells Board while he was working with Beecham at Covent Garden Dent found both obstructive and irritating, while there was an ongoing conflict of interests which only confused Lilian Baylis.

> G.T.'s aversion to Travelling Companion and Sir John is only explainable on the fact that he takes his ideas from what he thinks smart society thinks ... He is incapable of visualizing an opera from the score ... What I like are people who say 'I know everybody thinks Genoveva a rotten opera, but I believe in it, and I know I can interpret it in the right way and make everybody see that it is a masterpiece.' ... G.T. can only say at the best 'it was a success at Dresden or Monte Carlo, so we can make it a success here.' Also he is dead against the Vic–Wells being a 'Settlement' Opera. He would like to have dearer seats and a smarter audience. Well, by all menas [sic] raise the stalls from 6/- to 7/6 if you think you can get your audience, but don't interfere with the 6d. gallery ... you can have 'settlement opera' and yet do the works properly and do good works. She rightly fears Lady C. and party; but at the same time she wants the stalls filled.[139]

To complicate matters even further, at the same time the Carnegie Trust was putting pressure on the Vic–Wells to change its constitution, splitting the governing board into two: 'they propose that a small executive be appointed to run both the theatres and to have more control of everything'.[140] Dent was afraid that if the board was split, there would be fewer musicians on it and that he might be ousted in favour of Toye, so suggested to Clive that he, together with Muriel Gough, Sumner Austin, Jack and Lawrance Collingwood 'form a regular secret committee of your own', in order to get a solid music policy put together beforehand to 'push' decisions through the board. Thus the 'Soviet' came into being, an informal committee which knew how things ran and could discuss new ideas before running them past Lilian Baylis, exactly the kind of efficient if slightly covert operation Dent liked to employ. Throughout his travels in May and June 1934, Dent kept in touch with Jack and Clive, asking how things were shaping up for the next season; he wanted to study any definitely programmed operas over the next month, to think about translations: 'I have been careful not to worry Miss B. with too many suggestions, as I want her to make up her mind', he wrote to Jack Gordon. 'So I mentioned Cenerentola, Rigoletto, Freischütz and Arabella, as possibilities; these seem to be the ones you are most in favour of.'[141]

138 *Ibid.*

139 *Ibid.*

140 CC 22/06/1934.

141 JG 20/05/1934.

All that year, even with all his other commitments, Dent concerned himself with keeping up active discussions on future productions, feeling that if the ideas fizzled out, it was slow death for the Wells. So although the subjects might appear petty – for example, doing two 'English' operas, Lawrance Collingwood's *Macbeth,* which Dent thought 'not good, but Miss B is desperately anxious' to do it, and Vaughan Williams' *Sir John in Love,* an idea which 'horrified' Miss B. – they allowed even the most improbable ideas to breathe, and with them, concomitant points often more significant, raising practical questions: 'Can this be done in April, with a chorus depleted by loan to Cov. Gard. and possibly a tired company? … Is it necessary or desirable to produce a new opera towards the end of one season?'[142]

Through all the upheavals and uncertainties, the 1933–34 London opera seasons marked the beginnings of a new operatic order, with the main companies each establishing a distinctive style. What had threatened to become a destructive swallowing-up was developing into a healthy rivalry; the London opera world was really very small, interacting with its art world, and there was a great deal of overlap if not outright stealing, since good ideas are seldom mutually exclusive. So Covent Garden gave the British premiere of Strauss's recent opera *Arabella,* with Dent's old friend Clemens Krauss conducting the Vienna State Opera with his future wife singing the title role. Dent, noting the 'rather chilly reception at Covent Garden', thought it would suit Sadler's Wells better. He suggested contacting Strohbach, now back at Dresden, 'a great Strauss place', to enlist Strauss's advice. If they were going to take it on at the Wells, it was going to be done as well as possible.

The Sadler's Wells style was slowly emerging more along the lines Dent had envisaged, as a kind of opéra-comique foil to the grander style at Covent Garden; *Fra Diavolo* and Mozart as opposed to *Aïda.* Production standards could be maintained at relatively low cost, Dent continued to argue, with thought and care beside uncompromising musical standards, achieved through establishing a solid company who could maintain those standards. The Sadler's Wells audience was rather younger, more intelligent, capable of genuine response to the music, keen and not remotely stuffy, not a tiara in sight, a precursor of modern opera audiences at the Coliseum or Saffron Hall. Developing and sticking to that house style became a main preoccupation in those years, and Dent became mildly obsessive about it. Over and again, he discussed and refined with Clive and Jack what the Sadler's Wells style was, what they could do best, even with their limited resources, *A Theatre for Everybody,* as he later called it. Mostly Dent was delighted with the results of their efforts, *Fra Diavolo* in spite of Baylis thinking it a failure, and 'his' *Barber of Seville,* basking in the compliments from the foreign conductors who had seen it, Jalowetz from Cologne and Oppenheim from Prince Reuss's troupe.

Dent often sniped at the early John Christie style, averring that no one ever laughed at Glyndebourne, whereas there was always laughter to be heard at the Wells, while the extravagance of the operation never appealed to Dent, with its country-house setting, its upper-class overtones of exclusivity, expensive tickets and lavish production. But Christie knew his audience, who loved the studied formality of the

[142] JG 15/01/1934.

occasion as much as the productions. Although he often protested that he didn't go to Glyndebourne because he couldn't afford the tickets, Dent did help Christie when asked, as with the publication of some Glyndebourne editions of opera.[143] They never really saw eye-to-eye; egos grate, but Glyndebourne has long since taken up many of Dent's ideas for the Wells: the use of young, relatively unknown singers, the unusual and/or new productions beside the old repertoire, the high standards of singing and production.

That August Dent went as usual for a fortnight in the Dolomites with Carlo, to the Albergo Solda, near Bolzano, where he could work on a translation of Berlioz's *Les Troyens* for Erik Chisholm at Glasgow, 'especially as I hear that Beecham wants to do Les Troyens at Covent Garden in two years' time – so I shall rub the gilt off his gingerbread'. He had taken Dryden's *Virgil* along with him, 'for Dryden often puts in Alexandrines, and Berlioz of course writes a good many, so that Dryden has a certain affinity to the French style of poetry'.[144]

It was to be the last such idyllic time. Dent relaxed, entertained by Carlo's antics, dressing up as a prince to fool the tourists, and allowing his mind to range on the possibilities of the next year. The relaxation fed his determined optimism.

> We shall be there a fortnight or more, and then I want to go to Venice for the Festival; towards the end of September I must go to Prague, either via Vienna or via Budapest, to consult with the Prague people about the International Festival at Carlsbad (August 1935) and with this connected International Congress of Musical Education at Prague. The Congress is my attempt to revive on a more international basis the so-called 'Lausanne' conferences ... which have now come to grief owing to Anglo-American differences. I thought that if I could get to Prague to initiate another Conference and make it definitely international, it might solve the problem and produce good results. My own interest in it is owing to the book 'Music and the Community' – the Report of the Cambridgeshire Council of Musical Education on the Teaching of Music, which I nominally edited, and in part wrote ... We shall run the propaganda for the Prague Congress from our Cambridge office, so as to keep up my myth that Cambridge is the musical centre of England if not indeed of the world.
>
> I am feeling about tired out, but manage to keep going somehow. So I am being thoroughly extravagant and travelling to Milan by the Simplon-Orient (Constantinople) Express ... if I could afford it I think I should spend most of my holidays travelling in trains deluxe for 24 hours at a time; there are few things which refresh and rest me so successfully.[145]

But when he got to Venice, it was clear which way the wind was blowing. Strauss used the Biennale to publicly launch the new alternative international society, the Permanent Council; the future for German music would take place on very different lines from the ISCM, while its conservative, nationalistic elements appealed to the Italians. Dent always played by the fundamental rules, even as he tinkered at

143 CC 18/10/1934.

144 LH 04/08/1934.

145 *Ibid.*

the boundaries; he had stressed again and again the need for such flexible tactics in every dealing with either the ISCM or the ISMR, but he also wanted to demonstrate clearly what was unacceptable. Now the act of performing had become a political act, sometimes one of defiance, but certainly public. Since Germany had declared that its Jews and other undesirables would not be allowed to exist officially, Dent looked for ways to get round this repulsive stance, make an acceptable public statement and yet remain unexceptionable, and all in the greater cause of music, now an almost impossible undertaking.

While in Prague for the ISCM jury meeting that December 1934, he noted the rumblings, writing to Jack:

> Prague was full of rumours about Germany, but one never knows what to believe, and the Emigrant element is very strong here. But the German residents seem to be firm against Hitler, and to prefer the 'democracy' (about which the Czechs are never silent!) of Czechoslovakia under old Masaryk.[146]

Dent had had himself to pay 'most of the Jury's expenses at Carlsbad, owing to the dilatoriness of the Sections in sending in their subscriptions',[147] leaving him out of pocket until the London office could reimburse him. Still he remained over-optimistic, hoping for the spirit of *Simplicissimus* to be revived and these modern absurdities overthrown by satire. He enjoyed going to a satirical revue in Czech by Voskovec and Werich, 'the two comedians in it … The whole thing was a satire on dictatorship, with plenty of laughs at Hitler and Mussolini; the scene laid in an imaginary Central American state'. But soon it was not funny at all.

146 JG 05/01/1935.

147 LH 21/01/1935.

CHAPTER 13

The Beleaguered Diplomat 1935–1936

> I seem to be entering on a new period of life, and am not altogether attracted by it. It requires new efforts and energies, for which I feel myself very inadequately equipped. To some extent it flatters my vanity, and leads me to imagine that it is a duty to take these things on. At the same time, I feel myself growing lazier and lazier, both physically and mentally; probably if I did not take on these things I should degenerate rapidly into complete 'Acedia' and other such things.
>
> And all this building up a position as a celebrity is perfectly useless, for in spite of it all my books don't sell, and I can get nothing done at Sadler's Wells, which is inwardly my chief concern.
>
> However, don't imagine that I am in a state of depression, though depression is a notorious family failing! but I incline more and more to avoiding all society.[1]

Dent wrote this unusually reflective letter to Lawrence after his trip to Italy in April 1935. He was desperately tired, and the 'new period' in his life was throwing up challenges which undermined his usual self-confidence, replacing it with fears both vague and specific. Travelling abroad was not the escape or liberation it had been, and his other life was being forced back into the shadows. 'I am always getting calls [in Berlin and Prague] from total strangers, and when I ask their names they reply "Sie kennen mich nicht", which I find embarrassing, and always fear they are blackmailers.'[2] Such approaches, whether actually from blackmailers or (more likely) refugees, now upset him badly, confusing as they did the personal with the more distant threat. For the next year, up to the 1936 joint festival and congress at Barcelona, Dent was constantly battered by political forces, especially those government-backed internal ones in the ISCM and ISMR, mustered against him personally and against everything he stood for. The political storms blowing were anti-Semitic, homophobic and populist, the methods undermining, so Dent's depression at this point is entirely understandable, from both professional and personal standpoints.

The Italian trip had been intended partly to indulge Dent's usual methods of taking stock, partly to have a real break in congenial company, in this case with the young Nazi Friedl Friedrich, again. Although it could easily be construed as an example of Dent's 'blinkeredness', travelling with Friedl was Dent's way of testing the real, personal parameters of political doctrines he loathed; he would not drop old friends just because their politics were not his own, and how else could he understand the

1 LH 06/05/1935.

2 CC 07/03/1935.

extent of such Nazification? But self-deluding or not, it presents a disturbing picture. His letter to Lawrence before the trip shows him apparently being less concerned about the general militarisation and aggression than about Carlo's 'discomfort'.

> I am arranging to meet a young German architect from Hamburg in Rome about April 8, to go on to the Abruzzi for about 10 days, and after that I should like 10 days quiet at Venice. I feel slightly apprehensive about Italy, as everybody is being called up for military service. Carlo, who is 30 … was suddenly called up about 5 weeks ago, and spent 3 horrible weeks in training at Genoa and Naples, without uniform and in the greatest discomfort, expecting to be sent to Abyssinia any moment.[3]

By 1935, the ISCM had achieved enough international success to be considered a threat by the increasingly rigid regimes growing in power and influence. The musical politics at this difficult and uncertain time in world history were rapidly becoming more varied and more vicious while the propaganda being used more sophisticated: appearance and presentation masked the hidden message of conformity, playing on the need to belong. To that end fascist and communist regimes realised that the kind of public cultural credibility they needed to hide the real brutality came from such high cultural events as classical concerts and opera, and that centralised funding controlled the style of public events; hence the Permanent Council. Such control extended to performers and conductors, who would have no livelihood if they failed to do as they were told; composers were stonewalled. Many chose to compromise: Paul Hindemith gave in for a while, withdrawing a new piece from the Prague ISCM Festival, in order to have his music played in Germany, but even by 1934 he had compromised himself too much; his music returned to the ISCM London Festival in 1938 at the same time it was being condemned in Germany as 'degenerate'. The conductor of the Berlin Philharmonic, Wilhelm Furtwängler, famously wrote a defence of Hindemith in a public condemnation of the Nazi arts policies. He lost his job for a while and tried to leave the country, but even though he continued to conduct under protest and some threats, he was too important a public figure to let go. Public response to such artistic compromise in England was mixed, mostly for lack of information. The *Musical Times* columns continued to publish bland reports of German concerts: Furtwängler's expulsion was barely mentioned, and for several years German musicians continued to perform in London. Britain even provided a sympathetic base for the current German music, an English section of the Permanent Council set up later that year, run by composer Herbert Bedford.[4] Any retreat from the Second Viennese School was seen by some as a good thing.

Dent slogged on; his uncle had died, and closing down La Selva was an extra chore on a very long list.

3 LH 15/03/1935.

4 Herbert Bedford (1867–1945), married to Liza Lehmann, grandfather of composer David Bedford and violinist–conductor Steuart Bedford. His music was never chosen for the ISCM.

> I was horribly overworked at the end of term, and suffered badly from stomach trouble; the Scarborough doctor examined me and said I was on the verge of a breakdown, but one has to go on and do the best one can.[5]

Over April and May, he travelled to the jury meeting at Carlsbad, then Prague to plan the Congress of Musical Education, to Milan, to Nice to close up La Selva, then Lyon to inspect some Scarlatti manuscripts, Strasbourg and Brussels to plan for the *Fairy Queen* Boris was conducting in June. Until the London office reimbursed him for his Carlsbad trip, Dent had little money; his 'stomach trouble' was in fact the ulcer which nearly killed him, brought on by the unremitting stress this year. Still, he clung to his optimism, ploughing it into Sadler's Wells and Cambridge.

Somehow, probably through refugee Hans Strohbach, Jack Gordon had learnt that the writer Stefan Zweig was now in London for a few days prior to his departure for the United States. Zweig had just written a libretto for Richard Strauss, based on Ben Jonson's play *The Silent Woman*, but because Zweig was Jewish, official questions were being asked about the premiere that June in Dresden. To have such a figure working with Dent would be a propaganda coup for musical internationalism, undermining both anti-Semitism and anti-artistic policies. Ruthlessly bypassing Baylis, Jack and Dent immediately offered up Sadler's Wells for the premiere. Zweig, whom Dent had met before, was interested, but 'refused to take any part in the production of the Schweigsame Frau or to offer any suggestions about it', wanting it 'to be produced as a work of art and not as a political affair'.[6] But once Beecham's interest was discovered, the idea was dropped. The opera premiered in Dresden, with Zweig's name on the programme because Strauss refused to remove it, but without the significant presence of Joseph Goebbels. There were only three performances.

Instead, Dent concentrated on *Fra Diavolo*, writing an article for the house magazine,[7] and that January alone, five long, detailed letters to Jack Gordon on its production:

> Whoever conducts will have to be very careful with the orchestra and male chorus, for in almost all cases the violins have the real tune and it must be heard above the chorus: the RCM people [Jack Gordon's earlier production of the opera] sang too lustily! The same applies still more to the ensemble of male voices E major 6/8 at the end of Act II: it should be all or mostly sotto voce, so as to hear the tune in the orchestra.[8]

At the same time, Dent was encouraging Clive to travel to Berlin and Prague that spring for fresh inspiration on productions, dispensing detailed advice on where to stay and introductions to 'great friends', Dr Niedecken-Gebhardt of Charlottenburg, Georg Szell in Prague and Anton Mayer in Berlin.

> Anton Mayer might be useful to you – I have not heard from him for ages; possibly he considers me politically dangerous … as people like Springer and others

5 LH 21/01/1935.

6 JG 09/01/1935.

7 'Auber's Fra Diavolo', in *The Old Vic and Sadler's Wells Magazine*, vol. 2, no. 23, pp. 3–4.

8 JG 15/01/1935.

> were very severe on him for writing (to order) a 'Nazi' history of Music, in which he completely ignores all the 'moderns' – having before 1933 written another popular History of Music in which Johnny spielt auf [sic] was regarded as the final climax of German art![9]

'I expect regular work at Cambridge will be something of a rest!' he had written to Jack in early January. The Music Faculty had more students than ever, and the foundations, Dent could see, were being laid for a solid future: Winton Dean, Philip Radcliffe, Robin Orr, Rosamond Harding, James Denny; the next generation was in place. Dent had given Orr, a future Cambridge Professor and composer, the entrée to the Chigi-Saracini academy in 1932, and encouraged him to study for a while with Malipiero. He organised similar useful introductions for Rosamond Harding when researching her pioneering 1933 book *The Piano-Forte*.[10] The current standards were high enough to stretch the teaching resources; in 1934 only six out of fifteen students had passed under Vaughan Williams' stringent eye.[11] That June Dent wrote to Jack: 'I felt like a cat which has just delivered itself of a dozen kittens (many of which had to be drowned).'[12]

For the next two years, Dent's Cambridge life helped to steady the ship. His Handel work was being poured that summer into the Cambridge Handel festival, another town and gown affair, with a production of *Susanna* outside Gibbs Building at King's, produced by Dennis Arundell and Rootham, with Gwen Raverat and Elizabeth Vellacott doing the costumes. Dent himself was lecturing on what became his article in *Music & Letters*, 'Handel on the Stage'. Production was in a very healthy state at Cambridge, at least: with the support of Maynard Keynes and his wife Lydia Lopokova, and many King's dons – Dadie Rylands, Donald Beves, Jack Sheppard – the Arts Theatre opened in 1936.[13] Like Glyndebourne and Covent Garden, Cambridge was benefiting from the influx of refugees, and the Arts Theatre became a cultural refuge, with Kurt Joos's new ballet company taking up residence, supported by a board of locals, its offices above a tiny antiques shop opposite the Fitzwilliam Museum, started up as a retirement business by one of the dancers, Gabor Cossa.[14]

At the end of February Dent nipped across to Halle for a few days, to give a lecture there marking his honorary doctorate and see again how Handel was being

9 CC 05/03/1935.

10 Dent's correspondence with Orr on the subject is now in the Pendlebury Library. Rosamond Harding's book is barely mentioned anywhere by Dent, but her contacts were all Dent's, like the Broadwoods and Mme Pereyra.

11 LH 01/06/1934.

12 JG 05/06/1935.

13 Though Dent viewed its inception with some cynicism: 'The whole Glyndebourne business is really Mrs Christie; he built the theatre for her to sing in, just as that young man Csonka in Vienna ran an "International Opera" for the sake of his wife, and Maynard Keynes is building a theatre in Cambridge for dear Lydia to have as a "Dolls' House" – her favourite rôle, now that she is a good-humoured lady only in private life. Let us be thankful that Miss Baylis doesn't want to appear as Mélisande.' CC 05/03/1935.

14 It is still there.

co-opted in the name of German music.[15] Although he alludes to this arrogation in *Music & Letters* (July 1935),[16] he played it down, wryly remarking to Lawrence that trips to Halle always seemed to improve his health. In March he gave a lecture to the Musical Association on 'The Translation of Operas', with illustrations from *The Trojans* and other recent translations – *Don Giovanni, The Barber of Seville, Orpheus, Onegin,* sung by Muriel Gough and Clive Carey: 'Clive very well, and poor Miss Gough with a voice like a saw, but it was very kind of them, and the audience seemed to enjoy it.' Erik Chisholm at Glasgow was pressing him to do more Berlioz translations, but recovering Handel from his Germanised state had become more important. He sounded Jack about doing *Alcina,* in a production which would make the point:

> I have some hopes of our doing a Handel Opera at Sadlers Wells, and am pushing all I can to get it settled, and to choose the work and edit it myself; but of course Miss Baylis has not the remotest notion of the amount of scholar's work that has to be done first.[17]

After the Maggio Musicale in Florence later that spring – unusually for him, he left barely any record of this Italian trip apart from the resulting depression – he was certainly suggesting to Jack that they might consider Pizzetti's new opera, *Orseolo,* which had premiered there and which he had offered to translate, with ideas about *Hugh the Drover* and English operas by Percy Pinkerton and Stanford.

> The mere mention of new translations to her always sends her into hysterics … she merely screams about the expense and worry of getting them copied … I am sorry Miss B. is still so frightened about Fra Diavolo, She is an old woman, and always seems to trust the wrong people and mistrust the right ones. Your production promises well with Hans [Strohbach] and Berzlein to help.[18]

Then the old trouble: under the guise of collaboration, Covent Garden was still trying to poach from Sadler's Wells, putting on operas in English.

> I foresee complications with the new Beecham English company and fear that when the moment comes she [Baylis] will give way and leave her own really loyal friends and helpers in the lurch.[19]
>
> Miss G. [Muriel Gough] tells me dreadful stories about the new C.G. company & its intrigues … for Lilian's eternal hesitation will bring S.W. to ruin if

15 For a full account of this movement, see Potter, 'The Germanization of Composers: The Case of Handel', in *Most German of the Arts*, pp. 221ff.

16 The MT notes (April 1935), p. 362: 'the official ceremonies of the Handel "Gedenktage" … including Prof. Torrefranca from Italy and Prof. Dent from England … February 24 a ceremony at the Martin-Luther University, in the course of which Prof. Dent and Prof. Schneider (of Halle) made speeches preceded a tea-party of the Deutsch-Englischen Kulturaustausches and a gala performance of Handel's opera "Otto and Theophano".'

17 LH 15/03/1935.

18 JG 04/05/1935.

19 *Ibid.*

> something isn't done. If she wd only take decisions and plan things ahead she cd wipe the floor with TB [Beecham] & GT [Toye] & all the rest.[20]

In spite of such ongoing threats and his worsening health, Dent still planned to go to Brussels for Scherchen's production of *The Fairy Queen,* with Hartung and Boris Ord involved, before going on to Carlsbad.[21] 'Scherchen wants me to lecture there in July (in French) to his class, on Opera Productions & Illustrated by the study of Dido, Orpheus *&* D.G'.[22] He and Trend were travelling early, then going on afterwards to the Prague ISMR Congress on 7–11 September, with some 'vague plans' about going to Hungary before the start of term beside the education league he had become involved with, with Leo Kestenberg and Hermann Kretzschmar.

But Dent's plans and the ISCM were sent haywire that summer: on 17 July, 'the Carlsbad Town Council … suddenly cancelled the whole Festival ostensibly on financial grounds; but I suspect a Nazi intrigue.'[23] He went out immediately, staying a month in Prague to sniff the wind. Local elections had taken place after the jury meeting in December, and the 'Emigrant element', the Nazi-supported Sudeten German party, had made enormous gains. The Permanent Council was putting on its own alternative festival at Vichy, with a number of composers either rejected by the ISCM jury or who had given in to the regime, Philipp Jarnach and Paul Hindemith among them. When asked decades later what kind of music they were supporting, Gottfried von Einem said: 'The opposite of Schoenberg – music in C major.'[24] Only the year before, at the first Maggio Musicale in Florence, Dent had remarked,

> the only kind of (new) music which arouses international emotions on a large scale is generally of a quality which deprives it of all artistic interest. It is useless to offer music that is new and vital to popular audiences: it will appeal only to a certain international élite of artistic understanding.[25]

Having seen the new German 'international' in embryo at Hamburg the previous March, Dent was dismissive:

> I don't think the Nazi International is performing. Hamburg was rather a frost … and Frau Scherchen tells me that Roussel is very sceptical about the festival at Vichy. (Poulenc simply exploded with laughter when I told him (in February) that there was to be a Festival at Vichy).[26]

Only after weeks of uncertainty, not until late August, was the Prague Festival 'safe'. Finances had only been an excuse.

20 CC/27/05/1935.

21 JG 05/06/1935.

22 *Don Giovanni*. CC 27/05/1935.

23 JG 29/07/1935.

24 Michael Kater, *The Twisted Muse* (Oxford, 1997), p. 177. Kater interviewed him in 1994.

25 Quoted in MT (October 1935), p. 899.

26 JG 29/07/1935. Dent had himself been in Hamburg the previous year and seen the alternatives being presented.

> There was no shortage of money here for the Festival as now arranged; the government was ready to provide the third orchestral concert, but at such short notice it was impossible to get an orchestra and rehearse these difficult things. The alleged reason why the stodgy works have been kept in and the lighter works thrown out is that the two orchestras, Radio and Philharmonie, must play the things they know already, as far as possible.[27]

The issues had been further confused in July by a sudden offer from the Soviets to host the cancelled Carlsbad Festival in Moscow, with the extremely tempting assurance that all travel expenses would be paid by the government. After years of dithering about the place of Soviet music in the international sphere, the government was having a complete rethink, now urged on by the expatriate German communist Hans Eisler, who had been 'elected president of the Comintern's music division … and was expected to bring together a broad network of international musical organizations'.[28] In Eisler's view, such a move would serve the dual purpose of bringing more unfamiliar western music to the Soviet Union, while presenting to the world a reassuring vision of Soviet cultural life.

The Comintern was now very active in England; communism was currently fashionable with the young, mostly as a response to Oswald Mosley's Blackshirts;[29] the 'Cambridge spies' became politically committed at this time. In August 1935, around the same time that the Soviet Union was making its offer to host the cancelled Carlsbad (Karlovy-Var) Festival that November in Moscow, Dent's former pupil W.H. Kerridge was writing in the *Musical Times* on 'Musicians in Soviet Russia', presenting a rosy picture of cultural life there; this after the terrible famines of the previous three years and just at the beginning of the political purges which killed millions. In 1935 composer Alan Bush, a professed communist whose string quartet was being played at the Prague ISCM, wrote a review of the Festival for the *Musical Times*, one of his central points being that in a 'truly magnificent gesture … *The Soviet Union saved the Festival*'.[30] Partly true, since the Soviet offer to host the cancelled festival had provoked the Czechs to rescue it. Having had by this time more than enough politics in music, Dent distrusted the Soviet approaches and rejected the offer, using the practical excuses that November was inappropriate since it was in term-time and that Moscow was too far away for most members to get to, while exercising the more official reason that the Soviets did not have a formal Section.

> I have been obliged to agree to the programmes as altered & curtailed – it was not a question of money, but of getting an orchestra at all … They have to play

27 JG 30/08/1935.

28 Anne C. Schreffler, 'Modern Music and the Popular Front: The International Society for Contemporary Music and Its Political Context (1935)', in *Music and International History in the Twentieth Century,* ed. Jessica C.E. Gienow-Hecht (New York, 2015), p. 72. This chapter provides the fullest discussion of the Prague Festival in 1935, especially the background politics.

29 See, e.g., Nicholas Deakin, 'Middle-Class Recruits to Communism in the 1930s', Gresham College lecture 2013.

30 Alan Bush, 'The I.S.C.M. Festival at Prague', MT, October, 1935), p. 940. Italics in original.

> the works they mostly know already, to save time & rehearsals – hence the predominance of Czech works. There were also solid reasons for keeping Schönberg & Berg in – I shall hope to get Berkeley etc played at Barcelona & they will be useful for that programme as they are all short (about 8-12 min) and agreeable! ... All seems to be going well now. The Minister told me privately that he thought Carlsbad's refusal was due to Nazi influence – or at least to politics.[31]

The Prague Festival of 1935 was another mix of unknown and established composers with new pieces, the Czechs showing that in spite of the conspicuous Nazi demonstrations they could produce something special. The Second Viennese School was given the adulatory reception they rarely achieved elsewhere, except at Barcelona the following year, so there were Webern, Schönberg, Berg, beside Hába, a production of Janáček's *Jenufa* and performances of other contemporary music by Roman Palester, Lars-Erik Larsson and Carl Ruggles.

> Hába does in fact regard the Festival as a sort of football match ('match' was his own word to me!) between the Schönberg set and the Hába set, between the atonalists and the non-thematicists. These stodgy works will be better played here and more appreciated here than in Barcelona.[32]

At Dent's instigation, out of the near-shipwreck of the Prague Festival came a formal fresh declaration of the ISCM's aims, only after much internal debate about just how to frame the statement without compromising the integrity of a self-declared politically neutral society. As a working concept, they settled on the 'artistic freedom of the composer', regardless of race, nationality or religion, and that the music chosen need only be worthy of that choice.[33] What exactly constituted the 'most worthy' music could not be easily defined, but they were not going to allow themselves to be influenced by the Permanent Council, Dent's dismissive words at the 1934 Maggio Musicale coming to mind: 'The President then referred to the Conseil Permanent [Permanent Council] and its festivals. He expressed the view that we should not condescend officially to take notice of them.'

'I am adamantly of the opinion that the I.S.C.M shall remain a purely idealistic and artistic society – detached from all business or political matters.'[34] Scherchen chose to put that remark as a banner on the cover of his new journal, his 'Melos Redivivum' as he called it, *Musica Viva*.[35] Dent's words had 'carved out a separate, protected space for advanced, serious music'.[36] In this time of flux Dent continued to create ideological anchors for the institutions in his charge, never wavering

31 JBT 22/08/1935.

32 JG 30/08/1935.

33 This resolution is discussed in some detail in Schreffler, 'Modern Music and the Popular Front', pp. 76–80, and Haefeli, *IGNM*, pp. 190ff.

34 Ich bin definitiv der Meinung, dass die I.G.N.M. eine rein idealistische und künsterlerische Gesellschaft bleiben soll – von allem Geschäftlichen ebenso fern wie von allem Politischen. Quoted in Haefeli, *IGNM*, p. 190.

35 *Musica Viva* (1936) ed. Hermann Scherchen, p. 1. Quoted from a private letter, cited in Schreffler, 'Modern Music and the Popular Front', p. 79.

36 Schreffler, 'Modern Music and the Popular Front', p. 78.

from his public stance that the ISCM was a neutral, non-political organisation. Ernst Krenek for one felt that it was not enough to keep a neutral stance in the face of such egregious attacks on the ISCM; he wrote an article whose title 'Die Blubo-Internationale' excoriated the earnest 'Blut und Boden' (blood and soil) appeals to German music in particular. What worried Krenek and others was that many ISCM members were already involved with the Permanent Council:[37] how could compromise be avoided?[38] Krenek wrote Dent a conciliatory letter that November, thanking him for his friendly words, even though they disagreed about whether to condemn or pacify those separating themselves from the ISCM.[39]

The next festival and congress was to take place in Barcelona, far more neutral turf, with its own internecine wars, removed, it seemed at the time, from those of the European mainstream. As ever, Dent tried to keep the official discourse free of outside politics in order to protect musicians stuck in political quagmires and to obviate any possible political excuses for shutting it all down. Writing to Higini Anglès in early August 1935, Dent actually expressed his real thoughts about such 'politique à l'arrière-plan'.[40] In the same serious but easy vein, Dent continued to advise Anglès, right up to the Barcelona Congress and Festival in April 1936. But it was already far too late; the subversion of music too far gone.

❧ ❧ ❧

'I am completely in love with Sweden & Stockholm', Dent wrote to Clive in September 1935, '& wish I cd stay 6 weeks or more here'.[41] He was enchanted by the eighteenth-century theatre at Drottningholm, but going on to lecture at Copenhagen was also pleasant, free from politics. Knud Jeppesen, based there, was one of Dent's most stalwart supporters, and continued to be so over the next extremely difficult year, while spending time with JB in beautiful, neutral countries was a bonus.

Since they had first set up house together, J.B. Trend and Edward Dent had developed an extraordinary relationship around their busy, separate lives. Although they were so seldom together, the absences nurtured a vital correspondence which fed the creative and philosophical strains in either. Trend was probably the more committed, but he had been perfectly capable of building his own separate life; even Dent's constant infidelities were a part of the fabric of their shared understanding. So Dent continued to enjoy flirtations and affairs with his

37 Including Arthur Bliss, Malipiero, Casella, Sibelius, even Strauss himself was an honorary ISCM member; Pijper and especially Albert Roussel. Haefeli, *IGNM*, pp. 214–15.

38 Quoted in Haefeli, *IGNM*, p. 251 and p. 419 n. 127.

39 EK-EJD 29/11/1935 KCA.

40 There are political questions which are upstaging the main points, intrigues by the Nazis against the Jews. And once again I state the uncertainty of government support. In England, one never waits for government, never put your trust in Princes. HA 08/08/1935. Biblioteca de Catalunya.

41 CC 19/09/1935.

young Germans and Italians, while JB appears never to have minded these, and in turn entertained Dent with his own gentle exploits in Tangiers. But whenever he could, JB accompanied Dent to the ISCM festivals, Frankfurt, Salzburg, Venice, so he had first-hand knowledge of what was at stake and what actually went on; he knew how things were run and could help. Few people understood Dent's wider perspective better: his different experiences complemented Dent's work, especially the international aspects, so bringing Spain into the contemporary international musical sphere became their major joint project.

Since his initial *coup de foudre* in Spain, JB had spent much of his time there, building up friendships and working relationships, with Falla, with the poet–critic Eugenio d'Ors, and especially the people around the Residencia de Estudiantes in Madrid, which had nurtured Dalí, Lorca, Buñuel, and created an island of cultural vibrancy in what was a deeply conservative country. He had also made a series of remarkable musical discoveries, contemporary manuscripts of early Spanish music, initially as an offshoot of Dent's Scarlatti research, but quickly developing a life of its own.

JB's enthusiasm fired Dent to strengthen the Residencia's links with England and bring out more cutting-edge speakers to give a more up-to-date view of contemporary British culture: Keynes rather than Belloc. Trend is rarely given credit for Anglo-Spanish relations, but his letters to Dent over these years clearly show how deeply he was connected with Spain in the minds of his contemporaries. When Roger Fry, Lytton Strachey and Vanessa Bell went to Spain in 1923, it was Trend they asked to be their 'cicerone', which he did, rescuing them from a number of cultural mishaps.[42] But the musical connections sparked the real way forward with ideas Trend and Dent could work out together. Trend's friendship revived Falla's desire to compose and stimulated his relationship with the ISCM, while Trend continued to lobby locally to make sure that any Spanish Section was sympathetic to internationalist ideals and cultural openness. It took time and effort; some of the early submissions had been thought slight or conservative, while the acrimonious divisions between Spain and Catalonia had constantly to be navigated. It was not until 1935 when Dent finally came to Barcelona for the jury meeting that he fully realised what cultural riches were here. Liberal Barcelona was one of the few European cities to have new music and ideas at its heart and in its streets, and it embraced the event with real joy. The joint ISCM–ISMR festival and congress in April 1936 was a cultural high, the last for some time to come.

Madrid had fought the decision, arguing its own place as the centre of Spanish music, tacitly acknowledging Barcelona's insistence on its different, Catalan identity. But although Barcelona had a musical culture as lively as its architecture and fine arts, it too was split between conservative and avant garde, traditional and modern, and the joint festival quite naturally brought the divided elements together. In his preface to the ISMR programme, Dent had referred specifically to the recent joint festival at Liège, but in Barcelona he could see more of a general hunger for pure musical experience, an exuberance too often lacking elsewhere,

42 JBT–EJD 14/06/1923.

with a wealth of local talent and a desire to be part of international music. Unlike Vienna ten years before, Barcelona had already warmly embraced the Second Viennese School with packed concert halls; Schoenberg had seriously considered settling there. The two locals Trend had enlisted to help were cellist Pau Casals[43] and composer Roberto Gerhard.[44]

In Gerhard, Trend had a particularly important ally. Now the Minister for Culture in the Catalan government, a former pupil of Schoenberg, a civilised and cosmopolitan man, Gerhard's own writings on music are still fresh and lively and whose understanding and sympathy with contemporary music reflects the sophisticated backdrop for both the ISMR Congress and the ISCM Festival. He was entirely au fait with Viennese musical politics, and could write with ease and elegance on subjects dear to Dent's heart; for example, 'Music and Poetry':

> It is clear that the union of words and music is as old as poetry and music themselves ... A word dense in emotive content, allied to an exalted musical expression, to an interval or an apt and appropriate musical motif, to repetition, implies a whole series of strange roads leading to enchantment and magic.[45]

Both intellectual and creative, he worked with artists like Dalí to set up Amics de l'Art Nou; he composed, wrote about music and taught music, understood and loved both contemporary and traditional music, like Falla and Bartók employing traditional tunes and rhythms in his own music and writing. Webern had conducted the premiere of Gerhard's Catalan folksongs at the 1932 Vienna ISCM Festival. For ten years Gerhard had promoted links between the Second Viennese School and Barcelona as a bridge between the traditional and the modern, and his articles on Bartók and Schoenberg demonstrate why both composers felt so comfortable in Barcelona. In 1929 his own music had been performed by the Orfeó Català in the Palau de la Musica, and subjected to heavy criticism by the conservative critic who had founded the institution, Lluis Millet, whose idea of 'universal music' was limited to Beethoven and Wagner. So Gerhard knew first-hand the kinds of opposition and contradictions involved in running concurrent festivals.

It was also the last of the great prewar festivals, with violin concertos by Berg and Szymanowski, Frank Martin's first piano concerto, Bartók's fifth string quartet, a dazzling concert from the Spanish Section, conducted by Scherchen, Ansermet, Jacques Ibert, Casals, Arbós et al., with the new Hungarian Quartet, the Griller Quartet, all foreshadowing the later Prades Festivals run by Casals. Barcelona lapped it up, but the success had come at a cost.

43 Pau Casals (1876–1973), great Puerto Rican–Catalan cellist whose later Prades festivals carried on what was musically lost in the Spanish Civil War.

44 Roberto Gerhard (1896-1970), born in Catalonia to Swiss–Alsatian parents, educated in Switzerland, then Munich, then in Barcelona with Granados and Pedrell, before going to Vienna to study with Schoenberg. He married an upper-class Viennese girl, Leopoldina (Poldi) Feichtegger.

45 Gerhard, Music and Poetry', first published in *Quaderns de poesia*, no. 2 (July 1935), pp. 18–22. Translated by Meirion Bowen in *Gerhard on Music* (Farnham, 2000), p. 54.

Since the previous summer, Dent's gentle, insistent pressing of the joint festival issue had rubbed raw a number of festering grievances, especially in the ISMR, which unlike the ISCM still had German representation; the resentment seething in the Germanic ranks all that winter was not just against Dent, but against his stated ideas about musical 'hot-water bottles'. His case for Barcelona was seen in some touchy quarters, especially those with a political agenda, as being all of a piece in the way he had pushed through other ideas.

Dent's letter to Higini Anglès in August 1935 was both friendly and calculated; the German-trained Anglès had been an important ally in organising the congress. As he had done before with Casella and Malipiero, Dent appeared to bring the difficult issues out into the open. But even as Dent was writing this confidential, friendly, very personal letter to Anglès, German Heinrich Besseler[46] was also writing to enlist Anglès in a covert campaign to get rid of Dent as President and install instead a good German.[47] He was also busily writing to the other delegates, especially the Swiss secretary Merian, treasurer Speiser, Dent's old friend Johannes Wolf, and his severest critic, Jacques Handschin, besides any influential delegates sympathetic to Germanic musicology. He:

> handpicked only those colleagues who would present a strong and unified front against a perceived enemy alliance of Jewish émigrés and their sympathizers … planted the idea of an anti-German conspiracy in the minds of other participants … The German delegation came to envision an enemy camp consisting of Jews (Guido Adler, Otto Gombosi), German-Jewish émigrés (Curt Sachs, Alfred Einstein, Leo Kestenberg), and their supposed sympathizers, most notably the English president of the IMS, Edward Dent.[48]

Who has done more for musicology than Germany? he asked them. How long must we work under the cloud of the last war?[49] But this plot was no mere internal bickering and betrayal, rather an extension of official Nazi policy, with its stranglehold on music and the arts calculatedly reaching out to take over the international sphere. Fear was the key to his methods, the defensive fears many German musicologists had retained since the last war beside the new fear for their own jobs. Even those delegates supportive of Dent's liberal and internationalist views feared the kind of takeover they had already seen resulting in the mass expulsion of their German Jewish colleagues. Alfred Einstein wrote to Dent in February, praising his

46 Heinrich Besseler (1900–69), distinguished musicologist, whose major study *Die Musik des Mittelalters und der Renaissance* was published in 1931. In spite of his treatment of Jewish colleagues – perhaps most notably Manfred Bukhofzer – he survived the denazification process after the war, partly at least owing to the efforts of Johannes Wolf. The most comprehensive single reference about his life is Thomas Schipperges, *Akte Heinrich Besseler: Musikwissenschaftspolitik in Deutschland 1924 bis 1949* (Munich, 2005).

47 Their correspondence in 1935–6 consists of little else.

48 Potter, *Most German of the Arts*, p. 83.

49 From letters quoted in Schipperges, *Akte Heinrich Besseler*, p. 146.

officially neutral stance and damning those delegates who were doing nothing less than 'pimping' for Adolf Hitler.[50]

But it was impossible to speak openly, for fear of putting at risk the German delegates who had not been allowed to attend Barcelona. Johannes Wolf found himself right in the middle of it all; as Vice President of the society as well as German representative, he was in an important position, respected by all and loyal to the fundamental internationalist values of the ISMR. Besseler distrusted him because of his friendships with Dent and his Jewish colleagues, and wanted to get rid of him and replace him with Theodore Kroyer. But Kroyer, who was ill at the time, refused to go along with this, out of respect for Wolf.[51] In a poignant letter to Dent, Wolf described himself as a 'black sheep' as far as the authorities were concerned,[52] who had to keep his views secret to be in a position to help his Jewish colleagues and students.

Recognising that the 'Jewish question' was for many musicologists a sticking-point, Besseler with outrageous disingenuousness proposed to sideline it to the congress as simply a domestic political issue, nothing to do with musicology.[53] Sadly, some of Dent's ISMR colleagues – like Handschin, Anglès and the Swiss – not subject to that political duress showed themselves more than willing to get rid of him. Handschin later told Dent that he had withdrawn his endorsement, 'because I could not support your attitude to musicology'. Even Wolf had entertained doubts, later confiding to Anglès that he found it 'no longer bearable' that an Englishman should be the head of 'our' society,[54] how he had felt that Dent barely concealed his 'lack of interest' in the management of the Cambridge Congress, while at Barcelona he had pushed through the change of printer from the German Breitkopf & Härtel to the Danish firm Muncksgaard & Levin.[55]

Besseler played upon Dent's sometimes high-handed methods while carefully side-stepping any real issues, dividing the German sympathisers and waverers. What most annoyed Wolf, a longstanding and loyal friend, was what he felt to be Dent's arrogance in taking away from Germany the institution that had been German from its inception. Issues on the agenda were used as a stalking-horse: the apparently neutral questions of whether or not to change the publisher of the ISMR journal, *Acta Musicologica*, and of the society's precarious finances, both of which could be openly discussed via the official vehicle, the Protocol, while masking the real questions. In a letter to Dent that February, Jeppesen had already expressed his doubts about Speiser's abilities as treasurer,[56] but no-one could openly express the fear that

50 AE–EJD 02/02/1936. KCA.

51 Potter, *Most German of the Arts*, pp. 83–4.

52 JW–EJD 20/03/1936. KCA. Written from Jerusalem; Wolf did not make it to Barcelona.

53 Besseler to Handschin 17/03/1936. Cited in Schipperges, *Akte Heinrich Besseler*, pp. 146–7.

54 JW–HA 23/10/1941. Biblioteca de Catalunya.

55 JW–HA 23/10/1941. Biblioteca de Catalunya.

56 KJ–EJD 14/02/1936. He copies in a letter he has sent to Speiser outlining in detail a number of queries about the figures submitted, especially the figures to do with printing

if the *Acta* remained in the hands of its German publisher, the control of its editorial policy would be co-opted by the Third Reich. Instead, the excuse furnished was to do with the finances, the Danish Muncksgaard & Levin presented as a cheaper option.

The vast correspondence on this matter from October 1935 to March 1936 was mostly between Dent, Jeppesen, Speiser, Merian, Anglès, Wolf and André Pirro.[57] At the same time, Besseler was writing his own letters, urging Kroyer or Sandberg or Wolf, any serviceable German to replace Dent, while in the parallel correspondence Merian was getting the unmistakable impression that if Breitkopf & Härtel were abandoned for Muncksgaard & Levin, the German contribution to ISMR funds would be withdrawn, with hints that the German section would leave. No-one mentioned the fact that Muncksgaard & Levin was partly Jewish-owned.

The other open Protocol issue was related, the 'catastrophic' (Speiser's word) finances, with debts still carried over from Breitkopf & Härtel, an export-tax threatened on top, then increasingly desperate offers from Breitkopf & Härtel as it became clearer that it would indeed lose this useful contract and with it, precious foreign currency. It is not clear if it was under pressure from central government, but it is likely. These were the financial problems to which Jeppesen had drawn Dent's attention in February. What happened subsequently is described in a letter from Egon Wellesz to Guido Adler.[58] In a last attempt to clear the way, Dent himself stumped up the 150-pound shortfall, although he had little money of his own, a gesture which apparently floored Speiser,[59] especially as it was also discovered that Merian, who did not come to Barcelona, had been paying himself an inappropriately large honorarium as secretary. The resulting furore outraged even Handschin, a stickler for correct procedure, who wrote a remarkably conciliatory letter to Dent that May, saying that although he could not vote for him as President,

> you will surely understand this is not inconsistent with the esteem and the feelings which I had for you from the outset and which where [sic] corroborated by your benevolence to me at Cambridge and by my indebtedness to your 'Foundations of E. opera' and 'Scarlatti'.[60]

Higini Anglès vacillated, any loyalty to Dent dissolving in the barrage to his sense of elective affinity; as he told Handschin, he had felt besieged and alone in his responsibility for the congress, and as a Catholic cleric he may have been susceptible to homophobic excuses beside the narrow traditionalism. Jews were not the only group being targeted by the Nazis, and anti-Semitism was being matched by an equally aggressive homophobia. Up to 1936 Barcelona had appeared to be a haven for artists and homosexuals and other people being targeted. In March 1936, Dent

---

the *Acta*. Merian later wrote a furious rebuttal to Dent, denying any responsibility for 'keeping him in the dark' about the finances. 29/05/1936. KCA.

57 Dent archive KCA.

58 Wellesz to Guido Adler 14/08/1936. Wellesz archive, 1198 ÖNB.

59 *Ibid*: 'einen überwältigenden Eindruck machte'.

60 JH–EJD 08/05/1936. KCA.

CONGRÉS

de la Societat Internacional

de Musicologia

a

BARCELONA

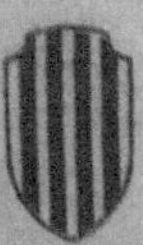

Programa de les sessions i festes

que es celebraran del 18 al 25 d'abril del 1936

FIGURE 19 (left and right). Programmes of the Barcelona ISCM and ISMR Joint Congress and Festival. By kind permission of the Provost and Fellows of King's College, Cambridge.

INTERNATIONALE GESELLSCHAFT FÜR MUSIKWISSENSCHAFT

DRITTER KONGRESS DER I.G.M.W.

BARCELONA 18.-25. APRIL 1936

Anlässlich des Kongresses zu Cambridge, im Jahre 1933, wurde Barcelona als nächste Kongresstadt bestimmt. Wir können heute endgültig mitteilen, dass der dritte Kongress unserer Gesellschaft in Barcelona stattfinden wird, und zwar vom 18. bis zum 25. april 1936. Wie es schon in Lüttich der Fall war, ist die gemeinsame Abhaltung unseres Kongresses mit dem Musikfest der Internationalen Gesellschaft für neue Musik vorgesehen.

Für die Versammlungen des Kongresses sind drei Sektionen vorgesehen: a) *Musikwissenschaft im allgemeinen;* b) *Volksmusik (Lied und Tanz);* c) *Die Choralforschung (fachwissenschaftlich). Die Referate können in deutscher, französischer, englischer, italienischer und in den spanischen Landessprachen gehalten werden. Für die beiden ersten Sektionen insbesondere, werden Studien bevorzugt, die mit der Musik Spaniens im Zuzammenhang stehen. Die Mitglieder, welche Mitteilungen zu machen wünschen, werden gebeten dieselben an Herrn Higini Anglès ehestens, jedenfalls vor dem Monat März, anzumelden. Die Mitteilungen dürfen eine Dauer von 15-20 Minuten nicht überschreiten.*

Für weitere Auskunft wolle man sich an Herrn Higini Anglès, Biblioteca de Catalunya, Apartat 1077, Barcelona, wenden. Im April-Heft der Acta wird die Liste der angekündigten Mitteilungen und Vorträge bekannt gegeben werden, sowie die für die Teilnehmer vorgesehenen Vergünstigungen.

Der Präsident der I.G.M.W. : Edward J. Dent.

PROGRAMM (Änderungen vorbehalten)

Samstag, 18. April.

Vormittag: Anmeldungen im Sekretariat.
Nachmittag: Eröffnung des Kongresses der I.G.M.W. und des Musikfestes der I.G.N.M. Empfang.
Abends: Konzert des *Orfeó Català* (weltliche und kirchliche spanische Mehrstimmigkeit des XIV. XV. und XVI. Jhrdt).

Sonntag, 19. April.

Vormittag: Konzert der *Banda Municipal de Barcelona* (moderne Musik für Bläser).
Nachmittag: Erstes Symphoniekonzert der I.G.N.M.

Montag, 20. April.

Vormittag: Sektionsvorträge der I.G.M.W.
Abends: Erstes Kammerkonzert der I.G.N.M.

Dienstag, 21. April.

Vormittag: Sektionsvorträge der I.G.M.W.
Nachmittag: Zweites Kammerkonzert der I.G.N.M.
Abends: «*Una cosa rara*», Oper des Vicenç Martin i Soler (1754-1806).

was expressing his relief to Jack Gordon that Hans Raab had left Germany and found a safe refuge in Barcelona with his Spanish partner, Modesto.

> I am glad you will be there too; and you will be able to have a good time in the company of Hans Raab, who is very happily settled there and doing well in his business, with several agreeable friends, English, Swiss and Spanish, who are rejoicing in the increased liberty afforded by the new government.[61]

Dent's optimism was short-lived; within months, Raab was on the run again.

In fact, Bessler might have spared his efforts: Dent was himself already making plans to quit, and devote his time and efforts to opera. 'As for me', he had written to Jack Gordon that March,

> I shall be so much worried with the affairs of two international societies that I shall never have a moment to myself, I fear ... I have had endless trouble over both of them, and I think I am now going to resign the presidency of the Contemporary for good; but probably shall have to stay on as President until the Paris Festival of 1937. Fifteen years has been about enough of it for me, and it is too exhausting to health, as well as to pocket.[62]

Dent never made it to the congress; he collapsed, vomiting, with a bleeding ulcer.[63] His place as Chairman was taken by Anglès, with Trend standing in for Merian. There were too few Germans there, so Besseler failed to achieve his aim of overthrowing Dent, and the *Acta* quietly migrated to Muncksgaard & Levin.

'Study the antique in order to understand the new.' The congress concerts were breathtaking. The 'conservative, bourgeois' Orfeó Català, 'modelled on Vincent d'Indy's Scuola Cantorum in Paris',[64] gave a concert of secular and sacred Spanish and Catalan music of the fourteenth to sixteenth centuries in its glass Palau de la Musica Catalana. Another local place more associated with conservative Catholicism was the picturesque monastery of Monserrat, about twenty miles out of Barcelona, where there was a concert of Spanish church music of the seventeenth and eighteenth centuries. Into this mix came the astonishing new music, which divided the local critics but enthused the local population. The local exponents included Pau Casals, whose orchestra played in the first of the three symphonic concerts on 19 April, and Roberto Gerhard. In spite of all this, the concept of a joint festival was seen by some critics as a failure; Anton Haefeli is probably expressing the German view when he says that 'the contact remained fruitless'.[65]

The 1936 ISCM–ISMR Congress on 18–25 April was a swan-song in every way. The city of Barcelona had done everything to show off Catalan music and culture, just when it was all poised to disappear in the Civil War only months later.

61 JG 16/03/1936.

62 *Ibid.*

63 See Appendix.

64 Bowen, *Gerhard on Music*, p. 41.

65 Haefeli, *IGNM*, p. 164 n. 372, p. 400; Cherbuliez, *Kongress in Barcelona*, p. 335.

CHAPTER 14

The Colonial Doctor 1936–1939

Dent's collapse and partial disengagement from the international societies brought liberation of sorts; his prolonged convalescence over the summer of 1936 gave him more time to focus on writing, research and on Sadler's Wells. That autumn he was to give an important lecture and receive his honorary doctorate from Harvard, his first trip to the USA and the first of several transatlantic voyages paid for by his lecture fees. With so many old friends and colleagues establishing themselves there, the way had already been paved, his reputation high. After all the ISCM–ISMR baggage his warm welcomes in the USA came as a pleasant surprise; by the time war threatened to break out again, Dent had considered seriously the idea of moving to the USA. Having survived the attempted ISMR coup and with no outside pressures, he even toyed with the idea of going back to Barcelona with JB. 'I have had no news from Barcelona, but I feel sure it is the safest and most reasonable town in Spain, whatever happens.' [1] Dent's wilful optimism about world affairs never left him, and he indulged this fantasy until August, when the news finally broke of the Spanish Civil War.

'I am getting better, but slowly', he had written to Jack Gordon in May. 'The doctor says it is all due to mental fatigue and worry and that rest and quiet are more important than diet restrictions – though I am still on a very quiet menu!'[2] Jack offered him his flat in Brunswick Square, Brighton, which Dent snapped up; he still had his Harvard lecture to prepare, his Cornell lectures on Romantic opera and several translations in train, Busoni's *Turandot* for Chisholm and *Rigoletto*. He craved company of the right sort, and Scott Goddard was currently sharing Jack's flat, commuting from London, while Brighton itself was full of established gay circles, often centred around its many excellent, often arcane bookshops; for years afterwards Dent did regular business with several of them. But however proximate, no Glyndebourne; Dent was disinclined, partly because of some unspecified disagreement with John Christie over his *Figaro* translation, but mostly because the antipathy was by now hard-wired. Another attraction presented itself in the unlikely shape of Montague Summers[3] 'and his most attractive (and even learned) acolyte!'.

1 LH 26/07/1936.

2 JG 28/05/1936.

3 Augustus Montague Summers (1880–1948), scholar of the 19th-century 'Gothick' and the occult, member of The Phoenix Society, which performed Restoration drama. His keen interests in pederasty and satanism forced him to keep a relatively low profile; he is perhaps best remembered for his landmark collections of ghost stories and his history

> Summers and I have kept up quite a correspondence ... he ... is much interested in various romantic opera libretti such as Zampa and La Nonne Sanglante etc ... We talked of many subjects, including Satanism and Black Masses; he told me that they were pursued even now in Brighton ... I am sure he would like me to think ... that he might possibly be celebrating Black Masses! ... He always pretends to assume the most orthodox of Catholic standpoints, knowing quite well that I don't believe for a moment in anything but his incontestable and marvellous erudition, which (as he knows) I deeply and sincerely respect.[4]

A self-professed satanist and pederast, remarkably knowledgeable about the origins of early Romanticism, Summers' erudite, offbeat company was just what Dent needed to perk him up, possibly a reaction to and retreat from the tacit homophobia quietly endured over the past two years. As ever, Dent's personal and professional selves were closely interlocked, sometimes a little too closely; his avoidance of John Christie was probably connected to a strong need for having things his own way right now, and in his own chosen company. Summers stimulated Dent's reading, especially the backgrounds for nineteenth-century opera librettos: Hugo's *Le roi s'amuse* ('I found that Blanche (Gilda) does at the end speak of "ma vertu en décombres" [my virtue is in ruins] so I suppose the dreadful deed was done'), and *Hernani*.

> It is all suitable matter for me to digest in preparation for my Cornell lectures in 1938. I am gradually collecting a lot of new ideas, or rather, new questions about the music of the Romantic Movement. I fear I shall have to make a careful study of various quite forgotten composers – and very poor stuff too, I fancy – Mercadante, Zingarelli, Guglielmi, Paer, Vaccaj, Pacini etc.[5]

Clearly stimulated by Summers' ideas on the Gothic and Romantic traditions, Dent rediscovered his love of musical research and began raising important questions about operatic history:

> when did composers begin to take it for granted that the trombones were to blaze away all through an opera as normal components of the orchestra (as in Rigoletto)? when did the chorus begin to have an important part? ... who invented the "choral ballad" – in which the chorus (invariably male, I think) tell a long story to explain something to the audience (as in Trovatore), and in verse, to a tune, not in recitative, though in the 18th century explanations of that kind would always have been given in recitativo secco. Why was there such a strong preference for the male chorus, rather than the mixed, or the female?[6]

The results can be seen in his Cornell lectures of 1938[7] and affected subsequent productions at the Wells.

---

of witchcraft. *The Supernatural Omnibus* (1931) is still in print. His correspondence with Dent is in the CUL, only recently discovered.

4 LH 26/07/1936.

5 *Ibid.*

6 *Ibid.*

7 Edited by Winton Dean and published as *The Rise of Romantic Opera* (Cambridge, 1976). Summers' contribution is not mentioned.

From August, the rumours and news from Spain began to come through, then a wave of more needy refugees, Spanish and Catalan. Dent escaped for the time being, sailing on the Cunard White Star *Georgic*, and spending his days on board translating *Rigoletto* and 'wrestling with my Harvard lecture … I feel that Harvard will expect a certain "virtuosity" of style at which I am sadly incompetent.'

Dent's Harvard lecture, 'The Historical Approach to Music',[8] is among his best, appropriately given on the occasion of his honorary doctorate, the first ever for Music from Harvard. His brief was to 'defend the dignity of Music as a subject of university study', with a prestigious public platform to explore some contentious musical issues so recently stirred up. He was still smarting from the onslaughts of German-backed musicologists, and Handschin's glib remark, 'your attitude towards musicology', had vexed him, so – serpentine – he used it as preface and reminder, referring to it several times.

Harvard was treated to pure Dent, subtle and controversial. He began by kindly pointing out the questions begged by 'that new and rather frightening word "musicology"', remarking that the English preferred to call it 'the Society for Musical Research … English people are notoriously illogical; I think their underlying reason for rejecting the word "musicology" was that, however keenly interested they might be in musical research, they refused to lose sight of the principle that music was an art.'[9] Dent's methods are those amusing, disingenuous ones developed by gay men to obviate any possible attackers, and easily co-opted for academic discourse. He raises questions and presents paradoxes, affecting an engaging, unthreatening passivity and a willingness to engage with new ideas, playfully citing the first number of the august *Bulletin of the American Musicological Society* as his inspiration, where the 'wise words' he finds in fact 'point out what a vast amount of musical research work has been done in the direction of what I would call mere excavation … What is the ultimate use of all this musical archaeology?'. But whatever Dent's audience thought might be coming in reply to this central question, Dent himself was already sidestepping any pat answers, instead pulling the useful academic's trick of citing another authority, his favourite Dr Burney, who in similar circumstances, 'found but little' in his own excavations, instead 'began to examine myself as to my musical principles … freedom of thought, unshackled by the trammels of authority'.'We must follow Dr Burney's example and examine ourselves as to our musical principles.'

Then Dent begins to pose the awkward questions, the 'embarrassing' questions about what those principles might be, what music means to us, harnessing awkward historical attitudes as a means to clarity, from Burney's apologetic stance – music as 'an innocent luxury' – to his favourite Cambridge don's 'a very harmless amusement for a man who could not afford to hunt', then to moderns for whom music was 'almost a religion', 'a doctrine which … has become something of a nuisance … "reverence for the classics"' and its paradoxical corollary:

8 E.J. Dent, 'The Historical Approach to Music', in Taylor, *Edward J. Dent: Selected Essays*, pp. 189–206. The lecture was first published in *Authority and the Individual* (Cambridge, MA, 1937), pp. 349–71, and in MQ, vol. 23, pp. 1–17.

9 All quotes taken from the version published in *Edward J. Dent: Selected Essays.*

> If in these two branches of imaginative production [novels and plays] we habitually demand the newest and latest, why is it that in music we almost invariably demand what is old-fashioned and out-of-date, while the music of the present day is often received with positive hostility?

He teases his audience with the 'thoroughly logical and reasonable doctrine' that contemporary music is for those who are alive, while antiquarians are spiritually dead: 'was there ever a time when pioneer music – the music which we now say made history – was popular with the multitude?', which brings him to his central idea. Music is an art, transitory in nature, so most music is by that definition 'old' music, and any attempt to fossilise music with a set 'reverent' attitude is ridiculous. So the function of musicology cannot be prescribed; the 'pure musicologist will go his own way', while some research might be put to use in educating a music-loving public and 'the university-trained musician'.

'I find Harvard delightful in every way', Dent wrote to JB, 'except that it disapproves of a jerry in one's bedroom, & I have to rise at odd hours & seek the beautiful bathroom in the passage! … it is a curious mixture of lavishness & puritanism'.[10] His lecture was given on 3 September, then after a few days' break in the country, he returned to Cambridge, Massachusetts, staying with Edward Burlingham, an old-fashioned Bostonian who had studied in Paris. On 18 September he received his doctorate in some style, with the 'great ceremonies' as five hundred delegates filed past in order of the foundation of their institutions, beginning with Cairo, c. 970 AD: 'Most of us were in academic dress, and there were some very strange and gorgeous robes, mostly Italian … the German universities have boycotted Harvard as a reprisal for their refusal to go to Heidelberg, I am told'.[11] Somewhat to his surprise, he enjoyed New York as well.

> All sorts of people – mostly German Jews – come up to me & remind me that they came to lunch with me in Cambridge: & I have not the foggiest idea who they are! I hear that Paul Ewald is here to-day: he wrote to me from Ann Arbor & I thought he was coming later. It is typical of the German government that he was allowed to come here, but forbidden to take part in the Mathematical & Astronomical conference, I suppose because Albert Einstein was to be here.[12]
>
> I am feeling better and stronger, physically and mentally every day: this visit to U.S. has done me incredible good. I am very much in love with America, especially after sampling American oysters.[13]

Just before he sailed home, a stark reminder arrived of what awaited him. Far from being the safe civilised haven of Dent's fantasies, Barcelona was one of the first war zones:

> a postcard from Anglès … he is safe. He escaped with his life in a great hurry on a French boat, and is now at the Institut der Englischen Fraülein, München … He

10 JBT 04/09/1936.

11 JG 18/09/1936.

12 JBT 04/09/1936.

13 JG 18/09/1936.

> is rather worried about the publication of the Proceedings of the Congress, and about my health – dear kind soul! ... Jack writes that Hans Raab is in Germany and Modesto with him: so there are 2 nice Spaniards safe, if no more. Here no-body has any news of Falla or the others.[14]

Hans and Modesto soon turned up in England, desperate and destitute, held up at Harwich under suspicion of being anarchists; Dent had to contact the Home Office to get permission for them to stay for a month at New Quebec Street, having promised their upkeep. So all that autumn Dent enjoyed having handsome Hans to squire him to the opera, his Nazi past sidelined. More gay men were now on the run and applying to Dent for help; Ernst Willer from Prague, and another Ernst from Riga, asking about a job in London. Jack now had a 'house full of refugees', the tide of supplicants showing no signs of slowing down. Between them, Dent and Jack were constantly sending the money and formal invitations now necessary even to enter the country. There was Hans Schoch, 'exhausted and suffering from his imprisonment', who Dent hoped would come to Cambridge and stay with Camille Prior, 'who would be glad of a new baby'. Schoch was a former lover of Raab, who was sticking by Modesto:

> What Hans himself wants himself really I do not know; but I am convinced that he is a man with a very high sense of honour. If he was not, he would have got rid of Modesto long ago ... but he is too honourable to let him down.[15]

So Dent put Schoch up at Panton Street. Dent's bookseller friend Kurt Engisch had fled Berlin, and Dent recommended him to Lawrence, currently applying for Sydney Cockerell's old job at the Fitzwilliam. 'The tale of refugees never ends', he wrote to Jack in October, telling him about Ernst Schmid, now turned out of both Graz and Tübingen after details of a 'small scandal at Graz (details unknown but guessable)'. Even the eminent Willibald Gurlitt was dismissed after eighteen years at Freiburg. Hermann Springer was in London now, too, staying with the Schoens in Belsize Park.

Jack Gordon continued his working trips to Berlin, checking on Frau Busoni, now seventy-two and going blind, and the fund they had raised from subscriptions, about two thousand pounds.[16] Dent himself now refused all offers to go to Germany again, even one to see Boris Ord conducting a German performance of *The Fairy Queen* being produced by Hans Strohbach, bankrolled by a Saxon Prince Schömberg, at his schloss near Chiemnitz, an 'ardent Nazi'.[17]

At Cambridge, Rootham was seriously ill, probably due to a stroke, and Dent had to fill in, with Boris taking over the conducting. 'I am trying to persuade Mrs R. that he might take a sabbatical year: the University wd gladly agree to that.'[18] Music in Cambridge was beginning to settle into Dent's vision of long-term high standards,

14 JBT 22/09/1936.

15 JG 10/02/1937.

16 Dent himself contributed £100; Jack Gordon £200.

17 CC 17/01/1937.

18 CC 01/10/1936.

with the facilities in Downing Place and the new Arts Theatre, the programming adventurous: Vaughan Williams' *The Poisoned Kiss* in 1936, *Riders to the Sea* in 1938, *Idomeneo*, the Handel series, the Greek Plays, Mrs Hackforth's weekly chamber concerts, opening up to The Ballets Joos, beside local efforts by the MDS with Dadie Rylands at the beginning of his long reign:

> it has been a roaring success so far ... Last night we had The Tempest in a very cleverly managed re-hash (by Dadie Rylands) of the Davenant–Dryden version of the play with Purcell's music. It was incredibly charming, and incredibly naughty, acted by our young people with supreme disinvoltura.[19]

In 1936, the local arts were being further enlivened by the latest refugees from Spain, Trend's musician friends Jesús and Rosita Bal y Gay, Alberto Jiménez,[20] and later, dozens of Basque children fleeing the bombing of Bilbao, who gave concerts of Basque music to raise funds and awareness.

Dent's academic work for his impending Cornell lectures on Romantic opera were also harnessed into his continuing translations and productions for Sadler's Wells. He finished *Rigoletto*, started on *Fidelio* while thinking about *Trovatore* for Sumner Austin, but Baylis vetoed the last two, suggesting instead *Don Pasquale*: 'the comic dialogue & recitatives good fun to translate, but the arias devilish'. But because it had flopped at Covent Garden, it was vetoed by the 'Soviet', still terribly wary of catching any of Covent Garden's colds. He revised *The Magic Flute* for Sadler's Wells and for Fritz Reiner at Philadelphia, as well as his old versions of *Figaro* and *Don Giovanni*, and Berlioz translations, beside Busoni's *Turandot* and *Doctor Faust*. The Sadler's Wells repertoire now included many of Dent's choices: *Fidelio, Falstaff, Madam Butterfly, The Magic Flute, Hugh the Drover,* even *Aïda,* directed by Gordon and Carey. He was 'thrilled' that they were to do *Fidelio* at last, and suggested Cherubini's *The Water Carrier* (*Les deux journées*) as a model, stressing the human rather than the heroic drama.[21] *Fidelio* was a project almost as close to Dent's heart as Mozart, and his letters to Jack that early summer are full of detailed ideas and suggestions. At Keynes' request, the Arts Theatre in Cambridge was to host its Sadler's Wells opera and ballet season, the first of many, it was hoped, for which Dent wrote the programme notes.

By 1937 the Vic and the Wells were in relatively good shape; the Sadler's Wells houses packed, but low seat prices meant that the finances were never settled and the musicians were still paid 'paltry' wages. The advent of Tyrone Guthrie[22] set the Vic on its legendary course, with Lawrence Olivier, Alec Guinness, Michael Redgrave and Edith Evans, and tightening up the company system, Guthrie now insisted on runs of less than three weeks.[23] 'Guthrie brings a new outlook to the opera, as regards

19 With supreme ease. JG 04/08/1938.

20 Cf Anstee, *An Unlikely Spanish Don*, pp. 168 ff. They later moved to Oxford and to Mexico.

21 JG 02/05/1937.

22 (Sir) William Tyrone Guthrie (1900–71), theatre director. He left the Vic after a year in 1934–35, but returned in 1936–37, becoming Director of both companies in 1939.

23 Gilbert, *Opera for Everybody*, pp. 56ff.

productions and dressings etc, and I think he will be a great help.' Only in 1935–36 had Lilian Baylis finally given in to what her board had been trying to tell her for years, that the two companies needed to be completely separated, with drama at the Vic and opera and ballet at the Wells, in order to focus on what either did best.[24] Before her death in November 1937, Baylis finally decided to look for an Intendant, asking both Carey, who declined, citing the lack of necessary 'ruthlessness',[25] but really, disliking Guthrie. Dent also refused, citing the loss of his Cambridge pension and his age.[26] Instead he was happy to let men like Guthrie take over at the production interface, preferring his own strong, established position behind the scenes, running his candidates like Evelyn Broadwood for the Sadler's Wells Board and introducing Kurt Joos to Ninette de Valois.

> JB has gone to Holland: I don't quite know where – but he has fallen in love with Holland lately, as a place to rest in, and it always does him good. He rather seemed to wish that I was coming with him, but I did not feel well enough, and I am sure that it is much better for both of us to get a little complete solitude now and then.[27]

A BBC broadcast on Busoni before the performance of *Doktor Faust* in March made Dent 'horribly nervous'; he was never entirely comfortable broadcasting his lectures.[28] After it was done, he returned to his Cornell lectures, 're-reading scores of Cherubini and Méhul with great pleasure'. 'Romantic Opera' had been on his mind since the summer, while translating *Rigoletto,* and now he had some time to muse on the 'Catholic' aspects of *Rigoletto,* the prayers, the conventions of religion on the stage, even recalling past conversations on the subject with Donald Tovey.

> I come to the conclusion that Cherubini's operas must have had an enormous influence on Schubert and Weber, as well as on Beethoven. The Germans as a rule don't like the idea of their great masters owing anything to a French-Italian like Cherubini … and the ordinary writers about music can't understand that a man like Chreubini [sic] may have been completely dull and uninspired but none the less an enormous influence in his time. I begin to see that what Schubert got from Cherubini was mainly his "longueurs" – the eternal repetitions of long sections, and those drawling melodies in which the smallest amount of inspiration is spread out thin so as to cover the largest area of paper! also certain habits of accompaniment figures which are common to Schubert and to Meyerbeer![29]

The ISCM Festival in Paris on 20–27 June 1937 had been sorted mostly without Dent's presence, but some involvement, with Edward Clark, Roberto Gerhard and

24 *Ibid.*, p. 57. The Charity Commission changed the terms of the trusts.

25 CC 18/02/1942, cited in Gilbert, *Opera for Everybody*, p. 60.

26 Gilbert, *Opera for Everybody*, p. 60 & n. 55.

27 LH 28/03/1937.

28 There are BBC sound archive recordings of several broadcasts. As might be expected, Dent's voice is patrician; deep, pleasant, with a slight Yorkshire flattening of some vowels. I am grateful to Dr Glen Leonard for this.

29 LH 28/03/1937.

Jacques Ibert on the jury, and Edwin Evans at the helm. Dent did the programmes as usual, but otherwise had more than enough to occupy him beside the continuous stomach troubles: committee meetings, consultations at the Royal Academy of Music, the odd performance of a Scarlatti opera at Longeton in July and lecturing to Kurt Joos's ballet class at Dartington, all while trying to finish his Oxford History of Music section and get on with his lectures for America. He sailed on 17 August for Montreal, aboard the *Duchess of York*: 'The Drunken Duchess, notorious for pitching and rolling.' After cruising down the St Lawrence, he spent a 'very restful and agreeable' week in Canada, visiting his cousin Doreen Brock, whom he had known as a child, at her lake house off the Ottawa River, before giving a talk in Toronto to a local music-teachers convention, its choir 'like one of those loud-speakers at a railway station which tell you where to change'.[30]

He needed the rest. After travelling by train with Earl V. Moore to Ann Arbor, the remainder of his trip was a series of whistle-stop lectures, at Northwestern University on 12 October, then to Chicago itself the following day, in a 'barn-like hall' with no desk for his notes, accompanied from underneath by the sounds of 'études d'execution transcendante on the pianoforte'.[31] After a week, he went on to Cleveland, then Rochester to give three lectures and two seminars at the Eastman School of Music, then across the state to Cornell. For the month he was in residence, Cornell put him up at the Telluride Association, 'half club half college' with 30 young men, 'a picked lot, with a certain intellectual arrogance'.[32] He discussed his latest opera, *A Dream of the East* with John Urich, even going along to a Columbia–Cornell football 'game', but glad to escape with the librarian for a musicological society meeting.

'The function of lectures is not to convey information, which we can now obtain far better from books, but to stimulate interest in a subject.'[33] The Messenger Lectures at Cornell[34] were delivered over that autumn and winter of 1937–38. Although they were not intended for publication,[35] Dent always meant to publish a book on the subject, possibly focusing on Weber, but never found the time to do so. Forty years later Winton Dean justified his decision to publish them:

> they explore an important turning-point in musical history … Comparatively little of Dent's work … has been overtaken by later research [written in 1976] … Dent reached conclusions that may still startle musicians and others brought up on accepted traditions: the the true initiators of Romantic Opera were the French; that it derived not from serious but from comic opera, and that it was the

30 CC 03/11/1937.

31 *Ibid.*

32 *Ibid.*

33 Dent, quoted by the editor, Dean, in *The Rise of Romantic Opera*, p. vii.

34 Founded in 1924 by Dr Hiram Messenger, a mathematician, 'a fund to provide a course of lectures on the Evolution of Civilization for the special purpose of raising the moral standard of our political, business, and social life'. Cornell University website. Dent was in the prestigious company of H.J.C. Grierson, Sir Arthur Eddington, later, Noam Chomsky, Richard Feynman and others.

35 As Dean makes clear in his preface to *The Rise of Romantic Opera.*

principal source of the nineteenth-century German symphonic and instrumental style … the lectures are full of characteristically sharp perception, clearly and often entertainingly expressed … Those who never knew him may discover … why he enjoyed a reputation as one of the world's foremost musicologists … their demonstration, implicit and explicit, of the methods of a great scholar and a great teacher … research was 'a training of the imagination', 'to cultivate imaginative experience for the enrichment of memory and life, and at the same time to develop a habit of perpetual scepticism and criticism as regards all so-called acknowledged masterpieces … reverence … is merely a polite mask for lazy-mindedness'.[36]

But the surprise of the trip was New York, which Dent enjoyed even more than he had expected, opening up for him the musical vistas happening in the USA, especially with the arrival of refugees. The Hotel Weston on Madison and East 50th St. was convenient for both the Metropolitan Opera and Carnegie Hall:

both of which have to be called hallowed spots because they are so shabby and dirty, especially as compared with the new concert halls at some provincial towns … the Carnegie-hall has dinginess and extreme plainness, but marvellous acoustics.[37]

He made friends with Lee Pattison, the assistant director of the Met, and with Deems Taylor, later doyen of New York opera critics: 'my idea is to develop an international recognition of S.W. as The National English Opera: and break up the legend of Covent Garden as far as we can.'[38] The contact stimulated him into considering 'the American outlook on music', referring to a recent article in *Music & Letters* 'on the absurdity of "just intonation"'.

it read, to me, as if the author just accepted the 'Metropolitan' type of singing as the only possible one. That, I think, is a fundamental difference of outlook: in England, there are people like ourselves, who question all that … we have a duty to question it all.[39]

Taylor had impressed him, though, with his independent concurrence that opera in English depended on 'singers who can act (and speak English decently): good translations: ensemble rather than stars: and cleverness rather than sumptuousness in production, scenery & costumes etc', beside some more pessimistic views found in the papers. America, Dent argued, should feature much more in international musical life:

some of the Europeans are rather sniffy. They don't realize the musical importance of the U.S. and they know that very few Europeans will be able to afford to go … But now that I have struck root here I feel differently and shall argue that if eucharistic Congresses etc are held in the U.S. why not musical ones? It wd do them all good to get right away from Hitler & Mussly & Co & from their silly

36 *Ibid.*, pp. viii–ix.

37 LH 29/11/1937.

38 JG 06/01/1938.

39 CC 01/01/1938.

ideas about Communism – to a country that has its own problems, but is at any rate going ahead to solve them peacefully.[40]

The news of Lilian Baylis' death only reached him in December: 'a shock, but no surprise. I felt sure she would go off suddenly some day when least expected'.

> Sir RR. [Reginald Rowe] is to be temporary head, with the 3 separate heads of department going on: Guthrie, Ninette, & (for this opera) the 'Soviet'. Very sensible, I think.: & I think the Soviet can & will do a great deal. It ought to start at once making plans for next season: & not wait until a new 'head' is appointed. We must be careful not to allow SW to be collared either by the Cov. Gard. set, or by the BBC. The BBC is always a potential danger, I think.[41]

JB joined him on 9 December, and they sailed to Cuba for a few weeks together. The Spanish Faculty at Cambridge was bitterly divided over current political issues, JB himself vehemently opposed to Franco. 'JB ... is very much obsessed with the Spanish war and can't get his mind away from that, or from the little war of the Spanish Department at Cambridge.'[42] This Cuban excursion boosted his 'intensified interest' in Spanish America, and he was now keen to go to Mexico, where many of the refugee academics would wind up.[43]

Havana was 'horribly noisy with trams, motors & loud-speakers, all enormously increased by the reverberation of colonnades everywhere ... It might be lovely to live in permanently, if one had a villa there in the new suburbs, which all look rather like the Riviera, with ... masses & masses of Bougainvillea – until one almost begins to like the colour of magenta'. It took twenty hours by train across the island to get to Santiago, Dent savouring the slow crawl through tropical valleys, hot and squalid, but not unattractive, with gardens everywhere and a sense of a deep culture. They stopped at Camaguey, one of the first towns founded by the Spanish, its Old Town run down but charming: 'there is a wonderful hotel, where one cd stay for a long period to write a book or a symphony or something ... the yard turned into a tropical garden full of palms, bougainvilleas, poinsettias and all sorts of lovely things'. The resident pianist playing out of tune 'Fumagalli & Golinelli – the sort of stuff Busoni used to play as a boy!'

In spite of some concerns over American income tax, it suited Dent to return home earlier, since Rootham was still not recovered, and there was much to be done at Cambridge. He was optimistic about the future of the Wells and of opera, feeling that if the Soviet could make solid plans now, any future Intendant would find things already up and running. But he remained suspicious of anyone not really in sympathy with the Vic–Wells style: Braithwaite, for example, he told Jack, wanted to put on

40 LH 04/01/1938.

41 CC 01/01/1938.

42 *Ibid.*

43 *Ibid.*

operas 'too big for our theatre',[44] leading to the 'heavyweight opera like the BNOC', which put too much pressure on the company.[45]

Back in Cambridge that Lent term 1938 Dent was kept busy with fourteen composition pupils and Rootham's lectures to give beside his own, but some good concerts: Francis Poulenc performing at one of Mrs Hackforth's chamber concerts, Dent teasing him about the 'very best slop' he chose to play, Fauré, Debussy and Poulenc. Rootham 'is now far worse', Dent wrote to Clive. 'He can't feed himself, and apparently can't lift his arms or hands at all.'[46] But he was cheerful, and insisting on finishing his symphony while the family kept up the sad fiction that it was all temporary. So although it was difficult to get down personally to Sadler's Wells, Dent kept the ideas buoyant through letters to Jack and Clive. On *Don Giovanni*: 'I do want to convey the impression that rape, murder, adultery & especially sacrilege are all great fun'.[47] And on the new *Trovatore* translation, was he making it 'too comic?' He put forward more suggestions for new productions – *Jenufa, L'Enfant et les sortilèges* – and urged the Cambridge tour.

When term finished in March, Dent sailed again to the USA on the *Manhattan*, to work at the Library of Congress, returning two weeks later to Paris for the congress meetings. On 12 March 1938, the 'Anschluss' between Germany and Austria, and the resulting Nuremberg laws, were sending even more people into exile.

> News reaches us here only in bare outline … What people think about it I do not know: I have not spoken to a soul. Half the passengers on the boat seem to be German Jews … who got on at Hamburg & I hear more German than American spoken.[48]

'Work gets on well, but I wish I had 3 months!' Dent wrote to JB.

> I am getting all sorts of new lights, and feel as if I was now just starting to work at my subject! it becomes more & more enormous – and I hardly dare attack it – feeling that I ought to read all the operas of incredibly prolific nonentities … like Fioravanti, Generati, Guglielmi & Carata who wrote about 50 operas each – in the hopes of just getting on the track of a 'romantic' idea.[49]
>
> They have astonishing things here – Hundreds of opera scores … of operas otherwise inaccessible: … often in MS or semi-MS … And only the other day they brought 300 scores (with Regie-Bücher) of German comic operas & operettas, never published at all, from a theatrical agent in Baden near Vienna … offered cheap, because they were so dirty & dilapidated. They are … conductors copies with all sorts of annotations – a unique collection. That is all due to Sonneck's interest in opera in the early 1900's.[50]

44 JG 06/01/1938. This was the conductor Warwick Braithwaite.

45 CC 01/01/1938.

46 CC 24/01/1938.

47 CC 01/02/1938.

48 JBT 18/03/1938.

49 JBT 24/03/1938.

50 *Ibid*. Regie-Bücher are opera-house production books.

Altogether, Dent's trip this time was far less satisfactory; Washington itself was 'dull', apart from a lunch with 'Arabella Pole', some of his lectures were being cancelled, and the disturbing and unclear news from Europe was bad enough for him to consult his advisor at the bank about keeping his money in the USA and to think seriously about the need for a bolt-hole.

> If one is to believe all the news one reads & hears, it really does look rather like what I imagine the collapse of the old Roman empire was … The education at Hitler's castles for young 'leaders' consists entirely of athletics and the works of Alfred Rosenberg! Shall you & I be able to carry on somewhere like Sidonius Apollinarius in the 6th century, a bishop somewhere in Gaul, writing copious letters in the language of Cicero, oblivious of the world around him? but it is more likely to be Mexico than Gaul, I fancy![51]

The return voyage was stormy, but there was excellent company on board, including 'a young American composer called Barber, about 25'.[52] He went immediately on to Paris for the International meetings and more opera research, trying to track down an Etty illustration to 'Mélidor et Phrosine', a poem by Gentil Bernard turned into an opera by Méhul based on the story by Guilbert de Pixérécourt, whom Dent credits with inventing 'melodrama'.

'Term comes to an end', he wrote to Lawrence in June, 'but one's duties never do; I am always having to see people, and always having to write letters about German refugees.' Since the Anschluss, another flow of applications burst, from friends of friends, requests to find jobs, places, sponsors for people desperate to get away:

> the trouble is that the new lot, from Vienna, are mostly very tiresome, and just the sort of people I cordially dislike: they almost make me anti-semite. The one exception is Egon Wellesz, and luckily he has got several friends who can help him.[53]

Dent did manage to help Wellesz, and his family as well.[54] Musicologist Otto Deutsch settled in Cambridge to work on his monumental Schubert catalogue during the war, though he would have preferred, as he told Dent, the Library of Congress.[55] But Dent's veiled, personal agenda was to try his best to help the hidden ones, especially homosexuals who were also being persecuted, sometimes escaping the net by marrying sympathetic women. The ones mentioned by name in Dent's letters are the tip of a big, hidden iceberg, and it was frustrating to be asked to help people he 'cordially disliked' while so many desperate old friends lacked any formal network to cling to and simply disappeared. The sense of helplessness was

51 JBT 18/03/1938.

52 This was Samuel Barber.

53 LH 07/06/1938.

54 Although Dent tried to get Wellesz a post at Cambridge, it was not to be, but he did go to Oxford, where he throve. Dent wrote to Jack Gordon in October about getting Elisabeth Wellesz a job at SW, and to Clive Carey in November; eventually she went to Rupert Doone and the Group Theatre.

55 Otto Eric Deutsch (1883–1967), Mozart and Schubert scholar; the Schubert 'D' numbers stand for Deutsch.

unfamiliar and terrible to him, and he lashed out at easy objects of his derision, like the 'fatuous' Congress of Modern Music, or at American music being taken over by arrogant old-school Germanic types he had been fighting for years. But through all this desperate time Dent's professionalism and concern for his students ensured that they never knew about his hidden demons; all that had to be kept secret, and having to keep such secrets while maintaining his public persona nearly killed him.

Dent prided himself on his tolerance, his exemplary courtesy to others, which had kept the two international societies ticking over, but perhaps failed to recognise the limits of such tolerance. Having witnessed first hand Nazi brutality in Berlin and the results of insane Nazi policies on his doorstep every day, at a time when Austria had just fallen to the Nazis and he was himself in poor health, Dent decided to go to Hungary in August with the Nazi Friedl Friedrich, to see Kodály's *Háry János* on the 13th and Liszt's Hungarian Mass on the 15th. Friedl had already expressed the fastidious desire not to accompany Dent to Budapest itself, 'as he fears compromising himself with Jewish society through me!' For several years Friedl had been a regular companion, possibly lover, and by now Dent, still fondly thinking that he could separate the personal from the political, should have been able to recognise the compromise. It is clear from his almost ingenuous remarks that he hated and feared the thought of another war; his life's work since the last war had been poured into internationalist movements and keeping the arts alive for everyone. But he was suffering a failure of the imagination, a failure to spot how his world was changing, and oddly for a man who set such great store by language, how destructive casual usage could be. By the time he actually set out in August, he was feeling completely besieged and exhausted, in constant pain or acute discomfort, his research into opera and his translation work even more of an escape from outside demands. JB was preoccupied with Spanish refugees; some had already moved on to Mexico.

Budapest was 'horribly' hot that August, but because of the Kodálys Dent enjoyed himself there. Writing to JB, Dent expresses what he chooses to believe is the prevailing mood:

> It is generally agreed that there will not be a war. Friedl Friedrich ... is the wildest of Nazis – and rather tiresome ... his view – wch is just that of the young enthusiast – is that Hitler doesn't want war (we are mostly agreed on that!) and that the Czech question will be settled (without war) in the course of this month: some of Cz. may be given back to Hungary (?) but most of it – including of course Prague & the Skoda works – will be annexed to Germany – the Czechs receiving as much autonomy as they have allowed to their minorities![56]

Dent continued to listen to the rumours flying around Budapest, about Admiral Horthy's visit to Hitler and Hitler's plans for a Hungarian revolt in Czechoslovakia to justify a German invasion there. 'Feeling here is naturally anti-Czech & therefore rather pro-German: but the Hungarians are quite clear they don't want to be Nazi, and they don't want to be invaded by Germany & annexed.'[57]

56 JBT 08/09/1938.

57 LH 16/09/1938.

Madame Kodály fussed over him, and Kodály took him out to try the sulphurous local waters, very enthusiastic about the undertaking to translate *Háry János*, and introducing him to a bossy baroness as tall as himself to help him with his Hungarian. Dent found Hungarian fascinating and irritating in turns, the syntax 'childish & primitive, almost like baby-talk', but he could almost forget his stomach problems in the joy of mastering a new and difficult language,[58] while the sheer gusto of the opera delighted him.

> Háry János (John Háry) is an old soldier of the Napoleonic wars. He relates his adventures in a public-house and is a copious liar. As in Tales of Hofmann, each adventure is put on the stage, but put on as Háry sees it in his imagination, wch is that of a primitive peasant ... You see how absurd it all is – & what a problem it is to translate it.[59]

He hit it off with the librettist Harsányi, an eminent and respected playwright and translator of *The Magic Flute*, and soon Dent was visiting him and his old mother, 'a great dear', meeting daily for long lunches. He found the whole process hilarious, since *Háry János* 'is crammed with dialect words and phrases, peasant speech, military jargon (half German and French): e.g. sarzs is charge spelt phonetically) etc.', in constant fits of laughter while they worked. 'When H. talks Hungarian, it is apt to sound like a motor-bicycle starting, but when she [his mother] talks it, it might be the voice of angels.' Dent was now excited about the real possibility of producing *Háry János*, writing enthusiastically to Jack: 'S.W. is the only place it could be done, I think: and I should like to think that we might attempt it.'[60]

Travelling back via Venice and Paris and picking up the gossip, he remained in denial about war: 'The Polish Minister here says Beck telegraphed to him that there would be no war!' But while Dent had been in Hungary, Neville Chamberlain had been meeting with Hitler to agree to the annexation of the Sudetenland. Four days before Kristallnacht, Dent was writing to Lawrence about everything except current affairs, about the recent deaths in his family: his brother Charles and his sister-in-law, Frank's wife, who had been committed to an asylum for the past twenty years, and the family gossip about Queen Mary's recent visit to Ribston while she had been staying nearby at Harewood House: 'my sister had to set to work and get a lot more flowers – such as there were – for the "saloon" and take all the cretonne covers off the state chairs and sofas'.[61]

❧ ❧ ❧

> Thank goodness I have been well since I came back this term; so I hope it will last the term out. I have only 8 pupils instead of 15 or 16, so I get more time to myself;

[58] He and JB had taken lessons already.

[59] LH 16/09/1938.

[60] JG 18/09/1938.

[61] LH 05/11/1938.

> and need it, for I am always having to write letters about refugees – that trouble never comes to an end; and one really can do next to nothing.

That autumn of 1938 Dent was lecturing on French Revolution Opera to Doone's Group Theatre; in London, he had a committee meeting at the Spanish Embassy about a Casals concert, lunch with Wellesz and his daughter, and went to hear Manfred Bukhofzer at the Musical Association. He met Sir Kenneth and Lady Clark, 'delighted' to find that they were 'keen enthusiasts for Sadlers Wells'.[62]

Encouraged by his spell of good health that term, Dent plunged again into research and travel, off to Paris for a few days to meet Jack Gordon and to see Berlioz's *La Prise de Troie*, having paved his way beforehand, offering Jack formal introductions to Louise Hanson-Dyer, Milhaud, Ibert and Roland-Manuel, and promising to have a word with Nadia Boulanger, before going on to Florence for a week. Florence itself he found dull and empty, with no opera going on, 'cold and miserable'; he read 'various scores of minor Italian composers about 1820 … all pretty dreadful', some early Meyerbeer, 'marvellously good imitations of Rossini with very careful orchestration … and two military bands on the stage!'[63] The old porter and the chambermaid at his hotel 'greeted him with immediate cordiality' and the waiters at the Campidoglio remembered him from four years ago. The Einsteins were there; they eventually bribed the border guards to let them into France and took ship via Gibraltar to New York. Smith College in Massachusetts snapped Einstein up; his 'struggles to learn the American language' coming as a relief.[64]

Travelling on to Rome, Dent eventually met up with Kurt Engisch, but things had changed:

> I find I like Paris more & more, and especially the old dirty Paris of quite uninteresting streets with here & there a a palace falling into ruin. Rome will soon be nothing but an outdoor museum: I think M.[ussolini] wants to destroy everything in old Rome except old Roman ruins … The ordinary houses are just being pulled down, and in front of St Peters colonnades there is a devastated area to the river.[65]

Opera under Mussolini was flourishing, but not in the way Dent liked; *L'arlesiana* by Cilea was 'gush'. They saw dancer Alexander von Swaine, a friend of Lydia and Maynard's, in *The Three-Cornered Hat*, soon to come to the Cambridge Arts Theatre. Swaine was yet another man who applied to Dent for help; from him they learned that Falla had died six months before.[66]

Using all his recent research, Dent's next project in the New Year 1939 was to write what he called his 'sixpenny book', *Opera*, for Pelican: 'I thought it might be made into good propaganda for Sadlers Wells.' Although it took him very little time,

62 Clark became a governor.

63 LH 26/12/1938.

64 AE–EJD 27/04/1939. KCA.

65 JBT 10/01/1939.

66 LH 26/12/1938.

he found it 'dreadfully hard to write', and it diverted him from working on what might have become his magnum opus, his major book on Romantic Opera.

> I wish I could have had your criticisms, but there was no time. After it was sent off I felt a great sense of relief and all sorts of new ideas came to me (wch I have now forgotten again) – but it was too late to use them.[67]

By the end of another difficult term, Dent's ulcer was playing up again, which was hardly surprising, but at least it furnished the excuse for avoiding the 'very Nazi and Fascist' Congress in Florence. And there was yet more trouble for the ISCM: Casella had sent an 'official' letter to say that the Italian Section was officially resigning 'because the Italian composers had been so badly represented':

> it is evident that this is a purely political matter, and that the Italian Section has been forced against its will to withdraw, probably under German pressure; it is typically Nazi to make the withdrawal just a week before the Festival ... It is an intrigue of Lualdi and others who don't get chosen by our juries.[68]

The 'best news' by far was that Dent had finally assembled all the permissions necessary to allow the Gerhards to leave Paris and come to Cambridge. With the support of Provost Sheppard and Richard Kahn, Gerhard was to be admitted to King's as a 'Refugee Student', with rooms in college and a stipend of 200 pounds. It meant two more lives saved, since Gerhard was now on several death lists. 'He is much delighted and most grateful', Dent wrote to JB, now in Yucatan. Dent had already sorted out accommodation for them at the Orrs and later at Thorneycreek, off Herschel Road, and had two instruments ready for Roberto's use.[69] By June Gerhard was installed at King's, having met most of musical Cambridge; in the next Michaelmas term of 1939 he wrote the music for a Lope de Vega play JB was producing.

> Gerhard has been an angel! he arranged all the music, finding tunes to fit Lope's words, and providing interludes whenever there was a pause before the curtain went up, he had piano, viola & oboe; a singer and a guitar! The music was rather more eclectic than usual, including things from Luis Milan (1536) to some Seguidillas manchegas in a very 18th century setting ... All the Spaniards who came, (including the Basque children, Fernández Shaw – & son of Falla's librettist of 'La vida breve' – the Catalan 'agent', and numerous others) were amused and enchanted.[70]

JB tried unsuccessfully to get pianist and composer Eduardo Torner a post at Christ's: 'There seems no chance of Christ's giving anything to a Spaniard – in spite of Raven and the strong minority which supports me!' He went to live with the Middleton Murrys. Other efforts that term, like those on behalf of Luis Gonzalez, were also unsuccessful. Kurt Engisch came to stay at Panton Street for an unspecified time, and with him in the house Dent found it difficult to work on his book, but

67 LH 19/06/1939.

68 JBT 07/04/1939.

69 One of these was the doctored square piano which inspired this biography.

70 JBT–EJD 19/04/1939.

he took to Mrs Prior's production of *Idomeneo*. One day Engisch simply cleared off, leaving no forwarding address and a puzzled but relieved host. Another transient was ambitiously pushing to set up a kind of British Salzburg Festival, refusing to acknowledge what had already been done and was being done locally, advocating only 'the very best', 'which', Dent gloomily reported to JB, 'I suppose means Bruno Walter and Mahler symphonies with the LSO or similar bodies'.

'I have had an extraordinarily interesting time', JB wrote from Mexico:

> After Spain, I began to think I should never want to go to any country to make 'contacts' & establish 'cultural relations' again; & that I should only go to Finland or Holland or somewhere to get right away, and see nobody. In Mexico, I felt that though I was beginning Spain all over again ... It was a Nueva España, of course: but una Nueva España con viejos amigos.[71]

An extended trip to Mexico was planned for that summer, before a musicological congress in New York in September. For Dent, the Warsaw ISCM Festival was now out of the question; the ISCM had been the source of too much physical and mental strain, while Dent's current leanings were now more towards the USA, where he felt the future lay. Randall Thomson, whom he had met at Eastman, now at the Curtis, held out the offer of some summer school work.[72] Hans Raab wrote from Brazil, asking Dent to come there to escape the inevitable war, but Dent persisted in his denial:

> I do not think there is any real danger of a war. The German and Italian newspapers will shriek more loudly than ever, and Hitler will do the same, but I think the King of Italy will keep Musso quiet, and I am pretty sure he does not mean to have a war with England. It would be thoroughly Italian, of course, to encourage Hitler to declare war, and then leave him in the lurch, asking high blackmail price from England and France.[73]

Dent sailed to New York on the *Mauretania*, where he spent the time on board translating *I quattro rusteghi* by Wolf-Ferrari after Goldoni, trawling through the Italian origins of the patter-song. 'I rather fear I have turned Wolf-Ferrari into something like Sullivan.'[74]

> Amusing & very light: the music is a sort of pastiche of Pergolesi and Schubert (the Schubert of Lilac Time): translation shows me how dreadfully cheap it all is – and much more Wolf than Ferrari, for all the tunes are German in rhythm and instrumentally conceived. Also the Goldoni is much 'Bearbeitet' [arranged] and fussed up, sometimes cleverly ... it is a relief to get away from Europe and also to have a week of complete inaccessibility.[75]

71 A new Spain with old friends. JBT–EJD 05/01/1939.

72 JBT 17/05/1939.

73 JBT 27/04/1939.

74 JG 22/07/1939.

75 LH 19/06/1939.

He enjoyed New York, even being taken out to a cocktail party and on to the World's Fair, before going on to see the *HOT MIKADO*, 'our old friend potted to an hour … a good deal jazzed up' with an all-Black cast. 'I thought it a great improvement'.[76]

Mexico was one of several Latin American countries opening their doors for those fleeing Spain, especially intellectuals, and expatriate colonies were already developing there. His contract as lector at Cambridge having expired in 1938, Jesús Bal y Gay had joined former colleagues already there, while his wife Rosita had gone to study in Paris with Nadia Boulanger,[77] the idea being that she would join him later, with JB. But assembling her visa, tickets and travel became a massive exercise in herding cats, reflecting what many refugees were being put through in order to escape. Dent noted that of the two hundred passengers on the *Siboney* headed for Vera Cruz via Havana, about two thirds were Jewish; his Jewish roommate owned a dress shop in Mexico City. The days on board passed pleasantly, working on his edition of Cavalieri's *Rappresentazione di anima e di corpo*, then by contrast going along for morning hymn-singing just to watch the scratch band, made up of mostly refugee musicians; 'the Jew pianist proved his Germanism by being unable to play any chord of the dominant without a 7th in it'.

At Vera Cruz Dent met up with JB and together, Dent reading D.H. Lawrence's *The Plumed Serpent*, they travelled across Mexico to Uruapan, founded by the Spanish in the sixteenth century.

> The great thing about Uruapan is the gardens … they looked really tropical as they were all dripping with rain. Parts of them must be quite old … Uruapan dates from about 1535 like most of the Mexican towns – & all laid out in square blocks.[78]

But he loved being in the warm climate, eating 'ate', a 'kind of damson cheese', seeing the intense redness of the earth after heavy rain. He was still grumpy and uncomfortable; his teeth and 'horrible neuralgia' bothering him in the high altitudes, irritated at the lack of civilised public café life, frowned on, he felt, because of the recent revolutions. JB, already in love with this New Spain, was drinking in local dialects and taking 'dozens and dozens of photographs (with his) marvellous camera full of German gadgets slung around his neck & worn on his abdomen – sometimes with his coat buttoned over it, so that the long telescopic lens sticks out by itself & looks as if his navel had turned into a Cyclopean eye'.

> I find Mexico very fascinating – & was enchanted with Puebla, where there are houses such as I never saw anywhere, a unique style of architecture in red & white, like tomato coloured cakes with elaborate white icing – all rather square & dumpy in form – doors & windows so broad that they look like mantelpieces. period probably 17th cent: but you can't date things easily here, as they went on building 'renaissance' into the 18th cent, with Aztec workmen repeating 'traditional' patterns – all very queer.

76 LH 30/07/1939.

77 Anstee, *An Unlikely Spanish Don*, pp. 172–3.

78 LH 19/08/1939.

They travelled back slowly by train, Dent's idea to trawl along the 'Sunset route' through the central and southern USA, stopping off at San Antonio, where Dent sent Jack a postcard of the opulent opera house there, and New Orleans.

> I wish we xould [sic] have had a month. The old French quarter [sic] now rather like Soho, arty, restauranty, negroid and slightly disreputable, is most picturesque, with marvellous florid iron balcnoies [sic] everywhere, dating, I think, from about 1840. Food also marvellous; and I also found there a Cruickshank print which is to illustrate my new book – 'An Exquisite at the Opera' several very effeminate yung [sic] dandies in a box, with a distant singer on the stage ... and under the sofa, coyly peeping out, a jerry![79]

He was almost as enchanted with 'adorable' Charleston, in South Carolina, but Williamsburg he felt was 'rather a pious fake'.

> It is a curious fate that wenevr [sic] JB and I explored a town we invariably got landed in the negro quarter ... eventually I got fascinated and I have come to like negroes very much, as far as I have seen them ... mostly very kind and friendly people, responding at once to any friendliness.[80]

Dent now loved the Americas, and the USA in particular, seeing in America the best ground for a new cultural future, his only reservation being about the baggage any refugees from Old Europe might bring with them. In his view, having been given this opportunity to begin afresh, too many of them were setting up shop with the same tired old wares.

The idyllic journey ended that September in New York with the ISMR Congress on 11 September: 'the Americans have selected their European guests with great care, and no Nazis are being asked to it!'[81] He was one of about half a dozen Europeans there, beside the resident refugees. It was a sombre occasion, taking place together with the Warsaw ISCM Festival just as the German tanks were plunging into Poland. Dent had continued to deny the possibility of war, writing to Jack on 31 August: 'I hope S.W. is not too much overcome by war scares: my own conviction at present is that there will not be a war at all.'

79 LH 01/11/1939.

80 *Ibid.*

81 JG 30/05/1939.

CHAPTER 15

Titurel 1939–1945

I feel rather like Titurel in Parsifal: he lies in his coffin & asks for a drink now & then but nobody takes any notice of him.[1]

1939–1943

For the first year of war, Dent was forcibly laid up in Cambridge, which in many ways suited him, a rare opportunity for undisturbed writing and research. But he had to be reminded to keep still. His ulcer had caught up with him again in November 1939, when on a trip down to London, he suddenly haemorrhaged badly: 'must have bled nearly to death; I certainly felt that I had got nothing left but a sense of humour!'[2] After a hasty operation he recuperated at New Quebec Street, looked after by one of his German refugees, the dancer Heinz Lander, also a trained nurse,[3] then returning to Cambridge to convalesce at the Evelyn Nursing Home. In spite of a night nurse who liked to give her captive audience ghoulish tales of previous patients, he gradually recovered, by January feeling well enough to move back into Panton Street, his ulcer reduced to a 'tiny spot', and extreme caution advised to obviate future flare-ups. For years this was to be another life pattern: haemorrhage, treatment, convalescence, then an excessive burst of activity which set it all off again.

Once again, war had changed everything. On his return from the USA that September, Dent had been 'horrified' to find London silent, in darkness, the theatres closed. 'I suppose it is good for the population to get accustomed to air-raid conditions a good long time before they begin.'[4] At Panton Street he found that two 'females', schoolteachers from St Martin's-in-the-Fields, had been billeted; some four thousand evacuees were now in the town and needing places to live. Exhausted, his stomach already giving him pain again, he needed his house to himself. But Hills, 'in one of her moods', made it very clear that she liked the two schoolteachers, who helped her around the house and were good company. He gave in: 'I was given a very good dinner to-night, probably as a sop to Cerberus.'[5]

1 EWW 24/06/1940.

2 JG 19/11/1939.

3 *Ibid.*

4 JG 18/09/1939.

5 JG 04/10/1939.

Cambridge had responded to war quickly and efficiently. In that first year of war the university had at least half its undergraduate population intact, and thanks to the infrastructure gradually put in place during Dent's tenure as Professor, Cambridge music could keep going. With twelve music students, all the staff were 'functioning', and there was a big local audience for any concerts, supplemented by interesting and engaged local refugees like Gerhards, the Hirsch family, Gustel and Wolff Scherchen, Eduardo Torner and musicologist Otto Deutsch, and evacuees from the London School of Economics, hospitals and colleges beside evacuated children. The local women had waded in, especially Camille Prior.

> Mrs P., like all middle-age women, is thoroughly enjoying the war. JB saw her and gave me a most comic account of how she organized the arrival at Cambridge of hundreds of evacuated children from London; before they were put into cars to go to their separate hosts and hostesses every child was made to make water, and as the station lavatories were insufficient, Mrs P. arranged for pails to be ranged all round the station square and then superintended the evacuation.[6]

The painstaking removal and storage of all the ancient glass in the King's College Chapel was overseen by Boris Ord, at the same time packing up the organ while keeping the college music going and conducting concerts; in 1941 he left to become a wireless operator in the RAF, replaced by Harold Darke and Patrick 'Paddy' Hadley, a future Professor of Music.

Regardless of blackouts, Dent insisted that the music facilities remain open, so, with the Guildhall, Downing Place was more or less constantly in use for rehearsals and concerts, while the Arts Theatre planned its series of Sunday afternoon concerts. He encouraged local organisations in his care like the Cambridge Philharmonic to keep going: 'In these troubled time people crave for music, and they want the moral support of serious music ... You are earning the real gratitude of the community by doing these things.'[7] He seized initiatives, to get 'both the Wells ballet and the Joos Ballet at the Arts' and to protect his students, all the time writing to Eric Walter White,[8] currently involved with what soon became the Committee for the Encouragement of Music and the Arts (CEMA), and one of Dent's most useful wartime connections.

> If I hear of youngish musicians whom I shd like to save from the fighting line, is it any good passing them on to your organization? I am of course completely in agreement with you that the cultural activities must be carried on – knowing only too well what happened in 1914–18. If I can help you in any way please let me know.[9]

6 *Ibid.*

7 Cambridge Philharmonic Society Minute Books, quoted in Knight, *Cambridge Music*, pp. 120–21.

8 Eric Walter White ((1905–85), music writer and critic.

9 EWW 03/10/1939.

At least one 'youngish musician' Dent had in mind was David Willcocks, who later took over the King's choir from Ord.[10] White himself was one of a number of talented younger men who shared Dent's postwar vision even in the early stages of the war; they had met when White, overseeing the music side of Toynbee Hall in the late 1930s, had asked Dent's permission to use his *Orpheus* translation. From 1940 White edited the *CEMA Bulletin*, and solicited hopeful articles about postwar opera from Dent.[11]

When the ulcer struck again that November, Dent had been casting about for illustrations for his Pelican *Opera* book, to be published in 1940, those he had already so carefully chosen from the Victoria & Albert Museum now dispersed around the country with the rest of its collections. He consulted Lawrence: 'anything at all suitable to illustrate a history of Opera, including scenery and librettos etc. Caricatures of opera would be most welcome.'[12] In desperation, he tried the British Museum, and photos of current 'ultra-modern' productions from Sadler's Wells, while young artist Kay Ambrose was commissioned to do some 'amusing' and informative drawings. In the New Year, Paul Hirsch called at Panton Street:

> with a wonderful assemblage of books & prints to let me use for further illustration – I have got from him two of the Schinkel designs for the Magic Flute (he has 2 exquisite aquatints): and a most comic caricature of Freischütz by George Cruickshank 1824 in a 'travestie' of the opera – coloured, drawn by G.C. after designs of an amateur.[13]

Since his removal to Cambridge, Hirsch had become a friend and colleague, and Dent had introduced him into his circles, lobbying to get him elected to the Reform Club.[14] Hirsch was more than grateful; he loaned his collection to the university, with the idea that it might remain in Cambridge permanently as the foundation of a major university music collection, an idea which had Dent's enthusiastic support, those vast Library of Congress collections in mind.

Dent's prolonged convalescence in Cambridge was another kind of escape, but he could still choose to have a few pupils, compose at leisure and keep in touch through letters, catch up on modern writers and some autobiography: Somerset Maugham[15] and J.S. Mill; later Rose Macaulay. His 'curious invalid life' went on throughout that winter and well into the summer, looked after by Hills, who faithfully cooked his strained carrots and fish. Lacking the energy he needed to get on with his Romantic Opera book, he found the composition of strict counterpoint

10 Sir David told me this in 2007. During one supervision at Panton Street, Dent advised him to sit his B Mus exams early and quickly because he was likely to be called up. Astonishingly he did both parts before the end of the year – something no one had ever done before. After the war he looked in his file to find that in February 1940, Dent had interceded with the Vice Chancellor to allow this to happen.

11 'The Future of Opera in England', *CEMA Bulletin*, no, 47 (March 1944), pp. 2–4.

12 LH 01/11/1939. Lawrence in fact did manage to recover some.

13 LH 29/01/1940.

14 EWW 22/04/1939.

15 Maugham became a friend, as his letters in KCA reveal.

restful, and that winter he began to compose again, the first pieces since 1920, the texts taken from Psalms 6, 23 and 50.

> Did I tell you that while I was in bed in London I composed 3 motets for unaccopd chorus as studies of fugue etc, especially of fugue as the expression of pain. I don't think any body will want to sing them, or print them![16]

'I am weary of my groaning' is usually for Holy Week, but Dent's subversive take is set as a classic fugue and refers to his chronic ulcer. Three more motets followed during that winter: settings of Blake, 'Holy Thursday', and Wesley's hymn 'O Thou who camest from above'. 'They are all rather queer stuff', he wrote to Lawrence.[17] Hubert Foss at Oxford University Press took all six, publishing the first three that year.[18] 'And I also wrote (& have had typed) my little tract of about 10,000 words on Fugue for Beginners. This I want to print here privately for personal distribution to pupils & friends.'[19] His 'little tract' remains one of the best introductions to the subject.

There was another haemorrhage in March, but with no need for a transfusion. By April his doctor allowed him 'in suitable weather' to 'potter' in the Botanic Gardens just across the road, but although he had 'no pain & no further signs of haemorrhage', such expeditions were a real strain. With Roberto Gerhard to support him, he attempted the short walk to the Fitzwilliam to see an exhibition of Eddie Marsh's pictures, but when faced with 'the hundreds of small pictures, my heart felt faint within me', and he turned back. He 'struggled' with his *Háry János* translation, especially the songs: 'a terribly difficult job any way: but wrestling with it in an invalid condition is almost beyond me'.[20] By May his medicine was giving him terrible pain, while the painkillers gave him severe diarrhoea, but he still read the proofs for his motets, and set exams in music history and composition; even taking the trouble to ask Lawrence to look after Daphne Bird, a former pupil who had taken a job at a girls' school near Manchester. He had hoped that Fred and Bou might be able to come up to help with the nursing and give him the company he craved, but Bou suddenly died in May; another blow. Letters and postcards poured in from around the world: from the Kodálys at a Hungarian health resort Dent immediately resolved to visit, from Lawrence and from Jack, keeping him in touch with current affairs. JB was preoccupied looking after both refugee Spaniards and the disruptive Franco supporters in his faculty. The Americas became their personal fantasy place of refuge.

> JB and I both feel that a time may come in our life-times when Europe becomes impossible: and we want to dig ourselves well in in the other hemisphere, both North, Central and South America. Alfred Einstein wrote me a cheery letter the

16 LH 29/01/1940.

17 LH 07/04/1940.

18 After OUP published the first three, in May Dent was expressing the hope that Humphrey Milford would do the second three, which he felt were the 'better compositions'. LH 11/05/1940.

19 LH 29/01/1940.

20 LH 07/04/1940.

> other day from Smith College, where he teaches exquisite American girls to sing shockingly improper Italian madrigal [sic] of the Cinquecento: he says Harvard will always give me a home whenever I want to go.[21]

Still shaky, Dent begged to be allowed down to London for the Sadler's Wells summer season, but his doctor, the Regius Professor of Physick, sharply told him to stay in bed for another six weeks and continue with his diet of baby-foods and 'perhaps junket or jelly'. 'I have certainly learned to appreciate the deliciousness of a plain potato, a vegetable most of us regard as a dull thing, often to be left out in favour of more exciting things such as asparagus or peas etc.'[22] So he continued for a while, examining, writing accompaniments for an edition of Purcell songs. When not over in Oxford visiting the Jiménezes,[23] JB kept him company, and Lawrence suggested that he use the time to write his autobiography, probably connected to Lawrence's own current undertaking, a catalogue of Dent's writings.

> I have no great desire to write my autobiography at present. A few years ago Chapman & Hall – a firm with which I had never had any dealings or connexion of any kind ... suddenly wrote & asked me to consider writing my memoirs – & added that if I agreed they wd send someone down to Cambridge to talk it over![24]

So he lay in his back garden on a new chaise-longue and fretted and read and did more desultory work on the Cavalieri *Anima e Corpo*.

> I do rather feel that I am degenerating mentally: any mental effort is tiring, and I feel less and less inclined to read – much less to work – and more willing to lie like a log in a state of vacuity. I think this is really what the doctors <u>want</u>.[25]

The Gerhards took pity on him, inviting him to stay with them at 'Southfields', the house loaned to them by Dent's former pupil Robin Orr, overlooking the fields of West Cambridge. Poldi Gerhard had told him tartly that he was far less likely to be bombed there than in Panton Street. The only local bombing episode he knew about tickled him: the captured German airman had been at Trinity and professed himself mortified to be bombing Cambridge.

> I moved in here yesterday – It is a new house in a new road behind the new Library, with a good sized garden and a sort of terrace in front of the house, a tennis lawn and a kitchen-garden beyond. Mrs Orr has inherited a vast quantity of good furniture & is the sort of person who 'likes everything nice' – so it is a curious contrast to my old bachelor establishment.[26]

He quickly settled in, even listening to German broadcasts on their wireless: 'I hate sitting by a box and being talked at', but illness had made him more accommodating.

21 LH 11/05/1940. The letter is dated 'March' but this must be May.

22 LH 19/05/1940.

23 They had moved there from Cambridge.

24 LH 08/06/1940.

25 LH 19/05/1940.

26 LH 22/06/1940.

> However, I suppose I ought to be thankful for this illness wch has kept me mostly a prisoner in my own house, & sheltered from all war-life and war mentality as if I were in a monastery. I wish I was in my own house still, in spite of all kindness here & the open garden.[27]

They were good company, especially Poldi. 'Everything goes very smoothly & happily here', he wrote to JB, 'I feel horrified that Mrs G. shd herself wash my shirts & pyjamas: but she insists, and nothing ever seems to be any trouble. Her cooking of my invalid meals is marvellous.'[28]

As Dent's spirits began to revive under the severe pampering, he began to work again, sending off his translation of Cavalieri's *Rappresentazione di anima e di corpo* to Lawrence: 'When I had finished it I was rather pleased, but could not quite make up my mind whether it was really good or only a collection of ill-created affectations and would-be quaintnesses.'[29] He had hopes of printing it at the Cambridge University Press, 'rather preciously' with woodcuts by Gwen Raverat, 'so that it wd make a really pretty little book & might eventually become a bibliographical rarity!' The translating was in this case pleasurable exercise, like the composition; Dent loved using old-fashioned English forms, hymns and folk-songs, and trawling through the Oxford Hymnal for ideas and models. He sent Lawrence one light-hearted effort he had done for 'a young friend … a High Church curate in Surrey':

> Only effort superhuman
> Can achieve the style of Newman:
> And it costs me fearful labour
> Just to write like Father Faber.
> So I very often take a
> Leaf from good Sir Henry Baker,
> Though I very seldom think worth
> While to crib from Catherine Winkworth.
> And the muse of [delete] Christina Miss Rossetti
> Often strikes me as rather petty.
> When I'm in a regular fix
> I reach to Chatterton Dix:
> Only when completely feeble
> Do I write like Mr Keble.
> When I'm feeling not so bright
> I remember H.F. Lyte.
> But I prefer my good old Tate & Brady
> To Augustus Montague Toplady![30]

Dent returned to Panton Street in late July 1940, having turned down invitations from the Hawards to stay with them in Manchester, anxious to get back to London,

27 *Ibid.*

28 JBT 01/07/1940.

29 LH 27/06/1940.

30 *Ibid.*

and considering taking over Fred and Bou's flat in Nottingham Place, Fred 'horribly depressed' after Bou's death and being looked after by Jack Gordon. But London was out of the question right now, with the bombing and the need to get into a shelter every night, the food shortages and no gas for cooking. Evelyn Broadwood advised against renting again, reckoning that it was a very good time to buy. When he retired in 1941, Dent firmly intended 'to leave Cambridge altogether', discussing with JB what their next move might be, and asking Jack to keep an eye out for a suitable house. 'If I was not chained up like a dog I would go to London and look about and talk to house-agents.'

The dormant ulcer continued to plague him, preventing any firm decisions about moving house and depleting his finances, but Dent was determined somehow to get back into harness; a wartime Vic–Wells now needed his services more than ever. His Penguin *Opera* had come out earlier that year to immediate success, raising public awareness even in terrible times. He had sent the proofs to Lawrence, confident about the worth of his little book, dismissing a rival paperback:

> I think there is a lot more meat in my book; more history, more analysis, more amusing stuff, and above all more passion and enthusiasm for opera. It is evident that Howes is rather bored with opera in general and has done this book for a commission.[31]
>
> It's an odd book – some of it dreadfully stodgy, I fear, and some of it possibly too frivolous – but I think frivolity is legitimate in a sixpenny, and it will lighten the stodge and tempt the ordinary reader to go on.[32]

Dent always said that he had written *Opera* as a piece of 'propaganda' for Sadler's Wells, and he smoothly manages to mention Sadler's Wells on nearly every page of his Introduction, finishing the book with a paean to Lilian Baylis and the Wells, so that, for the reader, Sadler's Wells equals opera. *Opera* may have been for popular consumption, but there is no condescension; Dent peppers his narrative with sharp, contentious ideas, and his little book is entertaining and just a bit exhausting, as if he had poured into its pages every ounce of energy he lacked in the rest of his frustrated life. He asks the reader why 'waste sixpence on this book?' Or, having seen their first opera, did they leave feeling 'that opera was to become the devotion of a lifetime?' Or agree with Tolstoy and Carlyle, that it was 'complete nonsense and a waste of time?'

> What makes opera difficult of access to the inexperienced listener is the fact that all operas are based on certain conventions not found in plays.[33]
>
> Monteverdi has gone down to posterity as the prototype of the daring revolutionary in music. He was nothing of the sort.[34]
>
> It is generally imagined that all opera librettos are nonsense and doggerel. This is not the case, for in the first operas the words were probably considered much

31 LH 01/11/1939. The book he dismissed was *A Key to Opera* by Frank Howes and Philip Hope-Wallace (London, 1939).

32 LH 03/02/1940.

33 E.J. Dent, *Opera* (London, 1940), p. 16.

34 *Ibid.*, p. 31.

> more important than the music. The dramas which Rinuccini wrote for musical setting were highly literary, one might almost say precious.[35]
>
> Strauss's chief quality has always been a robust energy and sensual exuberance; his later career shows that the 'perversities' of Salome and Elektra were artificial studies in technique. Hofmannsthal, on the other hand, was a Viennese aristocrat with a Jewish strain, the product of an over-refined and delicate culture derived largely from French and Italian sources.[36]
>
> All these experimental operas have confirmed the truth that can be learned from the operas of the past – that no opera can hold the interest of an audience unless the composer gives the innermost expression of his thought to the voices on the stage.[37]

And on Hindemith's *Neues vom Tage*:

> the sensation of the opera was a scene in which the heroine, lying in a bath at a hotel, sang the praises of electric heating – 'constant hot water, no horrid smell, no danger of explosion', etc. When the work was announced for performance at Breslau, the local gas company applied for and obtained an injunction, as this song was considered damaging to their trade. Opera is taken seriously in Germany.[38]

Any contentiousness is remarkably free from current politics, but in his offhand, inclusive manner serious points were tacitly made about the necessity for music to be free of ideological constraints.

After its initial closure just after the war broke out in September 1939, when staff had been laid off, Sadler's Wells was soon running again; an 'anonymous benefactor' stumping up a 'personal guarantee of £250' on the premise that there was still an audience happy to 'walk home in the dark'.[39] Tony Guthrie had taken over both companies in February 1939, and, Dent felt, shared the vision they had all been working to achieve: the need for rehearsal time, high production values, excellent texts, and in the long term, a 'national' theatre and opera.[40] But in spite of sold-out performances and favourable reviews, the finances of both companies were in a sorry state, so everyone was asked to take cuts in their already meagre salaries, especially Guthrie.[41]

Throughout the 1939–40 season, Sadler's Wells continued to turn out new productions, with *Otello* and *Die Fledermaus*, beside the 'Jubilee Performance of Wartime Opera',[42] but even with packed houses, its operating deficit was 8,000 pounds. Kurt Joos produced Handel's *Rodelinda* at the Vic, which both cheered and vexed Dent, as he had wanted it to be done at the Wells with Jack Gordon. For *The Wreckers*, Dame Ethel 'came on at the end and made a wonderful speech. Poor old

35 *Ibid.*, p. 113.

36 *Ibid.*, p. 132.

37 *Ibid.*, p. 139.

38 *Ibid.*, p. 138.

39 Dent, ATFE, p. 120.

40 Guthrie's article on 'Opera in English' in *Opera in English*, Sadler's Wells Opera Books, no. 1 (1945) reflects Dent's influence.

41 Cf Gilbert, *Opera for Everybody*, pp. 67–8.

42 *Ibid.*, pp. 68–9.

thing, she suffers from that form of deafness which makes one hear all music out of tune, so she got her ears well plugged and saw the performance only as a mute pantomime, but enjoyed it all very much'.[43] However ill, Dent had never let up on his opera work, continuing throughout to press Jack and Guthrie about productions which had failed owing to lack of rehearsal time, but also 'want of remitting care for detail on the part of singers and conductors as well as producers and scene-painters'.[44] He listed productions which might be revived and improved, *Onegin*, *Orpheus*, *Fra Diavolo*, *Bartered Bride*, having noted in *Opera* 'the popular repertory shows that lasting success is accorded only to those operas where the voices take the lead'.[45] With Jack especially he discussed how to improve current productions: *La traviata*, *The Barber of Seville* and *The Beggar's Opera*. The last had poor reviews, in spite of 'my dear friend Michael Redgrave' as Macheath, looking like 'a woman dressed up'.[46]

By September 1940, Dent was feeling 'much better', going out for a long walk each morning, free to use the library again, researching history and styles, his postponed *magnum opus* on Romantic Opera always at the back of his mind. He was keen to get working on productions, sending off his new edition of *Martha* to Oxford University Press, for future use at Sadler's Wells. But it was a rearguard action; the Blitz began, and Sadler's Wells had to close, the theatre handed over to the Borough of Finsbury to be used for homeless people.

'We're a *madhouse*', Guthrie wrote to Dent a few weeks later, 'five tours, either in the country or being organised, and hundred and sixty homeless people living in the theatre and giving a *lot of trouble*'.[47] Ever optimistic, Dent wrote to Lawrence, 'I expect the bombing will have to stop fairly soon, and the theatres will start again.' It didn't, but rescue came from the new Committee for the Encouragement of Music and the Arts (CEMA), a 'joint venture' of the Board of Education and the Pilgrim Trust,[48] which eventually became the Arts Council. Founded in January 1940, its immediate purpose was to address the 'collapse of all ordinary sources of theatre and music',[49] and to see to it that more isolated parts of the country were not neglected.[50]

43 JBT 27/04/1939.

44 JG 02/08/1940.

45 Dent, *Opera*, p. 140.

46 Dent kept very quiet about his friendships with a number of prominent actors and dancers, but letters in the 1930s and 40s are sprinkled with references to Michael Redgrave, John Gielgud, 'Bobby' Helpmann and 'Freddy' Ashton.

47 Dent, ATFE, p. 121. Dent quotes it in his letter to JG 03/10/1940.

48 The Pilgrim Trust is an important source of funding for the arts, but mainly painting and architecture. Founded in 1930 with a 2-million-pound grant from American philanthropist Edward Harkness (who had endowed Harvard), its board included John Buchan and Stanley Baldwin. It became the saviour of the Vic–Wells and its postwar transformation into the National Theatre, Ballet and Opera.

49 Dent, ATFE, p. 122.

50 'to help musicians, actors, artists, and artists whom air-raid precautions and bombing were likely to render unemployed, and to bring the "solace" of music and the arts to the bored, bombed-out, and evacuated'. Skidelsky, *John Maynard Keynes: Fighting for Britain*, pp. 286–7.

So at a time of chaos and fear, entertainment and a sense of cohesion were being provided; in the meantime, the two theatres were used as refuges for the bombed-out.

A governors' meeting at the New Theatre in St Martin's Lane decided the transfer that November 1940 of the entire Vic–Wells headquarters to the Victoria Theatre, Burnley in Lancashire, a decision which actually went against its constitution, so the governors themselves became personally liable for the finances, supported by the CEMA and the Carnegie Trust. His prolonged illness meant that over this difficult time Dent's attendance at the monthly board meetings was erratic; he missed the crucial November 1940 meeting, only finding out about Jack Gordon's dismissal in December. After Jack had had some kind of 'breakdown' that November, possibly brought on by all the upheavals and uncertainty, Guthrie decided in his pragmatic way to replace him with Sumner Austin, who could both sing and direct. From his fresh convalescence in Cambridge, Dent wrote urgently, advising him to stay in touch with Guthrie, keep in the loop and by no means give up on the Wells: 'you are the only opera producer there who is really any good … They seem to have treated you very badly, but please don't quarrel with them irrevocably'.[51]

Otherwise, the drastic move was a remarkable success, Dent crediting the 'friendly co-operation' of the local Burnley committee and the director of the theatre, Jess Lincott. From January 1941, three weeks of 'classical plays' followed three weeks of opera.[52] At Guthrie's request, Dent sent them *Martha*, and was working on Gluck's *Orfeo ed Eurydice*, glad to have the chance to re-work his previous translation, using the 1762 Viennese Italian version: 'I know a good deal more about Gluck and other things than I did in 1932.' The 'other things' included theatre history and a better sense of what worked on stage, especially the intensity of the relationship between Orpheus and Eurydice, and her sexuality.[53]

In fact, the Vic–Wells was already well placed to accommodate itself to wartime conditions, since all three companies – theatre, opera and ballet – had played in the provinces off-season, so the idea of touring was by no means novel, even if the conditions were far more difficult. The war forced it to do what had been discussed before, becoming more of a touring company.

> As long as practically all London theatres are shut, it won't matter if the Wells's shut too … I hear from friends at Newcastle-on-Tyne and Birmingham that they are longing to have the V.W. opera there & a tour might do a great deal (1) to build up audiences, (2) to pave the way for permanent branches of the Wells in provincial centres which is what you and I both want.[54]

51 JG 28/12/1940. To avoid confusion: Sumner Austin was taking over as singer and director; Frederic Austin had been an established singer and director since before WWI.

52 The Old Vic was 'badly damaged' in May 1941, and in June closed with a production of *The Tempest*, and was used as a refuge for bombed-out people. Dent recorded all of this in his history, *A Theatre for Everybody: The Story of the Old Vic and Sadler's Wells* (London, 1945, 2nd impression 1946, henceforth ATFE), p. 121, with Kay Ambrose illustration of 'homeless people living in the theatre'.

53 LH 15/10/1940.

54 JG 16/12/1940.

For the next two years Guthrie took his pared-down company, with its 'tiny cast of singers' and an orchestra of five players, to 'small mill towns' in Yorkshire and Lancashire, places which had not seen opera before. Buxton had its splendid opera house, but there was no place to stay since 'the town was packed with refugees', so the company were put up in the local hospital. The minimal scenery meant resourcefulness, as Dent had seen years before at the Deutsches Theater, but he hardly got to see any of the results.

The Carl Rosa Opera were already touring, coming to Cambridge, but Dent never viewed any of the other companies as rivals; rather as developing an 'entente cordiale'.[55] His letters to Jack played down the persistent illness, 'I was not very well recently', Dent instead enthusing on 'my big book on the Romantic Opera', his connected ideas on *Ballo in maschera,* always positive.

> If I were Intendant of the Wells, I should perform a number of 'Spieloper', like The Barber [of Seville], and try to develop a style of really good operatic acting, on the basis of comedy with spoken dialogue or secco recitative, as I think that style is eminently suited to English singers and audiences and to the English language and English voices.[56]

With the Wells so distant and himself so confined, Dent needed the outlet of these operatic letters while his mind was so active on the subject, so he continued to correspond with Jack, his eye on the future. Although he was in constant touch with Guthrie, who asked him to write some 'propaganda' articles for the Wells, it was far from the close personal working relationships Dent had enjoyed before. The secretary Evelyn Williams continued to keep him formally informed about the company's doings, but occasionally he read about them first in the newspaper, or was informed by Humphrey Procter-Gregg at Manchester. Only in December was Dent allowed to travel to London, staying at Gerry Cooper's 'Farm' for a week, hoping to get to the Randall Thompson symphony and to see the specialist again. 'Gerry nurses me like Florence Nightingale and cooks invalid food for me too – he is really angelic and the house very comfortable.'[57]

❧ ❧ ❧

> I go on always collecting material for my big book on the Romantic Opera, but write nothing of it.[58]

His recent 'correction of proofs' for Loewenberg's *Annals of Opera* had been an extremely useful exercise, both as a reference work and as a stimulus for the 'big book' he still hoped to write, but that was put on hold.

55 JG 19/01/1940.
56 JG 19/11/1940.
57 JG 28/12/1940.
58 JG 16/12/1940.

> At present I want to write my little popular book of propaganda for the Wells, to be called perhaps 'National Opera': what it has been and what it might be … Foss wants me to write it quickly and not to do too much research, but you know my ways.[59]

At first, 'National Opera' was simply to be a part of his bigger project on Romantic Opera, but he quickly realised that the scope of such a massive project, the mental and physical demands on his wracked body, made the larger undertaking impossible right now, so settling on the smaller one was a satisfying compromise. His intensive research over the past few years had revealed big gaps in the received knowledge and understanding of opera history.

> I find that the materials for the historical chapters are very scanty, and I, and I have had to do a fearful lot of reading and note-taking, merely to get a fairly complete record of (1) native English operas from 1656 onwards, and (2) foreign operas performed here in English (a) adaptations and pasticcios as most of them were up to about 1830 and (b) foreign operas given complete with all the original music. Also any manifestos in books or prefaces about the desirability of establishing a really national English opera. Allardyce Nicoll is of some help, but he is not much of a musician … the most useful book hitherto has been the autobiography of Fitzball, and I am amused to find that all the other biographers have pinched copiously from him! Planché's autobiography is fairly useful, but not what I really want … But although Carl Rosa did valuable work later, It seems to me that dreadful damage to the cause of English opera was done by (1) the gigantic success of Italian opera under Mapleson … and simultaneously, or almost, (2) the rise of 'Gilbertandsullivan'.[60]

The 'big book' never materialised, which is a tragedy. There were too many interruptions, from recurrent illness to the unceasing applications around refugees, which went on throughout the war. 'What wears me down is the never-ending correspondence about interned German refugees'.[61]

Another expensive trip to the 'duodenal specialist' in January 1941 included an X-ray: 'marvellous photographs of my inside, exquisitely arranged like a picture book or an old family album'.[62] Although by February he seemed clear of the ulcer (again), the doctor urged caution: '[he] says I suffer from chronic duodenitis, and I expect that will take a very long time to cure, if indeed it ever can be completely cured at my age … I must go on with the sieve diet etc and rest about half the day'.[63] Dent's 'half-invalid life' continued that winter, when concerts and theatres were 'quite impossible for me', the board meetings 'very tiring', while 'teaching is not quite so stimulating to me', and he was forced to resign his directorship of Arts

59 JG 19/11/1940. This became *A Theatre for Everybody*.

60 JG 19/11/1940. This letter is one of Dent's longest.

61 EWW 17/08/1943.

62 LH 11/02/1941.

63 *Ibid.*

Theatre. 'So you see', he wrote to Lawrence, 'it is not much of a life to get things done in; but I am always planning books and articles and trying to collect materials'.

But the research was another mode of escape, and Dent managed to work in the Rowe library at King's some mornings, 'I find it is very useful for Operas', looking for likely revivals for Sadler's Wells, especially good 'native' repertory, like Goring Thomas' *Esmeralda* and *Nadeschda*.[64] In April another attack put him back in bed for five weeks; sedatives to ease the pain only made him violently ill.[65] Roberto Gerhard loaned him *Don Quixote* but he found he couldn't get on with it: 'if I have not got the newspaper to read, I just lie like a log & rest ... I have never been a "reader-in-bed" – mainly owing to the difficulty of spectacles'.

> Colles wants me to write (though apparently not for publication) a complete record of the International Society for Contemporary Music, with all its inner history. I feel much too lazy to do anything of the sort at present.[66]

Meanwhile, Sadler's Wells was having other problems. That March, Guthrie approached two of the board members, Lord Lytton and Sir Reginald Rowe, to consider Dent's old idea of having an experienced Intendant to oversee artistic and managerial issues, even suggesting Rudolf Bing, now that Glyndebourne was shut for the war, backed by Joan Cross and Evelyn Williams. Other possible candidates were Geoffrey Toye and conductor Warwick Braithwaite. Although still very ill, Dent acted immediately, writing to everyone concerned and arranging to have a long talk with Guthrie. It was his recurring nightmare, expressed so often in those war years while he was ill and unable to act, that such a combination of events might force the Wells into apparently benign and necessary measures which would erode its essential character and purpose. Over and again through his letters he fought off such insidious solutions as amalgamation with Covent Garden – advocated by Procter-Gregg – or hiring ambitious people like Bing from outside, insensitive to the company's fundamental aims and who might after the war simply return to Germany. 'What I dread', he wrote to Jack,

> is the possibility of a complete catastrophe and the total closure of S.W. followed (when the war is safely over) by a reconstruction headed by John Christie and Fritz Busch! Busch would have no understanding at all of the old English repertory (Bo Girl etc) and Christie would have no use for a suburban theatre like the Wells, but would want (and G.T. also) nothing short of Cov. Gard. or Drury Lane – or at least His Majesty's.[67]

In the event, Guthrie agreed with Dent; their mutual purpose was to establish Sadler's Wells as *the* National Opera, with opera in English, English operas and modest but intelligent productions, and it was important to keep that long view alive. Guthrie was confident that after the war there would be a great demand for

64 JG 23/02/1941. Dent listed Macfarren's *Robin Hood*, Wallace's *The Amber Witch* and *Love's Triumph*, Goring Thomas' *The Golden Web* and Stanford's *Much Ado*.

65 LH 14/04/1941.

66 LH 01/07/1941. Dent did write a a short history, never published.

67 JG 02/04/1941.

music and opera, while by this time Dent had come to like and trust him, even through the difficult episodes with Clive and Jack and in spite of Dennis Arundell, who 'had not much good to say of Guthrie, who appears to have the Irish failing of saying one thing to one person and another to another – let us call it an excess of tact.'[68] Dent himself was by no means impervious to the Irish charm, but he recognised the vision and the operating pragmatism needed to achieve it: 'he knows very little about Opera, but he can understand my attempts to get down to principles about S.W. which the "practical people" of the company simply can't grasp'.[69]

The following season the company went out under the hopeful title of 'The National Opera', producing 'English' operas, *Dido and Aeneas* and Arne's *Thomas and Sally*. Guthrie had evidently instructed both conductors Collingwood and Lloyd to consult Dent, but Lloyd never bothered, and Collingwood 'had not the least desire to pick my brains'.[70] 'I expect they have already settled it all their own way, to do it without ballet, without chorus, without scenery, and almost without dresses. J. Cross as Belinda and that's enough.' He fretted constantly to Jack that despite the 'tremendous keenness' of the 'excellent audiences' up north, it would all disintegrate, a 'national disgrace'. Procter-Gregg, his 'cher confrère at Manchester'[71] meanwhile, had been writing corrosive reports of dropping production standards. Dent was dismissive: 'I am not continuing the correspondence at present … I might have asked what Manchester was doing in the way of operatic training.'[72]

Just before the Wells was due to play Cambridge in summer 1941, Guthrie called by to discuss some of the problems: 'The small opera travelling co. is horribly overworked & so much underpaid that they can't afford a holiday – so they get more & more on each other's nerves, travelling from one small town to another, & living in miserable commercial hotels.'[73] Coupon restrictions alone meant that new costumes were out of the question, and how could singers give six demanding performances a week while having to shift scenery at the same time? In Glasgow, Warwick Braithwaite conducted *Madam Butterfly* while the nearby shipyards were under attack; in one terrifying episode in Hull, they were bombed.[74] For two years and more the company struggled on: 'The weak points of S.W. now are scenery, chorus & orchestra: inevitably.'[75]

In May, while Dent was still recovering from more illness, with vomiting, heartburn and constantly recurring pain, Louis Clarke of the Fitzwilliam decided to commission a portrait – Dent had been in touch with Clarke about donating some Eric Gill sketches he had inherited from Maurice Ingram. E.X. Kapp, the same who had drawn 'a quite good caricature of me' in 1912, now commissioned by the government

68 JG 28/12/1940.

69 JG 02/04/1941.

70 JG 05/05/1941.

71 He had a lectureship there from 1935, becoming its first Professor of Music.

72 JG 07/02/1941.

73 LH 01/07/1941.

74 Gilbert, *Opera for Everybody*, p. 77.

75 JG 13/03/1942.

to draw pictures of people in wartime, came to Panton Street to do a series of sittings, sessions Dent found he enjoyed, in spite of pain and vomiting. 'The difficulty, as I knew, wd be that when I am quiet & silent my face all goes dead "like putty" as you used to say: and that I am only "interesting" when animated: and when animated I pass through a great number of different expressions.'[76] A string of visitors solved the problem; the result was a good likeness, if severe. He pottered in his tiny garden and tried to keep mentally primed with projects always at hand, most recently *The Beggar's Opera*.

The Wells touring company had undertaken a scaled-down version in Burnley that January, directed by Herbert Marshall, with Dent's scoring for a small 'chamber' band done to Frederic Austin's old version. A new edition was something Dent badly wanted in the Sadler's Wells repertoire, but he had been too ill all that winter to work with the company on it. Meanwhile, Frederic Austin had taken his old version on tour himself, and refused permission for the Wells to use it where he was on tour. To Dent's glee the production received terrible reviews, which in Guthrie's opinion put people off seeing it altogether; he wanted a new version done 'for the exclusive possession of the Wells', which Dent was happy to provide, having already begun his own version that March. 'I find it great fun', he wrote to Jack, now working in munitions, 'and have always wanted to do it for years. The small band offers good opportunities for ingenuity. I have got Austin's version from the library and I get more & more disgusted with its cheapness and its Philistinism. It is mostly in a degraded sort of bad Edward-German & Sullivan style.'[77] Roberto Gerhard advised him on scoring it for wind, and this condensed version was ready to show Guthrie when the Wells came to Cambridge in July.

Dent's new edition had actually been sparked by meeting another old friend, Katharine 'Katten' Thomson.

> On Saturday night I went to a sort of communist entertainment at the Cooperative Hall in Burleigh Street. Alan Bush ran it, and the music was provided by the Clarion Choral Society from Birmingham, conducted by Katharine Thomson … But the great event was scenes from Figaro (in my translation, of course) acted in costume with great spirit. The singers drove over from Birmingham in a lorry, & Figaro was the driver! I think Mozart wd have enjoyed it hugely as they were very musical & well in tune & time, and desperately keen. If that's communism I can only say Katharine's doing a great work in teaching those people to sing.[78]

The youngest of the three Stewart girls, Katharine had married George Thomson, a Fellow of King's, in 1934; he was now Professor at Birmingham and they had moved to one of the newer leafy suburbs in the south of the city. Like most of the extended Stewart clan, the couple had strong left-wing, internationalist convictions and exceptional musical talents, and the family had always entertained such visiting musicians as Alban Berg, Arthur Honegger, the Kodálys, and recently, refugees of all

76 LH 16/05/1941. The portrait was used for the cover of Taylor, *Edward J. Dent: Selected Essays.*

77 JG 17/06/1941.

78 LH 09/03/1941.

sorts. They were known and liked at Winterthur, at the Ewalds and others of Dent's wider circles; even the sour Merian sent his warm regards to Katharine via Dent. Once settled in Birmingham, the Thomsons set about working a small revolution in the music-making there, and Katharine's current project of grassroots opera in Birmingham, the Clarion Society, what Dent called her 'Red Opera', became a new focus for Dent's limited energies.

Dent had always held the whole family in great affection, with their attractive combination of conviction, generous spirit and musical talent, their liveliness and mutual affection. There were interesting conversations about Mozart's 'left-wing' tendencies, which Dent felt ought to be allowed out in a production, adding roughage to the more common view of his 'beautiful' music. When Katharine asked him about any operas of 'social significance' they might produce, and Dent mischievously suggested Bernard Snow's version of the *Ring*, before offering up Paisiello's *Il re Teodoro in Venezia* (c.1786), a 'rather Gilbertian comedy ... the music not nearly as good as Mozart, I fear: the libretto very funny'.[79] He mused on some 'French revolution opera', but it was clear that *Figaro* and and *The Beggar's Opera* best fitted the bill, subject to Guthrie's permission, which they got by October: 'I think he is quite pleased at the idea of an "ultra-red" production.'[80]

'Cambridge is full of music', Dent wrote to Jack in June 1941. Joan Cross sang in Paddy Hadley's May Week concert, Beethoven's Mass in D; Mrs Hackforth's weekly chamber concerts continued beside now-regular Sunday concerts at the Arts Theatre, also thriving. Beside the Wells visit in July, Norman Higgins of the Arts Theatre Trust wanted to spend their current 3000-pound profits on a Mozart Festival, with Sadler's Wells doing *The Magic Flute*. From his bed, Dent had 'pitched' the idea to Keynes of using Kurt Joos to produce it, with scenery by John Armstrong. 'The Trustees have made so much money this last year that they can afford to chuck some of it on a show of this sort.'[81] Not just the Vic–Wells but other companies found Cambridge congenial. The BBC was giving a series of orchestral concerts under Adrian Boult, broadcasting from the Arts Theatre, and Constant Lambert conducted some 'LPO 2' concerts of 'modern' music.[82] Of course he still had his grumbles: 'With all this professional orchestra performance the CUMS amateur orchestra cannot compete'.

The Wells's troubles over staffing and management continued all that summer and into the autumn. At the age of fifty Sumner Austin was called up, and now women were being called up as well; the company chorus suffered. Dent continued to revise his performing editions to suit the diminishing company and the varying theatres they played: *Rigoletto* and *The Barber of Seville* were especially popular, with *Madam Butterfly*. The BBC did Dent's *Onegin*, which Guthrie had vetoed as being too intimate and too intellectual for the bigger theatres.

79 KT 05/08/1941.

80 JG 09/10/1941.

81 JG 01/08/1941.

82 LH 15/02/1942.

After a meeting with Cross and Guthrie on 11 July, Dent felt well enough to travel down to London for the ENSA music committee meeting, his first since he had been appointed six months before: 'so I felt I ought to show I was alive'. ENSA (Entertainments National Service Association) had been set up by Parliament through the armed forces, and initially chaired by film director Basil Dean, father of Dent's pupil, Winton. Its initial brief was to provide entertainment for the armed forces and munitions workers; later in the war such entertainments went abroad as well. Dent grumbled that they were better funded than CEMA, but he warmly approved of the 'excellent' chairman, Sir Victor Schuster, and the rest: Vaughan Williams, 'strangely thin and almost haggard', Paddy Hadley, Arnold Goldsbrough. The brief was 'to organize good music', to run with the popular 'light and leggy' entertainment to keep the troops happy.[83]

For the rest of the war Dent was closely involved with both ENSA and CEMA, especially the latter. By the time Maynard Keynes became its Chairman in 1942, CEMA was bankrolled by the Pilgrim Trust, but R.A. Butler hinted to Keynes that it could develop into 'something that might occupy a more permanent place in our social organisation'. Like Dent, Keynes took the long view: 'Arts policy in Keynes's time at CEMA was closely bound up with his own personal philosophy.'[84] Especially latterly, while Dent was on the Arts Board, they had often talked informally about state-sponsored arts. Although Keynes had, in his biographer's words, 'no innate feeling for the visual arts' and 'only a moderate liking for music', he listened to trusted sources like Dent, and beside his understanding of the economics of the arts, Keynes possessed a strong belief in the power of the high arts to facilitate social good. According to his deputy, Kenneth Clark, 'he gave CEMA an electrifying sense of direction … he never dimmed his headlights'.[85] 'If Keynes & CEMA are still going strong, Sadler's Wells might really become a National Opera, whether at S.W. or at another theatre.'[86]

Throughout these difficult formative years for British arts funding, Dent was fighting his own battles with recurring illness, living with daily uncertainty, the pain and sudden vomiting, the enforced bed rest, and the lack of mental and physical energy. Although he spent so much of his day in bed, resting, he was exhausted, while any effort to take on the work he loved left him prostrated and in pain. His doctors had little real idea about the nature of his continual attacks, their advice often inconsistent. 'I certainly suspect strongly that the ulcer is still active', Dent had written to Lawrence in September 1941, 'and that I am liable to recurrence of the bad phases – so I am quite prepared to face an operation … The delay is tiresome, but I am not in the least worried about it, and am seizing the opportunity to get work finished.'[87] A few weeks later, another expensive consultation and X-ray made his doctor change his mind again, saying that there was no need for an operation. Dent

83 JG 01/08/1941

84 Skidelsky, *John Maynard Keynes: Fighting for Britain*, p. 287.

85 *Ibid.*, p. 289.

86 JG 13/03/1942.

87 LH 06/09/1941.

described how he made them all 'burst out laughing' by standing up in the X-ray frame, outlined in red, lights flashing, saying in his dry way 'this is rather like the *Crucifixion*'. He felt better most of that autumn, well enough to go down to London several times for Sadler's Wells Board meetings and to hear his motets being sung by the Fleet Street Choir, but after an extraction and some invasive dental work in January 1942, he was laid low again. He was still in bed throughout a cold February, any respite from the nagging pain 'a state of bliss!'.

> The pain that I get now is not so severe as it was, and is indeed bearable by itself: but any effort makes it worse, & in bed it prevents me sleeping – so that I have to take a lot of magnesia, wch produces diarrhoea, and I spend long periods lying still, trying to relax, feeling that I am on the verge of vomiting. But I do escape it, generally! so don't feel worried.[88]

The deafness which plagued his later years set in during the war. At the time, he blamed the cold winter, but by March 1942, he could not hear voices clearly on the telephone, while the 'big' acoustic in the Arts Theatre at a concert of 'modern' music made him uncomfortable. He made light of it all, refusing to dwell on any current setback or to consider that he might not recover, always battling to get back to normality, often having to pull out of concerts or meetings or pleasant dinners at the last minute. But he would not let himself be cast down, entertaining his friends with accounts drawn from all the informal bedside meetings he was having, where serious talk about production style was interlarded with gossip about why male opera singers 'flatly refuse to appear in bare legs, owing partly to the cold of the theatres, & partly (I suspect) to the fact that they never wash their feet'.

Determined, Dent went down to London for a few weeks in May, 'half the time in bed in considerable discomfort', and 'made a great explosion at the Wells Board which astonished the other members & delighted both Tony and Miss Glasgow'. The 'explosion' was about Sir George Dyson[89] 'forcing' Rudolf Bing onto Sadler's Wells as Manager. The long and disputatious meeting was underpinned by the need 'to keep the right side of, and perhaps give way to, certain unnamed people, friends of Chr. [John Christie] who supply the money & the political influences'.[90] Dent continued to argue for someone who knew the Wells and was sympathetic to its nature: 'J.C. [Joan Cross] has made such a success of this opera tour that I begin to think it might be a good plan to appoint her as Intendantin of Sadlers Wells, after the war is over'.[91] After three committee meetings (for ENSA, Sadler's Wells and the British Council) and a very congenial supper one evening at the Waldorf with Broadwood, he 'went home & vomited copiously'.[92]

Later that same week he still couldn't resist a lively lunch party at Flemmings Hotel with the entire Hirsch family; his doctor threatened him with a stomach

88 LH 07/03/1942.

89 Sir George Dyson (1883–1964), composer, Director of the Royal College of Music.

90 JG 25/05/1942.

91 JG 13/03/1942.

92 LH 24/05/1942.

pump if he didn't behave himself. Being forced back into a state of prostration he found 'most fatiguing', especially when his good manners dictated being unfailingly polite and apologetic to the nurses looking after him while he was throwing up. Poldi Gerhard brought the wireless around so he could listen to his translation of *Fra Diavolo* being sung; Lawrence Haward sent pots of honey and puddings; intimate friends like Broadwood made sure that there were young men at his bedside to cheer him up and tried to help with the practicalities of finding a place to live when he left Cambridge.

After a starvation diet and a few weeks of respite from sickness and pain, he was left too 'stupid and sleepy' to work, while his letters are full of enthusiastic, penetrating remarks about the current music which gave him so much pleasure through all the pain. CUMS had done an all-Mozart concert for May Week in King's Chapel, the 'Splendante te Deus' and the C minor Mass, which, with Paddy Hadley, Dent had edited for performance.

> It is a most astonishing work, with 2 immense & very academic fugues: one so dry-looking on paper, that both I and P. Hadley agreed it must be cut down – it really seemed more worthy of Ebenezer Prout. But when they sang it with the orchestra, complete, it sounded glorious & I wd not have missed a note. Tovey never cd understand ... that the academic "catholic" fugue – all strattos & inversions etc, with practically no episodes – wants the sound of human voices to make it alive.[93]

'The Wells opera seem to be doing well, & I get encouraging Press notices. The singers are at last beginning to see the advantages of my translations, and find that they get laughter & applause.'[94] The movement coaching he had advocated was now being addressed by Kurt Joos: 'I am very glad you liked the Flute & Joos's ideas', Dent wrote to Lawrence, 'I chose him because I wanted the opera to be more of a ballet'.

> He is now travelling regularly with the S.W. company, teaching them all movement etc and they seem to enjoy it very much. He likes the work too. It is amusing that this has come about without even my knowledge, for since 5 years ago I suggested that H. Lander ... shd be employed at S.W. to teach the singers how to move & stand etc the idea was very much rejected & it was supposed that the singers wd all resent it very much![95]

Joos's successful production of *The Magic Flute* was mostly sold out, and Dent was keen to do more in a similar vein: *Ballo in maschera, Orpheus, Bartered Bride*; he and JB came up with the novel idea of setting *Don Giovanni* in Mexico. 'Thirty years!' he exclaimed to Lawrence; it had taken thirty years for the idea to sink in that the words should be listened to:

93 LH 16/06/1942.

94 LH 24/05/1942.

95 LH 16/06/1942. This was the same Lander who nursed him.

> singers are incredible people: they really do think of nothing except their own individual voices, and the applause – applause not for the acting or interpretation, but just for the voice itself. We are still in the days of Halevy's La Juive, about 1836, where the Cardinal does hardly anything but demonstrate the power of his lungs on low E's and E flats![96]

Kalmus and Franckenstein tried to interest him in a scheme for 'a regular permanent Opera (if you can call it that!) with mainly refugees',[97] but Dent's objections were on the grounds of style ('Grosses Schauspielhaus minus the "Jackson boys"') and its fundamentally transient nature: such refugees would move on once the war was over and leave them stuck again. The refugees he did support, like the Gerhards or Kurt Joos, were part of the fabric.

He 'crashed' again in June while having tea with Joos, but to the despair of his doctor, flatly refused to go back into the Evelyn Nursing Home. He simply could not face the 'bedpans and enemas', and Hills, he decided could cook better food for him at home. 'And another thing that I find very exhausting in the nursing-home is the endless procession of the dear ministering angels, all so lady-like & so sweet & sympathetic (except perhaps the old dear who scrubs the floor).'

> I have missed the society of the young very much during these years of illness. I see someone perhaps one day & then hardly again for 3 or 4 months or more, & only hear of them through JB. I do not suffer from loneliness at all, and am very content to be alone, wch is rather a pity, perhaps. But I often find visitors, even JB, rather tiring.[98]

To give Hills a holiday, Dent went to stay with the Gerhards again in August, at Thorneycreek, where they had rented rooms out to JB, so it was easy and convenient for Dent simply to take up residence there and slip back into familiar routines. 'I am very tired of Cambridge … and I should love Cambridge if I could get to the libraries and work again. But I don't want to go to Concerts etc'.[99]

Now, Dent decided, was the time to move to London. He had officially retired from the Professorship in 1941, and the post was in abeyance. New Quebec Street was out of the question; Mrs Searl the housekeeper was negligent, possibly because the house itself was in such disrepair. Until his medical bills sucked up most of his savings, Dent had hoped to buy a house in the current deflated market; now he faced the bleak prospect of a retirement made uncertain by precarious health, not enough money, and no place to live in wartime. Although tempted by Hans Raab's repeated invitations to come out to Brazil, Dent decided against it, at least until the war was over and his health more settled. It was a difficult decision: he and JB had been increasingly predisposed towards the Americas, and Raab's current lifestyle was appealing to men who had been starved of a full social life for so long. But the decision had to be deferred yet again. All that autumn and into winter 1942–43, Dent

96 LH 16/06/1942.

97 JG 25/05/1942.

98 LH 16/06/1942.

99 JG 25/05/1942.

suffered terrible attacks, left prostrated, finally enduring another operation on 26 February, up in Manchester this time, being seen to by the father of one of his best pupils, W.R. Douglas, a surgeon far more expert and thorough.

> rather a nightmare as things had to be done in a bit of a hurry – a blood transfusion etc. and several stomach pumpings before the operation, and then for 2 days afterwards a good deal of pain & spasm, with a 'Ryle tube' [a thin rubber tube] down my throat into my stomach for 24 hours continuously, so that all the acid etc. could be pumped off every 2 hours or so … to prevent me from vomiting.[100]

But Douglas saved his life:

> when he saw my intestines, he was amazed that I should be alive at all & that no surgeon would have believed it possible for a man to write books & do continuous work with a duodenal ulcer of such a size and activity.[101]

His precarious finances notwithstanding, Dent decided to take a convalescent holiday for several weeks at the Methven Hotel at Grange-over-Sands, Lancashire. The Hawards saw him settled there before going back to Manchester, less than an hour away.

> I like the place, though so far we have had little sun … cooking excellent, and the manageress formerly a nurse & mistress of an nursing home, so that she knows exactly what I ought to have & allows me breakfast in bed. I have a ground floor room … as I am still horribly weak in the muscles of the waist & knees & always wanting to sit down. But I walk up & down the garden on the [?], with L.'s arm & a stick for about 1/4 hour twice a day & hope I am getting stronger.[102]

Three weeks of walks along the cold, windy beach, reading *Mein Kampf* along with the westerns he found in the local library, helped Dent rebuilt his strength, hoping that at long last the ulcer had been eradicated. Joan Cross wrote from Blackpool and Southport, where the Sadler's Wells company had been playing, asking Dent about the operas he had been advocating for ages, 'at considerable length', including *Der Freischütz*, *Orpheus* and *Don Giovanni*. 'I think', he wrote in his casually prescient way to Jack, 'if S.W. is going to attempt things on a larger scale now (NB thinking of Freischütz or Oberon) – as it well may, with the help of CEMA – I think it will have to start a second Ballet for employment only in opera.'

> If I do get back to really good health & strength, I want to go & see the S.W. company (and the Carl Rosa too) in London and if possible in other places – not the Arts Th. Cambridge, which is altogether exceptional in every way for many reasons. I should like to watch the reactions of a big provincial audience … to our shows.[103]

[100] JG 08/03/1943.

[101] JG 08/03/1943. See Appendix for more on this.

[102] JBT 26/03/1943.

[103] JG 09/04/1943.

He wrote to Jack about reviving *Fra Diavolo* now that there was a suitable tenor in the shape of young Peter Pears, 'a strong voice, great musicianship, & considerable good looks ... But I expect Collingwood has no use whatever for Auber, and ... no understanding of how to conduct him'.[104] Apart from a few attacks of lumbago that winter, for which he blamed the bitter cold, Dent was much better in mind and body for his enforced period of rest, and free of his Professorial responsibilities, his optimism returned and with it, his determination to pursue the long-term Sadler's Wells project.

While JB oversaw the entire removal, Dent stayed at Durrant's Hotel in Manchester Square, not far from his preferred part of town, seeing *Traviata* and *Figaro* at the New Theatre, and finally catching up with Douglas Hunt, one of his former Berlin crowd. At Dent's recommendation Hunt had made a living translating Hitler's early speeches, but fled to Britain with his German partner, Paul, settling in Pinner. As a German, Paul was interned and sent to an Australian camp, and Dent was keen to re-establish Hunt, getting Jack to look after him ('he is desperately poor but strictly honourable') and taking him to the opera.

As the bombing slowed down and his health improved, Dent spent part of his time in London house-hunting, with help of his niece Ruth Greenwood Richmond and his sister Catherine. By November Ruth had found something modest but suitable. 'I have got a flat – at 17 Cromwell Place S.W. 7. just opposite South Kensington Station. About 80 stairs and no lift!'

> 17 Cromwell Place will not be at all noisy I think as it is 3rd & 4th floors. No lift, and a good many stairs, but more of a view, & more sun & air both sides (east and west, more or less.) There are 4 good rooms, each 18 by 14, on 2 floors ... The big bedrooms are in an 'attic storey' with sloping walls ... No central heating ... The rooms are all very <u>low</u>. not much more than 8 ft – so I shd have to sacrifice my tall bookcase, or divide it. The 2 lower rooms are panellel ... very like College rooms![105]
>
> My niece advises me to make the lower east room my own bedroom, with a table for breakfast by the windows, wch I cd also use for other meals, for you & me together certainly, & there could be room to seat 4. Then I shd make the east room upstairs into a sort of study-workroom. You wd get quite a lot of western sun in your room: more than in Quebec St, I think ... I confess I disliked it all rather, at first, but I think I shd get accustomed to it, & cd make it cosy & comfortable. The total floor space of rooms (apart fr. kitchen & bath etc) is just over 1000 sq. ft: 50 sq feet more than my house in Panton Street.[106]

Immediately, Dent set to, taking a room in the nearby Rembrandt Hotel to 'direct workmen about decorations & electric fittings etc', besides keeping up with important committee meetings, ENSA or the Wells and going to the theatre. Having spent most of Christmas parcelling up books and music either to give away or to take with

104 JG 17/05/1943.
105 JBT 09/11/1943.
106 *Ibid.*

him – 'I have got rid of a huge lot, I am glad to say'[107] – he moved in on 31 January 1944, 'in spite of the fearful chaos'. It was another three weeks, though, before all the furniture from Cambridge was installed, the glass chandelier, another casualty of wartime conditions, sent off for repair. By March he was nearly normal, both his pianos now back from Broadwood's. 'Evelyn is very generous about other repairs & regulating etc. but I don't like to take advantage of it.'[108]

He now needed a 'manservant' to replace the retired Hills, and advertised in *The Times*. By now Dent had had enough of enforced female company; he wanted a man around, moreover one of the right sort. Hans Raab from Brazil recommended two possible candidates, one formerly in the Blues 'but I think he would be rather more than I could cope with'.[109] In the end he found a handsome former RAF pilot, 28-year-old H.A. Adie, immediately christened in the old angelic way 'Michael', who stayed with him for the rest of his life.[110]

1944–1945

> There are so many things I want to talk about, write about too, and more than that, I should like to do them and accomplish them – but I fear I must leave that to the next generation. I have become like Pfitzner – a tiresome old man with a grievance; one takes no notice of him.[111]

Dent's new flat, his new garden, meant a fresh start in every area of his daily life; from South Kensington he could easily get to concerts and meetings, have lunch with friends. His strength gradually returned, while his sense of purpose never deviated. With his London establishment up and running, 'Michael' efficiently assuming domestic control, Dent applied himself to the future of British opera. Even the bombs falling near enough to shatter the windows in his music-room didn't worry him; possibly he simply didn't hear, scorning to retreat down to the air-raid shelter. Scott Goddard reported 'the latest serpentism' to Jack Gordon in July: 'People of our class don't go to shelters.'[112]

1944 was a decisive year for the arts, especially opera, and all that winter and spring Dent began his real campaigning, not simply for reconstructing postwar arts, but revolutionising them. 'I am very good at drafting and getting things down on paper, as my father was, and I foresee that that is going to be one of my principal

[107] Quite a bit went to Cambridge or to the RCM library.

[108] JG 19/02/1944.

[109] JG 24/01/1944.

[110] Opinions seem to be mixed about him, although it is always difficult to assess such relationships from the outside. Christopher Raeburn encountered him when he visited Dent in the early 1950s, and felt that Michael was rather brusque and rough with Dent, who by then was becoming frail and almost completely deaf. Told to the author in 2007.

[111] EWW 03/09/1944.

[112] Goddard to Gordon 10/07/1944. Gordon correspondence.

jobs in the near future.'[113] The immediate problems were legion: 'it is hardly possible to make plans for a month ahead because nobody knows who will be available at the date to carry them out'.[114] Even with the war turning and a chance now to move back to a London base, the Vic–Wells companies were simply too exhausted and demoralised after years of relentless touring and constant improvising in the harshest conditions, juggling musicians and singers. Lawrence Collingwood was now 'practically a corpse';[115] Oliver Messel had done some 'sumptuous' designs for the projected *Queen of Spades*, but nothing could go forward until the the Wells had a settled place and finances; the building itself was still a mess. Guthrie had maintained the separation of drama and opera; the Vic continued at the New Theatre, while Dent and Guthrie looked out for a suitable alternative to the bombed-out Wells.

'I don't know what is actually going to happen at S.W.', Dent wrote to Jack that March:

> We don't want to go back to that theatre as long as it is so inaccessible and no food obtainable. Tony [Guthrie] wants to have the New Theatre all to himself for Drama, with a considerable scheme for a permanent Company ... We were offered the 65 year lease of the Piccadilly Th: but declined to buy. The price was enormous and T.G. [Guthrie] says the theatre is like a Pompadour's bedroom ... There is talk of getting the Savoy, which has a goodish orchestra pit & is suitable for opera – I hope we may come to terms. Failing that, I urge going to the King's Th. Hammersmith if we can get it to ourselves. It holds 1700 according to 'Who's Who in the Theatre' and is a pleasant looking house and very easily accessible by tube & rail & bus: also there are restaurants close by. Failing a real 'West End' Theatre, I think the King's Th. is the next best thing.[116]

For a year, the opera wound up shuffling between the New Theatre and Prince's. They needed a West End theatre, but it was the old story: West End theatres could get higher rents for popular shows. Moreover, the sources of funding – especially CEMA – were at the point of evolving painfully into their postwar entities; everyone concerned was beginning to think beyond the war without knowing exactly how to go about it.

> I wish these subsidizing bodies would co-operate and all help us together instead of being so jealous. CEMA is not loved anywhere very much – though I myself feel more at home with CEMA than with any of the other nymphs.[117]

The battles to establish an 'English' opera company were prolonged and messy. Dent remained clear in his own aims:

> As regards a National Opera – I hear from Dyson that the L.C.C. [London County Council] wish to develop Southwark and the Bankside as a sort of Art

113 CC 16/01/1944.

114 ATFE, p. 132 and CC 16/01/1944. Dent recycled much of what he wrote to Clive into ATFE. It was written in 1944 but not published until November 1945.

115 Dent made sure to praise Collingwood for his 'inestimable services' to the cause of English opera. ATFE, pp. 155–6.

116 JG 11/03/1944.

117 *Ibid.*

and Theatre centre; but even if they do it it will take them a great many years, and wherever the new Opera House is eventually to be, I think we must get started as soon as possible with a temporary one, already existing.

The 'mandarins' do not seem to be interested in Opera in the least, I find … The trouble about the Wells people is that they are terrified of embarking on any new scheme and any thing that is outside their Trust articles. Some of the, [sic] quite reasonably, cling to the old idea of cheap opera for the people and the ghost of Miss Cons. What I should like to see would be a really first-rate Royal and National Opera in English in an important central theatre, and elsewhere, either at the Vic or Wells, popular opera at cheap prices, as we are running it now. Singers and conductors etc would begin their career in the Popular Opera and graduate from that to the Royal Opera; there would also be the question of the provincial centres: should they have each their own permanent stock opera company, or should they be dependent on touring companies sent out by the Royal and the Popular Opera Houses in conjunction?[118]

From Dent's point of view the most serious threats to his vision for postwar opera were apathy and ignorance; he wrote article after article on 'The Future of Opera in England', 'The Future of British Opera', 'Rebuilding for Music',[119] and urged on by Guthrie, written in less than three months, *A Theatre for Everybody*, his history of the Vic and Wells – 'what I am trying to do is to show the Vic & Wells in the general perspective of London theatrical history'.[120] Its last chapter, 'The Prospect Before Us',[121] was written before the war had ended. The book covers theatre, ballet and opera in equal measure, with excellent potted histories of all three, but the central point is never left in doubt: to demonstrate the real need for 'national' theatre, ballet and opera, supported and sustained by the public, but not confined to London.

The difficulties of the war years have at least shown us the urgent importance of bringing both opera and drama to places where such things have perhaps hardly ever been seen or heard before. In developing our provincial tours we are educating new audiences to an understanding and love of the real theatre … many of us fear that a time may come when the living theatre will exist only as a highly specialised entertainment for a small coterie of intellectuals, or may even cease to exist at all.[122]

If the Old Vic and Sadler's Wells are to become truly national theatres they must achieve that status, subsidized or not, by their own creative efforts and the public's whole-hearted acknowledgement of them.[123]

Yet again Dent laid out his case against the old Covent Garden style of opera house, with opera given in a foreign language, its cult of the conductor and of the star singer, with often little regard for the quality of the music or the production; he

118 EWW 18/02/1944.

119 *CEMA Bulletin* (March 1944); MMR (December 1944).

120 JBT 28/06/1944.

121 ATFE.

122 *Ibid.*, p. 150.

123 *Ibid.*, p. 151.

argued for a fresh new approach for a fresh generation, shedding all the old baggage and looking to the future. The questions are raised, the answer left in no doubt even as the reader is carefully guided to the conclusions:

> the considerable body of persons who are seriously concerned with music and drama as indispensable factors in our cultural life, and since these persons are for the most part fairly young, they are precisely the section of the community for whom the future is most important and they are also the persons whose duty it is to take the lead in the shaping and ordering of that future.[124]

But even while he was exerting himself to present the case to the public, Dent knew that any real decisions about the future of the Vic–Wells would take place outside official committee meetings.

In 1944, Covent Garden was in poor shape again, surviving the war as a Mecca Café. John Christie had been keen to buy it and make it a London base for his Glyndebourne operas, 'a centre of cultural reconstruction' to be run along the same principles, but with a bid for government backing. He knew all the right people to approach for support, but he was thwarted. In April 1944, the Covent Garden Trust was created, which included publishers Boosey & Hawkes, agent Harold Holt and CEMA representatives Stanley Marchant and Kenneth Clark.[125] They took a five-year lease from Covent Garden Properties Ltd, with the view to producing opera and ballet, recreating an old-fashioned 'Italian' opera house with foreign stars and expensive seats, prestige and opulence in the old grand manner. In May the Covent Garden Trust invited an incorporation with Sadler's Wells, what Dent had always adamantly opposed, and after some heavy debate he won the day, the offer turned down by the Sadler's Wells governors. As Dent wrote to Clive, Boosey 'really had no use for English opera or opera in English sung by English singers at all'.[126] But by August, the Covent Garden Trust committee had expanded to include John Maynard Keynes, who had chaired CEMA so successfully throughout the war, steering it through the constant bickerings of 'captious and cantankerous people', and who had already been thinking seriously about its postwar nature – whether it should subsidise buildings or performers, be a grant-distributing body or an operating body.[127] He excluded from a revived Covent Garden Board 'anyone with any experience of producing opera before the war … from the planning, management

124 *Ibid.*, p. 133.

125 Gilbert, *Opera for Everybody*, pp. 90–91.

126 CC 25/05/1944.

127 Skidelsky, *John Maynard Keynes: Fighting for Britain*, p. 292. In September 1944, while he was also negotiating the Bretton Woods agreement and the postwar finances of the country and the world order, Keynes produced a memorandum outlining the 'Royal Council for the Arts', a panel of eleven, five of which were the executive committee. His proposals were taken up in January 1945, and The Arts Council of Great Britain was established: '"we soon found", Keynes said, "that we were providing what had never existed even in peacetime"'.

or artistic direction of the new venture: Beecham, Rudolf Bing, Carl Ebert, Eugene Goossens'.[128] He immediately asked Dent.

On the face of it Keynes's decision was understandable; he had known Dent, his politics and his musical principles, for a long time. Keynes was himself diffident about music and opera, but he had always known how to choose his advisers and listen to advice, and, quite apart from the fact that Keynes and John Christie loathed each other, Keynes had long been predisposed to support and promote Dent's principles.[129]

> What you say about the modern opera audiences being young is very important. They are young, and they enjoy opera because they hear it in English and can understand it and laugh when it is comic. 'Nobody ever laughs at Glyndebourne,' said Christie to me once, meaning that something must be very wrong at S.W. because people did laugh there.[130]

But Keynes had his own ideas about what constituted 'excellence', and to achieve this he decided that a revived Covent Garden, with big productions, the best singers and musicians and directors, was to be at the forefront of new 'national' opera: 'English performers ... building on the sound beginnings already made by Sadler's Wells'.[131] He wanted London's opera, a Royal Opera House, with resident ballet company, a centre of international importance, and according to his biographer, he was too afraid that Sadler's Wells, especially with its out-of-the-way theatre and its statutory commitment to low-cost, high-quality productions, was simply not up to the mark.[132] Over the next year the future of both institutions was thrashed out, with Keynes in the powerful background role pulling the strings. Once decided, it took just one note from Keynes to Second Secretary Sir Alan Barlow in January 1945 to secure the principle and the funding, 'drafted with the practised skill of one insider talking to another'.[133] Dent's own methods had been turned against him.

Dent accepted a compromise: a place on the Covent Garden Board and a voice in the decision-making of both opera companies. The board, now headed by Keynes, included Mary Glasgow of CEMA, another of Dent's allies, with Samuel Courtauld, music publishers Leslie Boosey and Ralph Hawkes, Kenneth Clark, Stanley Marchant and William Walton. Initially Dent was cautiously optimistic, while recognising that

128 *Ibid.*, p. 297. According to William Walton, Beecham was asked to be Music Director, but turned it down. Letter to Leslie Boosey 01/08/1944 in *The Selected Letters of William Walton 1936–1948* ed. Malcolm Hayes (London, 2002), p. 149.

129 As Skidelsky, *ibid.*, p. 297, points out, in blocking Christie's earlier bid to buy Covent Garden, Keynes did him 'a great service'; his focus on Glyndebourne built it into the most successful ever independent opera house. Interestingly, it became an exponent for many of Dent's principles: high production standards; excellent, often unknown singers; touring; and education. And the audience is encouraged to laugh.

130 EWW 03/09/1943.

131 KP:PP/84 (8) Keynes Papers in KCA, quoted in Skidelsky, *John Maynard Keynes: Fighting for Britain*, p. 296.

132 Skidelsky told me this in an e-mail.

133 Skidelsky, *John Maynard Keynes: Fighting for Britain*, p. 296.

battles still had to be fought – in fact the battles would go on for the rest of his life and beyond. He had discovered another important supporter in the well-fed shape of a jovial Liverpool draper called David Webster, the new Covent Garden manager. 'I am encouraging his self-confidence and love of power, because I want to be one of the experts whose advice he takes.'[134] Webster loved music and theatre, while his business experience running the Bon Marché department store was put to immediate use: he knew how the shop window attracts the patrons. Dent wrote to Clive that Webster agreed with his ideas about eschewing the 'old Covent Garden system of miscellaneous stars all singing in German or Italian with English singers allowed to do small parts, with no proper rehearsal or production'.[135] Like Guthrie, Webster was a consummate diplomat, shrewd enough to assess where his future lay. He devoted himself to Covent Garden and the revival of its past splendours, but from the outset determined that this time, it was going to last.

Throughout that autumn of 1944 the postwar identities of the two main opera houses were hotly debated, even as Dent and Guthrie drew up a 'memorandum' which clearly set out their vision. As he wrote to Clive, still in Australia, echoing what Keynes was saying about the Arts Council:

> I said to Tony [Guthrie] – and Tony did understand – 'What we are aiming at is something that has not yet been seen anywhere, and which only exists in our imagination, even if yours and mine don't exactly coincide, but these Covent Gardeners can't imagine anything; they can only remember what they have once seen, either at C.G. or at Vienna or elsewhere and want to set up that as a standard.'[136]

Dent and Guthrie presented the idea for a separate Sadler's Wells and Covent Garden, whereby the different styles could be exploited, with Sadler's Wells the 'Opéra Comique' of Dent's vision, and Covent Garden the home of 'grand' opera.[137] The two committees remained unconvinced, and the debate went on for nearly another year.

> October:
>
> Negotiations with S.W. and C.G. are still going on & I am now acting as the link between the two … I get on very well with Webster … I think that in practice S.W. will go on as before, but tending always more definitely to <u>Opéra-Comique</u> and abandoning all Wagner & noisy Verdi to C.G. C.G. will probably go on more or less as before: I don't see what else it can do. At best a new sort of BNOC, but I very much fear a Gerry Cooper season with foreign stars from all sorts of places & English singers in minor parts: no rehearsal or 'production' – Still, Webster <u>is</u> keen on production himself & may be able to effect improvements.[138]

134 CC 17/08/1944.

135 *Ibid.*

136 CC 25/09/1944.

137 Susie Gilbert in her history of English National Opera says that 'had it been adopted it might have saved many tears later'. *Opera for Everybody*, p. 92.

138 JG 25/10/1944.

November:

As regards Cov. Gard. I fear more & more that it is just going back to the old rut – Gerry will enjoy it. Sam Courtauld says 'the main thing is that we shd have a pedigree herd [of singers] – & that all small operas are perfectly suitable to Cov. Gard.'[139]

December:

I am going to a S.W. & C.G. meeting this aftn, rather doubtful as to my position. S.W. sent me no notice of it, expecting that C.G. would send me as one of their representatives: C.G. sent me no notice expecting that S.W. would summon me! Evelyn Broadwood only told me of the meeting on Tuesday night & said it was urgent that I should come.[140]

Dent travelled up to Liverpool to meet with Webster, Guthrie and Joan Cross. He loved the 'new' concert hall and was happy to travel up there from time to time, enjoying Webster's warm hospitality at his 'charming old house in the suburbs', and hearing Joan Cross in Michael Tippett's 'new' oratorio, *A Child of Our Time*.

Tippett's oratorio is a fine work … I went to hear it yesty rather prejudiced: but it is quite different from what I feared … It has a great contrapuntal austerity, expressive, not pedantic. And there are negro spirituals instead of chorales – wch I thought wd be absurd – but they are most beautifully arranged for the voices & sound very moving, very sincere & real.[141]

The encounter marked the beginning of his friendship with Tippett, while Liverpool had become the provincial cultural centre Dent had hoped to see emerging out of the war, after its kick-start from CEMA, a useful place for the Covent Garden Board to meet and engage with the Vic–Wells people there. Guthrie was there producing a play, Ninette de Valois was en route from Ireland, Walton was there to hear the Tippett. It was in Liverpool that musical history was made on 19 March, when Guthrie, Joan Cross and Lawrance Collingwood listened to Benjamin Britten play through his new opera *Peter Grimes* on the piano.

While in the middle of all these operatic wranglings, Dent was also enjoying overseeing his new edition of *The Beggar's Opera* being produced in a Birmingham tent that May by Katharine Thomson's Clarion Singers. 'I wish you could have seen my version of The Beggar's Opera at Birmingham last week', he wrote to Jack:

Saturday night brought a real Saturday night's audience, mostly female, who shrieked and howled with delight whenever they saw Macheath kiss a harlot on the stage – it must have been just like their own experiences with American soldiers … The performances were given in an old circus tent erected by the Corporation on a devastated area near the station … The singers … an allegedly Communist choral society were extremely good and acted far better than

[139] JBT 12/11/1944.
[140] JG 08/12/1944.
[141] JBT 12/11/1944.

> I had expected ... They knew the music marvellously and hardly made a single mistake, in spite of the chaos of the orchestra. The Corp. had promised us a professional orchestra, but the most professional thing about them was their reluctance to rehearse.[142]

Dent felt that his scoring had worked. 'The general effect of the strings was like girls who had just missed a bus and were vainly trying to catch it up ... I was especially pleased with the wind ensembles, which I had feared might go wrong altogether, as the scoring was rather experimental.' It was put on again at the 'People's Palace' in December, a vast, freezing barn of a place.[143] Under-rehearsed, 'arctic', and with a breakdown on the tube which meant that the orchestra had to walk the last mile to the hall and a reduced audience. Scott Goddard and Eric White had both liked it very much, and the small audience had given it a warm reception, 'so I don't much care whether it was a "success" in the commercial sense or not'.

❧ ❧ ❧

Then the war was over. Labour won the 1945 General Election by a landslide, the wartime coalition party led by Churchill consigned to history. Because of his battles to bring government to recognise the importance of the arts, Dent had long been predisposed to Labour, who alone of the three main parties showed itself prepared to engage with the arts at a public level.

> During the General Election of 1929 members of the British Drama League were invited by the committee of the League to ask Parliamentary candidates if they would pledge themselves to support a reasonable grant for a National Theatre, if and when the question was raised in the next Parliament.
>
> The Conservative candidate replied that while in sympathy with the arts there would be no funds available for such a purpose. The audience received the question and answer with laughter. The Liberal candidate said the he thought he could say yes. The audience received the question and answer in silence. The Labour candidate replied emphatically 'Yes' and devoted five minutes to explaining the need for a National Theatre and National Opera. The audience received the question and answer with applause. The sender of this information deduced from it (1) that the Labour candidate was the only one of the three who had given thought to the question put before him; (2) that the Labour audience was the only one alive to the fact that a National Theatre would aid the culture of the people.
>
> The reader may be interested to learn that the Conservative candidate on this occasion was the Right Honourable Winston Churchill.[144]

But the war had changed some fundamental attitudes. The Beveridge Report of 1942, drafted by the same man who had seen fit to rescue refugee academics in 1933, pre-

142 JG 29/05/1944.

143 In the Mile End Road in East London, now part of Queen Mary College, University of London.

144 ATFE, p. 8.

sented the vision of a welfare state, with equal opportunities for everyone in health, education and access to the ideas which lifted them out of poverty of the mind. Both Guthrie and David Webster had taken on some of Dent's ideas about future opera and theatre policy, as Guthrie's 'memorandum' shows, but in 1945 Webster had yet to commit himself, with his new responsibilities for Covent Garden as yet untested. The various interested parties ranged around Covent Garden and Sadler's Wells consisted of big personalities with impossibly strong views.

One critical point came in the winter of 1945, when Sadler's Wells was in the middle of acrimonious yet exciting rehearsals for the new opera which everyone believed was the bright new hope of 'English' opera. *Peter Grimes* was to be the first production back in Sadler's Wells, a statement of its future, so it was unthinkable that the company should have to fall back on its tattered old sets and costumes. In March 1945, the Sadler's Wells Chairman Lord Lytton had applied to Keynes for CEMA support of this promising but expensive new opera, an application by no means straightforward as Sadler's Wells and Covent Garden were still wrangling over the terms of their relationship, and Keynes was head of both CEMA and Covent Garden.

Then there was the question of the ballet. Ninette de Valois was keen to move to Covent Garden, and Keynes himself wanted the ballet company for Covent Garden, but not its 'weaker operatic sister'.[145] Basically, Keynes wanted everything achieved by the Wells so far except the Wells itself, with all its accumulated baggage; as far as he was concerned, the Wells would either be incorporated into Covent Garden or left to wither. When Sadler's Wells asked for compensation in view of the fact that they would lose revenue from the popular ballet and have to start up again from scratch, Keynes responded by saying that nothing could be done until Guthrie and Webster had sorted out between them what their respective companies' futures would be. On 1 May, Keynes wrote to the Sadler's Wells governors, the 'Keynes Letter', proposing that the Covent Garden Committee should take over the two Sadler's Wells companies, reserving the right to get rid of as many singers as it saw fit. As compensation, Sadler's Wells would get 2000 pounds per annum for four years; if they agreed, CEMA funds would be available to finance other activities, including an opera school. Sir George Dyson riposted with the proposal that both companies be managed by a joint committee with a single grant from CEMA, plus 30,000 pounds compensation paid to Sadler's Wells for the loss of the ballet company. 'There are endless complications as regards Cov. Gard. and also as regards S.W. & the S.W. companies themselves', Dent wrote to Jack in June. 'I expect you know more than I do. Luckily Dyson has suddenly thrown his weight onto the scales & come down heavily for English opera: & Clive returns this summer.'[146]

Some resolution came that August, when Keynes as Chair of the new Arts Council offered Lytton a guarantee of 5,000 pounds per annum; a derisory sum. At this most critical time, with the major premiere of *Peter Grimes* carrying the general hopes for the future, everyone was affected, Britten later recalling that he 'thought

145 Skidelsky, *John Maynard Keynes: Fighting for Britain*, p. 298.

146 JG 17/06/1945.

the whole thing would be a disaster'.[147] Morale was rock-bottom, even for a company that together had so recently endured so much. After three weeks of seeing how the uncertainty was undermining rehearsals at the Wells, Guthrie wrote to Dent that it was having 'a disintegrating effect' on everyone concerned, forcing him to produce a major restructuring of both companies – what is now called 'fire-fighting' – about which he wanted Dent's advice. He felt that the members of CEMA, and by implication, Keynes himself, really should not be taking artistic decisions and were compromised by their clashing responsibilities. With remarkable insensitivity – or calculation? – the mandatory contracts limited to six weeks were issued just before the opening night of this wonderful new opera, and the union representatives made their own positions clear. Now, together with most of the Sadler's Wells Board, including Dyson, Lytton, Dent and Dent's long-time allies, the company expressed its firm desire to remain at Sadler's Wells.

> I went to the first night of Peter Grimes & was much impressed with its originality & its dramatic force. I told P.P. [Peter Pears, singing Grimes] that he looked more like Struwwelpeter – and I also said the opera was out of Wozzeck by The Wreckers ... Anyway it is a great thing to have achieved a box-office success with new British opera and it will greatly strengthen the position of S.W.[148]

Although the war had ended in May, the battle for the Vic and Wells continued throughout 1945. Dent was heavily involved, but his increasing deafness meant that he quite literally did not hear everything that was going on. His constant writings on the subject, though, provided both testimony and reminder of what the aims had been for so long and what might now so easily be lost. First, there was the series of pamphlets, The Sadler's Wells Opera Books, produced that summer for the reopening season, one on each opera being produced, with the first one, *Opera in English*, a joint effort from Guthrie, Dent, Joan Cross, Ninette de Valois and Edwin Evans. They are less the usual kind of programme notes than a blueprint for educating and informing the audience, something Dent had been doing since the 1911 *Magic Flute.* Guthrie's article, 'Opera in English', is a lively and typical product of Guthrie's collaboration with Dent on the subject, a statement of intent and vision. He argues that fundamentally there needed to be more widespread knowledge about the art of opera; enthusiasm, while commendable, was not enough to sustain an art-form.

> This series of books is designed to supplement the performances given by the Sadler's Wells company; and, by making opera more intelligible, to relate it more closely to the life of every one of us. Without such a relation, opera must remain an exotic. It is our belief that if it does so remain, something valuable will be lost to our culture, and we shall be cut off from a source of great enjoyment and stimulation ... Opera is drama set to music: the dramatic element should be, and in the standard works is, the complement of the music – the one illuminates the other, and one without the other is a lamp without a battery.[149]

147 Quoted in Gilbert, *Opera for Everybody*, p. 98.

148 JG 17/06/1945.

149 'Opera in English', in *Opera in English*, p. 10.

Dent's article, 'The Future of British Opera', is much longer, a strong reminder of the basic questions being asked at this most critical time: Why has London, unlike other capital cities, 'never maintained a Royal or National Opera? This question has been asked so often by the foreign visitor to England that our musicians and musical critics have long become tired of it. They have become tired because they have never attempted to think out an answer.' Then why there was so little native tradition of composition, reiterating the history of Britain's 'fashionable' fascination for Italian opera to the exclusion of native talent. He credits 'idealistic' Carl Rosa and Moody-Manners with supporting the few British-born opera composers in the last century.

> Experiment in so elaborate a medium as opera must necessarily be expensive; and public contempt is all the more galling when it spells ruin … The time has come when we ought to consider a long-term policy for Sadler's Wells and for English opera in general. Can we honestly say that we have had any policy worthy of the name in the past? Can we indeed discover any such policy for English opera in the history of the last three centuries?[150]

But it was a rear-guard action. Reviews continued to highlight the lingering weaknesses, even of *Peter Grimes*. Guthrie's authority was being eroded; a tour of Hamburg and Germany that autumn, sponsored by ENSA, had been organised without his knowledge, undermining the planned recording of *Peter Grimes*. Dent was initially optimistic.

> I hope the Sadler's Wells ENSA tour will go through happily; I shan't feel quite secure till I hear of their opening night at Hamburg. There were endless worries and difficulties, and I had to do a great deal of peace-making … And it is much more important that I should be here when the question of the new Director comes up for discussion – that is, if Sir George will allow any sort of discussion. With him 'Mussolini ha sempre ragione!'[151]

The continental tour had mixed success, but artistic achievement was eroded by the company's shock at a trip to Belsen and the postwar devastation throughout Holland and Germany, on top of problems with casting and scenery. Those who had been most energetic in keeping it all together in the hardest times were now departing: Joan Cross resigned in late August, with Guthrie resigning at last on 12 December. Dyson, who had known Clive Carey at the Royal College of Music, was happy for him to replace Cross as Director for Sadler's Wells for the time being. Throughout that unsettling autumn Dent's attention was mostly taken up with lecturing at Liverpool and Leeds, but his persuasive writing continued unabated, with even more articles on the subject in 1946;[152] his advocacy would continue for the rest of his life. But Dent's had become a lone voice in support of the Wells as the

150 E.J. Dent, 'The Future of British Opera', in *Opera in English*, pp. 26–47.

151 Mussolini is always right! JG 22/08/1945.

152 'The Future of Opera in England', in *The Penguin Music Magazine* (December 1946); 'English Opera and Opera in English', in *Hinrichsen's Musical Year Book*, 1946. Haward, *Edward J. Dent: A Bibliography*, 153 and 164.

standard-bearer of English opera; all official attention was now on the revived, subsidised Covent Garden.

By the time its new season opened on Boxing Day 1945, the Wells company had been drained of everything and everyone that had kept it going so far, with only the departure of the ballet yet to happen in February, and the concomitant loss of income and worse, loss of prestige. Rebuilding yet again almost from scratch, the Wells was forced to exercise remarkable talent-spotting skills, yet again making a virtue of necessity, but by now its reputation was in shreds. Even former allies like Steuart Wilson, coming onto the Covent Garden Board from the BBC, argued against supporting Sadler's Wells any more. Many of its talented and devoted people were going either to the Garden or – like Joan Cross and Eric Crozier – off to join Britten's new English Opera Group. The lowest ebb was probably that December, after Guthrie's resignation, when everything pointed to the rise of Covent Garden, with its manifesto for everything Dent had tried to build up at the Wells: high production values, the nurturing of opera in English and of native talent. Dent had even felt the need to beg Desmond Shawe-Taylor to hold back on an article for *The New Statesman* which raised these issues. When Clive did at last return from Australia 'in roaring health – looking very pink & fresh and 10 years younger!',[153] he hesitated at taking on the near-impossible task of running the place, insisting that it was only temporary.

In spite everything thrown at it, the Wells did manage to survive, attracting new talent and new audiences, mostly through the energies of its dedicated board. The BBC had helped to educate the public palate for music, raising the bar against shoddy musical standards; ex-servicemen returning from Italy and Germany had been exposed to opera there and were getting up opera parties.[154] Dent's little book, *A Theatre For Everybody*, was a popular success, 'the whole edition (10,000) … sold already',[155] and helped to raise public awareness. 'James Agate says the book reads like Bradshaw.'[156] Five years later, it is clear that uncertainty had become the norm:

> The financial situation is dreadful. The theatre is often sold out and the average takings are about £385 out of a possible £400; but the Arts Council subsidy of £45,000 is not enough owing to the enormous expense of all overheads now – Covent Garden gets £145,000, but is not doing nearly so well (except on Ballet night) and is altogether on the wrong track. People are saying now that S.W. is much better than C.G. Webster still wants to get the beau monde and foreign stars: but the foreign stars that he does get are very poor stuff and the British singers really do far better – having mostly learned their job at S.W.[157]

The summer of 1945 had brought news of old friends in Europe. Camille Prior's son had 'released' Hans Strohbach from prison; Dent's nephew in the Coldstream Guards had met Philipp Jarnach at Bad Godesberg and forwarded a letter from him

153 JG 12/10/1945.

154 Gilbert, *Opera for Everybody*, p. 112 citing the *Daily Telegraph*.

155 JG 25/11/1945.

156 JG 15/12/1945.

157 LH 25/02/1950.

to Dent; by September Jarnach was reunited with his son in Munich. Boris Ord, stationed at Celle, 'much surprised to find that the organist of the church there knew me!'[158] The Sterns, Dent discovered, had escaped and were living in Hampstead. Letters gradually began to trickle through, from Curt Sembach, from Strohbach at the Braunschweiges Staatstheater, asking Dent to his German premiere of Vaughan Williams' 'Shepherds of the Delectable Mountains'.[159] Kurt Engisch was working at the American library and later at a big bookseller; his Berlin house had been burnt. Jack Gordon began to rebuild the old networks, asking Dent to put in a word for Strohbach at Covent Garden or the Wells: 'C.G. regards me with utter contempt (though very polite). Ditto Sadler's Wells (except that they are not contemptuous!).'[160] When Strohbach died in 1949, Engisch told Dent that 'wir hatten Ihn immer verdächtig, un malade imaginaire zu spielen' (we'd always thought his un malade imaginaire). Hans Raab and Eugene Szenkar were living in South America, Szenkar wishing to return to Europe. Fred Riley was running a hotel in Welshpool and had married. But although some former refugees had indeed returned to Germany, many were now settled abroad and helping to build music and theatre in their new homes; Europe's loss was the Americas' gain.

Dent was busy giving lectures at Liverpool and Leeds, revising an edition of *Mozart's Operas* for Oxford University Press and working with Clive on a new production of *Figaro* for Sadler's Wells that winter. More ghosts from the past appeared: after two wartime festivals in the USA, the ISCM was gradually returning to its European roots. Dent's successor, Edwin Evans, had died in 1945, and he was being recalled: 'I have got to tackle the problem of an ISCM Festival in London in 1946.'[161]

158 Dent, that is. JG 12/08/1945.

159 Strohbach to Dent 02/02/1945, KCA.

160 JG 10/01/1948.

161 JG 15/12/1945.

CHAPTER 16

Tityvillus 1946–1957

I go about like Onan, spilling my seed on the ground, and find that mostly very stony and barren, but a few seedlings occasionally come up and even flower.[1]

I know that in my old age I become more and 'possessed' by the devil – I call him Tityvillus, as I suspect he is that famous musical character of the English Middle Ages … who makes me see everything in a ridiculous light.[2]

Old age is not for the faint-hearted.[3]

Dent's seventieth birthday on 16 July 1946 was celebrated by a garden party at the Hirsch family home in west Cambridge, with friends and colleagues who were also 'tacitly expressing to him their gratitude for his inestimable service in helping to secure the Paul Hirsch Music Library for the nation'.[4] Dent had written an article in *The Times*, 'Need for a central music library: Value of the Hirsch collection',[5] stirring up public interest in the case. One of the world's great music collections was now in the British Museum, the cornerstone of a national music library, bought with a 'special grant' from the Treasury and a grant from the Pilgrim Trust of 120,000 pounds. 'At the end of the war, it was far from easy to raise such a very large sum of money, and the successful conclusion of the delicate negotiations was due in no small measure to Dent's powerful advocacy, both in public and behind the scenes.'[6] The Chancellor of the Exchequer was Dent's old Cambridge friend Hugh Dalton. Although offered a knighthood by the Attlee government, Dent turned it down, never mentioning it in his letters.

Cambridge finally rewarded Dent with an honorary doctorate in 1947, but far more important to him, Music was at last on the Tripos, with a solid curriculum in place. Visiting Cambridge was now unalloyed pleasure; each time Dent could see all around him just what he had been working to achieve there, with the Marlowe Society more active than ever, the Greek Play revived, and eventually the Cambridge

1 LH 29/03/1949.

2 LH 17/08/1949.

3 Marjorie Hewish to the author.

4 Alec Hyatt King, 'Paul Hirsch and his Music Library', *British Library Journal* (1981).

5 *The Times* (26 April 1946).

6 King, 'Paul Hirsch and his Music Library', p. 4.

University Opera Society thriving beside the CUMS and the CUMC. And his part was appreciated:

> An insistence on performance as the ultimate goal lay behind his approach to scholarship ... he consistently aimed at giving the curriculum greater breadth as a sound foundation, stressing particularly the study of music history and encouraging the performance of pre-19th century, especially Baroque, music.[7]

After his birthday celebrations Dent reconnected more with Cambridge, working on the Fellowship committee to examine Peter Tranchell's opera, lecturing the Musica Antica e Nuova Society on Stradella, finding yet another place for himself there. The new people like Thurston Dart delighted him, while old friends like Dadie Rylands kept him in touch with his past. He was pleased to be asked by his former pupil, Jill Vlasto, to advise on a production of Cavalieri's *Rappresentazione di anima e di corpo*, which Girton proposed to put on for a May Week show, 'as a part of the celebrations for Miss Butler's retirement as Mistress, and Miss Butler is a very great Italian scholar, so they think it will be appropriate'.[8]

> Mrs Vlasto (Jill Medway), one of my Girton pupils, now a lecturer in Music at Girton and married to A.P. Vlasto, an Etonian Greek who is a Fellow of King's, is arranging the music and producing the show. I stayed with the Vlastos, who are well off and have a very comfortable house in Adams Road – though my bedroom was rather cold! and had the advantage of the company of Robert Thurston Dart, who lodges with them; he is a recent importation to Cambridge, and lectures on Musical History. He is not much over thirty, I think, and quite incredibly learned; also a very good harpsichord player and a most amusing and attractive personality.[9]

The Vlastos were genuinely fond of Dent; he often stayed with them and is still remembered with awe and affection by the family.

His seventieth birthday also inspired Egon Wellesz to make a public testimonial:

> In normal times our Society would have presented you, its President, with the customary Festschrift ... this was impossible in the present circumstances. But you do not need such a conventional sign of affection. You have always done your work without éclat, and have found your satisfaction in furthering the appreciation of music as an essential part of our civilization, combining scholarly research with performances which made the music of the past accessible to the public.
>
> Speaking as one of your oldest friends, I should like to say that yours is a unique position among the great scholars who have advanced the study of the History of Music. You are the legitimate heir and successor of Dr Burney; like him, you visited the Continent and made contacts which were of value not only to your work but also to the musicians of many countries. But you did more than this: you succeeded in changing the musical climate of England. In the early days when you wrote your book on Scarlatti you made it clear to them what Opera

7 'Edward J. Dent' article in New Grove (2nd edn, 2001); by Nigel Fortune and Anthony Lewis, both former Dent pupils.

8 LH 12/02/1949.

9 LH 08/03/1949.

> meant to the people of Italy, France and Germany. Your masterly translations of libretti, beginning with those of Mozart, made Opera accessible to a wider public in England, and helped to create the atmosphere in which it was possible for it to take root in musical life. Your efforts, so long hindered by untoward circumstances, were finally crowned with success, and now you are taking part in the foundation of a permanent Opera, the fulfilment of your hopes.
>
> All these activities, however, represent only one side of your work. While you held the Chair of Music at Cambridge you gave the fruits of your knowledge to generations of young musicians and inspired them to follow in your path.
>
> Finally, when you had retired from Cambridge and settled in London you were able to devote yourself to Opera again, writing about it, translating libretti for Sadlers Wells and preparing scores for performances. The year of your seventieth birthday finds you collaborating in the planning of 'The New Oxford History of Music', where the youthfulness of your mind and the wide range of your knowledge are of inestimable value to your friends.[10]

Wellesz's warm tribute reflects Dent's stature at this time, retired but at the height of his career and reputation; for many, Dent *was* British music. In 1946, both the ISCM and the ISMR wanted him back at the helm to steer the societies into a postwar future; for once, everyone agreed that the only person possible for such responsibility was the man who had kept his integrity throughout what Wellesz had diplomatically called 'untoward circumstances'. 'I am trying (as a duty) to revive the activities of the International Society', Dent wrote to Lawrence, 'but here I find that I have changed, and I haven't the keenness at 70 wch I had at 50. I hope my presidency will be only ad interim.'[11] The old war-horse in him responded, though still deeply embroiled in the turbulent affairs of Sadler's Wells and Covent Garden.

> Once more Dent has taken over the task of building up an international world of music. This time it is an even more difficult task than it was after the first world war. But he has read the letters of the musicians of countries which have suffered under the catastrophe of this war, and his first impulse has been to help. He feels the responsibility of his task, but he must know that no one else has the authority to make the International Society for Contemporary Music work again.[12]

Although Dent's ISCM Presidency this time was really symbolic, his presence helped bring scattered Europeans back into the fold, and he enjoyed travelling abroad again and re-establishing contact with such old friends as Malipiero. He stayed with the ISCM for three years, steering through the BBC-backed London Festival in July 1946, and his final festival at Amsterdam in 1948, resigning at last in 1949.[13]

10 Egon Wellesz, 'Edward J. Dent – for his seventieth birthday', in *Acta Musicologica*, vol. 18–19 (1946–7). KCA offprint.

11 LH 23/08/1945.

12 Wellesz, 'E.J Dent and the International Society for Contemporary Music'; also Haefeli, *IGNM*, pp. 295–6, and Ana 407 Hartmann archive, Royal Library, Munich, correspondence over re-establishing the IGNM, letters from Karl Amadeus Hartmann to Max Butting, Josef Ruter, Boris Bladier.

13 LH 21/03/1949.

At the same time, May 1948, the revived ISMR begged him to become its interim President, 'much against my desires'.[14] But the next congress relaxed him, combined as it was with visits to the Hawards at Chamby, staying in Percy Scholes's little chalet there. 'I had a lazy time and a few little walks in picturesque country'.[15] At the congress itself he was excused any presiding duties 'owing to my deafness', but enjoyed watching Anglès in the chair: 'he did it quite well, in his extremely comic German, looking like an amiable elderly tom cat. I said I hoped he would be a Cardinal by the next Congress'.[16] Knud Jeppesen was elected President, Dent 'Honorary President'; his name on the stationery meant a great deal to him, but what gladdened his heart was to see the next generation there, Tony Lewis from Birmingham and Thurston Dart from Cambridge, 'so I had very agreeable company'.

Gradually, his international roles shifted to more ad hoc activities he could pick and choose. He became first President of the British Liszt Society; Leo Kestenberg asked his advice about setting up music in postwar Israel.[17] In 1947 he was asked with Michael Tippett to be on the jury for the Bartók competition in Budapest, going out in June 1948 and combining it with the ISCM jury meeting. Dent enjoyed it, 'as well as being a sort of venerable figure-head!' seeing many old friends, like the Kodálys and Aladár Toth, and giving two lectures. But it was a strain: 'I was very deaf & could not make out much of what was going on: and when the business passed into Hungarian I had a welcome rest'.[18] Tippett's subsequent account of Dent getting lost in Budapest, in spite of his vaunted familiarity with the place and the language, is cruel.[19] Far more likely is that his confusion was caused by deafness and general frailty: 'I feel I am altogether an ancient monument.'

That old friend and thorn in the flesh Gerry Cooper died suddenly in November 1947, leaving his collection to Dent, who gave it to the new Central Music Library, London. The deaths of family and friends Dent bore with calm regret, although in his later years Dent seemed to be closer to family members than ever before. When his sister Isabel died in October 1949, the whole family turned out for her funeral at Hunsingore, Dent's nephew Geoffrey 'looking rather like the undertaker in a very ancient and battered top-hat'.[20] Since Jack's death in 1944, Geoffrey had been busy rescuing Ribston from its near-derelict state; Jack had done 'everything for the land but nothing on the house'. Dent had feared it would be pulled down, like so many other country houses; instead it was being fitted up with modern plumbing and electricity, its beauties like the saloon, restored. Visiting Geoffrey, Dent recalled shaving in the brown water coming off the roof, the cold and damp. They examined the saloon, still intact, Dent amazed to find the old Broadwood grand still in tune (but he was deaf), then the vast wine cellar with 'hundreds of bottles with rotten

14 JG 26/04/1948.

15 JG 11/07/1949.

16 *Ibid.*

17 Their correspondence on the subject is in KCA.

18 LH 17/10/1948.

19 Tippett's biographer Meirion Bowen told me this.

20 LH 01/11/1949.

corks' which he offered to buy on spec. In the ruins and plaster-dust, he sat down with Geoffrey to drink a bottle of 1887 claret, 'the ghost of a good wine' in memory of Isabel, John and Jack.[21]

Ted Haynes's sudden disgrace and death in November 1948 came as a shock. That autumn he had been struck off the rolls, with vague hints of embezzlement, but he had appeared cheerful enough when Dent had lunch with him soon after. It was their last encounter; when he died only weeks later, Dent wondered if he hadn't killed himself.

Dent himself continued to look always to the future, writing more letters to old friends Clive, Lawrence and Jack, keeping up his punishing routines with his translation work, his research, going to every production he could. For a time he was still asked to speak at public functions like the Critics' Circle or Grove's lunches, but these talks had to be brief; deafness and chronic illness had drained his once-limitless energy. He complained about having to write for other people's books rather than his own neglected history of opera: Gerald Abraham invited him to contribute to his BBC *History of Sound in European Music*; he was writing five chapters for the *New Oxford History of Music.*

But in spite or in defiance of the deafness, Dent still kept up with current theatre and opera productions, his tall, stooped figure a fixture at Covent Garden and Sadler's Wells. He had heard and liked Roberto Gerhard's music for Stratford Shakespeare productions, but what bothered him was that instead using of live musicians, it was 'canned', which 'gave it all an unpleasant tinny resonance ... Poor Roberto was horribly upset about it ... the whole technical and artistic problem of modern incidental music for a modern production has not been solved'.[22] Dent never really took to the modern technology, mostly because of the inferior quality of the recorded music: 'Possibly my judgements are all quite wrong owing to my deafness; but I get more and more worried by acoustical conditions such as gramophone and wireless.'[23] Old age, his deafness and his resolute adherence to his own high standards in music and theatre militated against unreserved enjoyment. A visit to Stratford to see Barry Jackson and Peter Brook's new production of *Romeo and Juliet* echoed his reactions to Guthrie's 1944 *Hamlet*, which he had called 'an accumulation of dreadfulnesses': *Romeo and Juliet* he found 'too horrible for words ... painfully lacking in dignity, nobility and poetry: and there is a disgusting lot of kissing and cuddling: it all looks like a film advertisement!'.[24] With his ancient prepossessions, his ferocity was undiminished, his mind as active as ever with the command of his vast knowledge base, and younger men often found him 'terrifying'; the serpent had become the 'scorpion'.[25] Meeting up with Allardyce Nicoll again – 'It is an immense pleasure to meet a man so amazingly learned in the theatre and so full of enthusiasm for odd corners of theatrical history' – Dent immediately enlisted his support to put on some Gozzi

21 LH 12/05/1944.

22 JG 06/04/1947.

23 LH 17/08/1949.

24 JG 06/04/1947.

25 John Amis told me this.

at Birmingham. At the same time he was joining a syndicate with Arthur Bliss and Bobby Helpmann to run the Duchess Theatre.[26]

The summer of 1947 saw an unprecedented female invasion.

> We have been overrun with mice from the hotel next door, so my man obtained a kitten, but it was so small that I feared the mice would get a meal first. I proposed to call her Mimi as she was such a melancholy little wee thing when she arrived, but she is now frisky enough to be called Margot and fat enough to be called Eva (My man calls her Betty). Anyway she is the prima donna of the house, which stinks every day of fish for her dinner. She leaves her traces in most unsuitable places, but has her nose well rubbed in them, after which my man has quite a job washing it all off her face. The chairs will soon be torn to rags.[27]

Mimi–Betty quickly took over, was spoilt and indulged, nursed through her cat flu on warm milk and Marsala. The cat and his little garden outside gave Dent some pleasures away from his books, especially when his health began to deteriorate again.

'I have much enjoyed a quiet summer', he wrote to Lawrence in 1948, 'hearing no music, and seeing very few people ... Life becomes more & more expensive, and I begin to wonder how long I can afford the cost of this flat and life in London.'[28] As well as wasting his body, chronic illness had depleted his capital and eaten into his tiny pension, so an income from his books, translation royalties and the BBC talks was essential to keep the flat and Michael's services. 'I hope I may be able to keep it up: but it is hard work'.[29] His own poverty was a constant anxiety in Dent's final years; but his need to work was as much an assertion of independence and mental vigour as it was a source of income. 'I have quantities of stuff to write, mostly trivialities such as introductions to other people's books, but they bring in ten guineas or so and are welcome'.[30]

Dent did keep up his busy London life, supported by Michael and occasionally his friend David, who cooked, ironed, painted the flat (Dent called him 'Michaelangelo'), shifted the furniture, and who loved music and often reported back on operas he had seen. For a few years his health was good enough for Dent to sustain his heavy work-load, writing, lecturing, travelling, going to every production he possibly could. He continued to support amateur productions, especially of *The Beggar's Opera*.[31]

His deafness became worse; by 1950, when he took his niece Molly to Traviata: 'I am so dreadfully deaf that I cd hardly hear the orchestra at all when pianissimo, and the waltz music in Act I played off stage was a complete silence to me'.[32] But even as his faculties faded, his positive attitude never left him, and once again letter-writing

26 JG 06/04/1947.

27 GH 09/09/1947.

28 LH 10/09/1948.

29 LH 22/05/1948. He earned £1500 in that year.

30 LH 17/10/1955.

31 Besides Birmingham, Dent went to Oxford, Walthamstow, Colchester and other places.

32 LH 25/02/1950.

replaced other activities: dozens of letters to his old friends and the younger generation he hoped would take over, Winton Dean, Raymond Russell and Thurston Dart, but especially George Lascelles, later Lord Harewood.[33] Years later Lord Harewood recalled Dent with great affection, and his support a real boost to a young man at the beginning of his career, especially one who was the King's nephew and not really expected to have a career.[34] It was, he said, almost overwhelming to be taken seriously by a man of Dent's stature and gave him the confidence to continue.

> I have been reading your article in Tempo and found it full of sound criticism admirably expressed. I admire your literary style, as you cram a great deal into the fewest possible words. It is also very impartial and broad-minded. I am glad you take a firm stand at the end for opera in English and the foundation of a real national style of opera-singing.[35]

Dent continued to encourage Harewood, giving him introductions to Malipiero and other Italian opera people on his first visit there with David Webster in 1949. Like his other writings, Dent's letters in these latter years have a conversational quality, with the tacit assumption that the recipient is as familiar with Dent's vast knowledge base as Dent himself. On Harewood's Italian trip with Webster:

> I was not at all surprised to hear that you found all the companies rather second rate; some people seem to imagine that every Italian theatre is bursting with innumerable Pastas, Rubinis and Lablances; but even in their own way they were rarities, and to judge from Mapleson, Ebers and all the other operatic memoirs the 'golden age' of opera was mostly 'ma femme et cinq poupées' [my wife and five puppets] as Pasta's husband said.[36]

In the same letter Dent casually mentions listening to Flagstad rehearse, noting how she was 'really creating the rhythm herself instead of leaving it to the conductor', then Alfred Deller coming to lunch 'to have a little help over Handel opera songs for recording', before moving onto Guthrie's recent *Carmen* and a discussion of the place of historicism in opera production, the dead hand of tradition in *Figaro* and into costuming in ninetennth-century productions of *Traviata*. Harewood continued to be a strong supporter of the Wells, later extending its remit in ways Dent would have loved by founding Opera North.

The old asperity still manifested from time to time, usually in angry response to any backsliding from either opera company. Convincing the others on the intransigent Covent Garden Board to change their set views on production became almost a way of life.

33 George Henry Hubert Lascelles, 7th Earl of Harewood (1923–2011), Eton, King's College, Cambridge, Grenadier Guards, interned at Colditz, founded *Opera* magazine, on the boards of Covent Garden and English National Opera, edited *Kobbé's Complete Opera Book*.

34 He told me this in 2007.

35 GH 24/01/1948.

36 GH 09/03/1949.

I get infuriated at the C.G. idea that we must always do everything in the way it always has been done and never try to make any improvements ... Evidently scholarship and common sense have to be left in the cloakroom by anyone who enters C.G.

This was regarding Dent's proposed new production of *Un ballo in maschera*, which he had researched for years and seen 'half a dozen' times. He had for some time been pushing to replace the old 'Boston' version.

Kenneth Clark however seems definitely in favour of a 'Stockholm' BALLO and Jimmie Smith too; so if you share that view, as I gather you do, perhaps we shall succeed in getting it! Webster, and Steuart too, are both frightened of the 'people' who are supposed to know the opera by heart in the 'Boston' setting and will be horrified to see anything different. I should like to know who these 'people' are, and whether any of them ever pay for their seats. I asked Steuart if he thought they would open their programmes, read the names of Gustavus and Anckarstroem and Arvidson, and promptly go out and ask for their money to be returned ... If C.G. had any common sense they would make a splash with the Stockholm setting and all possible preliminary propaganda for it, as something new and as a way of making sense out of nonsense and a good opera out of a bad one.[37]

His letters to Winton Dean are conversations of another order, mostly written when Dean was at the beginning of his career. Dent warmly praised his essay on Puccini (and Dean knew Dent's views on Puccini): 'You always seem to get to the root of the matter ... without any literary frills'. He then moved into a conversation, expressing the wish that Dean had had time to address the 'question of Gozzi', comparing different musical treatments of Gozzi plays, one of Dent's own passions.[38] The next year, Dent invited Dean to take his place at the Vienna Congress and Festival: 'the proposed subjects offer every opportunity for windy nonsense, and they evidently expect me to give them some plain speaking: which you would do a great deal better than I should & without giving offence!'[39] He couldn't attend, but it was a rare compliment; Dent had told the organisers that Dean was 'the leading authority on Handel, Berlioz & Bizet if not on Benjamin Britten as well!'. It was probably at Dean's suggestion that Dent offered to translate *Deidamia* for 'an almost accidental presentation' in 1955 by Charles Farncombe and the Board of Trade choir, which 'resulted in the foundation of the very successful Handel Opera Society'.[40]

From December 1952, Dent wrote a series of long letters, initially prompted by Dean's article on *Orpheus* in *Opera*, but encompassing a history of the *Orpheus* setting, stage history, ideas, talking him through the 'fearful labyrinth of the various versions'. 'I don't know why you are so sniffy about the ballets'

I am drawn to the conclusion that you have not read the 1762 version, or compared it note by note & word by word with the French version of 1774 wch is

37 GH 15/07/1952.

38 WD 21/06/1951.

39 WD 24/04/1952.

40 Dean, *Handel and the Opera Seria*, p. 201 & n. 1.

> practically the same (except for transposition back to original keys) as the Berlioz version of 1858, now the 'standard' and most practicable version. … The original of 1762 was a timid attempt to make a 'French' opera to Italian words: hampered by the fact that it was in experiment (therefore short and with only 3 characters instead of 6 or 7) and by the fact that it was written for a court festivity as an afterpiece following a French play.[41]

There follow three more tightly packed pages. Their correspondence over that winter gave Dent something to get his teeth into during another bout of protracted illness and continued through a three months' convalescence in Portugal the winter of 1953.

> All these writers make the best of a bad job in one way or another. They all have to admit (except H. Abert who was impenitently in favour of the original 1762) that the French version of 1774 is a great improvement in many ways, and that it has Gluck's own authority: but they are all embarrassed by the same things – the frivolous overture, the anticlimax of Eurydice's resurrection and all that follows.[42]

He moves on to discuss how the ballet addresses the dramatic needs, especially the dramatic need to 'intensify' the personality of Eurydice and her sexuality. His next letter, on the 15th, apologises for having to miss Dean's Handel lecture at the Royal Musical Association, before sliding into a discussion of the drama to be found in Handel's oratorios, making the then little-known point that such works originated as 'substitutes for operas during Lent – in Italy they also had sacred operas in churches, and as late as 1830 (?) Donizetti's Il Diluvio Universale, in wch Noah & family march (praying) into the Ark to the tune afterwards employed in la fille du régiment'.[43] Citing the successful Cambridge performances (which Dean knew), he says 'on the stage they really come alive' and mentioning that in Handel's day 'it was not uncommon (certainly in Italy) to produce oratorios in costume against a scenic background … I certainly hope you will shock the RMA and all the conventional people'. At the same time, Dent shamelessly solicited Dean's support over wider opera matters, asking him to write a response to Gerald Abraham's editorial in the January *Monthly Musical Record* on the continuing imbalance in subsidies being given to Sadler's Wells and Covent Garden, 'destroying the subject'.

On rare occasions Dent's methods backfired, as in 1946 with Benjamin Britten over *Peter Grimes*, when his well-intended remarks about the production offended the prickly Britten. He wrote a long conciliatory letter: 'I'm afraid you didn't quite understand what I said to you … I dare say I expressed myself badly in the hurry of the moment (and you didn't give me much chance!).'

> I am sorry you don't feel satisfied with the Sadler's Wells performances … I hope I shall see it some day in a really large house, where you will have more strings to balance the wind and percussion, more space to blend, and more space on the stage altogether. However, don't be ungrateful; no English composer has ever

41 WD 31/12/1952.

42 WD 06/01/1953.

43 WD 15/01/1953.

had such chances before … but I don't think any composer in the world has ever had so much outward success with a first opera.[44]

Britten grudgingly responded, glad that Dent had 'changed [his] mind about Peter Grimes' and weighing in about how destructive such 'provincial' criticism can be. It took two years before friendly relations could be resumed, but Dent never stopped writing his 'extremely kind letter[s]'[45] about productions of Britten's version of *The Beggars' Opera*, *Albert Herring*, a performance in Budapest of *Peter Grimes*, and in 1951, of *Billy Budd*. 'Benjamin was extremely friendly and agreeable, and I was glad to find that he had quite cast off any idea that I was his enemy, as he seems to have imagined for a long time.'[46]

Throughout his final, grim decade, Dent never let up his drives to establish opera as a part of everyday life and to keep Sadler's Wells fit for purpose. If in 1946 the principles behind the establishment of the two main opera houses had been put in place, the wrangling that continues to this day, about funding, the different roles of either house, the repertoire, production styles and most recently, location, might have been obviated from the outset. As governor and trustee, Dent continued to suggest repertoire, translate librettos and write programme notes; when Sadler's Wells was 'forming a S.W. library', starting from the collection Novello's 'deposited' there, Dent approached Jack Gordon about doing something similar with his own collection. He knew the importance of a well-maintained archive for any active institution.

'I am always trying to stir', he said over and again about the board meetings. The principles had never varied: he wanted intelligent productions where the music and the ideas were clear and appropriate, the singing good but a part of the whole, the words clear to the audience. To Dent, this meant for an English audience, opera in English, and his prepossession on this point often made him impatient of productions he saw at Covent Garden or Glyndebourne where the language being sung was 'poor'. The audience should be given every chance to enjoy what they were seeing and hearing, but he hoped for *intelligent* enjoyment. In his old age the point became mildly obsessive; John Amis recalled him shaking his fist at the crowds leaving Victoria to go to Glyndebourne.[47] His letters to Jack and to Clive reflect his concerns and his partisanship for the Wells. 'It was a monument of stupidity and ignorance', he wrote furiously to Jack about the recent Covent Garden *Magic Flute* which in his view had mangled his translation:

nobody seemed to have studied the opera as a whole, or to have any understanding of it – it might have been an Italian performance in the 1860's at Her Majesty's … I had rather a row with Webster about it, for I was treated abominably over it all – it really constituted a breach of contract with my publishers.

He urged Sadler's Wells 'to make up their minds that S.W. is a permanent national Opera … and look ahead for 50 years and more, instead of working on the Baylis

44 BB 27/02/1946.

45 BB to EJD 14/03/1946 and 16/06/1948. Copyright Britten–Pears Foundation.

46 LH 29/03/1949.

47 This might have been a joke; Amis was young and more earnest then.

week to week system as if the whole thing might crack at any moment'.[48] Then, 'to go into the whole problem of copyright' of editions and translations arising from a projected *Carmen*: 'I said at once that I hoped they would make up their minds to perform it as at Paris always since 1875, i.e. with spoken dialogue as printed in the standard French libretto ... P.G. had made a translation of it'. But the copyright was unclear, so the production was held up. Any cultural historian now would appreciate the points he was trying to make.

> They all think they are so practical & that I am a cranky pedant with no sense of the stage: but I find that in the long run it is always the most practical thing to go back to the original MSS or editions if possible & work things out in a scholarly way. Tinkering here & there only makes one mess worse than the previous one.[49]
>
> I never can get anybody interested in performing these old operas except people who have no organization behind them.[50]
>
> I had lunch with Peter Brook two days ago; the difficulties at C.G. are endless, mainly owing to bad management and doing things in a hurry, and also I think to the employment of too many foreigners. Sadler's Wells on the other hand gets better and better, and draws surprisingly good audiences, indeed averaging about 80 per cent of capacity instead of 65 as last season. At C.G. there are all sorts of private confabs going on about making changes in the management ... There is a persistent attitude in certain quarters of hankering after the old glamour of the International seasons, and mildly condescending patronage towards S.W. as a mere 'people's opera'. C.G. would do better to spend less on scenery and more on rehearsals. If I were an active critic with a paper to write in, I could say a good deal, but as a Trustee my tongue is tied ... And I get tired of writing, as I find that whatever I write it is always some sort of scolding, either of audiences or managements.[51]

However little he liked himself for doing so, he continued to rail in public and private against Glyndebourne and against the Covent Garden affectations:

> Did you see Idomeneo? it was like an international Congress of Esperantists; I never heard such ludicrous attempts at the Italian language. But as you know I have little use for the Christie Minstrels altogether, nor for Ebert and his stunts, nor (I regret to say) for my venerable friend Busch, who still goes on beating VON, two three, four, all the time, like the old German governess of one's youth.[52]

A fall in October 1950[53] kept him mostly bedridden for a few weeks, but still able to work at home, reading Goldoni and Martelliani. He made a special effort to get to Covent Garden for Vaughan Williams' *Pilgrim's Progress* in April, and

48 JG 10/01/1948.

49 JG 10/01/1948.

50 LH 17/08/1949.

51 LH 12/02/1949.

52 GH 24/08/1951.

53 'carrying a rather heavy bag of soil for the garden into the house', JBT 25/10/1950.

wrote VW a long and warm appreciation of a work he would far rather had been given at the Wells.

> I hope you were pleased with the performance of the Pilgrim last night, and with the way in which the audience were completely absorbed by it and gave it the tribute of a definite silence at the end. I felt very conscious all the time of the audience's tense concentration on the work. As I have myself a deep-rooted inherited Quakerism (though I have never been able to live up to it!) I can very willingly make a complete surrender to a work of that kind, although most of my friends would not think it possible.[54]

VW was grateful, and wrote a reply he knew Dent would appreciate, asking his views on several points of staging. It was much more than a kind gesture; Dent's collaboration was still appreciated by those old friends who mattered.

By the following August, Dent was feeling well enough for his first trip to Italy in thirteen years: 'I am always happy wandering about the unfrequented quarters of Venice and watching the normal life of the place.'[55] He 'wanted to avoid music altogether', either at Verona or Venice, fearing a 'super-Glyndebourne-cum-Salzburg', but felt that generally, Italy had changed for the better since the war: 'there seems to be much less horrible poverty, no begging, no dishonesty, and a general sense of independence and self-respect which produces a wonderful kindness and friendliness everywhere'.[56] Another trip to Venice in 1952 with Raymond Russell was much shorter; his last.

In the end, Dent was probably brought down by his own hyperactivity. In January 1952, he was working on the 'libretto' article for Grove's, excited by the ideas emerging from it:

> between 1860 & 1870 there are 4 composers in 4 different countries, all utterly independent of each other, who suddenly take libretto-writing quite seriously, write their own librettos and evolve something quite new which eventually makes all composers from 1900 onwards take librettos seriously in a new way: Wagner with Tristan, Berlioz with Les Troyens, Boito with Mefistofele and Mussorgsky with Boris Godunov.[57]

But soon after, he contracted 'influenza', which brought on his old stomach troubles. By April he was in bed for weeks, cancelling his engagements at Utrecht, Vienna and Salzburg.

> Michael is a severe nurse & keeps me strictly on the diet, but very agreeably – cauliflower passed through a sieve, with cheese sauce, is a most succulent dish. I am

54 EJD–RVW 27/04/195.1 Printed in *Letters of Ralph Vaughan Williams 1895–1958*, ed. Hugh Cobbe (Oxford, 2008), pp. 480–81. Also in Kennedy, *Catalogue of the Works of Ralph Vaughan Williams*. Kennedy considered the advice as important to VW.

55 GH 24/08/1951.

56 *Ibid.*

57 LH 06/01/1952.

> quite happy without alcohol, but miss my black coffee, and boredom tempts me to smoke too much.[58]

The Harewoods sent him eggs and butter, the Kleibers sent him clotted cream from Switzerland, which cheered him. Lawrence's doctor son Adrian looked after him sympathetically, and to give Michael a break, he went for several weeks in May and June to the Hotel Mount Ephraim in Tunbridge Wells to recuperate, the first of many such enforced stays in his final years. The hotel was by no means his first choice; he found it 'dull', devoid of any congenial company, but it was convenient and all he could afford.

Although poorly all summer 1952, Dent continued at his *Seraglio* translation, and in October lectured at the Barber Institute in Birmingham. In spite of a 'black haemorrhage' on the 18th, just before he was to give his Presidential address to the Society for Theatre Research, he ploughed on. Then he went to see the new production of *Ballo*, which he thought good, although the singers appeared 'nervous'. By December he was laid up again with another 'duodenal ulcer' and forced to stay in bed for a month at least, mitigated by his correspondence with Winton Dean. Seeing his frustration, JB organised a stay in Lisbon, and Dent flew out with Michael, remaining there in the warmth until spring. His letters all that winter from the Hotel Tivoli describe the long walks in that hilly, 'fascinating' city: 'I am getting stronger every day and the weather is mainly quite delightful.' The opera was starting up, but Dent didn't yet feel up to 'sit out an opera from 9 p.m. to about 2 a.m. … let alone the bother of having to dress up for it'.[59] Lisbon bucked him temporarily, as his long letters to Winton Dean at this time demonstrate. But by December he was ill again, 'wrestling with C.G. over Freischütz'.

When the lease for Cromwell Place came up for renewal, Dent considered returning to Cambridge and sharing a house there with JB, who retired in 1953. But by now he was too ill and too poor from the constant medical and nursing bills, not quite in time to benefit from the new NHS.

The last four years of Dent's life were miserable, but he was not. In pain or discomfort much of the time he nevertheless continued to forge ahead with ideas and projects, actively encouraging the young, like the great recording producer Christopher Raeburn, who was helped to get the British Council grant which launched his career and given introductions to European musicians.

> Christopher Raeburn, a bright young man who has got a B.C. and Leverhulme scholarship to do research in Vienna, writes that he gave a lecture at Salzburg on Mozart in England, but thought his audience did not know that there was any connexion at all between England and Mozart.[60]

Dent's astonishing mental energy continued until his death. He needed to keep working, writing, in the public eye; the one thing he hated was loneliness, and the isolation his illness and deafness imposed.

58 LH 03/05/1952.

59 WD 11/02/1952.

60 LH 06/02/1956. Raeburn told me about Dent issuing him with advice about Vienna.

> I managed to see a really charming performance of Werther and found that my hearing seemed to have improved. Freischütz seems to have been successful at Cardiff … I had fearful tussles with Christopher West over the spoken dialogue. Steuart Wilson wanted to cut it down to practically nothing, & tried to take advantage of my bad collapse at the end of October to make me give him a free hand. I protested volcanically from my bed & at once go the OUP to support me: I was not going to have a repetition of the Magic Flute trouble … I had to give way sometimes & allow myself to be retranslated into RAF English, but I think he got the right general idea of Freischütz as a roaring romantic melodrama for a popular public, not for Glyndebourne connoisseurs![61]

He never ceased to praise Michael's kindness and patience: 'All I can do for him is to give him money to buy silk pyjamas and such things, which are a great pleasure to him.'[62]

In the last ten years of his life Dent wrote 140 articles, translations, programme notes and lectures; the letters never ceased to flow, full of ideas and the knowledge of a long lifetime's application and enthusiasm. The activity 'held him together' as the Scarlatti book had years before. He was made a Fellow of the British Academy in 1956 and elected an 'Honorary Member' of the Haendel Gesellschaft in July 1955 at the behest of his old friend Ernst Meyer.[63] He was delighted when Rafael Kubelik and John Piper trudged up the stairs at Cromwell Place to discuss a new production of the *Flute*, happy to talk about Renishaw and the Sitwells with Piper. But such visits were increasingly rare. As one who had always thrived on socialising and needed the stimulus of company, Dent's isolation hit him hardest: 'I see nobody … I write nothing', he wrote to Lawrence, who continued to keep in touch with letters.[64] His ulcer persisted:

> bad intestinal haemorrhage and had to be taken to a very expensive nursing home at 99 Cromwell Road … horribly bored … but it is a slow business, as they thought it dangerous to give me a blood transfusion, and I have to build up my iron supply by taking iron pills.[65]

For his eightieth birthday he was driven in style up to Cambridge for a lunch in his honour at King's. The Provost had thoughtfully provided paper and pencils, so there was some of the old Cambridge conversation he enjoyed, a rare treat now. 'I give up all concerts and most operas now, so I feel a good deal cut off from life.'[66] But Dent never lost his curiosity, his love of scholarly exploration; his last letters are full of optimism, the ideas never cease flowing. The rare times he gave in to gloom were when, to give Michael a break, he had to stay in the drab hotel in Tunbridge

61 JG 01/04/1954.

62 LH 25/05/1955.

63 I am indebted to Toby Thacker for this information.

64 LH 04/08/1955.

65 JG 06/06/1956.

66 LH 09/03/1956.

Wells, more of a hellish final departure lounge, where there was no conversation, no company, no music.

> Royal Mount Ephraim Hotel. I am rather bored and horribly lonely ... As usual I seem to live in the dark ... It is autumnal anyway, and my eyes are always rather bad ... I am very shaky on my legs and found it hard work coming up ... carrying Sitwell's book ... The company here is is usual, and very dull: besides, I speak to no one and can hear nothing ... full of middle-aged and elderly women mostly very 'sensible shoes' ... schoolmistressy ... There is a suggestion that I shd translate Idomeneo as a present for Dr Veko, a refugee who has lived here since about 1930 or so ... I can't tackle Idomeneo at present, as it is always dark here, and my eyes are bad ... I feel I may last till 90 or longer, or drop down any moment.[67]

It was his last letter to Lawrence, the confident, flowing handwriting crabbed and uneven. Optimism and mental energy could not drive a broken body, and Dent died in London on 22 August 1957.

At his memorial service in King's Chapel they played *The Dream of Gerontius*. Dent *would* have been amused.

67 LH 24/07/1957.

Afterword

The obituaries came thick and fast. The *Yorkshire Evening Post* revealed that 'one of Yorkshire's most distinguished authorities on music' was also 'vice-president of the Leeds New Canal Society',[1] but most focused on music and theatre. Harold Rutland in the *Musical Times* called him 'a man of the theatre ... His influence on the presentation of opera, as on musical scholarship generally, was incalculable, and was by no means confined to this country'.[2] Desmond Shawe-Taylor went deeper: 'The truth was perhaps that Dent, growing up in a period rich in great singers but often unpardonably careless in ensemble and production, took the singing for granted and concentrated his fire on the defects of the old tradition.'[3] There were a few understatements: 'He rather liked upsetting people's complacency.'[4] His old friends had warmer memories: Steuart Wilson remembered how Dent would politely preface any reproof with 'my dear so and so', and how he had inherited his father's precision of speech, saying, 'I'm not my father's son if I can't draft a resolution'. Wilson remarked on Dent's unpopularity with his colleagues, how Rootham had openly disliked him, 'but Dent never spoke evil of any of them'. Dent was, he ended, 'the most painstaking of friends'.[5] Rolf Gardiner wrote: 'Edward Dent simply showered helpfulness, complete with shrewd and sometimes merrily malicious comments on personalities.'[6] Trend wrote a restrained and personal piece for *The Score*.

The Times obituary mentions the Beethoven centenary, when Dent's remarks had shocked people: 'In truth he was alive to Beethoven's greatness, far more keenly so than most of the eulogists, but he was not interested in what was common knowledge. He wanted to get at something which the rest of the world had not seen.'[7] But possibly the most characteristic view of Dent was in *Music and Musicians*. The BBC had produced an opera for which Dent had done the translation, but a 'musician from abroad' in charge of production took exception to Dent's translation:

> 'Zis translation', declared the producer, 'she is all wrong – eet is terreeble – eet must all over again at this passage be done!' Edward Dent, quiet and polite, replied softly, 'I'm so sorry. Let me see – where have I made a mistake? Have I

1 *Yorkshire Evening Post* (23 August 1957).

2 *Musical Times* (October 1957).

3 *The New Statesman* (14 September 1957).

4 *Liverpool Daily Post* (27 August 1957).

5 James Steuart Wilson in *Opera* (November 1957). Wilson had written an earlier appreciation in the MMR (2 June 1930), pp. 163–4.

6 Letter in *The Times* (24/08/1957).

7 *The Times* (23 August 1957).

translated something badly?' 'Ach, no,' replied the producer. 'Ze translation is right, but ze English – she is terreeble!' 'Ah,' said Dent blandly, 'there you have the advantage of me. You see – you studied English. I merely – ah – picked it up!'[8]

Dent's other, wider achievements and contributions are not mentioned.

Everything he had not already given away – books, music, furniture – Dent left to J.B. Trend, who died suddenly the following April, so many of Dent's possessions went up for auction at Sotheby's, his books and music sold mostly to dealers.[9] His papers might have gone the same way, but for the strenuous efforts of Jill Vlasto, who secured them for King's, with a long-term view to collecting as many of his letters as possible.[10] She was met with opposition from the outset; Dent's homosexuality was only one point of contention. Lawrence Haward's widow felt that some of the material was 'too confidential to be made use of'.[11]

> The great difficulty I suspect, apart from finding a biographer, will be to get the owners' or executors' permission to publish yet awhile, for, judging from those letters of Dent's that I have read both to myself & other people, he did not spare those performances or persons about whom he wrote in confidence to his friends. Why should he? He was not the man to have his eye on posterity, or rather, on the public; I think he would enjoy the sight of his potential biographers rejecting such a delicate & dangerous task![12]

Dent's own modesty and reticence had precluded any autobiography:

> I am going through old diaries to find information about HP Allen for a memoir wch Cyril Bailey of Oxford is writing. It makes me feel rather like being psycho-analyzed. They are useful for odd facts & a few anecdotes, but I must be careful to destroy the lot before I die. There are no indiscretions, but it all reads very childishly.[13]

Many of Dent's closest friends died around the same time. Lawrence had finished his monumental bibliography of Dent's writings[14] in time for his eightieth birthday, using materials Dent had sent him over the years. In his own final years, Clive Carey had begun notes for a biography. Jill Vlasto had favoured Winton Dean as the best possible biographer, but he was far too busy to do a proper job, he felt; he always regretted not having taken it on.[15] His 'Centenary Tribute' in *Music & Letters* is still the best single piece on Dent, which, taken together with his Introduction to

8 *Music and Musicians* (October 1957).

9 Sotheby & Co, 'Catalogue of Printed Books and Music comprising music and books on music and musicians, with some manuscripts. The Property of the late Professor E.J. Dent / The Property of Professor J.B. Trend … Second day's sale; Tuesday, January 21st, 1958'.

10 Letter to Katharine Thomson 04/04/1962.

11 *Ibid.*

12 *Ibid.*

13 LH 20/03/1947. He didn't destroy it.

14 Lawrence Haward, *Edward J. Dent: A Bibliography* (Cambridge, 1956).

15 Told to the author.

The Rise of Romantic Opera, gives a vivid personal sketch of Dent's personality and scholarship.

> Dent had the intense professionalism of the serious scholar who began as an amateur, but he never lost the freshness of his early vision or underrated the role of the amateur performer.[16]
>
> Further causes of prejudice and intolerance were Dent's homosexual inclinations and his political radicalism, curiously blended with a fastidious and aristocratic conservatism that remained central to his character.[17]
>
> Dent was … a highly idiosyncratic character, and in some respects, a bundle of contradictions. This not only delighted his friends and students, and irritated his opponents; it coloured the tone of his more popular writings, and to some degree his approach to musical history, and is therefore more important than might appear at first glance.[18]

Eventually, the time lapse grew too big; the people who had known and appreciated Dent, those best qualified to address his remarkably eclectic life story, died, and some terrible gaps appeared. Philip Radcliffe's *E.J. Dent: A Centenary Memoir* of 1976 is the most complete portrait, although brief, but Radcliffe died before he could write another, more comprehensive piece. Clive Carey's nephew, Hugh Carey, wrote his charming 'informal biography', but limited his scope to their correspondence, carefully side-stepping Dent's sexuality, so fundamental in understanding his complex character. But as has been discussed earlier, the gross misunderstanding of strangers persists. The limited picture presented of Dent in some recent books shows a particular kind of deeply engrained myth at work. According to one he was 'nothing if not a creature of fashion … a socialist who revelled in the good life'.[19] Another averred that he only did his opera translations 'with unerring self-interest', 'an amateur at everything, fixed in his scholarly prejudices'.[20] But other recent scholarship from Philip Brett, John Deathridge and the recent winner of the Royal Musical Association Dent Medal, Annegret Fauser,[21] is more elastic and comprehensive, beginning to touch on his elusive, multilayered life. Philip Brett:

> Dent would have no doubt been horrified by the mispronunciation and dismemberment of works characteristic of the British radio station Classic FM, but the astounding rise of musical literacy after the war and the marketing of classical

16 Winton Dean, 'Edward J. Dent: A Centenary Tribute', M&L (October 1976), p. 357.

17 *Ibid.*, p. 355.

18 *Ibid.*, p. 354.

19 Richard Osborne, *Music and Musicians of Eton: from 1440 to the Present* (London, 2014), p. 114.

20 Norman Lebrecht, *Covent Garden: the Untold Story – Dispatches from the English Culture War, 1945–2000* (London, 2000), pp. 97–8.

21 Annegret Fauser, 'The Scholar behind the Medal: Edward J. Dent (1876–1957) and the Politics of Music History', *Journal of the Royal Musical Association*, vol. 139 (2014), pp. 235–60.

music in Britain today as a music of the people is the result of something he worked hard for. It was no mean achievement.[22]

What exactly is Dent's legacy? Although some of his writing might too easily be dismissed these days as patronising or dated, it is always worth reading for his style alone, while his scholarship is still remarkable by any standard, and many of the points he raised nearly a century ago continue to confound. His internationalism and his belief in the high arts for everyone are ideals still valid and still under attack; he would have loathed current apologetics and 'dumbing down'. Dent would not have seen surtitles as a substitute for words being sung clearly, but as the distraction they are. His Penguin *Opera* remains an excellent introduction, and is much more entertaining than many more recent examples. Sadly, his arguments for national theatre and opera in *A Theatre for Everybody* continue to be as relevant today as they were in his lifetime, not for lack of application on the part of his cultural descendants. A glance at the comments on any 'classical music' columns in the press show how opinion is still sharply divided about the high arts, their purpose and their funding. As I write this in 2021, live music, theatre and opera are again under threat by the twin forces of the Covid-19 pandemic and crass government attitudes to 'the arts industry', faring far better in the other European countries where they are properly subsidised. Only time will tell if the cultural institutions Dent worked so hard to establish survive in the UK. A fresh Dent for our age is desperately needed.

While there is yet to be any English Heritage Blue Plaque, much less any memorial next to those of Lilian Baylis and Reginald Rowe in the London Coliseum – home to English National Opera (ENO), as Sadler's Wells Opera is now known – there are many other, more appropriate living reminders of Dent's life and work. Here are just a few: a flourishing National Youth Orchestra, a Marlowe Production at the Cambridge Arts Theatre, a Cecilia Bartoli recording of Scarlatti from a manuscript Dent gave to the Fitzwilliam Museum; every other book in the Rowe Library at King's College; early scores in the Pendlebury Music Library and the Fitzwilliam Museum; the thriving Music Faculty at West Road, with its small Dent Room and excellent, flourishing concert hall; a production of Rameau at ENO, Handel at Glyndebourne, English Touring Opera and its clever, engaging productions in English of early opera. You have only to look and listen.

22 Brett 'Musicology and Sexuality', p. 425.

Appendix: Dent's Ulcer

It is mostly likely that Dent suffered from what is now known to be a duodenal peptic ulcer caused by the bacterium Helicobacter Pylori (*H. pylori*), only discovered in 1983, and now easily treatable by antibiotics and acid suppression. But in Dent's day treatment was mostly guesswork, and the results could be prolonged and extremely uncomfortable; apart from the physical pain and disruption, the mental strain of never knowing when it might blow up again did not add to the quality of life. The operations often had long-term side-effects, as did Dent's, and he was lucky not to have died from a perforation of the ulcer, a common side-effect. Judging from his reported symptoms, he must have had continuous inflammation of the duodenum (duodenitis), of various degrees of severity, causing symptoms of abdominal pain in between the acute ulceration phases, which would have been very debilitating. Aspirin may have been one of his painkillers, terrible for his ulcer; even Alka-Seltzer contained aspirin. The milk of magnesia he took may have given him his severe diarrhoea.

Dent's lifelong smoking would have been a major contributing factor to his ulceration. In the early twentieth century, stress was considered to be the main cause of peptic ulcers. Treatment – as Dent's by Conway Davies – was medical: bed rest and bland diet, especially milk. Judging by the comments of his surgeon W.R. Douglas, Dent's was a large duodenal ulcer, and he probably had a partial gastrectomy, removing the part of the stomach which secretes acid, but it could have been something different. The stomach-pumping tube beforehand was fairly standard, keeping the stomach as free as possible of acid to try to heal the ulcer, and he would have had a drip to keep him hydrated. Severe haemorrhage from duodenal ulcers was a dangerous complication. This could manifest itself, as it did in 1939 – when it may have been treated by 'oversewing' the ulcer, darning it to stop the vessel from bleeding – by the patient vomiting up the blood; or, as it did in 1952, by 'melaena', where the blood is not vomited but passes through the bowel and is passed as a black tarry stool, called melaena, which is possibly what Dent meant by 'black haemorrhage'.

With thanks to Dr Judith Murray-Rust and Dr Carol Evans

Select Bibliography

Dent's Writings

The fullest bibliography is Lawrence Haward, *Edward J. Dent: A Bibliography* (Cambridge, 1956), henceforth LH. The below is a selection only.

Books and Pamphlets

Alessandro Scarlatti (London: Edward Arnold, 1905)

Mozart's Opera 'The Magic Flute': its History and Interpretation (Cambridge: W. Heffer & Sons, 1911)

Mozart's Operas: a Critical Study (London: Chatto & Windus, 1913); German edn, translated by Anton Mayer (Berlin: Erich Reiss Verlag, 1923); 2nd English edn, rev. (Oxford University Press, 1947)

'Musical Illustrations of History and Literature: Lecture Recitals for Schools and Colleges by Mr Edward Dent and Miss Gladys Moger' (Cambridge University Press, privately printed, 1919)

Terpander, or Music and the Future (London: Kegan Paul, Trench, Trübner & Co., n.d. [1926])

Foundations of English Opera:A Study of Musical Drama in England during the 17th century (Cambridge University Press, 1928)

Ferruccio Busoni: a Biography (London: Oxford University Press, 1933)

Handel, Great Lives series (London: Duckworth, 1934)

Händel in England (Halle: Max Niemeyer Verlag, 1936)

Ferruccio Busoni (Philadelphia: Prospectus of the Busoni Society, 1939)

Opera (Harmondsworth: Penguin Books, Ltd. 1940); two more edns, 1942, 1949; Spanish edn, translated by Eduardo Warshaver (Buenos Aires, 1947)

Notes on Fugue for Beginners (Cambridge University Press, privately printed, 1941)

A Theatre for Everybody: The Story of the Old Vic and Sadler's Wells (London: T.V. Boardman & Co., 1945); 2nd edn, 1946

Franz Liszt (London: Prospectus of the Liszt Society, 1950)

Translations

Dent translated 39 operas, most of which were published by Oxford University Press. He also translated 18 shorter pieces, by Mussorgsky, Goldoni, Mozart, Scarlatti, Kodály, Gozzi, Vecchi, *et al.*

Miscellaneous

Dent wrote articles for many musical reference books (LH 139–52), including *The Oxford History of Music* (Oxford, 2nd edn, 1938); *The New Oxford History of Music* (Oxford, unfinished); *Grove's Dictionary of Music and Musicians*, 2nd edn, ed. Fuller Maitland (London, 1904–10), 4th edn, ed. H.C. Colles (London, 1940), 5th edn, ed. Eric Blom (London, 1954); *Encyclopaedia Britannica*, 11th edn (1910). Dent also wrote numerous prefaces and introductions (LH 119–38), programme notes (LH 233–71), including programmes for the ISCM festivals every year, many for CUMS, for the Royal Philharmonic Society, for productions at Sadler's Wells and Covent Garden.

Compositions

Only three of Dent's songs were published, but the two sets of three motets he composed in 1940–41 were published by OUP. KCA has MSS of 18 songs he composed, mostly c.1900, and MS versions of Overture in C minor (1895), Variations for Pianoforte ... in E minor (1895), Serenade in F for Small Orchestra (1897, rev. 1899); Serenade in G minor for Small Orchestra (1900), 'Orchestral Prelude, and Setting for Voices and Orchestra ... from Shelley's *Hellas*' (1901); Incidental Music to *The Christening of Rosalys* (1905) and *Princess Fragoletta* (1906) by Netta Syrett; String Quartet (one movement, 1908); Fugue in Two Parts for Pianoforte (1940).

Primary Sources

Unpublished

Augustiner Bibliothek, Vienna; early operas
Biblioteca National de Catalunya, Barcelona: Anglès archive
Birmingham City Library: Thomson archive
British Library: Rutland Boughton; Adrian Boult; Edwin Evans; Ralph Vaughan Williams; Christopher Raeburn papers; Hirsch Library. Add MSS 52256, 72627
Britten–Pears Archive, Snape: Britten–Dent letters
Cambridgeshire Collection, Cambridge Central Library: photos and documents
Cambridge University Library: Add MSS 7973; Add MSS 8089, 8505, 8786, 8654, 8371; 9193, 9194; Minute Books CUMC XVI.1.1.
Fitzwilliam Museum, Cambridge: Berg letters, music given by Dent, Sargent painting of Mozart
Fondazione Giorgio Cini, Venice: Casella, Chilesotti, Malipiero archives
Gesellschaft der Musikfreunde archives, Vienna: Mandezcyski archive
Gonville & Caius College Library: Charles Wood archive
King's College, Cambridge, Archive Centre: Dent: Diaries 1897–1922 EJD/3/1; letters, EJD/4; MS music; Busoni and ISCM/ISMR collections; unpublished writings. Collections: Carey, Forster, Moorsom, Felkin, Forster, Kahn, Browning, James, Sheppard, Brooke, Dickinson, Keynes
Magdalene College, Cambridge, Pepys Library: Benson archive, A.C. Benson diaries, using David Newsome's index of the diaries

Österreichische Nationalbibliothek archives, Vienna: F 13/1198: Wellesz, Berg, Adler
Royal College of Music, London: Carey archive.
Royal Library, Munich archives: ana 407, Hartmann, Karl Amadeus
Schoenberg Institut, Vienna
Staatsbibliothek, Berlin: Busoni archive
Stadtbibliothek, Winterthur: Werner Reinhart archive Dep MK 326/52
Letters from private collections: Robert Ponsonby, The Earl of Harewood, George Dannatt, Winton Dean, Robin Orr, Jack Gordon, Katharine Thomson, Meirion Bowen, Christopher Raeburn
Interviews with the Earl of Harewood, Christopher Raeburn, Professor Robin Orr, Katharine Thomson, Nigel Fortune, John Amis, Sir David Willcocks, Winton Dean

Published

Ackerley J.P., *My Father & Myself* (London, 1968)
Asquith, Cynthia, *The Diaries of Lady Cynthia Asquith 1915–1918* (London, 1968)
Baedeker's Northern Germany (Leipzig, 1904)
Baedeker's Southern Germany (Leipzig, 1902)
Baedeker's Northern Italy (E.M. Forster's copy in KCA)
Baedeker's Southern Italy (E.M. Forster's copy in KCA)
Beecham, Thomas, *A Mingled Chime* (London, 1944, 1979)
Berg, Alban, *Letters to his Wife*, edited, translated and annotated by Bernard Grun (London, 1971)
The Blaue Reiter Almanac, ed. Wassily Kandinsky and Franz Marc; repr. ed. Klaus Lankheit (London, 2006)
Bliss, Arthur, *As I Remember* (London, 1970)
Britten, Benjamin, Donald Mitchell, Philip Reed, Mervyn Cooke, ed., *Letters from a Life: Selected Letters of Benjamin Britten* Vol. III 1946-51 (London, 2004)
Brooke, Rupert, *Friends and Apostles: The Correspondence of Rupert Brooke and James Strachey* ed. Keith Hale (New Haven, 1998)
BSSSP pamphlet no. 1 (written by Laurence Housman) 'Policy and principles, general aims' (London, 1914)
Burke's Landed Gentry, 18th edn
Busoni, Ferruccio, *Letters to his Wife*, translated by Rosamund Ley (London, 1938)
—*Selected Letters*, edited and translated by Antony Beaumont (New York, 1987)
Clark, Kenneth, *Another Part of the Wood: A Self-Portrait* (London, 1974)
—*The Other Half: A Self-Portrait* (London, 1977)
A Dictionary of Modern Music & Musicians, ed. Eaglefield Hull and others (London, 1924)
The Dictionary of National Biography
Haward, Lawrence, *Edward J. Dent: A Bibliography* (Cambridge, 1956)
Haynes, E.S.P., *Life, Law & Letters* (London, 1936)
—*The Case for Liberty* (London, 1919)
—*The Lawyer: A Conversation Piece Selected from the Lawyer's Notebooks and other writings by E.S.P. Haynes 1877–1949*, ed. Renée Haynes (London, 1951)

Kelly, F.S., *Race Against Time: The Diaries of F.S. Kelly*, ed. Therese Radic (Canberra, 2006)
King's College Register (1919–1958) (London, 1963)
Klemperer, Victor, *I Shall Bear Witness: The Diaries of Victor Klemperer 1933–1941*, translated Martin Chalmers (London, 2006)
Lascelles, George H.H., Earl of Harewood, *The Tongs and the Bones: the Memoirs of Lord Harewood* (London, 1981)
Lutyens, Elisabeth, *A Goldfish Bowl* (London, 1972)
Luxmoore, H.E., *Letters* (Cambridge, 1929)
Music and the Community: the Cambridgeshire Report on the Teaching of Music (Cambridge, 1933)
Nichols, Beverley, *The Unforgiving Minute* (London, 1978)
Ordinances of the University of Cambridge to the End of the Easter Term 1927 (Cambridge, 1927)
Orr, Robin, *Musical Chairs: An Autobiography* (London, 1998)
Pemberton, Antony, 'A Trip Round my Dining Room Walls' (Cambridge, 2011)
Raverat, Gwen, *Period Piece: A Cambridge Childhood* (London, 1952)
Sotheby & Co., 'Catalogue of Printed Books and Music comprising Music and books on music and musicians, with some manuscripts: The Property of the late Professor E.J. Dent / The Property of Professor J.B. Trend … Second day's sale; Tuesday, January 21st, 1958.'
Strachey, Lytton, *The Letters of Lytton Strachey* ed. Paul Levy (New York, 2005)
Taylor, Hugh, ed., *Edward J. Dent: Selected Essays* (Cambridge, 1979)
Toye, Francis, *For What We Have Received* (London, 1950)
Vansittart, Robert, *Black Record: Germans Past and Present* (London, 1941)
Williams, Ralph Vaughan, *Letters of Ralph Vaughan Williams*, ed. Hugh Cobbe (Oxford, 2008).
Withers, John J., *A Register of Admission to King's College Cambridge 1797–1925 …* (London, 1929)
Walton, William, *The Selected Letters of William Walton 1936–1948*, ed. Malcolm Hayes (London, 2002)

Secondary Sources

Aldrich, Robert, *The Seduction of the Mediterranean: Writing, Art and Homosexual Fantasy* (London, 1993)
Alpers, Anthony, *The Life of Katherine Mansfield* (Oxford, 1982)
Annan, Noel, *The Dons: Mentors, Eccentrics and Geniuses* (London, 1999)
Anstee, Margaret, *An Unlikely Spanish Don: the Life and Times of Professor John Brande Trend* (Eastbourne, 2013).
Anstruther, Ian, *Oscar Browning* (London, 1983)
Arundell, Dennis, *The Story of Sadler's Wells 1683–1964* (London, 1965)
Beaumont, Antony, *Busoni the Composer* (London, 1985)
Benson, E.F., *David of King's* (London, 1924)
Blackshaw, W.S., *'More than a school to us': A History of Bilton Grange* (Rugby, 1997)

Boulestin, X. Marcel, 'Le Problématique avenir de l'Opéra en Angleterre' in *Société Internationale de Musique Journale* (April 1911), pp. 52–61
Bowen, Meirion, ed., *Gerhard on Music: Selected Writings* (Farnham, 2000)
Brett, Philip, 'Are You Musical?', *Musical Times*, vol. 135 (1994), pp. 370–76
— 'Musicology and Sexuality: The Example of Edward J. Dent' in *Proceedings of the SIM* (London, 1997) pp. 418–27
Bush, Alan, 'The I.S.C.M. Festival at Prague', *Musical Times* (October 1935)
Carey, Hugh, *Duet for Two Voices: an Informal Biography of Edward Dent compiled from his letters to Clive Carey* (Cambridge, 1979)
—*Mansfield Forbes and his Cambridge* (Cambridge, 1984)
Carpenter, Edward, *Love's Coming-of-Age* (London, 1909)
—*The Intermediate Sex* (London, 1908)
Cole, Michael, 'Rosamond Harding: Author and Musicologist', *The Galpin Society Journal*, vol. 60 (April 2007), pp. 71–84
Cork, Richard, *Wild Thing: Epstein, Gaudier-Brzeska, Gill* (London, 2010), Exhibition catalogue
— *Art Beyond the Gallery in Early Twentieth-Century England* (New Haven, 1984)
Cornford, Francis, *Microcomosgraphia Academica* (Cambridge, 1908)
Cribb, Tim, *Bloomsbury & British Theatre: The Marlowe Story* (Cambridge, 2007)
d'Arch Smith, Timothy, *Love in Earnest: Some Notes on the Lives and Writings of English 'Uranian' Poets from 1889–1930* (London, 1970)
Davidson, Jim, *Lyrebird Rising: Louise Hanson-Dyer of Oiseau-Lyre 1884–1962* (Melbourne, 1994)
Dean, Winton, *Handel and the Opera Seria* (Berkeley, 1969)
—'Edward J. Dent: A Centenary Tribute', *Music & Letters*, vol. 57, no. 4 (October 1976) pp. 353–61
Deathridge, John, 'Music Historiography, Critical Theory, and Other Tales', *Proceedings of the 16th International Congress, London, 1997* (Oxford, 2000), pp. 230–38
Delany, Paul, *Fatal Glamour: The Life of Rupert Brooke* (Montreal, 2013)
— *The Neo-Pagans: Friendship and Love in the Rupert Brooke Circle* (London, 1987)
Dibble, Jeremy, *Charles Villiers Stanford: Man and Musician* (Oxford, 2002)
Dobler, Jens, *Von anderen Ufern: Geschichte der Berliner Lesben und Schwulen in Kreuzberg und Frierichshain* (Berlin, 2003)
Doctor, Jennifer, *The BBC and Ultra-Modern Music: Shaping a Nation's Tastes* (London, 1999)
Egremont, Max, *Siegfried Sassoon: A Biography* (London, 2005)
Eldorado: Homosexuelle Frauen und Männer in Berlin 1850–1950: Geschichte, Alltag und Kultur (Berlin, 1984)
Elkin, Robert, *Queen's Hall 1893–1941* (London, 1944)
Ellis, H. Havelock and J.A. Symonds, *Sexual Inversion 1897: A Critical Edition*, ed. Ivan Crozier (London, 2008)
Faulks, Sebastian, *The Fatal Englishman: Three Short Lives* (London, 1996)
Fauser, Annegret, 'The Scholar behind the Medal: Edward J. Dent (1876–1957) and the Politics of Music History' *Journal of the Royal Musical Association*, vol. 139 (2014), pp. 235–60

Fillion, Michelle, *Difficult Rhythms: Music and the Word in E.M. Forster* (Champaign, IL, 2014)

Firbank, Ronald, *Valmouth, Prancing Nigger, The Eccentricites of Cardinal Pirelli* (London, 1961)

Furbank, P.N. *E.M. Forster: A Life. Volume One: The Growth of the Novelist (1879–1914); Volume Two: Polycrates' Ring (1914–1970)* (London, 1977, 1978)

Fussell, Paul, *The Great War and Modern Memory* (Oxford, 1975).

Gilbert, Susie, *Opera for Everybody: the Story of English National Opera* (London, 2009)

Grant, Joy, *Harold Monro and the Poetry Bookshop* (London, 1967)

Haefeli, Anton, *IGNM: Die Internationale Gesellschaft für Neue Musik: Ihre Geschichte von 1922 bis zur Gegenwart* (Zurich, 1982)

Harding Rosamond, *The Piano-Forte: Its History Traced To The Great Exhibition of 1851* (Cambridge, 1933, rev. edn 1978)

Hassall, Christopher, *Edward Marsh: Patron of the Arts* (London, 1959)

— *Rupert Brooke: A Biography* (London, 1964)

Hastings, Michael, *The Handsomest Young Man in England: Rupert Brooke* (London, 1967)

Hewitson, Robert, *Footlights! A Hundred Years of Cambridge Comedy* (London, 1984)

Hibbert, Dominic, *Harold Monro: Poet of the New Age* (London, 2001)

Hill, W.H. and A.F. Hill, *The Violin-Makers of the Guarneri Family (1626–1762)* (London, 1931)

Hoare, Philip, *Noel Coward: A Biography* (London, 1995)

— *Wilde's Last Stand: Decadence, Conspiracy and the First World War* (London, 1997)

Holroyd, Michael, *Lytton Strachey* (London, 1994)

Hull, A. Eaglefield, 'A Few Words about the British Music Society', *Musical Times* (1 February 1919), p. 71

Humphrey, George, *Guide to Cambridge: The Town, University & Colleges* (Cambridge, 1895)

Hyatt-King, Alec, 'Paul Hirsch and his Music Library', *British Library Journal* (1981)

Hynes, Samuel, *The Edwardian Turn of Mind* (London, 1998)

— *A War Imagined: the First World War and English Culture* (London, 1990)

Jackson-Stops, Gervase, 'Ribston Hall, Yorkshire–II', *Country Life* (18 October 1973)

Jones, Nigel, *Rupert Brooke: Life, Death & Myth* (London, 1999)

Kater, Michael H., *The Twisted Muse* (Oxford, 1997)

Keilson-Lauritz, M., *Die Geschichte der eigenen Geschichte* (Berlin, 1997)

Kennedy, Michael, *Adrian Boult* (London, 1987)

— *Richard Strauss: Man, Musician, Enigma* (Cambridge, 1999)

—*The Works of Ralph Vaughan Williams* (Oxford, 1964)

Kniazeva, Janna, ed., *Jacques Handschin in Russland: Die neu aufgefundenen Texte* (Basel, 2011)

Knight, Frida, *Cambridge Music* (Cambridge, 1980)

Laurence, Dan H. ed., *Shaw's Music: The Complete Musical Criticism of Bernard Shaw*, 3 volumes (London, 1981)

Law, Joe, 'The Precariously Homosexual Art: Music and Homoerotic Desire in *The Picture of Dorian Gray* and Other Fin-de-Siècle Fiction', in *The Idea of Music in Victorian Fiction*, ed. Sophie Fuller and Nicky Losseff (Farnham, 2004)
Lebrecht, Norman, *Covent Garden: the Untold Story – Dispatches from the English Culture War, 1945–2000* (London, 2000)
Lee, Hermione, *Virginia Woolf* (London, 1997)
Leslie, Shane, *The Oppidan* (London, 1922)
Levi, Erik, 'Those Damn Foreigners: Xenophobia and British Musical Life during the First Half of the Twentieth Century', in Fairclough, P., ed., *Twentieth Century Music and Politics: Essays in Memory of Neil Edmunds* (Farnham, 2013), pp. 81–96
Levy, Paul, *G.E. Moore and the Cambridge Apostles* (London, 1979)
Lloyd, Stephen, *Constant Lambert: Beyond the Rio Grande* (Woodbridge, 2013)
Lucas, John, *Thomas Beecham: An Obsession with Music* (Woodbridge, 2008)
Magee, Bryan, *Wagner and Philosophy* (London, 2000)
Marcard, Micaela von, 'Die Staatsoper Unter den Linden 1919–1997' in *Das 'Zauberschloss'. Unter den Linden: Die Berliner Staatsoper. Geschichte und Geschichten von den Anfängen bis heute* (Berlin, 1997)
Martin, Benjamin G., *The Nazi–Fascist New Order for European Culture* (Cambridge, MA, 2016)
Masters, Brian, *Great Hostesses* (London, 1982)
Metzger, Rainer and Christian Brandstätter, *München: Die grosse Zeit um 1900: Kunst, Leben und Kultur 1890–1920* (Munich, 2008)
Moffatt, Wendy, *E.M. Forster: A New Life* (London, 2010)
Moore, Gerald, *Am I Too Loud?: Memoirs of an Accompanist* (London, 1962)
Newsome, David, *On the Edge of Paradise: A.C.Benson, Diarist* (London, 1980)
Nicoll, Allardyce, *The World of Harlequin: A Critical Study of the Commedia dell'Arte* (Cambridge, 1963)
Ollard, Richard, *An English Education: A Perspective of Eton* (London, 1982)
Orrey, Leslie, and Rodney Milnes, *Opera, A Concise History* (London, 1987)
Osborne, Richard, *Music and Musicians of Eton: From 1440 to the Present* (London, 2012)
Palmier, Jean-Michel, *Weimar in Exile: the Anti-Fascist Emigration in Europe and America* translated D. Fimbach (London, 2006)
Panayotova, Stella, *I Turned it into a Palace: Sydney Cockerell and the Fitzwilliam Museum* (Cambridge, 2008)
Pimlott, Ben, *Hugh Dalton* (London, 1985)
Potter, Pamela, *Most German of the Arts: Musicology and Society from the Weimar Republic to the End of Hitler's Reich* (New Haven, 1998)
Power, Eileen, *Medieval People* (London, 1924, 1986)
Radcliffe, Philip, *E.J. Dent: A Centenary Memoir* (Rickmansworth, 1976)
Riley, Matthew, *Edward Elgar and the Nostalgic Imagination* (Cambridge, 2006)
Rodmell, Paul, *Charles Villiers Stanford* (Farnham, 2002)
Rowe, P.R.R., 'The Old Vic', *Music & Letters*, vol. 12 (April 1932), pp. 141–6
Rowbotham, Sheila, *Edward Carpenter: A Life of Liberty and Love* (London, 2008)
Sadie, Stanley, ed., *The New Grove Dictionary of Music and Musicians* (London, 2001)
Saltmarsh, John, *King's College: A Short History* (Cambridge, 1958)

Schafer, Elizabeth, *Lilian Baylis: A Biography* (Hatfield, 2006)
Scheijen, Sjeng, *Diaghilev: A Life* (London, 2010)
Schipperges, Thomas, *Akte Heinrich Besseler: Musikwissenschaftspolitik in Deutschland 1924 bis 1949* (Munich, 2005)
Scholes, Percy, *The Mirror of Music 1844–1944*, 2 volumes (London, 1947)
Schreffler, Anne C., 'Modern Music and the Popular Front: The International Society for Contemporary Music and Its Political Context (1935)', in *Music and International History in the Twentieth Century*, ed. Jessica C.E. Gienow-Hecht (New York, 2015)
Seabrook, Jeremy, *The Refuge and the Fortress: Britain and the Flight from Tyranny* (London, 2008)
Sellers, Leonard, *The Hood Battalion* (Barnsley, 1995).
Shedlock J.S., 'Mozart's "Magic Flute"', *Monthly Musical Record* (July 1909)
Skidelsky Robert, *John Maynard Keynes: Hopes Betrayed 1883–1920* (London, 1983); *John Maynard Keynes: Fighting for Britain 1937–1946* (London, 2000)
Spalding, Frances, *Gwen Raverat: Friends, Family and Affections* (London, 2004)
Stansky, Peter, *On or About December 1910: Early Bloomsbury and its Intimate World* (Cambridge, MA, 1996)
Streatfeild, R.A., *The Opera: A Sketch of the Development of Opera. With full Descriptions of all Works in the Modern Repertory*, with an introduction by J.A. Fuller-Maitland (London, 1896; 5th edn, 1925, revised, enlarged and brought up to date by Edward J. Dent)
Tierney, N., *William Walton: His Life and Music* (London, 1984)
Toye, Francis, 'Opera in England', *The English Review* (December 1910)
Trend, J.B., 'Dent', *The Score*, no. 22 (1958), pp. 49–55.
Tyrrell, John and Rosemary Wise, *A Guide to International Congress Reports in Musicology 1900–1975* (London, 1979)
Wainwright, David, *Broadwood By Appointment: A History* (London, 1982)
— *The Piano Makers* (London, 1975)
Walton, Susannah, *Behind the Façade* (Oxford, 1988)
Wellesz, Egon, 'E.J. Dent and the International Society for Contemporary Music', *The Music Review* (1946), pp. 205–8
White, Eric Walter, *The Rise of English Opera* (London, 1951)
Wilkinson, L.P., *A Century of King's* (Cambridge, 1980)
Wilson, Jean Moorcroft, *Siegfried Sassoon: The Making of a War Poet* (London, 1999)
Wilson, Margaret, *English Singer* (London, 1970)
The Wipers Times: the complete series of the famous wartime trench newspaper (London, 2006)
Wingfield-Stratford, Esmé, *Before the Lamps Went Out* (London, 1945)
Wortham H.E., *Oscar Browning* (London, 1927)

Index

Abraham, Gerald, 503
Academic Assistance Council, 409, 410
Acta Musicologica (ISCM journal), 374, 412, 440–1, 444
Adie, H. A. ('Michael'), 486
Adler, Guido, 162, 162n114, 336, 379, 388, 441
Albert, Eugen d', 65, 301, 306–7, 306n140
Allan, Maud, 102, 203, 265–6, 289
Allatini, Rose, 266
Allen, Hugh: appointment of Cambridge Professor of Music, 348–9, 367; Bach Festival, 172, 292; at Cambridge, 30, 32, 42, 189; conductor of CUMS, 33, 40; conducts Bach Choir, 147; friendship with Dent, 45, 51; in Germany, 59; and the IMG/IMS, 167; Petersfield choral competition, 149, 172, 178; at the Royal College of Music, 269
Ambrose, Kay, 466
Amelli, Dom Ambrogio, 79, 92, 97, 162
Amis, John, 508
Anglès, Higini, 410, 439, 440, 441, 444, 448–9, 502
Annunzio, Gabriele d', 343, 416
Ansermet, Ernest, 284, 288, 331, 335, 380, 405, 438
anti-semitism: in 1930s Germany, 409–10; and the ISCM, 341, 440–1
Anzoletti, Emilio, 132
Apostles, The, 24–5
Arányi, Jelly d', 268, 359
Arici, Max, 103
Arkwright, G. E. P., 152, 165
Armstrong, George Cyril, 16, 35, 54–5, 241
Arts Council, 472, 491, 494
Arundell, Dennis, 158, 291, 345, 349, 357–8, 371, 380, 385, 431, 477
Asquith, Lady Cynthia, 266
Athenaeum, The (journal), 273, 275–7, 283–4, 304, 315
Atkin, William 'Gabriel', 254, 271
Auber, Daniel, *Fra Diavolo*, 63, 423, 425, 430, 482, 485
Austin, Sumner, 421, 424, 450, 473, 479

Bacchia, Emilio ('EB), 78
Bach Choir, 53, 53n167, 147
Bainbrigge, Philip, 193, 200, 239, 241, 246, 250, 252, 256, 266, 271, 272
Baird, James, 103, 257
Bal y Gay, Jesús and Rosita, 450, 462
Balfour, Arthur, 188
Balfour Gardiner, H., 195, 195n84
Balkwill, Violet, 334
Ballets Russes, 195, 210, 271–2, 275, 284, 391
Bantock, Granville, 166–7, 210, 290
Barber, Samuel, 456
Barber, William ('The Saint'), 206, 220
Barber Institute, Birmingham, 511
Barcelona, ISCM-ISMR festival (1936), 401, 437–44
Barger, Florence, 150
Barger, George, 86, 87, 118
Barker, Harley Granville, 123, 138, 195, 206, 230, 275, 307n141, 406
Barlow, Sir Alan, 490
Barratt, W. A., 43
Barrie, J. M., 15
Barrios, Angel, 286, 286n51
Bartholomew, Theo, 106, 144, 173, 214, 229, 232, 238, 241, 251, 260
Bartok, Bela, 164, 370, 374, 438; *Bluebeard's Castle*, 323
Barwell, Noel ('The Little Wretch'), 106, 207, 254, 259
Bax, Arnold, 182, 207, 252, 328, 338-9, 350, 353n
Bax, Clifford, 350
Baylis, Donald, 231
Baylis, Lilian, 184, 279–81, 291, 373, 384, 391–3, 400, 402, 404, 423–4, 432, 450, 451, 454
Bayreuth Festival, 17, 38, 46
BBC Symphony Orchestra, 383, 396
Beaton, Cecil, 362
Beaumont & Fletcher, *The Knight of the Burning Pestle*, 158, 163, 164, 173n169, 179, 187
Beavan, John, 350, 362
Bechert, Paul, 356
Bechet, Sidney, 288
Beckmann, Max, 300
Bedford, Hubert, 429

Beecham, Joseph, 181–2
Beecham, Sir Thomas: affair with Maud Cunard, 257; and the British Music Society, 292; against the broadcasting of music, 383n70; conducting during the First World War, 216, 222; conducts *The Wreckers*, 163; contribution to British opera scene, 182, 282–3; at Covent Garden, 181, 402–5, 423; and Dent's Mozart translations, 210, 233, 247; differences with Dent, 181–2, 247; Imperial League of Opera, 402; and the Royal Philharmonic Orchestra, 382
Beethoven, Ludwig, *Fidelio*, 60, 172, 175–6, 178, 415, 450
Behmer, Marga, 131, 132
Bekker, Paul, 157n85, 304, 311, 312, 334, 336
Bell, Clive, 87
Bell, Hugo, 38, 57 n183
Bellincioni, Gemma, 78, 148
Belloc, Hilaire, 139, 147, 437
Bennett, Arnold, 255
Benson, A. C., x, xiii, xvi, 33, 104, 110 n128, 117 n159, 191, 250
Bentoft, Fred, 223
Berenson, Bernard and Mary, 5, 55, 99–100, 104 n103, 119, 174, 185
Berg, Alban, 200, 334, 379, 393–4, *394*, 411, 435, 438; *Wozzeck*, 386, 396
Berlin: Busoni in, 101–2; Dent on, 160, 186–7; gay sub-culture in, 129–30, 135–7, 301, 303–4; music scholarship in, 129; opera house closures (1930s), 389–90; post First World War, 295–6; public shootings (1934), 419; Secession exhibitions, 137; theatre, film and music in (1920s), 296–310
Berlin Philharmonic, 382
Besseler, Heinrich, 439–41, 439n46, 444
Beveridge, William, 409, 480
Beveridge Report (1942), 480–1
Beves, Donald, 385
Bie, Oscar, 308-9
Bilton Grange prep school, 12–14
Binyon, Laurence, 221
Birch, Frank, 200, 214, 249, 278, 358
Birrell, Francis, 60 n5, 205, 313
Bliss, Arthur, 190, 200, 242, 245–6, 252, 269, 275, 288, 291, 349, 504
Bliss, Howard, 245, 402
Bliss, Kennard, 200, 222, 241, 244–5, 247
Blom, Eric, 412
Blonay, André de, 420
Bloomsbury Group, 276
Blue Review (journal), 195, 196, 210
Bologna, Italy, 80–1, 101, 139
Bonavia, Ferrucio, 412
Boosey, Leslie, 490
Bossi, Enrico, 124, 133
Bötticher, Rita, 131
Boughton, Rutland, 166, 232, 232n79, 248, 273n2, 275, 288, 292
Boulanger, Nadia, 418
Boulenger, C. L.('Bou'), 241, 331, 362, 467, 470
Boulestein, X. Marcel, 116 n152, 185, 188, 194, 199 n102, 244
Boult, Adrian, 252, 252n161, 261, 261–2, 268, 269, 271, 284, 321, 382, 383, *394*, 396, 479
Bragg, W. H., 409
Brahms, Johannes, 17, 42, 59
Braithwaite, Warwick, 476, 477
Braunfels, Walter, 314
Brecher, Gustav, 300
Brett, Philip, 208, 516–17
Bridge, Frank, 250, 261, 267, 292
Bridge, Sir Frederick, 147
Bridges, Robert, 152, 191
Bridges-Adams, William, 178–9, 179n10, 241, 275, 302
British Broadcasting Corporation (BBC), 359, 381, 382–3, 401, 451, 479, 497, 501
British Music Society, 269–71, 273, 292, 329, 334, 359
British Society for the Study of Sexual Psychology (BSSSP), 172, 207–9, 215, 221, 231
Britten, Benjamin, 419, 497; *Peter Grimes*, 492, 494–5, 496, 507–8
Broadwood, Evelyn, 254, 289, 399, 451, 470, 482, 486
Brodorotti, Frau von, 61, 73, 82
Brodorotti, Hermann von, 61, 126
Brook, Peter, 503
Brooke, Alfred, 200, 214, 220, 229
Brooke, Justin, 141–2, 158, 164, 168
Brooke, Rupert: and the *Blue Review*, 195; at Cambridge, 142, 142n16, 158, 164–5, 168–9; correspondence with Dent, 241; death, 225–7; Dent's obituary for, 140, 225; enthusiasm for war, 214, 217; and the Fabians, 184; friendship with Dent, 145–6, 150–2; 'The Soldier', 225
Brown, Horatio, 101, 167
Browne, (William) Denis, 145, 158, 167, 171, 173, 195, 196, 206, 213, 214, 222–3, 225, 227–8
Browning, Oscar, 22–4, 25, 31, 35, 52, 65n33, 69, 177n4

Buckley, Frank, 16, 61, 148, 230, 231, 232
Budapest, 88, 90–1, 101 n20, 407, 426, 457, 502, 508
Bukhofzer, Manfred, 459
Burkhard, Heinrich, 326
Burlingham, Edward, 448
Burnley, Lancashire, 473, 478
Burton, Harry, 128, 152, 220 & n
Busch, Adolph, 334
Busch, Fritz, 310, 310n161, 312
Bush, Alan, 434, 478
Busoni, Ferruccio: concert at the Philharmonic (1898), 52; Dent's friendship with, 102, 130–3, 163, 204–5, 289; influence on Dent's criticism, 157, 197–8; conducts at the Newcastle Festival (1909), 166; at CUMS concert in Cambridge, 174, 176; in Zurich in the First World War, 264; London recital (1919), 290; in post-war Berlin, 304–8; death, 352; Dent's biography of, 352–3, 360, 377; *Die Brautwahl*, 203; *Doktor Faust*, 360, 361, 374
Busoni, Gerda, 130, 206, 360, 370, 377, 389, 449
Butler, R. A., 480
Butterworth, George, 17, 147, 152, 172, 210, 214, 215, 241, 246, 262
Butting, Max, 416

Calvocoressi, Michel Dmitri, 231
Camargo Society, 391–2
Cambridge: ISMR Congress (1933), 407–8, 410–13; during the Second World War, 465–6, 479; at the turn of the 20th century, 25–7
Cambridge Antiquarian Society, 221
Cambridge Arts Theatre, 431, 450, 465, 479
Cambridge Magazine, 198–9, 213, 218–19, 226, 233–4, 235, 240, 251, 255, 272, 275
Cambridge Philharmonic, 114n143
Cambridge Report, on music education, 397–8
Cambridge Review, 35, 48, 50, 104, 158, 169
Cambridge spies, 434
Cambridge University, and music, 23n20, 29, 367
Cambridge University Musical Club (CUMC), 22, 31, 32–3, 40, 44, 86, 87, 115, 170, 196
Cambridge University Musical Society (CUMS), 22, 27, 29, 31, 32–3, 74, 115, 149, 215, 237, 252, 411, 482
Cambridge University Opera Society, 499–500
Cameron, Ernest, 268
Cannan, Gilbert, 218
Caplet, André, 331
Carey, Clive: at Cambridge, 87, 97, 104, 116; Dent's correspondence with, 222, 228, 247, 249, 251–2, 256, 260–1, 269; Dent's friendship with, 106–10, 127; directs opera at the Vic-Wells, 404, 420; emigrates to Australia, 343, 385; in Germany, 121–2; lecture to the Music Association, 432; in *The Magic Flute*, 179, *192*, 193; in the Marlowe Dramatic Society, 141, 142; notes for Dent biography, 515; and the Old Vic, 279–80, 290–1, 319; in Paris, 148; producer and director, 195, 197, 275, 369; on Rupert Brooke, 227; wartime service, 214, 231, 256
Carey, Hugh, 5, 516
Carl Rosa Opera Company, 196, 345, 474
Carpenter, Edward, 128, 172, 207, 208, 212, 223
Carreño, Teresa, 62
Carreras, Guido, 205
Carse, Adam, 166–7
Casals, Pau, 438, 444
Casella, Alfredo, 355, 362, 381, 393, 394, 460
Casement, Roger, 265n225
Casper, Johann Ludwig, 135
Cavalli, Carlo, 385, 416–17, 426, 429
CEMA (Committee for the Encouragement of Music and the Arts), 465, 472, 480, 487, 494–5
Certani, Alessandro, 138–9, 138n57, 152, 185
Chadfield, H., 269
Chamberlain, Neville, 458
Champion, Hubert H. ('Cham'), 36–8, 45, 46, 53, 64–5
Charlton, General L.E.O., 260
Chester's (music publisher), 287, 287n54, 332
Chigi, Prince (Count Guido Chigi Saracini), 77, 97 n66, 376, 379
Chilesotti, Oscar, 205, 294
Chisholm, Erik, 420, 432
Chisholm, Hugh, 129
Christie, John, 139, 415, 425–6, 445, 446, 489, 490n129
Chudadhij, Prince, 221
Church Music Society, 152, 165, 172, 196
Churchill, Winston, 165 n131, 214, 225, 480
Clarion Singers, 478, 479, 492
Clark, Edward, 288, 288n60, 318, 394, 396, 451
Clark, John Willis, 51, 155
Clark, Kenneth, 480, 489, 490
Clarke, Louis, 477
Coates, Albert, 284

Cobbett, W. W., 269
Cockerell, Kate, 154, 173, 188, 189, 210, 290
Cockerell, Sydney, 123, 154, 158, 232
Cohen, Harriet, 353
Cole, Horace, 116, 116n151
Colefax, Sybil, 257, 258
Colles, H. C., 233
Collingwood, Lawrance, 392, 402, 424, 477, 487, 492
Combarieu, Jules, 224, 368
communism, 434
Compton, Bishop Lord Alwyne, 51
Compton, Lady Alwyne, 51, 121
Condamine, Robert, 166
Cons, Emma, 184, 280
Contemporary Music Centre, London, 331, 335, 359
Cooke, A. H., 21, 27, 50
Coolidge, Elizabeth, 376
Cooper, Gerald, 331, 356, 361, 374, 386, 399, 401–2, 474, 502
Cooper, Lady Diana, 243
Corder, Frederick, 188
Cornford, Francis, 45, 51, 142, 146, 153, 175
Corri, Charles, 402
Cortot, Alfred, 289
Cossa, Gabor, 431
Courtauld, Elizabeth, 383
Courtauld, Samuel, 490
Covent Garden opera house, 183, 402–3, 404, 414, 423, 425, 432–3, 489–92, 505–6
Coward, Henry, 166
Coward, Noël, 259n195, 260
Cox, Ka, 146
Crace, John, 48
Craig, Gordon, viii, 143, 148, 151, 166, 195, 241, 251, 264, 318n197
Creighton, Basil, 203
Creighton, Ursula, 131, 203, 289, 399
Cribb, Tim, 141
Cross, Joan, 476, 479, 481, 492, 496
Cuba, 454
Cunard, Maud, 247, 257, 403
Cust, Robert Hobart, 69, 78, 94, 103, 128, 166, 220

Dalcroze, Emile Jacques, 274n8
Dalcroze Society, 274
Dale, Benjamin, 262
Dalton, Hugh, 146, 165, 173, 184, 196, 200, 241, 262, 499
Darke, Harold, 465
Darling, Malcolm, 299
Dart, Robert Thurston, 500, 502
Darwin, Frances, 146, 150, 151, 153, 505
Darwin, George 169, 170, 211
Darwin, Gwen *see* Raverat, Gwen
Darwin, Horace, 171, 193
Darwin family, 24, 32n67, 146, 151, 152, 168, 169
Davies, Walford, 30
Day, Timothy, 22n
De Falla, Manuel, 261, 283–7, 333, 334, 347–8, 359, 364, 459; *The Three-Cornered Hat*, 284
Dean, Basil, 480
Dean, Winton, 323, 368, 421, 423, 431, 452, 505, 506–7, 515
Deathridge, John, 516
Defauw, Desiré, 216 n16, 223, 264, 393, 394
Del Re, Arundel, 357
Delius, Frederick, 17, 134, 135, 182, 275
Deller, Alfred, 505
Denman, John, 345
Denny, James, 431
Dent, Catherine, 7, 9, 12, 47, 139, 145, 188, 191, 205, 248, 290, 485
Dent, Charles, 57, 205
Dent, Charles Jonathan, 7, 9
Dent, Edward Joseph: appearance, 19n; elected to The Athenaeum Club, 420; attempts to establish music as academic subject, 114; trips to Bayreuth, 38–9, 46; BBC broadcast, 451, 451n28; in Berlin, 128–39, 295–310; witnesses public shootings in Berlin, 419; President of the British Liszt Society, 502; correspondence with Britten, 507–8; membership of BSSSP, 207–9; relationship with Busoni, 130–3, 204–5, 304–8, 352–3, 360; home in Cambridge, 143–5; musical life in Cambridge, 22, 28, 31–3, 40–2, 44–5, 53, 57, 74, 87; Cambridge lectures, 97, 105; appointed Professor of Music at Cambridge, 367–9, 371–2; writes for the *Cambridge Magazine*, 198, 251, 255, 266, 270; elected to Cambridge Musical Board, 105; honorary doctorate from Cambridge, 499–500; Cambridge Report on music education, 397–8; Classics scholarship at King's College, Cambridge, 19–22, 27–8, 49–50; adjudicates choral competitions, 149; composition, 41–2, 48, 48n140, 54, 64, 87–8, 120–1, 155, 467; Cornell lectures (1938), 446, 450, 451, 452–3; deafness, 41, 481, 495, 503, 504; diaries of, 33–5; early compositions, 17–18; early musical experiences, 10–12;

interest in early musical instruments, 43, 45, 55, 74, 112, 117; education, 12–18; controversial remarks on Elgar, 388–9; involvement with ENSA, 480; family background, 6–10; friendship with E. M. Forster, 91–6; visits to France, 209–10; visits to Germany, 59–68, 72–3, 82, 96–7, 101–2, 121–2, 125, 160–3, 201, 203–5, 205–6, 310–16; honorary doctorate from Harvard, 445, 447–8; at the Haydn centenary in Vienna, 161–3; homosexuality, 33–6, 43–4, 77–8, 129–30, 135–7, 155–6, 173, 207–9, 266–7; visit to Hungary (1938), 457–8; and the ICSM, 327–34, 336–43, 351–2, 360–5, 369–71, 501–2; campaign against in the ISCM, 439–44; ill health, 344, 354, 356, 361, 381, 395, 430, 444, 445, 460, 510–13; illness and convalescence in Cambridge, 464–70, 475–6, 480–1, 483–4; offered teaching post in Illinois, 196; President of ISMR, 387, 399, 502; visits to Italy, 51–2, 68–71, 70–2, 75–81, 97–101, 103–4, 124–5, 128, 139, 148, 166, 173–4, 205; journalism on music and theatre, 274–7, 292–5, 317–23; studies for BMus at King's, 27–8, 40, 44, 56–7; King's Fellowship, 65–7, 69–70, 83–5, 86–8, 139; legacy, 517; moves to London, 249; production of *The Magic Flute*, 176, 177–8, 187–94; medical exemption from war service, 236, 261; misogyny, 131–2, 150, 174; Mozart research, 155, 166; campaigning for national opera and theatre, 486–92, 508–9; championing of national opera house, 181–4, 247–8; visit to New York, 453; obituaries and tributes, 514–16; involvement in the 'Old Vic', 279–82; appointed governor of the Old Vic, 372–3; opera editions, 357–8, 361, 373, 395, 450, 478; opera translations, 172, 178–9, 179–80, 231, 232–3, 420, 426, 432, 450, 467, 469; President of the Philharmonic Society, 383–4; portrait commissioned, 477–8; retires from Professorship, 483; friendship with Siegfried Sassoon, 231–2, 237–9, 271; Scarlatti research, 71–2, 75, 76–7, 82–5, 88, 88–90; 70th birthday celebrations, 499–501; move to South Kensington, 485–6; relationship with J. B. Trend, 153, 153n69, 165, 218, 241, 249, 436–7; trip to US and Mexico, 461–3; lectures in Vienna, 344; visits to Vienna and Prague, 201–3; 'blinkered' attitude to approaching war, 415–16, 428–9, 457–8, 461, 463; on outbreak of war, 212; wartime correspondence, 240–7; and Vaughan Williams, 169–70, 170–1, 510; writing style, 171–2

Dent, Edward Joseph, writings: 'Academic Teaching: A Defence and a Criticism', 224; *Alessandro Scarlatti*, 105, 111–13; *Ferruccio Busoni, a Biography*, 369–71, 377, 385, 397; *Foundations of English Opera* (1928), 209, 366, 369; *Handel* (1938), 421–3; 'Hans Pfitzner', 316–17; *Hellas*, 73, 80, 83–4; 'Letters from Germany', 299–300, 304, 316; 'Looking Backward' (1949), 328–9; *Mozart's Opera The Magic Flute: its History & Interpretation* (1911), 189–90, 194; *Mozart's Operas*, 196, 201–3, 205, 498; *Notes on Fugue for Beginners*, 467; obituary of Rupert Brooke, 140, 225; *Opera* (1940), 459–60, 466, 470–1, 517; 'Revaluations', 100, 294–5; *Terpander*, 368–9; *'The Baroque Opera'*, 167–8; 'The Future of British Opera', 496; 'The Pianoforte and its Influence on Modern Music', 224–5; 'The Willow-Tree Bough' (song), 262, 263; *A Theatre for Everybody*, 488, 497, 517

Dent, Francis ('Frank'), 7, 9, 175, 249

Dent, Geoffrey, 502–3

Dent, Henry, 8

Dent, Isabel, 7, 9, 10, 11–12, 38, 44, 237, 502

Dent, John Dent, 6, 8, 14

Dent, John William ('Jack'), 7, 8

Dent, Joseph (*formerly* Tricket), 7

Dent, Laura Freshfield, 7

Dent, Mary Hebden Woodall, 6, 8, 10, 20, 47, 256–7

Dent, Reverend Joseph, 7

Deutsch, Otto, 456, 465

Diaghilev, Sergei, 195, 271–2, 284, 362

Dickinson, Goldsworthy Lowes ('Goldie'), 24, 25, 86, 104, 172, 219, 299, 301, 303, 371

Diestel, Meta, 117, 125

Dohnanyi, Ernst von, 87

Dolmetsch, Arnold, 289

Donaldson Collection, 45

Donaueschingen, Baden, 320, 326, 329

Doncaster, Leonard, 241

Doone, Rupert, 369–70, 456 n54, 459

Douglas, Norman, 350
Douglas, W. R., 484
Draber, H. W., 353, 362
Drach, Fritz, 136, 137, 161, 302
Drama League movement, 274, 302
Dresden, Germany, 59–65, 72–3, 82, 125, 161
Duncan, Isadora, 152
Dunhill, Thomas, 248
Durnford, Walter, 168
Dussek, Franz, 203
Dyer, Louise Hanson, 407
Dyson, Sir George, 481, 494, 496

Earle, Reverend Walter, 12–13
Ebert, Carl, 415
Écorcheville, Jules, 209
Edschmidt, Cosimus, 312
Edward Arnold (publisher), 105, 111, 124
Einem, Gottfried von, 433
Einstein, Albert, 410
Einstein, Alfred, 314, 374, 409, 410, 439–40, 459
Eisler, Hans, 434
Eitner, Robert, 75
Elgar, Edward: Dent's appreciation of, 386; Dent's controversial remarks on, 388–9; Dent's reservations about, 124, 166; *The Dream of Gerontius*, 513
Eliot, T. S., 258, 272, 276
Ellis, F. B., 172, 176, 214
Ellis, Havelock, 36, 207, 208
Engisch, Kurt, 449–50, 459, 460–1, 498
English National Opera, 184, 517
English Opera Group, 497
English Singers, 231, 321
ENSA (Entertainments National Service Association), 480, 496
Erdmann, Eduard, 308, 363
Erhardt, Otto, 376–7, 413–14
Esmarch, Bernard, 128, 135, 160
Eton College, 14–18
Evans, Edith, 450
Evans, Edwin, 230, 230n72, 291; and the ISCM, 329, 330, 331, 351, 353, 362, 395, 397, 452, 498
Ewald, Clara, 137, 138n57, 313
Ewald, Paul, 313, 314

Fabian Society, 184
Fairbairn, T. C., 230, 230n68, 232-3, 247, 251, 281, 292
Fassbender, Max, 303
Fauré, Gabriel, 46, 131n27, 133, 316, 361, 455
Fauser, Annegret, 516
Fellerer, Karl Gustav, 410
Fellowes, Edmund, 399
Festing-Jones, Henry, 238, 249, 251, 254
Figgis, W., 48, 51
Fight for Right movement, 255, 255n
Firbank, Ronald, 153, 165, 224, 288–9
First World War: initial responses to, 212–14; Belgian relief operations, 215; Defence of the Realm Act (DORA), 212, 219, 234, 241, 253, 266; impact on musical activities, 216–17; Gallipoli campaign, 222–3; death of friends, 225–9, 245–7; Military Service Act (1916), 236; Armistice, 272
Fisher, H. A. L., 262, 409
Fitelberg, Gregor, 393, *394*
Fitzwilliam Museum, Cambridge, 54, 75, 123, 154
Fitzwilliam Virginal Book, 72
Flesch, Carl, 134
Fletcher, Maisie, 121, 121n179, 179, 197
Florence, Italy, 5, 52, 55, 69, 76–7, 93, 97–9, 103, 128, 166, 173–4; ISCM festival (1934), 416–19
Footlights, Cambridge, 87
Forbes, Mansfield 'Manny', 252, 278
Forster, E. M.: at Cambridge, 22, 116; diaries, 33n75; friendship with Dent, 48, 69, 73, 87, 91–6, 191; Italian novels, 54–5, 74, 95; wartime service, 239, 241; *The Longest Journey*, 139; *Maurice*, 36, 96, 208, 221, 259; *A Room With a View*, 92, 94–5, 153; *"The Machine Stops"*, 159; *Where Angels Fear to Tread* (originally *Monteriano*), 93, 95, 96, 118–19, 184
Foss, Hubert, 344, 354, 357, 361, 362, 364, 372, 375, 395, 467
Foss, William, 230, 261, 274, 354
Fothergill, John, 262
Fox Strangways, W. H., 261, 261n211, 374, 403, 412
Franckenstein, Baron Clemens von und zu, 314
Freemasonry, in *The Magic Flute*, 180–1
Fried, Oskar, 138
Friedlaender, Max, 97–8, 98n68, 101–2, 129, 162, 185, 196, 204, 300, 310, 313, 356, 389
Friedrich, Friedl, 416, 428, 457
Frommel, Wolfgang, 416, *417*
Fry, Geoffrey, 220, 231
Fürstenberg, Prince Max Egon zu, 326
Furtwängler, Wilhelm, 429
Fussell, Paul, 274

Gandarillas, Antonio de, 258n193
Gandolfi, Riccardo, 55, 76, 97

Gardiner, Rolf, 395, 514
Gardner, Edmund, 423
Garrett, Harry, 148, 232
Gaselee, Stephen, 407
Gatty, C. T., 54
Gatty, Nicholas, 30, 34, 37, 43, 45, 173–4, 248, 261, 262, 278, 292, 319
Gatty, René, 195n85, 197, 262
Gay, John, *The Beggar's Opera*, 478, 479–80, 504
General Election (1945), 480
Georgian Poetry (anthology), 195, 238, 257
Gerhard, Poldi, 468–9, 482
Gerhard, Robert, 401, 438, 444, 451, 460, 467, 468, 476, 503
Germany: annexation of Sudetenland, 458; Anschluss with Austria, 455; appointment of Hitler as Chancellor, 407; Degenerate Art and Music exhibitions (1938), 409; Nazi policy towards the arts, 439; Permanent Council for the International Cooperation of Composers, 420, 429, 433, 436; public shootings (1934), 419; Third Reich, 407, 408; Weimar Republic, 386, 390, 406, 409 *see also* Berlin; First World War
Gibbs, Cecil Armstrong, 153, 196, 200, 246, 277, 288, 350
Gibson, Thornely 'Gibby', 160, 185, 189, 322, 350, 404
Gielgud, John, 390
Giesecke, Carl Ludwig, 190, 202
Gillett, Maud and Katherine, 48
Glasgow, Mary, 490
Glazunov, Alexander, 45
Glyndebourne, 415, 425–6, 445, 489, 490n129, 508
Goddard, Scott, 331, 362, 445, 480, 486, 493
Goebbels, Joseph, 409
Goldsbrough, Arnold, 480
Goldschmidt, Ernst, 115, 153, 173, 201, 289
Goldschmidt, Hugo, 88
Gombosi, Otto, 410
Goodhart-Rendel, Harry 'Hal', 123, 159–60, 187, 249, 256, 264, 404
Goodricke, Sir Henry, 6
Goossens, Eugène, 290, 331, 336, 338, 339, 490
Gordon, Cosmo, 123, 141, 144, 147, 158
Gordon, Jack, ix, xi, 133n32, 259n193, 345, 361, 362, 369–70, 375, 386, 393, 395, 404, 413, 414, 420–1, 424, 430, 444, 445, 449, 450, 456n54, 459, 470, 471, 473, 486, 498, 508
Gosse, Edmund, 152, 238
Gough, Muriel, 279, 280, 404, 421, 424, 432
Gow, Andrew, 142, 278
Grainger, Percy, 15n23, 102, 195n84, 314
Graves, Robert, 249
Gray, Alan, 30, 32, 41, 83–4, 115, 127, 149, 150, 213
Gray, Arthur, 241
Greek Play (at Cambridge), 21, 50–1, 74, 106, 141, 142, 168–70, 385, 499
Greenwood, L. H. G., 87
Greenwood, Margaret ('Maggie'; *née* Dent), 7, 9
Griller Quartet, 419, 438
Grissell, H. D., 77
Grosz, George, 300
Gruenberg, Louis, 363–4, 376
Grützmacher, Friedrich Wilhelm, 62
Guinness, Alec, 450
Gurlitt, Willibald, 449
Guthrie, Tyrone 'Tony', 450–1, 471, 472, 473, 476–7, 492, 494, 495, 496

Hába, Alois, 419, 435
Hadley, Patrick 'Paddy', 465, 479, 480, 482
Hadow, Henry, 88, 165, 262
Haefeli, Anton, 320n207, 338n49, 375, 396, 444
Halliburton, Richard, 399
Hamilton, Eddie, 231
Hamilton, Rowan, 61
Hammerschlag, Hans, 407
Hamsen, Knut, 312
Handbuch der Musikgeschichte, 388
Handel, Georg Friedrich: Dent's research on, 322–3, 358, 421–3, 431–2; *Samson*, 398–9; *Semele*, 358
Handschin, Jacques, 410–11, 439, 440, 441
Harding, Rosamond, 380, 431
Hardy, Thomas, 152, 255; *The Dynasts*, 240
Harewood, George Lascelles, 7th Earl of, 25, 505
Haring, Jessie, 131, 132
Harman, Charles, 220, 229, 241, 242, 243–4, 278, 279
Harman, Eddy, 279, 345
Harrison, Beatrice, 353
Harrison, Jane, 142, 146, 150, 165, 175, 217, 255, 267
Harsányi, Zsolt, 458
Hart-Davis, Dick, 16
Hartung, Gustav, 302, 311, 312
Harty, Sir Hamilton, 383
Haslam, W.H. 'Michael', 253, 278, 345

Hatchlands (house), 159n102
Haward, Lawrence: at Cambridge, 48–9, 69, 97, 104; Dent's correspondence with, 52, 61, 148–9, 174; in Dresden, 72–3, 82; friendship with Dent, 48–9, 482; at Manchester City Art galleries, 223; marriage, 174; music critic at *The Times*, 105, 194; travel with Dent, 344, 379–80
Hawkes, Ralph, 490
Haydn, Joseph, centenary, 161–3
Haynes, E.S.P. ('Ted'): and civil rights, 207, 220, 266; death of Alfred Brooke, 229; disgrace and death, 503; at Eton with Dent, 15–16, 16n; friendship with Dent, 46–7, 87, 99, 103, 193; in the Heretics, 217; marriage, 122–3; play staged in London, 211
Headlam, Walter, 21, 48, 151
Headlam family, 9
Heffer, William, 290
Heller, Hugo, 328, 340
Helpmann, Sir Robert 'Bobby', 504
Henry, Leigh, 318, 319n198
Heretics (Cambridge society), 217, 236
Herrmann, Max, 302n127
Hertzka, Emil, 328
Herzog, Wilhelm, 136, 136n48, 138, 160, 296
Heseltine, Philip (aka 'Peter Warlock'), 318, 353
Hewlett, Maurice, 79
Hierl-Deronco, Alois and Otto, 81
Higgins, Norman, 479
Hill, Arthur, 264
Hill, Octavia, 280
Hill, Philip, 414
Hindemith, Paul, 310n161, 326, 328, 333, 334, 341, 363, 365n175, 379, 396, 419, 429, 433, 471
Hirsch, Paul, 374, 466, 481, 499
Hirsch Music Library, 413, 499
Hirschfeld, Magnus, 135–6, 172–3, 185, 207, 208, 301, 302–4
Hitler, Adolf, 386, 407, 458
Hoefert, Franz Konrad, 301
Hoesslin, Franz von, 311
Holland, Henry, 103
Holst, Gustav, 45, 87, 262
Holt, Harold, 489
homosexuality: in the armed forces, 244; and the Billing trial, 265–7; and the BSSSP, 207–9; and German cinema, 303; Hirschfeld's research on, 135–6, 172–3; in Nazi Germany, 419, 441
Hopper, Victoria (aka Sylvia Nelis), 179, 189, 193
Hornbostel, Eric von, 138, 138n59, 185
Horner, David, 257n185, 362
Hovingham Hall, 11, 58
Howard de Walden, Lord, 264, 264n218, 292, 331
Howells, Herbert, 267
Höxter, Tommy, 136, 137, 186, 302
Hudson, Canon Thomas Percy(later Pemberton), 11
Hughes, Dom Anselm, 410–11
Hull, Arthur Eaglefield, 269–70, 271, 286n51, 339, 359, 374
Hungary, 410, 433, 457–8, 502
Hunt, Douglas, 485
Hutchings, Arthur, 273n1
Huxley, Aldous, 276
Hynes, Samuel, 212

Ibert, Jacques, 438, 452
Idell, Cecil, 231
Indy, Vincent d', 112n139, 133-4, 135, 222, 264, 287n52, 318, 444
Inge, Dean William, 138, 138n60, 225
Ingram, Bruce, 317
Ingram, Maurice, 220, 257, 257n186, 377
International Congress of Musical Education, 398
'International Conservatoire of Music', 268–9, 278
International Music Society (IMG/IMS): dissolved during First World War, 221; English committee, 124, 167; London Congress (1913), 188; Rome Congress (1903), 97–8; Vienna Congress (1927), 365, 373–4
International Society for Contemporary Music (ISCM): birth of, 327–34; German section, 415, 419–20; and international politics, 429, 435–6; Spanish section, 334, 347–8, 376, 437; Amsterdam festival (1948), 501; Barcelona festival (1936), 437–44; Florence festival (1934), 416–19; Frankfurt festival (1927), 374–6; Geneva festival (1929), 380; Liège-Brussels festival (1930), 386; London festival (1946), 501; Oxford-London festival (1931), 383, 387, 393–7; Paris festival (1937), 451–2; Prague festival (1924), 351–2; (1925), 360–1; (1935), 426–7, 433–6; Salzburg festival (1923), 335, 338–43; (1924), 353–5; Siena

festival (1928), 379; Venice festival (1925), 362–4; Vienna festival (1932), 405–6; Zurich festival (1926), 364–5
International Society for Musical Research (ISMR): Cambridge Congress (1933), 407–8, 410–13; New York Congress (1938), 463; Dent elected President, 399, 502
Inwards, Haydn, 33
Ireland, John, 258–9, 262
Isaacs, Lea, 268
Ives, George, 207, 231

Jachimecki, Zdzislaw, 163, 163n124
Jackson, Barry, 345, 345n83, 503
Jackson, Kains, 207
James, M. R., 21, 24, 47
Janácek, Leos: *The Cunning Little Vixen*, 360; *Glagolithic Mass*, 380; *Jenufa*, 435
Jarnach, Philipp, 305, 360, 361, 370, 374, 433, 497–8
Jekyll, Francis 'Timmy', 16, 69, 82, 147, 172, 200, 207, 213, 220, 229, 242, 243, 253, 274, 293, 345–6, 386
Jenkinson, Daisy, 32, 157, 197
Jenkinson, Francis, 32, 47, 74, 87, 197, 350
Jeppesen, Knud, 412, 436, 440, 502
Jewish musicians, displaced from Germany, 409–10, 413–15
Jezek, Jaroslav, 419
Jiménez, Alberto, 450, 468
Joachim, Joseph, 11, 68
Joachim, Marie, 59
Joachim Quartet, 29, 59
John, Augustus, 165
Johnson, John St Anthony, 36–7, 43, 45, 78, 105
Jones, Bernard, 52, 232, 246, 250, 256
Jōos, Kurt, 392, 395, 414, 431, 450, 451, 471, 482
journals, post-war, 273–4
Joyce, James, 264–5

Kandinsky, Wassily, 68, 96
Kapp, E. X., 477
Kardorff, Konrad von, 136, 136n48, 137, 138, 154, 160, 174, 185
Kekewich, Hilda, 38
Kekewich family, 8–9, 17, 47–8, 51–2, 58
Kelly, F. S., 17, 48n140, 88, 172, 213, 214
Kempff, Wilhelm, 376
Kerridge, W. H., 196, 256, 264, 265, 271, 434
Kestenberg, Leo, 131, 131n22, 398, 502
Keynes, Florence, 215
Keynes, Geoffrey, 141–2, 158, 197
Keynes, John Maynard: and the Academic Assistance Council, 409; and the Camargo Society, 391; at Cambridge, 115–16, 118, 159, 172, 191, 193, 219, 380; and the Cambridge Arts Theatre, 431; Chairman of CEMA, 480, 494; on the Covent Garden Trust committee, 489–90; at Eton College, 16; and *The Nation & Athenaeum*, 317; *The Economic Consequences of the Peace*, 217, 301
Keyserling, Hermann, Graf von, 312
King's College, Cambridge, 19–22
King's College Chapel, 465, 513
King's College Musical Society (KCMS), 22, 25
Kipnis, Alexander, 414
Kirchner, Ludwig, 300
Klee, Paul, 68, 409
Klein, Sigmund, 185
Klemm, Oswald, 60, 61, 73
Knox, Collie, 259, 260
Knox, Ronald, 252
Kodály, Zoltán, 457–8, 502
Koechlin, Charles, 394
Korngold, Julius, 328, 329, 341
Kraus, Alessandro, 55-7, 76-7, 97, 122
Krauss, Clemens, 425
Kreisler, Fritz, 134, 206
Krenek, Ernst, 326, 370, 418–19, 436
Kretzschmar, Hermann, 79, 129, 129n10, 162
Kronfeldt, Dr, 303, 309
Kroyer, Theodore, 440
Kruse, Johann, 11
Kubelik, Rafael, 512

Labour Government (1945), 480
Labroca, Mario, 362, 363
Lambert, Constant, 365, 372, 391, 393, 396, 479
Lander, Heinz, 464, 482 & n95
Landowska, Wanda, 162, 162n121, 320
Larsson, Lars-Erik, 435
Lascelles family(see also Harewood), 9
Lawes, Henry, 146–7
Lawford, Raymond, 350
League of Nations, 379
Lee, Hermione, 34
Lee, Vernon (Violet Paget), 58, 122, 129, 148, 150, 219, 229, 248, 324
Leeds Festival, 210
Lehmann, Lotte, 414
Leichtentritt, Hugo, 186, 308, 309, 421
Leigh, Augustus Austen, 21, 65, 83
Leo, Leonardo, 70, 102, 125, 129
Lewis, Anthony 'Tony', 500, 502
Lewis, Percy Wyndham, 195n85, 274, 317

Linde-Walther, Heinrich, 137, 137n55
Little, William, 241
Littleton, Alfred, 209
Livingstone, Dr T. H., 209
Lloyd, Charles Harford, 16–17, 18, 53, 69, 105, 112, 368
Lloyd, E. Bertram, 172, 207
Lomer, Sydney, 259, 260, 267
London Philharmonic Orchestra, 383, 401
London Symphony Orchestra, 382, 383
Longo, Alessandro, 112, 117, 148
Lopokova, Lydia, 271, 391, 431
Lorenz, Robert, 388
Lübbecke-Job, Emma, 363
Lubbock, Percy, 53, 104, 107, 109–10, 191, 278, 279
Lytton, Lord, 409, 476, 494

MacCarthy, Desmond, 249
MacDonald, Ramsay, 267, 402
Mackay, Robert, 200
Mackenzie, Sir Alexander Campbell, 143, 143n, 161–2, 188
Maclean, Charles Donald, 76, 76n85, 143, 156, 161, 166, 167, 188
Maddalena, Edgardo, 98, 98n71, 126, 143, 148, 163, 202
Maddison, Adela, 131, 131n27
Magray, George, 103
Maitland, J.A. Fuller, 72, 75, 102, 114, 148, 154, 170
Malipiero, Gian Francesco, 415–16, 501–2
Malleson, Miles, 158, 250
Mallory, George, 144, 151–2, 195
Maltby, Charles R. C. 'Bob', 179, 179n11, 211, 231, 234, 241, 247, 251
Mandycyzki, Eusebius, 202
Mann, A. H. ('Daddy'), 22, 22n, 30, 42–3, 48, 73, 127, 371, 380
Mansfield, Katherine, vii, 195, 276
Marchant, Stanley, 489, 490
Marconi, Alfonso, 268
Marlowe, Christopher, *Dr Faustus*, 141–3
Marlowe Dramatic Society, 27, 140, 141–3, 141n7, 146–7, 158, 164, 168, 170, 175, 178, 278, 385, 401, 450, 499
Marsh, Sir Edward 'Eddie', 165, 165n131, 195, 214, 228, 229, 229n65, 238–9, 251
Marshall, Douglas, 289
Marshall, Herbert, 478
Marshall, M. O., 236, 256
Martin, Frank, 438
Marx, Joseph, 328
Massine, Leonide, 271, 272
Massingham, W. H., 317, 320, 322, 325
Mathews, Edgar, 249
Mathews, Mrs Lee, 269, 271, 362
Matthias, Helena, 274
Maussel, Roland, 351
Mayer, Anton, 324, 360, 369, 385, 430–1
Mayer, Sir Robert, 334
Meiklejohn, Roderick, 345
Meiningen, Germany, 59
Melbourn Choral Society, 42, 53
Meredith, Hugh, 69, 73, 86, 87, 104, 116, 117
Merrill, George, 172, 208
Messel, Oliver, 487
Mexico, 461–3
Meyer, A. R. 'Munkepunke', 301
Meyer, Ernst, 410, 512
Meyer, Hermann, 413
Meyer, Kathi, 374, 410, 412, 413
Mikota, Jan, 362
Miles, Philip Napier, 345, 348
Milner, Augustus, 289
Milton, John, *Comus*, 146–7, 150–2, 179
Mimbelli, Guido, 101, 104, 119, 121
Moger, Gladys, 250–1, 259, 262, 264, 267, 278
Mollison, Will, 32, 69, 87, 126, 164
Monro, Harold, 57, 238, 239–40
Monte Cassino monastery, 78–9, 92
Monthly Musical Record, 157, 171, 181, 187
Moodie, Alma, 334, 377
Moore, Earl V., 452
Moore, G. E., 24, 53, 86
Moorsom, Rainsley, 48
Morales, Pedro, 261, 261n206, 268, 284, 347
Morello, Giovanni, 79, 98, 119
Morley, Samuel, 280
Morley College, 280, 282
Morris, May, 158
Morris, R. O., 230, 276
Moser, Hans Joachim, 313, 313n173
Mosley, Sir Oswald, 434
Moulton, Dorothy (Lady Mayer), 322, 334
Mozart, Wolfgang Amadeus, *The Magic Flute*, 176, 177–8, 210, 290
Mühlfeld, Richard, 59
Munich, 66–8, 96–7, 201, 205–6
Murdoch, William, 258
Murry, John Middleton, viii, 195, 275, 276, 283, 290, 299, 315, 460
Music & Letters (journal), 273, 403, 453
music academies, in Britain, 183, 183n39
Musical Association (*later* Royal Musical Association), 87, 97n65, 105, 114
Musical League, 154
Musical Quarterly (journal), 224–5

Musical Times (journal), 270, 274, 383, 429
musicology, 28–9, 209, 327, 439, 440, 447, 448
Mussolini, Benito, 416, 418, 459

Naples, 79
Nash, Paul, 271
Nation & The Athenaeum, The (journal), 317–18, 331
National Theatre, 184
Naylor, Edward, 30, 97, 177, 371; *The Angelus*, 148, 158
Newcastle, music festival, 166–7
Newman, Ernest, 216
Nichols, Beverley, 253, 267
Nichols, Robert, 49, 258
Nicoll, Allardyce, 503
Niczy, Rolf, 96–7
Nikisch, Arthur, 185, 210
Nixon, J. E., 21, 24, 31, 41, 50, 73, 218, 247
Noble, Humphrey, 200
Noble, Tertius, 44, 50–1
Novello (publisher), 209
Novello, Ivor, 248

Oatfield, William, 200
Ogden, Charles Kay, 198, 198n101, 213, 217, 219, 226, 229, 234, 272
Old Vic and Sadler's Wells company, 390–3, 402–5, 420–1, 424–5, 450, 481–2, 487, 494–7; move to Burnley during the war, 473–4, 478
Old Vic Magazine, 344
Old Vic theatre, 184, 279–82, 290, 291, 372–3, 384
Olivier, Laurence, 450
Olivier sisters, 146
Ord, Boris, 319, 349, 362, 364, 369, 375, 380, 411, 449, 465, 498
Orlandi, Valentino, 110–11, 119–20, 124–5, 136
Orr, Robin, 380, 431
Ors, Eugenio d', 286, 347–8
Owen, Wilfred, 239, 271, 272
Oxford University, 114
Oxford University Press, 395

Paganini, Niccolò, 76
Palester, Roman, 435
Parratt, Sir Walter, 17, 18, 38, 69
Parry, Sir Hubert, 16, 16n, 74, 83–4, 87–8, 188, 216, 268
Pater, Walter, 36
Pattison, Lee, 453
Paul, Louis, 43, 47, 52, 68
Pavlova, Anna, 160n106
Pears, Peter, 485
Pechstein, Max, 160
Pedrell, Felip, 286, 286n48, 347
Pemberton-Billing, Noel, 265–6
Pendlebury Library, Cambridge University, 86
Perutz, Max, 24
Perzynski, Friedrich, 336
Petersfield, choral competition, 45, 149, 172
Petri, Egon, 62, 131, 131n21, 132, 166, 203, 385
Pfitzner, Hans, 307, 311, 316
Phalanx group, 96
Philharmonic Society, 382, 383–4, 401
Phillips, O'Neill, 129, 136, 140–1, 164
Pijper, William, 380
Pilgrim Trust, 386, 413n101, 472, 472n48, 480, 499
Pinkerton, Percy, 432
Pinsent, Cecil, 174
Piper, John, 512
Pirro, André, 399, 407
Pitt, Percy, 166, 383, 384
Pizzetti, Ildebrando, 331, 423, 432
Playfair, Nigel, 58, 275, 293
Plunkett-Greene, Harry, 87, 197, 261
Poetry Bookshop, 238, 239–40
Pohl, C. Ferdinand, 178
Pole, Reginald, 158, 175, 217
Polignac, Princesse de, 362
Pollock, Jack, 16, 69, 87, 138
Poulenc, Francis, 318, 328, 330, 338, 433, 455
Power, Eileen, 229
Praelinger, Melanie, 385
Prague, 202–3, 321, 335; International Congress of Musical Education (1935), 398, 426; ISCM festival (1924), 343, 351–2; (1925), 360–1; (1935), 429, 433–5
Praz, Mario, 400
Prerauer, Curt, 414
Prior, Camille, 356, 398, 449, 465
Procter-Gregg, Humphrey, 221, 221n37, 365, 385, 474, 476, 477
Proms (concerts), 250, 288
Prunières, Henry, 190, 351, 354–5
Pugin, Augustus Welby, 13
Purcell, Henry: *Dido and Aeneas*, 357n138, 373; *The Fairy Queen*, 209, 210–11, 278, 290–1, 395, 433; *King Arthur*, 371
Purcell Society, 124, 209
Purves, Chester, 173, 175, 200, 218, 220, 241, 242, 256, 322, 324, 331, 337, 345, 361, 379

Quilter, Roger, 15, 17, 127, 250

Raab, Hans, 416, *418*, 444, 449, 483, 498

Radcliffe, Philip, 380, 385, 388n6, 389, 431, 516
Raeburn, Christopher, 511
Ranalow, Frederick, 233
Rasi, Luigi, 98, 98n69, 143, 148, 178, 195
Rausch, Hans, 302, 315
Ravel, Maurice, 45n125, 222, 230, 237, 261, 306, 328, 332, 338, 378, 379, 380, *381*
Raverat, Gwen (*née* Darwin), 121, 121n180, 146, 150, 164, 168, 173, 189, 214, 399, 431, 469
Redfern, W. B., 27
Redgrave, Michael, 450, 472
refugees: from Nazi Germany, 409–10, 413–15, 431, 448–9, 455, 456, 462, 498; from the Spanish Civil War, 450, 460
Reger, Max, 126
Reichl, Otto, 312
Reinhardt, Max, 202, 243, 297, 302n123, 345
Reinhart, Werner, 333–4, 341, 353, 407
Respighi, Ottorino, 80, 139, 152, 160, 284
Réti, Rudolf, 327–8, 329n13, 333, 340
Reznicek, Emil von, 307
Rhythm (literary journal), 195, 210
Ribston Hall, Yorkshire, 6, 153, 215, 502–3
Richardson, Ralph, 390
Richmond, Ollife, 97, 127, 165
Richmond, Ruth Greenwood, 485
Richter, Hans, 157, 203, 205, 209
Richter, Sviatoslav, 52
Rickett, Jerry, 52
Riemann, Hugo, 158–9
Riisager, Knudage, 419
Riley, Fred, 362, 498
Riley, Matthew, 388n6
Robert, Eugen, 298
Robertson, Denis, 175, 385
Robinson, Henry, 402
Rokseth, Yvonne, 407
Rolland, Romain, 213, 219
Rootham, Cyril, 30, 178, 189, 211, 213, 221, 291, 348, 371, 372, 399, 411, 431, 449, 455
Ross, Robert, 220, 232, 238, 239, 248, 252, 257, 301
Rostand, Edmond, 58
Rothenstein, Albert (*later* Rutherstone), 151, 152, 187–8, 220, 230, 254
Rottenburg, Harry, 57, 69, 87
Rouché, Jacques, 230, 230n71
Rowe, L. T., 126, 262
Rowe, Reginald, 403, 454, 476
Rowntree, Arnold, 276
Royal Academy of Music, 411, 452
Royal College of Music, 268–9, 348, 393
Royal Philharmonic Orchestra, 382
Royal Victoria Coffee and Music Hall, 184
Royston Choral Society, 53
Rubens brothers, 57, 69, 87
Rubenstein, Arthur, 290
Ruggles, Carl, 435
Russell, Bertrand, 24, 212, 216, 219, 234
Russell, Raymond, 505, 510
Russell, Sydney, 384, 392–3
Rutland, Harold, 514
Rylands, George 'Dadie', 279, 450, 500

Sadler's Wells: origins of, 184, 373; and Covent Garden, 491–2; Dent's involvement in, 384, 403–5, 420, 423–5, 450–1, 481, 508–9; and the ENO, 517; financial difficulties, 402; opening and teething troubles, 390–3; Opera Books, 495–6; première of *Peter Grimes*, 494–5; during the Second World War, 471–4, 476–7; tour of Germany (1945), 496
Saerchinger, César, 309, 309n156, 321, 335
Salazar, Alfonso, 325,334, 337, 347
Salzburg: chamber music festival (1922), 327–8; ISCM festival (1923), 338–43; ISCM festival (1924), 353–5
Sammons, Albert, 258
Sanden, Irene, 131, 203
Sandrock, Adele, 298
Santayana, George, 45, 217
Santini Library, Münster, 89, 102, 122
Sassoon, Siegfried, 231–2, 234, 237–9, 240, 249–50, 254, 257, 271
Sayle, Charles, 41, 44, 49, 51, 87, 144, 151, 153, 188, 201, 226
Scarlatti, Alessandro, Dent's research on, 65–7, 69–70, 83–5, 88, 111–13
Schade, Richard, 205, 241, 308
Scherchen, Hermann, 305, 308–9, 309n153, 331, 334, 336, 337, 338, 342, 353, 364n172, 396, 419, 433, 435, 438
Schillings, Max von, 302, 309
Schmidt, Leopold, 363
Schmitt, Florent, 351
Schnabel, Artur, 133–4, 203, 360, 363, 385
Schneider, Otto, 305
Schoch, Hans, 449
Schoenberg, Arnold, 333, 335, 363, 364, *401*, 409, 435, 438
Scholes, Percy, 388, 388n5, 398, 502
Scholfield, Alwyn, 107, 142, 188, 189, 196, 350
Scholz, Wilhelm von, 302
Schreker, Franz, 306n136, 309, 310, 311, 314, 326
Schulz-Dornburg, Rudolf, 357, 357n137, 395
Schuster, Sir Victor, 480

Schütt, Kurt, 301
Schwimmer, Franciska, 91
Scontrino, Antonio, 77, 97, 98
Scott, Geoffrey, 174
Scott, Marion, 262
Scott-Moncrieff, Charles, 200, 239, 250, 262
Secession exhibitions, 68, 81, 96, 137, 160, 203
Second Viennese School, 435
Second World War, 464–5
Serkin, Rudolf, 334
Shaw, George Bernard, 113, 177n4, 184, 190, 195, 207, 216, 274, 292, 388
Shawe-Taylor, Desmond, 497, 514
Sheppard, Sir John Tresidder 'Jack', 104, 144, 193, 215, 229, 278, 279, 371, 380
Shield, William ('Billy'), 8, 47
Shove, Gerald, 173, 371
Sickert, Bernard, 69
Sidgwick, Adam, 169
Siegel, Rudolf, 314
Sitwell, Edith, 257–8
Sitwell, Osbert, 257–8, 271, 274, 294
Sitwell, Sacheverell, 257–8, 290
Sitwell, Sir George and Lady Ida, 417
Slevogt, Max, 68
Smyth, Ethel, 17, 182, 289, 393, 400, 471–2; *The Wreckers*, 163
Société Internationale de la Musique (SIM), 399
Somerset, Henry, 103, 148, 166
Somervell, Arthur, 362
Sommariva, Marchese di ('Claudio'), 78, 379
Sonneck, Oscar, 162, 224, 331, 376
Sonnenkamp, Fritz von, 215, 241
Southward, W. T., 41
Soviet Union, music in, 434
Spain: Catalan music and culture, 444; Civil War, 445, 448–9; ISMC/ISMR festival (1936), 437–44; J B Trend's musical research in, 283–7
Sparrow, Sylvia, 264, 267
Spens, Will, 127
Speyer, Sir Edgar, 261
Speyer, Ferdy, 250
Spottiswoode, Jane, 61, 65, 82, 161, 203
Springer, Hermann, 449
Sprott, W.J. 'Sebastian', 253, 271, 279, 380
Squire, Barclay, 72, 73–4, 124, 157, 163, 191, 268–9
Squire, J. C., 255, 282, 356
Stamer, Arthur, 12
Stamer, Carrie, 46
Stamer, Ellen (*née* Dent), 8
Stamer, Reverend Lovelace, 8, 12, 47, 138
Stanford, Charles Villiers: Cambridge Professor of Music, 27, 28–31, 56, 97, 149–50; conducts Bach Choir, 53; at Hovingham music festival, 58; advises Dent on Fellowship, 69–70; and Cambridge politics, 197, 199; death, 348; *The Critic* (opera), 248–9
Steegman, John, 279, 291
Stefan, Paul, 360, 396
Steinbach, Fritz, 59
Stephen, Adrian, 116
Stephen, Thoby, 87
Stern, Ernst, 137, 137n50, 143, 160, 301-2, 498
Sterndale Bennett, William, 97
Stewart, Bruce Hylton, 123, 277
Stewart family, 356–7, 394, 478
stock market crash (1929), 386, 394
Strachey, James, 144, 279
Strachey, Lytton, 35n80, 104, 276
Strachey, Oliver, 104
Strauss, Richard, 62, 67, 264, 420; *Arabella*, 425; *Der Rosenkavalier*, 201–2; *Elektra*, 160; *Salome*, 134, 148
Stravinsky, Igor, 409
Streatfeild, Philip, 259n195
Streatfeild, Richard A., 73, 105, 157, 163, 167, 191, 194, 336, 421
Strindberg, August, 374
Strindberg, Frida Uhl, 195n85
Strohbach, Hans, 414, 497
Summers, Montague, 445–6
Swaine, Alexander von, 459
Symonds, John Addington, 49, 167, 208
Syrett, Netta, 120–1
Szenkár, Eugene, 365, 498
Szigeti, Joseph, 419
Szilard, Leo, 409
Szymanowski, Karol, 386, 438

Tagliapietra, Gino, 131
Tanner, Laurence, 264
Taruskin, Richard, 273n1
Taylor, Deems, 453
Taylor, Sedley, 32, 41, 53, 59, 127, 213, 292
Tertis, Lionel, 123, 125, 248, 264, 353
Thern, Vilmos 'Willi' and Lajos 'Louis', 125–6
Thoma, Hans 68&n
Thoma, Ludwig, 96–7
Thompson, Herbert, 166, 412
Thomson, George, 478–9
Thomson, J. J., 24
Thomson, Katharine (*née* Stewart), 357, 478–9, 492
Thomson, Randall, 461
Tiessen, Heinz, 334, 380
Tilley, A. A., 21

Tippett, Michael, 492, 502; *A Child of Our Time*, 492
Torchi, Luigi, 79, 80, 97, 98
Torggler, Hermann, 81
Torner, Eduardo, 460, 465
Torrefranca, Fausto, 188, 205
Tovey, Donald, 17, 48n140, 53–4, 59, 135, 188, 312, 388, 451
Toye, Francis, 36, 116, 116n152, 123, 168, 185, 197, 205, 231, 261, 270, 325, 423
Toye, Geoffrey, 215, 230, 231, 261, 269, 289, 402, 404–5, 424
Tranchell, Peter, 500
transvestism, 303, 310
Tree, Viola, 248
Trend, John Brande ('JB'): at Cambridge, 153; relationship with Dent, 153n69, 165, 218, 223, 241, 249, 436–7; on Dent's hearing, 41n97; in Munich, 205; on the outbreak of WWI, 212n2; letter published in the *Cambridge Magazine*, 234; correspondence with Dent, 242, 325; and the ISCM, 331; and Spanish music, 283–7, 334, 347–8, 358–9; applies for Oxford Spanish Professorship, 400–1; and Anglo-Spanish relations, 437; visits Cuba with Dent, 454; in Mexico with Dent, 461–3; support for war refugees, 467; obituary for Dent, 514; death, 515
Trevelyan, G. M., 423
Trotsch, Uli, 301
Trowell, Brian, 388n6
Turina, Joaquim, 287, 334, 347, 375–6
Turner, W. J., 382

Ulrichs, Karl, 135, 208
Universal Edition (music publisher), 332
Unruh, Fritz von, 324

Vacaresco, Hélène, 379
Valéry, Paul, 379
Valois, Ninette de, 373, 391–2, 391n18, 451, 492, 494
Vandervelde, Lalla, 261, 262, 264, 267, 271
Vansittart, Robert, 64
Vansittart family, 9, 47
Vecchio, Orazio, *Amfiparnoas*, 179–80, 184–5, 186
Veidt, Conrad, 303, 303n129
Vellacott, Elizabeth, 431
Venice, 68, 70–2, 76, 88, 93, 101, 103-4, 109, 161, 257n187, 324-5, 345–7, 350-1, 355, 356, 360, 362-4, 377, 385, 426, 429, 458, 510
Victoria, Queen, 18
Vienna, 81–2, 125–6, 201–2; ISCM festival (1932), 405–6
Villa I Tatti, 99–100, 174
Vlasto, Jill (*née* Medway), 500, 515
Vlieger, Emile de, 268
Volzogen, Ernst von, 122, 122n183

Wadham, Helen, 374
Wagner, Peter, 356
Walker, Frank, 112
Walston, Charles (changed from 'Waldstein'), 21
Walter, Bruno, 205–6, 314, 324
Walton, William, viii, 289, 338, 375, 379, 388, 391, 490, 492
Warlich, Reinhold von, 153, 153n73
Warlock, Peter (see Heseltine, Philip), 388
Waterlow, Sydney, 16, 16n, 20, 48, 53, 69, 70–1
Webb, Philip, 38
Webern, Anton, 435
Webster, David, 491, 492, 494
Weckerlin, Jean Baptiste, 57, 125
Wedd, Nathaniel, 21
Wedekind, Frank, 72, 96n62, 138, 160, 296, 297, 312
Wedgwood, Ralph, 43
Wegelius, Martin, 80
Weingartner, Felix, 202
Weissmann, Adolf, 334, 336, 339, 340, 362-3
Wellesz, Egon, 202, 305, 308–9, 308n152, 314, 329, 330, 406, 441, 456, 500–1
Wells, John, 253–4, 260, 262, 267
West, Rebecca, 255
Weston, George, 78, 88, 139, 150, 165
Whistler, Rex, 415
White, Eric Walter, 465–6, 480; *The Rise of English Opera*, 183
Whitman, Walt, 36
Whittaker, W. G., 375, 375n36
Whitworth, Geoffrey, 274, 317
Wilde, Oscar, 301, 303
Willcocks, David, 466, 466n10
Willer, Ernst, 449
Williams, Evelyn, 476
Williams Iolo, 200
Williams, Ralph Vaughan: at Cambridge, 30; chamber music concert, 170–1, 174–5; on ENSA committee, 480; friendship with Dent, 45; at the IMG conference (1913), 188; and Purcell's The Fairy Queen, 197; wartime service, 214–15, 221; Hugh the Drover, 211; 'London' Symphony, 261; Pastoral Symphony, 360–1; Pilgrim's Progress, 509–10;

Sea Symphony, 171; Towards the Unknown Region, 147, 149; The Wasps (incidental music), 154, 168–70
Wilson, Hugh, 141–2, 144
Wilson, John Dover, 223–4
Wilson, Steuart, 153, 168, 171, 175, 179, 214, 218, 222, 228, 228n59, 230, 247, 277–8, 345, 398–9, 497, 514
Wing, W. H., 28, 42
Wittgenstein, Ludwig, 196–7
Wittgenstein, Paul, 419
Wolf, Johannes, 88, 129, 158, 162, 179, 299, 399, 409, 410, 413, 439, 440
Wood, Charles, 28, 30, 31, 31n61, 41, 97, 105, 168–9, 176, 178, 348, 349, 350, 356, 365
Wood, Henry, 216, 273n2, 401
Woodall, Edward ('Ted'), 8, 46, 75, 125, 356, 361, 429
Woodall, John, 8
Woodman, Richard, 262
Woolf, Leonard, 104, 276
Worsley family, 9, 11
Wotquenne, Alfred, 81, 82, 89
Wright, Sir Thomas, 103

Yeatman, Frank, 222
Young, Hilton, 73
Younghusband, Francis, 255n176
Ysäye, Eugène, 87, 248

Zadora, Michael von, 130
Zanello, Alfredo, 78
Zemlinsky, Alexander von, 331, 335
Zweig, Stefan, *Die Schweigsame Frau*, 430